DATE DUE

Feb 23 '67			
Feb 10 '68			
GAYLORD			PRINTED IN U.S.A.

THE RACES OF EUROPE

A SOCIOLOGICAL STUDY

(Lowell Institute Lectures)

BY

WILLIAM Z. RIPLEY, Ph. D.

ASSISTANT PROFESSOR OF SOCIOLOGY,
MASSACHUSETTS INSTITUTE OF TECHNOLOGY ;
LECTURER ON ANTHROPOLOGY AT COLUMBIA UNIVERSITY
IN THE CITY OF NEW YORK

ACCOMPANIED BY A SUPPLEMENTARY BIBLIOGRAPHY
OF THE ANTHROPOLOGY AND ETHNOLOGY
OF EUROPE, PUBLISHED BY THE
PUBLIC LIBRARY OF THE CITY OF BOSTON

NEW YORK
D. APPLETON AND COMPANY
1899

JOHNSON REPRINT CORPORATION
111 Fifth Avenue, New York, N.Y. 10003

JOHNSON REPRINT COMPANY LIMITED
Berkeley Square House, London, W. 1

Landmarks in Anthropology, a series of reprints in cultural anthropology

General Editor: Weston La Barre

First reprinting, 1965, Johnson Reprint Corporation

Printed in the United States of America

TO MY CHILDREN

CORRIGENDA.

Page 54, second footnote should read Bertholon, *1891*.

Page 81, third footnote should be Zampa, 1886 *a*.

Page 81, third footnote should read *Kopernicki*, 1889, p. 50.

Page 85, third line from bottom, should read *on* page 86.

Page 106, third footnote should be Beddoe 1867–'69 a, *reprint*, p. 171.

Page 106, fifth footnote should read Collignon, 1890 a, *reprint*, p. 15.

Page 124, footnote, should be Lagneau, *1873 c* and *1879 b*.

Page 208, seventh line, should be spelled Jøderen.

Page 358, second footnote should be 1895 B, p. 70.

Page 428, eighteenth line, should read, the *Slavs* were of fair complexion.

Page 433, tenth line, should be, portraits at page *364*.

Pages 462 and 466, footnotes, should be spelled *Schaaffhausen*.

Page 523, second line, should read, *their* best friends, etc.

PREFACE.

THIS work is the outgrowth of a course of lectures upon "physical geography and anthropology" in the School of Political Science at Columbia University in the city of New York; delivered before the Lowell Institute in the fall of 1896. It originally comprehended, in a study of aboriginal societies and cultures, an analysis of the relation of primitive man to his physical environment. Gradually, with a growing appreciation of the unsuspected wealth of accumulated data, it has expanded along lines of greater resistance, concentrating attention, that is to say, upon Europe—the continent of all others wherein social phenomena have attained their highest and most complex development. Containing little that may be called original, strictly speaking, it represents merely an honest effort to co-ordinate, illustrate, and interpret the vast mass of original material—product of years of patient investigation by observers in all parts of Europe—concerning a primary phase of human association: that of race or physical relationship.

An earnest attempt has been made to bring this abundant store of raw material into some sort of orderly arrangement, and at the same time to render it accessible to future investigators along the same line. The supplementary bibliography under separate cover has, it is hoped, materially contributed to both of these results. The intimate relationship between the main volume and the bibliographical list, as explained in the preface to the latter, is too apparent to need further explanation. It will be noted at once that all citations according to author and date may be immediately identified in full, by reference to the supplementary list of authorities at the appropriate place.

To secure a graphical representation of facts by maps which should conform to strictly scientific canons, was an indispensable requisite in a geographical work of this kind. By rare good fortune it has been possible to develop a chance suggestion from my artist friend, Mr. Frank B. Masters, into a definite and simple system of map construction, whereby the work could be done by our own hands. The sacrifice of artistic finish incident thereto, was deemed unimportant beside the manifest advantage of a close adaptation of the maps to the text, both being prepared in unison. To secure this result a number of the maps have been entirely redrawn; in several cases they have been experimentally prepared even to the engraving of the plates, three times over. Many of the maps in this volume—probably the majority—are the handiwork of my wife, to whose constant material aid as well as inspiration, reference has elsewhere been made. From these all extraneous details have been purposely omitted. Moreover, the various maps have been co-ordinated with one another, with the adoption of a common scheme for all. Thus, for example, dark shades invariably denote the shorter statures, and similar grades of tinting, so far as possible, designate equal intensities of the phenomena in question. In the maps of head form this co-ordination has been applied most consistently. In respect of maps of stature and pigmentation, the diverse anthropometric methods employed and the extraordinary range of variation, have rendered it a more difficult matter to preserve a strict uniformity.

In several cases in the reproduction of standard maps it will be noticed that the graphical system has been considerably modified from the original. Sometimes, as in the map of Limousin on page 83, the author's scheme has been simplified; in others, as in Broca's classical map of Brittany on page 100, the number of degrees of shading has been greatly increased, it is believed to good effect; and oftentimes, as in the map on page 143, an entire rearrangement of the graphical representation has been made to conform to precise statistical methods; for it is a cardinal principle in graphic statistics that the visual impression must, so far as possible, conform to the represented facts. To denote one grade of variation of ten per cent by a single tint, and to make the succeeding shade designate a range three times as great, involves almost as serious misrepresentation as an actual misstatement in the text. At times, as in the evidently misleading scheme used on Odin's map on page 525, where equal shades of tint are used for widely different ranges of variation, the original scheme has been left, because of difficulties in a proper rearrangement from the published data.

Another detail upon these sketch maps will certainly attract attention—viz., the apparent lack of system employed in the lettering, French, German, Italian, or English orthography being alike employed. The rule—unfortunately not invariably observed—has been to apply the spelling native to each country in question wherever the map was a direct copy: thus Bretagne for Brittany in maps of France, Roma instead of Rome in Italy, and Sachsen, not Saxony, on maps of the German Empire. When it is an original one, constructed herein from statistical data for the first time, English transliterations have been used. The purpose of this confessedly awkward arrangement has been to permit of a possible adaptation of these selfsame maps to foreign translation. It is the only possible international arrangement, that each country should preserve its indigenous spelling. As for the legends and titles, they lie outside the drawing proper, and necessarily must correspond to the language of the text.*

It would be disingenuous not to confess pride in the collection of portrait types inclosed between these covers. This is the more pardonable, inasmuch as a failure thus to recognise its value and completeness would be to reflect lesser credit upon those to whose entirely disinterested efforts the collection is really due. Without the earnest co-operation and never-failing interest of the eminent authorities in all parts of Europe, to whom specific reference is made at appropriate places in the body of the text, as well as by name in the index list of portraits, this work of scientific illustration of the dry matter of the text would have been almost impossible. For the proper selection of portrait types necessitates an intimate knowledge of the people of each country, not possible to the observant student but only to those who have lived and worked among them often for months at a time. Words are inadequate fully to express the deep measure of obligation of which I am sensible for assistance along these lines.

Among all the European authorities to whom I am indebted in various ways, there is no one to whom the obligation is so great as to my friend Dr. John Beddoe, F. R. S., late president of the Anthropological Institute of Great Britain. From first to last, his interest in the work—especially evidenced by way of candid criticism upon all points of detail—

---

* In this connection we may note a few *errata* indelibly fixed in the engravings : viz., on page 170, for Basse Navarra in France, read Basse Navarre ; on page 169, for Medoc, read Médoc ; on page 189, for Bilboa and Plamplona, read Bilbao and Pamplona respectively ; on page 225, it should obviously be Schleswig ; and on page 517, Savoie ; at page 318 possibly Edinburgh ; and on the folding map at page 222, Tyrol should be Tirol and Würtemburg should properly be Würtemberg.

has been a constant source of inspiration. Without the sure guidance of such criticism, many more errors than now remain for future elimination, must surely have occurred.

The courtesy manifested by the officers and council of the Anthropological Institute of Great Britain, in intrusting the valuable albums of British photographs belonging to the Society to my charge, merits the deepest gratitude. As an act of international courtesy it is peculiarly worthy of note at this time. Professor A. C. Haddon, of Cambridge University, and Dr. C. R. Browne, of Dublin, Ireland, have also, among English authorities, rendered important service. In Germany, I have continually turned to Dr. Otto Ammon, of Carlsruhe, for aid, and have not failed in any instance to find a ready response.

A goodly share in the preparation of this volume has been performed by my wife—fully enough to warrant my own personal desire that two names should appear upon the title-page, instead of one. For a large part of the drawing of the maps, much wearisome reading of proofs, interminable verification of references and of bibliographical details have fallen to her share of the work: and in addition, the invaluable service has been rendered of remorseless criticism in all matters of style as well as of fact. The six years required for the completion of the work by our joint labour must have been greatly prolonged, and the final product would surely have been far more imperfect, had it not been for her constant and devoted aid.

W. Z. R.

BOSTON, *April 25, 1899.*

CONTENTS.

xi

CHAPTER V.

STATURE.

CHAPTER VI.

THE THREE EUROPEAN RACES.

CHAPTER VII.

FRANCE AND BELGIUM.

CHAPTER VIII.

THE BASQUES.

CHAPTER IX.

THE TEUTONIC RACE: SCANDINAVIA AND GERMANY.

CHAPTER X.

THE MEDITERRANEAN RACE: ITALY, SPAIN, AND AFRICA.

CHAPTER XI.

THE ALPINE RACE: SWITZERLAND, THE TYROL, AND THE NETHERLANDS.

CHAPTER XII.

THE BRITISH ISLES; IBERIAN ORIGINS (?).

CHAPTER XIII.

RUSSIA AND THE SLAVS.

CHAPTER XIV.

THE JEWS AND SEMITES.

CHAPTER XV.

EASTERN EUROPE: THE GREEK, THE TURK, AND THE SLAV; MAGYARS AND ROUMANIANS.

CHAPTER XVI.

WESTERN ASIA: CAUCASIA, ASIA MINOR, PERSIA, AND INDIA.

CHAPTER XVII.

EUROPEAN ORIGINS: RACE AND LANGUAGE; THE ARYAN QUESTION.

CHAPTER XVIII.

EUROPEAN ORIGINS (*continued*): RACE AND CULTURE.

CHAPTER XIX.

SOCIAL PROBLEMS: ENVIRONMENT *versus* RACE.

CHAPTER XX.

MODERN SOCIAL PROBLEMS (*continued*): STRATIFICATION AND URBAN SELECTION.

CHAPTER XXI.

ACCLIMATIZATION : THE GEOGRAPHICAL FUTURE OF THE EUROPEAN
RACES.

LIST OF PORTRAIT TYPES

WITH ANTHROPOMETRIC DATA AND INDICATION OF ORIGIN.

NOTE.—Figures refer to the separate portraits as individually numbered, six on a page.

| | HEAD. | |
Number.	LENGTH. Millimetres.	BREADTH. Millimetres.
67–68. Original ; loaned by Dr. Ammon, of Carlsruhe.....	200	151
69–70. Original ; loaned by Dr. Ammon, of Carlsruhe.....	...	...
71–72. Original ; loaned by Dr. Ammon, of Carlsruhe.....	179	155
73–74. Original ; loaned by Dr. Janko, of Buda-Pesth.....	182	155
75–76. Original ; loaned by Dr. Janko, of Buda-Pesth.....	174	154
77–78. Original ; loaned by Dr. Beddoe....	...	...
79–80. Original ; loaned by Captain Dr. Livi, of Rome....	195	178
81–82. Original ; loaned by Captain Dr. Livi, of Rome....	188	157
83–84. Original ; loaned by Captain Dr. Livi, of Rome....	193	147
85–86. Original ; loaned by Captain Dr. Livi, of Rome....	189	156
87–88. Original ; loaned by Captain Dr. Livi, of Rome....	187	158
89–90. Original ; loaned by Captain Dr. Livi, of Rome ...	...	...
On page 256. Original ; loaned by Captain Dr. Livi, of Rome	182	155
91. Original ; loaned by Dr. Bertholon, of Tunis	193	152
92. Original ; loaned by Dr. Collignon (from his 1896 b)	...	...
93–94. Original ; loaned by Dr. Collignon...............	186	138
95–96. Loaned by Dr. Collignon. Original in his 1887 a..	...	...
97–98. From Defregger's Aus Studienmappen deutscher Meister. (Courtesy of Prof. Kollmann.)........	...	...
99. Original ; loaned by Prof. Kollmann, of Basle......	...	...
100. Original ; loaned by Dr. Beddoe	...	...
101–102. Original ; loaned by Prof. Kollman, of Basle	205	140
On page 298. Original ; loaned by Dr. De Man, of Middelburg, Holland	...	...
103–110. Original ; loaned by the Anthropological Institute of Great Britain and Ireland...................	...	...
111–112. Original ; loaned by Prof. A. C. Haddon, of Cambridge University. Described in his 1897........	...	...
113. Original ; loaned by the Anthropological Institute..	...	...
114. Original ; loaned by Dr. Beddoe	197	152
115–119. Original ; loaned by the Anthropological Institute..	...	...
120. Original ; loaned by Dr. Beddoe	...	...
121–126. Original ; loaned by the Anthropological Institute..	. .	...
127–128. Original ; loaned by Dr. Beddoe	...	...
129–131. Original ; loaned by the Anthropological Institute..	...	...
132. Original ; loaned by Dr. Beddoe	...	...
133–134. Original ; loaned by Prof. A. C. Haddon (1893)	198	163
135–136. Original ; loaned by the Anthropological Institute..	...	...
137. Original ; loaned by Dr. Beddoe................ .	...	...
138. Original ; loaned by the Anthropological Institute..	...	...
139–140. From Zograf, 1892 a...........................	190	160
141–142. From Zograf, 1892 a	195	160
143–144. From Zograf, 1892 a.......................	182	156
145–146. Original ; loaned by Dr. Beddoe	...	...

	HEAD.	
	LENGTH.	BREADTH.
Number.	Millimetres.	Millimetres.
147–148. Original ; taken for me by Mr. David L. Wing	...	...
149. Original ; taken for me by Mr. David L. Wing ..	187	157
150. Original ; taken for me by Mr. David L. Wing	202	152
151–152. From Szombathy ; Mitt. Anth. Ges., Wien, xvi, p. 25	...	...
153–154. From A. N. Kharuzin, 1889, plate v	...	...
155–156. From Sommier, 1889	...	...
157–158. From A. N. Kharuzin, 1890 d....................	...	...
159–162. From Sommier, 1886 and 1888...............	...	...
163–164. Loaned by Major Dr. Collignon. Original in his 1887 a	...	...
165–166. Original ; loaned by Dr. Bertholon, of Tunis	200	150
167–168. Original ; loaned by Dr. Bertholon, of Tunis	192	144
169–170. From de Ujfalvy, 1878–'80, by permission..........	...	...
171. Original ; loaned by Prof. de Lapouge, of Rennes..	...	...
172. Original ; loaned by Dr. S. Weissenberg, of Eliza-bethgrad.	...	...
173. Original ; loaned by Major Dr. A. Weisbach, of Sarajévo, Bosnia...............	...	...
174. Original ; loaned by Dr. Weissenberg.............	...	...
175–176. Original ; loaned by Dr. Achilles Rose, of New York	...	...
177–180. Original ; loaned by Dr. Janko, of Buda-Pesth.....	...	...
181–186. From F. Ritter von Luschan, 1889, by permission ..	...	...
187–188. From A. N. Kharuzin, 1890 d, by permission.......	...	...
189–192. From F. Ritter von Luschan, 1889, by permission ..	...	...
193–194. Original ; loaned by Dr. Janko, of Buda-Pesth.....	182	162
195–196. Original ; loaned by Dr. Janko, of Buda-Pesth.....	174	158
197–198. Original ; loaned by Dr. Janko, of Buda-Pesth.....	...	...
199–210. From Chantre, 1885–'87, vol. iv, by permission.....	...	...
211–216. From F. Ritter von Luschan, 1889, by permission..	...	...
217–218. From Chantre, 1895	...	...
219–220. From Danilof, 1894	180	140
221–222. From Danilof, 1894	194	145

LIST OF MAPS AND DIAGRAMS.

LIST OF PORTRAIT PAGES.

NOTE.—Footnotes in this volume give, wherever possible, the pagination according to the original publication. In cases of bibliographical disagreement, page numbers have been taken from reprints separately and independently paged.

THE RACES OF EUROPE.

CHAPTER I.

INTRODUCTION.

"HUMAN history," says Taine in the introduction to his History of English Literature, "may be resolved into three factors—environment, race, and epoch." This epigrammatic statement, while superficially comprehensive, is too simple to be wholly true. In the first place, it does not distinguish between the physical environment, which is determined independently of man's will, and that social environment which he unconsciously makes for himself, and which in turn reacts upon him and his successors in unsuspected ways. The second factor, race, is even more indefinite to many minds. Heredity and race may be oftentimes synonymous in respect of physical characteristics; but they are far from being so with reference to mental attributes. Race, properly speaking, is responsible only for those peculiarities, mental or bodily, which are transmitted with constancy along the lines of direct physical descent from father to son. Many mental traits, aptitudes, or proclivities, on the other hand, which reappear persistently in successive populations may be derived from an entirely different source. They may have descended collaterally, along the lines of purely mental suggestion by virtue of mere social contact with preceding generations. Such characteristics may be derived by the individual from uncles, neighbours, or fellow-countrymen, as well as from father and mother alone. Such is the nature of tradition, a very distinct

3   I

factor in social life from race.* It is written in history, law, and literature; it is no less potent, though unwritten, in national consciousness, in custom and folklore. M. Taine's third factor, epoch, what the Germans call the *Zeitgeist*— the spirit of the times, the fashion of the hour—is perhaps the most complex of all. A product of the social environment, it is yet something more than this. There may be a trace of tradition in it, a dash of race; to these being added the novel impulses derived from immediate contact with one's fellow-men. This means something different from slavish imitation of the past; it generally arises from a distinct desire for self-assertion in opposition to it. Style in literature, schools of art, fashions in dress, fads, parties in politics, panic in the mob—all alike spring from the imitative instinct in man. If his imitation be of the past, we term it custom, conservatism, tradition; if imitation of his present fellow-men—reciprocal suggestion, or what Giddings terms " like-mindedness "—it generates what we call the spirit of the times.

Human society is indeed an intricate maze of forces such as these, working continually in and through each other. The simplest of these influences is perhaps that of the physical environment, the next being race. The task before us is to disentangle these last two, so far as possible, from the complex of the rest, in all that concerns Europe; and to analyze them separately and apart, as if for the moment the others were non-existent.

The history of the quasi-geographical study of environment as a factor in human history and progress may roughly be divided into three periods, conditioned by the rise and varying fortunes of the evolutionary hypothesis.† This first of these periods preceded the appearance of Darwin's Origin of

---

* Bertillon distinguishes this from the "mesologic" influences of environment as "hereditary social forces" (De l'Influence des Milieux, Bull. Soc. d'Anth., 1872, p. 711).

† For additional references and details, consult our Geography and Sociology in Political Science Quarterly, x, 1895, pp. 636–655, with bibliography.

Species. Its great representatives were Ritter, Guyot, and Alexander von Humboldt. They completed the preliminary work of classification and description in geography which Agassiz, Owen, Prichard, and Dawson performed in other kindred natural sciences. The results of all these systematists were subject to the same limitation—namely, the lack of a general co-ordinating principle. They perceived the order of natural phenomena, but explained it all on the teleological basis. Africa and Asia were practically unknown; no sciences of anthropology or sociology had accumulated data; and the speculations as to human affairs of these earlier geographers, therefore, were necessarily of a very indefinite, albeit praiseworthy, nature. From lack of proper material they were constrained merely to outline general principles. Whenever details were attempted, they were too often apt to lead to discouraging absurdities. Price's [29] theory that the black eyes of the Welsh peasantry were due to the prevalence of smoke from their coal fires is a case in point. The only other studies of a similar nature in this early period were those of Quetelet and Bernard Cotta. These were, to be sure, definite and specific; they contained to some degree the ideas of mass and average, but they were each limited to a narrow field of investigation.

The literature produced in the period just noticed was exclusively continental. The decade following 1859, which we may call the probational period for the doctrine of evolution, at first promised well for the extension of geographical studies into the English field. Ritter's works were received with great favour in translations, and Guyot's Lowell Lectures awakened intense interest in America. No one thought of the lurking danger for the teleological idea. But suddenly "the gloomy and scandalous" theories of Thomas Buckle's History of Civilization cast a deep shade over the field; the alarm awakened by the lectures of Vogt and the claims of Darwin and Huxley as to man's origin became intensified; and the sudden outburst all over Europe of interest in anthropological studies excited new fears. Moreover, the younger advocates of the doctrine of environmental influence in human affairs insisted upon taking the apparently harmless general principles of the founders of modern geography and carrying them out into all details of social life. Long before the proper data existed, Buckle, Crawfurd, Pellarin, and their fellows tried in vain to imitate the precision of the older and exact natural sciences. It must be confessed also that the exaggerated claims of the economists and the generalizations of the utilitarian philosophers also contributed in some degree to bring the study of physical environment as a factor in social life into disrepute.

Uprooted in England, the new environmental hypotheses found on the Continent a congenial soil, that had long been prepared for their reception by Bodin, Montesquieu, and Quetelet. Cuvier had not hesitated to trace the close relation borne by philosophy and art to the underlying geological formations. The French inclination to materialism offered a favourable opportunity for the propagation of the environmental doctrines. They were kept alive in anthropology by Bertillon *père* and Perier; in literature by Taine; and in the study of religions by Renan. It appears to be true that where the choice lies between heredity and environment, the French almost always prefer the latter as the explanation for any phenomenon. In Germany during this second period the earlier work of Cotta and Kohl was continued by Peschel, Kirchhoff, and Bastian, and in later days with especial brilliancy by Ratzel.

The last decade has witnessed a marked revival of interest among English scholars in the study of the environmental influences which play upon man individually and upon human society at large. Buckle's errors have been forgiven. Antagonism to the doctrine of evolution has passed away. A new phase of geographical research—in short, its purely human aspects—is now in high favour among historians and students of social affairs. The apostles of the movement have been the late historian Freeman and the eminent author of The American Commonwealth.* Payne, in his History of the

* An interesting sketch of the geographical work of Mr. Freeman will be found in the Geographical Journal, London, for June, 1892. The

New World called America, has shed a flood of new light upon an old theme by the appeal to environmental factors. Justin Winsor, in The Mississippi Basin, shows the geographical idea logically developed " with such firm insistence and with such happy results that he almost seems to have created a science for which as yet we have no name—which is capable of development even to the predictive stage," to quote the words of a reviewer. The movement has even invaded the sacred precincts of biblical literature in Smith's Geography of the Holy Land, which is in itself a wonderfully suggestive commentary upon the influence of physical environment during the course of Jewish history.

The real significance of this tendency in historical writing lies not in its novelty, for it merely revives an old idea; but in the fact that the initiative comes this time from the historians rather than from the geographers or the economists. Geography has heretofore appeared in the guise of a suppliant for recognition at court. The burden of proof in maintaining the value of geographic science for the historian and sociologist has therefore rested mainly in the past upon the geographers and students of purely natural science. Notwithstanding all manner of discouragement, however, Wallace, Geikie, Strachey, Mill, Keltie, and others have at last succeeded in making their claims good, both in the English universities and in the learned world outside as well. The tendency to broaden the scope of economics and the new interest in sociology have together served as an encouragement. Cliffe-Leslie and Roscher pointed the way; Meitzen, Ravenstein, and Kirchhoff brought the use of statistics to its aid; until to-day geography stands ready to serve as an introduction, as well as a corrective, to the scientific study of human society.

The geography that is attracting the attention of historians

province of geography in its relation to history is also discussed by him in the Methods of Historical Study; and his uncompleted History of Sicily shows the extreme development of the ideas found in his Historical Geography of Europe. Despite this tendency, we find a late reviewer (Nation, July 18, 1895, p. 50) declaring that "after all his everlasting insistence on the great external facts of the history of the Western world, [he] erred chiefly in going no further."

to-day is that which is defined by Gonner as "the study of
the environment of man." It is the geography of Guyot and
Ritter, stimulated and enlightened by the sciences of anthropology, archæology, sociology, and even statistics. No one
of these contributory branches of investigation antedates the
middle of this century. Call it " physiography," defined by
Huxley as the science of man in relation to the earth; as distinct from geography, the science of the earth in its relations
to man : " anthropo-geography," with Ratzel : or even " histo-
geography," as some one has proposed. These names all
convey the same general meaning. It is neither political,
commercial, administrative, nor economic geography; it is
something more than the science of the distribution of races.
It overlaps and includes them all. It is not merely descriptive.
It is able to formulate definite laws and principles of its own.
In fact, geography in any of the familiar senses, is, after all,
only a single element in this new field of research. It represents primarily the attempt to explain the growing convic-
tion, so well expressed by Giddings, that " civilization is at
bottom an economic fact."

The scope and purpose of this new phase of geography—
the study of physical environment in its influence upon man—
are certain and well defined. It is a branch of economics,
with a direct bearing upon both history and sociology. " It
is the point of contact," observes Bryce,* " between the sciences of Nature taken all together and the branches of inquiry which deal with man and his institutions. Geography
gathers up, so to speak, the results which the geologist, the
botanist, the zoölogist,† and the meteorologist have obtained,
and presents them to the student of history, of economics, of
politics—and, we might even add, of law, of philology, and
of architecture—as an important part of the data from which

---

* Cf. The Relations of History and Geography, Contemporary Review, xlix, pp. 426–443 ; also, The Migrations of the Races of Men
considered Historically, ibid., lxii, pp. 128–149, reprinted in Smithsonian
Reports, 1893, p 567.

† See Payne's masterly discussion, in his History of America, of the
influence of the zoölogical poverty of the Western hemisphere upon
Aztec civilization.

he must start, and of the materials to which he will have to refer at many points in the progress of his researches." By reason of its very comprehensiveness, this study of geography may be entitled, perhaps, merely a mode of sociological investigation, allied to the graphical method in statistics. Thus Schiffner exemplifies it in treating of the relations between geography and jurisprudence.* "Every relation of life," he says, "which exists upon the earth and which may be plotted upon a map belongs, in one sense, to geography." Mill's definition, that "geography is the science of distribution," expresses the same idea. In this sense we have applied it to all manner of social phenomena in our subsequent chapters on Social Problems. Economic tendencies may be illustrated by it.† In linguistics and ethnology there is no limit to its suggestiveness.‡ In the analysis of political phenomena, in tracing the migrations of civilization—in fact, in almost every branch of science—the value of this mode of statistical or cartographical investigation is bound to become more and more fully recognised.

In every science which deals with man we may discover some trace of a division of opinion, similar to that which is responsible for the great controversy in which the biologists have recently been engaged. Two schools of investigators almost everywhere appear. One of these attaches the greatest importance to race, to transmitted characteristics or heredity; while the other regards this factor as subordinate to the influences of environment. This antagonism is clearly marked in the science of physical anthropology, and especially, for example, in the discussions over the causes of variations in stature among the different populations of the world. In the early days, when race was an adequate explanation for every-

---

* Ueber die Wechsel-Beziehungen zwischen der geographischen und der Rechts-Wissenschaft (Mitt. Geog. Gesell., Wien, 1874, pp. 100–113). Schroeder's Erläuterung zur Rechtskarte von Deutschland, Petermann Geog. Mitt., xvi, 1870, Tafel 7.

† Ashley, Introduction to English Economic History, ii, p. 304.

‡ Gerland's Atlas der Völkerkunde, for example.

thing, the problem was simple.   But since the doctrine of
evolution has shaken faith in what Cliffe-Leslie * terms " the
vulgar theory of race," another competent explanation is to
be found in the mere influence of outward circumstances.
Too often, however, the choice between these two possible
causes of the phenomenon, or their relative importance when
both are recognised as effective, will vary, in absence of more
definite proof, with the personal bias of the observer.   Thus
in France we find among the advocates of environmental
influence Villermé, Sanson, Bertillon, Durand de Gros,
Boudin, and De Quatrefages; while Broca, Lagneau, and
Topinard as strenuously maintain the priority of racial factors.
Endless examples of such diversity of opinion might be given:
In Italy it is Pagliani and Sormani *versus* Cortese and Lombroso; in Switzerland, Dunant *versus* Carret; in Germany,
to a lesser degree perhaps, Ranke *versus* Virchow; and in
Russia, Zograf *versus* Anutchin and Erismann.   Fortunately,
however, there is in anthropology a tendency among all the
later authorities—Beddoe, Collignon, Livi, and others—to
admit both causes as alike efficient according to circumstances.

The predisposition of observers to take these opposing
views on the same or similar evidence in respect of social
phenomena, may be shown by a few illustrations chosen at
random.   It appears at once in all discussions over the various forms of village community and of architectural types in
Europe.   Thus Meitzen ('95), as we shall see later, divides Germany into several sections, dominated respectively by what
he terms the German, the Celtic, the Roman, and the Slavic
type of village.   In comparing these, the haphazard grouping
of dwellings in the Germanic village is sharply contrasted with
the regular arrangement in the Slavic community, with its
houses about a central court or along a straight street: and
the regular division of the land into hides (*Hufenverfassung*)
owned in severalty, which characterizes the German type, is
as sharply differentiated from the holding of lands in com-

---

* Fortnightly Review, xvi, 1874, p. 736.

mon among the Slavs. Distinct from each in many respects is the Celtic type, which rules in South Germany and Bohemia. Approaching the subject in this way, the statistician may help in solving the vexed question of the origins of these populations, provided the village types are the constant accompaniment of certain racial types. But if these differences are merely the result of local circumstances, all their ethnological significance vanishes, and their study becomes of importance merely for purposes of reform or administration. In a similar investigation in France, the predilection for environmental explanations has apparently led to this latter conclusion.* Apply this method of reasoning to Germany. May not the utter lack of variety in the quality of plots for cultivation in the open plains inhabited by the Slavs, have led to habits of communal ownership, which are perpetuated in a new land through the selection of localities for habitation where such customs may persist unchanged? May not even the laws of inheritance be affected by the environment in the sandy sterile regions, to the end that primogeniture, and not equal division of the land among heirs, may be the only form of inheritance which will survive? Is not emigration of all the children but one a physical necessity? These are some of the questions which the geologist Cotta would answer in the affirmative,† and Baring-Gould acquiesces in his opinion.‡ The truth, probably, is a mean between these extremes, but in the absence of some recognised criterion our judgment will depend to a great extent upon personal predilections. Precisely the same conflict of opinion may prevent a final acceptance of some of the theories of Gomme with regard to the early inhabitants of Great Britain; for we may emphasize the ethnic

---

* Enquête sur les Conditions de l'Habitation en France. Les Maisons Types. Min. de l'In. Pub., des Beaux-Arts et des Cultes, Paris, 1894. Introduction by A. de Foville. *Vide* pp. 9–18, especially.

† Deutschlands Boden, sein Geologischer Bau und dessen Einwirkung auf das Leben des Menschen, Leipzig, 1858. In part ii, p. 63 *et seq.*, the geological factor in the distribution of the village community in Germany is fully discussed.

‡ History of Germany, p. 74.

element, as he is inclined to do, or we may prefer to interpret the form of the village more nearly in terms of environment, as does the geologist Tapley.*

A distinction must be made at this point between social
and physical environment. This is especially important because it is closely related to a further distinction between
the direct and the indirect effects of the *milieu*. Thus, that in
general under a system of peasant proprietorship, the size
of agricultural holdings should be larger on an infertile soil
than on rich bottom lands, is a direct result of environment;
for the size of holdings tends to vary according to their capacity for giving independent support to a household. But
the influence of environment is no less important, even though
less direct, when the infertile region produces social isolation, and thereby generates a conservative temperament which
resists all attempts at a subdivision of the patrimony.† The
result—a holding above the average size—is in each case the
same; and the ultimate cause, although in the second instance
working indirectly, is physical environment.

The importance of emphasizing the distinction between
the direct and the indirect influence of environment lies in the
fact that with advance in culture it is the latter, subtler aspect
of the *milieu* which becomes progressively of greater importance. All students would agree with Spencer that " feeble
unorganized societies are at the mercy of their surroundings ";
or with Kidd, that " the progress of savage man, such as it
is, is born strictly of the conditions in which he lives." Nature sets the life lines for the savage in climate; she determines his movements, stimulates or restrains his advance in
culture by providing or withholding the materials necessary
for such advance. The science of primitive ethnology is a

---

* The Village Community in Great Britain, p. 133 *et seq.*, and Jour-
Anth. Inst., iii, p. 32 *et seq.*, especially p. 45. All of the references on
this subject are accompanied by diagrams, maps, or illustrations. The
peculiarities of land tenure in the south Midland and other counties may
likewise be the product of a double set of causes.

† This is the cause assigned by Cliffe-Leslie for certain peculiarities in
land tenure in parts of France. Fortnightly Review, xvi, p. 740.

constant illustration of this fact even in the smallest details.*
It is only when we come to study peoples in more advanced
stages of culture that we find environment marking the line
of cleavage between two opposing views. One set of think-
ers—Ward, for example, in his Dynamic Sociology †—affirms
that at a certain point natural selection seizes upon mind as
the dominant and vital factor in progress. Society passes
from the " natural " to the " artificial " stage. Based upon this
thesis, the study of environment, and even of race, becomes
more and more retrospective—even, so to speak, archæological.

The opponents of this optimistic view take the ground that
civilization is merely a result of adaptation to environment,
physical as well as political. Once more to quote Mr. Bryce :
" The very multiplication of the means at his [man's] disposal for profiting by what Nature supplies, brings him into
ever closer and more complex relations with her. The variety of her resources, differing in different regions, prescribes
the kind of industry for which each spot is fitted ; and the
competition of nations, growing always keener, forces each
to maintain itself in the struggle by using to the utmost
every facility for the production or for the transportation of
products." ‡

It would be easy to multiply examples of the effect of
progress in thus compelling specialization—the utilization of
each advantage to the last degree—thus illustrating the force
of environment even in the highest civilization. When the
vine was introduced into California the settlers tried to cul-
tivate it in the north and in the south, along the rivers and
on the hillsides, near the coast and in the interior. The grape
rapidly took root and grew, but its very prosperity in some

---

* This is ingeniously worked out by Shaler in his Nature and Man in
North America.

† Cf. Patten's Theory of Social Forces, in his discussion of race and
physical environment.

‡ A new chapter on this subject added to the third edition of The
American Commonwealth, ii, p. 450. The same view is well expressed
by Strachey in Proc. Roy. Geog. Soc., xxi, p. 209 et seq.; by Geikie in
ibid., 1879, p. 442, and in Macmillan's Magazine for March, 1882.

places threatened its culture in others.*   Some valleys soon
proved too hot to produce wine which would sell in competition with the best; some soils were too heavy, others too
moist.   Certain regions produced sherries, while others served
better for port wines.   To insure success, the conditions had
to be most diligently investigated each year, and it was precisely because all were successful that specialization was bound
to follow as a matter of course.

A similar example is the progressive differentiation in
agriculture taking place all over the United States to-day.
Once it was possible to point to the corn, cotton, wheat, and
rye belts, and to show a massing of each crop, regardless of
local circumstances.   But, in virtue of the severe international
competition, these great aggregations of similar crops are
breaking up, and local specialization is the rule.†   It is precisely because nearly all Japan is favoured as a silk-producing
country that her best silk culture is forced to localize itself.‡
Less than a quarter of a century ago a difference of an inch
in the length of the cotton staple was of slight importance;
but in 1894, with improved manufactures, Egypt found a ready
market in the United States—the home of cotton—for thirty-
five million pounds of her product.   The same principle holds
true of mechanical industry.   When the manufacture of cotton was introduced into the United States it was indiscriminately prosecuted wherever there were water power and
labour.   At last it was perceived that climatic influences were
of great importance in the finer fabrics, and to-day there are
indications that the work of this grade is tending to localize
itself along the south shore of New England.#   Here, again,
it is not any lack of ability to manufacture in the less favoured
spots, but the conspicuous advantages in the new localities,
that finally produce the new results.   Each advance in skill
makes the influence of local peculiarities more keenly felt.   In
short, we have here merely another illustration of the eco-

---

* Fortnightly Review, vol. liii, p. 401 *et seq.*
† Publications Amer. Stat. Assoc., December, 1893, p. 492 *et seq.*
‡ Jour. Royal Geog. Soc., xl, p. 340.
# New York Evening Post, March 30, 1895.

nomic advantages of division of labour. Viewed in this wise, environment assumes a greater measure of importance with each increment of progress and civilization. The fact seems to us to be incontestable.

With all its possibilities, this study of physical environment must at the outset clearly recognise its own limitations, arising from the power of purely historical elements, of personality, of religious enthusiasm, and of patriotism. By all the laws of geographical probability, England's historical influence on France ought to have been greatest in Normandy, while in reality Aquitaine was the centre of English continental activity. That Yorkshire and not Kent should to-day exhibit the strongest infusion of Norman blood in England is also a geographical anomaly. Again, take the following case in connection with the distribution of population: In Brittany a primitive, non-absorbent rock formation affords numerous natural reservoirs to hold the abundant rains, and the population is scattered broadcast in little hamlets. In the department of the Marne, on the other hand, where a calcareous soil quickly absorbs the scanty rainfall, the people are bunched about the springs and rivers. Accordingly, the two districts differ widely in their percentages of urban population and in all the social characteristics dependent thereon.* It would seem as if the relation of geological and social conditions here discovered might be formulated into a general law, through which the course of settlement in a new country might be predicted. But the United States promptly sets such a law at defiance. For here it is on the primitive rock formations, in the area of plentiful rains, that the New England village is at home. It is in the drier areas of the West, and even on their clayey soils, that population is most widely scattered. Thus the force of custom and tradition proves itself fully able to withstand for a time the limitations of physical conditions.

Yet, even if it does not reach the grade of a predictive science, the study of the *milieu* can not be neglected. One

---

* For illustrations in detail, see Levasseur, Bulletin de l'Inst. Internat. de Statistique, iii, liv. 3 (1888), p. 73.

of its aims will always be " to discover whether the historical development of a people is in harmony with its environment, and, if not, whether it is a plus or minus factor in progress." Viewed in this light, geography derives a new significance from the standpoint of human interests. It deserves a primary place in all departments of research which have to do with man or with his institutions. This we hope to be able to prove in detail for the continent of Europe.

CHAPTER II.

THE historian of The Norman Conquest of England was very fond of contrasting the east and the west of Europe. He maintained that the political unrest which underlies the Eastern question was partly due to the utter lack of physical assimilation among the people of the Balkan states; that, in other words, nationality had no foundation in race. This was undoubtedly true to some extent; and yet even in the west the formation of these boasted nationalities is so recent that it accords but slightly with the lines of physical descent. All over the continent there exist radical differences of blood between the closest neighbours, so that the west is merely a step in advance of the east after all. It is a trite observation that all over Europe population has been laid down in different strata more or less horizontal. In the east of Europe this stratification is recent and distinct. West of the Austro-Hungarian Empire the primitive layers have become metamorphosed, to borrow a geological term, by the fusing heat of nationality and the pressure of civilization. The population of the east of Europe structurally is as different from that of the west to the naked eye as, to complete our simile, sandstone is from granite; nevertheless, despite their apparent homogeneity, on analysis we may still read the history of these western nations by the aid of natural science from the purely physical characteristics of their people alone.

To the ordinary observer a uniform layer of population is spread over the continent as waters cover the earth. In reality, while apparently at rest, this great body of men reveals itself to-day in constant motion internally; * for population is as certain to follow social and economic opportunity as water is to run down hill. Currents and counter-currents sweep hither and thither, some rising and others falling, with now and then a quiet pool or eddy where alone population is really in a quiescent state. These movements are not transient. Some, to be sure, may be of local and special origin, but others are due to the operation of great natural causes. These latter have been at work for centuries, determined by the unchanging economic character and the geography of the continent. They are shifting suddenly now with modern industrial life, but they have persisted until the present through generations. Proof of this antiquity we have; since, where Nature has isolated little pools of population, we may still find men with an unbroken ancestral lineage reaching back to a time when the climate, the flora and fauna of Europe were far different from those which prevail to-day. This may be shown, not by historical documents, for these men antedate all written history; but by physical traits which are older than institutions and outlast them all as well.

This varied population, as we see it to-day, is in its racial composition the effect of a long train of circumstances, historical upon the surface, social it may be in part, but at bottom also geographical. From the study of this population as it stands, and from the migrations even now going on within it, we may analyze these permanent environmental influences—many of which have hitherto been neglected by students of institutions—which have been operative for centuries, and which have persisted in spite of political events or else have indirectly given rise to them. Progress in social life has not been cataclysmic; it has not taken place by kangaroo-leaps of political or social reforms on paper; but it has gone on slowly, painfully perhaps, and almost imperceptibly, by the constant pressure of slight but fixed forces. Our problem is to examine certain of these fundamental mainsprings of movement,

---

* Ravenstein, 1885, for the British Isles, and Rauchberg, 1893, for Austria-Hungary, give interesting graphical representations of these undercurrents of migration at the present time.

especially the influence of the physical environment; and to do it by means of the calipers, the measuring tape, and the colour scale. Science proceeds best from the known present to the remote past, in anthropology as in geology or astronomy. The study of living men should precede that of the dead. This shall be our method. Fixing our attention upon the present population, we shall then be prepared to interpret the physical migrations and to some extent the social movements which have been going on for generations in the past.

Let us at the outset avoid the error of confusing community of language with identity of race.* Nationality may often follow linguistic boundaries, but race bears no necessary relation whatever to them. Two essentials of political unity are bound up in identity of language: namely, the necessity of a free interchange of ideas by means of a common mental circulating medium; and, secondly, the possession of a fund of common traditions in history or literature. The first is largely a practical consideration; the second forms the subtle essence of nationality itself. For these reasons we shall find language corresponding with political affiliations far more often than with ethnic boundaries. Politics may indeed become a factor in the physical sense, especially when re-enforced by language. It can not be denied that assimilation in blood often depends upon identity of speech, or that political frontiers sometimes coincide with a racial differentiation of population. The canton of Schaffhausen lies north of the Rhine, a deep inset into the grand duchy of Baden, yet its people, though isolated from their Swiss countrymen across the river, are intensely patriotic. In race as in political affairs they are distinctly divided from their immediate German neighbours.

---

* A full discussion of this point is offered by Broca, 1862 c ; Sayce, 1875 ; Freeman, 1879 ; and in the brilliant essay on Race and Tradition, in Darmesteter, 1895. See also Taylor, 1890, p. 204. The first protest against the indiscriminate use of the word " race " came from Edwards, 1829, in his letters to Thierry, author of the Histoire des Gaulois. It led to the foundation of the first Société d'Ethnologie at Paris as a result.

4

Mentally holding to the Swiss people, they have unconsciously preserved or generated during three hundred years of political union a physical individuality akin to them as well.* Thus it is possible that a sense of nationality once aroused may become an active factor through selection in the anthropological sense. Nevertheless, this phenomenon requires more time than most political history has at its disposition, so that

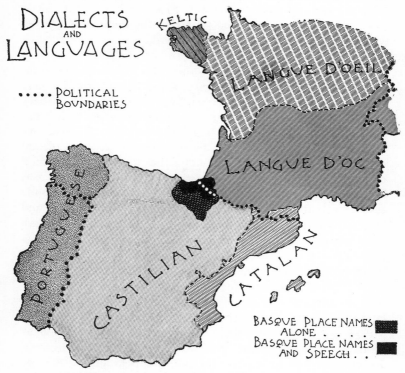

in the main our proposition remains true. Despite the political hatred of the French for the German, no appreciable effect in a physical sense has yet resulted, nor will it until the lapse of generations.

---

* Kollmann, 1881 a, p. 18, finds the blonde types among them less than half as frequent as in Baden. Schaffhausen affiliates with Switzerland in stature also, as we shall show.

Consideration of our linguistic map of the southwest of Europe will serve to illustrate some of the potent political influences which make for community of language without thereby indicating any influence of race. The Iberian Peninsula, now divided between two nationalities, the Spanish and the Portuguese, is, as we shall subsequently show, in the main homogeneous racially—more so, in fact, than any other equally large area of Europe. The only exception is in the case of the Basques, whom we must consider by themselves. This physically uniform population, exclusive of the Basque, makes use to-day of three distinct languages, all Romance or Latin in their origin, to be sure; but so far differentiated from one another as to be mutually unintelligible. It is said, for example, that the Castilian peasant can more readily understand Italian than the dialect of his neighbour and compatriot, the Catalan. The gap between the Portuguese and the Castilian or true Spanish is less deep and wide, perhaps; but the two are still very distinct and radically different from the language spoken in the eastern provinces of Spain. The Catalan speech is, as the related tints upon our map imply, only a sub-variety of the Provençal or southern French language. The people of the eastern Balearic Islands speaking this Catalan tongue differ from the French in language far less than do the Corsicans, who are politically French, though linguistically Italian.*

At first glance all this seems to belie our assertion that unity of language is often an historical product of political causes. For it may justly be objected that the Portuguese type of language, although in general limited by the political boundary along the east, has crossed the northern frontier and now prevails throughout the Spanish provinces of Galicia; or again, that the French-Spanish political frontier has been powerless to restrain the advance, far toward the Strait of

---

* Morel-Fatio is best on Catalan. Its limits in France are given by Hovelacque, 1891. See also Tubino, 1877, p. 108. For the Basque, Broca, 1875, is best; and for Langue d'Oc., Tourtolon and Bringuier, 1876. Gröbers's Grundriss gives many interesting details on Spanish and Portuguese.

Gibraltar, of the Catalan speech, closely allied as we have said, to the dialects of Provence in southern France; that not even the slight line of demarcation between these last two lies along the Pyrenean political boundary, but considerably to the north of it, so that Catalan is to-day spoken over nearly a whole department in France; and, lastly, that the Basque language, utterly removed from any affiliation with all the rest, lies neither on one side nor the other of this same Pyrenean frontier, but extends down both slopes of the mountain range, an insert into the national domains of both France and Spain. . These objections are, however, the very basis of our contention that language and nationality often stand in a definite relation to one another: for, if we examine the history of Spain and Portugal, we shall discover that historical causes alone have determined this curious linguistic distribution. The sole discoverable influence of language upon race appears in the Iberian character of the Catalan corner of France. It really seems as if intercourse around the eastern end of the Pyrenees, facilitated by community of language, had produced a distinctly Iberian type of population on French soil.*

The three great languages in the Iberian Peninsula—Castilian or Spanish, Portuguese, and Catalan—correspond respectively to the three political agencies which drove out the Moorish invaders from the ninth century onward, from three different directions and from distinct geographical centres. The mountains of Galicia, in the extreme northwest, served as the nucleus of the resistant power which afterward merged itself in the Portuguese monarchy. Castile in the central north was the asylum of the refugees, expelled from the south by the Saracens, who afterward reasserted themselves in force under the leadership of the kings of Castile. Aragon in the northeast, whose people were mainly of Catalan speech, which they had derived from the south of France, during their temporary forced sojourn in that country while the Moors were in active control of Spain, was a base of supplies for the third

---

* Olóriz, 1894 a, p. 180. See also p. 165, *infra*. Schimmer, 1884, p. 8, finds similar evidence of a reaction of language upon race in Austria-Hungary.

organized opposition to the invaders. Each of these political units, as it reconquered territory from the Moors, imposed its official speech upon the people, where it remains to-day. Were the present Spanish nation old enough and sufficiently unified; were the component parts of it more firmly knitted together by education, modern means of transport, and economic interests, this disunity of speech might disappear. Unfortunately, the character of the Iberian Peninsula is such—arid, infertile, and sparsely populated in the interior—that these languages socially and commercially turn their backs to one another.* Of necessity, they do this also along the frontier between Spain and Portugal. The eyes of each community are directed not toward Madrid, but toward the sea; for there on the fertile littoral alone is there the economic possibility of a population sufficiently dense for unification. Thus the divergence of language is truly the expression of natural causes working through political ones, which promise to perpetuate the differences for some time. The modern political boundaries in the Iberian Peninsula are even less important than the linguistic ones as a test of race. For, as Freeman says, if in the fifteenth century Isabella of Castile had married the King of Portugal instead of the King of Aragon, the peninsula would to-day be divided, not into Spain and Portugal; but into two kingdoms of Spain and Aragon respectively, and Portugal as such would have disappeared from the map. As for the Basques, they have been politically independent both of the French and the Spaniards until within a few years, and have been enabled to preserve their unique speech largely for this reason. But now that their political autonomy has begun to disappear, the official Spanish is pressing the Basque language so forcibly that it seems to be everywhere on the retreat.

Friction is generally incident to a divergence of political from linguistic boundaries. Especially is this the case where a small minority of alien speech is rudely torn up by the roots and transferred in its political allegiance. Alsace-Lorraine

---

* Fischer's map in Verh. Ges. für Erdkunde, xx, 1893, map 3, brings out this coast strip clearly.

exemplifies this contingency. Turn to our map on page 231, and it will be seen that the frontier between France and Germany follows the bounds of speech approximately along the west of southern Alsace. It departs widely from it all across Lorraine, which is about equally divided in its language. There can be little doubt that the acute unrest in this province would be greatly relieved if the two frontiers, linguistic and political, were the same. The natural boundary of nationality would certainly seem to lie where the people are set apart from one another in respect of this primary element of social intercourse. This linguistic boundary has, moreover, persisted in its present form for so many generations as to give decided proof of its permanence. And yet, despite this persistence through many political changes, it has absolutely no ethnic significance. The boundary of racial types bears no relation to it in any way, as we shall see.

We have seen that community of language is often imposed as a result of political unity. Thus it is, after all, rather a by-product, so that it often fails even here to indicate nationality. Its irresponsibility in respect both of nationality and of race is clearly indicated by the present linguistic status of the British Isles.* As our map shows, the Keltic language is now spoken in the remote and mountainous portions of Wales, Scotland, and Ireland, as well as across the English Channel in French Brittany. It is everywhere on the retreat before the English language, as it has been ever since the Norman Conquest. Are we to infer from this that in these several places we have to do with vestiges of a so-called Keltic *race* which possesses any physical traits in common? Far from it! For, although in a few places racial differences occur somewhere near the linguistic frontiers, as in Wales and Brittany, they are all the more misleading elsewhere for that reason. Within the narrow confines of this spoken Keltic language are to be found populations characterized by all the

---

* For exact details and maps of the spoken languages, *vide* Ravenstein, 1879. For France, Broca, 1868 a; Andree, 1879 b and 1885 a; and Sebillot, 1886, give maps and details. See our map on p. 100. Andree gives the boundary in France in the twelfth century, showing the retreat clearly.

extremes of the races of Europe. The dark-haired, round-faced Breton peasant speaking the Kymric branch of the Keltic tongue in France is, as we shall hope to demonstrate, physically as far removed from the Welshman who uses the same language, as from the tall and light-haired Norman neighbour at home who knows nothing of a Keltic speech at all.

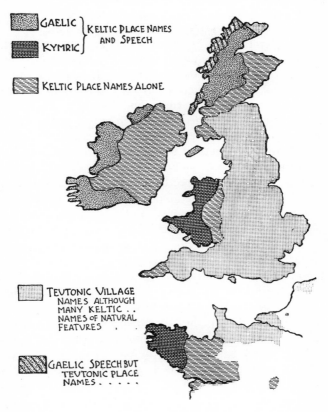

The Welshman in turn is physically allied to the Irish and distinct from many of the Gaelic-speaking Scotch, although these last two speak even the same subtype of the Keltic language. Such racial affinity as obtains between certain of these people is in utter defiance of the bonds of speech. The

Breton should be more at home among his own folk in the
high Alps in respect of race, even although he could hold no
converse with the Swiss people in their own tongue.

A sense of nationality, "memories of the past and hopes
for the future," may indeed become highly developed in absence of any community of language at all. The Walloons
and Flemish are equally ardent Belgian patriots, despite their
linguistic differences.* Switzerland offers us an interesting
illustration of the same phenomenon. While the greater part
of the confederation is of German speech, as our map on page
284 shows, both Italian and French coexist peacefully alongside of it, to say nothing of the primitive Romansch, of which
we shall speak later.† There is no such linguistic repulsion in
Switzerland as between German and Czech in Bohemia, or
Italian and Slavonic in the Adriatic provinces of the Austrian
Empire. This exception to our law, that nationality and language are alike products of social contact, is not hard to explain. Primarily, Swiss nationality exists despite linguistic
differences, because the three languages exist on terms of entire equality. The confederated form of government, with a
high degree of local autonomy in the cantons, leaves each
linguistic contingent in no fear of annihilation by its neighbour. The Italian in Ticino, moreover, is entirely isolated
by the Alpine chain ; the boundary of speech runs along the
mountain crests, so that geographical and political circumstances alike insure its perpetuation free from disturbance.
The reason for the present boundary of French and German
is more difficult to explain. It runs often at right angles to
the topography, as where, for example, our map shows it cutting off the upper Rhone Valley in Valais. Historical factors,
as in Spain, must be invoked as a cause. The Burgundian
kingdom, radiating its influence from Geneva, undoubtedly
imposed its French speech upon the whole western highlands ;
and the present boundaries of the French language undoubt-

---

* See p. 162, *infra*.

† On languages in the Alps, see Charnock, 1873 ; Schneller, 1877 ;
Bresslau, 1881 ; Galanti, 1885 ; Bidermann, 1886 ; Zemmrich, 1894 a;
Andree, 1879 a and 1885 b, etc.

edly are a heritage from this Burgundian rule.* The Swiss nation is indeed an artificial one, as Freeman says; it offers an example of both political and linguistic adoptions of a unique sort. One point is certain. Such racial differences as exist in Switzerland are absolutely independent of all these linguistic boundaries. We seek in vain for any evidence of physical differences along these lines. South of the Alps to-day there are considerable communities still bearing the German speech and customs, evidence of the Teutonic invasions of historic times. These people have become so completely absorbed that they are not distinguishable physically from their Italian neighbours.† There are indeed spots in Italy where German racial traits survive, but they are quite remote from these islets of Teutonic language, as we shall see.

If we turn to the east of Europe, we encounter all sorts of linguistic anomalies, beside which European ethnography west of Vienna appears relatively simple.‡ The Bulgarians have entirely abandoned their original Finnic speech in favour of Slavic. The Roumanian language, Latin in its affinities, is entirely a result of wholesale adoption: and a new process of change of speech like that in Bulgaria threatens now to oust this Roumanian and replace it also by a Slavic dialect.# Magyar, the language of the Hungarians, spreading toward the east, displaced by German, which is forcing its way in from the northwest, is also on the move. Beneath all this hurry-skurry of speech the racial lines remain as fixed as ever. Language, in short, as a great philologist has put it, "is not a test of race. It is a test of social contact." Waves of language have swept over Europe, leaving its racial foundations as undisturbed as are the sands of the sea during a storm. The linguistic status of the British Isles, above described, shows us one of these waves—the Keltic—which is, to put it somewhat flippantly, now upon its last lap on the shores of the western ocean.

---

* The French language also extends far across the Italian frontier into Piedmont, perhaps for the same reason. (Pullé, 1898, p. 66, and map ii.)

† Livi, 1896 a, p. 147, and 1886, p. 70 (reprint).

‡ Topinard, 1886 c, is fine on this. See also chap. xv, *infra*.

Xenopol, 1895.

We may discover how slippery speech is upon men's tongues in yet another way—namely, by observing it actually on the move in a physically quiescent population, leaving a trail behind to mark its passage. Language becomes truly sedentary when a distinctive name is given by men to a place of settlement; it may be a clearing in the virgin wilderness or a reconstructed village after a clearing away by conquest of the former possessors. In either case the result is the same. The name, be it Slavic, Keltic, or other, tends to remain as a permanent witness that a people speaking such a tongue once passed that way. A place name of this kind may and often does outlive the spoken language in that locality. It remains as a monument to mark the former confines of the speech, since it can no more migrate than can the houses and barns within the town. Of course, newcomers may adapt the old name to the peculiar pronunciation of their own tongue, but the savour of antiquity gives it a persistent power which is very great. For this reason we find that after every migration of a spoken language, there follows a trail of such place names to indicate a former condition. Our maps, both of the British Isles and of Spain, show this phenomenon very clearly. In the one case, the Keltic speech has receded before the Teutonic influence, leaving a belt of its peculiar village names behind. In the other, the Basque place names, far outside the present limits of the spoken Basque, even as far as the Ebro River, indicate no less clearly that the speech is on the move toward the north, where no such intermediate zone exists.* Similarly, all over Russia, Finnic place names still survive as witness of a language and people submerged by the immigrant Slavs.†

Then, after the village names have been replaced by the newcomers, or else become so far mutilated as to lose their identity, there still linger the names of rivers, mountains, bays, headlands, and other natural features of the country. Hallowed by folklore or superstition, their outlandish sounds only serve the more to insure them against disturbance. All over

---

* Broca, 1875, p. 43; Bladé, 1869, p. 381. See also chap. viii, *infra*.
† Smirnov, 1892, p. 105.

England such names are not uncommon, pointing to a remote past when the Keltic speech was omnipresent. Nay more, not only from all over the British Isles, but from a large area of the mainland of Europe as well, comes testimony of this kind to a former wide expansion of this Keltic language. Such geographical names represent the third and final stage of the erosion of language prior to its utter disappearance. Nevertheless, as we shall show, the physical features of men outlive even these, so inherent and deep rooted have they become. It is indeed true, as Rhys [84], himself a linguist, has aptly put it, that " skulls are harder than consonants, and races lurk behind when languages slip away."

It appears that language rests even more lightly upon men than do traditions and folk customs. We find that it disappears first under pressure, leaving these others along with physical traits, perhaps, as survivors. There are several reasons for this mobility of speech. One is that languages rarely coalesce.* They may borrow and mutilate, but they seldom mix if very distinct in type. The superior, or perhaps official, language simply crowds the other out by force. Organization in this case counts for more than numbers. In this way the language of the Isle de France has prevailed over the whole country despite its once limited area, because it had an aggressive dynasty behind it. Panslavism in Russia at the present time, with the omnipotence of officialism, is, in a similar way, crowding the native Finnic and Lithuanian languages out of the Baltic provinces; although less than ten per cent of the inhabitants are Russians.† Language, moreover, requires for its maintenance unanimous consent, and not mere majority rule ; for, so soon as the majority changes its speech, the minority must acquiesce. Not so with folk tales or fireside customs. People cling to these all the more pertinaciously as they become rare. And still less so with physical

---

* *Vide* interesting discussion of this point in detail in A. H. Keane, Ethnology, pp. 198 *et seq*. Taylor, 1890, p. 275, gives examples of difficulties in pronunciation which seem to be hereditary.

† Leroy-Beaulieu, 1893–'96, i, p. 70. See also on Little Russia, ibid., p. 120. On the Tatar adoptions of language by Finns, see p. 360 *infra*.

traits of race. Many of these last are not apparent to the eye.
They are sometimes unsuspected until they have well-nigh
disappeared. Men mingle their blood freely. They inter-
marry, and a mixed type results. Thus, racially, organization
avails nothing against the force of numbers. In linguistic
affairs nothing succeeds like success; but in physical anthropology impetus counts for nothing.

It is impossible to measure race by the geographical distribution of arts or customs; for they also, like language,
migrate in complete independence of physical traits. With the
Keltic language spread the use of polished stone implements
and possibly the custom of incineration, but this did not by
any means imply a new race of men. The best opinion to-day
holds the Keltic culture and language to have represented
merely a dominant aristocracy, forming but a small proportion
of the population. It is not unlikely that this ruling class introduced new arts along with their speech, although it is still
not directly proved. At times a change of culture appears,
directly accompanied by a new physical type, as when bronze
was introduced into Britain,* or when the European races
brought the use of iron to America. More often are the ad-
vents of a new culture and a physical type merely contemporaneous. Such an event occurred when the domestication
of animals seemed roughly to coincide with the appearance in
Europe of a brachycephalic population from the east. No
one is competent to affirm, notwithstanding this fact, that the
new race actually introduced the culture.† Of course, contact is always implied in such migration of an art, although
a few stragglers may readily have been the cause of the spread
of the custom. This may not be true in respect to the migration of religions, or in any similar case where determined
opposition has to be overcome and where conquest means
substitution; but in simple arts of immediate obvious application, copying takes place naturally. The art spreads in direct proportion to its immediate value to the people concerned.
No missionaries are needed to introduce firearms among the

---

* Thurnam, 1863, p. 129 *et seq.*
† *Cf.* Mortillet, 1879 a, p. 232.

aborigines. The art speedily outruns race. Moreover, cultures like languages seldom mix as men do. Parts may be accepted here and there, but complete amalgamation seldom results. The main effect of the contact of two distinct cultures is to produce stratification. The common people become the conservators of the old; the upper classes hold to the new. It is a case of folklore and superstition *versus* progressive ideas. Here, as in respect of language, arts and customs become reliable as a test of race only when found fixed in the soil or in some other way prevented from migration.

Always be careful lest you attach too much importance to the statements of historical and classical writers in their accounts of migrations and of conquests.* They wrote of men organized in tribes; it is our province to study them individually in populations. We should beware of the travellers' tales of the ancients. Pliny describes a people of Africa with no heads and with eyes and mouth in the breast—a statement which to the anthropologist appears to be open to the suspicion of exaggeration. Even when conquest has undoubtedly taken place, it does not imply a change of physical type in the region affected. We are dealing with great masses of men near the soil, to whom it matters little whether the emperor be Macedonian, Roman, or Turk. Till comparatively recent times the peasantry of Europe were as little affected by changes of dynasty as the Chinese people have been touched by the recent war in the East. To them personally, victory or defeat meant little except a change of tax-gatherers.

In this connection it should be borne in mind that conquest often affected but a small area of each country—namely, its richest and most populous portions. The foreigner seldom penetrated the outlying districts. He went, as did the Spaniards in South America, where gold was gathered in the great cities. France, as we know, was affected very unevenly by the Roman conquest. It was not the portion nearest to Rome, but the richest though remote one, which yielded to the Roman rule to the greatest extent. At all events, the

---

* Bertrand, 1873, is fine in criticism of these; also Bertrand and Reinach, 1894, chapter i.

Roman colonists in Gaul and Brittany have disappeared, to leave no trace. The Vandals in Africa have left no sign— neither hide nor hair, in a literal sense.* Aquitaine was held by the English for three centuries, but no anthropological evidence of it remains to-day.† The Tatar rule in Russia and the Saracen conquest of Spain were alike unproductive of physical results, so far as we can discover. Both alike constituted what Bryce aptly terms merely a "top dressing" of population. The Burgundian kingdom was changed merely in respect of its rulers; and spots in Italy like Benevento, ruled by the Lombards for five hundred years, are, in respect of physical characteristics, to-day precisely like all the region round about them.‡

The truth is that migrations or conquests to be physically effective must be domestic and not military. Wheeler rightly observes, speaking of the Eastern question, that "much that has been called migration was movement not of peoples, but power." Guizot's eighth lecture upon the History of Civilization in France contains some wholesome advice upon this point. Colonization or infiltration, as the case may be, to be physically effective must take place by wholesale, and it must include men, women, and children. The Roman conquests seldom proceeded thus, in sharp contrast to the people of the East, who migrated in hordes, colonizing incidentally on the way. The British Isles, anthropologically, were not affected by the Roman invasion, nor until the Teutons came by thousands. There is nothing surprising in this. In anthropology, as in jurisprudence, possession is nine points of the law. Everything is on the side, physically speaking, of the native. He has been acclimated, developing peculiarities proper to his surroundings. He is free from the costly work of transporting helpless women and children. The immense majority of his fellows are like him in habits, tastes, and circumstances. The invader, if he remains at all, dilutes his blood by half as soon as he marries and settles, with the prospect that it will be quartered in the next generation. He can not

---

* Broca, 1876.   † Collignon, 1895, p. 71.   ‡ Livi, 1896 a, p. 166.

exterminate the vanquished as savages do, even if he would. Nay more, it is not to his advantage to do so, for servile labour is too valuable to sacrifice in that way. Self-interest triumphs over race hatred. The conqueror may indeed kill off a score or two of the leading men, and the chroniclers may call it exterminating a tribe, but the probability is that all the women and most of the men will be spared. In the subsequent process of acclimatization, moreover, the ranks of the invading host are decimated. The newcomer struggles against the combined distrust of most of his neighbours, as well as with the migratory instinct which brought him there in the first place. If he excels in intelligence, he may continue to rule, but his line is doomed to extinction unless kept alive by constant re-enforcements. It has been well said that the greatest obstacle to the spread of man is man. Collignon is right in his affirmation that " when a race is well seated in a region, fixed to the soil by agriculture, acclimatized by natural selection, and sufficiently dense, it opposes an enormous resistance to absorption by newcomers, whoever they may be."

Population being thus persistent by reason of its indestructibility, a peculiar province of our study will be to show the relation which has arisen between the geography of a country and the character of its people and its institutions. Historians have not failed in the past to point out the ways in which the migrations and conquests of nations have been determined by mountain chains and rivers. They have too often been content merely to show that the immediate direction of the movement has been dependent upon topographical features. We shall endeavour to go a step further in indicating the manner in which the real ethnic character of the population of Europe has been determined by its environment, not only directly, but indirectly as well, entirely apart from political or historical events as such, and as a result of social forces which are still at work. Thus, for example, we shall show that the physical character of the population often changes at the line which divides the hills from the plains. The national boundary may run along the crest of the mountain chain, while the ethnic lines skirt its base where the economic character of the country changes. In other cases, the racial may be equally far from the political boundary, since the river bed may delimit the state, while the racial divisions follow the watershed.*

Modern political boundaries will, therefore, avail us but little; they are entirely a superficial product; for, as we insist, nationality bears no constant or necessary relation whatever to race. It is an artificial result of political causes to a great extent. Political boundaries, moreover, may not even be national; they are too often merely governmental. From the moment an individual is born into the world, he finds himself exposed to a series of concentric influences which swing in upon him with overwhelming force. The ties of family lie nearest: the bonds and prejudices of caste follow close upon; then comes the circle of party affiliations and of religious denomination. Language encompasses all these about. The element of nationality lying outside of them all, is as largely the result of historical and social causes as any of the others, with the sole exception of family perhaps. Race may conceivably cut across almost all of these lines at right angles. It underlies them all. It is, so to speak, the raw material from which each of these social patterns is made up. It may become an agent to determine their intensity and motive, as the nature of the fibre determines the design woven in the stuff. It may proceed in utter independence of them all, being alone freed from the disturbing influences of human will and choice. Race denotes what man *is;* all these other details of social life represent what man *does.* Race harmonizes, at all events, less with the bounds of nationality than with any other—certainly less so than with those either of social caste or religious affiliation. That nearly a half of France, while peopled by ardent patriots, is as purely Teutonic racially as the half of Germany itself, is a sufficient example of the truth of our assertion. The best illustration of the greater force of religious prejudices to give rise to a dis-

---

* Regnault, 1892, offers an interesting discussion of the relation of topography and race.

tinct physical type is afforded by the Jews. Social ostracism, based upon differences of belief in great measure, has sufficed to keep them truer to a single racial standard, perhaps, than any other people of Europe.* Another example of religious isolation, re-enforced by geographical seclusion, may be seen among the followers of the mediæval reformer, Juan Valdés. Persecuted for generations, driven high up into the Alps of northwestern Italy, these people show to-day a notable difference in physical type from all their neighbours.† The Huguenot colony about La Rochelle, together with English influence, seems also to have left its impress in the present blondness of the department of Charente Inférieure.‡ The Armenians also, constituting an island of Christianity surrounded by alien beliefs, are, as we shall see, highly individualized physically. Religious isolation is the cause beyond doubt.

Political geography is, for all these reasons, entirely distinct from racial and social geography, as well in its principles as in its results. Many years ago a course was delivered before the Lowell Institute by M. Guyot, the great geographer, subsequently published under the caption The Earth and Man. It created a profound sensation at the time, as it pointed out the intimate relation which exists between geography and history; but it was of necessity extremely vague, and its results were in the main unsatisfactory. Its value lay mainly in its novel point of view. Since this time a completely new science dealing with man has arisen, capable of as great precision as any of the other natural sciences. It has humanized geography, so to speak, even as M. Guyot did in his time and generation; and it has enriched history and sociology in a new and unexpected way.

We have now to bring still other elements—anthropology and sociology—into touch with these other two, to form a combination possessed of singular suggestiveness. It affords at once a means for the quantitative measurement of racial

---

* Renan, 1883, offers a brilliant discussion of this. See also our chapter on the Jews, later.

† Mendini, 1890; Livi, 1896 a, p. 135.

‡ Topinard, 1889 a, p. 522.

5

migrations and social movements; and it yields a living picture of the population—the raw material—in and through which all history must of necessity work. Studying men as merely physical types of the higher animals, we are able to trace their movements as we do those of the lower species. We may correlate these results with the physical geography and the economic character of the environment; and then, at last, superpose the social phenomena in their geographical distribution. We attempt to discover relations either of cause and effect, or at least of parallelism and similarity due to a common cause which lies back of them all—perhaps in human nature itself. Science advances by the revelation of new relationships between things. In the present case the hope of perhaps striking a spark, by knocking these divers sciences together, has induced men to collect materials, often in ignorance of the exact use to which they might be ultimately put. To show the results which have already been achieved is the task to which we have to address ourselves.

The observations upon which our conclusions for Europe are to rest cover some twenty-five million or more individuals, a large fraction being school children, a goodly proportion, however, consisting of conscripts taken from the soil directly to the recruiting commissions of the various European armies. The labour involved in merely collecting, to say nothing of tabulating, this mass of material is almost superhuman; and we can not too highly praise the scientific zeal which has made possible our comfortable work of comparing this accumulated data. As an example of the difficulties which have been encountered, let me quote from a personal letter from Dr. Ammon, one of the pioneers in this work, who measured thousands of recruits in the Black Forest of Germany. " One naturally," he writes, " is reluctant to undertake a four or six weeks' trip with the commission in winter, with snow a metre deep, living in the meanest inns in the little hamlets, and moving about every two to five days. The official inspectors must not be retarded in their work, as the Ministry of War attaches that condition to their permission to view the recruits. Many of those rejected for service are dismissed by the surgeons at a glance, but I must make measurements on all alike. Only when the doctor stops to make an auscultation or to test the vision do I have a moment's respite. They are sent to my room from the medical inspector at the rate of two hundred in three hours, sometimes two hundred and forty; and on all these men I must make many measurements, while rendering instant decision upon the colour of the hair and eyes. The mental effort involved in forming so many separate judgments in such quick succession often brings me near fainting at the close of the session."

Of course, where observations are privately made, to obtain the consent of the owner of the characteristics is the main obstacle to be overcome. To make the subject understand what is wanted, is impossible; for it would involve a full discussion of the Keltic question or of the origin of the Aryans, which, after the first one hundred cases, becomes tiresome. The colour of the hair and eyes, of course, may be noted in passing, and observers may station themselves on crowded thoroughfares and easily collect a large mass of material. I have myself found profit and entertainment on the Fall River boats in running up some columns from my unsuspecting fellow-passengers. But to make head measurements is another matter. Dr. Beddoe adopted an ingenious device which I will describe in his own words: "Whenever a likely little squad of natives was encountered the two archæologists got up a dispute about the relative size and shape of their own heads, which I was called in to settle with the calipers. The unsuspecting Irishmen usually entered keenly into the debate, and before the little drama had been finished were eagerly betting on the sizes of their own heads, and begging to have their wagers determined in the same manner."

The figures gathered in this way from the schools and the armies have a peculiar value. They represent all classes of the population, but more especially the peasantry in all the nooks and corners of Europe wherever the long arm of the *Polizei Staat* reaches. The only difficulty is that research upon adults is almost entirely confined to the men; observations upon

adult women are exceedingly scarce.   Fortunately, such as
we have tends to agree with those taken upon males in all important respects.   We shall have to note but a few exceptions
to this law.*   The upper classes are less fully represented oftentimes than the peasantry, since they attend private schools
or are better able to evade the military service by money payment or by educational test.   This simplifies the matter, since
it is the *proletariat* which alone clearly reflects the influence
of race or of environment.   They are the ones we wish to
study.   In this sense the observations upon these populations
may aid the sociologist or the historian; for the greatest obstacle, heretofore, to the prosecution of the half-written history of the common people has been the lack of proper raw
materials.   There is a mine of information here which has
barely been opened to view on the surface.

---

* *Cf.* remarks at page 399 *infra*.

CHAPTER III.

THE HEAD FORM.

THE shape of the human head—by which we mean the general proportions of length, breadth, and height, irrespective of the " bumps " of the phrenologist—is one of the best available tests of race known. Its value is, at the same time, but imperfectly appreciated beyond the inner circle of professional anthropology. Yet it is so simple a phenomenon, both in principle and in practical application, that it may readily be of use to the traveller and the not too superficial observer of men. To be sure, widespread and constant peculiarities of head form are less noticeable in America, because of the extreme variability of our population, compounded as it is of all the races of Europe; they seem also to be less fundamental among the American aborigines. But in the Old World the observant traveller may with a little attention often detect the racial affinity of a people by this means.

The form of the head is for all racial purposes best measured by what is technically known as the cephalic index. This is simply the breadth of the head above the ears expressed in percentage of its length from forehead to back. Assuming that this length is 100, the width is expressed as a fraction of it. As the head becomes proportionately broader—that is, more fully rounded, viewed from the top down—this cephalic index increases. When it rises above 80, the head is called brachycephalic; when it falls below 75, the term dolichocephalic is applied to it. Indexes between 75 and 80 are characterized as mesocephalic. The accompanying photographs illustrate the extent of these differences as they appear upon the skull. They are especially notable in the view from the

37

top downward. These particular crania, with the indexes of
73 and 87 respectively, are, it may be observed, typical of the
general limits of variation which occur among the races of
Europe at the present time. In very rare instances the cephalic
index may run in individuals as low as 62, and it has been

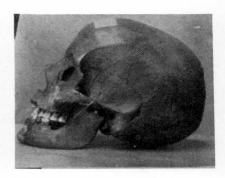

Brachycephalic type.   Index 87.
Zuid-Beveland, Holland.

Dolichocephalic type.   Index 73.
Zeeland, Holland.

observed as high as 103—that is to say, the head being broader
than it is long.   In our study, which is not of individuals
but of racial groups, the limits of variation are of course much
narrower.*

* See Appendix A for technical details.

1.   SWISS, Basle.   Index 64.   Index 75. NORWEGIAN, Aamot.   2.

3.   GERMAN, Baden.   Index 83.   Index 88.5. HUNGARIAN, Thorda. 4.

5.   LAPP, Scandinavia.   Index 94.   Index 96. FRENCH, Savoy.   6.

(Illustrating the relation between the form of face and the proportions of head, measured by the cephalic index.)

A factor which is of great assistance in the rapid identification of racial types, is the correlation between the proportions of the head and the form of the face. In the majority
of cases, particularly in Europe, a relatively broad head is
accompanied by a rounded face, in which the breadth back
of the cheek bones is considerable as compared with the height
from forehead to chin. Anthropologists make use of this relation to measure the so-called facial index; but a lack of
uniformity in the mode of taking measurements has so far
prevented extended observations fit for exact comparison.*
It is sufficient for our purposes to adopt the rule, long head,
oval face; short head and round face. Our six living types on
the opposite page, arranged in an ascending series of cephalic
indices from 64 to 96, make this relation between the head
and face more clearly manifest. In proportion as the heads
become broader back of the temples, the face appears relatively shorter. We are here speaking, be it noted, of those
proportions dependent upon the bony structure of the head,
and not in any sense of the merely superficial fleshy parts. A
rounded face due to full cheeks should be carefully distinguished from one in which the relative breadth is due either
to prominence of the cheek bones or to real breadth of the
head itself. It is the last of these alone which concerns us
here. Only a few examples of widespread disharmonism, as
it is called, between head and face are known. Among these
are the Greenland Eskimos, which resemble the Lapp shown
in our portrait in squareness of face, notwithstanding the fact
that they are almost the longest-headed race known. The
aborigines of Tasmania are also disharmonic to a like degree,
most other peoples of the earth showing an agreement between the facial proportions and those of the head which is
sufficiently close to suggest a relation of cause and effect.
In Europe, where disharmonism is very infrequent among the
living populations, its prevalence in the prehistoric Cro-
Magnon race will afford us a means of identification of this
type wherever it persists to-day. At times disharmonism arises

---

* Topinard, Éléments, p. 917. Weissenberg, 1897, gives a convenient
outline of the various systems.

in mixed types, the product of a cross between a broad and a long headed race, wherein the one element contributes the head form while the other persists rather in the facial proportions.*   Such combinations are apt to occur among the Swiss, lying as they do at the ethnic crossroads of the continent.   Several clear examples of it are shown among our portraits at page 290.

An important point to be noted in this connection is that this shape of the head seems to bear no direct relation to intellectual power or intelligence.   Posterior development of the

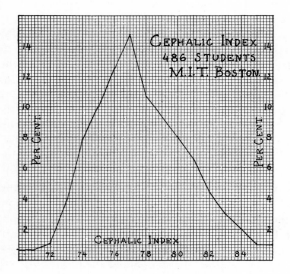

cranium does not imply a corresponding backwardness in culture.   The broad-headed races of the earth may not as a whole be quite as deficient in civilization as some of the long heads, notably the Australians and the African negroes.   On the other hand, the Chinese are conspicuously long-headed, surrounded by the barbarian brachycephalic Mongol hordes; and the Eskimos in many respects surpass the Indians in cul-

---

* Boas (Verh. Berl. Anth. Ges., 1895, p. 406) finds among Indian half-breeds that the facial proportions of one or the other parent are more apt to be transmitted entirely than that an intermediate form results.

ture. Dozens of similar contrasts might be given. Europe offers the best refutation of the statement that the proportions of the head mean anything intellectually. The English, as our map of Europe will show, are distinctly long-headed. Measurements on the students at the Massachusetts Institute of Technology are fairly typical for the Anglo-Saxon peoples. Out of a total of 486 men, four were characterized at one extreme by an index below 70; the upper limit was marked by four men with an index of 87. The series of heads culminated at an index of 77, possessed by 72 students. The diagram herewith represents the percentage distribution of the several indexes. It points to a clear type at a head form quite near the lower limits of variation of the human races; those, namely, of the African negroes and the Australian aborigines. This example, together with a moment's consideration of our world map of the cephalic index, will show how impossible is any relation between the head form of a people and its civilization or average intelligence. Comparisons have been instituted in parts of Europe between the professional and uncultured classes in the same community for the further elucidation of this fact. The differences in head form are as apt to fall one way as another, depending upon the degree of racial purity which exists in each class. Dr. Livi * finds that in northern Italy the professional classes are longer-headed than the peasants; in the south the opposite rule prevails. The explanation is that in each case the upper classes are nearer a mean type for the country, as a result of greater mobility and ethnic intermixture.† In our study of the proportions of the head, therefore, as a corollary of this principle, we are measuring merely race, and not intelligence in any sense. How fortunate this circumstance is for our various purposes will appear in due time.

---

* 1896 a, pp. 86–95.

† We have discussed this more fully in our 1896 c and 1896 d. See also Boas, 1896; Beddoe, 1894; Broca, 1872 b; Niederle, 1896 a, p. 100, etc.; and the works of Ammon, Lapouge, Muffang, and other social anthropologists. Venn, 1888, believes to have discovered a tendency among his Cambridge students, but our own results belie it.

MICRONESIA

MELANESIA

W.Z.R. feet

DIVISION of FLORA
AND
FAUNA

79-81

76-8

73-5 — LONG HEADS

88-9—BROAD HEADS

85-7

82-4

POLYNESIA

CEPHALIC INDEX

Equally unimportant to the anthropologist is the absolute size of the head. It is grievous to contemplate the waste of energy when, during our civil war, over one million soldiers had their heads measured in respect of this absolute size; in view of the fact that to-day anthropologists deny any considerable significance attaching to this characteristic. Popularly, a large head with beetling eyebrows suffices to establish a man's intellectual credit; but, like all other credit, it is entirely dependent upon what lies on deposit elsewhere. Neither size nor weight of the brain seems to be of importance. The long, narrow heads, as a rule, have a smaller capacity than those in which the breadth is considerable; but the exceptions are so common that they disprove the rule. Among the earliest men whose remains have been found in Europe, there was no appreciable difference from the present living populations. In many cases these prehistoric men even surpassed the present population in the size of the head. The peasant and the philosopher can not be distinguished in this respect. For the same reason the striking difference between the sexes, the head of the man being considerably larger than that of the woman, means nothing more than avoirdupois; or rather it seems merely to be correlated with the taller stature and more massive frame of the human male.

Turning to the world map * on the opposite page, which

---

* This map is constructed primarily from data on living men, sufficient in amount to eliminate the effect of chance. Among a host of other authorities, special mention should be made of Drs. Boas, on North America; Sören-Hansen and Bessels, on the Eskimos; von den Steinen, Ehrenreich, Ten Kate, and Martin, on South America; Collignon, Bérenger-Féraud, Verneau, Passavant, Deniker, and Laloy, on Africa; Sommier and Mantegazza, on northern, Chantre and Ujfalvy, on western Asia; Risley, on India; Lubbers, Ten Kate, Volz, Micklucho-Maclay, and Maurel, on Indonesia and the western Pacific. For special details, *vide* Bälz, on Japan; Man, on the Andamans; Ivanovski and Yavorski, on the Mongols, etc. For Africa and Australia the results are certain; but scattered through a number of less extended investigations. Then there is the more general work of Weisbach, Broca, Pruner Bey, and others. All these have been checked or supplemented by the large collections of observations on the cranium. It will never cease to be a matter of regret that observers like Hartmann, Fritsch, Finsch, the Sarasin

shows the geographical distribution of the several types of head
form which we have described, the first fact which impresses
itself is of the violent contrasts in the eastern hemisphere between Europe-Asia and the two southern continents Africa and
Australia. A few pages further on in this chapter will be
found two sheets of portraits representing the differences between these regions. The broad heads and square faces of
the Asiatic types are very different from the long oval of the
dolichocephalic negro, or of the Berber populations north of
the Sahara, which in head and face so strongly resemble them.
In profile the posterior development of the negro skull should
be compared with the bullet-shaped head of the Asiatic. It
will appear that differences in length are as remarkable as in
the breadth. With these contrasts in mind, turn to our world
map. The line of division of head forms passes east and west
just south of the great continental backbone extending from
the Alps to the Himalayas. Thus the primitive natives of
India, the black men of the hill tribes, who are quite distinct
from the Hindu invaders, form part of this southern long-
headed group. The three southern centres of long-headedness
may once have been part of a single continent which occupied
the basin of the Indian Ocean. From the peculiar geographical localization about this latter centre of the lemurs, a species allied to the monkeys, together with certain other mammals, some naturalists have advocated the theory that such
a continent once united Africa and Australia.* To this hypothetical land mass they have assigned the name Lemuria. It
would be idle to discuss the theory in this place. Whether
such a continent ever existed or not, the present geographical
distribution of long-headedness points to a common derivation of the African and the Australian and Melanesian races,
between whom stand as a connecting link the Dravidian or

brothers, Stanley, and others, offer no material for work of this kind.
For the location of tribes, we have used Gerland's Atlas für Völkerkunde.
It is to be hoped that Dr. Boas's map for North America, now ready for
publication, may not long be delayed; our map has benefited from his
courteous correction.

* Ernst Haeckel, 1891, gives an interesting map with a restoration of
this continent as a centre of dispersion for mammals.

7.   UZBEG, Ferghanah.   8.

 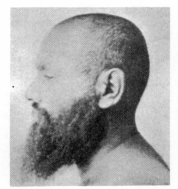

9.   KIPTCHAK.   10.

11.   KARA-KIRGHEZ.   12.

BRACHYCEPHALIC ASIATIC TYPES.

13.   BERBER, Tunis.   Dark brunet.   Index 69.   14.

15.   BERBER, Tunis.   Dark brunet.   Index 72.   16.

17.   SÉRÈRE, Negro.   Index 75.   18.

DOLICHOCEPHALIC AFRICAN TYPES.

aboriginal inhabitants of India. The phenomena of skin colour and of hair only serve to strengthen the hypothesis.

The extremes in head form here presented between the north and the south of the eastern hemisphere constitute the mainstay of the theory that in these places we find the two primary elements of the human species. Other racial traits help to confirm the deduction. The most sudden anthropo-geographical transition in the world is afforded by the Himalaya mountain ranges. Happily, we possess, from Ujfalvy * and others, pretty detailed information for parts of this region, especially the Pamir. This " roof of the world " is of peculiar interest to us as the land to which Max Müller sought to trace the Aryan invaders of Europe by a study of the languages of that continent. It is clearly proved that this greatest mountain system in the world is at the same time the dividing line between the extreme types of mankind. It is really the human equator of the earth. Such is as it should be. For while the greatest extremes of environment are offered between the steaming plains of the Ganges and the frigid deserts and steppes of the north, at the same time direct intercourse between the two regions has been rendered well-nigh impossible by the height of the mountain chain itself. In each region a peculiar type has developed without interference from the other. At either end of the Himalayas proper, where the geographical barriers become less formidable, and especially wherever we touch the sea, the extreme sharpness of the human contrasts fails. The Chinese manifest a tendency toward an intermediate type of head form. Japan shows it even more clearly. From China south the Asiatic broad-headedness becomes gradually attenuated among the Malays, until it either runs abruptly up against the Melanesian dolicho-cephalic group or else vanishes among the islanders of the Pacific. Evidence that in thus extending to the southeast, the Malays have dispossessed or absorbed a more primitive population is afforded by the remnants of the negritos. These black people still exist in some purity in the inaccessible up-

---

* Les Aryens au Nord et au Sud de l'Hindou-Kouch. Paris, 1896.

lands of the large islands in Malaysia, and especially in the Philippine Archipelago.

Compared with the extreme forms presented in the Old World, the Americas appear to be quite homogeneous and at the same time intermediate in type, especially if we except the Eskimo; for in the western hemisphere among the true Indians the extreme variations of head form are comprised between the cephalic indices of 85 in British Columbia and Peru, and of 76 on the southeast coast of Brazil. Probably nine tenths of the native tribes of America have average indices between 79 and 83. Many American peoples among whom customs of cranial deformation prevail, are able artificially to raise their indices to 90 or even 95; but such monstrosities should be excluded for the present, since we are studying normal types of man alone. Translated into words, this means that the American aborigines should all be classified together as, in a sense, a secondary and more or less transitional racial group.

With them we may place the great group of men which inhabits the islands of the Pacific. These people manifest even clearer than do the American Indians that they are an intermediate type. They are, however, more unstable as a race, especially lacking in homogeneity. They seem to be compounded of the Asiatic and Melanesian primary racial elements in varying proportions. It is the most discouraging place in the world to measure types of head, because of their extreme variability. We shall have occasion shortly to compare certain of their characteristics other than the head form with those of the people of Europe. This we shall do in the attempt to discover whether these Europeans are also a secondary race, or whether they are entitled to a different place in the human species. We shall then see that one can not study Europe quite by itself without gaining thereby an entirely false idea of its human history.

Before proceeding to discuss the place which Europe occupies in our racial series, it may be interesting to point out certain curious parallelisms between the geographical localization of the several types of head form and the natural dis-

tribution of the flora and fauna of the earth.* Agassiz a half
century ago commented upon the similar areas of distribution
of mammals and of man. His observations are confirmed by
our data on the head form. Where, as in Africa and Australia, there is marked individuality in the lower forms of life,
there is also to be found an extreme type of the human species. Where, on the other hand, realms like the Oriental
one which covers southeastern Asia and the Malay Archipelago, have drawn upon the north and the south alike for both
their flora and fauna, several types of man have also immi-
grated and crossed with one another. Often the dividing lines
between distinct realms for varieties of man, animal, and plant
coincide quite exactly. The Sahara Desert, once a sea, and
not the present Mediterranean, as we shall show, divides the
true negro from the European, as it does the Ethiopian zoölogical and botanical realm from its neighbour. Thus do the
African Berbers in our portraits belong of right to the European races, as we shall soon be able to prove. The facial resemblance is enough to render such proof unnecessary. The
Andes, the Rocky Mountains, and the Himalayas, for a similar
reason divide types of all forms of life alike, including man.
Even that remarkable line which Alfred Russel Wallace so
vividly describes in his Island Life, which divides the truly
insular fauna and flora from those of the continent of Asia,
is duplicated among men near by. The sharp division line
for plants and animals between Bali and Lombok we have
shown upon the map. It is but a short distance farther east,
between Timor and Flores, where we suddenly pass from
the broad-headed, straight-haired Asiatic Malay to the long-
headed and frizzled Melanesian savage—to the group which
includes the Papuans of New Guinea and the Australian.†

Following out this study of man in his natural migrations
just as we study the lower animals, it can be shown that the
differences in geographical localization between the human

---

* Beddard, Lyddeker, Sclater, are best on geographical zoölogy. Brinton, 1890 a, p. 95, gives many references on this.

† A good ethnological map of this region is given in Ratzel, 1894–'95,
vol. i.

and other forms of life are merely of degree. The whole matter is reducible at bottom to terms of physical geography, producing areas of characterization. Where great changes in the environment occur, where oceans or mountain chains divide, or where river systems unite geographical areas, we discover corresponding effects upon the distribution of human as of other animal types. This is not necessarily because the environment has directly generated those peculiarities in each instance; certainly no such result can be shown in respect of the head form. It is because the several varieties of man or other mammals have been able to preserve their individuality through geographical isolation from intermixture; or contrariwise, as the case may be, have merged it in a conglomerate whole compounded of all immigrant types alike. In this sense man in his physical constitution is almost as much a creature of environment as the lower orders of life. Even in Europe he has not yet wholly cast off the leading strings of physical circumstance, as it is our purpose ultimately to show.

By this time it will have been observed that the differences in respect of the head form become strongly noticeable only when we compare the extremes of our racial series; in other words, that while the minor gradations may be real to the calipers and tape, they are not striking at first glance to the eye. Let us carefully note that in observing the proportions of the head, we have absolutely nothing to do with those features by which in Europe we are accustomed to distinguish nationalities. Nine times out of ten we recognise an Irishman, a Swede, or an Italian by means of these lesser details. They are in reality more often national or local than wholly racial. Let us also rigidly eliminate the impressions derived from mere facial expression. Such belongs rather to the study of character than of race. It seldom becomes strongly marked before middle life, while the more fundamental traits are fully apparent much earlier. As a matter of fact, it is the modesty of the head proportions—not forcing themselves conspicuously upon the observer's notice as do differences in the colour of the skin, the facial features, or the bodily stature—

which forms the main basis of their claim to priority as a test of race. Were this head form as strikingly prominent as these other physical traits, it would tend to fall a prey to the modifying factor of artificial selection: that is to say, it would speedily become part and parcel among a people of a general ideal, either of racial beauty or of economic fitness, so that the selective choice thereby induced, would soon modify the operation of purely natural causes.

However strenuously the biologists may deny validity to the element of artificial selection among the lower animals, it certainly plays a large part in influencing sexual choice among primitive men and more subtly among us in civilization. Just as soon as a social group recognises the possession of certain physical traits peculiar to itself—that is, as soon as it evolves what Giddings has aptly termed a "consciousness of kind"—its constant endeavour thenceforth is to afford the fullest expression to that ideal. Thus, according to Bälz, the nobility in Japan are as much lighter in weight and more slender in build than their lower classes, as the Teutonic nobility of Great Britain is above the British average. The Japanese aristocracy in consequence might soon come to consider its bodily peculiarities as a sign of high birth. That it would thereafter love, choose, and marry—unconsciously perhaps, but no less effectively—in conformity with that idea is beyond peradventure. Is there any doubt that where, as in our own Southern States, two races are socially divided from one another, the superior would do all in his power to eliminate any traces of physical similarity to the menial negroes? Might not the Roman nose, light hair and eyes, and all those prominent traits which distinguished the master from the slave, play an important part in constituting an ideal of beauty which would become highly effective in the course of time? So uncultured a people as the natives of Australia are pleased to term the Europeans, in derision, "tomahawk-noses," regarding our primary facial trait as absurd in its make-up. Even among them the "consciousness of kind" can not be denied as an important factor to be dealt with in the theory of the formation of races.

Such an artificial selection as we have instanced is peculiarly liable to play havoc with facial features, for which reason these latter are rendered quite unreliable for purposes of racial identification. Because they are entirely superficial, they are first noted by the traveller and used as a basis of classification. A case in point is offered by the eastern Eskimos, who possess in marked degree not only the almond eye, so characteristic of the Mongolian peoples, but also the broad face, high cheek bones, and other features common among the people of Asia. Yet, notwithstanding this superficial resemblance, inspection of our world map of the head form shows that they stand at the farthest remove from the Asiatic type. They are even longer-headed than most of the African negroes. The same phenomenon confronts us in our analysis of the aborigines of Russia. We shall find many of the dolichocephalic Finns, who are superficially Mongols in every facial characteristic. They remain Finns nevertheless, although their faces belie it. Equally erroneous is it to assume, because the Asiatic physiognomy is quite common among all the aborigines of the Americas, even to the tip of Cape Horn, that this constitutes a powerful argument for a derivation of the American Indian from the Asiatic stock. We shall have occasion to point out from time to time the occurrence of local facial types in various parts of Europe. On the principle we have indicated above, these are highly interesting as indications of a local sense of individuality; though they mean but little, so far as racial origin and derivation are concerned.

Happily for us, racial differences in head form are too slight to suggest any such social selection as has been suggested; moreover, they are generally concealed by the head-dress, which assumes prominence in proportion as we return toward barbarism. Obviously, a Psyche knot or savage peruke suffices to conceal all slight natural differences of this kind; so that Nature is left free to follow her own bent without interference from man. The colour of skin peculiar to a people may be heightened readily by the use of a little pigment. Such practices are not infrequent. To modify the shape of the cranium itself, even supposing any peculiarity were detected, is quite a different matter. It is far easier to rest content with a modification of the headdress, which may be rendered socially distinctive by the application of infinite pains and expense. It is well known that in many parts of the world the head is artificially deformed by compression during infancy. This was notably the case in the Americas. Such practices have obtained and prevail to-day in parts of Europe.* Bodin tells us that the Belgæ were accustomed to compress the head by artificial means. The people about Toulouse in the Pyrenees are accustomed, even at the present time, to distort the head by the application of bandages during the formative period of life. This deformation is sometimes so extreme as to equal the Flathead Indian monstrosities which have been so often described. Fortunately, these barbarous customs are rare among the civilized peoples which it is our province to discuss. Their absence, however, can not be ascribed to inability to modify the shape of the head; rather does it seem to be due to the lack of appreciation that any racial differences exist, which may be exaggerated for social effect or racial distinction. More important to-day are the customs, such as the use of hard cradles, which indirectly operate to modify the shape of the cranium. Our portraits of Armenians and other peoples of Asia Minor at page 444 show the possible effect of such practices. These deformations not being clearly intentional, can not be reckoned as evidence of a selective process.

Westermarck † develops the interesting law that deformative practices generally tend to exaggerate the characteristics peculiar to a people. It is true, indeed, that a flattening of the occiput seems to be more prevalent among the naturally

---

* For a full account of such deformation, *vide* L'Anthropologie, vol. iv, pp. 11–27. The illustrations of such deformation, of the processes employed, and of the effect upon the brain development, are worthy of note. Other references concerning Europe are Lagneau, 1872, p. 618; Luschan, 1879; Lenhossek, 1878; Perier, 1861, p. 26; Davis and Thurnam, 1865, pp. 34, 42; Thurnam, 1863, p. 157; Bertholon, 1892, p. 42; Globus, lix, p. 118, after Delisle in Bull. Soc. d'Anth., 1886, p. 649. Anutchin, 1887 and 1892, on Russia, is particularly good.

† History of Human Marriage, second edition, p. 262.

brachycephalic aborigines of America and Asia. We have an African example of a recognition of the opposite cephalic peculiarity. It seems highly suggestive. The naturally long-headed Ovambo shave all the head save at the top, it is said, in order to bring their prominent occiputs into greater relief. One can not deny the effectiveness of such a custom in the case of our African portraits in this chapter. They certainly exaggerate the natural long-headedness to a marked degree. Such phenomena are, however, very rare; cranial individuality is very seldom subject to such modification, being in so far free from disturbance by artificial selection.

Another equally important guarantee that the head form is primarily the expression of racial differences alone lies in its immunity from all disturbance from physical environment. As will be shown subsequently, the colour of the hair and eyes, and stature especially, are open to modification by local circumstances; so that racial peculiarities are often obscured or entirely reversed by them. On the other hand, the general proportions of the head seem to be uninfluenced either by climate, by food supply or economic status, or by habits of life; so that they stand as the clearest exponents which we possess of the permanent hereditary differences within the human species. Ranke, of Munich, most eminent of German authorities, has long advocated a theory that there is some natural relation between broad-headedness and a mountainous habitat.* He was led to this view by the remarkable Alpine localization, which we shall speedily point out, of the brachycephalic race of Europe. Our map of the world, with other culminations of this type in the Himalayan plateau of Asia, in the Rocky Mountains, and the Andes, may seem to corroborate this view. Nevertheless, all attempts to trace any connection in detail between the head form and the habitat have utterly failed. For this reason we need not stop to refute this theory by citing volumes of evidence to the contrary, as we might. Our explanation for this peculiar geographical phenomenon, which ascribes it to a racial se-

---

* *Cf.* Moschen, 1892, p. 125, for criticism of this. Beiträge zur Anthropologie Bayerns, i, 1877, pp. 232–234; ii, 1879, p. 75.

lective process alone, is fully competent to account for the fact. The environment is still a factor for us of great moment, but its action is merely indirect. In the present state of our knowledge, then, we seem to be justified in ruling out environment once and for all as a direct modifier of the shape of the head.

Having disposed of both artificial selection and environment as possible modifiers of the head form, nothing remains to be eliminated except the element of chance variation.* This last is readily counterbalanced by taking so many observations that the fluctuations above and below the mean neutralize one another. Variation due to chance alone is no more liable to occur in the head than in any other part of the body. Rigid scientific methods are the only safeguard for providing against errors due to it. It is this necessity of making the basis of observation so broad that all error due to chance may be eliminated, which constitutes the main argument for the study of heads in the life rather than of skulls; for the limit to the number of measurements is determined by the perseverance and ingenuity of the observer alone, and not by the size of the museum collection or of the burial place. It should be added that our portraits have been especially chosen with a view to the elimination of chance. They will always, so far as possible, represent *types* and not *individuals*, in the desire to have them stand as *illustrations* and not merely *pictures*. This is a principle which is lamentably neglected in many books on anthropology; to lose sight of it is to prostitute science in the interest of popularity.

The most conspicuous feature of our map of cephalic index for western Europe † is that here within a limited area all the extremes of head form known to the human race are crowded together. In other words, the so-called white race of Europe is not physically a uniform and intermediate type in the proportions of the head between the brachycephalic Asiatics and the long-headed negroes of Africa. A few years ago it was be-

---

* Ranke, 1897 b. See also chapter vi for further discussion.
† See Appendix A for technical details.

lieved that this was true.* More recently, detailed research
has revealed hitherto unsuspected limits of variation. They
are roughly indicated by our portraits of living European
types at page 39. In the high Alps of northwestern Italy are
communes with an average index of 89, an extreme of round-
headedness not equalled anywhere else in the world save in
the Balkan Peninsula and in Asia Minor. This type of head
prevails all through the Alps, quite irrespective of political
frontiers. These superficial boundaries are indicated in white
lines upon the map to show their independence of racial limits.
There is no essential difference in head form between the
Bavarians and the Italian Piedmontese, or between the French
Savoyards and the Tyrolese.

From what has been said, it will appear that these Alpine
populations in purity exceed any known tribes of central Asia
in the breadth of their heads. Yet within three hundred miles
as the crow flies, in the island of Corsica, are communes with
an average cephalic index of 73.† These mountaineers of inland Corsica are thus as long-headed as any tribe of Australians, the wood Veddahs of Ceylon, or any African negroes
of which we have extended observations. A little way farther
to the north there are other populations in Scotland, Ireland,
and Scandinavia which are almost as widely different from
the Alpine peoples in the proportions of the head as are the
Corsicans. An example of extreme individual variation downward is shown in our Teutonic type at page 39, which has a
lower index than any recorded for the longest-headed primitive
races known. Nor is this all. Pass to northern Scandinavia,
and we find among the Lapps, again, one of the broadest-

---

* Sir W. H. Flower, in his classification of human types, asserted it as
late as 1885 ; it is reaffirmed in Flower and Lyddeker's great handbook
(1891) ; yet A. Retzius, as early as 1864, in his map of cephalic index,
practically represented the modern proved facts, which detailed research
has been slowly confirming ever since.

† Lapouge, 1897 c, describes, perhaps, the broadest-headed contingent
in Europe. Jaubert and Mahoudeau are best on Corsica. Bertholon,
1892, found an average below 74 for 358 Berbers in Khoumirie. Portugal,
as we shall see, is equally long-headed, according to data furnished by
Ferraz de Macedo. *Cf.* Closson, 1896 a, p. 176.

headed peoples of the earth, of a type shown in our series
of portraits.

So remarkably sudden are these transitions that one is
tempted at first to regard them as the result of chance. Further examination is needed to show that it must be due to
law. Proof of this is offered by the map itself; for it indicates a uniform gradation of head form from several specific
centres of distribution outward. Consider Italy, for example,
where over three hundred thousand individuals, from every
little hamlet, have been measured in detail. The transition
from north to south is, as we shall see, perfectly consistent.
The people of the extreme south are like the Africans among
our portraits, at page 45 in respect of the head form; gradually the type changes until in Piedmont we reach an extreme
perfectly similar to that depicted on our other page of brachycephalic Asiatic types. So it is all over the continent. Each
detailed research is a check on its neighbour. There is no
escape from the conclusion that we have to do with law.

Two distinct varieties of man, measured by the head form
alone, are to be found within the confines of this little continent. One occupies the heart of western Europe as an outpost of the great racial type which covers all Asia and most
of eastern Europe as well. The other, to which we as Anglo-
Saxons owe allegiance, seems to hang upon the outskirts of
Europe, intrenched in purity in the islands and peninsulas
alone. Northern Africa, as we have already observed, is to
be classed with these. Furthermore, this long-headed type
appears to be aggregated about two distinct centres of distribution—in the north and south respectively. In the next
chapter we shall show that these two centres of long-headedness are again divided from one another in respect of both
colour of hair and eyes and stature. From the final combination of all these bodily characteristics we discover that in
reality in Europe we have to do with three physical types,
and not two. Thus we reject at once that old classification
in our geographies of all the peoples of Europe under a single
title of the white, the Indo-Germanic, Caucasian, or Aryan
race. Europe, instead of being a monotonous entity, is a

most variegated patchwork of physical types. Each has a
history of its own, to be worked out from a study of the living
men. Upon the combination of these racial types in varying
proportions one with another the superstructure of nationality has been raised.

Among other points illustrated by our map of Europe is
the phenomenon paralleled in general zoölogy, that the extreme or pure type is normally to be found in regions of
marked geographical individuality. Such areas of characterization occur, for example, in the Alpine valleys, in Corsica
and Sardinia, somewhat less so in Spain, Italy, and Scandinavia. The British Isles, particularly Ireland, at least until
the full development of the art of navigation, afforded also a
good example of a similar area of characterization. Europe
has always been remarkable among continents by reason of
its "much-divided" geography. From Strabo to Montesquieu political geographers have called attention to the advantage which this subdivision has afforded to man. They
have pointed to the smooth outlines of the African continent,
for example; to its structural monotony, and to the lack of
geographical protection enjoyed by its social and political
groups. The principle which they invoked appears to hold
true in respect of race as well as of politics. Africa is as uniform racially as Europe is heterogeneous.

Pure types physically are always to be found outside the
great geographical meeting places. These, such as the garden of France, the valleys of the Po, the Rhine, and the
Danube, have always been areas of conflict. Competition,
the opposite of isolation, in these places is the rule; so that
progress which depends upon the stress of rivalry has followed as a matter of course. There are places where too
much of this healthy competition has completely broken the
mould of nationality, as in Sicily, so ably pictured by Freeman. It is only within certain limits that struggle and conflict make for an advance forward or upward. Ethnically,
however, this implies a variety of physical types in contact,
from which by natural selection the one best fitted for survival may persist. This means ultimately the extinction of

extreme types and the supersession of them by mediocrity. In other words, applying these principles to the present case, it implies the blending of the long and the narrow heads and the substitution of one of medium breadth. The same causes, then, which conduce socially and politically to progress have as an ethnic result mediocrity of type. The individuality of the single man is merged in that of the social group. In fine, contrast of race is swallowed up in nationality. This process has as yet only begun in western Europe. In the so-called upper classes it has proceeded far, as we shall see. We shall, in due course of time, have to trace social forces now at work which insure its further prosecution not only among the leaders of the people, but among the masses as well. The process will be completed in that far-distant day when the conception of common humanity shall replace the narrower one of nationality; then there will be perhaps not two varieties of head form in Europe, but a great common mean covering the whole continent. The turning of swords into ploughshares will contribute greatly to this end. Modern industrial life with its incident migrations of population does more to upset racial purity than a hundred military campaigns or conquests. Did it not at the same time invoke commercial rivalries and build up national barriers against intercourse, we might hope to see this amalgamation completed in a conceivable time.

CHAPTER IV.

BLONDS AND BRUNETS.

THE colour of the skin has been from the earliest times regarded as a primary means of racial identification. The ancient Egyptians were accustomed to distinguish the races known to them by this means both upon their monuments and in their inscriptions. Notwithstanding this long acquaintance, the phenomenon of pigmentation remains to-day among the least understood departments of physical anthropology. One point alone seems to have been definitely proved: however marked the contrasts in colour between the several varieties of the human species may be, there is no corresponding difference in anatomical structure discoverable.

Pigmentation arises from the deposition of colouring matter in a special series of cells, which lie just between the translucent outer skin or epidermis and the inner or true skin known as the cutis. It was long supposed that these pigment cells were peculiar to the dark-skinned races; but investigation has shown that the structure in all types is identical. The differences in colour are due, not to the presence or absence of the cells themselves, but to variations in the amount of pigment therein deposited. In this respect, therefore, the negro differs physiologically, rather than anatomically, from the European or the Asiatic. Yet this trait, although superficial so to speak, is exceedingly persistent, even through considerable racial intermixture. The familiar legal test in our Southern States in the *ante-bellum* days for the determination of the legal status of octoroons was to look for the bit of colour at the base of the finger nails. Under the transparent outer skin in this place the telltale pigmentation would remain, despite a long-continued infusion of white blood.

58

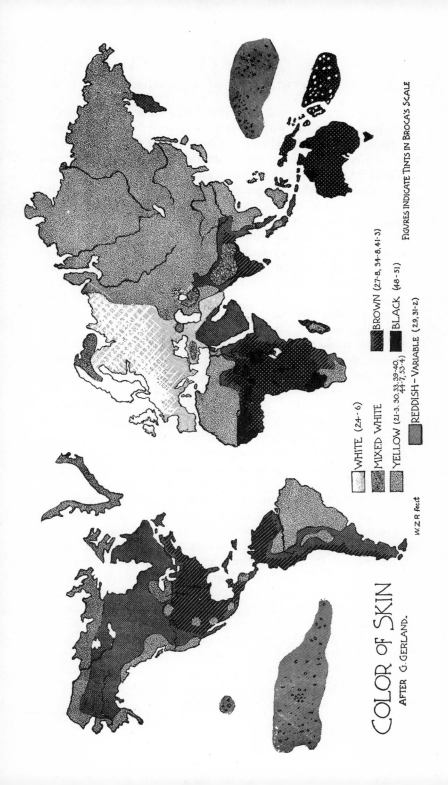

COLOR OF SKIN

AFTER G. GERLAND.

W. Z. R. fecit

WHITE (24 – 6)

MIXED WHITE

YELLOW (21-3, 30, 33, 39-40, 44-7, 53-4)

REDDISH – VARIABLE (29, 31-2)

BROWN (27-8, 34-8, 41-3)

BLACK (48-51)

FIGURES INDICATE TINTS IN BROCA'S SCALE

In respect of the colour of the skin, we may roughly divide
the human species into four groups indicated upon our world
map.   The jet or coal black colour is not very widespread.
It occurs in a narrow and more or less broken belt across
Africa just south of the Sahara Desert, with a few scattering
bits farther south on the same continent.   Another centre
of dissemination of this characteristic, although widely separated from it, occurs in the islands southeast of New Guinea
in the Pacific Ocean, in the district which is known from this
dark colour of its populations as Melanesia.   Next succeeding this type in depth of colour is the main body of negroes,
of Australians, and of the aborigines of India.   This second
or brownish group in the above-named order shades off from
deep chocolate through coffee-colour down to olive and light
or reddish brown.   The American Indians fall within this class,
because, while reddish in tinge, the skin has a strong brown
undertone.   In the Americas we find the colour quite variable, ranging all the way from the dark Peruvians and the
Mexicans to the aborigines north of the United States.   The
Polynesians are allied to this second group, characterized by
a red-brown skin.   A third class, in which the skin is of a
yellow shade, covers most of Asia, the northern third of Africa,
and Brazil,* including a number of widely scattered peoples
such as the Lapps, the Eskimos, the Hottentots and Bushmen
of South Africa, together with most of the people of Malaysia.
Among these the skin varies from a dull leather colour,
through a golden or buff to a muddy white.   In all cases the
shading is in no wise continuous or regular.   Africa contains
all three types of colour from the black Dinkas to the yellow
Hottentots.   In Asia and the Americas all tints obtain except
the jet black.   There are all grades of transitional shading.
Variations within the same tribe are not inconsiderable, so
that no really sharp line of demarcation anywhere occurs.

The fourth colour group which we have to study in this
paper is alone highly concentrated in the geographical sense.
It forms the so-called white race, although many of its mem-

---

* K. E. Ranke, Zeits. f. Eth., xxx, 1898, pp. 61–73.

bers are almost brown and often yellow in skin colour. As we shall show, its real determinant characteristic is, paradoxically, not the skin at all but the pigmentation of the hair and eyes. Nevertheless, so far as it may be used in classification, the very light shades of skin are restricted to Europe, including perhaps part of modern Africa north of the Sahara, which geologically belongs to the northern continent. There is a narrow belt of rather light-skinned peoples running off to the southeast into Asia, including the Persians and some high-caste Hindus. This offshoot vanishes in the Ganges Valley in the prevailing dark skin of the aboriginal inhabitants of India. The only entirely isolated bit of very light skin elsewhere occurs among the Ainos in northern Japan; but these people are so few in number and so abnormal in other respects that we are warranted in dismissing them from further consideration in this place.

Anthropologists have endeavoured for a long time to find the cause of these differences in the colour of the skin.* Some have asserted that they were the direct effects of heat; but our map shows that the American stock, for example, is in no wise affected by it. A consideration of all the races of the earth in general shows no correspondence whatever of the colour of the skin with the isothermal lines. The Chinese are the same colour at Singapore as at Pekin and at Kamchatka. Failing in this explanation, scientists have endeavoured to connect pigmentation of the skin with humidity, or with heat and humidity combined; but in Africa, as we saw, the only really black negroes are in the dry region near the Sahara Desert; while the Congo basin, one of the most humid regions on the globe, is distinctly lighter in tint. Others have attempted to prove that this colour, again, might be due to the influence of the tropical sun, or perhaps to oxygenation taking place under the stimulation of exposure to solar rays. This has at first sight a measure of probability, since the colour which appears in tanning or freckles is not to be distinguished

---

* Waitz: Anthropologie der Naturvölker, vol. i, p. 55 *seq*., contains some interesting remarks on this subject. Topinard, Ranke, De Quatrefages, and all standard authorities devote much attention to it.

physiologically from the pigment which forms in the main body of the skin of the darker races. The objection to this hypothesis is that the covered portions of the body are equally dark with the exposed ones: and that certain groups of men whose lives are peculiarly sedentary, such as the Jews, who have spent much of their time for centuries within doors, are distinctly darker than other races whose occupations keep them continually in the open air. This holds true whether in the tropics or in the northern part of Europe. This local coloration in tanning, moreover, due to the direct influence of the sun is not hereditary, as far as we can determine. Sailors' children are not darker than those of the merchant, even after generations of men have followed the same profession. Each of these theories seems to fail as a sole explanation. The best working hypothesis is, nevertheless, that this coloration is due to the combined influences of a great number of factors of environment working through physiological processes, none of which can be isolated from the others. One point is certain, whatever the cause may be—that this characteristic has been very slowly acquired, and has to-day become exceedingly persistent in the several races.

Study of the colour of the skin alone has nothing further to interest us in this inquiry than the very general conclusions we have just outlined. We are compelled to turn to an allied characteristic—namely, the pigmentation of the hair and eyes —for more specific results. There are three reasons which compel us to take this action. In the first place, the coloration of the hair and eyes appears to be less directly open to disturbance from environmental influences than is the skin; so that variations in shading may be at the same time more easily and delicately measured. Secondly; the colour or, if you please, the absence of colour, in the hair and eyes is more truly peculiar to the European race than is the lightness of its skin. There are many peoples in Europe who are darker skinned than certain tribes in Asia or the Americas; but there is none in which blondness of hair and eyes occurs to any considerable degree. It is in the flaxen hair and blue eye that the peculiarly European type comes to its fullest physical expression. This at once reveals the third inducement for us to focus our study upon these apparently subordinate traits. Europe alone of all the continents is divided against itself. We find blondness in all degrees of intensity scattered among a host of much darker types. A peculiar advantage is herein made manifest. Nowhere else in the world are two such distinct varieties of man in such intimate contact with one another. From the precise determination of their geographical distribution we may gain an insight into many interesting racial events in the past.

The first general interest in the pigmentation of the hair and eyes in Europe dates from 1865, although Dr. Beddoe began nearly ten years earlier to collect data from all over the continent. His untiring perseverance led him to take upward of one hundred thousand personal observations in twenty-five years.* During our own civil war about a million recruits were examined by Gould ('69) and Baxter ('75), many being immigrants from all parts of Europe. The extent of the work which has been done since these first beginnings is indicated by the following approximate table:

Number of Observations.

	School children.		Adults.
Germany................	6,758,000	Italy.................	299,000
Belgium.............	608,000	France..............	225,000 ±
Switzerland..........	497,000	British Isles :	
Austria..............	2,304,000	General...........	53,000
Others..............	50,000 ±	Criminals, etc.......	12,000
		United States.........	1,000,000
		Remainder of Europe..	50,000 ±
	10,217,000		1,639,000

It thus appears that the material is ample in amount. The great difficulty in its interpretation lies in the diversity of the systems which have been adopted by different observers. It is not easy to give an adequate conception of the confusion which prevails. Here are a few of the obstacles to be encoun-

* Mainly published in his monumental Races of Britain, London, and Bristol, 1885.

tered. As the table indicates, the countries north of the Alps
have been mainly studied through their school children. In
the Latin half of Europe adults alone are included. It is a
matter of common observation that flaxen hair and blue eyes
are characteristic of childhood. As it has been proved that
from ten to twenty per cent of such blond children at maturity
develop darker hair or eyes, the fallacy of direct comparison
of these figures for the north and south of Europe becomes
apparent.* Secondly; some observers, like Beddoe, rely primarily upon the colour of the hair; others place greater reliance upon the tints of the iris, as in the case of the Anthropometric Committee. It is, indeed, certain that brunetness is
not equally persistent in the two. Dark traits seem to reappear with greater constancy in the hair, while a remote
blond cross more often leaves its traces in the eyes.† Thus
we have the characteristic blue eye in the dark-haired Breton
peasantry. The opposite combination—that is to say, of dark
eyes with light hair—is very uncommon, as the Anthropometric Committee [83] found in the British Isles. The normal
association resulting, as we shall see, from a blond cross with
a primitive dark race is of brownish hair and gray or bluish
eyes.‡ In the third place, it is not easy to correct for the personal equation of different observers. A seeming brunet in
Norway appears as quite blond in Italy because there is no
fixed standard by which to judge. The natural impulse is to
compare the individual with the general population round
about. The precision of measurements upon the head is
nowise attainable. Some observers take the colours as they
appear upon close examination, while the majority prefer to
record the general impression at a distance. And, finally, after
the observations have been taken in these different ways, some

---

* Consult Anthropometric Committee, 1883, p. 28 ; Virchow, 1886 b, p.
291 ; Zuckerkandl, 1889, p. 125 ; Livi, 1896 a, p. 67 ; Pfitzner, 1897, p. 477.
Bordier's observations in Isère, 1895, are particularly good for comparison.

† Topinard, 1889 a, pp. 515 and 523 ; 1889 c ; Collignon, 1890 a, p. 47 ; Virchow, 1886 b, p. 325. If the hair be light, one can generally be sure that the
eyes will be of a corresponding shade. Bassanovitch, 1891. p. 29, strikingly confirms this rule for even so dark a population as the Bulgarian.

‡ Sören Hansen, 1888, finds this true in Denmark also.

authorities in their computations reject neutral tints which are neither clearly blond nor brunet, and give the relative proportions of the two types after this elimination. The resultant difficulty in drawing any close comparisons under such circumstances can readily be appreciated.

The general rule is that eyes and hair vary together, both being either lightish or dark, as if in correspondence.* Nevertheless, such ideal combinations do not characterize a majority of most European populations. Thus, in Germany, of six million school children observed on a given day, not one half of them showed the simple combination of dark eyes and dark hair or of light eyes and light hair.† In the British Isles, according to the Anthropometric Committee ('83), it appears that over twenty-five per cent of persons measured have fair eyes and dark hair—in other words, that the hair and the eyes do not accompany one another in type. Of nearly five hundred students at the Institute of Technology, sixty-five per cent were of this mixed type. Even among the Jews, Virchow found less than forty per cent characterized by the same tinge of hair and eyes. In parts of Russia the proportion of pure types is scarcely above half; ‡ in Denmark, less than forty per cent were consistently pure.#

Under these trying circumstances, there are two principal modes of determining the pigmentation of a given population. One is to discover the proportion of so-called pure brunet *types*—that is to say, the percentage of individuals possessed of *both* dark eyes and hair. The other system is to study brunet *traits* without regard to their association in the same individual. This latter method is no respecter of persons. The population as a whole, and not the individual, is the unit. North of the Alps they have mapped the pigmentation in the main by types; in France, Norway, Italy, and the British Isles they have chosen

---

* Ammon, 1899, p. 157, is fine on this. Among 6,800 recruits in Baden, sixty-three per cent of blue-eyed men had light hair, while eighty-four per cent of dark-eyed men had brown or black hair. Cf. also Livi, 1896 a, p. 63 ; Weisbach, 1894, p. 237 ; Arbo, 1895 b, p. 58.

† Virchow, 1886 b, p. 298.

‡ Talko-Hryncewicz, 1897 a, p. 278; Anutchin, 1893, p. 285.

Sören Hansen, 1888.

to work by dissociated traits. Here again is a stumbling-block in the way of comparisons. The absolute figures for the same population gathered in these two ways will be widely different. Thus in Italy, while only about a quarter of the people are pure brunet types, nearly half of all the eyes and hair in the country are dark. That is to say, a large proportion of brunet traits are to-day found scattered broadcast without association one with another. In Europe, as a whole, upward of one half of the population is of a mixed type in this respect. In America the equilibrium is still further disturbed. Nor should we expect it to be otherwise. Intermixture, migration, the influences of environment, and chance variation have been long at work in Europe. The result has been to reduce the pure types, either of blond or brunet, to an absolute minority. Fortunately for us, in despair at the prospect of reducing such variant systems to a common base, the results obtained all point in the same direction whichever mode of study is employed. In those populations where there is the greatest frequency of pure dark types, there also is generally to be found the largest proportion of brunet traits lying about loose, so to speak. And where there are the highest percentages of these unattached traits, there is also the greatest prevalence of purely neutral tints, which are neither to be classed as blond or brunet. So that, as we have said, in whichever way the pigmentation is studied, the results in general are parallel, certainly at least so far as the deductions in this paper are concerned. Our map on the next page is indeed constructed in conformity with this assumption.*

By reason of the difficulties above mentioned, this map is intended to convey an idea of the relative brunetness of the various parts of Europe by means of the shading rather than by concrete percentages. It is, in fact, impossible to reduce all the results to a common base for exact comparison. What we have done is to patch together the maps for each country, adopting a scheme of tinting for each which shall represent, as nearly as may be, its relation to the rest. In the scale at the left the shades on the same horizontal line are supposed

---

* See Appendix B.

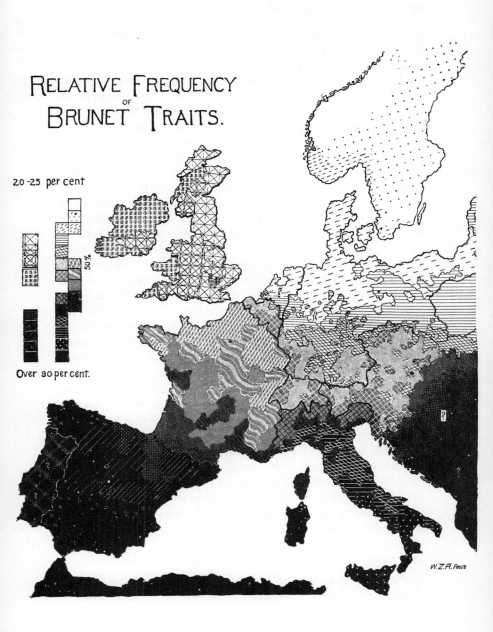

RELATIVE FREQUENCY
OF BRUNET TRAITS.

20-25 per cent

50%

Over 90 per cent.

W.Z.R. Fecit

to represent approximately equal degrees of pigmentation. The arrangement of the colours in separate groups, it will be observed, corresponds to national systems of measurement. Thus the five tints used in Germanic countries and the six in Italy are separately grouped, and are each distinct from those used for the coloration of France. It will be observed that these separate national groups often overlap at each end. This arrangement indicates, for example, that the darkest part of Scandinavia contains about as many brunet traits as the lightest portion of Germany, and that they are both lighter than any part of Scotland; or that the fourth zone of brunetness in Germany contains about as high a proportion of dark traits as the lightest part of France, and that they are both about as dark areas as the middle zone in England. As the diagram shows, central France is characterized by a grade of brunetness somewhat intermediate between the south of Austria and northern Italy. In other words, the increase of pigmentation toward the south is somewhat more gradual there than in the eastern Alps. To summarize the whole system, equally dark tints along the same horizontal line in the diagram indicate that in the areas thus equally shaded there are about the same proportions of traits or types, as the case may be, which are entitled to be called brunet.

In a rough way, the extremes in the distribution of the blond and brunet varieties within the population of Europe are as follows: At the northern limit we find that about one third of the people are pure blonds, characterized by light hair and blue eyes; about one tenth are pure brunets; the remainder, over one half, being mixed with a tendency to blondness.* On the other hand, in the south of Italy the pure blonds have almost entirely disappeared. About one half the population are pure brunets, with deep brown or black hair, and eyes of a corresponding shade; and the other half is mixed, with a tendency to brunetness.† The half-and-half line seems to lie about where it ought, not far from the

---

* Topinard, 1889 c, for Norway; Hultkrantz, 1897, for 699 Swedes gives twenty-six per cent pure blonds.

† Livi, 1896 a, p. 60.

Alps. Yet it does not follow the parallels of latitude. A circle, described with Copenhagen as a centre, sweeping around near Vienna, across the middle of Switzerland, thence up through the British Isles, might serve roughly to indicate such a boundary. North of it blondness prevails, although always with an appreciable percentage of pure brunets. South of it brunetness finally dominates quite exclusively. It should not fail of note that toward the east there is a slight though constant increase of brunetness along the same degrees of latitude, and that the western portion of the British Isles is a northern outpost of the brunet type.

Thus we see at a glance that there is a gradual though constant increase in the proportion of dark eyes and hair from north to south. Gould's data ('69) on our recruits during the civil war, for example, represents about sixteen per cent of dark hair in Scandinavia, the proportion rising to about seventy-five per cent among natives of Spain or Portugal. There are none of those sharp contrasts which appeared upon our maps showing the distribution of the long and broad heads in Europe. On that map the extremes were separated by only half a continent in either direction from the Alps; whereas in this case the change from dark to light covers the whole extent of the continent. It is as if a blending wash had been spread over the map of head form, toning down all its sharp racial division lines. Some cause other than race has evidently exerted an influence upon all types of men alike, tending to obliterate their physical differences. It is not a question of Celt, Slav, or Teuton. It lies deeper than these. The Czechs in Bohemia are as much darker than the Poles to the north of them, both being Slavic; as the Bavarians exceed the Prussians in the same respect, although the last two are both Germans. It would be unwarranted to maintain that any direct relation of climate to pigmentation has been proved. The facts point, nevertheless, strongly in that direction. We do not know in precisely what way the pigmental processes are affected. Probably other environmental factors are equally important with climate. To that point we shall return in a few pages. We may rest assured at this writing that our map

for Europe corroborates in a general way testimony drawn
from other parts of the earth that some relation between the
two exists.

It seems to be true that brunetness holds its own more
persistently over the whole of Europe than the lighter characteristics. Probably one reason why this appears to be so,
is because the dark traits are more striking, and hence are
more apt to be observed. Yet, after making all due allowance
for this fact, the relative persistency, or perhaps we might say
penetrativeness, of the brunet traits seems to be indicated.
Our map shows that, while in Scandinavia seldom less than
one quarter of all the eyes and hair are dark, in the south
the blond traits often fall below ten per cent of the total.
Thus in Sardinia there are only about three per cent of all the
eyes and hair which are light. The same point is shown with
added force if we study the distribution of the pure blond
or brunet types, and not of these traits independently. In
the blondest part of Germany there are seldom less than seven
per cent of pure brunet children. Among adults this would
probably not represent less than fifteen per cent of pure brunets, to say the least. As our table shows, in Scotland direct
observations on adults indicate nearly a quarter of the population to be pure brunets. On the other hand, the pure

Percentage of—

	PURE BRUNETS.		PURE BLONDS.	
	Children.	Adults.	Children.	Adults.
North Germany	7–11	..	33–44	..
Middle Germany	12–15	..	25–32	..
South Germany	15–25	..	18–24	..
Scotland	.....	22	.....	50
Ireland	.....	23	.....	48
Wales	.....	27	.....	34
Belgium	.....	27	.....	..
England	.....	31	.....	40
Switzerland	26	..	11	36
Austria	23	18	20	18
Italy	.....	25	.....	3
Sardinia	.....	49	.....	0.5
Croatia	.....	57	.....	..
Greece	.....	96	.....	..

blonds become a negligible quantity long before we reach the bottom of the table at the south. Thus, among two thousand and fifty natives of Tunis in North Africa, true Europeans as we must repeat, Collignon * found that, while blond hair or eyes were noticeable at times, in no single case was a pure blond with both light hair and eyes to be discovered. Similarly, in Sardinia, less than one per cent of the population was found by Livi to be of this pure blond type.† Dr. Ferraz de Macedo has courteously placed the results of an examination of eighteen hundred Portuguese men and women at our disposition. Less than two per cent of these were characterized by light hair of any shade; about one fifth were black-haired, the remainder being of various dark chestnut tints. The interest and significance of this extreme rarity of blondness in the south lie in its bearing upon the theory, propounded by Brinton, that northern Africa was the centre of dispersion of the blond invaders of Europe, who introduced a large measure of its culture.‡ We shall return to this theory at a later time. It is sufficient here to notice how completely this blond type vanishes among the populations of the south of Europe and northern Africa to-day. Such blonds do occur; they are certainly not a negligible quantity in some districts in Morocco. A portrait of one is given, through the courtesy of Dr. Bertholon, of Tunis, in our series at page 278. Each one in so dark a general population as here prevails, however, is a host itself in the observer's mind. The true status is revealed only when we consider men by hundreds or even thousands, in which case the real infrequency of blond traits becomes at once apparent.

Thus far we have been mainly concerned with the pigmentation of the hair and eyes as a result of climatic or other environmental influences. Let us now consider the *racial aspect* of the question. Is there anything in our map which might lead us to suspect that certain of these gradations of

---

* 1888, p. 3.   † 1896 a, p. 60.
‡ Keane, in his recent Ethnology, acquiesces in the same view.

pigmentation are due to purely hereditary causes? In other words, do the long heads and the short heads differ from one another in respect of the colour of the hair and eyes, as well as in cephalic index? In the preceding chapter we took occasion to point out in a general way the remarkable localization of the round-headed element of the European population in the Alps. The great central highland seemed indeed to constitute a veritable focus of this peculiar physical type. In this way it divided two similar centres of long-headedness— Teutonic in the north, Mediterranean in the south—one from another. This geographical characterization of the broad-headed variety entitled it, in our opinion, to be called the Alpine type, in distinction from the two others above mentioned. It will now be our purpose to inquire whether or not the physical traits of pigmentation stand in any definite and permanent relation to the three types of head form we have thus separated from one another in the geographical sense.

Many peculiarities in our colour map point to the persistence of racial differences despite considerable similarity of environment. Thus the Walloons in the southeastern half of Belgium, with a strip of population down along the Franco-German frontier, are certainly darker than the people all about. Among these Walloons, as our map on page 161 shows, brunet traits are upward of a third more frequent than among the Flemish in northern Belgium. This is especially marked by the prevalence of dark hair in the hilly country south of Brussels. The British Isles offer another example of local differences in this respect which can not be ascribed to environment. Wales and Ireland, Cornwall and part of Scotland, as we shall see, are appreciably brunet in comparison with other regions near by. The contrast between Normandy and Brittany in France is of even greater value to us in this connection. Dark hair is more than twice as common in the Breton cantons as it is along the English Channel in Normandy. These differences can not be due to the Gulf Stream mildness of the western climate or to the physical environme in any other way. In the other direction, among the

Hungarians, we begin to scent an Asiatic influence in the dark population of the southeast of Europe.

Perhaps the most conspicuous example of the racial fixity of this trait of pigmentation is offered by the Jews. They have preserved their Semitic brunetness through all adversities.* Socially ostracized and isolated, they have kept this coloration despite all migrations and changes of climate. In Germany to-day forty-two per cent of them are pure brunets in a population containing only fourteen per cent of the dark type on the average. They are thus darker by thirty per cent than their Gentile neighbours. As one goes south this difference tends to disappear. In Austria they are less than ten per cent darker than the general population; and finally in the extreme south they are even lighter than the populations about them. This is especially true of the red-haired type common in the East. To discover such differences requires minute examination. The reward has been to prove that pigmentation in spite of climate is indeed a fixed racial characteristic among the people of Europe. We are therefore encouraged to hope that great racial groups of population may still yield us evidence of their relationship or lack of it in respect of the colour of their hair and eyes, as well as in the head form.

It must be confessed that ethnically the study of pigmentation for Europe has heretofore yielded only very meagre and somewhat contradictory results. Huxley's famous theory of two constituent races, light and dark respectively, intermingled all across middle Europe, seems alone at first glance to represent adequately the facts for these traits.† It is only by consideration of other physical characteristics—notably the head form—that we see how complex it is in reality. No clear-cut demarcation of blond or brunet types is anywhere apparent. This we might indeed ascribe to intermixture were it not for the sharp definition of the boundaries of head form. A second reason for this apparent obliteration of racial char-

---

* Consult chapter xiv for details.

† 1870; his map is reproduced in Ranke's Mensch. It is adopted by Flower and Lyddeker as a final classification.

acteristics in the matter of pigmentation lies at hand apparently. We hope to be able to prove that, while the Alpine racial type is intermediate in the colour of the hair and eyes between the Teutonic populations on the north and the Mediterranean at the south, at the same time this physical trait is open to profound modification by the direct influences of environment. We shall hope to prove directly what we have already inferred from consideration of our general map of Europe—namely, that certain factors, either. climate, economic status, or habits of life, are competent to produce appreciable changes in the colour of the hair and eyes.

Since, at this point, we are venturing forth upon an uncharted sea, it behooves us to move slowly. Two theses we hope to prove respecting those portions of central Europe which are characterized by the broad-headed Alpine type of population. The first is that this racial element being the most ancient, becomes relatively more frequent in the areas of isolation, where natural conditions have been least disturbed by immigrants. In the byways, the primitive inhabitant; in the highways, the marauding intruder! This principle is as old as the hills. It is certainly true of languages and customs, why not likewise of race? We shall be able to establish its verity for all parts of Europe in due time. It forms the groundwork of our socio-geographical theory. The second thesis, no less important, is that this primitive Alpine type of population normally tends to be darker in hair and eyes than the blue-eyed, flaxen-haired, and long-headed Teutonic peoples on the north; and that, on the other hand, by its grayish hazel eyes and brownish hair, this broad-headed type in the highlands of central Europe is to be distinguished from its more thoroughly brunet neighbour at the south. The geographical evidence afforded by our map of Europe all gives tenability to this view that the Alpine type is intermediate in the colour of hair and eyes. It will serve as proof provisionally at least. In a succeeding chapter we shall discuss the matter of the association of separate traits into racial types from another point of view. We shall run up against some contradictory evidence, to be sure, but satisfactory disposition may be made of this when it appears. In the meantime we assume it to be geographically, if not indeed as yet anthropologically, proved beyond question.

What deduction is to be made from these two theses we have just outlined? The third side of our logical triangle seems to be fixed. If the areas of isolation are essentially Alpine by race, and if this ethnic type be truly intermediate in pigmentation, the byways, nooks, and corners of central Europe ought normally to be more brunet than the highways and open places all along the northern Teutonic border. Contrariwise, toward the south the indigenous undisturbed Alpine populations ought to be lighter than the heterogeneous ones, infused with Mediterranean brunet blood, if we may use the term. Since mountainous areas are less exposed to racial contagion by virtue of their infertility and unattractiveness, as well as by their inaccessibility or remoteness from dense centres of population, we may express our logical inference in another way. Where the Teutonic and the Alpine racial types are in contact geographically, the population of mountainous or isolated areas ought normally to contain more brunets than the people of the plains and river valleys, since blond traits have had lesser chance of immigration. The opposite rule should obtain south of the Alps. If we find this relation to fail us, we shall be led to suspect environmental disturbance of a serious kind. Fortunately for our contention, we are able to prove that it does so fail in various parts of Europe, notably in the Black Forest, the Vosges Mountains, and Switzerland. In all of these regions the populations at considerable altitudes, who ought racially to be more brunet than their neighbours, are in fact appreciably more blond, and no other reason for this blondness than that it is a direct result of physical circumstances is tenable.*

In order, before dismissing this subject, to make our point clear, let us adduce one example in detail tending to prove that in mountainous areas of isolation some cause is at work which tends to disturb racial equilibrium in the colour of the hair and eyes. This is drawn from Livi's monumental treatise

---

* See pages 234 and 288 *infra*.

8

on the anthropology of Italy. In entire independence of my
own inferences, he arrived at an identical conclusion that
blondness somehow is favoured by a mountainous environment. From a study of three hundred thousand recruits, he
found that fourteen out of the sixteen *compartimenti* into which
Italy is divided conformed to this law. There was generally
from four to five per cent more blondness above the four-
hundred-metre line of elevation than below it.* The true significance of these figures is greater than at first appears, for
we have again to consider the contrasts in the light of racial
probability. In northern Italy the mountains ought to be
lighter than the plains, because the Alps are here as elsewhere
a stronghold of a racial type relatively blond as compared
with the Mediterranean brunets. Environment and race
here join hands to produce greater blondness in the mountains. It is in the south of Italy that the two work in opposition, and here we turn for test of our law. In the south the
mountains should contain the Mediterranean brunet type in
relatively undisturbed purity; for the northern blonds are
more frequent in the attractive districts open to immigration.
Even here in many cases this racial probability is reversed or
equalized by some cause which works in opposition to race,
so that we find comfort at every turn.

The law which we have sought to prove is not radically
new. Many years ago Waitz asserted that mountaineers
tended to be lighter in colour of skin than the people of the
plains,† educing some interesting evidence to that effect from
the study of primitive peoples. Among a number of very
dark populations elsewhere, blonds occur in this way in ele-

---

* Antropometria Militare, p. 63 *seq.*; also in 1896 b, p. 24. We have
discussed this in Publications of the American Statistical Association.
vol. v, pp. 38 and 101 *seq.* This law is shown by study of provinces also.
There are sixty-nine of these available for comparison. Twelve of these
contain no mountains : thirty-two show manifestly greater blondness in
both hair and eyes ; fifteen show it partially ; in two, mountain and plain
are equal ; and in the remaining seven the law is reversed. Several of
these latter are explainable by local disturbances.

† 1859–1872, i, p. 49. Prichard hints at the same law, and Peschel
exemplifies it among primitive peoples

vated regions. Thus the Amorites in Palestine, and especially the numerous blonds in the Atlas Mountains in Morocco, may conceivably be due to such causes.* It is not certain that the true cause lies in the modifying influences of climate alone. Much of the data which we have here collected does not prove this. In fact, climatic changes can not be related to some of the variations in blondness which have been outlined. It seems as if some other factor had been at work. Livi, for example, ascribes the blondness of his mountaineers rather to the unfavourable economic environment, to the poor food, unsanitary dwellings, and general poverty of such populations. This explanation fits neatly into our social theory: for we assert that the population of mountains is relatively pure because there is no incentive for immigration of other types. Thus a pure population implies poverty of environment—a poverty which may stand in direct relation to the lack of pigmentation. It is yet too early to assert that this is the main cause. For the present it will suffice to have proved that appreciable differences in pigmentation exist, leaving the cause for future discussion. Much interesting material drawn from comparisons of urban with rural populations may help to throw light upon it. Our main purpose here has been to prove that pigmentation is a trait which is affected by environment. If, as we hope to have shown, the shape of the head is not open to such modification, we shall know where to turn when conflict of evidence arises. We shall pin our faith to that characteristic which pursues the even tenor of its racial way, unmoved by outward circumstances.

---

* Sayce, 1888 a and 1888 b. Sergi, 1897 a, p. 296, after a masterly analysis, expressly adopts this explanation for the African blonds. Majer and Kopernicki, 1885, p. 45, find the mountaineers lighter if the mixed types be excluded, but not otherwise.

CHAPTER V.

STATURE.

THE average stature of man, considered by racial groups or social classes, appears to lie between the limits of four feet four inches and five feet ten inches; giving, that is to say, a range of about one foot and a half. The physical elasticity of the species is not, however, as considerable as this makes it appear. The great majority of the human race is found restricted within much narrower limits. As a matter of fact, there are only three or four groups of really dwarfed men, less than five feet tall. Our map of the world shows a considerable area inhabited by the diminutive Bushmen in South Africa. Another large body of dwarfs occurs in New Guinea. The line of demarcation in the first case between the yellowish African Bushmen and the true negroes is very sharp; but in the East Indies the very tall and light Polynesians shade off almost imperceptibly in stature through Melanesia into the stunted Papuans. Other scattering representatives of true dwarf races occur sporadically throughout the Congo region and in Malaysia, but their total number is very small. On the whole, considerably more than ninety-nine per cent of the human species is above the average height of five feet and one inch; so that we may still further narrow our range of variation between that limit and five feet ten inches. We thereby reduce our racial differences of stature to about nine inches between extremes. These variations in size, it will be observed, are less than those which occur among the lower animals within the same species. Compare, for example, the dachshund, the St. Bernard, the Italian greyhound, and the smallest lapdog, and remember that they are all as-

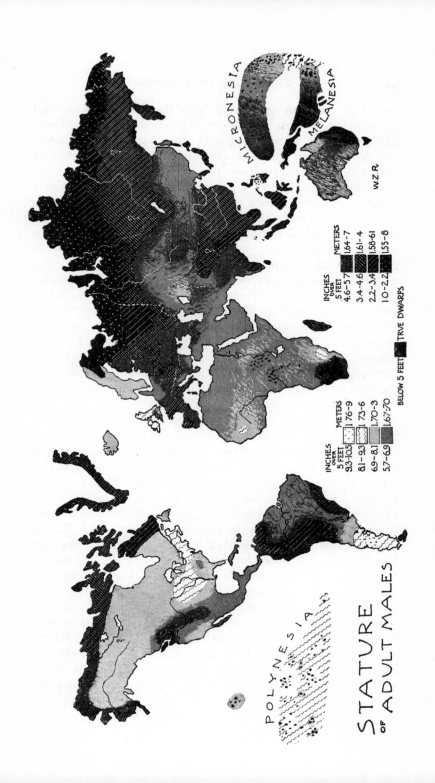

MICRONESIA

MELANESIA

W.Z.R.

METERS
INCHES
OVER
5 FEET
4.6–5.7   1.64–7
3.4–4.6   1.61–4
2.2–3.4   1.58–61
1.0–2.2   1.55–8

BELOW 5 FEET   TRUE DWARFS

INCHES
OVER
5 FEET   METERS
9.3–10.5   1.76–9
8.1–9.3   1.73–6
6.9–8.1   1.70–3
5.7–6.9   1.67–70

POLYNESIA

STATURE
OF ADULT MALES

cribed to the same species; or that the Shetland pony and the Percheron horse are likewise classified together. These abnormities are, to be sure, partly the result of artificial selection by man; but the same variation holds to a considerable extent among the wild animals.

The bodily height of a group of men is the resultant of a number of factors, many of which are as purely artificial as those concerned in the domestication of animals. These causes are quite as truly social or economic as they are physical or physiological. Among them we may count environment, natural or artificial selection, and habits of life. Beneath all of these, more fundamental than any, lies the influence of race which concerns us ultimately. This is overlaid and partially obscured by a fifth peculiarity manifested as a result of the sportiveness of Nature, whereby a large number of variations are due to chance, seemingly not caused by any distinct influences whatever. By scientific analysis we may eliminate this last factor, namely chance variation. The other four causes besides race are more important and deserve consideration by themselves.

Among savages it is easy to localize the *influence of environment*, as it acts directly through limitation of the food supply. In general the extreme statures of the human species are found either in regions where a naturally short race, like the Bushmen of South Africa, are confined within a district of great infertility like the Kalahari Desert; or, on the other hand, where a naturally tall race, like the Polynesians in the Pacific Ocean, enjoys all the material bounties which Nature has to bestow. It is probable that the prevalent shortness of the Eskimo and other inhabitants of the arctic regions is largely due to this factor. It is also likely that the miserable people of Terra del Fuego are much shorter than the Patagonians for the same reason. Scarcity or uncertainty of food limits growth. Wherever the life conditions in this respect become changed, in that place the influence of environment soon makes itself felt in the average stature of the inhabitants. Thus the Hottentots, physically of the same race as the Bushmen, but inhabiting a more fertile region; and, moreover, possessed of a regular food supply in their flocks and herds, are appreciably taller from these causes alone. All the aborigines of America seem to be subject to this same influence of the fertility of their environment.* In the Mississippi Valley, for example, they are much taller than in the desert lands of Arizona and New Mexico.† In the mountains on either side of the Mississippi basin they are as a rule distinctly shorter, although living the same life and belonging to the same race. The Creeks and the Iroquois exceed the Pueblos by several inches, probably because of the material bounty of their environment; and where we find a single tribe, such as the Cherokees, inhabiting both the mountains and the plains, we find a deficiency of stature in the mountains quite marked by comparison.

Among civilized peoples likewise this direct influence of environment acts through the food supply to affect the stature of any given group of men. Thus, in Europe, as among the aborigines of America, it may be said that the populations of mountainous districts are shorter, as a rule, than those which enjoy the fertility of the plains and the river basins. Italy has been most carefully studied in this respect, the law being established clearly all along the Apennines.‡ The people in the Vosges Mountains # and in the Black Forest ‖ are characterized by relatively short stature, partly for the same reason. Our map on page 236 brings this relation into strong relief. In this case, however, we shall be able to show that purely ethnic tendencies are also responsible in a measure for the phenomenon. Along the Carpathian chain a similar shortness of stature of the mountaineers has been proved, especially in the growing period of youth.△ In the Austrian Alps the same rule holds

---

* D'Orbigny, i, p. 95.

† Boas in Verh. Berl. Anth. Gesell., Sitzung, May 18, 1895, p. 375.

‡ Lombroso, 1879; Zampa, 1881 and 1886, p. 191; Livi, 1883, and especially 1896 a, pp. 39–47.

Collignon, 1881, p. 10; Brandt, 1898, p. 10.

‖ Ecker, 1876, and Ammon, 1890.

△ Majer and Kopernicki, 1877, p. 21, and 1889, p. 50. Lebon, 1881, p. 230, in the Podhalian mountaineers, finds an average stature as low as 1.59 metres.

good.* Our map of Switzerland (page 285) brings out very clearly the shortness of stature in the Bernese Oberland. Almost every other Swiss administrative division overlaps both valley and mountain in such a way as to render comparisons impossible. The testimony, however, is not at all unanimous. In the Bavarian Alps, Ranke † finds the mountaineers appreciably taller than the peasantry in the plains. Along the northern slopes of the Pyrenees in France, the population in the inner valleys is also well above the average for the plains of Béarn.‡ We are able to explain a similar phenomenon all over Thuringia,# through the later occupation of the valleys by the relatively short Slavs, invaders from the east.

The influence of environment is, in any case, not at all as simple as it would appear. In addition to the direct effect of this environment, a selective process is also at work. Only thus can we account for the fact that while the populations at moderate altitudes seem to be physically depressed by their surroundings, those from regions of the greatest elevation seem to be rather above the normal stature.‖ It seems permissible, indeed, to assume with Ranke △ that only those of decided vigour are able to withstand the rigours and privations in this latter case, leaving an abnormally tall, selected population as a result. This may account for the high average stature found by Carret [(’83)] and Longuet [(’85)] in Savoy,

---

* Weisbach, 1894, p. 234.

† 1881 ; see our map on p. 227, *infra*.

‡ Chopinet, 1890 ; and Collignon, 1895, p. 92. The tallness of the Basques we have discussed on p. 201.

Reischel, 1889, pp. 138–142. In the British Isles the data of the Anthropometric Committee (Final Report, 1883, p. 14) is too limited to give force to its generalizations. Scheiber, 1881, p. 257, finds no differences in Hungary, but the mountains are all too low there in any case. Dunant found no such relation either in Geneva or Freiburg ; nor does Bedot in Valais apparently.

‖ Collignon, 1895, p. 93, and Livi, 1896 a, p. 39, confirm this for France and Italy respectively. Majer and Kopernicki, 1877, p. 23, found adults in the Carpathians taller than in the plains although shorter by six centimetres at twenty years of age, this difference gradually diminishing with growth.

△ 1881, p. 14.

shown on our maps of France. Toldt [91] finds a high proportion of very tall in the Tyrol also, perhaps for the same reason,
although here again we run afoul of racial complications of
importance.*

Wherever the geology of a district has produced a soil
which yields with difficulty to cultivation, or where the climate is unfavourable to prosperity, the influence is reflected

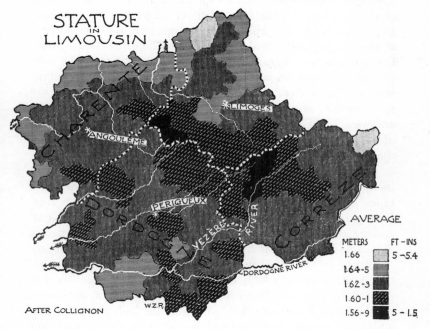

in the physical characteristics of the population.† All over
Europe we may locate such "misery spots," one of which
will, however, serve as an example. It is depicted in the
accompanying map.‡ This spot is likewise indicated in the
south central part of France upon our general map for Eu-

---

* Page 101.

† Durand de Gros, 1868, first suggested such an explanation. His
later work confirms it, especially with Lapouge, 1897–'98 (rep., p. 61).
Beddoe, 1867–'69 a, discusses it (rep., p. 174).

‡ From Collignon, 1894 b, pp. 26 *et seq.*

rope, facing page 96. In this district we find a general average stature of five feet and two to three inches—a low level not elsewhere touched in France save in a little spot to the southwest of this, where similar conditions prevail. Here in Limousin there is a barren range of low hills which lies along the dividing line between the departments of Dordogne, Corrèze, and Haute-Vienne, about half-way between Périgueux and Limoges. The water courses on our map show the location of these uplands. They extend over an area about seventy-five miles long and half as wide, wherein average human misery is most profound. Dense ignorance prevails. There is more illiteracy than in any other part of France. The contrast in stature, even with the low average of all the surrounding region, is clearly marked by the dark tint. There are sporadic bits of equal diminutiveness elsewhere to the south and west, but none are so extended or so extreme. Two thirds of the men are below five feet three inches in height in some of the communes, and the women are three or more inches shorter even than this. One man in ten is below four feet eleven inches in stature. This is not due to race, for several racial types are equally stunted in this way within the same area. It is primarily due to generations of subjection to a harsh climate, to a soil which is worthless for agriculture, to a steady diet of boiled chestnuts and stagnant water, and to unsanitary dwellings in the deep, narrow, and damp valleys. Still further proof may be found to show that these people are not stunted by any hereditary influence, for it has been shown that children born here, but who migrate and grow up elsewhere, are normal in height; while those born elsewhere, but who are subject to this environment during the growing period of youth, are proportionately dwarfed.*

There is a second "misery spot" in France, a little farther to the southwest from the Limousin hills. It extends along the west coast in the triangle between the Garonne River and the Spanish frontier. The cause is here the same. The department of Landes derives its name from the great expanse of flat country, barely above the sea level, which stretches

---

* Collignon, 1894 b, pp. 32 *et seq.*

away south of Bordeaux. There is no natural drainage slope.
The subsoil is an impervious clay. In the rainy season, water
accumulates and forms stagnant marshes, covered with rank
vegetation. At other times the water dries away, and the
vegetation dies and rots. Malaria was long the curse of the
land. Government works are to-day reclaiming much of it
for cultivation and health, but it will be generations before
the people recover from the physical degeneration of the past.
One may follow, as Chopinet [98] has done, the boundary of
this unhealthful area by means of the degenerate physique of
the peasantry, especially marked in its stature. Influences
akin to these have undoubtedly been of great effect in many
other parts of Europe, especially in the south of Italy and Sardinia, where the largest area of short statures in Europe prevails to-day. Meisner is thus able to account for the relatively short population of Stade, in the sandy plains between
Hamburg and Bremen.* The Jews in Lithuania are below the
Jewish average for the fertile Ukraine and Bessarabia for the
same reason,† even as the Great Russian falls below the Little
Russians in this respect, as we shall show subsequently.

Environment thus acts directly upon stature through the
food supply and economic prosperity. The second modifying influence lies in so-called *artificial selection*—a cause which
is peculiarly potent in modern social life. The efficiency of
this force depends upon the intimate relation which exists between bodily height and physical vigour. Other things being
equal, a goodly stature in a youth implies a surplus of energy
over and above the amount requisite merely to sustain life.‡
Hence it follows that, more often than otherwise, a tall population implies a relatively healthy one. Our double map,
of the westernmost promontory of Brittany, opposite page 86,
shows this most clearly. In the interior cantons, shorter on
the average by an inch than in the population along the sea-

---

* 1889, p. 115 ; 1891, p. 323. See our map on p. 225.

† Talko-Hryncewicz, 1892, pp. 8 and 59–60.

‡ Broca, 1868 a, p. 201, although Baxter and Erismann show it to be
not always true. Chopinet, Myrdacz, and others give many maps, both
of stature and disease, which confirm the law regionally at all events.

coast, there is a corresponding increase of defective or degenerate constitutional types. The character of the environment is largely responsible for this. The barren, rocky tableland is strongly contrasted with the " ceinture dorée " described by Gallouédec [93]. The fishing industry is of great material value to the coast population as well. The parallelism between our two maps is broken in but three or four instances. The map, in fact, illustrates the truth of our assertion far better than words can express it.

This relation between stature and health is brought to concrete expression in the armies of Europe through a rejection of all recruits for service who fall below a certain mini-

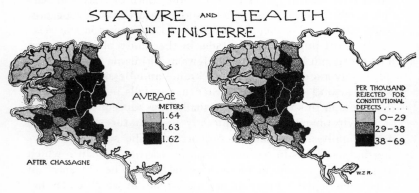

mum standard of height, generally about five feet.* The result of this is to preclude the possibility of marriage for all the fully developed men, during their three years in barracks; while the undersized individuals, exempted from service on this account, are left free to propagate the species meanwhile. Is it not apparent that the effect of this artificial selection is

* Military selection of this kind is first mentioned by Villermé, 1829, p. 385 ; the effect of the Napoleonic wars is discussed by Dufau, 1840, p. 169, and Tschouriloff, 1876, pp. 608 and 655. See also Lapouge, 1896 a, pp. 207–242 ; Broca, Sur la prétendue dégénérescence de la population française, Bull. Acad. de Méd., Paris, xxxii, 1867, pp. 547–603 and 839–862 ; and Bischoff, Ueber die Brauchbarkeit der in verschiedenen europäischen Staaten veröffentlichen Resultate des Recruterings-Geschäftes, München, 1867.

to put a distinct premium upon inferiority of stature, in so far as future generations are concerned? This enforced postponement of marriage for the normal man, not required of the degenerate, is even more important than at first sight appears. It implies not merely that the children of normal families are born later in life—that would not be of great moment in itself —it means far more than this. The majority of children are more often born in the earlier half of married life, before the age of thirty-five. Hence a postponement of matrimony means not only later children but fewer children.* Herein lies the great significance of the phenomenon for us. Standing armies tend in this respect to overload succeeding generations with inferior types of men. This selection is in operation akin to the influence which Galton has invoked as a partial explanation for the mental darkness of the Middle Ages. This he ascribes to the beliefs and customs by which all the finer minds and spirits were withdrawn from the field of matrimony by the Church, leaving the entire future population to the loins of the physically robust and adventurous portion of the community. Mind spent itself in a single generation of search for knowledge; physique, bereft of intellect, was left to its own devices among the common people.

The intensity of this military selection, potent enough in time of peace, is of course highly augmented during the prosecution of a war. At such periods the normal men are not only isolated for an indefinite period; their ranks are permanently decimated by the mortality at the front. The selective influence is doubly operative. Fortunately, we possess data which appear to afford illustration of its effects. Detailed investigation in various parts of France is bringing to light certain curious after-effects of the late Franco-Prussian War. We do not always fully realize what such an event means for a nation, quite irrespective of the actual mortality and of the direct economic expenditure. Every family in the land is affected by it; and the future bears its full share with the con-

* Marriage at an average age of twenty years insures an increasing population; if postponed until the age of twenty-nine, population is bound to decrease (Beddoe, 1893, p. 15, citing Galton, 1883).

temporaneous population. In France, for example, during the year of the war, there were seventy-five thousand fewer marriages than usual. In 1871 upon its conclusion, an unprecedented epidemic of them broke out, not equalled in absolute numbers since the veterans returned from the front in 1813, on the cessation of hostilities at that time.*

Two tendencies have been noted, from a comparison of the generations of offspring severally conceived before, during, and after the war. This appeared in the conscripts who came before the recruiting commissions in 1890–'92, at which time the children conceived in war times became, at the age of twenty, liable for service. In the population during the progress of the war the flower of French manhood, then in the field, was without proportionate representation. There must have been an undue preponderance, not only of stunted men rejected from the army for deficiency of stature alone, but of those otherwise physically unfitted for service. Hence the population born at this time ought, if heredity means anything, to retain some traces of its relatively degenerate derivation. This is indeed the case. In Dordogne this contingent included nearly seven per cent more deficient statures than the normal average.† Quite independently, in the distant department of Hérault, Lapouge discovered the same thing.‡ He found in some cantons a decrease of nearly an inch in the average stature of this unfortunate generation, while exemptions for deficiency of stature suddenly rose from six to sixteen per cent. This selection is not, however, entirely maleficent. A fortunate compensation is afforded in another direction. For the generation conceived of the men returned to their families at the close of the war has shown a distinctly upward tendency almost as well marked. Those who survived the perils and privations of service were presumably in many cases the most active and rugged ; the weaker portion having succumbed in the meanwhile, either to wounds or sickness. The result was that the generation conceived directly after the war was as much above the average, especially

---

* De Lapouge, 1896 a, p. 233.   † Collignon, 1894 b, p. 36.
‡ 1894 a, pp. 353 *et seq.*

evinced in general physique perhaps more than in stature, as their predecessors, born of war times, were below the normal.

Another illustration of the operation of artificial selection in determining the stature of any given group of men appears in the physique of immigrants to the United States. In the good old days when people emigrated from Europe because they had seriously cast up an account and discovered that they could better their condition in life by coming to America; that is, before the days when they came because they were overpersuaded by steamship agents, eager for commissions on the sale of tickets; or because of the desire of their home governments to be rid of them—in those days investigation revealed that on the average the immigrants were physically taller than the people from whom they sprang.* This difference, in some instances, amounted to upward of an inch upon the average. Among the Scotch, a difference of nearly two inches was shown to exist by the measurements taken during our civil war. These immigrants were a picked lot of men—picked, because it required all the courage which physical vigour could give to pull up stakes and start life anew. This law that *natural* emigrants, if I may use the term, are taller than the stay-at-home average was again exemplified during the civil war in another way. It was found that recruits hailing from States other than those in which they were born were generally taller than those who had always remained in the places of their birth—that is to say, here again physical vigour and the adventurous migratory spirit seemed to stand in close relation to one another.

In times of peace, perhaps the most potent influence of this form of artificial selection bears upon the differences in stature which obtain between different *occupations* or *professions*.†

* Gould, 1869, pp. 126 and 179. Baxter, 1875, i, p. 16, holds age differences largely accountable for it, however.

† The only authorities which classify statures by occupations are: J. C. Majer, 1862, pp. 365–372, for Franconia; Beddoe, 1867–'9 a, p. 150, and Roberts, 1878, p. 104, for the British Isles; J. Bertillon, 1886, p. 13, and Needon, 1867–'8, on Saxony; Olóriz, 1896, pp. 47 and 61, for Madrid; and Livi, 1897 a, pp. 14 and 27, on Italy. Schweizerische Statistik, Tab. 10, since 1887 are also very good. Lagneau, 1895, is fine on this also.

This is strikingly exemplified by the accompanying table, based upon the examination of nearly two hundred thousand Swiss conscripts. An almost uninterrupted increase in the proportion of the undersized, with a coincident decrease in the relative numbers of the tall men, will be seen to take place from the top of the table toward the bottom. While nearly half the professional men and ecclesiastics are tall men ; but about one tenth of the cobblers, tailors, and basket-weavers, at the opposite extreme, attain the moderate height of 1.7 metres (five feet seven inches). The table is a complete demonstration of this law in itself. It needs no further description.

Stature by Occupations. Switzerland, 1884–'91.
(Schweizerische Statistik, 1894.)

OCCUPATION.	PER CENT OF STATURES.	
	Under 156 cms. (5 ft. 1.4 in.).	170 cms. and above (5 ft. 7 in.).
Professions...........................	2	47
Priests or ministers......................	4	45
Teachers	3	35
University students	2	44
Brewers	3	36
Machinists.............................	4	39
Blacksmiths............................	6	21
Merchants and clerks....................	6	31
Masons................................	13	17
Farm labourers.........................	14	20
Spinners and weavers...................	21	11
Chemical industries	20	18
Basket-weavers	23	12
Cobblers...............................	20	11
Chimney-sweeps........................	23	12
Tailors................................	33	7
Factory operatives in general.............	24	11

Two causes may be justly ascribed for this phenomenon of differences in stature according to occupation. The first one is, as we have said, that of an artificial selection. The physically well-developed men seek certain trades or occupations in which their vigour and strength may stand them in good stead; on the other hand, those who are by nature weakly, and coincidently often deficient in stature, are compelled to make shift with some pursuit for which they are fitted. Thus, workers in iron, porters, firemen, policemen, are taller as a class than the average, because they are of necessity recruited from the more robust portion of the population. In marked contrast to them tailors, shoemakers, and weavers, in an occupation which entails slight demands upon the physical powers, and which is open to all, however weakly they may be, are appreciably shorter than the average. Moreover, certain diseases fall upon this second class in a way which tends still further to lower the average stature among them. Thus, consumption is uncommonly prevalent in these particularly sedentary industrial classes, and it is also more common among tall youths. It seems, therefore, that this disease weeds out, as if by choice, those who within this relatively stunted class rise above its average. As an extreme example of this selective influence exercised in the choice of an occupation we may instance grooms, who as a class are over an inch shorter than the British population as a whole. This is probably because men who are light in build and short in stature find here an opening which is suited to their physique. Their weight may nevertheless be often greater than the stature implies, because of an increase which has taken place late in life. The diminutiveness of chimney-sweeps, shown by our table for Switzerland, is certainly a result of such a process of selection. Sailors also are generally undersized. Gould [69], noticing this among both negroes and whites during the civil war, ascribed it, however, to the privations and exposure incident to a seafaring life, rather than to any selective process.

The final effects of this influence of artificial selection are highly intensified by reason of the fact that, as soon as the choice of occupation is once made, other forces come into play which differentiate still further the stature of the several classes. This is the last of our modifying influences in respect of stature; namely, the direct effect of *habits of life or of the nature of the employment*.* Thus, the weakly youth who

---

* Instructive parallels between physical development and morbidity in the several occupations may be drawn. Consult our review of Westergaard and Bertillon (Jour. Soc. de Stat., Paris, Oct.–Nov., 1892) in Pubs. Amer. Stat. Ass., iii, 1892-'93, pp. 241–44.

enters a sedentary occupation immediately becomes subjected
to unfavourable circumstances as a result of his choice.   If he
chooses to take up the tailor's trade because he is physically
unfitted for other pursuits, all the influences of the trade tend
to degenerate his physique still further.   Among these we
may count the cramped position in which he works, the long
hours, the unsanitary surroundings, etc.   The physical degeneracy among bakers and metal-workers seems to be quite
constant; brewers and butchers, on the other hand, are more
often tall as a class.   Perhaps the best example of all is offered
by the Jews, of whom we shall speak in detail later.   An active
life conduces to growth and vigour, especially an active life
in the open air.   Denied all these advantages, everything
operates to exaggerate the peculiarities which were due to
natural causes in the preceding generation alone.   For the
choice of occupation is to a large extent in Europe a matter of
hereditary necessity; as, for example, among the potters and
lead-miners in Great Britain.*   This direct influence of the nature of the employment is probably the second principal cause
of the great differences in stature which we observe among the
several social classes in any community.   A patent example
is offered by our data for the British Isles.   At the head stand
the liberal professions, followed in order as our tables show,
by the farmers and the commercial group, then by the industrial open-air classes, and finally by those who are engaged
in indoor and sedentary occupations.   The difference between

Average Stature in Inches (British Isles).†

No. of ob-servations.	Age (males).	Professional class.	Commercial class.	INDUSTRIAL CLASS.	
				Open air.	Indoors.
3,498	15 years.	63.6	62.2	61.8	61.3
592	23 "	68.7	67.4	67.4	66.4
1,886	30–40 "	69.6	67.9	67.6	66.8

* Anthropometric Committee, 1883, p. 20; and Beddoe, 1867–'9 a, pp. 182
and 221.

† Anthropometric Committee, British Association, 1883, p. 38.   Olóriz.
1896, p. 61, gives for Madrid the following heights in metres for these
four classes : 1.639, 1.611, 1.607, and 1.598 respectively.

Averages by Occupations (British Isles).*

No. of observations.	Occupation.	Stature (inches).	Weight (pounds).
174	Miscellaneous outdoor........	67.6	142.0
242	Clerks	67.3	136.7
834	Labourers	67.1	140.0
209	Iron-workers...............	67.1	140.0
135	Tailors and shoemakers	66.9	134.5
235	Miscellaneous indoor.........	66.7	132.5
101	Grooms	66.5	138.7

these last two—namely, those who work in the open air and those who are confined within doors—amounts in Great Britain to upward of one half an inch upon the average, if we consider masons, carpenters, and day labourers as typical of the first class, and tailors and shoemakers of the second. In Madrid, according to Olóriz's figures given in our footnote, the fourth industrial class is more than an inch and a half shorter than the first professional one. As our table shows, the differences during the period of growth often amount to upward of two inches, greater among girls than among boys. As extreme examples of divergencies of this kind, we may instance a difference of seven inches between boys of fourteen in the well-to-do classes and those who are in the industrial schools in Great Britain; or the difference in average stature of four inches and a half between extreme classes of English girls at the age of ten years. Later in life this disparity becomes less, as it appears that the influence of factory life is more often to retard growth than to cause a complete cessation of it.† This influence of industrialism must always be borne in mind in comparing different districts in the same country. Derby and Yorkshire are below the average for England, as our later maps will demonstrate, probably for no other reason.‡

---

* Beddoe, 1867–'9 a, p. 150.

† Porter, 1894, p. 305, finds the children in St. Louis of the industrial classes relatively defective in height at all ages after fourteen. Erismann, 1888, pp. 65–90, found the same true of factory operatives in Russia; the defectiveness of textile workers was especially marked. Riccardi, 1885, p. 123; Uhlitzsch, 1892, p. 433; Anthropometric Committee, 1883, p. 38; and Drs. Bowditch, Boas, and West all confirm this.

‡ Favier, 1888, and Carlier, 1893, have analyzed such industrial districts in France with similar conclusions.

Interesting deductions might also be drawn from the relation of the height to the weight in any class, by which we
may determine to some degree when and how these degenerative influences become effective.* Thus clerks, as a class, are
above the average stature, but below it in weight. This follows because these men are recruited from a social group
where the influences during the period of growth are favourable. The normal stature was attained at this time. The unfavourable circumstances have come into play later through
the sedentary nature of the occupation, and the result is a
deficiency in weight. The case of grooms given above is exactly the reverse of this; for they became grooms because they
were short, but have gained in weight afterward because the
occupation was favourable to health.

These differences in stature, indicative of even more profound differences in general physical development within the
community offer a cogent argument for the protection of our
people by means of well-ordered factory laws. The Anthropometric Committee of the British Association for the Advancement of Science [83] declares, as a result of its detailed investigation, that the protection of youth by law in Great Britain
has resulted in the gain of a whole year's growth for the factory children. In other words, a boy of nine years in 1873
was found to equal in weight and in stature one of ten years of
age in 1833. This is Nature's reward for the passage of laws
presumably better than the present so-called "beneficent"
statute in South Carolina which forbids upward of eleven
hours' toil a day for children *under* the age of fourteen. In
every country where the subject has been investigated—in
Germany, in Russia, in Austria, Switzerland, or Great Britain
—the same influence is shown. Fortunately, the advance out
of barbarism is evidenced generally by a progressive increase
in the stature of the population as an accompaniment of the
amelioration of the lot of the masses. This is certainly going
on decade by decade, absolutely if not relatively. Evidence
from all over Europe is accumulating to show that the

---

* Livi, L'indice ponderale, Atti Soc. Romana di Antrop., v, fasc. 2, 1896,
is good on this.

standard of physical development is steadily rising as a
whole.* There is no such change taking place among the
prosperous and well-to-do. It is the masses which are, so to
speak, catching up with the procession. It offers a conclusive argument in favour of the theory that the world moves
forward.

One of the factors akin to that of occupation which appears to determine stature is the unfavourable *influence of city
life*. The general rule in Europe seems to be that the urban
type is physically degenerate. This would imply, of course,
not the type which migrates to the city on the attainment
of majority, or the type which enjoys an all-summer vacation
in the country, but the urban type which is born in the city
and which grows up in such environment, to enter a trade
which is also born of town life. The differences in stature
which are traceable to this influence of city life are considerable. Glasgow and Edinburgh offer an extreme example
wherein the average stature of the poorer classes has been
found by Dr. Beddoe ('67) to be four inches less than the average for the suburban districts. The people, at the same time,
are on the average thirty-six pounds lighter. On the other
hand, it must be confessed that this unfavourable influence
of city life is often obscured by the great social selection
which is at work in the determination of the physical type of
the population of great cities. While the course of the town
type by itself is downward, oftentimes the city attracts another class which is markedly superior, in the same way that
the immigrants of the United States have been distinguished
in this respect. The problems of urban populations are, however, complicated by various other processes. Discussion of

---

* For France, earlier contentions of Broca and Boudin are confirmed
by detailed investigations ; as by Carret, 1882, and Longuet, 1885, for
Savoy ; Hovelacque, 1894 b for the Morvan, and 1896 a, with especial
clearness, for Provence ; Collignon, 1890 a, for Côtes-du-Nord ; and de
Lapouge, 1894 a, for Hérault. The Anthropometric Committee, 1883, shows
increasing stature in Great Britain ; J. Bertillon, 1886, p. 12, represents it
as true in Holland ; while Arbo, 1895 a, asserts an average increase of
over half an inch in recent years in Norway. Hultkrantz, 1896 a, finds
the same true in Sweden.

these we defer to a later chapter, where the entire subject will be treated by itself at length.

It would be interesting to inquire in how far the relative height of the *sexes* is due to a similar selective process. Certain it is that among us in civilization, women average from three to four inches below men in stature, a disparity which seems to be considerably less among primitive peoples. Brinton * has invoked as a partial explanation, at least, for this, the influence of the law of sexual division of labour which obtains among us. This law commands, in theory, that the men should perform the arduous physical labour of life, leaving the more sedentary portion of it to the women. If the conscious choice of mates had followed this tendency, its effect would certainly be unfavourable to the development of an increasing stature among women, while it might operate to better the endowment of men in that respect. It is impossible, owing to the paucity of selected data as to sexual differences, to follow this out. The only discoverable law seems to be the one formulated by Weisbach, that sexual differences in height are more marked in the taller races. Probably this difference of stature between the sexes is partially due to some other cause which stops growth in the woman earlier than in the man. For the clearest evidence is offered by developmental anthropometry that the female of the human species is born smaller; grows more slowly after puberty; and finally attains her adult stature about two years earlier than man. The problem is too complex to follow out in this place. So far as our present knowledge goes, the question has no ethnic significance.

From the preceding array of facts it would appear that stature is rather an irresponsible witness in the matter of race. A physical trait so liable to disturbance by circumstances outside the human body is correspondingly invalidated as an indication of hereditary tendencies which lie within. We are compelled for this reason to assign the third place

---

* 1890 a, p. 37. Rolleston, 1884, ii, pp. 254 and 354, discusses this, adducing most interesting archæological evidence. Havelock Ellis's Man and Woman offers a most convenient summary also.

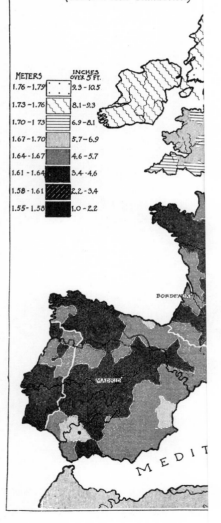

AVERAGE STATURE
EUROPE

(WITHOUT AGE CORRECTION.)

METERS		INCHES OVER 5 FT.
1.76 – 1.79		9.3 – 10.5
1.73 – 1.76		8.1 – 9.3
1.70 – 1 73		6.9 – 8.1
1.67 – 1.70		5.7 – 6.9
1.64 – 1.67		4.6 – 5.7
1.61 – 1.64		3.4 – 4.6
1.58 – 1.61		2.2 – 3.4
1.55 – 1.58		1.0 – 2.2

BORDEAUX

MADRID

MEDIT

to this characteristic in our series of racial tests, placing it below the colour of the hair and eyes in the scale. This does not mean that it is entirely worthless for our ethnic purposes. There are many clear cases of differences of stature which can be ascribed to no other cause; but it bids us be cautious about judging hastily. It commands us to be content with nothing less than hundreds of observations, and to rigidly eliminate all social factors. The best way to do this is to take the broad view, by including so many individuals that locally progressive and degenerative factors may counterbalance one another. Turning back to our map of the world, it will at once appear that we can not divide the human species into definite continental groups characterized by distinct peculiarities of stature. The so-called yellow Mongolian race comprises both tall and short peoples. The aborigines of America are, as a rule, tall; but in the Andes, the basin of the Columbia River, and elsewhere they are quite undersized. The only two racial groups which seem to be homogeneous in stature are the true African negroes and the peoples of Indonesia and the Pacific. In Africa the environment is quite uniform. In the other cases racial peculiarities seem to be deeply enough ingrained to overcome the disturbances due to outward factors. The Malays are always and everywhere rather short. The Polynesians are obstinately inclined toward tallness. With these exceptions, racial or hereditary predispositions in stature seem to be absent. Let us turn to the consideration of Europe by itself, and inquire if the same rule holds here as well.

The light tints upon this map * indicate the tall populations; as the tint gradually darkens, the people become progressively shorter. Here again we find that Europe comprehends a very broad range of variations. The Scotch, with an average height of five feet nine inches, stand on a level with the tall Polynesians and Americans, both aboriginal and modern white. At the other extreme, the south Italians, Sicilians, and Sardinians range alongside the shortest of men,

---

* See Appendix, C.

if we except the abnormal dwarf races of Africa. From one
to the other of these limits there is a regular transition, which
again points indubitably to racial law. Two specific centres
of tall stature appear, if we include the minor but marked
tendency of the Dalmatians, Bosnians, and Montenegrins along
the Adriatic Sea. The principal one lies in the north, culminating in the British Isles and Scandinavia. In Britain, economic prosperity undoubtedly is of importance, as the level
of material comfort is probably higher than on the Continent.
But even making allowance for this fact, it appears that the
Teutons as a race are responsible for the phenomenon. Our
map slightly exaggerates, perhaps, the physical superiority in
the north. Conscription in the southern countries of Europe
usually takes place at the age of twenty, so that our results
in this region do not represent fully matured statures. For
Scandinavia and the British Isles, the ages of men observed
were greater. Nevertheless this slight correction affects in
nowise the proposition that the Teutons are a race of great
height. Wherever they have penetrated, as in northern
France, down the Rhone Valley, or into Austria, the population shows its effects. The light area along the Adriatic, indicating a very tall population, is difficult to account for.
Deniker ('98) ascribes it to the presence of a gigantic Dinaric
race ; a point which we shall discuss later.

Central Europe is generally marked by medium height.
The people tend to be stocky rather than tall. The same
holds true as we turn to the Slavic countries in the east of Europe. Across Austria and Russia there is a progressive although slight tendency in this direction. The explanation of
the extreme short stature of Sardinia and southern Italy is
more problematical. Our map points to a racial centre of
real diminutiveness, at an average of five feet and one or two
inches. Too protracted civilization, such as it was, is partly to
blame. It is undeniable that, as Lapouge and Fallot assert,
while the average height of the other populations of Mediterranean race is low, a goodly proportion of the people are of
fair stature. It is the presence of a heavy contingent of abnormally stunted men which really depresses the average in

places below mediocrity.* This would seem to indicate physical degeneracy, rather than a natural diminutiveness as the
cause. A notable difference of stature confronts us in Africa.
All along the coast from Morocco to Tunis the Berbers and
Arabs are finely developed men.† Nor is Spain below the
general standard for most of France or Switzerland. It is indeed difficult to explain the variations in height which we
meet about the Mediterranean on any other theory than that
of environmental disturbance, although Livi and Deniker assert it to be purely a matter of race.‡

We may demonstrate the innate tendency of the Teutonic
peoples toward tallness of stature more locally than by this
continental method. We may follow the trait from place to
place, as this migratory race has moved across the map.
Wherever these " greasy seven-foot giants," as Sidonius Apol-
linaris called them, have gone, they have implanted their stature upon the people, where it has remained long persistent
thereafter. Perhaps the clearest detailed illustration of a persistency of this racial peculiarity is offered by the people
of Brittany. Many years ago observers began to note the
contrasts in the Armorican peninsula between the Bretons
and the other French peasantry, and especially the local differences between the people of the interior and those fringing
the seacoast. The regularity of the phenomenon is made manifest by the map on the next page. This is constructed from observations on all the youth who came of age during a period
of ten years from 1850–'59. There can be no doubt of the

---

* The theory of a so-called "pygmy" race in Europe, even with the
support of such distinguished authorities as Kollmann, Sergi, and others,
seems to me entirely untenable. All populations contain a very few
dwarf types, as a normal result of variation or degeneracy, as Virchow
also asserts. To dignify them with the name of a race entirely miscon-
ceives the meaning of the term ; nor does Sergi's hypothesis that these
dwarfs represent vestiges of immigrants from the pygmy races of central
Africa seem more probable. Consult Kollmann, in Jour. Anth. Inst.,
1895, p. 117 ; Sergi, 1895 a, p. 90: Niceforo, 1896.

† Collignon, 1887 a, p. 208 ; Bertholon, 1892, p. 10 ; at p. 13 a heavy
contingent of very short types seems to be present even in Africa.

‡ 1896 a, p. 183. Cf. Appendix, D.

facts in the case. It has been tested in every way. Other measurements, made twenty years later, are precisely parallel in their results, as we have already seen (page 86 *supra*) in the case of Finisterre.*

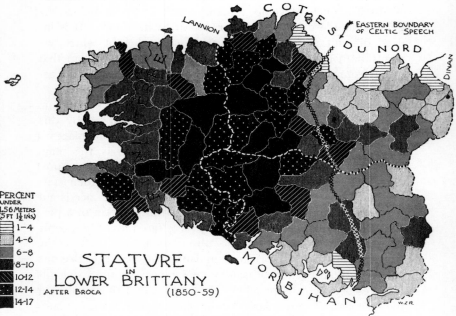

STATURE in LOWER BRITTANY
AFTER BROCA   (1850-59)

PERCENT
UNDER
1.56 METERS
(5 FT 1½ INS)
- 1–4
- 4–6
- 6–8
- 8–10
- 10–12
- 12–14
- 14–17

The average stature of the whole peninsula is low, being only about five feet five inches; yet in this "*tache noire*" it descends more than a full inch below this. This appreciable difference is not wholly due to environment, although the facts cited for Finisterre show that it is of some effect. The whole peninsula is rocky and barren. The only advantage that the people on the coast enjoy is the support of the fisheries. This is no insignificant factor, to be sure. Yet we have direct proof beyond this that race is here in evidence. This is afforded by other physical differences between the population of the coast and that of the interior. The people of the littoral are lighter in hair and eyes, and appreciably

---

* Broca, 1868 a ; and Chassagne, 1881.

longer-headed; in other words, they show traces of Teutonic intermixture. In ancient times this whole coast was known as the "*litus Saxonicum*," so fiercely was it ravaged by these northern barbarians. Then again in the fifth century, immigrants from Britain, who in fact bestowed the name of Brittany upon the country, came over in hordes, dispossessed in England by the same Teutonic invaders. They were probably Teutonic also; for the invaders of Britain came so fast that they literally crowded themselves out of the little island.

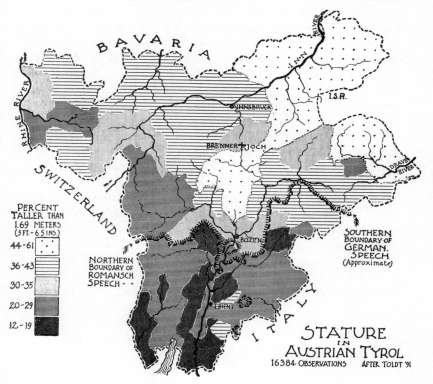

The result has been to infuse a new racial element into all the border populations in Brittany, while the original physical traits remain in undisturbed possession of the interior. The Normans to the northeast are, on the other hand, quite purely

Teutonic, especially marked in their height.   In this case environment and race have joined hands in the final result, but the latter seems to have been the senior partner in the affair.

One more detailed illustration of the persistence of stature as a racial trait may be found in the people of the Austrian Tyrol.   The lower Inn Valley (uppermost in our map) was the main channel of Teutonic immigration into a primitively broad-headed Alpine country by race, as we shall later see. From the south, up the Adige Valley by Trient came the second intrusive element in the long-headed brunet Mediterranean peoples.   This map at once enables us to endow each of these types with its proper quota of stature; for the environment is quite uniform, considered as in this map by large districts covering valley and mountain alike.   Each area contains all kinds of territory, so that we are working by topographical averages, so to speak.   Moreover, the whole population is agricultural, with the exception of a few domestic industries in the western half.   Such differences as arise must be therefore in large measure due to race.   The regular transition from the populations at the northeast with generally a majority of the men taller than five feet six inches, to the Italian slopes where less than one fifth attain this moderate height, is sufficient proof. One of those rare examples of a parallelism of physical traits and language is also afforded.   Both tall stature and the German language seem to have penetrated the country from the northeast, crossing the Alps as far as Bozen.   Could demonstration in mathematics be more certain that here in the Tyrol we have a case of an increase of stature due to race alone?

CHAPTER VI.

THE THREE EUROPEAN RACES.

IT may smack of heresy to assert, in face of the teaching of all our text-books on geography and history, that there is no single European or white race of men; and yet that is the plain truth of the matter. Science has advanced since Linnæus' single type of *Homo Europæus albus* was made one of the four great races of mankind.* No continental group of human beings with greater diversities or extremes of physical type exists. That fact accounts in itself for much of our advance in culture. We have already shown in the preceding chapters that entire communities of the tallest and shortest of men as well as the longest and broadest headed ones, are here to be found within the confines of Europe. Even in respect of the colour of the skin, hair, and eyes, responsible more than all else for the misnomer " white race," the greatest variations occur.† To be sure, the several types are to-day all more or less blended together by the unifying influences of civilization; there are few sharp contrasts in Europe such as

---

* The progress of classification, chronologically, is indicated in our supplementary Bibliography, under the index title of Races. It is significant of the slow infiltration of scientific knowledge into secondary literature that the latest and perhaps best geographical text-book in America still teaches the unity of the European or " Aryan " race. Zoölogical authorities also in English seem to be unaware of the present state of our information. Thus Flower and Lyddeker in their great work on the mammals make absolutely no craniological distinctions. They have not advanced a whit beyond the theory of the " oval head " of a half century ago.

On the latest and most elaborate classification, that by Deniker, consult our Appendix D.

† Huxley's (1870) celebrated classification into Melanochroi and Xanthochroi is based on this entirely.

those between the Eskimo and the American Indian, or the Malay and the Papuan in other parts of the world. We have been deceived by this in the past. It is high time for us to correct our ideas on the subject, especially in our school and college teaching.

Instead of a single European type there is indubitable evidence of at least three distinct races, each possessed of a history of its own, and each contributing something to the common product, population, as we see it to-day. If this be established it does away at one fell swoop with most of the current mouthings about Aryans and pre-Aryans; and especially with such appellations as the " Caucasian " or the " Indo-Germanic " race. Supposing for present peace that it be allowed that the ancestors of some peoples of Europe may once have been within sight of either the Caspian Sea or the Himalayas, we have still left two thirds of our European races and population out of account. As yet it is too early to discuss the events in the history of these races; that will claim our attention at a later time. The present task before us is to establish first of all that three such racial types exist in Europe.

The sceptic is already prepared perhaps to admit that what we have said about the several physical characteristics, such as the shape of the head, stature, and the like, may all be true. But he will continue to doubt that these offer evidence of distinct races because ordinary observation may detect such gross inconsistencies on every hand. Even in the most secluded hamlet of the Alps, where population has remained undisturbed for thousands of years, he will be able to point out blond-haired children whose parents were dark, short sons of tall fathers, and the like. Diversities confront us on every hand even in the most retired corner of Europe. What may we not anticipate in more favoured places, especially in the large cities?

Traits in themselves are all right, our objector will maintain: but you must show that they are hereditary, persistent. More than that, you must prove not alone the transmissibility of a single trait by itself, you must also show that combina-

tions of traits are so handed down from father to son. Three
stages in the development of our proof must be noted: first,
the distribution of separate *traits;* secondly, their association
into *types;* and, lastly, the hereditary character of these types
which alone justifies the term *races.** We have already taken
the first step: we are now essaying the second. It is highly
important that we should keep these distinct. Even among
professed anthropologists there is still much confusion of
thought upon the subject—so much so, in fact, that some
have, it seems to us without warrant, abandoned the task in
despair. Let us beware the example of the monkey in the
fable. Seeking to withdraw a huge handful of racial nuts
from the jar of fact, we may find the neck of scientific possibility all too small. We may fail because we have grasped
too much at once. Let us examine.

There are two ways in which we may seek to assemble
our separate physical traits into types—that is, to combine
characteristics into living personalities. The one is purely
anthropological, the other inferential and geographical in its
nature. The first of these is simple. Answer is sought to a
direct question. In a given population, are the blonds more
often tall than the brunets, or the reverse? Is the greater
proportion of the tall men at the same time distinctly longer-
headed or otherwise? and the like. If the answers to these
questions be constant and consistent, our work is accomplished. Unfortunately, they are not always so, hence our
necessary recourse to the geographical proof: but they at
least indicate a slight trend, which we may follow up by the
other means.

Let it be boldly confessed at the outset that in the greater
number of cases no invariable association of traits in this
way occurs. This is especially true among the people of the
central part of Europe. The population of Switzerland, for
example, is persistently aberrant in this respect; it is everything anthropologically that it ought not to be. This should
not surprise us. In the first place, mountainous areas always

---

* Consult our Appendix D concerning Deniker's definition of races in
this connection.

contain the "ethnological sweepings of the plains," as Canon Taylor puts it. Especially is this true when the mountains lie in the very heart of the continent, at a focus of racial immigration. Moreover, the environment is competent to upset all probabilities, as we hope to have shown. Suppose a brunet type from the south should come to Andermatt and settle. If altitude, indeed, exerts an influence upon pigmentation, as we have sought to prove; or if its concomitant poverty in the ante-tourist era should depress the stature; racial equilibrium is as good as vanished in two or three generations. It is therefore only where the environment is simple; and especially on the outskirts of the continent, where migration and intermixture are more infrequent; that any constant and normal association of traits may be anticipated. Take a single example from many. We have always been taught, since the days of Tacitus, to regard the Teutonic peoples—the Goths, Lombards, and Saxons—as tawny-haired, "large-limbed giants." History is filled with observations to that effect from the earliest times.* Our maps have already led us to infer as much. Nevertheless, direct observations show that tall stature and blondness are by no means constant companions in the same person. In Scandinavia, Dr. Arbo asserts, I think, that the tallest men are at the same time inclined to be blond. In Italy, on the other edge of the continent, the same combination is certainly prevalent.† Over in Russia, once more on the outskirts of Europe,‡ the tall men are again said to be lighter complexioned as a rule. In the British Isles,# in Holstein,‖ in parts of Brittany △ and southern France,◊ in Savoy,‡ and in Würtemberg ‡ it is more often true

---

* Hervé, 1897, gives many texts. *Cf.* also references in Taylor, 1890, p. 108. † Livi, 1896 a, pp. 74, 76, 143.

‡ Zograf, 1892 a, p. 173 ; though denied by Anutchin, 1893, p. 285, and Eichholz, 1896, p. 40.

Beddoe, 1867-'69 a, p, 171 ; also Rolleston, 1884, i, p. 279. Not true so often in Scotland.

‖ Meisner, 1889, p. 118 ; but contradictory, p. 111 ; also 1891, p. 323.

△ Collignon, 1890 a, p. 15,

◊ Lapouge, 1894 a, p. 498 ; 1897-'98, p. 314.

‡ Carret, 1883, p. 106.

‡ Von Hölder, 1876, p. 6 ; Ecker, 1876, p. 259, agrees.

than otherwise. But if we turn to other parts of Europe we are completely foiled. The association in the same individual of stature and blondness fails or is reversed in Bavaria,* in Baden,† along the Adriatic,‡ in Poland,# and in upper Austria and Salzburg,‖ as well as among the European recruits observed in America during our civil war.△ It seems to be significant, however, that when the association fails, as in the highlands of Austria; where the environment is eliminated, as in lower Austria, the tall men again become characteristically more blond than the short ones. In this last case environment is to blame; in others, racial intermixture, or it may be merely chance variation, is the cause.◊

In order to avoid disappointment, let us bear in mind that in no other part of the world save modern America is such an amalgamation of various peoples to be found as in Europe. History, and archæology long before history, show us a continual picture of tribes appearing and disappearing, crossing and recrossing in their migrations, assimilating, dividing, colonizing, conquering, or being absorbed. It follows from this, that, even if the environment were uniform, our pure types must be exceedingly rare. Experience proves that the vast majority of the population of this continent shows evidence of crossing, so that in general we can not expect that more than one third of the people will be marked by the simplest combination of traits. We need not be surprised, therefore, that if we next seek to add a third characteristic, say the shape of the head, to a normal combination of hair and eyes, we find the proportion of pure types combining all three traits in a fixed measure to be very small indeed. Imagine a fourth trait, stature, or a fifth, nose, to be added, and our proportion of pure types becomes almost infinitesimal. We are thus reduced

---

* Ranke. Beiträge zur Anth. und Urg. Bayerns, v, 1883, pp. 195 *seq.* ; and 1886–'87, ii, p, 124.

† Ammon, 1890, p. 14 ; 1899, pp. 175–184.   # Elkind, 1896.

‡ Weisbach, 1884, p. 26.   ‖ Weisbach, 1895 b, p. 70.

△ Baxter, 1875, i, pp. 23 and 38 ; with exception of the Germans, however.

◊ In Appendix E, the association of the other primary physical traits in individuals is discussed.

10

to the extremity in which my friend Dr. Ammon, of Baden, found himself, when I wrote asking for photographs of a pure Alpine type from the Black Forest. He has measured thousands of heads, and yet he answered that he really had not been able to find a perfect specimen in all details. All his round-headed men were either blond, or tall, or narrow-nosed, or something else that they ought not to be.

Confronted by this situation, the tyro is here tempted to turn back in despair. There is no justification for it. It is not essential to our position, that we should actually be able to

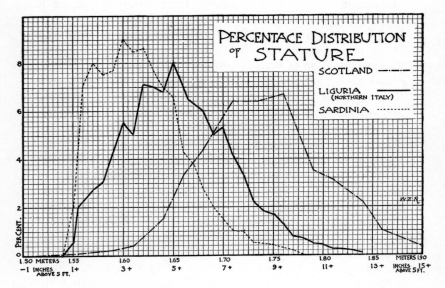

isolate any considerable number, nor even a single one, of our *perfect* racial types in the life. It matters not to us that never more than a small majority of any given population possesses even two physical characteristics in their proper association; that relatively few of these are able to add a third to the combination; and that almost no individuals show a perfect union of all traits under one head, so to speak, while contradictions and mixed types are everywhere present. Such a condition of affairs need not disturb us if we understand ourselves aright. We should indeed be perplexed were it otherwise.

Consider how complex the problem really is! We say the people of Scotland are on the average among the tallest in Europe. True! But that does not exclude a considerable number of medium and undersized persons from among them. We may illustrate the actual condition best by means of the accompanying diagram.* Three curves are plotted therein for the stature of large groups of men chosen at random from each of three typical parts of Europe. The one at the right is for the tall Scotch, the middle one for the medium-sized northern Italians, and the one at the left for Sardinians, the people of this island being among the shortest in all Europe. The height of each curve at any given point indicates the percentage within each group of men, which possessed the stature marked at the base of that vertical line. Thus eight per cent of the Ligurian men were five feet five inches tall (1.65 metres), while nine per cent of the Sardinians were fully two inches shorter (1.60 metres). In either case these several heights were the most common, although in no instance is the proportion considerable at a given stature. There is, however, for each country or group of men, some point about which the physical trait clusters. Thus the largest percentage of a given stature among the Scotch occurs at about five feet nine inches and a half. Yet a very large

---

* The curve for the Scotch, taken from the Report of the Anthropometric Committee of the British Association for the Advancement of Science for 1883, has been arbitrarily corrected to correspond to the metric system employed by Dr. Livi in the other curves. A centimetre is roughly equal to 0.4 of an inch. It is assumed that in consequence only 0.4 as many individuals will fall within each centimetre class as in the groups of stature differing by inches. The ordinates in the Scotch diagram have therefore been reduced to 0.4 of their height in the original curve.

The best technical discussion of such curves among anthropologists will be found in Goldstein, 1883 ; Stieda, 1883 ; Ammon, 1893 and 1896 c ; Livi, 1895 and 1896 a, pp. 22 et seq.; and in the works of Bowditch, Galton, etc. Emme, 1887, gives a pointed criticism of the possible fallacy in mere averages. Dr. Boas has contributed excellent material, based upon the American Indians for the most part.

number of them, about five per cent, fall within the group of
five feet seven inches (1.70 metres)—that is to say, no taller
than an equal percentage of the Ligurians—and even in Sardinia there is an appreciable number of that stature. We
must understand, therefore, when we say that the Scotch are
a tall people or a long-headed or blond one; that we mean
thereby, not that all the people are peculiar in this respect even
to a slight degree, but merely that in this region there are
more specimens of these special types than elsewhere. Still
it remains that the great mass of the people are merely neutral.
This is a more serious obstacle to overcome than direct contradictions. They merely whet the appetite. Our most difficult problem is to separate the typical wheat from the non-
committal straw; to distinguish our racial types from the general mean or average which everywhere constitutes the overwhelming majority of the population.

We have now seen how limited are the racial results attainable by the first of our two means of identification—that
is, the purely somatological one. It has appeared that only
in the most simple conditions are the several traits constant
and faithful to one another in their association in the same
persons. Nor are we justified in asking for more. Our three
racial types are not radically distinct seeds which, once planted
in the several parts of Europe, have there taken root; and,
each preserving its peculiarities intact, have spread from those
centres outward until they have suddenly run up against one
another along a racial frontier. Such was the old-fashioned
view of races, in the days before the theory of evolution had
remodelled our ways of thinking—when human races were held
to be distinct creations of a Divine will. We conceive of it
all quite differently. These types for us are all necessarily
offshoots from the same trunk. The problem is far more
complex to us for this reason. It is doubly dynamic. Upbuilding and demolition are taking place at the same time.
By our constitution of racial types we seek to simplify the
matter—for a moment to lose sight of all the destructive
forces, and from obscure tendencies to derive ideal results.
We picture an anthropological goal which might have

been attained had the life conditions only been less complicated.

Are we in this more presumptuous than other natural
scientists? Is the geologist more certain of his deductions,
in his restoration of an ideal mountain chain from the de-
nuded roots which alone bear witness to the fact to-day? In
this case all the superstructure has long since disappeared.
The restoration is no less scientific. It represents more clearly
than aught else, the rise and disappearance, the results and
future tendencies of great geological movements. We take
no more liberties with our racial types than the geologist
with his mountains; nor do we mean more by our restora-
tions. The parallel is instructive. The geologist is well
aware that the uplifted folds as he depicts them never existed
in completeness at any given time. He knows full well that
erosion took place even as lateral pressure raised the con-
torted strata; that one may even have been the cause of the
other. If indeed denudation could have been postponed until
all the elevation of the strata had been accomplished, then the
restoration of the mountain chain would stand for a once real
but now vanished thing. This, the geologist is well aware, was
not thus and so. In precisely the same sense do we conceive of
our races. Far be it from us to assume that these three races
of ours ever, in the history of mankind, existed in absolute
purity or isolation from one another. As soon might the
branch grow separate and apart from the parent oak. No
sooner have environmental influences, peculiar habits of life,
and artificial selection commenced to generate distinct varieties of men from the common clay; no sooner has heredity
set itself to perpetuating these; than chance variation, migration, intermixture, and changing environments, with a host
of minor dispersive factors, begin to efface this constructive
work. Racial upbuilding and demolition, as we have said,
have ever proceeded side by side. Never is the perfect type
in view, while yet it is always possible. " Race," says Topinard [79], " in the present state of things is an abstract conception, a notion of continuity in discontinuity, of unity in diversity. It is the rehabilitation of a real but directly unattain-

able thing." In this sense alone do we maintain that there are three ideal racial types in Europe to be distinguished from one another. They have often dissolved in the common population; each particular trait has gone its own way; so that at the present time rarely, if indeed ever, do we discover a single individual corresponding to our racial type in every detail. It exists for us nevertheless.

Thus convinced that the facts do not warrant us in expecting too much of our anthropological means of isolating racial types, we have recourse to a second or inferential mode of analysis. In this we work by geographical areas rather than by personalities. We discover, for example, that the north of Europe constitutes a veritable centre of dispersion of long-headedness. Quite independently, we discover that the same region contains more blond traits than any other part of Europe, and that a high average stature there prevails. The inference is at once natural, that these three characteristics combine to mark the prevalent type of the population. If one journeyed through it, one might at first expect to find the majority of the people to be long-headed and tall blonds; that the tallest individuals would be the most blond, the longest-headed most tall, and so on. This is, as we have already shown, too good and simple to be true, or even to be expected. Racial combinations of traits, indeed, disappear in a given population as sugar dissolves—or rather as certain chemical salts are resolved into their constituent elements—when immersed in water. From the proportions of each element discovered in the fluid, quite free from association, we are often able to show that they once were united in the same compound. In the same manner, finding these traits floating about loose, so to speak, in the same population, we proceed to reconstitute types from them. We know that the people approach this type more and more as we near the specific centre of its distribution. The traits may refuse to go otherwise than two by two, like the animals in the ark, and they may change partners quite frequently; yet they may still manifest distinct affinities one for another nevertheless.

The apparent inference is not always the just one, although it tends to be. Suppose, for example, that one observer should prove that sixty per cent of ten thousand natives of Holland were blonds; and another, studying the same ten thousand individuals, should prove that a like proportion were very tall—would this of necessity mean that the Hollanders were mainly tall blonds? Not at all! It might still be that the two groups of traits merely overlapped at their edges. In other words, the great majority of the blonds might still be constituted from the shorter half of the population. Only twenty per cent need necessarily be tall and blond at once, even in this simple case where both observers studied the same men from different points of view. How much more confusing, if each chanced to hit upon an entirely different set of ten thousand men! This, be it noted, is generally the case in practice. Nevertheless, although there is always danger in such inferences, we are fortunate in possessing so many parallel investigations that they check one another, and the tendencies all point in one direction.

These tendencies we may discover by means of curves drawn as we have indicated above on page 108. By them we may analyze each group in detail. Every turn of the lines has a meaning. Thus, the most noticeable feature of the Sardinian curve of statures is its narrowness and height the Ligurian one is broader at the base, with sloping sides and the Scotch one looks as if pressure had been applied at the apex to flatten it out still farther. The interpretation is clear. In Sardinia we have a relatively unified type. Nearly all of the people are characterized by statures between five feet one inch (1.56 metres) and five feet five inches (1.65 metres). They are homogeneous, in other words: and they are homogeneous at the lower limit of human variation in stature. The curve is steepest on the left side. This means that the stature has been depressed to a point where neither misery nor chance variation can stunt still further; so that suddenly from seven per cent of the men of a height of five feet one inch and a half (more frequent than any given stature in Scotland) we drop to two per cent at a half inch shorter stature. A moment's consideration shows, moreover, that the narrower the pyramid, the higher it must be. One hundred per cent of the people must be accounted for somewhere. If they are not evenly distributed, their aggregation near the middle of the curve will elevate its apex, or its shoulders at least. Thus a sharp pyramid generally denotes a homogeneous people. If they were all precisely alike, a single vertical line one hundred per cent high would result. On the other hand, a flattened curve indicates the introduction of some disturbing factor, be it an immigrant race, environment, or what not. In this case the purity of the Sardinians is readily explicable. They have lived in the greatest isolation, set apart in the Mediterranean. A curve drawn for the Irish shows the same phenomenon. Islands demographically tend in the main to one or the other of two extremes. If unattractive, they offer examples of the purest isolation, as in Corsica and Sardinia. If inviting, or on the cross-paths of navigation, like Sicily, their people speedily degenerate into mixed types. For if incentive to immigration be offered, they are approachable alike from all sides. The Scotch, as we have observed, are more or less mixed in type, and unequally subjected to the influences of environment; so that their curve shows evidence of heterogeneity. Scotland combines the isolation of the Highlands with a great extent of seacoast. The result has been that in including the population of both kinds of territory in a single curve we find great variability of stature manifested.

It will repay us to analyze a few more seriation curves, for they illustrate graphically and with clearness the complex facts in the situation. These diagrams are based not upon statures, but upon cephalic indices. The same principles apply, however, in either case. The first one deals, as will be noted, with a very large number of individuals. It illustrates the difference in contour between a curve drawn for a relatively simple population and one in which several distinct types are coexistent. The narrowness and height of the percentage pyramids for the two extremes of Italy, culminating at indexes of 79 and 84 respectively, are notable.* The two regions are severally quite homogeneous in respect of the head form of their population; for the apex of such curves rarely exceeds the limit of fourteen per cent reached in these instances. The curve for all Italy, on the other hand, is the resultant of compounding such seriations as these for each district of the country. It becomes progressively lower

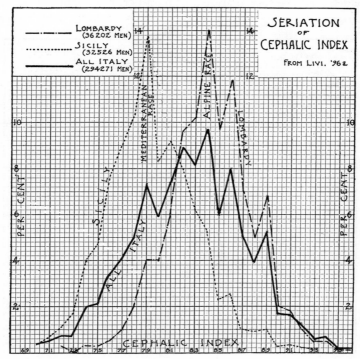

and broader with the inclusion of each differently character-ized population. It will be observed, however, that even this curve for a highly complex people, preserves vestiges, in its minor apexes, of the constituent types of which it is com-pounded. Thus its main body culminates at the broadened head form of the Alpine race; but a lesser apex on the left-

* The geographical distribution of these is shown upon our map on page 251.

hand side coincides with the cephalic index of the Mediterranean racial type; that which entirely dominated in the simple curve for Sicily alone.

The second diagram contains examples of a number of erratic curves. The Swiss one represents a stage of physical heterogeneity far more pronounced than that of all Italy, which we have just analyzed. Or rather, more truly, it is the product of an intermixture upon terms of entire equality of

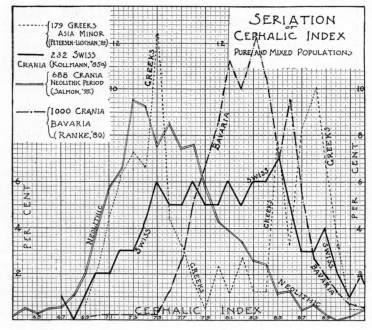

a number of types of head form. In Italy, as we have seen, the broader head form so far outweighed the Mediterranean one, that a single culminating point of maximum frequency still remained, with a lesser one corresponding to the minority partner. In this second diagram Bavaria represents about the same condition as all Italy, with, however, the proportions of the two constituent types reversed; for, being north of the Alps, the culminating apex of greatest frequency lies toward the longer-headed side of the curve. Therein does the predominant dolichocephaly of the Teutonic race make itself manifest.

Compared with these curves for Italy and Bavaria, the Swiss seriation is seen to be devoid of any real apex at all. It represents a population in no wise possessed of distinct individuality so far as cephalic index is concerned. Broad and long heads are about equally common. This corresponds, of course, to the geographical probabilities for two reasons: inasmuch as Switzerland not only lies at the centre of the continent; but also, owing to its rugged surface, comprises all extremes of isolation and intermixture within its borders. A state of heterogeneity absolutely unparalleled seems to be indicated by still another of our curves—that drawn for the Greeks of Asia Minor. It culminates at the most widely separated cephalic indexes—viz., 75 and 88 respectively —known in the human species. The lower index corresponds to the primitive long-headed Greek stock; the other is probably a result of intermixture with Turks, Armenians, and others. Or perhaps it is nearer the truth to say that the only bond of unity in the entire series is that of language; in other words, that the broad-headed apex represents Turks, Armenians, and others, still physically true to their original pattern, yet who have chanced to adopt the speech of the Greeks. Here again is the heterogeneous ethnic composition of eastern Europe fully exemplified by a seriation curve of cephalic index.

By the second geographical method which we have described we constitute our racial types as the archæologist, from a mass of broken fragments of pottery, restores the designs upon his shattered and incomplete vases. Upon a bit of clay he discovers tracings of a portion of a conventionalized human figure. A full third—let us say the head of Thoth or some other Egyptian deity—is missing. The figure is incomplete to this extent. Near by is found upon another fragment, a representation of the head and half the body of another figure. In this case it is the legs alone which lack. This originally formed no part of the same vase with the first bit.

It is perhaps of entirely different size and colour. Never-theless, finding that the portions of the design upon the two fragments bear marks of identity in motive or pattern, data for the complete restoration of the figure of the god are at hand. It matters not, that from the fragments in his posses-sion the archæologist can reconstruct no single perfect form. The pieces of clay will in no wise fit together. The designs, notwithstanding, so complement one another that his mind is set at rest. The affinity of the two portions is almost as clearly defined as the disposition of certain chemical elements to combine in fixed proportions; for primitive religion or ornament is not tolerant of variation.

We copy the procedure of the archæologist precisely. In one population, colour of hair and stature gravitate toward certain definite combinations. Not far away, perhaps in an-other thousand men drawn from the same locality, the same stature is found to manifest an affinity for certain types of head form. It may require scores of observations to detect the tendency, so slight has it become. In still another thousand men perhaps a third combination is revealed. These all, how-ever, overlap at the edges. Granted that an assumption is necessary. It is allowed to the archæologist. Our conclu-sions are more certain than his, even as the laws of physical combination are more immutable than those of mental asso-ciation. For it was merely mental conservatism which kept the primitive designer of the vase from varying his patterns. Here we have unchanging physical facts upon which to rely. Of course, we should be glad to find all our physical traits definitely associated in completeness in the same thousand re-cruits, were it not denied to us. The archæologist would like-wise rejoice at the discovery of one perfect design upon a single vase. Both of us lack entities; we must be contented with affinities instead.

A final step in our constitution of races—that is to say, of hereditary types—is to prove that they are persistent and transmissible from one generation to the next.* Of direct

---

* Consult in general the works of Perier; E. Schmidt, 1888; Virchow, 1896; Kollmann, 1898; and also Science, New York, 1892, pp. 155 *et seq.*

testimony upon this point so far as concerns normal physical characteristics, we possess little that is authoritative; although the anthropological journals abound in examples of the inheritance of monstrous peculiarities. Von Hölder * claims to have followed certain traits in Esslingen down through four generations. Von Luschan † gives some interesting data concerning the transmission of peculiarities of head form in two collaterally related families, although his number of observations is too limited to form a basis of generalization. The same objection applies to Goenner's work [95]. An indication of the possibilities of research along these lines, is offered by a very recent study at Stockholm of some six hundred women, and an equal number of their new-born infants.‡ Several traces of direct hereditary transmission appear statistically to be indicated, especially in respect of the cephalic index. The proportions of the mother's head seem even in these newly born children, often with abnormal or deformed crania at so tender an age, to betray an appreciable tendency to reappear in like form. One of the most valuable contributions by De Candolle [84] concerns the inheritance of the colour of the iris. He found, for example, that where both parents were brown-eyed, eighty per cent of the children were characterized by an iris of the same shade. The proportion of blue-eyed children in the succeeding generation was as high as 93.6 per cent when both parents were alike in this respect. When they differed, one being blue-eyed the other having a brown iris, the shade of the father's eyes seemed to be slightly more persistent (fifty-three to fifty-six per cent), but great variability was manifested.# Some interesting calculations by Miss Fawcett [98] on the inheritance of the head form, according to Boas's observations on American aborigines, are also in progress. Galton's

---

* 1876, p. 10.

† 1889, p. 211.

‡ Johanssen and Westermark, 1897, p. 366. The infantile index, as a whole (80.3), however, is far above the mean for the mothers (76.5), probably in conformity with Boas's (1896) rule that frontal development with growth tends to lower the index progressively.

Pfitzner, 1897, p. 497, gives other data on pigmentation, based upon the population of Alsace.

studies relating to the transmissibility of stature are also well known to English readers. The difficulty in the prosecution of extended investigations in this line, is that the lifetime of a single observer is too brief to comprehend more than three generations at most; and even where this is possible, the unreliability of a comparison of the phenomena of childhood with old age vitiates many of the conclusions. One law alone, to which we have already made reference, seems to be verified. It is this; viz., that *types*, which are combinations of separate traits, are rarely if ever stable in a single line through several generations. The physical characteristics are transmitted in independence of one another in nine cases out of ten. The absolute necessity of studying men in large masses, in order to counteract this tendency is by this fact rendered imperative.

Our proof of the transmissibility of many of the physical peculiarities with which we have here to deal must of necessity be indirect. The science of prehistoric archæology affords testimony of this kind plentifully. From all parts of Europe comes evidence as to the physical characteristics of the people from which the living one has sprung. Our volume abounds in it. Viewed broadly—that is to say, taking whole populations as a unit—the persistence of ethnic peculiarities through generations is beyond question. We know, for example, that in the north of Europe, as far back as archæology can carry us, men of a type of head form identical with the living population to-day were in a majority. Likewise the lake dwellers in Switzerland in the stone age, little more civilized than the natives of Africa, were true ancestors of the present Alpine race. Even since the earliest period of history made known to us in Egypt, there has been no appreciable change in the physical character of the population, as Sergi * has proved. Prehistoric archæology thus comes to our aid, with cumulative proof that at all events traits are hereditary in populations, even if not always plainly so in families. In truth, we here enter upon a larger field of investigation than the anthropological one. The whole topic

---

* 1897 a, p. 65.

19.   *Teutonic types.*   Norway.   Pure blond.   20.

21.   *Alpine type.*   Austrian.   Blue eyes, brown hair.   Index 88.   22.

23.   *Mediterranean type.*   Palermo, Sicily.   Pure brunet.   Index 77.   24.

THE THREE EUROPEAN RACIAL TYPES.

of heredity opens up before us, too immense to discuss in this place. Suffice it to say that in the main no question is entertained upon the subject, save in the special cases of artificially acquired characteristics and the like. Even here, in a few isolated cases, as among the Jews, our evidence upon this contested question seems to be indubitable.*

After this tedious summary of methods, let us turn to results. The table on this page shows the combinations of traits into racial types which seem best to accord with the facts. It speaks for itself.

European Racial Types.

		Head.	Face.	Hair.	Eyes.	Stature.	Nose.	Synonyms.	Used by.
1	TEUTONIC.	Long.	Long.	Very light.	Blue.	Tall.	Narrow ; aquiline.	Dolicho-lepto. Reihen-gräber. Germanic. Kymric. Nordic. Homo-Europæus.	Koll-mann. Ger-mans. English. French. Deniker. Lapouge
2	ALPINE (Celtic).	Round.	Broad.	Light chest-nut.	Hazel-gray.	Medium, stocky.	Variable ; rather broad ; heavy.	Celto-Slavic. Sarmatian Dissentis. Arvernian. Occidental Homo-Alpinus. Lappanoid	French. Von Hölder. Germans Beddoe. Deniker. Lapouge Pruner Bey.
3	MEDITER-RANEAN.	Long.	Long.	Dark brown or bl'k	Dark.	Medium, slender.	Rather broad.	Iberian. Ligurian. Ibero-Insular Atlanto-Med.	English. Italians. Deniker.

The first of our races is perhaps the most characteristic. It is entirely restricted to northwestern Europe, with a centre of dispersion in Scandinavia. Each of the other types extends beyond the confines of the continent, one into Asia, the other into Africa. Lapouge's name of *Homo Europæus* is by no means inapt for this reason. Our portraits, chosen as typical by Dr. Arbo of the Norwegian army, show certain of the

---

* Page 393.

physical peculiarities, especially the great length of the head, the long oval face, and the straight aquiline nose. The face is rather smooth in outline, the cheek bones not being prominent. The narrow nose seems to be a very constant trait, as much so as the tendency to tall stature. This race is strongly inclined to blondness. The eyes are blue or light gray, and the hair flaxen, tawny, reddish, or sandy. The whole combination accords exactly with the descriptions handed down to us by the ancients. Such were the Goths, Danes, Norsemen, Saxons, and their fellows of another place and time. History is thus strictly corroborated by natural science.

A distinctive feature of the Teutonic race, which we have not yet mentioned, is its prominent and narrow nose. This is notable, in general, as a fact of common observation, but it is very difficult of anthropometric proof.* The range of individual variation in the fleshy parts seems to be very great, even in the same race. There is some indication, moreover, that the nasal bones are influenced by the structure of the face.† The lack of any international agreement as to the system of measurement renders statistical comparisons doubly difficult. Nevertheless, enough has been done to show that from the north of Europe, as we go south, the nose betrays a tendency to become flatter and more open at the wings. Especially where the Alpine and Teutonic types are in contact do we find the flatter nose of the broad-headed race noticeable.‡ Arbo # has observed it in the southwestern corner of Norway. Houze [88] proves it for Belgium in a comparison of Flemings and Walloons; it is certainly true in France that the Teutonic elements are more leptorhin (narrow-nosed) than the Alpine.|| The association of a tall stature with a narrow nose is so close as to point to a law. Italy shows a regular increase in fre-

---

* In general consult Topinard, 1891 b ; Collignon, 1887 d ; and Hovorka, " Die äussere Nase," Wien, 1893.

† Collignon, 1883, p. 47 ; 1887 a, p. 237 ; Livi, 1896 a, p. 114.

‡ Topinard, 1885, Elements, p. 305.

1897, p. 57.

|| Collignon, 1883, p. 508 ; 1892 b, pp. 48 and 54 ; 1894 a, Calvados, p. 24 ; and 1894 b, Dordogne, p. 41.

quency of the broad and flat nose from north to south; and Collignon's law of the association of the form of nose to stature seems again to be confirmed.* From this point south, even from the Mediterranean coast in Tunis toward the interior, the broad and open form of nose, extremely developed in the negro race, becomes more common.† Our Sardinian portraits (page 251), compared with those of the various Teutonic types, will strongly accentuate this change. A distinct,

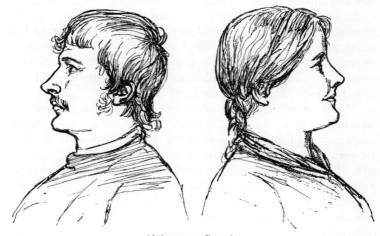

Alpine types, Bavaria.

though distant, affinity of the Mediterranean stock with the negro is surely the only inference to be drawn from it.

Our second racial type is most persistently characterized by the shape of the head. This is short and at the same time broad. The roundness is accompanied by a broad face, the chin full, and the nose rather heavy. These traits are all shown more or less clearly in our portraits of the Austrian German, and of the two Bavarian peasants. The side views in the latter cases show the shortness of the head as con-

---

* Livi, 1896 a, pp. 104–112; with maps XIV, XV, in atlas; as also Mori, 1897.

† Collignon, 1887 a, Tunis, pp. 229–232. Even here the tall blonds are more leptorhin.

trasted with the Teutonic type above described. At the same time the cranium is high, the forehead straight, sometimes almost overhanging. It seems as if pressure had been applied front and back, the skull having yielded in an upward direction. This type is of medium height, decidedly inclined toward stockiness in build. Its whole aspect is rather of solidity than of agility. The colour of the hair and eyes is rather neutral, at all events intermediate between the Teutonic and Mediterranean races. There is a tendency toward grayish eyes, while the hair is more often brown. In these respects, however, there is great variability, and the transition to the north and south is very gradual. Climate or other environmental influence has in these traits eliminated all sharp division lines. These peculiarities appear only when the type is found in extreme isolation and purity.

What name shall we apply to this second race, characterized primarily by its great breadth of head, and which has its main centre of dissemination in the Alpine highlands of midwestern Europe? The most common name applied to it is that of Celtic. This seems without doubt most adequately to harmonize the results contributed to our knowledge of the subject by the various sciences of history, philology, archæology, and physical anthropology. Nevertheless, a very grave objection to its use pertains. To make this clear we must for a moment examine historically the so-called *Celtic question*, than which no greater stumbling-block in the way of our clear thinking exists. It is imperative to make the matter definite before we proceed.*

The leading ethnologists prior to 1860, relying entirely upon the texts of the classical writers, generally agreed in affiliating the Celts of early history with the tall, blond peoples of northern Europe. In other words, they interpreted literally

---

* In our complete Bibliography, see under "Celts," in the index, a chronological outline of the discussion, containing full titles of all papers by Broca, Bertrand, and others not specifically given here. Among the best references will be found Bertrand and Reinach's masterly work of 1894; Lagneau, especially 1877 b; Topinard, article "Français," in the Nouveau Dictionnaire de Géographie; Collignon's extended review (1893 b) of Arbois de Jubainville's latest work. Von Hölder, 1876, discusses it well.

Cæsar's well-known passage in the Commentaries, "All Gaul is divided into three parts, one of which the Belgæ inhabit, the Aquitani another, those who in their own language are called Celts, in ours Gauls, the third." This statement was interpreted to mean that the Gauls and Celts were of the same race, although of course we see to-day that Cæsar was speaking not necessarily of races at all, but of peoples or political units. Moreover, ammunition for endless controversy was afforded by the conflicting statements of other ancient historians, no one of them in fact until Polybius, as Bertrand ('73) has shown, really, using the words Celts and Gauls with any discrimination whatever.

A new phase of the matter was presented by Broca's celebrated researches concerning the physical characteristics of the French people in the decade following 1860, especially those among the peasants in Brittany. Here were the only Celtic-speaking people on the continent, and they were of a brunet and short race. Then, in 1865, came the monumental work of Davis and Thurnam, the *Crania Britannica*, with added proof that a large part of the Celtic-speaking population of the British Isles, particularly the Welsh, were equally short and of dark complexion. Broca ('64b) and Beddoe ('65b) among anthropologists at once grasped the situation; they perceived the inconvenience attendant upon the use of the term. Nevertheless, the advocates of the old view of tall blond Celts still counted eminent authority among their number, such as von Baer, with His ('64b) and Rütimeyer.

Proof of a widespread short and dark population through central Europe, even in southern Germany, meanwhile accumulated rapidly at the hands of Ecker, von Hölder, Welcker, and others; they, however, dodged the issue by applying new names to this broad-headed, un-Teutonic population which they discovered in the recesses of the Black Forest and the Alps. These people they called Ligurian, Sarmatian, Slavic or Sion types. Finally, however, the close parallel between the area characterized by Celtic place-names, as analyzed by Bacmeister or described as Celtic by the ancients, and that occupied by this newly discovered physical type, forced an issue between the anthropologists on the one hand and the philologists and old-fashioned ethnographers on the other. The years 1873–'74 brought the matter to a head. It was a battle of the giants indeed, marked especially by the brilliant flashes between Bertrand and Arbois de Jubainville, Omalius d'Halloy and Lagneau, with Broca, master of them all, against the field. The controversy extended over a number of years, Henry Martin,* Rawlinson ⁽⁷⁷⁾, and others being involved; they, with the ethnographers, still contending for the tall blondness of the Celts of history. Whatever be the present state of opinion among students of other cognate sciences; there is practically to-day a complete unanimity of opinion among physical anthropologists, that the term *Celt*, if used at all, belongs to the second of our three races—viz, the brachycephalic, darkish population of the Alpine highlands. Such is the view of Broca, Bertrand, Topinard, Collignon, and all the French authorities. It is accepted by the Germans, Virchow ⁽⁹⁵⁾, Kollmann,† and Ranke ‡ as well; by the English, foremost among them Dr. Beddoe,# and by the most competent Italians.||

Despite the agreement among anthropologists as to the connotation of the term Celt, its use involves us in interminable difficulty, so long as the word is applied separately to a definite language. The philologers properly insist upon calling all those who speak the Celtic language, Celts. With less reason the archæologists follow them and insist upon assigning the name Celt to all those who possessed the Celtic culture; while the physical anthropologists, finding the Celtic language spoken by peoples of divers physical types, with

---

* 1878 ; and especially in Bull. Soc. d'Anth., 1877, p. 483.

† 1877, p. 154.

‡ Der Mensch, 1890, ii, pp. 261–268, is conclusive.

See also Rudler, 1880, for a very good summary. Dissident alone is Lapouge, L'Anthropologie, iii, p, 748. *Cf.* Zampa, 1892, on Italy. Hoyos Sáinz and Aranzadi, 1894, p. 429, may be right in asserting the Celtic invaders of Spain to be blond. They would certainly appear so, compared with the Iberians, while yet being dark alongside the Teutonic peoples.

|| *Cf.* Sergi, 1883 b, p. 139, and 1895 a, p. 93.

equal propriety hold that the term Celt, if used at all, should be applied to that physical group or type of men which includes the greatest number of those who use the Celtic language. This manifestly would operate to the exclusion of those who spoke Celtic, but who differed from the linguistic majority in physical characteristics. The practical result of all this was, for example, that anthropologists called the tall and blond people of northern France and Belgium, Gauls or Kymri; and the broad heads of middle and southwestern France, Celts; while Cæsar, as we saw, insisted that the Celt and the Gaul were identical. The anthropologists affirmed that the Celtic language had slipped off the tongues of some, and that others had adopted it at second hand. Their explanation held that the blond Belgæ had come into France from the north, bringing the Celtic speech, which those already there speedily adopted; but that they remained as distinct in blood as before. These anthropologists, therefore, insisted that the Belgæ deserved a distinctive name, and they called them Gauls, since they ruled in Gaul; in distinction from the Celts, who, being the earlier inhabitants, constituted the majority of the Celtic-speaking people. This was a cross-division with the philologists, who called the Belgæ Celts, because they brought the language; reserving the name Gaul, as they said, for the natives of that country; but both philologists and anthropologists alike differed from the historians, who held to Cæsar's view that the Gauls and the Celts were all one.

Still greater confusion arises if we attempt to discuss the origin of the people of the British Isles, where this Celtic question enters again. Thus the people of Ireland and Wales, of Cornwall and the Scottish Highlands, together with the Bretons in France, would all be Celtic for the linguist because they all spoke the Celtic language. For the anthropologist, as we shall see, the Breton is as far from the Welsh as in some respects the Welsh are from the Scotch. And after all, the best opinion to-day is entirely in accord with Belloguet's original suggestion of thirty years ago, that the Celts of the historians never, in fact, formed more than the ruling class all through central Europe.

It is not for us to say the final word upon these moot points. If we have shown what confusion may result from the use of this term, Celt, or Kelt if you please, we are content. Our own view is that the linguists are best entitled to the name *Celt;* but that they should be utterly denied the use of the word *race.* Then, if we can adopt a distinctive word for the first stage of iron culture, such as that of *Hallstatt,* long used by the Germans and recently adopted by Bertrand and Reinach as applicable to the civilization most generally co-ordinated with the Celtic language, our terminology will be adequate to the present state of knowledge. The word *Alpine* seems best to fit this second racial type which we have isolated. This name, proposed by Linnæus, has been revived with profit by De Lapouge. It seems to be free from many objections to which others are open. Especially is it important to avoid misunderstandings by the use of historical names, such as Ligurian or Iberian.* In many respects Deniker's name of Nordic would be better than Teuton, which we have applied to our first type, for this reason. Geographical names are least equivocal. We shall, therefore, everywhere call the broad-headed type Alpine. It centres in that region. It everywhere follows the elevated portions of western Europe. It is, therefore, pre-eminently a mountain type, whether in France, Spain, Italy, Germany, or Albania; it becomes less pure in proportion as we go east from the Carpathians across the great plains of European Russia.† By the use of it we shall carefully distinguish between language, culture, and physical type. Thus the Celtic language and the Hallstatt culture may spread over the Alpine race, or *vice versa.* As, in fact, each may migrate in independence of the others, so in our terminology we may distinctly follow them apart from one another. No confusion of terms can result.

We now come to the last of our three races, which is generally known as the Mediterranean or Iberian type. It prevails everywhere south of the Pyrenees, along the southern

---

* *Cf.* page 261, *infra.*

† The significance of the term Slavic and of Celto-Slavic, applied to this race, is discussed in our chapter on Russia.

coast of France and in southern Italy, including Sicily and
Sardinia.   Once more we return to a type of head form almost
identical with the Teutonic.   Our portraits (facing page 121)
exemplify this clearly, in the oval face and the prominent occiput of this third type.   The cephalic index drops from 87
and above in the Alps to about 75 all along the line.   This
is the primary fact to be noted.*   Coincidently, the colour of the hair and eyes becomes very dark, almost black.
The figure is less amply proportioned: the people become light,
slender, and rather agile.† As

to the bodily height of this third
race two varieties are to-day
recognised: the group north of
the Mediterranean is exceedingly short, while the African Berbers are of goodly size.‡   Authorities are, however, divided
as to the significance of this.
It has been shown that while
the average height of the Sardinians, for example, is low, a
considerable number, and those
of the purest type in other respects, are of goodly stature.
Our seriation curve on page 108
illustrates this persistency of a
taller contingent very well.   Lapouge ('94a), especially, discovers a marked tendency in south-

Mediterranean Type, Corsica.
Index 72.3.

ern France away from this excessive shortness.   It may indeed
be that, as we have already suggested, too protracted civilization is responsible for this diminutiveness on the northern

---

* A subdivision of this type, the Cro-Magnon, preserves the same head
form, as we shall show, but the face becomes much broader.   Collignon
recognises these two as subvarieties of a common race.

† Collignon, 1883, p. 63.

‡ Deniker calls them Ibero-Insular and Atlanto-Mediterranean, respectively.   Consult our Appendix D on his system.

shore of the Mediterranean.   At all events, despite this sub-division, the substantial unity of the southern dolichocephalic group is recognised by all authorities.*

It would be interesting at this time to follow out the intellectual differences between these three races which we have described.   The future social complexion of Europe is largely dependent upon them.   The problem is too complicated to treat briefly.   In a later chapter, devoted expressly to modern social problems, we shall return to it again.   Our physical analysis is now complete.   The next task is to trace the origin of nationalities from the combination of these elements.

---

* Sergi, 1895 a, best proves this fact and summarizes its characteristics.

CHAPTER VII.

FRANCE AND BELGIUM.

It is difficult to give satisfactory references on the anthropology of France as a whole. It has seemed more expedient, owing to the richness of the literature, to give specific authorities for each of the distinct quarters of the country, as they have been separately treated.

SEVERAL reasons combine to make France the most interesting country of Europe from the anthropological point of view. More is known of it in detail than of any other part of the continent save Italy. Its surface presents the greatest diversity of climate, soil, and fertility. Its population, consequently, is exposed to the most varied influences of environment. It alone among the other countries of central Europe is neither cis- nor trans-Alpine. It is open to invasion from all sides alike. Lying on the extreme west coast of Europe, it is a place of last resort for all the westward-driven peoples of the Old World. All these causes combine to render its population the most heterogeneous to be found on the continent. It comprises all three of the great ethnic types described in our preceding chapter, while most countries are content with two. Nay, more, it still includes a goodly living representation of a prehistoric race which has disappeared almost everywhere else in Europe.*

Thirty years ago observers began to perceive differences in

---

* It would be ungracious not to acknowledge publicly my great indebtedness to the foremost authority upon the population of France, Major Dr. R. Collignon, of the École Supérieure de Guerre, at Paris ; and to Prof. G. V. de Lapouge, of the University of Rennes, in Brittany, as well. Invaluable assistance in the preparation of this and the following chapter has been rendered by each. No request, even the most exacting, has failed of a generous response at their hands.

central France between the people of the mountains and of the plains. As early as 1868 Durand de Gros noted that in Aveyron, one of the southern departments lying along the border of a mountainous area, the populations of the region thereabout were strongly differentiated. On the calcareous plains the people were taller, of light complexion, with blue or grayish-blue eyes, and having fine teeth. In the upland areas of a granitic formation, the people were stunted, dark in complexion, with very poor teeth. These groups used distinct dialects. The peasants differed in temperament: one was as lively as the other was morose; one was progressive, the other was backward in culture and suspicious of innovations. This same observer noted that the cattle of the two regions were unlike; on the infertile soils they were smaller and leaner, differing in bodily proportions as well. He naturally, therefore, offered the same explanation for the differences of both men and cattle—namely, that they were due to the influences of environment. He asserted that the geology of the districts had determined the quality of the food and its quantity at the same time, thereby affecting both animal and human life. When this theory was advanced, even the fact that such differences existed, was scouted as impossible, to say nothing of the explanation offered for them. As late as 1889 we find Frech, a German geologist, in ignorance of the modern advance of anthropology, strongly impressed by these same contrasts of population, and likewise ascribing them to the direct influence of environment as did the earlier discoverer. These differences, then, surely exist even to the unpractised eye. We must account for them; but we do it in another way. The various types of population are an outcome of their physical environment. This has, however, worked not directly but in a roundabout way. It has set in motion a species of social or racial selection, now operative over most of Europe. Since it is most clearly expressed in France, an additional reason appears for according a primary place to this country in our analysis.

Before we proceed to study the French people, we must cast an eye over the geographical features of the country.

These are depicted in the accompanying map, in which the deeper tints show the location of the regions of elevation above the sea level. At the same time the cross-hatched lines mark the areas within which the physical environment is unpropitious, at least as far as agriculture—the mainstay of economic life until recent times—is concerned. These lines

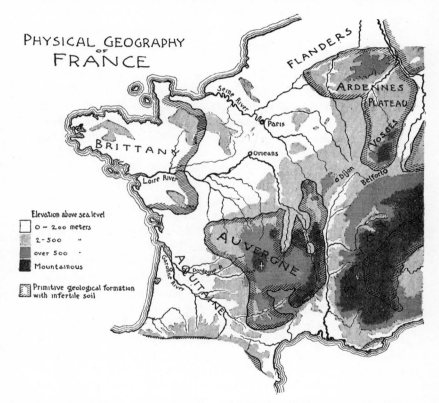

PHYSICAL GEOGRAPHY
of
FRANCE

Elevation above sea level
0 - 200 meters
2 - 500 "
over 500 "
Mountainous

Primitive geological formation
with infertile soil

indicate the boundary of the regions of primitive geological formation, those in which the granitic substrata are overlaid by a thin and stony soil.

A glance is sufficient to convince us that France is not everywhere a garden.* Two north and south axes of fertility

* Collignon, 1890 b, is suggestive on this.

divide it into three or four areas of isolation. These differ in degree in a way which illustrates the action of social forces with great clearness. Within these two axes of fertility lie two thirds of all the cities of France with a population of fifty thousand or over. The major one extends from Flanders at the north to Bordeaux in the southwest. Shaped like an hourglass, it is broadened about Paris and in Aquitaine, being pinched at the waist between Auvergne and Brittany. The seventy-five miles of open country which lie between Paris and Orleans have rightly been termed by Kohl * " the Meso- potamia of France." This district is not only surpassingly fertile; it is the strategic centre of the country as well. At this point the elbow of the Loire comes nearest to the Seine in all its course. An invader possessed of this vantage ground would have nearly all of France that was worth having at his feet. If the Huns under Attila, coming from the East in 451, had captured Orleans, as Clovis did with his Frankish host at a later time, the whole southwest of France would have been laid open to them. The Saracens, approaching from the south along this main axis of fertility had they been victorious at Tours, could in the same way have swarmed over all the north and the east, and the upper Rhone Valley would have been within reach. The Normans in their turn, coming from the northwest, must needs take Orleans before they could enter the heart of the country. Finally, it was for the same reason that the English fought for the same city in 1429, and the Germans took it twice, in 1815 and again in 1870. This dis- trict, then, between Paris and Orleans, is the key to the geo- graphical situation, because it lies at the middle point of this backbone of fertility from north to south.

The second axis, lying along the river Rhone, is of some- what less importance as a centre of population because of its extreme narrowness. Yet it is a highway of migration be- tween the north and the south of Europe, skirting the Alps; and it is easily accessible to the people of the Seine basin by the low plateau of Langres near the city of Dijon. This ren-

---

* 1874, p. 140 *et seq.* His analysis of the geographical features of France is very suggestive also.

ders it the main artery of communication from Paris to the Mediterranean. Down its course Teutonic blood has flowed. The culture of the south has spread into northern Europe in the contrary direction.* Such is the normal exchange between the two climates in human history, the world over. The great fertility of the Rhone axis, moreover, is in strong contrast to the character of the country upon either side. Judged by its population, it merits the important position we have here assigned to it.

The two axes of fertility above described set apart three areas in France which exhibit the phenomena of social isolation in different degrees. East of the Rhone lies Savoy, exceedingly mountainous, with a rigorous Alpine climate, and of a geological formation yielding with difficulty to cultivation. This region combines two safeguards against ethnic invasion. In the first place, it is not economically attractive; for the colonist is unmoved by those charms which appeal to the tourist to-day. We reiterate, the movement of peoples is dependent upon the immediate prosperity of the country for them. It matters not whether the invading hosts be colonists, coming for permanent settlement, or barbarians in search of booty; the result is the same in either case. Savoy, therefore, has seldom attracted the foreigner. It could not offer him a livelihood if he came. In the second place, whenever threatened with invasion, defence of the country was easy. Permanent conquest is impossible in so mountainous a district. Combining both of these safeguards in an extreme degree, Savoy, therefore, offers some of the most remarkable examples of social individuality in all France.

The second area of isolation lies between our two north and south axes of fertility—that is to say, between the Rhone on the east and the Garonne on the southwest. It centres in the ancient province of Auvergne, known geographically as the *Massif Centrale*. This comprises only a little less than two thirds of France south of Dijon. In reality it is an outpost of the Alps cut off from Savoy by the narrow strip of the

---

* *Cf.* Montelius, 1891.

Rhone Valley. Much of it is a plateau elevated above two thousand feet, rising into mountains which touch three thousand feet in altitude. Its climate is unpropitious; its soil is sterile; impossible for the vine, and in general even for wheat. Rye or barley alone can be here successfully raised. At the present time this region is almost entirely given over to grazing. It has vast possibilities for the extractive arts; but those meant nothing until the present century. For all these reasons Auvergne presents a second degree of isolation. It was until recently entirely devoid of economic attractiveness; but it is not rugged enough in general to be inaccessible or completely defensible as is Savoy.

Brittany or Armorica, the third area of isolation, is perhaps somewhat less unattractive economically than Auvergne. It is certainly less rugged. Extending in as far as the cities of Angers and Alençon, it is saved from the extreme infertility of its primitive rock formation by the moisture of its climate. Neither volcanic, as are many parts of Auvergne, nor elevated—seldom rising above fourteen hundred feet—it corresponds to our own New England. For the farmer, it is more suited to the cultivation of Puritan religious propensities than to products of a more material kind. It is the least capable of defence of the three areas of isolation; but it redeems its reputation by its peninsular position. It is off the main line. It is its remoteness from the pathways of invasion by land which has been its ethnic salvation.

In order to show the effect which this varied environment, above described, has exerted upon the racial character of the French people, we have arranged a series of three parallel maps in the following pages, showing the exact distribution of the main physical traits. For purposes of comparison certain cities are located upon them all alike, including even the map of physical geography as well. A cross in the core of Auvergne in each case; the Rhine shown in the northeast; the location of Paris, Lyons, Belfort, etc., will enable the reader to keep them in line at once. It should not fail of notice, in passing, that maps like these are constructed from averages for each department as a unit. These last are mere-

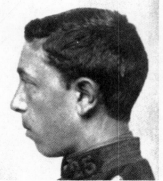

25.   *Teutonic type.*   Cotentin, Normandy.   Blond.   Index 79.   26.

27.   *Alpine type.*   Landes.   Brunet.   Index 90.   28.

29.   Lodève.   Index 76. Montpellier. Brunet. 30.

Mediterranean types.

12   FRANCE.

ly administrative districts, entirely arbitrary in outline, and entirely in dissonance with the topography of the country. The wonder is that, in view of this, the facts should still shine out so clearly. Thus all the Rhone departments lie half up among the mountains on the east. Their averages are therefore representative neither of the mountains nor the valleys. Between Dijon and Lyons the departments completely span the narrow valley, entirely obliterating its local peculiarities.

Earlier in our work we have seen that the several physical traits which betoken race vary considerably in their power of resistance to environmental influences. This resistant power is greatest in the head form; less so in the pigmentation and stature. As we are now studying races, let us turn to our most competent witness first. This is a reversal of the chronological order in which knowledge of the anthropology of France has progressed. Its peculiarities in the matter of stature were the very first to be studied; the facts concerning that were proved thirty years ago. Study of the head form has been the latest of all to awaken interest; yet it has rendered definite testimony of paramount importance. It will be remembered, from our third chapter, that we measure the proportions of the head by expressing the breadth in percentage of the length from front to back. This is known as the cephalic index. We have also seen, thereafter, that a high index—that is, a broad head—is the most permanent characteristic of the so-called Alpine race of central Europe. This type is bounded on the north by the long-headed and blond Teutons, on the south by a similarly long-headed Mediterranean stock, which is, however, markedly brunet. It is with all three of these racial types that we have to do in France. Passing over all technicalities, our map of cephalic index shows the location of the Alpine racial type by its darker tints; while, in proportion as the shades become lighter, the prevalence of long and narrow heads increases.

The significance of these differences in head form to the eye is manifested by the three portraits at hand. The northern long-headed blond type, with its oval face and narrow chin, is not unlike the Mediterranean one in respect of its cranial conformation. Ours is, I am informed by Dr. Collignon, a good type of the Norman peasant, with lightish though not distinctly blond hair and eyes. The Alpine populations of central France are exemplified by rather an extreme type in

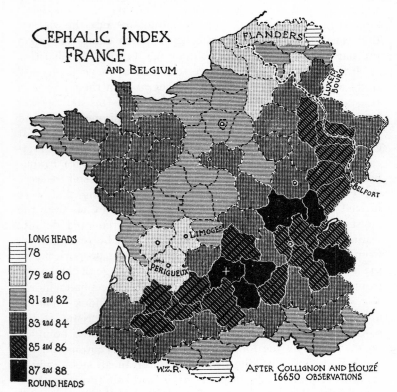

CEPHALIC INDEX FRANCE AND BELGIUM

LONG HEADS
78
79 and 80
81 and 82
83 and 84
85 and 86
87 and 88
ROUND HEADS

W.Z.R.   AFTER COLLIGNON AND HOUZÉ
                      16650 OBSERVATIONS

This map, after Collignon, '96 a, is slightly modified from his earlier ones published in '90 b, and also in Appendix to Bertrand and Reinach, '91. It is more authoritative, being based upon nearly twice the original number of observations. Later researches of his own in the southwest; of Lapouge in Hérault, Aveyron, and Brittany; Brandt in Alsace-Lorraine, Hovelacque and Hervé, Labit and others, confirm his results here shown.

our middle portrait, in which the head is almost globular, while the face is correspondingly round. Such extremes are rare. They indicate the tendency, however, with great distinctness. The contrast between the middle type and those above and below it is well marked. Even with differences but half as great as those between our portrait types, it is no wonder that Durand de Gros and other observers should have insisted that they were real and not the product of imagination.

Recalling the physical geography of the country, as we have described it, the most patent feature of our map of cephalic index is a continuous belt of long-headedness, which extends from Flanders to Bordeaux on the southwest. It covers what we have termed the main axis of fertility of France.* A second strip of long-headed population fringes the fertile Mediterranean coast, with a tendency to spread up the Rhone Valley. In fact, these two areas of long-headed populations show a disposition to unite south of Lyons in a narrow light strip. This divides the dark-coloured areas of Alpine racial type into two wings. One of these centres in the Alpine highlands, running up to the north; the other, in Auvergne, extends away toward the Spanish frontier on the southwest. At the present time let us note that this intrusive strip of long heads cutting the Alpine belt in two, follows the exact course of the canal which has long united the head waters of the Loire with the Rhone. It is an old channel of communication between Marseilles and Orleans. Foreigners, immigrating along this highway, are the cause of the phenomenon beyond question.

The long-headed populations, therefore, seem to follow the open country and the river valleys. The Alpine broad-headed type, on the other hand, is always and everywhere aggregated in the areas of isolation. Its relative purity, moreover, varies in proportion to the degree of such isolation enjoyed, or endured if you please. In Savoy and Auvergne it is quite unmixed;† in Brittany only a few vestiges of it remain, as we shall soon see. These few remnants are strictly confined within the inhospitable granitic areas, so that boundaries geographical and physical correspond very closely. The spoken Celtic

---

* Atgier, 1895, finds an even lower index (80) in Indre and Vienne. This would still more accentuate the contrasts here shown.

† Hovelacque, 1877–'79, is good on Savoy; Lapouge, 1897–'98, on Auvergne.

tongue has also lingered here in Brittany for peculiar reasons, which we shall soon discuss.   The main one is the isolation of the district, which has sheltered the Alpine race in the same way.   For it is now beyond question that the Breton, the Auvergnat, and the Savoyard are all descendants of the same stock.   The facial resemblance between the Bretons and the Auvergnats is said to be particularly noticeable.*   In nearly every case the Alpine race is found distributed, as Collignon says, " by a mechanism, so to speak, necessary, and which by the fatal law of the orographic condition of the soil ought to be as it is."   In the unattractive or inaccessible areas the broad-headedness centres almost exclusively ; in the open, fertile plains the cephalic index falls as regularly as the elevation.   So closely is this law followed, that Collignon affirms of the central plateau, that wherever one meets an important river easily ascended, the cephalic index becomes lower and brachycephaly diminishes.

The two-hundred-metre line of elevation above the sea seems most nearly to correspond to the division line between types.   This contour on our map on page 133 is the boundary between the white and first shaded areas.   Compare this map with that of the cephalic index, following round the edge of the Paris basin, and note the similarity between the two. There is but one break in the correspondence along the eastern side.   This exception it is which really proves the law. It is so typical that it will repay us to stop a moment and examine.   We have to do, just south of Paris, on our map of cephalic index, with that long tongue of dark tint, that is of relative broad-headedness, which reaches away over toward Brittany.   It nearly cuts the main axis of Teutonic racial traits (light-tinted) in two.   This is the department of Loiret, whose capital is Orleans.   It is divided from its Alpine base of supplies by the long-headed department of Yonne on the east.   This latter district lies on the direct route from Paris over to Dijon and the Rhone Valley.   Teutonic peoples have here penetrated toward the southeast, following as always

---

* Topinard, 1897, p. 100.

the path of least resistance. Why, you will ask, is Loiret about Orleans so much less Teutonic in type? The answer would doubtless appear were the country mapped in detail. The great forest of Orleans, a bit still being left at Fontainebleau, used to cover this little upland between the Seine and the Loire, east of Orleans. It was even until recently so thinly settled that it was known as the *Gatinais*, or wilderness.* Its insular position is for this reason not at all strange. The Teutons have simply passed it by on either side. Those who did not go up the Seine and Yonne followed the course of the Loire. Here, then, is a parting of the ways down either side of Auvergne.

Another one of the best local examples illustrating this law that the Alpine stock is segregated in areas of isolation and of economic disfavour is offered by the Morvan.† This *mauvais pays* is a peninsula of the Auvergne plateau, a little southwest of the city of Dijon. It is shown on our geographical map (page 133). Here we find a little bit of wild and rugged country, about forty miles long and half as wide, which rises abruptly out of the fertile plains of Burgundy. Its mountains, which rise three thousand feet, are heavily forested. The soil is sterile and largely volcanic in character; even the common grains are cultivated with difficulty. The limit of cultivation, even for potatoes or rye, is reached by tilling the soil one year in seven. This little region contains at the present time a population of about thirty-five thousand—less to-day than fifty years ago. Until the middle of the century there was not even a passable road through it. It affords, therefore, an exceedingly good illustration of the result of geographical isolation in minute detail. Its population is as strongly contrasted with that of the plains round about as is its topography. The people, untouched by foreign influence to a considerable

---

* *Cf.* Gallouédec, 1892, p. 384, on the neighbouring Sologne, west of Orleans, also. While its infertility has always been an unfavourable element, its proximity to Orleans, focus of all military disturbances, has been even more decisive.

† Hovelacque and Hervé, 1894 b, give an ideal anthropological study of this interesting bit of country.

extent, have intermarried, so that the blood has been kept quite pure.   The region is socially interesting as one of the few places in all France where the birth rate long resisted the depressing influences of civilization.   For years it has been converted into a veritable foundling asylum for the city of Paris. Its mothers, famous wet-nurses, have cared for innumerable waifs besides their own offspring.   This isolated people is strongly Alpine, as our portraits show herewith, the boy on the right being a peculiarly good type; the other one has a strain of Teutonic narrow-headedness from all appearances. Beyond a doubt here is another little spot in which the Alpine race has been able to persist by reason of isolation alone.*

Types in the Morvan.

The law which holds true for most of France, then, is that the Alpine race is confined to the areas of isolation and economic unattractiveness.   A patent exception to this appears in Burgundy—the fertile plains of the Saône, lying south of Dijon.   A strongly marked area of broad-headedness cuts straight across the Saône Valley at this point.   A most desirable country is strongly held by a broad-headed stock, although it is very close to the Teutonic immigration route up

---

* It should be noted that this relation does not appear upon our map of head form, because this represents merely the averages for whole departments.   The Morvan happens to lie just at the meeting point of three of these, so that its influence upon the map is entirely scattered.

along the Rhine. Here we have a striking example of the reversion of a people to its early type after a complete military conquest. It serves as an apt illustration of the impotency of a conquering tribe to exterminate the original population. The Burgundians, as we know, belonged to a blond and tall

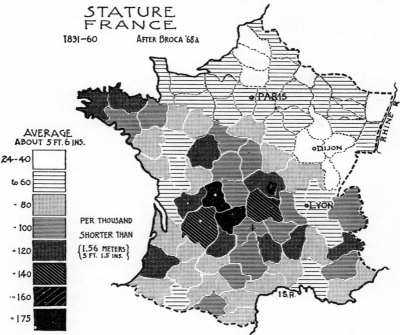

STATURE
FRANCE
1831–60   AFTER BROCA '68a

AVERAGE
ABOUT 5 FT. 6 INS.

24 – 40
6o 60
– 80
– 100   PER THOUSAND
        SHORTER THAN
– 120   {1.56 METERS}
        {5 FT. 1.5 INS.}
– 140
– 160
– 175

NOTE.—Savoy, for which Broca had no data, owing to its recent annexation, appears to occupy about the relative place here assigned to it. We have interpolated it for unity in comparison, following Carret and Longuet's data. It will be observed that our statistical representation is entirely different from the one originally employed by Broca.. This present mode of grouping is the only one which graphically corresponds to the facts in the case. For other details and maps consult Levasseur, '89, I, pp. 377-397.

race of Teutonic lineage, who came to the country from the north in considerable numbers in the fifth century.* The Romans welcomed them in Gaul, forcing the people to grant them one half of their houses, two thirds of their cultivated

* Lagneau, 1874 a, is good on this. Boudin first proved its existence a half century ago ; it was afterward confirmed by Broca.

land, and a third of their slaves.   For about a thousand years
this district of Burgundy took its rule more or less from the
Teutonic invaders: and yet to-day it has largely reverted to
its primitive type of population.   It is even more French
than the Auvergnats themselves.   The common people have
virtually exterminated every trace of their conquerors.   Even
their great height, for which the Burgundians have long been
celebrated, is probably more to be ascribed to the material
prosperity of the district than to a Teutonic strain.   This
physical peculiarity of the people of this region appears clearly
upon both our maps of stature.   The peasantry are among the
tallest in all France to-day.   According to our first map, in the
region about Dijon short men under five feet one inch and a
half in height are less frequent than almost anywhere else
in the country.   The same tallness appears, as we shall see,
among the western Swiss; those who inhabit the ancient
Burgundian territory.   This latter fact would lead us to suspect that race was certainly an important element in the matter.   The complexity of the problem is revealed when we
compare this Teutonic giantism of the people with their extreme Alpine broad-headedness.   A curiously crossed type
has been evolved, found in Alsace-Lorraine as well.   Here in
Burgundy the present currents of migration are quite strong.
Perhaps they may account for it in part.   One factor contributing to the result we observe, is that the fertile country
of the Saône Valley is open to constant immigration from
Switzerland and the surrounding mountains.   The Rhine has
drawn off the Teutons in another direction, and political ha-
treds have discouraged immigration from the northeast.   The
result has been that the Alpine type has been strongly re-
enforced from nearly every side, while Teutonic elements have
been gradually eliminated.   The tallness of stature once due
to them may nevertheless have persisted, because of the great
fertility of the district.*

---

* By reference to Deniker's map in our Appendix D, it will appear
that he attributes this curious cross of a tall stature with brachycephaly
to the presence of his so-called Adriatic or Dinaric race.   This we have
discussed in describing his classification elsewhere.

Another and perhaps even more potent explanation for this localization of the Alpine type in Burgundy also lies at hand. This fertile plain is the last rallying point of a people repressed both from the north and the south. The general rule, as Canon Taylor puts it, is that the " hills contain the ethnological sweepings of the plains." This holds good only until such time as the hills themselves become saturated with population, if I may mix figures of speech. Applying this principle to the present case, it appears as if the original Alpine stock in Burgundy had been encroached upon from two sides. The Teutons have overflowed from the north; the Mediterranean race has pressed up the Rhone Valley from the south. Before these two the broad-headed Alpine type has, as usual, yielded step by step, until at last it has become resistant, not by reason of any geographical isolation or advantage, but merely because of its density and mass. It has been squeezed into a compact body of broad-headedness, and has persisted in that form to the present time. It has rested here, because no further refuge existed. It is dammed up in just the same way that the restless American borderers have at last settled in force in Kansas. Being in the main discouraged from further westward movement, they have at last taken root.* In this way a primitive population may conceivably preserve its ethnic purity, entirely apart from geographical areas of isolation as such.

What is the meaning of this remarkable differentiation of population all over France? Why should the Alpine race be so hard-favoured in respect of its habitat? Is it because prosperity tends to make the head narrow; or, in other words, because the physical environment exerts a direct influence upon the shape of the cranium? Were the people of France once completely homogeneous until differentiated by outward circumstances? There is absolutely no proof of it. Nevertheless, the coincidence remains to be explained. It holds good in every part of Europe that we may have to examine—in Swit-

* Perhaps the peculiar concentration of Russians about Moscow described by Zograf, 1892 a, may be a similar phenomenon of social aggregation.

zerland, the Tyrol, the Black Forest, and now here in great detail for all France. Two theories offer a possible and competent explanation for it all. One is geographical, the other social.

The first theory accounting for the sharp differences of population between the favourable and unpropitious sections of Europe, is that the population in the uplands, in the nooks and corners, represents an older race, which has been eroded by the modern immigration of a new people. In other words, the Alpine race may once have occupied the land much more exclusively, being the primitive possessor of the soil. From the north have come the Teutonic tribes, from the south the Mediterranean peoples, in France just as in other parts of Europe. The phenomenon, according to this theory, is merely one of ethnic stratification.

A second explanation, much more comprehensive in its scope and pregnant with consequences for the future, is, as we have said, sociological. The phenomenon may be the outcome of a process of social selection, which rests upon racial or physical differences of temperament. This theory is advanced by the so-called school of social anthropologists, whose theories we shall have to consider in our later chapter on Social Problems. Briefly stated, the explanation is this: In some undefined way the long-headed type of head form is generally associated with an energetic, adventurous temperament, which impels the individual to migrate in search of greater economic opportunities. The men thus physically endowed are more apt to go forth to the great cities, to the places where advancement in the scale of living is possible. The result is a constant social selection, which draws this type upward and onward, the broad-headed one being left in greater purity thereby in the isolated regions. Those who advocate this view do not make it necessarily a matter of racial selection alone. It is more fundamental for them. It concerns all races and all types within races. This is too comprehensive a topic to be discussed in this place. Personally, I think that it may be, and indeed is, due to a great process of *racial* rather than purely *social* selection. I do not think it yet

proved to be other than this. The Alpine stock is more primitive, deeper seated in the land; the Teutonic race has come
in afterward, overflowing toward the south, where life offers
greater attractions for invasion. In so doing it has repelled
or exterminated the Alpine type, either by forcible conquest or
by intermixture, which racially leads to the same goal.

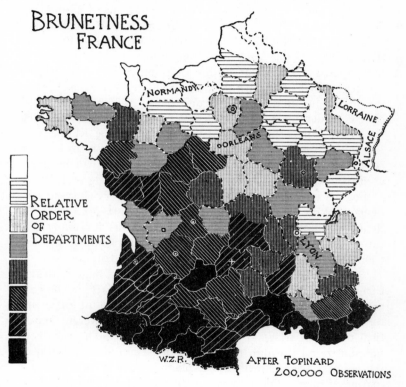

BRUNETNESS
FRANCE

RELATIVE
ORDER
OF
DEPARTMENTS

W.Z.R.

AFTER TOPINARD
200,000 OBSERVATIONS

Before we proceed further let us examine the other physical traits a moment. Our map of the distribution of brunetness shows these several Alpine areas of isolation far less distinctly than that of the cephalic index.* It points to the

* Topinard (1886 b, 1887, 1889 a, 1889 b, and 1893 a) is the authority
on this. Many maps showing the exact proportions of each trait, together
with their combinations in each department, are given. Pommerol, 1887;

disturbing influence of climate or of other environment. If
the law conducing to blondness in mountainous areas of infertility were to hold true here as it appears to do elsewhere,
this factor alone would obscure relations.   Many of the populations of the Alpine areas should, on racial grounds, be
darker than the Teutonic ones; yet, being economically dis-
favoured, on the other hand, they tend toward blondness.
The two influences of race and environment are here in opposition; to the manifest blurring of all sharp racial lines and
divisions.   Despite this disturbing influence, the Auvergnat
area appears as a great wedge of pigmentation penetrating
the centre of France on the south.   This is somewhat broken
up on the northern edge, because of the recent immigration
of a considerable mining population into this district which
has come from other parts of the country.   The Rhone Valley appears as a route of migration of blondness toward the
south.   Little more than these general features can be gathered from the map of colour, except that the progressive brunetness as we advance toward the south is everywhere in evidence.   Were we to examine the several parts of France in
detail we should find competent explanations for many features which appear as anomalous—as, for example, the extreme blondness upon the southwest coast of Brittany.

Comparing our map of stature on the next page with our
earlier one on page 143, it will appear that the facts in the case
are beyond controversy.   Two authorities, working at an in-
terval of twenty years apart and by entirely different statistical methods, arrive at identical conclusions.   The relatively
tall stature all through the historically Teutonized portion of
the country needs no further explanation; it is indubitably a
matter of race.   The tallness of the population of the Rhone
Valley is probably due to a double cause.*   The Teutons followed it as a path of invasion, while relative fertility still fur-

---

Bordier, 1895; and other local observers referred to in our other footnotes
give more details concerning special localities.

    * Cf. Hovelacque, 1896 a, on the recent augmentation of stature in
Provence.   Lapouge, 1894 a, ascribes the relative tallness of Hérault to
ethnic immigration down the Rhone.

ther accentuated its contrast with the mountainous districts
on either side, as in the Garonne Valley as well. Our three
areas of isolation appear upon both our maps. Savoyards,
Bretons, and particularly Auvergnats are relatively much
shorter than the populations round about them. In this case
the process is again cumulative; for the infertile regions pro-

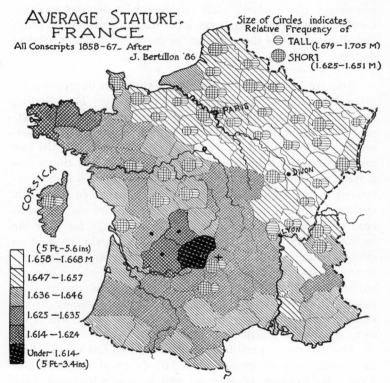

ductive of decreased bodily height at the same time tend to discourage immigration for the Teutonic race, which always carries a tall stature wherever it goes. The main axis of fertility
from Paris to Bordeaux, which was so clear upon our map of
cephalic index, does not appear for two reasons. The area
about Limoges and Périgueux, with the shortest population of
all, is the seat of a prehistoric people which we shall describe

shortly; and north of it toward Orleans, local causes such as
the Sologne and the infertility of the Limousin hills, which we
examined in detail in our chapter on Stature, are in evidence.
Perhaps the fertility of Charente and Bordelais, contrariwise,
is responsible for the light shade—that is to say, the tall stature which we observe just north of the Garonne mouth on
our map.*   As a whole, while less useful for detailed analysis,
owing to such disturbance by local causes, our stature maps
yet afford proof of the influence of racial causes to a marked
degree.

Brittany and *Normandy* are two of the most interesting regions in Europe to the traveller and the artist.   The pleasing
landscapes and the quaint customs all serve to awaken interest.   To the anthropologist as well the whole district possesses a marked individuality of its own.   Within it lie the two
racial extremes of the French people—the old and the new—
closely in contact with one another.   Attention was first attracted to the region because of the persistence of the Celtic
spoken language, now vanished everywhere else on the mainland of Europe—quite extinct, save as it clings for dear life
to the outskirts of the British Isles.   Here again, we find an
ethnic struggle in process, which has been going on for centuries, unsuspected by the statesmen who were building a
nation upon these shifting sands of race.   This struggle depends, as elsewhere in France, upon the topography of the
country.   The case is so peculiar, however, that it will repay
us to consider it a little more in detail.†

The anthropological fate of Brittany, this last of our three
main areas of isolation, depends largely upon its peninsular
form.   Its frontage of seacoast and its many harbours have
rendered it peculiarly liable to invasion from the sea; while
at the same time it has been protected on the east by its re-

---

* Collignon, 1896 b, p. 166.
† On Brittany and Normandy an abundant literature exists : given in
our complete Bibliography, under those index-subjects most important,
are those of Broca, 1868 a ; Lagneau, 1875 b ; Chassagne, 1881 ; Collignon,
1890 a and 1894 a ; Lapouge, 1895 a and 1896 b ; and Topinard, 1897.

moteness from the economic and political centres and highways of France. This coincidence and not a greater purity
of blood has preserved its Celtic speech. Since the foreigners
have necessarily touched at separate points along its coast,
concerted attack upon the language has been rendered impossible. This fact of invasion from the sea has not divided its
people into the men of the mountain, distinct from those of
the plain—a differentiation of population, by the way, as old as
the reforms of Solon and Cleisthenes. The contrast has arisen
between the seacoast and the interior. This differentiation is

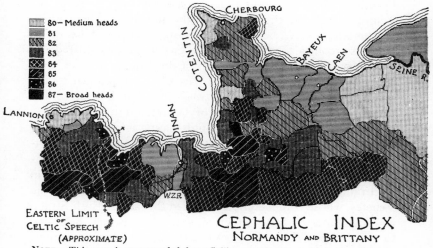

80 – Medium heads
81
82
83
84
85
86
87 – Broad heads

CHERBOURG
COTENTIN
BAYEUX
CAEN
SEINE R.
LANNION
DINAN
W.Z.R.

EASTERN LIMIT
OF
CELTIC SPEECH
(APPROXIMATE)

CEPHALIC INDEX
NORMANDY AND BRITTANY

NOTE.—This map is compounded from Collignon's sketches in his '90 a and '94 a.

heightened by the relative infertility of the interior uplands,
compared with the " *ceinture dorée* " along parts of the coast.*
The people of the inland villages contain a goodly proportion
of the Alpine stock; although, as our maps show, it is more
attenuated than in either Savoy or Auvergne. To the eye
this Alpine lineage in the pure Breton appears in a roundness
of the face, a concave nose in profile, and broad nostrils.
Along the coast intermixture has narrowed the heads, light-
ened the complexion, and, perhaps more than all, increased

* Gallouédec, 1893–'94.

the stature.* Our portraits illustrate this contrast, if we take
the Norman types as characteristic of the coast population.
Our Normans show plainly the elongated face and the high
and thin nose so peculiar to them. The varying degrees of
ethnic intermixture and their distribution will be seen from
an examination of our maps. Concerning those of stature at
pages 86 and 100 we have already spoken in detail. The dark
shading in both cases indicates the primitive population; the
lighter ones betray intermixture.

In view of the nature of these physical changes induced
by ethnic crossing along the seacoast, we must look to the
Teutonic race for the lineage of the invaders. They must,
on the whole, have been light and long-headed. History, in
this case, comes to our aid. The Saxon pirates skirted the
whole coast around to the mouth of the Loire. In fact, they
were so much in evidence that part of it was known to the
old geographers as the *litus Saxonicum*. The largest colony
which has left permanent traces of its invasion in the character
of the present population—although Cæsar assured us that he
exterminated it utterly—is located in Morbihan. This department on the south coast of the peninsula, as our map of relative brunetness on page 147 showed, is one of the blondest in
all France. Its capital, Vannes, derives its name from the
Venetes, whose confederation occupied this area. Both Strabo
and Diodorus of Sicily asserted that these people belonged
to the Belgæ (Teutonic stock), although modern historians
of Gaul seem inclined to deny it. Our anthropological evidence is all upon the side of the ancient geographers.† It
should be observed, however, that there are certain indications
in the Breton peasantry of a blond cross at a very early prehistoric period. Nowhere is the Alpine race found in such
purity as in our other areas of isolation. The persistence of
the " frank blue Breton eye " is in itself a heritage from this
primitive blond ethnic element, dating perhaps, as Broca asserts, from many centuries before the Christian era.

---

* Topinard, 1897, gives very good descriptions of these types.

† Lagneau, 1875 b, p. 627 ; Collignon, 1890 b, p. 221 ; and Beddoe,
1893, p. 31.

From a different source, although due indirectly to these same Teutonic barbarians, are derived the physical characteristics of the people in the north of Brittany near Dinan, in the valley of the Rance. Its location appears upon both of our maps of Brittany (pages 100 and 151). This little district is very distinct from the surrounding country. The landscape also is peculiar in many respects. The cottages are like the English, with hedgerows between the several plots of ground. All these outward features corroborate the anthropological testimony that this was a main settlement of the people who came over from Cornwall in the fifth century, ousted by the Anglo-Saxons. They, in fact, gave the name Brittany to the whole district. They spoke the Celtic language in all probability, but were absolutely distinct in race. They seem to have been largely Teutonic. The Saxons soon followed up the path they laid open, so that the characteristics of the present population are probably combined of all three elements. At all events, to-day the people are taller, lighter, narrower-nosed, and longer-headed than their neighbours.* A similar spot of narrow-headedness appears upon our map at Lannion. The people here are, however, of dark complexion, short in stature, characterized by broad and rather flat noses. Here is probably an example of a still greater persistence in ethnic traits than about Dinan; for the facts indicate that here at Lannion, ante-dating even the Alpine race, is a bit of the prehistoric population which we shall shortly seek to identify and locate.

Normandy is to-day one of the blondest parts of France. It is distinctly Teutonic in the head form of its people. In fact, the contrast between Normandy and Brittany is one of the sharpest to be found in all France. The map of cephalic index on page 151 shows the regularly increasing long-headedness as we approach the mouth of the Seine. In the Norman departments from thirty to thirty-five per cent of the hair colour is dark; in the adjoining department of Côtes-du-Nord in Brittany, the proportion of dark hair rises from forty to

---

* Collignon, 1892 b, p. 45 ; Taylor, 1863, p. 89. Meitzen, 1895, Atlas, Anlage 66 b, shows the Teutonic forms of settlement in this part of France.

sixty and in some cases even to seventy-five per cent.* In
stature the contrast is not quite as sharp, although the people
of the seacoast appear to be distinctly taller than those far inland.   The ordinary observer will be able to detect differences
in the facial features.   Our page of portraits, as we have said,
illustrates this clearly.   The Norman nose is high and thin;
the nose of the Breton is broader, opening at the nostrils.
This difference is no less marked than the contrast in the
contour of the face and the general proportions of the
head.

Normandy, on the whole, is an example of a complete ethnic conquest.   At the same time while a new population has
come, the French language has remained unaffected, with the
exception of a spot near the city of Bayeux, where the Saxons
and Normans together combined to introduce a bit of the
Teutonic tongue.   This conquest of Normandy has taken
place within historic times.   It is probably part and parcel
of the same movement which Teutonized the British Isles;
for it appears that the Normans were the only Teutonic invaders who can historically be traced to this region.   Wherever they left the country untouched, the population approaches the Alpine type, being darker, broader-headed, and
shorter in stature.   This indicates that the tribes, such as the
Caletes (the city of Caux), the Lexovii (Lisieux), and the
Baiocasses (Bayeux) in Cæsar's time were probably of this
latter type; in other words, that the district was Alpine in
population until the Normans came with Rollo in the tenth
century.   Freeman † takes note of the marked tallness of the
modern population of Bayeux, ascribing it to the intensity of
the Norman occupation.   The Romans appear to have allowed
the Saxons to settle at places along the seacoast, but they
had never penetrated deeply into the interior.   The " Otlinga
Saxonica," the dotted area upon our map of place names, for
example, dates from the third century.

The correspondence between the map of Norman place
names and that of cephalic index is sufficiently close to attest

---

* Collignon, 1894 a, p. 20.   See also Lagneau, 1865 ; and Beddoe, 1882 b.
† Norman Conquest, i, p. 119.

to the value of each.* One of the common features of the Teutonic village names is " ville," from " weiler," meaning an abode; not, as has been asserted, from " villa," of Romance origin. This suffix appears, for example, in Hacon*ville*, or in a corrupted form in Hardi*villiers*. Another common ending of place names is *bœuf*, as· in Marbœuf. Collignon has traced a considerable number of such place names of Norman origin, all of which point to the Cotentin—that distinct peninsula which juts out into the English Channel—as a centre of Norman dispersion. Certain it is that Cherbourg at

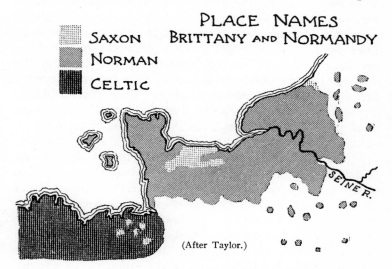

PLACE NAMES
BRITTANY AND NORMANDY

SAXON
NORMAN
CELTIC

(After Taylor.)

its extremity shows the Norman element at its maximum purity. Our Norman portraits are taken from this region as being most typical. Probably this was a favourite base of supplies, protected by its isolation and in close proximity to the island of Jersey, which the Normans also held. The Saxon colony near Caen was a factor also which determined this location. The extension of the Normans to the west

* Canon Taylor, 1863, is best on this; his map we have reproduced by permission of the publishers. Collignon, 1894 a, p. 14, gives corroborative testimony.

seems to have been stopped by the human dike set up by the English and Saxons about Dinan, and by " Norman Switzerland," the hilly region just east of it. Follow the similarity between the boundary of long and narrow heads on our map of cephalic index of Brittany, and the cross-hatched lines and tints on the map of physical geography (pages 133 and 151). Note how they both cut across diagonally from northwest to southeast, parallel to the course of the Seine. Here the economic attraction in favour of the invasion of Brittany ceased, and at the same time the displaced natives found a defensible position. Prevented from extension in this direction, the Normans henceforth turned toward the Seine, where, in fact, their influence is most apparent at the present time. They also pushed to the south into Berri, occupying the present departments of Cher and Indre in force.* Probably the wedge of relative blondness, appearing upon our map on page 147, which seems to penetrate nearly to Orleans, may be due to this later Norman immigration. Paris and Orleans, the Mecca of all invaders, toled them away, and Brittany was saved.

The northeastern third of France and half of Belgium are to-day more Teutonic than the south of Germany. This is clearly attested by the maps which show the distribution of each of the physical characteristics of race, especially, as we have seen, that of stature. It should not occasion surprise when we remember the incessant downpour of Teutonic tribes during the whole historic period. It was a constant procession of Goths—from all points of the compass—of Franks, Burgundians, and others. France was entirely overrun by the Franks, with the exception of Brittany, by the middle of the sixth century. All through the middle ages this part of Europe was not only ethnically Teutonic: it was German in language and customs as well. The very name of the country is Teutonic. It has the same origin as Franconia in southern Germany. In 813 the Council of Tours, away down south, ordained that every bishop should preach both in the Romance

---

* Hovelacque and Hervé, 1893. Collignon suggests that the low index in Cher is also due to Norman influence.

31. TEUTONIC TYPES. 32.

33. DEUX-SÈVRES. Index 87. Index 86. AVEYRON. 34.

ALPINE TYPES.

35. Cephalic Index 67. MONTPELLIER. 36.

MEDITERRANEAN TYPES.

FRANCE.

and the Teutonic languages.* The Franks preserved their German speech four hundred years after the conquest; even to-day after the cession of Alsace-Lorraine, a last vestige of Teutonic language, the Flemish, still persists on French territory along the Belgian frontier. Charlemagne was a German; his courtiers were all Germans; he lived and governed from outside the limits of modern France. The Abbé Sieyès uttered an ethnological truism when, in the course of the French Revolution, he cried out against the French aristocracy: " Let us send them back to their German marshes whence they came! " Even to-day the current of migration between France and Germany sets strongly to the south, as it has ever done, in virtue of economic laws deeper than national prejudice or hostile legislation.†

Why is Belgium entitled to a separate national existence among the states of modern Europe? Ireland and even Wales have tenfold stronger claims to political independence on the score both of race and religion. One half of this little state is topographically like Holland; the other is not to be distinguished in climate, geography, or soil from Alsace-Lorraine—that shuttlecock among nations. Belgium is father to no national speech. The Flemings can not hold common converse with their fellow-countrymen, the Walloons; for the first speak a corrupted Dutch, the second an archaic French language. Nor are the people more highly individualized in the anthropological sense. In fact, in a study of races Belgium is not to be considered apart from either northern France or southwestern Germany. It is closely allied to both. Of course, even despite the lack of all these elements of national-

---

* " Et ut easdem homilias quisque aperte transferre studeat in rusticam Romanam linguam aut Theotiscam (German) . . . quo facilius cuncti possint intelligere quaie dicuntur."—Hardouin, p. 1026, article xvii. *Cf.* Revue Mens. de l'École d'Anth., x, 1898, pp. 301–322.

† Kitchen, History of France, i, pp. 118 *et seq.* Taylor, Words and Places, 1893, p. 94, gives place names by map. See also Lagneau, 1874 b. Levasseur, 1889, i, p. 393, as also Andree, 1879 b, give convenient map of languages and dialects. Meitzen, 1895, i, pp. 516 and 532, with map in Atlas 66 a, traces this German intrusion by the village types. Turquan and Levasseur show the course of immigration.

ity, there is still a reason for the separate political existence of the Belgians. There must have been, for the sense of nationality is very intense among them. There is no sign of its abatement at the present time. It has made them a dominant power in Africa and elsewhere abroad. Their nationality is a geographical as well as an historical product. We shall deal with that presently. In the meantime we must consider the Belgians together with the whole population of northern France. It is befitting to do so; for Cæsar informs us that the Belgæ in his time controlled the whole region.* Roman Gaul, properly speaking, extended only as far north as the Seine and the Marne. In Cæsar's time the frontier of Belgium—the land of the Belgæ—lay near Paris. Has its recession to the north produced any appreciable change upon the people? Certainly not in any physical sense, as we shall attempt to point out.

The movement of population racially has been strongly influenced by the geography of the country. Were it not for the peculiar conformation of this part of Europe, there would be no geographical excuse for the existence of Belgium as a separate political entity, as we have said; and northern France would be far more thoroughly Teutonized than it is to-day. In order to make this clear, we must recall the topography of the district for a moment.† From the Alps in western Switzerland a spur of mountainous country of very indifferent fertility, known as the Ardennes plateau, extends far out to the northwest, its axis lying along the Franco-German frontier, as indicated upon our map at page 133. This area is triangular in shape with its apex touching Switzerland, the Rhine forming its eastern edge, and its base lying east and west across Belgium a little north of Brussels. This base is the geographical boundary between Flanders and the rugged uplands. Near the southern point, this Ardennes

---

* The Celtic question, involving the ethnic affinities of the Belgæ, is discussed in Chapter VI. Henri Martin, Arbois de Jubainville, and Desjardins assert the Gauls to be Celts; while Thierry, Bertillon, and Lagneau as strenuously deny it.

† Auerbach, 1890.

plateau rises into the Vosges Mountains. The major part of it consists of an elevated table-land, of little use in agriculture. Its uplands are heavily forested; its valleys are deep and very narrow. This plateau is divided from the main body of the Alps by a low pass about twenty-five miles wide, known as the Gap of Belfort. This has always formed the main pathway of communication between the valleys of the Seine, the Rhone, and the Rhine, from the time of Attila to that of the Emperor William I. It is the strategic key to central Europe. The only other routes from France to Germany cut straight across the rugged and difficult Ardennes plateau, following the valleys either of the Meuse or the Moselle. These valleys are both extremely fertile, but narrow and easy of defence. Sedan commands the one and Metz the other. This depression at Belfort has played quite a unique part in the natural history of Europe as well as in its military campaigns. It is the only route by which southern flora and fauna could penetrate to the north, since they could not traverse the Alpine highlands. The parallel is continued by the constant counter-migration of southern culture over the same way, evinced in archæology and history. It is not surprising that in anthropology this Gap of Belfort should be equally important.*

The Ardennes plateau is the core of a considerable population, which is primarily of the Alpine racial type.† It is an anthropological table-land of broad-headedness, surrounded on every side except the south, where it touches the Alps, by more dolichocephalic populations. Turn for a moment to our map on page 231. Notice the core of brachycephalic population in the Vosges and stretching out in two wings, either side of Metz on the Moselle. Gradually over in Belgium on the northwest this disappears at the edge of the plateau among the Flemings, as we shall see in a moment. Observe how it is eroded on the east along the Rhine Valley; and toward Paris, beginning in Marne and Haute-Marne,

---

* Kohl, 1841, p. 140; Marshall, 1889, p. 256; and Montelius, 1891.

† Consult Collignon, 1881, 1883, 1886 b, 1890 b, and 1896 a; also Hovelacque, 1896 b. For further references, see chapter on Germany.

toward the fertile plains of the Isle of France.*   The Germanic tribes in their ceaseless wanderings are the cause of that phenomenon beyond question.   It is evident that for Teutonism to enter France, it must pass through the Gap of Belfort, around north through Flanders, or follow the valleys of the Meuse or the Moselle.   All three of these it has certainly done in the anthropological sense.   It has overflowed along each of these channels, traversing the Alpine racial barrier.   It has done even more.   Its influence is manifest even in the nooks and byways.   For the people of the whole region are well

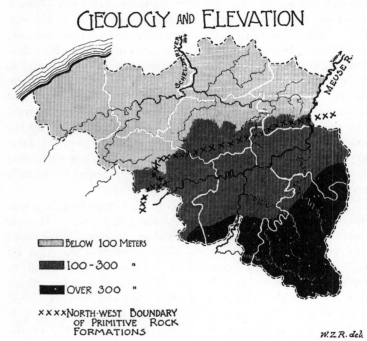

GEOLOGY AND ELEVATION

BELOW 100 METERS
100 - 300   "
OVER 300   "

××××NORTH-WEST BOUNDARY
     OF PRIMITIVE ROCK
     FORMATIONS

W. Z. R. del.

above the average French in stature.   They are quite Teutonic in this respect.   This we shall again emphasize in speaking of Germany later.   But the invaders have not been able

* This is shown in detail in the excellent study of the department of Ardennes by Labit, 1898, whose maps show both the increasing brachycephaly and the variations of stature along the edge of the plateau.

to efface that most persistent trait of the primitive population
—the broad, round head.   Here, as in the Black Forest just
across the Rhine, this physical characteristic remains as a
witness of priority of title to the land.

In Belgium itself, lying on the northwestern edge of the
Ardennes plateau, the contrast between the upland and the

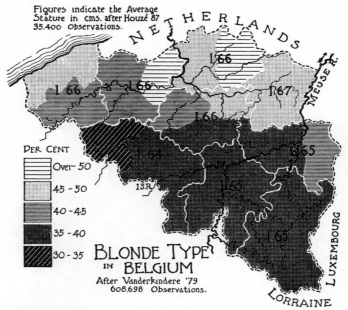

BLONDE TYPE
IN BELGIUM
After Vanderkindere '79
608,698 Observations.

plain is so distinct, and it coincides so closely with the racial
boundary between the Flemings and the Walloons, that it
merits special attention.*   Language here follows closely in
the footsteps of race.   As our three maps of the country show
in detail, the Walloons in the uplands are broader-headed than
the Flemings.   They are distinctly shorter in stature.   Our
map shows how much more infrequent blond types are among

* Authorities upon Belgium are Houzé, 1882, Ethnogénie de la Belgique; also his work of 1887 and 1888; Vanderkindere, 1879, Enquête
anthropologique sur la couleur—en Belgique.   Linguistic boundaries in
Belgium are mapped by Vandenhoven, 1844; Böckh, 1854; and Brämer,
1887.

them than among the Flemings.   It is curious to notice this
Teutonism of Flanders and the Low Countries.   It denotes
the utter extermination of all traces of the Spaniards, despite
their whilom political activities.   Belgium is sharply divided,
therefore, into halves, following the topographical boundary
of the plateau exactly, except in the department of Hainaut,
where Walloons are found in the plains.   The two halves of
Belgium thus indicated differ in politics, language, and in
many social customs.   One, Flanders, is cultivated largely by

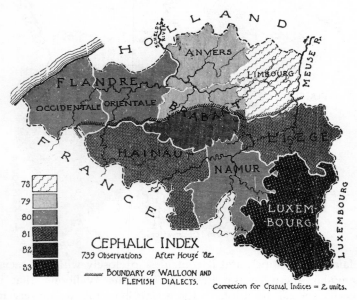

CEPHALIC INDEX
739 Observations   After Houzé '82.
BOUNDARY OF WALLOON AND
FLEMISH DIALECTS.
Correction for Cranial Indices = 2 units.

tenant farmers, the other tilled by peasant proprietors.   So
clearly drawn is the line of division that many interesting sociological problems may best be investigated here.   These, for
the moment, we pass by.   For us, at this time, the significance
of the division is, to put it in Dr. Beddoe's words [72], that
"the Walloons and their hilly, wooded country are a Belgic
cliff against which the tide of advancing Germanism has
beaten with small effect, while it has swept with comparatively
little resistance over the lowlands of Flanders and Alsace, and

penetrated into Normandy and Lorraine." Had it not been for this geographical area of isolation, political boundaries would have been very different from those of to-day. Belgium is a piece-of-pie shaped stop-gap between France and Germany. Being internationally neutralized in the military sense, it protects the main line of communication over the plains of Flanders between its two powerful neighbours. This is, in the eyes of the natural scientist, its main excuse for separate existence as a political entity. The Franco-German hatred is nothing but a family quarrel, after all, from our point of view. It is a reality, nevertheless, for historians. The only country whose population is really homogeneous is the tiny duchy of Luxemburg in the very centre of the plateau, scarcely more than a dot on the map. It deserves its independence for a like reason with Belgium. Were Alsace-Lorraine also a neutralized and separate kingdom, the prices of European government bonds would be considerably higher than they are to-day.

Let us now return to France again. We have still to cover the most interesting part of all in many ways. Cæsar's third division of Gaul from the Loire River southwest to the Pyrenees was inhabited, as he tells us, by the Aquitani. Strabo adds that these people were akin to the Iberians of Spain, both in customs and race. Detailed study, however, reveals a population far less homogeneous than these statements of the ancients imply.*

A glance at our map of the physical geography of France, on page 133, shows that this southwestern section is centred in the broad, fertile valley of the Garonne. From Bordeaux in every direction spreads one of the most productive regions in France, favoured alike in soil and in climate. Ascending the river valley, it narrows gradually until we reach a low pass, leading over toward the Mediterranean. This little axis of fertility, along which will run the projected canal to unite the two seacoasts of France, divides the plateaus of Auvergne from the highlands which lie along the Pyrenees. In this

---

* Authorities on this part of France are Lagneau, 1872 ; Castaing 1884 ; and especially Collignon, 1894 b, 1895, and 1896 a.

latter region fertility decreases as we approach the Spanish
frontier in proportion to the increase in altitude, although
most of the region is fairly capable of supporting a considerable population.   The only extensive area which is extremely unfavourable in character is the seacoast department of
Landes, along the Bay of Biscay south of Bordeaux.   This region is a vast sandy plain, but little raised above the sea level.
It is a flat district underlaid by an impermeable clay subsoil,
which is, except in midsummer, a great fen covered with rank
marsh grasses.   Without artificial drainage, it is unfit for cultivation, so that it remains to-day one of the most sparsely
populated sections of the country.*   As a whole, then, the
southwest of France presents the extremes of economic attractiveness, at the same time being devoid of those geographical barriers which elsewhere have strongly influenced the
movements of races.

The first impression conveyed by the general map of the
cephalic index for all France on page 138 in respect of this
particular region above described, is that here at last all correspondence between the nature of the country and the character of the population ceases.   A wedge of the broad-headed
Alpine stock centreing in the uplands of Auvergne pushes its
way toward the southwest to the base of the Pyrenees.   This
Alpine offshoot extends uninterruptedly from the sterile plateau of Auvergne, straight across the fertile plains of the Garonne and deep into the swamps and fens of Landes.   While
the geographical trend of the country is from southeast to
northwest parallel to the Garonne, the population seems to be
striped at right angles to it—namely, in the direction of the
Paris-Bordeaux axis of fertility.   At the northwest appears
the lower edge of the broad-headedness of the area of Brittany; then succeeds a belt of long heads from Paris to Bordeaux, to the south of which comes the main feature—a central strip of the Alpine type pushing its way to the extreme
southwest, as we have said.   The middle portrait at page 137
is a good example of the last-named round-headed type, which

---

* Chopinet, 1897, well describes this region and its people.

forms the bulk of the population. We are confronted by a racial distribution which appears to be utterly at variance with all the laws which elsewhere in France determine the ethnic character of its population.

One point is certain: either conditions have changed wonderfully since Strabo's time, or else the old geographer was far from being a discriminating anthropologist, when he described the people of Aquitaine as uniformly Iberians, both in race and in customs. A large element among them is as far removed from the Spaniards in race as it is possible in Europe to be. There is, as our map shows, a strip all along the Mediterranean which is Iberically narrow-headed and oval-faced, of a type illustrated in our portraits. Especially is this true in the department of Pyrénées-Orientales, shown on our map by the banded white area. This is the only part of France where the Catalan language is spoken to-day, as we took occasion to point out in our second chapter. This population in Roussillon, while truly Iberian in race, is Provençal in language; all the other peoples of Aquitaine differ from the Spaniards in both respects.

As regards the physical characteristics other than the head form, the population of Aquitaine is quite uniformly dark. On the whole, the brunet type outnumbers the blonds. About one seventh of the hair and eyes is light, whereas in Normandy blondness is represented by about one third of the traits.* In stature the general average is very low, well toward the shortest in Europe.

Turn back for a moment to the map of head form on page 138, and notice the curious light-tinted area in the heart of this southwestern region. It seems to be confined to four departments, lying between Limoges on the northeast and Bordeaux at the southwest. This peculiar little island of long-headedness has for years been a puzzle to anthropologists. It is a veritable outcrop of dolichocephaly close to the great body of broad-headedness which centres in Auvergne.† It lies, to

---

* Collignon, 1894 b, p. 20. *Cf.* map p. 147 *supra*.

† Atgier, 1895, finds a lower index than Collignon in Indre and Vienne, as we have said. The transition thence to the brachycephaly of Brittany on the north is quite sudden.

be sure, at the southwestern extremity of that axis of fertility from Paris to Bordeaux which we have already described. In conformity with the law of differentiation of populations which holds all through the north, a long-headed people is found in the plains. The trouble here is that the people are altogether too extreme in type. The general law is out-proved by it. The remoteness of this spot from any, other great centre of long-headedness constitutes the main point of interest. Such a trait ought to have been derived either from the north or the south of Europe. Teutonic inter-mixture is not a competent explanation for two reasons. In the first place, the heads are often more Teutonic in form than those of the peoples of direct Germanic descent along the Belgian frontier; nay more, in some cantons the people outdo the purest Scandinavians in this respect. This region is also separated from all Teutonic centres across country by several hundred miles of broader-headed peoples. That disposes of the theory of colonization from the north across France. Could the Teutons have come around by sea, then, follow-ing the *litus Saxonicum* already described? Obviously not so; for, as we shall see, the deepest pit of long-headedness lies far inland, about the city of Périgueux. If this be due to immigrants, they certainly could not have come in ships. Is it possible, then, that the people of these departments could have come from the south, an offshoot of the Mediterranean type? If so, they must have come over the Pyrenees or else across the low pass down the course of the Garonne. In either case a dike of brachycephaly must have been heaped up behind them, cutting off all connection with any Spanish base of racial supplies. And then, after all, we do not place too much reliance in any case upon theories of such whole-sale bodily migration that populous departments among the largest in France are completely settled in a moment. Hu-man beings in masses do not, as my friend Major Livermore has put it, play leap-frog across the map in that way, save under great provocation or temptation. We look for slow-moving causes, not cataclysms, just as the geologists have long since learned to do.

The reality of this peculiar island of long-headedness is best shown by the map on the next page, in which the same region is charted in great detail. The head form is here given by cantons, small administrative divisions intermediate between the department and the commune or township. The location of the capital cities of Limoges and Périgueux, on both maps, will enable the reader to orient himself at once. The "key" shows the boundaries of the departments. It is clear that a series of concentric circles of increasing long-headedness—that is, of light tints upon the map—point to a specific area where an extreme human type is prevalent.

History offers no clew to the situation. The country in question, in Cæsar's time, was occupied by a number of tribes of whose racial affinity we know nothing. On the west dwelt the Santones by the present city of Saintes (ancient Saintonge). The city of Périgueux, which gave its name to the ancient province of Périgord, marks the territory of the Petrocorii of Roman times. The province of Limousin to the northeast of it was the home of the Lemovici, with their capital at the modern city of Limoges. Around the ancient city at Bordeaux lay the Bituriges and their allies the Medulli (Médoc).* Along the east lay the Arverni, whence the name Auvergne; together with a number of minor tribes, such as the Cadurci, giving name to the district of Quercy to-day. Unless the population has shifted extensively, contrary to all ethnological experience, the people whose physical origin is so puzzling to us included the tribes of the Lemovici and especially the Petrocorii. For these two covered the main body of narrow-headedness shown upon our map, extending over two thirds of the department of Dordogne, and up into Haute-Vienne and Charente beyond the city of Angoulême. It appears as if we had to do with two tribes whose racial origin was profoundly different from that of all their neighbours. The frontier on the southeast, between the Petrocorii and the Arverni, seems to-day to have been the sharpest of all. In places there is a sudden drop of over five units in cephalic index at the

---

* Collignon, 1894 b, p. 69; 1895, pp. 74 and 85.

boundary lines. This means a change of type almost as great as that indicated between our several portrait types at page 156. This is especially marked at the frontiers of the two modern departments of Corrèze and Dordogne, as our "key" map shows. This racial boundary finds no parallel in distinctness elsewhere in France, save between the Bretons and Normans. In this present case, the people are distinct because the modern boundaries coincide exactly with the ancient ecclesiastical and political ones. For centuries the Arverni in Corrèze have turned their backs upon the Petrocorii in Périgord on *fête* days, market days, at the paying of taxes, or examination of conscripts. This they did as serfs in the middle ages,

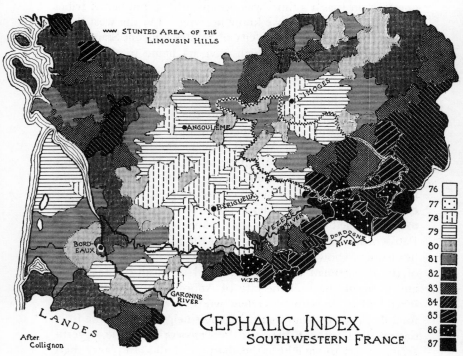

CEPHALIC INDEX
SOUTHWESTERN FRANCE

After Collignon

and they do it to-day as freemen when they go to the polls to vote. Each has looked to its capital city for all social inspiration and support. The result has been an absence of intercourse, with its attendant consequences. Artificial selection has sharpened the contrasts imposed in the first instance by differences of physical descent. It is one of those rare cases where political boundaries are competent to perpetuate and even to accentuate natural peculiarities due to race.

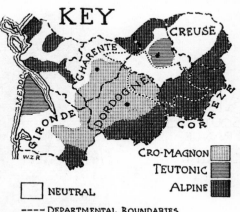

Let us now concentrate our attention upon these two peoples clustering about the modern cities of Périgueux and Limoges respectively — separated alike from all their neighbours by their long-headedness. Closer inspection of the map reveals that each of these two cities is to-day the kernel of a distinct subcentre of dolichocephaly; for two very light-coloured areas surround each city, the two being separated by a narrow strip of darker tint upon our map. Along this latter line the cephalic index rises appreciably. Thus, for example, while only 78 about Limoges, and 76 or 77 in Dordogne, it rises on this boundary line to 80 and 81. In other words, a bridge of relative broad-headedness cuts across the map, setting apart the descendants of the Lemovici, at Limoges, from those of their contemporaries, the Petrocorii, about Périgueux. This means that we have to do with two distinct spots of long-headedness—a small one about Limoges, and a major one extending all about Périgueux and Angoulême. There can be no doubt about this division. The boundary is a purely natural one, and deserves a moment's attention.

This frontier between Limousin and Périgord lies along the crest of the so-called " hills of Limousin," made familiar to us already in another connection. It marks the watershed between the two great river systems of western France, the Garonne and the Loire. Turn back for a moment to our stature map of Limousin, on page 83, which indicates the courses of these streams. Here is a true parting of the

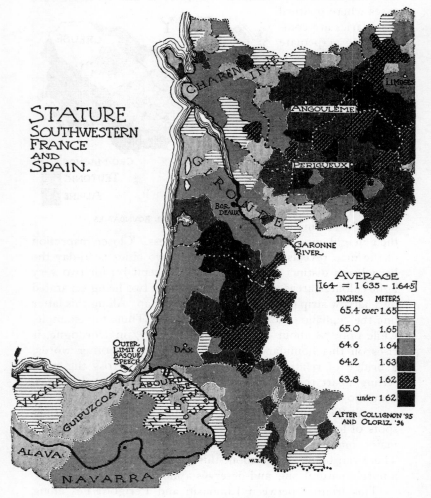

STATURE
SOUTHWESTERN
FRANCE
AND
SPAIN.

AVERAGE
[164 = 1 635 – 1.645]

INCHES	METERS	
65.4 over	1.65	
65.0	1.65	
64.6	1.64	
64.2	1.63	
63.8	1.62	
	under 1.62	

AFTER COLLIGNON '95
AND OLORIZ '96

waters; for the Charente flows directly to the sea on the west; the affluents of the Loire run to the north; and the Vézère, part of the system of the Garonne, to the south. These hills of Limousin are the western outposts of the granitic area of Auvergne; and just here the country changes abruptly to a calcareous formation along the south and west. The district is accounted the very poorest in all France. Its soil is worthless even for grazing; the water is bad and the climate harsh and rigorous.

These hills of Limousin, as we pointed out in our former discussion, are, so to speak, a veritable watershed of stature as well.* The bridge of relative broad-headedness we have described as lying along this line is but one among several peculiarities. The people of these hills are among the shortest in all Europe. Imagine a community whose members are so dwarfed and stunted by misery that their average stature is only about five feet two inches! Many cantons exist in which over thirty per cent of the men are under five feet three inches tall; and a few where two thirds of them all are below this height, with nearly ten per cent shorter than four feet eleven inches. About three men in every eight were too diminutive for military service, as Collignon measured them. With women shorter than this by several inches, the result is frightful. Around this area we find concentric circles of increasing stature as the river courses are descended and the material prosperity of the people becomes greater. Within it the regular diet of boiled chestnuts and bad water, with a little rye or barley; the miserable huts unlighted by windows, huddled together in the deep and damp valleys; and the extreme poverty and ignorance, have produced a population in which nearly a third of the men are physically unfit for military service. This geographical barrier, potent enough to produce so degenerate a population, lies, as we have said, exactly along the boundary between the descendants of the Lemovici about Limoges and the Petrocorii about Périgueux. To make it plain beyond question, we have marked the stunted area upon our map of cephalic index. The correspondence is exact. It also shows beyond doubt that this short stature is a product of environment and

---

* Collignon, 1894 b, p. 26 *et seq.*; also 1896 a, p. 165.

not of race; for our degenerate area overlies all types of head form alike, whether Alpine or other.

Here, then, is an anthropological as well as a geographical boundary, separating our long-headed tribes from one another. Without going into details, let it suffice to say that complexions change as well. To the north and east about Limoges the blond characteristics rise to an absolute majority, especially among the women; in the contrary direction about Périgueux, the proportion of brunets increases considerably. In short, the general association of characteristics is such as to prove that among the Lemovici there is a considerable infusion of Teutonic blood. They are the extreme vanguard of the Germanic invaders who have come in from the northeast. That accounts at once for their long-headedness. Similar to them are the populations west of Bordeaux in Médoc (*vide* key map). They also are remnants of the same blond, tall, long-headed type; but they have come around by sea. They are part of the Saxon hordes which have touched all along the coast of Brittany. These last people, settled in the beautiful Médoc and Bordelais wine country, protected by their peninsular position, are among the tallest peasantry of the southwest. They are, without doubt, the legitimate descendants of the Medulli and of the Bituriges Vivisci of early times. But between these two colonies of the Teutons, about Limoges and in Médoc respectively, lies the one whose origin we have not yet traced. The Petrocorii about Périgueux, who are they? If they also are of Teutonic descent, why are they not blond? This they most certainly are not: for a noticeable feature of the population of Dordogne is the high proportion of black hair, rising in some cantons to twenty-seven per cent.* This is very remarkable in itself, as even in Italy and Spain really black hair is much less frequent. This characteristic for a time gave colour to the theory that this great area of dolichocephaly was due to the relics of the Saracen army of Abd-er-Rhaman, shattered by Charles Martel at the battle of Tours. It is not improbable

---

* Collignon, 1894 b, p. 23.

37. DORDOGNE. 38.

39. DORDOGNE. 40.

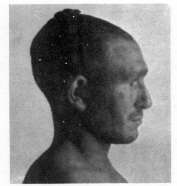

41. BERBER, Tunis. Eyes and hair very dark. Index 69. 42.

CRO-MAGNON TYPES.

that some Berber blood was thereby infused into the peasantry; but this explanation does not suffice to account for other peculiarities, which a detailed investigation reveals.*

The most curious and significant trait of these long-headed people in Dordogne remains to be mentioned. A harmonic long and narrow head ought normally to be accompanied by an elongated oval visage. In the Teutonic race especially, the cheek bones are not prominent, so that an even smooth outline of the face results. Inspection of our Norman faces, or of any other Teutonic peoples will exemplify this. In the Dordogne population, on the other hand, the faces in many cases are almost as broad as in the normal Alpine round-headed type. In other words, they are strongly disharmonic. To make this clear, compare the heads shown on the opposite page of portraits.† Notice at once how the Cro-Magnon head is developed posteriorly as compared with the Alpine type. This is noticeable in nearly every case. Observe also how in the front view the cranium narrows at the top like a sugar loaf, at the very place where the Alpine type is most broad. Yet despite this long head, the face is proportioned much more like the broad-visaged Alpine type than after the model of the true Mediterranean ones at page 156. These latter are truly normal and harmonic dolichocephalic types. This Cro-Magnon one is entirely different.

In our Dordogne peasant there are many other minor features which need not concern us here. The skull is very low-vaulted; the brow ridges are prominent; the nose is well formed, and less broad at the nostrils than in the Alpine type. These, coupled with the prominent cheek bones and the powerful masseter muscles, give a peculiarly rugged cast to the countenance. It is not, however, repellent; but more often open and kindly in appearance.‡ The men are in no wise pe-

---

* G. Lagneau, 1867 a.

† For the French Cro-Magnon portraits I am indebted to Dr. Collignon himself. These are the first, I think, ever published, either here or in Europe. The African type is loaned by Dr. Bertholon, of Tunis. It is described in his paper of 1891.

‡ Cf. Verneau's description in Bull. Soc. d'anth., 1876, pp. 408–417.

culiar in stature. They are of medium height, rather stocky than otherwise. In this latter respect they show the same susceptibility to environment as all their neighbours; they are tall in fertile places and stunted in the less prosperous districts. Lying mainly south of the dwarfed areas of Limousin, they are intermediate between its miserable people and their taller neighbours in the vine country about Bordeaux. Let it be clearly understood that they are not a degenerate type at all. The peasants are keen and alert; often contrasting favourably with the rather heavy-minded Alpine type about them.

The people we have described above agree in physical characteristics with but one other type of men known to anthropologists. This is the celebrated Cro-Magnon race, long ago identified by archæologists as having inhabited the southwest of Europe in prehistoric times.* As early as 1858 human remains began to be discovered by Lartet and others in this region. Workmen on a railway in the valley of the Vézère, shown on our map, unearthed near the little village of Les Eyziès the complete skeletons of six individuals—three men, two women, and a child. This was the celebrated cave of Cro-Magnon. In the next few years many other similar archæological discoveries in the same neighbourhood were made. A peasant in the upper Garonne Valley, near Saint-Gaudens, found a large human bone in a rabbit hole. On excavating, the remains of seventeen individuals were found buried together in the cave of Aurignac. At Laugerie Basse, again in the Vézère Valley, a rich find was made. In the cave of Baumes-Chaudes, just across in Lozère, thirty-five human crania with portions of skeletons were unearthed. These were the classical discoveries. The evidence of their remains has been completely verified since then from all over Europe. In no district, however, are the relics of this type so plentiful as here in Dordogne. Eight sepulchral caves have been dis-

---

* Authorities on this are E. and L. Lartet, 1861 ; and subsequently : De Quatrefages and Hamy, 1882. pp. 46 *et seq.*; also Verneau, 1886, and Hamy, 1891, especially. Bertrand and Reinach, 1891, give a suggestive map showing the areas of greatest frequency of Cro-Magnon remains. Its correspondence with Collignon's map of cephalic index is very close. Consult also Salmon, 1895, and Hervé, 1894 b.

covered within as many miles of the village of Les Eyziès alone in the Vézère Valley. Because of the geographical concentration of a peculiar type in this region, it has become known by the name of the Cro-Magnon race, since in the cave of this name the most perfect specimens were found.

The geographical evidence that here in Dordogne we have to do with the real Cro-Magnon race, is fully sustained by a comparison of the physical characteristics of the crania here discovered in these caves in the valley of the Vézère, with the peculiar living type we have above described. The original Cro-Magnon race was extremely dolichocephalic; as long-headed, in fact, as the modern African negroes or the Australians. The cranial indices varied from 70 to 73, corresponding to a cephalic index on the living head between 72 and 75. This was and is the starting point for the theory that the Mediterranean populations are an offshoot and development from the African negro. The only other part of Europe where so low an index has been located in the living population is in Corsica, where it descends almost to this level.* The people of Dordogne do not to-day range quite as long-headed as this, the average for the extreme commune of Champagnac being 76. This difference need not concern us, however, for within the whole population are a large proportion with indexes far below this figure. Close proximity to the very brachycephalic Alpine type, just over the line in Corrèze, would account for a great deal larger difference even than this. Probability of direct descent becomes almost certainty when we add that the Cro-Magnon head was strongly disharmonic, and very low-skulled. The modern population does not equal its progenitors in this last respect, but it approaches it so distinctly as to show a former tendency in this direction. The skull was elongated at the back in the same way—a distinguishing trait which appears prominently upon comparison of the profile view of a modern Cro-Magnon type with that of its Alpine neighbours, as we have already observed. The brows were strongly developed, the eye orbits were low, the

---

* *Cf.* page 54 *supra.*

chin prominent. The noted anthropologist, De Quatrefages, prophesied what one of these types ought to look like in the flesh. I give his description in his own words, that its agreement with the facial type above represented may be noted: " The eye depressed beneath the orbital vault; the nose straight rather than arched, the lips somewhat thick, the maxillary (jaw and cheek) bones strongly developed, the complexion very brown, the hair very dark and growing low on the forehead—a whole which, without being attractive, was in no way repulsive."

The prehistoric antiquity of the Cro-Magnon type in this region is attested in two distinct ways. In the first place, the original people possessed no knowledge of the metals; they were in the same stage of culture as, perhaps even lower than, the American aborigines at the coming of Columbus. Their implements were fashioned of stone or bone, although often cunningly chipped and even polished. They were ignorant of the arts, either of agriculture or the domestication of animals, in both of which they were far below the culture of the native tribes of Africa at the present day. Additional proof of their antiquity was offered by the animal remains found intermingled with the human bones. The climate must have been very different from that of the present; for many of the fauna then living in the region, such as the reindeer, are now confined to the cold regions of northern Europe. To be sure, the great mammals, such as the mammoth, mastodon, the cave bear, and hyena, had already become extinct. They were contemporaneous with the still more ancient and uncultured type of man, whose remains occur in a lower geological stratum. This Cro-Magnon race is not of glacial antiquity, yet the distribution of mammals was markedly different from that of to-day. Thus of nineteen species found in the Cro-Magnon cave, ten no longer existed in southern Europe. They had migrated with the change of climate toward the north. The men alone seem to have remained in or near their early settlements, through all the changes of time and the vicissitudes of history. It is perhaps the most striking instance known of a persistency of population unchanged through thousands of years.

It should not be understood that this Cro-Magnon type was originally restricted to this little region alone. Its geographical extension was once very wide. The classical skull of Engis, in Belgium, so well described by Huxley,[*] was of this type. It has been located in places all the way from Tagolsheim and Bollwiller in Alsace to the Atlantic on the west. Ranke [†] asserts that it occurs to-day in the hills of Thuringia, and was a prevalent type there in the past. Its extension to the south and west was equally wide. According to Verneau, it was the type common among the extinct Guanches of the Canary Islands. Collignon [('87a)] and Bertholon [('91)] have identified it in northern Africa. Our third Cro-Magnon portrait is representative of it among the Berbers. From all these places it has now disappeared more or less completely. Only in two or three other localities does it still form an appreciable element in the living population. There is one outcrop of it in a small spot in Landes, farther to the southwest; and another away up north, in that peculiar population at Lannion [‡] which we mentioned in our description of Brittany, with a promise to return to it. So primitive is the population here, in fact, that nearly a third of the population to-day is of this type. On the island of Oléron off the west coast there seems to be a third survival.[#] A very ancient type has also been described by Virchow[||] in the islands of northern Holland, which is quite likely of similar descent.

In all these cases of survival above mentioned, geographical isolation readily accounts for the phenomenon. Is that also a competent explanation for this clearest case of all in our population in Dordogne? Why should these peasants be of such direct prehistoric descent as to put every ruling house in Europe to shame? Has the population persisted simply by virtue of numbers, this having been the main centre of its dispersion in prehistoric times? Or is it because of peculiarly favourable circumstances of environment? It certain-

---

[*] 1863 and 1897.   [†] Der Mensch, 1887, ii, p. 446.

[‡] See maps, pp. 100 and 151 *supra*.

[#] Collignon, 1890 a, p. 58 ; and 1895, p. 95.

[||] 1876 a.

ly is not due to isolation alone; for this region has been overrun with all sorts of invaders, during historic times at least,
from the Romans to the Saracens and the English.   Nor is
it due to economic unattractiveness; for, be it firmly fixed
in mind, the Cro-Magnon type is not localized in the sterile
Limousin hills, with their miserable stunted population.   It
is found to-day just to the southwest of them in a fairly open,
fertile country, especially in the vicinity of Bordeaux.   These
peasants are not degenerate; they are, in fact, of goodly height,
as indeed they should be to conform to the Cro-Magnon
type.   In order to determine the particular cause of this
persistence of an ancient race, we must broaden our hori-
zon once more, after this detailed analysis of Dordogne, and
consider the whole southwest from the Mediterranean to Brittany as a unit.   It is not impossible that the explanation for
the peculiar anomalies in the distribution of the Alpine stock
hereabouts may at the same time offer a clew to the problem
of the Cro-Magnon type beside it.

   The main question before us, postponed until the conclusion of our study of the Dordogne population, is this: Why
has the Alpine race in the southwest of France, in direct opposition to the rule for all the rest of Gaul, spread itself out
in such a peculiar way clear across the Garonne Valley and
up to the Pyrenees?   It lies at right angles with the river valley instead of along it.   In other words, why is not the Alpine
type isolated in the unattractive area of Auvergne instead of
overflowing the fertile plains of Aquitaine?   The answer is, I
think, simple.   Here in this uttermost part of France is a last
outlet for expansion of the Alpine race, repressed on every
side by an aggressive alien population.   It has merely expanded along the line of least resistance.   The Alpine type in
Auvergne, increasing in numbers faster than the meagre means
of support offered by Nature, has by force of numbers pushed
its way irresistibly out across Aquitaine, crowding its former
possessors to one side.   Certainly this is true in the Pyrenees.
For here at the base of the mountains the population changes
suddenly, as we shall see in our next chapter on the Basques.
On the other side at the north lies, as we have just seen, a

second primitive population, less changed from the prehistoric type than any other in Europe. This Cro-Magnon race has been preserved apparently by the dike of the Limousin hills with their miserable population; for these hills have cut across the Paris-Bordeaux axis of fertility and have stopped the Teutonic race at the city of Limoges from expanding farther in this direction—that is to say, economic attraction having come to an end, immigration ceased with it. The intrusive Teutonic race has therefore been debarred from this main avenue of approach by land into Aquitaine. The competition has been narrowed down to the Alpine and Cro-Magnon types alone. Hence the former, overflowing its source in Auvergne, has spread in a generally southwestern direction with slight opposition. It could not extend itself to the south; for the Mediterranean type was strongly intrenched along the seacoast, and was in fact pushing its way over the low pass into Aquitaine from that direction. The case is not dissimilar to that of Burgundy. In both instances a bridge of Alpine broad-headedness cuts straight across a river valley open to a narrow-headed invasion at both ends. It is not improbable that in both, this bridge is a last remnant of broad-headedness which would have covered the whole valley had it not been invaded from both sides by other competitors.

Enough has been said to show the complexity of the racial relations hereabouts. We have identified the oldest living race in this part of the world. The most primitive language in Europe—the Basque—is spoken near by. It will form the subject of the next chapter.

CHAPTER VIII.

THE BASQUES.

THE Basques, or *Euskaldunak*, as they call themselves, on account of the primitive character of their institutions, but more particularly because of the archaic features of their language, have long attracted the attention of ethnologists. Few writers on European travel have been able to keep their hands off this interesting people. Owing to the difficulty of obtaining information from the original Basque sources, a wide range of speculation has been offered for cultivation. Interest for a long time mainly centred in the language; the physical characteristics were largely neglected. The last ten years have, however, witnessed a remarkable change in this respect. A series of brilliant investigations has been offered to science, based almost entirely upon the study of the living population. As a consequence, this people has within a decade emerged from the hazy domain of romance into the clear light of scientific knowledge. Much yet remains to be accomplished; but enough is definitely known to warrant many conclusions both as to their physical origin and ethnic affinities.*

---

* The best modern authorities on the Basques are R. Collignon, Anthropologie du sud-ouest de la France, Mém. Soc. d'Anth., série iii, i, 1895, fasc. 4 ; De Aranzadi y Unamuno, El pueblo Euskalduna, San Sebastian 1889 ; Hoyos Sáinz and De Aranzadi, Un avance à la antropologia de España, Madrid, 1892 ; Olóriz y Aguilera, Distribución geográfica del índice cefálico en España, Madrid, 1894 ; Broca, Sur l'origine et la répartition de la langue Basque, Revue d'Anth., série i, iv, 1875. De Aranzadi has also published a most interesting criticism of Collignon's work in the Basque journal, Euskal-Erria, vol. xxxv, 1896, entitled Consideraciones acerca de la raza Basca. For ethnography the older standard work is by T. F. Bladé, Étude sur l'origine des Basques, Paris, 1869. The works of Web-

Thirty years ago estimates of the number of people speaking the Basque language or *Euskara* ran all the way from four to seven hundred thousand. Probability pointed to about a round half million, which has perhaps become six hundred thousand to-day; although large numbers have emigrated of recent years to South America, and the rate of increase in France, at least, is very slow. About four fifths of these are found in the Spanish provinces of Vizcaya (Biscay), Navarra, Guipuzcoa, and Alava, at the western extreme of the Pyrenean frontier and along the coast. (See map, page 170.) The remainder occupy the southwestern third of the department of Basses-Pyrénées over the mountains in France. The whole territory covered is merely a spot on the European map. It is by quality, therefore, and not in virtue either of numbers or territorial extension, that these people merit our attention. In the preceding chapter we aimed to identify the oldest living population in Europe—a direct heritage from prehistoric times. We found it to lie about the city of Périgueux in the department of Dordogne, east of Bordeaux. Here, less than two hundred miles to the southwest, is probably the most primitive spoken language on the continent. Is there any connection discoverable between the two? Whence did they come? Why are they thus separated? Which of the two has migrated? Or have they each persisted in entire independence of the other? Or were they never united at all? Such are some of the pertinent questions which we have to answer.

These people derive a romantic interest from the persistence with which, both in France and Spain, they have maintained until the last decade their peculiar political organization, despite all attempts of the French and Spanish sovereigns through centuries to reduce them to submission.* Their

---

ster, Dawkins, Monteiro, and others are of course superseded by the recent and brilliant studies above outlined.

To my constant friend Dr. Collignon I am obliged for the portrait types of French Basques reproduced in this chapter.

* Herbert, 1848, pp. 316–322 ; Bladé, 1869, p. 419 *et seq*.; Louis-Lande, 1878, p. 297 ; and more recently, W. T. Strong, The Fueros of northern Spain, in Political Science Quarterly, New York, viii, 1893, pp. 317–334.

political institutions were ideally democratic, worthy of the enthusiasm bestowed by the late Mr. Freeman upon the Swiss folk-moot.   In Vizcaya, for example, sovereignty was vested in a biennial assembly of chosen deputies, who sat on stone benches in the open air under an ancestral oak tree in the village of Guernica.   This tree was the emblem of their liberties.   A scion of the parent oak was always kept growing near by, in case the old tree should die.   These Basques acknowledged no political sovereign; they insisted upon complete personal independence for every man; they were all absolutely equal before their own law; they upheld one another in exercising the right of self-defence against any outside authority, ecclesiastical, political, or other; they were entitled to bear arms at all times by law anywhere in Spain; they were free from all taxation save for their own local needs, and from all foreign military service: and in virtue of this liberty they were accorded throughout Spain the rank and privileges of *hidalgos* or noblemen.

Along with these political privileges many of their social customs were equally unique.*   On the authority of Strabo, it was long asserted that the custom of the *couvade* existed among them—a practice common among primitive peoples, whereby on the birth of a child the father took to his bed as if in the pains of labour.   This statement has never been substantiated in modern times; although the observance, found sporadically all over the earth, probably did at one time exist in parts of Europe.   Diodorus Siculus asserted that it was practised in Corsica at the beginning of the Christian era. There is no likelier spot for it to have survived in Europe than here in the Pyrenees; but it must be confessed that no direct proof of its existence can be found to-day, guide books to the contrary notwithstanding.†   The domestic institutions are remarkably primitive and well preserved.   Every man's house is indeed his castle.   As Herbert puts it in his classical

---

* Cordier, 1868–'69; Bladé, 1869, 419–444, also 525.   Demolins, 1897, and Dumont, 1892, are particularly good on their present demography, economic institutions, etc.

† *Cf.* Hovelacque, Études de Linguistique, 1878, pp. 197 *et seq.*

Review of the Political State of the Basque Provinces, speaking of Vizcaya: " No magistrate can violate that sanctuary; no execution can be put into it, nor can arms or horse be seized; he can not be arrested for debt or subjected to imprisonment without a previous summons to appear under the old oak of Guernica." The ties of blood are persistently upheld among all the Basques. Communal ownership within the family is frequently practised. The women enjoy equal rights before the law in many places. Customs vary from place to place, to be sure, and primitive characteristics are not always confined to the Basques alone. They are, however, well represented, on the whole. In some places the eldest daughter takes precedence over all the sons in inheritance, a possible relic of the matriarchal family which has disappeared elsewhere in Europe. Demolins [97] gives a detailed analysis of one of these communal families, presided over by the eldest daughter. It would lead us astray to enlarge upon these social peculiarities in this place. It will be enough in passing to mention the once-noted mystery plays, the folklore, the dances, the week consisting of but three days (as Webster asserts), and a host of other facts, each capable of inviting attention from the ethnological point of view. Many of these, according to Dumont [92], have now become things of the past, owing to the persistent opposition of the clergy, to whom the people are entirely subservient. Their dislike of town life is even to-day proverbial.* The only detail which it will repay us to elaborate is the language. To that we turn for a moment.

To the ordinary observer many peculiarities in the Basque language are at once apparent; x, y, and z seem to be unduly prominent—to play leading parts, in fact. There are more consonants alone, to say nothing of the vowels and double characters, than there are letters in our entire alphabet. For the linguist the differences from the European languages are of profound significance. The Basque conforms in its structure to but two other languages in all Europe, each of which is akin to the linguistic families of Asia and aboriginal Amer-

---

* Jour. Anth. Inst., ii, 1872, p. 157.

ica. It is formally like the Magyar or Hungarian; but this
we know to be an immigrant from the east within historic
times. It is also fashioned after the model of the speech of
the Finns in Russia. These people are likewise quite foreign
to western Europe; they are akin to tribes which connect them
with the Asiatic hordes. The Basque alone of the trio is mys-
terious as to its origin; for it constitutes a linguistic island,
surrounded completely by the normal population and languages of Europe.

In place of inflection, the Basque makes use largely of the
so-called principle of agglutination.* The different meanings
are expressed by the compounding of several words into one,
a device not unknown, to be sure, in Aryan tongues; but in
the Basque this is carried much further. The verb habitually
includes all pronouns, adverbs, and other allied parts of speech.
The noun comprehends the prepositions and adjectives in a
like manner. As an example of the terrific complexity possible as a result, Bladé gives fifty forms in the third person
singular of the present indicative of the regular verb *to give*
alone. Another classical example of the effect of such agglutination occurs in the Basque word meaning " the lower field
of the high hill of Azpicuelta," which runs

Azpilcuelagaraycosaroyarenberecolarrea.

This simple phrase is an even match for the Cherokee word
instanced by Whitney:

" *Winitawtigeginaliskawlungtanawneletisesti,*"

meaning " they will by this time have come to the end of
their (favourable) declaration to you and me." Sayce † gives
a similar example of agglutination from the Eskimo:

" *Aglekkigiartorasuarnipok,*"

whose significance is " he goes hastily away and exerts him-

---

* On language consult Pruner Bey, 1867; Gerland, 1888, in Gröber's
Grundriss; Bladé, 1869, pp. 237 *et seq.*; and the recent researches of Van
Eys, Vinson, Von der Gabelentz, and others. Titles of these will be
found in our extended Bibliography.

† Contemporary Review, April, 1876, p. 722.

self to write." This agglutinative characteristic, common to primitive languages the world over, justifies the proverb among the French peasants that the devil studied the Basque language seven years and learned only two words. The problem is not rendered easier by the fact that very little Basque literature exists in the written form; that the pronunciation is peculiar; and that the language, being a spoken one, thereby varies from village to village. There are in the neighbourhood of twenty-five distinct dialects in all. No wonder a certain traveller is said to have given up the study of it in despair, claiming that its words were all "written Solomon and pronounced Nebuchadnezzar."

Several features of this curious language psychologically denote a crudeness of intellectual power. The principle of abstraction or generalization is but slightly developed. The words have not become movable " type " or symbols, as the late Mr. Romanes expressed it. They are sounds for the expression of concrete ideas. Each word is intended for one specific object or concept. Thus there is said to be a lack of such simple generalized words as " tree " or " animal." There are complete vocabularies for each species of either, but none for the concept of tree or animal in the abstract. They can not express " sister " in general; it must be " sister of the man " or " sister of the woman." This is an unfailing characteristic of all undeveloped languages. It is paralleled by Spencer's instance of the Cherokee Indians, who have thirteen distinct words to signify the washing of as many different parts of the body, but none for the simple idea of " washing " by itself. The primitive mind finds it difficult to conceive of the act or attribute absolved from all connection with the material objects concerned. Perhaps this is why the verb in the Basque has to include so many other parts of speech. The Arabic language is similarly primitive. It has words for yellow, red, green, and other tints, but no term exists to express the idea of " colour," apart from the substance of the thing on which, so to speak, the colour lies.

A second primitive psychological characteristic of the Basque is found in the order of the words. These follow the

natural sequence of ideas more closely than in European languages.   The importance of the idea determines precedence.
Thus, instead of saying " of the man," the Basque puts it
" man, the, of."   Nouns are derived from one another in this
manner.   From *buru*, head, comes *buruk*, " head-for-the," or
bonnet.   Many of the words thus contain traces of their derivation, which have long since vanished from the Aryan.
Sayce gives some good examples.   Thus *orzanz*, thunder,
comes from *orz*, cloud, and *azanz*, noise.   The word for month
is *illabete*, derived from *illargi-bete*, meaning " moon-full."
And the word for moon is again divisible into *il*, death, and
argi, light.   In this manner we can trace the process of reasoning which induced the combination in many more cases than
in our own languages.   We have still some, like *twilight;* or
hidalgo, which in Spanish signifies " son-of-somebody," a no-
bleman ; but these are the exception.

Probably the most primitive element in the Basque is the
verb, or the relative lack of it.*   It was long asserted that no
such part of speech existed in it at all.   This, strictly speaking,
is not true.   Most of the verbs are, however, really nouns :
" to give " is in fact treated as if it were " donation " or the
" act of giving."   It is then declined quite like a noun, or
varied to suit the circumstances.   This is indeed truly· primitive.   Romanes has devoted much time to proving that the
verb requires the highest power of abstraction of all our parts
of speech.   Certain it is that it is defective in most primitive
languages, from the Chinese up.   Its crudity in the Basque
is undeniable evidence of high antiquity.

The archaic features of these Basque dialects in the days
when language and race were synonymous terms led to all
sorts of queer theories as to their origin and antiquity.   Bladé
describes these in great detail.   Flavius Josephus set a pace
in identifying the people as descendants of Tubal-Cain and
his nephew Tarsis.   In the middle ages they were traced to
nearly all the biblical heroes.   Such hypotheses, when comparative philology developed as a science, gave way to a num-

---

* Vinson, 1875–'95, is an authority.

ber of others, connecting the Basques with every outlandish language and bankrupt people under the sun. Vogt [63] and De Charency [67] connected them directly with the American Indians, because of the similarity in the structure of their language. Then De Charency [89] changed his mind and derived them from Asiatic sources. Sir William Betham [42] made them kin to the extinct Etruscans, a view to which Retzius subscribed. Bory de Saint-Vincent proved that they were the sole survivors of the sunken continent of Atlantis; of the type of the now extinct Guanches of the Canary Islands. Avezac said they were Sicani; Molon that they were Turanian.* Max Müller gives some evidence of similarity to the Lapps, the Finns, and the Bulgarians. Others said the ancient Egyptians were related to them. We have no space to mention more. Little by little opinion crystallized, especially among the historians, about the thesis originally upheld by Wilhelm von Humboldt,[17] that the Basque was a survival of the ancient Celt-Iberian language of Spain; and that these people were the last remnants of the ancient inhabitants of that peninsula. Pictet was the only linguistic dissident from this view, holding that the Basques were of even greater antiquity; being in fact the prehistoric race type of Europe, antedating the Aryan influx altogether. More recently we have Fita's [93] identification of the Basques with the Picts, a theory apparently not repugnant to such distinguished authority as Rhys [92]; together with Bertholon's [96] sustained attempt to trace a relationship to the ancient Phœnicians. As for affinity to the Hamitic or Berber languages of northern Africa, von der Gabelentz [93] proves it, while Keane [96] as strenuously denies the possibility.† So much, then, for the conclusions of the philologists. Not very satisfactory, to be sure!

It will be observed that all these theories rested upon the assumption that racial derivation could be traced by means of language. A prime difficulty soon presented itself. Some thirty years ago the Basque language was found by Broca[75]

---

* Nicolucci, 1888, p. 4; Issel, 1892, ii, p. 76.

† Cf. Boyd Dawkins's (1874 b) attempt to prove Berber, Basque, and Breton affinity; with Webster's criticism, 1875.

to be drifting toward the north, despite the apparent immobility of the people themselves.   It seemed to be losing ground rapidly in Spain, with no indication of doing so, rather the reverse, in France.   Nor was this apparently a new development. Everything denoted that it had been going on for many years. The mode of proof is interesting as Broca used it.   There are two independent sources of evidence.   In the first instance the place names all over Navarra as far south as the Ebro River are of Basque origin.   The language, as our map at page 18 shows, does not to-day extend nearly as far.   This indicates that the Basque speech prevailed when the villages, the mountains, and the rivers were named.   No such zone of place names lies outside the speech line in France, save in one canton, just over the Pyrenees.   There the Basque place names extend out as far as the broad white line upon our larger and more detailed map on the next page.   The inward bend of the curve of present speech at this place points to a retrogression of language.   Everywhere else in France the division line of place names coincides very closely with that of speech.

No less important proof that Basque is losing ground in Spain but holding its own in France is at hand.   Notice on the map that the Spanish language is to-day in use considerably within the Basque limit.   In other words, there is an intermediate zone in Spain where both languages are understood and spoken by the peasants.   This zone varies considerably in width.   By the city of Pamplona there is a deep recess cut in the Basque.   Castilian being the official language, and Pamplona the capital of the province, the people in its vicinity have been compelled to adopt this language.   They have forgotten their native Basque tongue entirely.   At Bilbao, also an official city, the Spanish is actively forcing its way in; although the Basque language has more persistently held its own along this side.   All along the frontier in Spain the Basque is on the retreat, much of the movement having taken place since the sixteenth century.   In France, on the other hand, the Basque tongue holds its own.   The line of demarcation between the Basque and the Béarnais-French *patois* is clean and clear cut.   There is no evidence of an invasion of

territory by the outsider. This is equally true in respect of
customs and folklore; so that the Basque frontier can be detected all along the line from village to village. The present

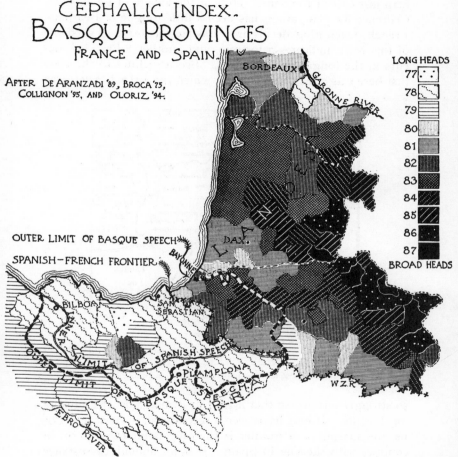

CEPHALIC INDEX.
BASQUE PROVINCES
FRANCE AND SPAIN.

AFTER DE ARANZADI '89, BROCA '75,
COLLIGNON '95, AND OLORIZ '94.

LONG HEADS
77
78
79
80
81
82
83
84
85
86
87
BROAD HEADS

OUTER LIMIT OF BASQUE SPEECH
SPANISH—FRENCH FRONTIER

NOTE.—Collignon, 1897, and Chopinet, 1898, give additional data for the departments
of Gers and Landes respectively, with maps in each case.

boundary is of such a form that it denotes a complete equality
of the two rival tongues. It has remained immovable for
many generations.

The clearness of this frontier in France is interestingly illustrated by a bit of detail on the accompanying map. It concerns that loop which is roughly indicated upon the larger map just east of Bayonne. Here at the village of La Bastide-Clairence for generations has been a little tongue of Béarnais-French penetrating deeply into Basque territory. The name of this town indicates a fortress, and another " Bastide " occurs in the tongue farther north. Broca inclines to the view that here was a bit of territory in which the French *patois* was

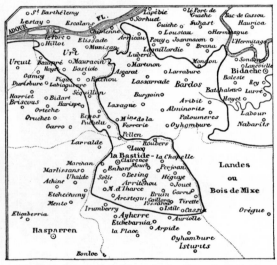

DETAIL.—Basque-French boundary.   (From Broca, '75.)

so strongly intrenched that it held its own against the advancing Basque. It may have been a reconquest, to be sure. For us, the sharpness of frontier is the only point of concern, in contrast with the one in Spain. It is an undoubted instance of linguistic invasion toward the north.

Another difficulty, no less insuperable than the fact that their language was on the move in a quiescent population, lay in the way of the old assumptions that the Basques were pure and undefiled descendants of some very ancient people.

Study of the head form precipitates us at once into it.* No
sooner did physical anthropologists take up the matter of
Basque origins than they ran up against a pair of bars. Study
of the cephalic index yielded highly discordant results. Those
who, like Broca [63] and Virchow, measured heads or skulls
of the Basques in Spain discovered a dolichocephalic type,
with an index ranging about 79 on the living head. Equally positive were those like Pruner Bey [67], who investigated the head form on the French slopes of the Pyrenees,
that the Basque was broad-headed. The indexes obtained in
this latter case clustered about 83. The difference of four
units and over was too great to ascribe to chance variation or to defective measurement. The champions of the
broad heads, such as Retzius and Pruner Bey, affirmed an
Asiatic origin; while their opponents, following Broca, as ve-
hemently claimed that, whatever the Basques might be, they
certainly were not Mongolian. They generally asserted an
African origin for them. The often acrimonious discussion
has been settled finally by proof that both sets of observers
were right, after all. Strange as it may seem, the people on
the two opposite slopes of the Pyrenees, both alike speaking
the same peculiar language distinct from all others in Europe,
were radically different in respect of this most fundamental
racial characteristic. No proof of this, beyond a glance at our
map of cephalic index, on page 189, is necessary. From preceding chapters the broad heads in France, denoted by the dark
tints, will be recognised as the extreme vanguard of the Alpine
race of central Europe. Spain, on the other hand, is a stronghold of the long-headed Mediterranean type.† Here we have
the point of contact between the two.

Bearing in mind now that the crest of the Pyrenees runs
along the political frontier, it seems as if, on the whole, the
line of division between broad-headed and long-headed types

---

* Collignon, 1895, p. 13, for France; Olóriz, 1894, pp. 167–175, with
map, for Spain.

† Aranzadi, while contesting many of Collignon's theses, shows in his
curve of seriation, 1889, p. 17, two constituent elements even among the
Spanish Basques.

lay at the northern base rather than along the summits of the
mountains. This is indeed true. Apparent exceptions prove
the rule ; for where, in the heart of the Basque territory, the
broad heads seem to penetrate to the Spanish frontier, there
is the ancient pass of Roncesvalles, celebrated in history and
literature. The broad-headed type would naturally have invaded here if at all. Everywhere else the long-headed type
seems to prevail, not only on the Spanish slopes, but clear over
to the foothills of the Pyrenees on the other side in France.
This the reader may roughly verify for himself by consideration of the five-hundred-metre contour line shown upon the
map at page 194. Assuming that this marks the lower edge
of the mountains, our proposition will at once be demonstrated.

If these facts be all true, what has become of our Basque
physical type? Where are our philological theories of purity
of racial representation? If the Basques are indeed an unmixed race, there must be one of these two types which is
spurious. At first the anthropologists sought thus to reject one
or the other, French or Spanish, for this reason. Then they
laid aside their differences ; they abandoned entirely the old
theory of purity of descent. The Basque became for them the
final complex product of a long series of ethnic crosses. Each
of the conflicting characteristics was traced to some people,
wherever found it mattered not. The type was compounded
by a formula, as a druggist puts up a prescription. Bladé
wrote in the light of such views. Canon Taylor, in his Origin
of the Aryans, holds that the broad-headed French Basque is
only a variation of the Alpine type which, as we have seen, prevails in all the southwest of France, with a dash of Lapp
blood. For him the Spanish Basque was, on the other hand,
a sub-type of the long-faced Iberian or Spanish narrow head.
The result of the crossing of the two was to produce a peculiarity of physical feature which we shall shortly describe—
namely, a broad head and a long, narrow face. Aranzadi,*
himself a Basque, assigns an equally mixed origin to his people. His view is that the Basque is Iberian at bottom, crossed

---

* 1889, p. 42.

 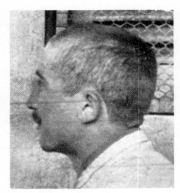

43.   FRENCH BASQUE, Basses-Pyrénées.   44.

45.   FRENCH BASQUE, Basses-Pyrénées.   46.

47.   HARMONIC TYPES.   Inner Pyrenees.   48.

BASQUES.

with the Finn or Lapp, and finally touched by the Teuton.
All these views resemble Renan's celebrated formula, cited by
Dr. Beddoe for a Breton, "a Celt, mixed with a Gascon and
crossed with a Lapp."

Is there, after all, a Basque physical type corresponding to
the Basque language? Enough has already been said to cast
a shadow of doubt upon the assumption. Can it be that all
which has been written about the Basque *race* is unwarranted
by the facts? Examine our Basque portraits collected from
both slopes of the Pyrenees. They appear in two series in
this chapter. At once a peculiar characteristic is apparent in
nearly every case. The face is very wide at the temples, so
full as to appear almost swollen in this region.* At the same
time the chin is very long, pointed, and narrow, and the nose
is high, long, and thin. The outline of the visage becomes
almost triangular for this reason. This, with the eyes placed
somewhat close together, or at least appearing so from the
breadth of the temples, gives a countenance of peculiar cast.
It resembles, perhaps, more than anything else the features of
so-called infant prodigies, in which the frontal lobes of the
brain have become over-developed. This resemblance is only
superficial. These people are notably hardy and athletic.
"To run and jump like a Basque" has become a proverb in
France. The facial contrast appears especially strong when
we compare this Basque type with that of its neighbours. The
people all about, in the plain of Béarn, are distinctly Alpine in
racial type; they have very well-developed chins and regular
oval features, in many cases becoming almost squarish, so
heavily built is the lower jaw. A Basque may generally be
detected instantly by this feature alone. The head is poised
in a noticeable way, inclining forward, as if to balance the
lack of chin by the weight of forehead. The carriage is always erect, a little stiff perhaps. This may be because bur-
dens are habitually carried upon the head. On the whole,
the aspect is a pleasant one, despite its peculiarities, the glance

---

* Collignon, 1895, p. 37; Aranzadi, 1889, p. 33; 1894 a, p. 518 ; 1896,
p. 70.

16

being direct and straightforward, the whole bearing agreeable yet resolute.

The peculiar triangular facial type we have described—characteristic both of Spanish long-headed or French brachycephalic Basques—has been mapped by Dr. Collignon for the north slope of the Pyrenees with great care. We have reproduced his map on this page. It is very suggestive. It shows a distinct centre of distribution of the facial Basque wherein over half the population are characterized by it. Con-

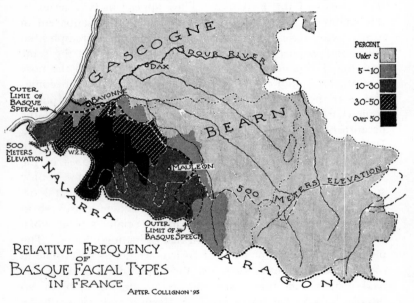

RELATIVE FREQUENCY
OF
BASQUE FACIAL TYPES
IN FRANCE
AFTER COLLIGNON '95

centric circles of diminishing frequency lie about it, vanishing finally in the plains of Béarn and Gascogne. The most noticeable feature is the close correspondence of this distribution of a physical type with the linguistic boundary. It is exact, save in one canton, Aramitz, at the eastern end southeast of Mauléon.* Here it will be remembered was the one spot in France where there was evidence in the place names of a retrogression of the Basque speech before the French. The light-dotted line

---

* On the local type here, *cf.* Collignon, 1895, p. 86.

shows the former boundary. It is the one French-speaking canton, with nearly a quarter of the population of the Basque facial type. The exception proves the rule. Some relation between language and racial type is proved beyond a doubt.

Another significant fact is illustrated by this map. It appears that instead of being refugees isolated in the recesses of the Pyrenees, the Basque physical type is really most frequent in the foothills and open plains along the base of the mountains. In order to emphasize this point we have indicated the lay of the land upon our map by means of the five-hundred-metre contour line of elevation above the sea. It shows that in the Basque country the mountains are much narrower than farther to the east. The Pyrenees, in fact, dwindle away in height down to the seacoast. The only canton in the mountains proper with upward of half the population of the Basque facial type lies at the famous pass of Roncesvalles. At this point the contour line sweeps far south, well toward the frontier. Of the three cantons with the maximum frequency of triangular faces among conscripts, Dr. Collignon found two and a half to be outside the mountains proper. The area of their extension is shaped like a fan, spreading out toward the plain of Béarn. The two wings of the fan are the cantons which form the core of the ethnic group. This region, Basse-Navarre, has always enjoyed a considerable political autonomy. Quite probably the ethnic segregation is due in part to this cause, as well as to the peculiarities of language. This fact that the Basques are not an ethnic remnant barely holding their own in the fastnesses of the Pyrenees, as is generally affirmed; but that they have politically and ethnically asserted themselves in the open fertile country, reverses their status entirely. It confirms an impression afforded by a study of their language, that however it may be in Spain, these people are a positive factor in the population of France.

In reality we have here in the department of Basses-Pyrénées a complex ethnological phenomenon, the Basques constituting the middle one of three distinct strata of population lying on the north slope of the Pyrenees. Our map of cephalic index, on page 189, serves to illustrate this. The plains of

Béarn are occupied by the extreme western outpost of the broad-headed, round-faced Alpine type of central Europe. Portraits characteristic of these are given in the preceding chapter. Then come the Basques proper, with their broad heads and triangular faces. These lie mainly along the foothills, although at Roncesvalles extending back into the mountains proper. Behind them, in the recesses of the Pyrenees, is the third layer of population. These mountaineers are distinctly and harmonically dolichocephalic—that is to say, being long-headed they are equally long- and narrow-faced. Conscripts with this characteristically narrow head, the long and smoothly oval face, are depicted in the lowest pair of portraits at page 193. These last people are really Mediterranean in type, overflows from the true Iberian stock, which forms the bulk of the Spanish population. Their ethnic segregation has probably been preserved in the innermost valleys of the Pyrenees because of the political independence of the people during many generations. These three groups of population above described of course merge into one another imperceptibly; but on analysis their differentiation has now been clearly established.

How has it come to pass that our Basques are thus left interposed between two neighbouring populations so entirely distinct in respect of these important racial traits? Is it permissible to suppose that the intermediate zone in which the triangular face occurs most commonly is really peopled by a simple cross between the two ethnic types on either side? This would be similar to Canon Taylor's supposition that a brachycephalic parent stock determined the head form of the Basques, while the narrow lower face and chin was a heritage from a dolichocephalic long-visaged ancestry. Such disharmonic crania arise sometimes from crossing of the two types of head form, especially in Switzerland where the Teutonic and Alpine races come into contact with one another. An objection to this theory of secondary origin by intermixture is close at hand. It is fatal to the assumption. It is an important fact that the Basques are relatively broader-headed than even the neighbouring peasantry of Béarn, and of course even

more so than the long-headed Spanish population across the
Pyrenees. Turning back to our map on page 189 this will
appear. Of course, the Basques are not more extreme in this
respect than the pure Alpine type; we mean that they rise in
cephalic index above their immediate and adulterated Alpine neighbours in the plains of Béarn.* This implies, of
course, that they are at the same time far broader-headed than
the Spanish Basques over the mountains. Thus we dispose at
once of the explanation offered both by Canon Taylor and De
Quatrefages for the broad-headedness of the French over the
Spanish Basque. Taylor accounted for this marked difference
between the people of the two opposite slopes of the Pyrenees
on the supposition that in invading Béarn from Spain the
Basques intermarried with the broad-headed Alpine stock there
prevailing, and so deviated from their parent type. This fact
that we have mentioned, that in France in their greatest
purity the Basques are broader-headed than the Béarnais about
them, proves beyond question that they are brachycephalic by
birth and not by intermixture with their French neighbours.
In Spain, on the other hand, the facial Basque, if we may use
the term, is slightly broader-headed than his purely Spanish
neighbour. Surrounded thus on all sides by people with
longer and narrower heads, we are forced to the conclusion
that this people is by nature of a broad-headed type. An
important corollary is that the pure Basque is to-day found
in France and not in Spain, although they both speak the
same language. This exactly reverses Taylor's theory. It is
the Spanish Basque which is a cross-type—in other words,
narrower-headed by four units than the French Basque because of intermixture with the dolichocephalic Spaniards.
Those who are found here in Spain are probably stragglers;
they have merged their physical identity in that of their Spanish neighbours. Their political autonomy on this south side
of the mountains being less marked, the power of ethnic resistance vanished quickly as well.

Having disposed of the explanation of origin by inter-

---

* *Cf.* Aranzadi, 1896, pp. 34–36.

mixture, the only hypothesis tenable is that these Basques are immigrants—that they are an intrusive people.   Dr. Collignon's explanation is so simple and agrees so well both with history and with anthropological facts that we give it as nearly as possible in his own words.*   During the Roman imperial rule a number of petty Iberian tribes, by virtue of the same tenacity which enables their descendants to enjoy political autonomy to this day, had preserved a similar independence south of the Pyrenees.   Such were the Vardules, Caristes, Autrigons, and the Vascons (Basque—by no means physically identical with the Gascons, although derived from the same root word).   These last occupied the upper course of the Ebro —that is to say, modern Navarra in Spain.   The barbarian invasions ravished all Gaul with fire and sword.   The Visigoths, controlling for a time the two slopes of the Pyrenees, were finally expelled from Aquitaine by the Franks, greater barbarians even than they.   It is readily conceivable that these Visigoths about this time began to covet the rich territory of the Vascons over in Spain, especially the environs of Pamplona, which were of great strategic importance.   History furnishes no details of the conflict, except that the Vascons were completely subjugated and partly driven into the Pyrenees.   Here they speedily found their way over into Béarn in France, meeting no opposition since the country there had mainly been depopulated by constant wars.   This occupation by the Vascons, according to Gregory of Tours, took place in the year 587—that is to say, some time after the fall of the Roman Empire.†   The invasion was accelerated later through the pressure exerted by the Spaniards, fleeing before the Saracen conquerors in the south.   Remnants of all the Spanish peoples took refuge at this time in the north.   Impelled by this pressure from behind, the Vascons were driven out of the Pyrenees and still farther north into France, retaining their political autonomy under Frankish rule.   Here they remained

---

* Collignon, 1895, pp. 50 *et seq.*; better in 1894 c ; also Aranzadi, 1896, p. 131, who denies his conclusions.

† For historical material, consult Bladé, 1869, p. 42 ; and Broca, 1875, p. 27, as well as Collignon, *op. cit.*

undisturbed by the Saracens, save by the single army of Abd-er-Rahman. Hence on this northern side of the Pyrenees they have preserved their customs and physical characteristics intact, while in Spain intermixture has disturbed the racial type to a greater degree. The language alone has been better preserved south of the mountains because it was firmly fixed there before the Spanish refugees came in such numbers. Of our three layers of present population the dolichocephalic type in the fastnesses of the Pyrenees to-day represents the primitive possessors of Aquitaine. Here, driven to cover by the advancing wave of the Alpine stock on the north long before the fall of Rome, they have remained protected from disturbance by the later invaders from the south. The Vascons or Basques have simply passed through their territory, with eyes fixed upon the fertile plains of Aquitaine beyond. They spread out in two wings as soon as they were out of the mountains, as we have seen. In the course of time they have intermarried with the primitive population of the Pyrenees; and the latter have adopted the Basque language and customs: for they were penned in by them all along the base of the mountains and had no other option. This community of language and customs could not fail to encourage intermarriage; to the final end that to-day even in the mountains the Basque is considerably crossed, as our map shows. In the plains, on the other hand, the line of demarcation of blood is as sharp as that of speech. Purity of type on this side was made possible by the political independence which Basse-Navarre has always enjoyed.

We have still to inquire as to the physical origin of this curious people. We have traced them back to Spain. Whence did they come into this country in the first place? Are they of African descent, following Broca's theory, or are they offshoots from Mongolian stock as Pruner Bey would have it? Or must we class them with the lost tribes of Israel? We already know the physical type of the prehistoric Cro-Magnon race. Let us compare it with our Vascons and test the theory of descent from it. The Basque head is disharmonic—that is, it is broad, while the face is extraordinarily narrow. This is in contravention of the general law that the face and the head usually participate alike in the relative proportions of breadth and length. Thus, as our portraits have shown, the broad-headed Alpine stock in Béarn has a round, short face; while the dolichocephalic population of the Pyrenees, lying behind the Basque, has a correspondingly long, oval visage. The Cro-Magnon race offers the only other example of a widespread disharmonic head in Europe. Are our Basques derived from this pure ethnic source? Curiously enough, these two cases of disharmonism so near to one another cross at right angles. In the Basque the head is broad and the face narrow; in the Cro-Magnon it is the head which is narrow while the face is broad. In view of this flat contradiction, the hypothesis of the Basque as a direct and pure descendant of the most primitive prehistoric population of Europe becomes completely untenable. Thus we dispose of one possible source for this people. We have already rejected the theories based upon intermixture. The broad head of our Basque with its narrow face is explained by De Aranzadi,* himself a Basque, by the supposition of an admixture of Lapp blood to give the broad head with Iberian or Berber blood for the narrow face. Modern research is, however, inimical to such hasty assumptions of migration across continents and over seas: for the inertia of simple societies is immense. Causes of variation nearer at home are regarded as more probable and potent, and there is none more powerful than social selection.

The difficulty of placing the Basque is solved by Collignon in a novel and yet simple way which has won favour already among anthropologists. It is of great significance for the student of sociology. His explanation for the Basque type is that it is a sub-species of the Mediterranean stock evolved by long-continued and complete isolation, and in-and-in breeding primarily engendered by peculiarity of language. The effects of heredity, aided perhaps by artificial selection, have generated local peculiarities and have developed them to an extreme. The objection to this derivation of the Basque from

---

* Briefly stated in his 1894 a.

50. Zamudio,
Guipuzcoa.

51. Tolosa, Guipuzcoa. 52.
SPANISH BASQUES.

53. FRENCH BASQUE, Basses-Pyrénées. 54.
BASQUES.

the Mediterranean stock which at once arises is that the latter
is essentially dolichocephalic, while the Basques, as we have
shown, are relatively broad-headed. It appears, however, that
the Basque is broad-headed in the main pretty far forward near
the temples. The cranium itself at its middle point is of only
medium width and the length is merely normal. The proportions, in fact, excluding the frontal region, are very much like
those of the Mediterranean stock in Spain across the Pyrenees. They approach much nearer to them, in fact, than to
the Alpine or broad-headed stock. It is thus only by its abnormal width at the temples that the cranium of the Basques
may be classed as broad-headed.* Collignon regards the type,
therefore, as more or less a variation of the Mediterranean variety, accentuated in the isolation which this tribe has always
enjoyed. It approaches in stature and in general proportions
much nearer also to the Mediterranean than to the Alpine stock
in France.

That the Basque facial type—that which is recognised as
the essential characteristic of the people, both in France and
Spain—is a result of artificial selection, is rendered probable
by another bit of evidence. The Basques, especially in France
where the type is least disturbed by ethnic intermixture as we
have seen, are distinguishable from their Béarnais neighbours
by reason of their relatively greater bodily height.† This appears upon our map of stature on page 170. The lighter tints
denoting taller statures are quite closely confined within the
linguistic boundary. This is not due to any favourable influence of environment; for the Basque foothills are rather below
the average in fertility. The case is not analogous to that of
the tall populations of Gironde, farther to the north, light
tinted upon the map. They, as we took occasion to point out

---

* On true and false brachycephaly of this kind elsewhere, consult
Lapouge, 1891 b; and Lapouge-Durand, 1897–'98 (rep.), p. 16; as also
Ujfalvy, 1896 a, pp. 84 and 398.

† The same superiority of stature, as compared with the rest of Spain,
appears on the map at p. 170. Olóriz in Navarra made no distinction between Spanish and Basques; else perhaps the northern half of that province would have been revealed as equal to Guipuzcoa or Vizcaya in
stature.

in the preceding chapter, are above the average either in Dordogne on the north or in Landes on the south. The contrasted tints show this clearly. These differences are in great measure due to the surpassing fertility of the valley of the Garonne as compared with the sterile country upon either flank. No such material explanation is applicable to the Basque stature. Some other cause must be adduced. Ought not artificial selection, if indeed it once became operative in a given ethnic group, to work in this direction? Goodly stature is earth-wide regarded as a type of beauty. We know that the Basques are proud of this trait. May they not have evolved it, or at least perpetuated it, by sexual choice perhaps? This, of course, is merely supposition on our part, but it seems to be worthy of mention.

The development of a facial type peculiar to certain localities is by no means a rare phenomenon. We shall have occasion to call attention to it later in other portions of Europe, particularly where isolation prevails. The form of the nose, the proportions of the face, nay, at times the expression, seem to be localized and strongly characteristic. Thus among the Finnic peoples in Russia, however much they may differ in head form, a characteristic physiognomy remains.* It is easy to conceive of artificial selection in an isolated society whereby choice should be exercised in accordance with certain standards of beauty which had become generally accepted in that locality. It is merely an illustration of what Giddings, in his Principles of Sociology, aptly terms a recognition of " consciousness of kind "; or, as Dr. Beddoe puts it, of " fashion operating through conjugal selection." † An example of the effect of selection of this kind in producing strongly individual types is offered by the Jews. They as a race vary greatly in the proportions of the head, and in colour of eyes and hair to a lesser degree. Nevertheless, despite all variations in these characteristics, the prominent facial features remain always the same.‡ The first, being inconspicuous traits, are allowed to run their natural course; the latter are seized upon

---

* Beddoe, 1893, p. 40.
† Beddoe, 1893, p. 12, discusses this.   ‡ *Vide* p. 49 *supra*.

and accentuated through the operation of sexual preference for that which has become generally recognised either as beautiful or ethnically individual.

In the attempt to justify this interesting sociological explanation for the peculiarities of the Basques, causing them to differ from their parent Mediterranean stock, several corroborative facts have come to light. In the first place the people themselves are fully conscious of their peculiarities. Collignon gives an interesting illustration of this in the ease with which a Basque is recognised at a glance.* Certain customs among the peasants seem to imply a recognition of their facial individuality. These all tend to accentuate the peculiarities which have now apparently become hereditary among them. The chin is almost invariably shaven in the adults, with the effect of exaggerating its long and pointed formation.† More conclusive still, it is said that in early manhood side whiskers are often grown upon the broadest part of the cheeks. This would obviously serve still more to exaggerate the peculiar form which the face naturally possesses. A neighbouring people, the Andalusians, differ in their way of adorning the face in such wise as to heighten the contrast between themselves and the Basques. Among them chin whiskers are grown, which serve to broaden their already rounded chins and to distinguish them markedly from the pointed-chinned Basques. All this fits in perfectly with much of the evidence brought forward by Westermarck, in his History of Human Marriage, serving to show that the fashions in adornment which prevail among various peoples are largely determined by the physical characteristics which they naturally possess. Thus the North American aborigines, having a skin somewhat tinged with a reddish hue, ornament themselves almost entirely with red pigment, heightening still more their natural characteristics. Among the negroes a similar fact has been observed, in each case the attempt being to outdo nature.

Is it not permissible to suppose that here the same process has been at work gradually remoulding the physical type?

---

* 1894 c, p. 281. † Aranzadi, 1896, pp. 70, 101.

A far-reaching and bold hypothesis this, to be sure. It would have less probability in its favour did we not observe in modern society many phenomena of fashion and custom closely akin to it in their immediate effects. We have but to suppose a fashion arising by chance, or perhaps suggested by some casual variation in a local hero or prominent family. This fashion we may conceive to crystallize into customary observance, until finally through generations it becomes veritably bred in the bone and part of the flesh of an entire community. A primary requisite is isolation—material, social, political, linguistic, and at last ethnic. No other population in Europe ever enjoyed all of these more than the Basques. If such a phenomenon could ever come to pass, no more favourable place to seek its realization could be found than here in this uttermost part of Europe.

CHAPTER IX.

THE TEUTONIC RACE: SCANDINAVIA AND GERMANY.*

SCANDINAVIA, by reason of its geographical remoteness from the rest of Europe, and also because of its rigorous climate and the infertility of its soil, contains naturally one of the most highly individualized populations in Europe. We have already seen that it is the home of the Teutonic race in its maximum purity. Representatives of this type in its several varieties are given in the accompanying portrait pages. It will be observed that the head form, in every case where our subjects have been measured, is of the long and narrow type already made familiar to us in the earlier chapters. The cephalic index falls, as a rule, well below 78. This degree of long-headedness, however, judging by our map of cephalic index on the next page, is almost entirely confined to the interior of the country. It is especially marked in the long, narrow valley of the Glommen, known as Osterdal, and also about Vaage in the upper Gudbrandsdal.† These two regions, according to our map, are the purest Teutonic districts in Norway, which means by implication, perhaps, in all Europe. Our two portrait types from this region, Vaage and Hedalen, are clear examples of this tall, oval-faced, straight-nosed, and clear blond variety. It is not without interest, especially in its bearing upon our future contention ‡ that the Scandinavian peo-

---

* To Major Dr. C. O. E. Arbo, of Christiania, I am deeply indebted for assistance both in the matter of personal notes and of photographs in all that concerns Norway. From Sweden science has much to hope from the extensive investigations now proceeding under the personal direction of Prof. Hultkrantz, of Stockholm. Full lists of the literature are given in our Bibliography.

† Arbo, 1891, especially pp. 4, 28.

‡ Page 364.

ples are of the same race as the Lithuanians and Finns across
the Baltic on the east, to note that the blondness of these
purest Teutons very often assumes a reddish cast.   In one
place, Aamlid, Arbo found the remarkable proportion of nineteen per cent of red hair, for example, a frequency unequalled

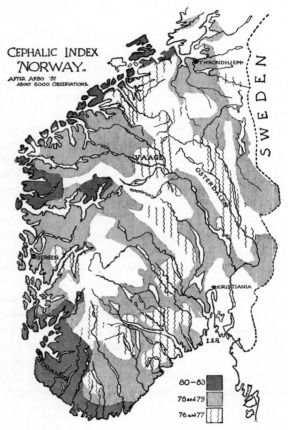

elsewhere in Europe, either in Finland or Lithuania.   Among
the Scotch, notable for this rufous characteristic, the proportion is seldom above half of this.*   It seems as if Topinard's
law that the rufous shades are but varieties of the blond type

---

* Arbo, 1891, pp. 28, 36 ; 1898, pp. 10 and 28.   Beddoe, 1885, pp. 151–156.

were again verified in Norway, as it apparently has also been in Germany * and Italy.†

The most striking feature of our map, perhaps, is that all along the seacoast, with the exception of the neighbourhood of Bergen and of the southeastern coast, a strong tendency to very prevalent broad-headedness appears. This is especially marked, even far inland in the southwest angle of the coast by Stavanger. From this town south for quite a distance the character of the coast differs entirely from the fiord-like and deeply indented shore-line on either side. There are no mountains here breaking away abruptly down to the sea. The coast is low and sandy, especially noticeable being the absence of those protected waters, highly favourable to coastal navigation, so characteristic of Scandinavia as a whole. This district, Jøderen, is sparsely populated, deriving no economic advantages either from fishing in the sea, or from mining industry or farming on land. It has, nevertheless, been populated since a very early period. Evidence of settlement in both the stone and the bronze age is abundant.‡ In this region, despite the purely Teutonic character of the main body of Norway, a population of decidedly Alpine affinities occurs. Arbo finds, as our map shows, an average index often as high as 83. In isolated places it rises to an extreme of brachycephaly, in fact scarcely exceeded by central Europe.# Nor is this a recent phenomenon. Barth ‖ has investigated crania from about the thirteenth century, finding the same broad-headed folk to be present. Among our portraits several of these types appear, especially good being the round-faced ones from Jøderen.

This brachycephalic coast population in Norway is appreciably darker than the pure Teutonic ones which, as we have said, occur in the interior. Oftentimes the children may

---

* Topinard, 1893 a ; Virchow, 1886 b, p. 337.   † Livi, 1896 a, p. 73.
‡ Arbo, 1887, p. 263 ; 1894, pp. 167–178.
# 1895 b, p. 12 ; 1894, p. 168.
‖ 1896, p. 79, finds a curve of cranial index with two maxima, one at 75 and one at 80, measured horizontally. It is very different for his curve for Tønsberg which is clearly Teutonic, culminating at 73 with almost no indices above 80.

17

still be light, even tow-haired; but with advancing years distinctly brunet tendencies are revealed, especially in the hair.* In the colour of the eyes the differences from place to place are far less noticeable. Thus, while in the purest Teutonic populations in northern Osterdal and Gudbrandsdal about sixty per cent of the hair was light, with less than twenty per cent of really dark or black hair; in Joderen, Arbo found the blond and the really dark hair to be about equally represented, with forty per cent of each, the remainder being neutral in colour.† More than this has been proved. Not only are the broad-headed coast districts darker as a whole; in them the brachycephalic individuals actually tend to be darker than the other types, as Arbo has clearly shown.‡ Finally, while, as our map of stature indicates, the population of this southwestern corner of Norway is not distinctively shorter than the remainder of the country, nevertheless, in this region the broadest-headed types incline to shortness of stature.# In temperament these people, un-Teutonic in all of the ways we have described, are also peculiar. They seem to be more emotional, loquacious, and susceptible to leadership, in contradistinction to the stolid, reserved, and independent Teutons.||

We may profitably consider the stature of Scandinavia as a whole. Fortunately for comparisons with the rest of Europe, each of the two common methods of showing the distribution of this trait have been adopted for Norway and Sweden respectively. On the other hand, direct comparison of one with the other is rendered impossible. All that we know with certainty, is that the general average for the two countries is about the same—viz., 5 feet 6.7 inches (1.695 metres). This is, as we have already shown, considerably below the level for the British Isles, but it is superior to that of any other portion of Europe. Little direct relation of the local variations to the environment occur. In Norway, for example, while the district west of Vaage shows by its dark tint a relatively short

---

* On pigmentation in general, consult Topinard, 1889 c.

† 1891, pp. 16 and 48 ; 1895 b, p. 49 ; 1898, p. 20.

‡ 1898, p. 68.   # Arbo, 1895 a, p. 506 ; 1895 b, p. 51.

|| Arbo, 1891, p. 49 ; 1894, p. 173.

55.   VAAGE.   Index 75.   Index 76.   HEDALEN.   56.

57.   JØDEREN.   TEUTONIC TYPES.   NORWEGIAN.   58.

59.   Stature 1.46 m.   Index 87.5.   Index 87.5.   Stature 1.43 m.   60.

LAPPS.

SCANDINAVIA.

61.   AAMOT.   Index 77.   Index 76.   TRYSIL.   62.

63.   SØNDRE FRON.   Index 78.   JØDEREN.   64.

65.   NORWAY.   JØDEREN.   66.

NORWAY.

population, the highlands east of it, especially those in the upper Osterdal, do not seem to be depressed by their rugged environment. Nevertheless, it should be noted that this region is the habitat of the purest Teutonic population in the

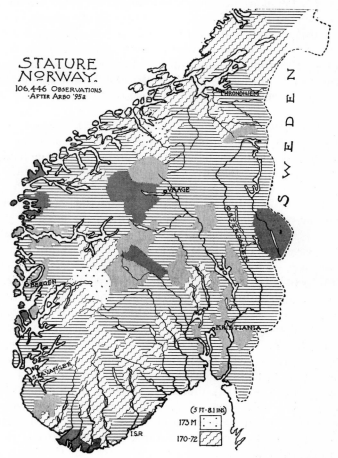

STATURE
NORWAY.
106,446 Observations
·After Arbo '95a

country, measured both by blondness and head form. It ought to excel, on racial grounds alone, many other districts, especially along the coast, where populations with intermixture of a shorter type prevail. Perhaps, indeed, the rigorous environment may have been competent to hold these purest Teutons down in stature to the level of their neighbours.* The dark shade, denoting a short-statured population on the eastern frontier, next to Sweden, seems to be of peculiar origin. The people of Trysil are not only abnormally short for Scandinavia; they seem to be quite dark, often being characterized in features by a Mongolian cast.† This appears in our subject from this valley, whose portrait is surely of such a type. Who shall say that this bit of long-headed but broad-faced and dark population is not again an outcrop of that Cro-Magnon type, so nearly extinct elsewhere in Europe save in southern France? As for Sweden, the depression of stature north of Jemtland and Helsinge where tallness culminates, may be due to either of two causes, as Hultkrantz ('97) suggests. Intermixture with the Lapps would inevitably tend to depress the average height, and the poverty of the environment would have a tendency in the same direction.

What explanation can be offered for the curiously un-Teutonic population which seems to fringe the coast of Norway, especially centreing in the southwest? It is an untenable hypothesis, as, in fact, Nilsson found it, to ascribe this to the persistence of a substratum of Lapps from the stone age. These people, to be sure, are characterized by all the traits noted in the southwest of Norway, and this, moreover, to an extraordinary degree. They are almost dwarfed in stature; they are dark-haired and swarthy; and, as our two portraits illustrate, they are broad-headed to an extreme. Their squat faces prove this, even in absence of anthropometric data; no contrast could be more striking than that between the Lapps and the Teutons. The difficulty, however, in holding them responsible for the cross of physical traits in the southwest is a very positive one, albeit, mainly, geographical in character. The Lapps lie at the remotest distance from this district; there is no evidence in place names or otherwise that they ever occupied the country even as far south as Vaage.‡ Arbo, realizing the impossibility of this hypothesis, has not apparently

---

* Arbo, 1895 a, p. 511.   † Arbo, 1891, p. 14.
‡ Arbo, 1895 a, p. 512; Dueben, 1876.

hit upon the explanation which seems to us to be perfectly simple. It is this: that here in the southwest of Norway we have an outlying lodgment of the Alpine racial type from central Europe. This view is greatly strengthened by virtue of

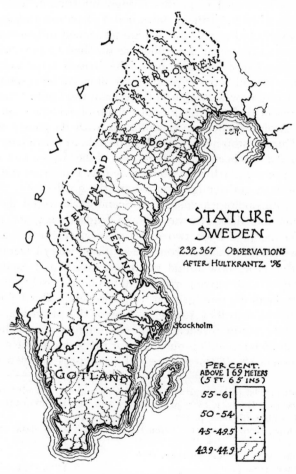

STATURE
SWEDEN
232,367 OBSERVATIONS
AFTER HULTKRANTZ '96

PER CENT.
ABOVE 1 69 METERS
(5 FT. 6 5 INS)

55 - 61	
50 - 54	
45 - 49.5	
43.9 - 44.9	

the fact that Denmark, just across the Skager Rack, so far as our indefinite knowledge goes, seems to be peopled by a type not unlike that of Jøderen. The peninsula is far less purely

Teutonic than Schleswig-Holstein, as we shall see,[*] this being especially true of the islands off the coast.[†] The name Borreby denotes a distinctly brachycephalic stone-age type, which was long characteristic of this region. The modern peasantry have somewhat recovered from this foreign infiltration, and have seemingly reverted to their aboriginal Teutonism, judging by the head form.[‡] Perhaps this Alpine settlement in Denmark is only a part of the expansion which, as we shall see, exerted for a time a profound influence upon the British Isles as well.[#] The same Round Barrow people may likewise be responsible for the strong representation of the type in the Faröe Islanders at the present time.[||] Nor does our chain of evidence connecting the Alpine element in Scandinavia with its congeners in middle Europe stop here. We shall be able to prove later that Holland also has been a stepping-stone of the Alpine race in its extension to the northwest; so that we may thus trace the type throughout its entire migration toward the north.

The anthropological history of Scandinavia would then be something like this: Norway has, as Undset suggests, probably been peopled from two directions, one element coming from Sweden and another from the south by way of Denmark. This latter type, now found on the seacoast, and especially along the least attractive portion of it, has been closely hemmed in by the Teutonic immigration from Sweden. This being so, we are tempted to look to the interior of the peninsula, as at Vaage and over in Sweden in the celebrated Dalarna district just south of Jemtland on our map, for the Teutonic race in its purest essence.[△] Thus we are led to expect Sweden as a

---

[*] Beddoe (1885, pp. 16 and 233, and 1867-'69 c) gives an index of 80.5 for the Danes. Deniker, 1897, p. 197, holds it to be lower than this. *Cf.* Ranke, Beiträge, iii, 1880, p. 165.

[†] Virchow, 1870, pp. 64–71. Sören-Hansen, 1888, gives data on brunetness.

[‡] Ranke, 1897 a, p. 54 ; Dueben, 1876.

[#] Beddoe, 1885, p. 16.   [||] Arbo, 1893.

[△] Johanssen and Westermarck, 1897, found an index of 76.5 for 654 women in Stockholm. Thirty-nine Swedes from the lumber camps of Michigan averaged 76.9. Hultkrantz finds no averages above 79, most of them being 77 or 78. Dueben, 1876, confirms it.

whole to be more homogeneous racially than Norway, although, perhaps, further investigation may demonstrate that Gottland has been infected from Denmark as the coast of Jøderen in Norway has been. Everything leads us to look toward the Baltic Sea as a centre of dispersion for this Teutonic race; for we shall find it represented along the opposite coast in Finland and Lithuania to a marked degree as well.

Germania! A word entirely foreign to the Teutonic speech of northern Europe. Deutschland, then, the country of the Deutsch—not Dutch, for they are really Netherlanders. What do these words mean? What territories, what peoples do they comprehend? The Austrians speak as pure German as the Prussians; yet the defeat of Königgratz, barely a generation ago, left them outside of Germany. On the other hand, the Polish peasants of eastern Prussia, with their purely Slavic language, are accounted Germans in good standing to-day.*

Ambiguous linguistically, do these words, German or Deutsch, imply any temperamental or religious unity? This can not be, for the main participants in the Thirty Years' War—

> " Fighting for conciliation,
> And hating each other for the love of God "—

were Germans. Historians are accustomed to identify the division line of belief in this conflict with that of racial origin. They are pleased to make the independent, liberty-loving spirit of the Teutonic race responsible for the Protestant Reformation. Let us not be too sure about that. Such bold generalizations are often misleading. Racial boundaries are not so simple in outline. The Prussians and the Prussian Saxons— Martin Luther was one—were anything but pure Teutons racially; this did not prevent them from siding with Prince Christian and Gustavus Adolphus. And then there were the Bohemians who began the revolt, and the Swiss Calvinists, and the rebels of the Peasants' War in Würtemberg! None

---

* Von Fircks, 1893, gives the latest linguistic map of this region. Langhans, 1895, maps the whole Empire.

of these were ethnically Teutons. Let us beware of such as-
criptions of a monopoly of virtue or intellect to any given race,
however comforting they may be to us who are of Teutonic
descent. Modern Germany, to be sure, is half Catholic and
half Protestant, but the division was not of ethnic origin in
any sense. Thus the word German is even more nondescript
religiously than linguistically. In short, it applies to-day to
an entirely artificial concept—nationality—the product of
time and place. Religious, linguistic, and in large measure
political differences have merged themselves in a sympa-
thetic unity. Thus has the original meaning of the word
Deutsch—a people or nation—come to its truest expression
at last.

The fact is that nationality need not of necessity imply any
greater uniformity of ethnic origin than of either linguistic or
religious affiliations. Such we shall soon see is the case in
Italy, as in France. Especially clear are the two distinct racial
elements in the former case. And in Germany, on the northern
slopes of the main European watershed, we are confronted
with a great nation, whose constituent parts are equally divergent in physical origin. With the shifting of scene, new
actors participate, although the plot is ever the same. It is not
a question of the Alpine and Mediterranean races, as in Italy.
The Alpine element remains, but the Teuton replaces the other.
Briefly stated, the situation is this: Northwestern Germany—
Hanover, Schleswig-Holstein, Westphalia—is distinctly allied
to the physical type of the Swedes, Norwegians, and Danes.
All the remainder of the Empire—no, not even excluding
Prussia, east of the Elbe—is less Teutonic in type; until finally
in the essentially Alpine broad-headed populations of Baden,
Würtemberg, and Bavaria in the south the Teutonic race passes
from view. The only difference, then, between Germany and
France in respect of race is that the northern country has a
little more Teutonic blood in it. As for that portion of the
Empire which was two generations ago politically distinct from
Prussia, the South German Confederation, it is in no wise
racially distinguishable from central France. Thus has political history perverted ethnology; and, notwithstanding, each

nation is probably the better for the blend, however loath it may be to acknowledge it.*

First, and always, as to the physical geography of the country: everything ethnically depends upon that. It is depicted upon the map on the next page, which represents elevation above sea level by means of darkening tints, the mountainous regions being generally designated by the broad bands of shading. Draw a line from Breslau, or, since that lies just off our map, let us say from Dresden to the city of Hanover, and thence to Cologne (Köln). Such a line roughly divides the uplands

---

* It is to be regretted that so many of the authorities on Germany have relied upon craniometric investigations rather than study of the living population. Even more grievous is the paucity of evidence regarding the northeastern third of the empire. With the exception of Baden, Bavaria, and Würtemberg, less is known of the German Empire than of any other part of Europe—far less even than of Spain or Scandinavia. In our supplementary Bibliography we have indexed all authorities, where they may be found *in extenso*. In this place we may merely mention the larger standard works arranged chronologically: H. Welcker, Kraniologische Mittheilungen, Archiv f. Anth., i, pp. 89–160, 1866. A. Ecker, Crania Germaniæ meridionalis occidentalis, Freiburg i. B., 1865. H. von Hölder, Zusammenstellung der in Württemberg vorkommenden Schädelformen, Stuttgart, 1876. R. Virchow, Beiträge zur physischen Anthropologie der Deutschen, u. s. w., Abh. kön. Akad. Wiss., Berlin, 1876; and also Gesammtbericht über die Erhebungen über die Farbe der Schulkinder in Deutschland, Archiv f. Anth., xvi, pp. 275–475, 1886. J. Gildemeister, Ein Beitrag zur Kenntniss nordwest deutscher Schädelformen, Archiv f. Anth., xi, pp. 26–63, 1879. J. Ranke, Beiträge zur physischen Anthropologie der Bayern, München, 1883–'92. Ranke, also in Der Mensch, Leipzig, 1886–'87, ii, pp. 254–269, gives the completest short summary of the anthropology of Germany extant. O. Ammon, Natürliche Auslese beim Menschen, Jena, 1893, and especially his superb Anthropologie der Badener, 1899—one of the most complete regional monographs extant. Equally important, although not restricted to Germany alone, are the papers by Prof. J. Kollmann, especially his Schädel aus alten Grabstätten Bayerns, in Beit. zur Anth. Bayerns, München, i, 1877, pp. 151–221. Certain technical points concerning these writers we have discussed in L'Anthropologie, Paris, vii, 1896, pp. 519 *seq.* For ethnographic details the older work of Zeuss (*vide* bibliography) is now supplanted by that of K. Müllenhof, which may confidently be relied upon. Howorth, in Jour. Anth. Inst., London, vi and vii, is also good. For a convenient *résumé* of our knowledge, both ethnographic and anthropological, consult also Hervé, 1897.

from the plains. To the north stretches away the open, flat, sandy expanse of Hanover, Oldenberg, Pomerania, Branden-burg, and Prussia. This vast extent of country is mainly below one hundred metres in elevation above the sea. South of our

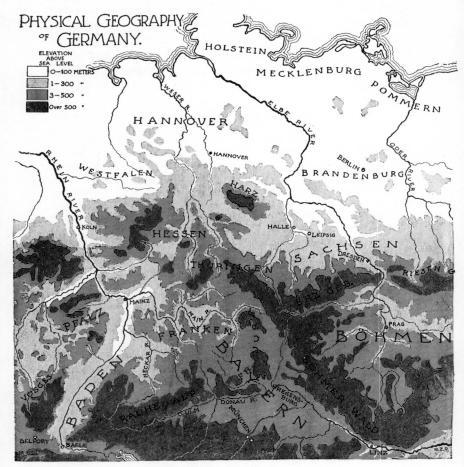

division line the land rises more or less abruptly to a region upward of a thousand feet in altitude. In Bavaria, Würtem-berg, and Bohemia lie extensive table-lands fully five hundred feet higher even than this; giving place finally to the high

Alps. The transition from north to south is particularly emphasized along our artificial division line by the fringe of mountains which lie along it, including the Riesen and Erzgebirge bounding Bohemia, the heavily wooded mountains of Thüringen, and farther west the Harz, the Waldgebirge, and the Westerwald by Cologne. On this side the highlands across the narrow gully of the Rhine River have already been described in speaking of the Ardennes uplands in France and Belgium. Their extension in Germany is known as the Rhenish plateau.

For the sake of unity of treatment, preserving the general form of argument adopted for other countries of Europe, let us consider the head form of the people first. At once we perceive a progressive broadening of the heads—that is, an increase of cephalic index—as we travel outward from the northwestern corner of the empire in the vicinity of Denmark.* Thus we pass from a head form identical with that of the Scandinavians, to one in the south in no wise distinguishable from the Swiss, the Austrian, and other Alpine types in France and northern Italy. Our three accompanying portraits on the next page will serve to illustrate this gradual change of physical type.† The first is a pure blond Teuton, blue-eyed, fair-haired, with the characteristically long head and narrow, oval face of his race. The features are clear cut, the nose finely moulded. Such is the model common in the upper classes all over Germany. Among the peasants it becomes more and more frequent as we approach the Danish peninsula.‡

---

* In L'Anthropologie, vii, 1896, pp. 513–525, we have given detailed citation of all authorities, with their data. Ranke, Der Mensch, ii, p. 264, is best among Germans.

† For these photographs I am indebted to my very good friend Dr. Otto Ammon, of Karlsruhe i. B., whose work we have noted elsewhere.

‡ Von Hölder, 1876, p. 15. On this region consult Gildemeister, 1879; Meisner, 1883 et seq.; Virchow, 1872 b; Sasse, 1876 a, etc. Virchow's great work, 1876 a (also 1872 b), attempting to prove the existence of a low-skulled dolichocephalic Frisian population in this region, antedating the true Teutonic long-headed Franks, has not apparently been confirmed by later observers. Consult especially, von Hölder, 1880, and A. Sasse, 1879, and our chapter on the Netherlands.

Here in these northwestern provinces it predominates, but gives place slowly to a mixed and broader-headed type as we pass eastward into Prussia. The intermediate type of head form prevalent in regions of ethnic intermixture is depicted in our middle portrait. In this particular case the eyes were still blue, but the hair was brown. This variety occurs all along the division line between upland and plain, which we traced a few moments ago. It appears that it is indigenous in Thüringen, the Hesses, and, in fact, all the isolated bits of highland down to the Baltic plain. Oftentimes the result of intermixture is a disharmonism, in which the broad Alpine head is conjoined with the longish face of the Teuton; less often the reverse. This is quite common in Bavaria and the Alpine highlands, as our portraits from these regions will show. Mixed types of this kind occurring everywhere in the south prove that the Teutonic invaders were finally outnumbered by the indigenous Alpine inhabitants. The pure, unmixed Alpine race finds its expression in the plateaus of Bavaria and Würtemberg, in the Schwarzwald, the Rauhe Alp, and parts of the Thüringerwald. Such is our third type, with its rounded face and skull foreshortened from front to back.* Our representative here photographed was dark brown both in hair and eyes, nose rather irregular, less finely moulded perhaps; certainly considerably broader at the nostrils than in the Teutons. At the same time the stature was short, only five feet one inch and a half, with a correspondingly stocky figure. The facts speak for themselves. There can be no doubt of two distinct races of men.

It is especially important to emphasize the fact that the heads broaden not only from the neighbourhood of Denmark southward but toward the east as well. This raises what was once a most delicate question. What is the place of the Prussians among the other peoples of modern Germany? The political supremacy of the house of Hohenzollern in the Diet of

---

* Whether there is a universal tendency in the south toward a relatively high-vaulted crania seems doubtful. Virchow, 1876 a, p. 53 *et seq.*, emphasizes the low flat skulls in Frisia; while Ranke proves the existence of high heads with steep foreheads in Bavaria. (Beiträge, ii, 1879, p. 53; iii, 1880, p. 172; v, 1883, p. 60.)

67. *Teutonic type.* Hair light, eyes blue. 68.
Stature 1.72 m. (5 ft. 7.7 in.). Ceph. Index 75.

69. *Mixed type.* Hair brown, eyes blue. 70.
Stature 1.62 m. (5 ft. 3.8 in.). Ceph. Index 83.

71. *Alpine type.* Eyes and hair dark brown. 72.
Stature 1.59 m. (5 ft. 2.6 in.). Ceph. Index 86.

GERMANY.

the Empire; and the whilom rivalry and jealousy of the other states, made it once a matter of some concern to determine this point. Happily for us, such questions have no terrors to-day. We have already seen how securely nationality may rest upon heterogeneity of physical descent. Be that as it may, it seems to be certain that the peasantry of Prussia is far from being purely Teutonic in physical type. We should expect this to be the case, of course, in those eastern provinces, Posen and Silesia, which still retain their Slavic languages as evidence of former political independence. These ought normally to be allied to Russia and eastern Europe, as we have already observed. But as to Brandenburg—the provinces about Berlin. How about them? Do they also betray signs of an intermixture with the broad-headed Alpine race, of which the Slavs are part? It seems to be so indeed. Germany on the east shades off imperceptibly into Silesia and the Polish provinces of Russia. Little by little the heads broaden to an index rising 83. Whether this is a product of historic expansion we may discuss later. For the present we may accept it as a fact.*

The race question in Germany came to the front some years ago under rather peculiar circumstances. Shortly after the close of the Franco-Prussian War, while the sting of defeat was still smarting in France, De Quatrefages, an eminent anthropologist at Paris, promulgated the theory, afterward published in a *brochure* entitled The Prussian Race, that the dominant people in Germany were not Teutons at all, but were directly descended from the Finns. Being nothing but Finns, they were to be classed with the Lapps and other peoples of western Russia. As a consequence they were alien to Germany—barbarians, ruling by the sword alone. The political effect of such a theory, emanating from so high an authority, may well be imagined. Coming at a time of profound national humiliation in France, when bitter jealousies were still rife among the Germans, the book created a profound sensation. It must be confessed that the tone of the work was by no means judi-

---

* Virchow admits it himself, Alte Berliner Schädel, 1880 b, p. 234. *Cf.* Bernstein on stature also; Lagneau, 1871, gives ethnology; confirmed by Howorth.

cial, although it was respectably scientific in its outward form. Thus the chapter in it describing the bombardment of the Musée d'Histoire Naturelle, of which De Quatrefages was the director, intended to prove the anti-civilized proclivities of the hated conquerors, could not in the nature of things be entirely dispassionate. The Parisian press, as may be imagined, was not slow to take advantage of such an opportunity. Articles of De Quatrefages in the Revue des Deux Mondes were everywhere quoted, with such additions as seemed fitting under the circumstances. The affair promised to become an international incident.

A champion of the Prussians was not hard to find. Professor Virchow of Berlin set himself at work to disprove the theory which thus damned the dominant people of the Empire. The controversy, half political and half scientific, waxed hot at times, both disputants being held victorious by their own people.* One great benefit flowed indirectly from it all, however. The German Government was induced to authorize the official census of the colour of hair and eyes of the six million school children of the Empire which we have so often mentioned in these pages. One of the resultant maps we have reproduced in this chapter. It established beyond question the differences in pigmentation between the north and south of Germany. At the same time it showed the similarity in blondness between all the peoples along the Baltic. The Hohenzollern territory was as Teutonic in this respect as the Hanoverian. Thus far had the Prussians vindicated their ethnic reputation. It is profoundly to be regretted that the investigation was not extended by a comprehensive census either of stature or of the head form of adults, similar to those conducted in other countries. Such a project was, in fact, sidetracked in favour of the census of school children. Whether politically inspired, or whether considered derogatory to the noble profession of arms, the Prussian army is forbidden for all scientific investigations of this kind, despite the efforts of

---

* Under the dates of 1871-'72, the articles by the two principal disputants will be found in our Bibliography. *Cf.* Hunfalvy, 1872, also.

Virchow and other eminent authorities in that direction; so that knowledge of this most important region is to-day almost entirely lacking.*

To an American the apparent unwillingness of some of the Germans boldly to own up to the radical ethnic differences which exist between the north and south of the Empire is incomprehensible. It seems to be not improbable that the Teutonic blond race has so persistently been apotheosized by the Germans themselves as the original Aryan civilizer of Europe, that to acknowledge any other racial descent has come to be considered as a confession of humble origin. Or, more likely still, this prejudice in favour of Teutonism is an unconscious reflection from the shining fact that this type is widely prevalent among the aristocracy all over Europe. Whether Aryan or not, it certainly predominates in the ruling classes to-day. At all events, the attempt is constantly being made to prove that the ethnic contrasts between north and south are the product of environmental influences, and not a heritage from widely different ancestry. This is not an impossibility in respect of pigmentation; but it can not be pushed too far. Thus Ranke of Munich, most eminent authority, has striven for years to account for the broad-headedness of the Bavarian population by making it a product of the elevated and often mountainous character of the country. This being proved, it would follow that the Bavarians still were ethnically Teutonic, merely fallen from dolichocephalic grace by reason of change of outward circumstances. This theory seems to be completely incapable of proof; for, as Ranke himself has shown,† the effect of the malnutrition generally incident to an abode at considerable altitudes is entirely in the opposite direction. Among poorly nourished children in factory towns, for example, the immediate effect is to cause an arrest of development about the temples, exactly where the broad-headed Alpine race is so well en-

---

* Virchow, 1876 a, p. 10. Reischel, 1889, is positively the only observer working on the living population in all of Prussia.

† Beiträge zur Anth. Bayerns, i, 1877, pp. 232 *seq.*, and 285 ; also ibid., ii, 1879, p. 75 ; iii, 1880, p. 149. H. Ranke, 1885, p. 110, asserts the Bajovars to have been originally brachycephalic.

dowed. It is strange to us in America to find how important such matters may become by reason of a social differentiation between races. Another patent example is offered in Russia. The late Professor Zograf of Moscow, than whom none stood higher as an anthropologist in Russia, confronted by the same division of ethnic types as Germany contains, has positively identified the blond long-headed one as the original Slav.* This may or may not be true; it may be gratifying to have it so. To us the evidence apparently points the other way. In Russia, however, no other conclusion than this is likely to be generally popular. Pan-Slavism prevails there with a vengeance.

After this *excursus*, let us come back to statistics and examine the evidence from the study of blonds and brunets among the school children. Our double-page map, as will be observed, includes not only the German Empire but Switzerland, Belgium, and Austria, down to the Adriatic as well—exclusive, however, of Hungary. Censuses were taken in all these countries in quick succession.† The system employed was identical in all, save in Belgium; and even here the definition of brunets was the same, although the term blond was made more comprehensive. For this reason the results are strictly comparable so far as our map is concerned. A great defect in all such investigations on children, as we have already stated, lies in the tendency to a darkening of hair and eyes with growth. This is probably intensified in the more southern countries, so that our shading probably fails to indicate the full extent of the progressive brunetness in this direction. North of the Alps, however, we may accept its evidence, provisionally, at all events.

One or two points on this map deserve mention, after noting the general contrast between northern and southern Germany. Observe how sharp the transition from light to dark becomes, all around the mountainous boundaries of Bohemia. Here we pass suddenly from Germanic into foreign territory;

---

* *Cf.* p. 355.

† Virchow's report on Germany, 1886 b; for Austria, Schimmer, 1884; for Switzerland, Kollmann, 1883; and for Belgium, Vanderkindere, 1879.

for the Bohemian Czechs are truly Slavic in origin as in speech.* One wonders if it is purely chance that so accentuated a brunet spot occurs about Prague. That is the capital city, the nucleus of the nation. As for the German-speaking Austrians, they are in no wise distinguishable in pigmentation from the Slovaks, Slovenes, Czechs, or other Slavic neighbours all about them. The second point which we would emphasize is the striking way in which blondness seems to have trickled down, so to speak, through Würtemberg, and even as far as the Swiss frontier.† We have already called attention to this in a preceding chapter. It will bear repetition here. The Rhine Valley bears no relation to it. At first sight, the infiltration seems to have taken place directly across country. Closer inspection shows that it coincides with other evidence derived from the study of the head form in the same district. Especially noteworthy are the peculiarities of Franconia (Franken), the southern edge of which appears as the light-dotted area on our map on page 233. This Franconian long-headed district extends over nearly the whole basin of the Main River well into Bavaria, and, as our map shows, up along the Neckar. It constitues by far the clearest case of wholesale Teutonic colonization south of the Baltic plain. This is probably the cause of the wedge of blondness upon our large map. Historians tell us the Franks were Teutons, and here is where they first settled. Their further extension into Switzerland will be a matter for discussion hereafter.

It is interesting to observe how this Teutonization of Franconia, manifested in our map of brunet traits, tallies with geographical probability.‡ Here is just where we should be led to expect a settlement in any case. Turn back for a moment to our map of physical geography (page 216). As the invaders pushed southward, they would naturally avoid the infertile uplands bordering Bohemia, and on the west the difficult,

---

* Schimmer, 1884, pp. viii, xi, and xix.
† Virchow, 1886 b, p. 317.
‡ J. Ranke, Beiträge, iii, 1880, p. 144 to 148, proves by the cephalic index that the Main Valley was a centre of dolichocephaly. The contrast of the fertile valley with the Spessart, for example, is of great interest.

heavily forested Rhenish plateau. Each of these wings of the
German upland are of a primitive geological formation, agri-
culturally unpropitious, especially as compared with Thuringia
—rugged, but well watered and kindly, as it is.. Suppose our
Teutonic tribes to ascend the Weser and its affluents, the
Fulda and Werra, or perhaps the narrow gully of the Rhine
to Mainz. There would be little to tempt them to turn back
to the wooded country, either of Hesse or Thuringia. What
was more natural, however, than that sedimentation should
take place on reaching the fertile valley of the Main? Its
basin, light dotted on our map, with that of the Neckar just
south of it, forms as a consequence the great Teutonic colony
in the Alpine highlands. Corroborative testimony of place
names also exists. Canon Taylor,* for example, states that this
district is a hotbed of Teutonic, mainly Saxon, village and local
names. It closely resembles parts of England in this respect.
Further wholesale colonization to the south seems to have been
discouraged by the forbidding Rauhe Alp or Swabian Jura.
The Teutonic characteristics have heaped up all along its
northern edge, as our map on page 233 shows; but the mountains themselves remain strongholds of the broad-headed type.
A considerable colony of dolichocephaly lies on the other side
of them, seemingly bearing some relation to the Allgäuer dialect. Beyond this all is Alpine in type. Allemanni and Hel-
vetii have left no trace of their Teutonism in the living population. Viewed in the light of these geographical facts, the contrast in brunetness between Würtemberg and Bavaria is readily
explained. The fluvial portals of the Bavarian plateau open
to the east, not the north. We know that the Boii (Bohemians)
and the Bajovars or ancient Bavarians came from this side,
following up the course of the Danube. Their names are Keltic, their physical characteristics seem to have been so as well.†

One more physical trait remains for consideration before we
pass from the present living population to discuss certain great
historic events in Germany which have left their imprint upon

---

* 1864 (ed. 1890), pp. 99–102.
† *Vide* H. Ranke, Zur Craniologie der Kelten, 1885, pp. 109–121 ; J.
Ranke, in Beiträge zur Anth. Bayerns, iii, 1880, pp. 149 *seq*.; and Pič, 1893.

the people. We refer to stature. The patent fact is, of course, that the areas of blondness and of dolichocephaly are also centres of remarkably tall stature. Our three portrait types illustrated this relation in the individual combinations clearly. The first grenadier was five feet nine inches in height (1.75 metres); the mixed type was shorter by about five inches (1.62 metres), while the conscript from the recesses of the Black Forest in Baden stood but five feet two inches in his stockings (1.59 metres). This last case is a bit extreme; averages seldom

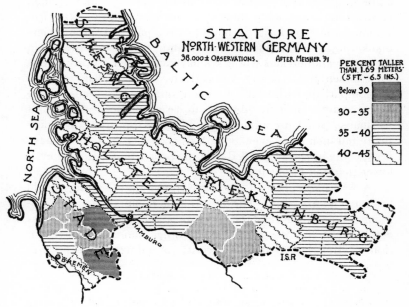

fall in Germany below five feet five inches. Local variations are common, as elsewhere; crowded city life depresses the average, prosperity raises it; but underneath it all the racial characteristic, so inherent in the " sesquipedal " Teutons, makes itself felt wherever they have penetrated the territory of the short and sturdy Alpine race. An idea of the contrast between north and south Germany is afforded by considera-tion of our various maps of stature on the accompanying pages. As will be seen, difficulty arises in direct comparison, owing to the two systems of calculation—one of averages, the other of proportions above a given height.   Our tints are adopted, however, to give a rough idea of the relations by means of the shading alone, dark tints always denoting the shorter population.*   The most Teutonic quarter of Germany, Schleswig, averages about five feet six and a half inches (1.69 metres), while the Bavarians as a whole are fully two inches shorter (1.63 metres).   The Rhine, on the other hand, a pathway for Teutonic invasions, has generated a considerably taller population in the southwest, noticeably in Alsace-Lorraine.†   Baden seems to be appreciably shorter, as our map shows.   Notwithstanding the superiority in height of the purest Teutonic Germans, they still exhibit the phenomenon to a less degree than the real Scandinavians whom we have examined.   Fortunately, for Sweden and Norway, respectively, we have data suitable for comparison with both systems of our German maps.   Norway averages an inch or more above even these very tallest Germans ; Sweden contains a far higher proportion of abnormally tall men also ; even as high as sixty per cent, as we have seen, while in Bavaria and Baden the proportion descends even lower than ten per cent.‡

A few particulars in the distribution of this trait should be noted in passing.   The law that a mountainous environment tends to depress the average stature seems to be exemplified in the Vosges.   On the other hand, in contravention of this law that the severity of climate and poverty

---

* It would appear that from 20 to 30 per cent of statures above 1.69 m. (170 m. and above) corresponds to an average of about 1.63 metres ; 10 to 19 per cent. represents an average of 1.61 metres ; and 30 to 39 per cent. to an average of 1.66 metres.

† Reischel, 1889, finds a stature about Erfurt of about 1.66 metres ; not far from the average for Alsace-Lorraine (166.6).   Kirchhoff, 1892, gives data about Halle.   See also Sick, 1857, on Würtemberg ; and Engel, 1856, on Saxony.   Ranke's (Beiträge, v, 1883, p. 196) average of 1.676 metres for 256 men seems to be above that indicated by his map.

‡ Comparisons may be continued internationally, by turning to our maps of Italy (page 255) and the Tyrol (page 101), both constructed on the same system of proportions above 1.69 metres ; that is to say, of 1.70 metres and above.   Brandt, 1898, gives parallel maps on both systems for Alsace-Lorraine.

of environment in mountainous districts exert a depressing influence upon stature, the Alps and the Böhmerwald in Bavaria, contain a population distinctly above the general average in the great plateau about Ingolstadt. This is all the more extraordinary, since these mountaineers are Alpinely

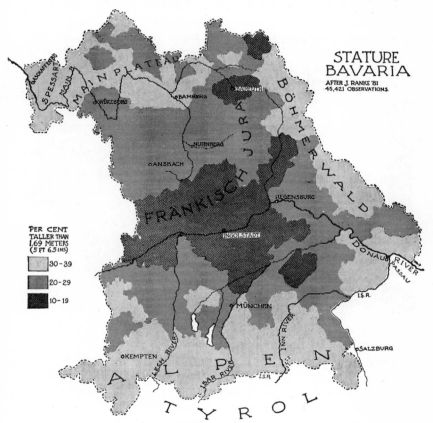

STATURE
BAVARIA
AFTER J. RANKE '81
45,421 OBSERVATIONS.

PER CENT
TALLER THAN
1.69 METERS
(5 FT 6.5 INS)

30 – 39
20 – 29
10 – 19

broad-headed and relatively brunet to an extreme. It would be a highly discouraging combination did we not remember that the great Bavarian plateau is itself of considerable altitude. Even then one is led to suspect, with Ranke,* that some process

* 1881, p. 14.

of selection has been at work to compass such a result. For if we turn to the Schwarzwald in Baden again, we there find that our law holds good. Wolfach, from which our portrait type was taken, exemplifies it completely. Here, on the high plateau known as Die Baar, the average stature falls below five feet four inches, the lowest recorded, I believe, in the Empire.

Austria proper, with the province of Salzburg, constitutes an isolated outpost of Teutonic racial traits, surrounded on three sides by populations of alien speech and of very different physical characteristics.* We shall speak of them later, in connection with the Slavic people among whom they reside;†

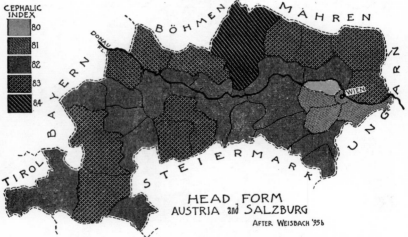

HEAD FORM
AUSTRIA and SALZBURG
AFTER WEISBACH '95 b

but it is not without significance at this point to notice the physical resemblances between the Bavarians and the Austrian Germans. Both alike are Germanized members of the Alpine race. Both betray their mixed origin in the same fashion. To the Alpine race they owe their prevalent broad-headedness, while they have derived their relative superiority in stature over the Slavs and Hungarians, as well as their blondness, from a Teutonic strain. The same tendency to a disharmonic type

---

* Weisbach, 1892, 1894, 1895 b. Consult also Auerbach, 1898 ; Petermann and Zuckerkandl.

† Page 349.

73.   AUSTRIAN. Blue eyes, chestnut hair. Index 85.   74.

75.   HUNGARIAN. Blue eyes, brown hair. Index 88.   76.

77.   MORLACHIAN, Bressa.   78.

AUSTRIA–HUNGARY.

of head and face, as among the Bavarians, is also apparent.* Such a union of a long face with a broad and round head is illustrated by our portraits herewith (*cf.* also page 290). A truly harmonic head is shown in the case of the Hungarian type, with which the Austrian may profitably be compared as respects the facial proportions. In pigmentation, the attenuated Teutonic strain is to-day most apparent in the lightness of the eyes, the hair being far more often of a dark shade. Vienna seems, judging by our little map, to have served as a focus about which the immigrant Teutonism has clustered. It is also curious to note how the immediate valley of the Danube denotes the area of Germanic intensity of occupation. The head form increases rapidly in breadth on leaving the river. The influence of the Bohemian and Moravian brachycephaly is clearly manifest on our map. In the other direction, south of the Danube, the increase is less sudden. It is also important to notice that this Teutonism is not only local; it is quite recent and superficial. Archæology reveals the presence of an earlier population, distinctly allied to another race in its characteristics.† This region was the seat of the very important early Hallstatt civilization, of which we shall have more to say. At present it is sufficient to emphasize the fact that the kingdom of Austria to-day is merely an outpost of Teutonic racial occupation, betraying a strong tendency toward the Alpine type.

Two great events in the history of northern Europe have profound significance for the anthropologist. The first is the marvellous expansion of the Germans, about the time of the fall of Rome; the second is the corresponding immigration of Slavic hordes from the east. Both of these were potent enough to leave results persistent to this day.

We know nothing of the German tribes until about 100 B. C. Suddenly they loom up in the north, aggressive foes of the Romans. For some time they were held in check by the stubborn resistance of the legions; until finally, when the restraining hand of Rome was withdrawn, they spread all over

---

* Beiträge zur Anth., Bayerns, v, 1883, p. 200.
† *Vide* p. 498 *infra.*

western Europe in the fourth and fifth centuries of our era. Such are the well-known historic facts. Let us see what archæology may add to them.* The first investigators of ancient burial grounds in southern Germany unearthed two distinct types of skulls. The round-headed variety was quite like that of the modern peasantry roundabout. The other dolichocephalic type was less frequent, but strongly marked in places. An additional feature of these latter was noted at once. They were generally found in burial places of a peculiar kind. An easterly sloping hill was especially preferred, on which the skeletons lay with feet toward the rising sun—probably a matter of religious importance. The bodies were also regularly disposed in long rows, side by side, a circumstance which led Ecker to term them *Reihengräber*, or row-graves. Other archæologists, notably Lindenschmidt, by a study of the personal effects in the graves, succeeded in identifying these people with the tall, blond Teutonic invaders from the north. Such graves are found all through Germany as far north as Thüringia. They bear witness that Teutonic blood infiltrated through the whole population. The relative intensity of intermixture varied greatly, however, from place to place. Our map on page 233 shows in a broad way its geographical distribution in Würtemberg and Baden, so far as it can be measured by the head form. *Reihengräber* and cephalic index corroborate one another. The most considerable occupation seems to have been, as we have said, in Franconia. We have already adduced some geographical reasons for the settlement in this place. Still another one remains to be noted. The Frankish race spot seems to lie just outside the great wall, the *Limes Romanus*, which the Emperor Tiberius and his successors built to hold the barbarians in check. Von Hölder has indicated the relation between the long-headed Teutonic areas and this ancient political boundary. Our map on page 233 is adapted from his.† The

---

* Von Hölder, 1876, p. 26 ; and 1880 ; Virchow, 1876 a, pp. 48 *et seq.*; Ranke, Beiträge, v, 1883, pp. 215–247. Bulle, 1897, gives reproductions of early representations of these types.

† From Ammon's data we have roughly extended the area of brachycephaly, on this map, over into Baden. Von Hölder's original map

modern limits of the Frankish dialect also coincide with it in great part. Here, just outside the Roman walls, the Burgundians, Helvetians, and Franks undoubtedly were massed for a long time.

The Black Forest in southwestern Germany affords us so good an opportunity for the comparison of relatively pure and mixed populations that a word more may be said respecting

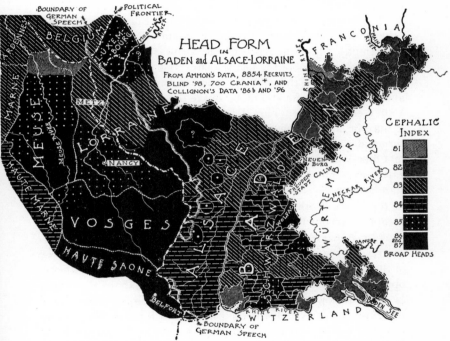

HEAD FORM
IN
BADEN and ALSACE-LORRAINE
FROM AMMON'S DATA, 8854 RECRUITS,
BLIND '98, 700 CRANIA +, AND
COLLIGNON'S DATA '86b AND '96

CEPHALIC INDEX

81
82
83
84
85
86 and 87
BROAD HEADS

it. This mountainous, heavily wooded district, shown on our map herewith, lies close by the upper courses of the two principal rivers of Europe, which have both formed great channels of racial migration. The Rhine encircles it on the west and south, and an important affluent of the same river bounds it on

stopped at the frontier. The whole extent of the Roman wall in Germany is shown upon our subsequent map (on page 242) of village types, by means of a similar heavy black line. Its relation there to the Germanic village type can not fail to be observed.

the east; for the Neckar drains the fertile plains of Würtemberg, or Swabia, which lie about Stuttgart. This capital city,
it should be observed, lies not far from the point of that blond
Teutonic wedge which, we have already shown, penetrates
central Europe from the north. The Danube also takes its
source in the southeastern part of the Forest, and has therefore opened up still another route of racial immigration from
this quarter.*

There is every evidence that here in the Black Forest is another mountainous area of isolation containing a people which
is distinctly Alpine in type of head form as compared with the
mixed populations of the fertile plains and valleys round about
it. For example, the cephalic index in Wolfach in its centre is
above 86, three units and more above the average for the Rhine
Valley communes.† This difference is appreciable to the eye;
it may be approximately shown by the three portraits in our
series at page 218. Our pure Alpine type, in fact, is a native
of Ober-Wolfach, where, as the black tint on our map indicates, extreme brachycephaly is prevalent. Judged by this
standard, there is every indication that the innermost recesses
of the Black Forest contain the broad-headed Alpine type in
comparative purity.

For Würtemberg and the Neckar Valley we have no modern researches upon living men to offer as evidence. In place
of them we possess the results of which we have spoken above,
obtained upward of thirty years ago from a study of the crania
of modern populations. At that time von Hölder discovered
the existence of two distinct types of head form in the population of Swabia, and he found them severally clustering about·
the two areas outlined upon his map on the next page. In the
northern one, lying mainly beyond and north of the old Roman

---

* Authorities upon this region are, primarily, Ecker, 1865, 1866, and
1876 ; and Ammon, 1890, 1893, and 1894. A comprehensive work by Ammon, based upon extensive observations, is now in press (1899).

† This relation is obscured on our map because the administrative
divisions nearly all extend from the river deep into the Forest, thus
obliterating all local differences. The innermost recesses, moreover, with
the exception of Wolfach, all lie across in Würtemberg ; in Neuenburg,
Calw, and Freudenstadt, for example, all shown upon our map.

wall, he found traces of a long-headed population, deemed by him typical of the barbarians of Germany. Within the *Limes Romanus* were mixed populations infused with Roman characteristics, but pointing to an isolated centre of broad-

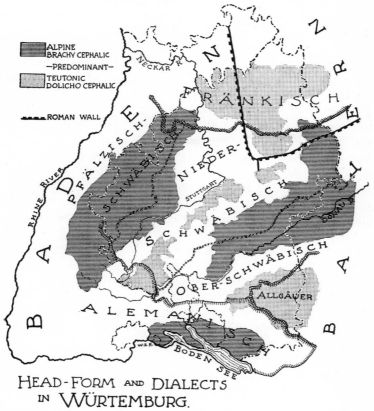

HEAD-FORM AND DIALECTS
IN WÜRTEMBURG.

AFTER VON HÖLDER '76.

Plain white, the absence of shading on this map denotes an intermediate type of head form incident upon intermixture.

headedness. This is shown by the dark-shaded areas. It will be observed at once that his results for Würtemberg and those of Ammon in Baden are a check upon one another, despite the fact that the two researches were made over thirty years apart—one upon skulls, the other upon living men. That in this Black Forest area of isolation we have to do with an island of the Alpine type is also rendered more probable by the relative shortness of its people.* This third physical trait helps, therefore, to confirm us in our deduction.

A curious point here deserves mention. This population of the inner Black Forest being Alpine, ought normally to be darker in the colour of the hair and eyes than the Teutonic peoples round about. Nevertheless, the evidence all goes to show that, instead of being darker, it really manifests a distinct tendency toward blondness. Here, again, we are able to draw proof from two separate sources which serve as a check upon one another. Virchow † showed that a considerable part of the "Alpine area" in Würtemberg contained an abnormal number of blond children. For example, forty-two hundred children in this Alpine area comprised but fifteen per cent of blond types, as compared with an average of nearly twenty-five per cent in the Rhine and Neckar Valleys. For Baden, however, the blondness of the upland interior region does not appear upon his map. Fortunately, we possess detailed results for this region of even greater value, since Dr. Ammon has studied the adult population. He asserts that there is a regularly increasing blondness toward the centre of the Forest.‡ Why did this not appear among the thousands of school children in Baden studied by Virchow? To venture a rash hypothesis, may it not have been because the influences of environment had not had time to produce their effects so strongly in childhood, and that they appeared in accentuated form at a later period of life? At all events, it would appear that this surprising reversal of racial probability pointed to a disturbing influence of environ-

---

* Compare our map showing Wolfach, on page 236.

† 1886 b, pp. 404 and 428. It clearly appears on our map of relative brunetness at page 222.

‡ For example, Wolfach, in the southern part of the "Alpine area," with the broadest heads in Baden, contains thirty-three per cent of blonds among adults. (Ammon, 1899, Tafel xii.) In this commune sixty-four per cent of the cephalic indices were above 85. Curiously, however, Oberndorf, near by, has fewer blonds than any other part of southern Germany. (Virchow, 1886 b, p. 307.)

ment. We have already taken occasion to note the effect of a
mountainous or infertile habitat in the production of relative
blondness. Perhaps we have another such case here in the
Schwarzwald.

Before we take leave of this most interesting quarter of Germany, let us cross the Rhine and consider briefly the populations of Alsace-Lorraine.* This lies on the debatable land between German and French influence. Geographically it extends from the Rhine up on to the eastern side of the Ardennes
plateau, of which we have treated in speaking of France
and Belgium. Turning back to our map of head form on
page 231, we observe at once how Alsace in particular is
bounded on the west by the Vosges area of extreme brachycephaly. Here is a solid mass of Alpine population protected
again in this instance against Teutonic submergence by the
rugged nature of its territory. Investigation is bound to show
a prevalent broad-headedness immediately on leaving the narrow river plain of the Rhine. At all the points throughout
Alsace where Blind has examined crania in large numbers—and
these towns are shown on our map by distinctive tints within
the small white circles—this fact has been established beyond
question. At the same time the Teutonic influence, spreading from the Rhine, has been powerfully exerted in the matter
of stature. Our map on the next page seems at first sight to
indicate a much taller population in Alsace than in Baden. The
main cause of the contrast is merely technical. Brandt's figures
are for the soldiery only, after rejection of all the undersized
men; while in Baden the averages are for all the recruits, without distinction. This would superficially make the Alsatians
seem far taller than the general population really is. Nevertheless, there can be no doubt of an appreciable superiority of
stature west of the Rhine, and no other explanation than that

---

* Schwalbe, of Strassburg, has recently inaugurated a brilliant series
of monographs upon this region. Blind's data on the cranial index are
embodied in our map on page 231; that of Brandt on the stature is
reproduced on page 236. On Lorraine, Collignon, 1886 b, is best. The
ground tints for Alsace are adopted from this latter authority; Blind's
local observations are shown separately within small white circles.

of Teutonism can readily be invoked for it. Apparently, also, where, as in the inner valleys of the Vosges Mountains, the immigrant race is less strongly represented, the stature decreases as a consequence. The dark shades on this part of the map are highly significant for this reason. Brandt * has

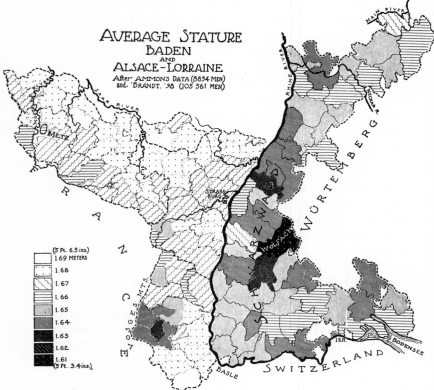

AVERAGE STATURE
BADEN
AND
ALSACE-LORRAINE
After AMMON'S DATA (8854 MEN)
and BRANDT. '98 (105 561 MEN)

(5 Ft. 6.5 ins.)
1.69 METERS
1.68
1.67
1.66
1.65
1.64
1.63
1.62
1.61
(5 Ft. 3.4 ins.)

NOTE.—The apparent superiority of stature west of the Rhine seems to be due to the fact that Brandt's data is for the accepted recruits only, excluding all the undersized ; while Ammon's figures for Baden include the entire male population.

also shown, as an interesting corollary, that, as a rule, the German-speaking communes exceed the French in height, with very few exceptions. Thus do we in a slight degree detect

* 1898, p. 21.

the relation between the language and the physical traits of a people.

The Teutons, in invading the territory of the indigenous Alpine population, only succeeded in displacing the aborigines in part. They followed up the rivers, and took possession of the open plains; but everywhere else left the natives in relative purity. This accounts in some measure for the great differentiation between people of mountain and plain all over this part of Europe, to which we have constantly adverted. It endows the whole event with the character of a great social movement, rather than of a sudden military occupation. We can not too fully guard against the hasty assumption that this Teutonic expansion was entirely a forcible dispossession of one people by another. It may have been so on the surface; but its results are too universal to be ascribed to that alone.* A revolution of opinion is taking place among anthropologists and historians as well, to-day, similar to that which was stimulated in geology many years ago by Sir Charles Lyell. That is to say, conceptions of terrific cataclysms, human or geological, producing great results suddenly, are being supplanted by theories of slow-moving causes, working about us to-day, which, acting constantly, almost imperceptibly, in the aggregate are no less mighty in their results. In pursuance of this change of view, students look to-day to present social slow-working movements for the main explanation of the great racial migrations in the past.

We can not resist the conclusion that the Teutonic expansion must be ascribed in part to the relative infertility of the north of Europe; possibly to differences in birth rates, and the like. Population outran the means of support. For a long while its overflow was dammed back by the Roman Empire, until it finally broke over all barriers. It is conceivable that some such contrast as is now apparent between the French and Germans may have been operative then. The Germans are to-day constantly emigrating into northern France—all over the world, in fact—and why? Simply because popula-

---

* Guizot, in his History of Civilization in France, lecture viii, offers an interesting discussion of this.

tion is increasing very rapidly; while in France it is practically at a standstill.   Another effective force in inducing emigration from the north may have been differences in social customs indirectly due to environmental influences.   Thus Baring-Gould * has called attention to the contrast in customs of inheritance which once obtained between the peasants of northern and southern Germany.   In the sandy, infertile Baltic plain the land is held in severalty, inheritance taking place in the direct line.   The oldest son, sometimes the youngest, remains on the patrimony, while all the other children go forth into the world to make their way alone.   Primogeniture prevails, in short.   In the fertile parts of Würtemberg, on the other hand, where the village community long persisted, all the children share alike on the death of the father.   Each one is a constituent element in the agrarian social body, for which reason no emigration of the younger generation takes place.   The underlying reason for this difference may have been that in the north the soil was already saturated with population, so to speak.   The farms were too poor to support more than a single family, a condition absent in the south.   The net result of such customs after a few generations would be to induce a constant Teutonic emigration from the north.   Military expeditions may have been merely its superficial manifestation. It would, of course, be unwarranted to suggest that any one of these factors alone could cause the great historic expansion. Nevertheless, it is far from improbable that they were contributory in some degree.

When all the Teutonic tribes broke over bounds and went campaigning and colonizing in Gaul and the Roman Empire, a second great racial wave swept over Germany from the east. Perhaps the Huns and other Asiatic savages may have started it; at all events, the Slavic hordes all over the northeast began to move.   Here we have another case of a widespread social phenomenon, military on the surface, but involving too many people to be limited to such forcible occupation.   There is abundant evidence that these Slavs did not always drive out

---

* History of Germany, p. 78.

the earlier population. They often merely filled up the waste lands, more or less peaceably, thus infiltrating through the whole country without necessarily involving bloodshed.

There are several ways in which we may trace the extent of this Slavic invasion before we seek to apply our criteria of physical characteristics. Historically, we know that the Slavs were finally checked by Karl the Great, in the ninth century, at the so-called *Limes Sorabicus*. This fortified frontier is shown on our map on page 242, bounding the area ruled in large squares diagonally. The Slavic settlements may also be traced by means of place names. Those ending in *itz* are very common in Saxony; *zig* also, as in Leipzig, " city of lime trees"; *a* in Jena; *dam* in Potsdam—all these cities were named by Slavs. Indications of this kind abound, showing that the immigrant hordes penetrated almost to the Rhine. To the northwest they occupied Oldenburg. As Taylor says, Slavic dialects were spoken at Kiel, Lubeck, Magdeburg, Halle, Berlin, Leipzig, Dresden, Salzburg, and Vienna.*

It seems impossible that the movements of a people should be traced merely by the study of the way in which they laid out their villages; yet August Meitzen, the eminent statistician, has just issued a great four-volume work, in which this has been done with conspicuous success.† It appears that the Slavic peoples in allotting land almost always followed either one of two plans. Sometimes they disposed the houses regularly along a single straight street, the church near the centre, with small rectangular plots of garden behind each dwelling. Outside this all land was held in common. Such a village is that of Trebnitz, whose ground plan is shown in our first cut on the next page.‡ In other cases it was customary to lay out the settlement in a circular form, constituting what is known as the Slavic round village. In such case there is but one opening to the common in the centre, and the hold-

* Consult Lagneau, 1871; Virchow, 1878 c; Bidermann, 1888; Reischel, 1889, p. 143; Haupt, 1890.

† 1895. Seebohm gives a good outline in Economic Journal, vii, p. 71; as also criticism by Ashley in Political Science Quarterly, xiii, p. 150.

‡ Ibid., i, p. 52.

ings in severalty extend outward in triangular sectors. Beyond these, in turn, lie the common pasture and woodlands.

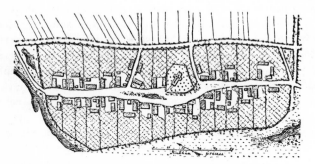

Slavic Long Village.   Trebnitz, Prussian Saxony.

Our second diagram represents one of these village types.
Contrast either of these simple and systematic settlements with
the one plotted in our third map.   This Germanic village is

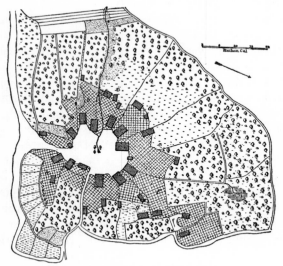

Slavic Round Village.   Witzeetze, Hanover.

utterly irregular.   The houses face in every direction, and
streets and lanes cross and recross in delightfully hop-scotch

fashion.* Nor is the agrarian organization of this Germanic village by any means simple. Divided into small plots or " hides," so called, a certain number of each kind are, or were once, assigned by lot in rotation to the heads of households. These " hides " were scattered all about the village, so that a peasant might be cultivating twenty or more parcels of land at one time. The organization was highly complex, including ordinances as to the kind of crops to be raised, and other similar matters of detail. We shall not attempt even to outline such a " Hufenverfassung "; for us it must suffice to note the complexity of the type, as opposed to the Slavic form.

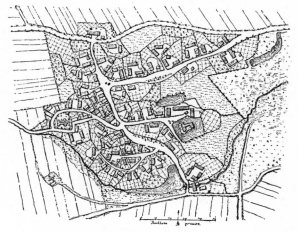

Germanic Village. Geusa, Prussian Saxony.

Our large map on the next page shows the geographical distribution of these several village types. The circumscribed area of the original Germanic settlements is rather remarkable. It shows how far the Slavs penetrated in number sufficient thus to transform the landscape. It will be observed that on this map the small squares and triangles denote the areas into which the German tribes transplanted their peculiar institutions. That they were temporarily held in check by the Romans appears from the correspondence between the Roman

* Ibid., i, p. 47.

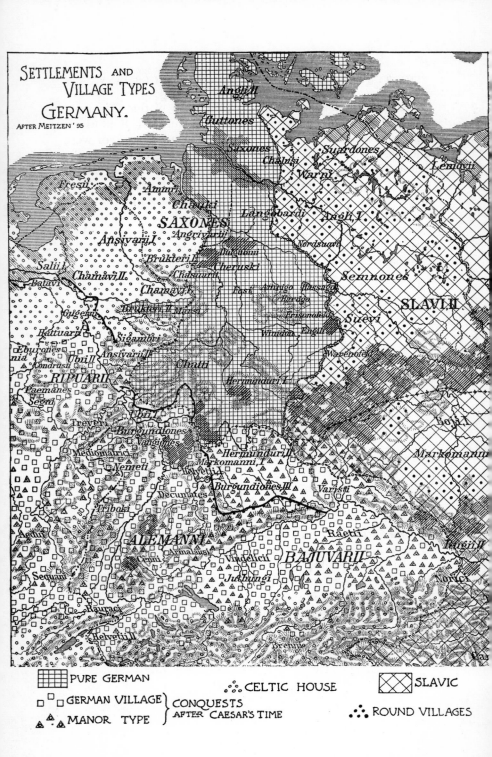

SETTLEMENTS AND
VILLAGE TYPES
GERMANY.
AFTER MEITZEN '95

Angelii
Guttones
Saxones   Chaluši   Suardones
                              Lemovii
Fresii   Warni
        Ammri   Angli. I
      Chauci
SAXONES   Langobardi   Avion. I
      Angrivarii   Nordsuavi
    Brukterii I.
  Saliik Chidsuarii Cheruski   Semnones
Chamavii II.   Brukterii II Marsi   Faši Aviago Pharodini SLAVI II
Batavi   Fosi Aviago Harigi
  Gugerni   Frisenabuli Suevi
  Hattuari   Winidan Engli
Eburones   Ubii Ansivarii II.   Wapenoteni
nid Condrusi   Chatti
    RIPUARII   Hermunduri I
Paemanes
Segni   Boja I.
      Treveri   Burgundiones Vangiones   Markomanni
    Nemomarci   Hermundurii II
      Nemeti   Markomanni, I
                  Helveti I Varisti
    Triboki   Decumates   Buroundiones III
Aduii   Raeti   Taifri II
  ALEMANNI   Vindelici BAJUVARII   Norici
Sequani   Venni Armalausi
                Juthungi
  Raurac
    Helvetii II   Brenna

PURE GERMAN   CELTIC HOUSE   SLAVIC

GERMAN VILLAGE } CONQUESTS
MANOR TYPE   } AFTER CAESAR'S TIME   ROUND VILLAGES

wall, shown by a heavy black line on the map, and the southern boundary of the Germanic villages. Of course, when they spread abroad, a considerable change in the agrarian organization was induced by the fact that the emigrants went as a conquering class. The institutions became less democratic, rather approaching the feudal or manorial type; but they all preserved sufficient peculiarities to manifest their origin. Such hybrid village types, covering all northern France and eastern England, are as good proof of Teutonization as we could ask.*

It will be observed that all the village types we have so far illustrated are closely concentrated and compact. A remarkably sudden change in this respect takes place west of the original Germanic village area. The whole economic character of the country changes within a few miles. It is of great historic importance. Our map shows the transition to occur strictly along the course of the Weser River. A large district is here occupied by the Celtic house, so called. The small circles denote that there are no closely built villages at all in the region so marked. Each house stands entirely by itself, in the middle of its farm, generally in no definite relation to the highroads. These latter connect market places and churches perhaps, about which are sometimes dwellings for the schoolmaster, the minister, or storekeeper; but the peasantry, the agricultural population, is scattered entirely broadcast. This resembles the distribution of our American farmers' dwellings in the Western States. We have no time to discuss the origin of these peculiarities. The opinion prevails that they stand in some relation to the clan organization of the Kelts, who are said to have once occupied this territory. The nearest prototype is, as our map shows, in the high Alps.

It is high time to take up once more the main thread of our argument—how far did the Slavic invasion, which so profoundly influenced the agrarian institutions, the place names, and the speech, affect the physical type of the people of Germany? We may subdivide the Slavic-speaking nations of eastern Europe, as we shall prove subsequently, into two

* *Vide* map in Meitzen's Atlas to volume iii, Anlage 66 a.

groups, which, however, differ from one another and from the pure Alpine race only in degree. The northern Slavs include the Russians, Poles, Slovaks, Czechs, and Wends; the southern is composed of the Serbs, Croatians, Slovenes, and Bulgarians. Both of these are broad-headed, the southern group being rather taller and considerably darker than the one which surrounds Germany. All the modern Slavic peoples of northern Europe approximate to the Alpine type; from which it follows that intermixture of them with the Teutons ought normally to produce shorter stature, darker hair and eyes, and, most persistently of all, an increased breadth of head. The district where these changes have been most clearly induced is in the region of Saxony, especially about Halle. A noticeable contrast is apparent between this district and the protected hills of Thuringia. The peasants in the plain of the Saale are appreciably shorter in stature and broader-headed than their neighbours. All over Thuringia the rule is that the population on the hills is taller, contrary to environmental influences, than that of the valleys. The explanation is that a short immigrant type has ousted the primitive and taller Teutons.* This Slavic invasion penetrated Bavaria from the northeast, the intruders apparently taking possession of the upland districts, which had been thinly peopled before. So well marked was this that the region south of Baireuth was long known as Slavonia.† The same people also seem to have been in evidence in Würtemberg.‡ In places, as at Regensburg and Berlin, we may trace the Slavic intrusion in the different strata of crania in the burial places.# The general extent of this Slavonization of Germany is indicated upon our large double-page map of brunet types. The wedge of colour which seems to follow down the Oder and over nearly to Holstein is undoubtedly of such origin.‖ Because of this historic movement Saxony, Brandenburg, and Mecklenburg are less

---

* Reischel, 1889, especially pp. 138, 143 ; Kirchhoff, 1892.
† Ranke, Beiträge, iii, 1880, p. 155.
‡ Von Hölder, 1876, pp. 15 and 27.
# Von Hölder, 1882 ; Virchow, 1880 a.
‖ Meisner, 1891, p. 320 ; Virchow, 1878 b.

SAXONS. Individual portraits and composite.

Loaned from the collection of Dr. H. P. Bowditch.

WENDS, Saxony. Individual portraits and composite.

From the collection of Dr. H. P. Bowditch.

purely Teutonic to-day than they once were in respect of pigmentation. The whole east is, as we have already seen, broaderheaded, shading off imperceptibly into the countries where pure Slavic languages are in daily use. Thus the contrast in customs and traditions between the eastern and western Germans, which historians since Cæsar have commented upon, seems to have an ethnic basis of fact upon which to rest. Moreover, a hitherto unsuspected difference between the Germans of the north and of the south has been revealed, sufficient to account for many historical facts of importance.

CHAPTER X.

THE anthropology of Italy has a very pertinent interest for the historian, especially in so far as it throws light upon the confusing statements of the ancients. Pure natural science, the morphology of the genus *Homo*, is now prepared to render important service in the interpretation of the body of historical materials which has long been accumulating. Happily, the Italian Government has assisted in the good work, with the result that our data for that country are extremely rich and authentic.* The anthropological problems presented are not as complicated as in France, for a reason we have already noted—namely, that in Italy, lying as it does entirely south of the great Alpine chain, we have to do practically with two in-

---

* The best authority upon the living population is Dr. Ridolfo Livi, Capitano Medico in the Ministero della Guerra at Rome. To him I am personally indebted for invaluable assistance. His admirable Antropometria Militare, Rome, 1896, with its superb atlas, must long stand as a model for other investigators. Titles of his other scattered monographs will be found in our Bibliography, as well as full details concerning the following references, which are of especial value: G. Nicolucci, Antropologia dell' Italia nell' evo antico e nel moderno, 1888; G. Sergi, Liguri e Celti nella valle del Po, 1883, giving a succinct account of the several strata of population; Arii e Italici, 1898, of which a most convenient summary is given by Sergi himself in the Monist, 1897 b; R. Zampa, Sulla etnografia dell' Italia, Atti dell' Accademia pontificia de' Nuovi Lincei, Rome, xliv, session May 17, 1891, pp. 173–180; and Crania Italica vetera, 1891. Many details concerning primitive ethnology will be found in Fligier, 1881 a; and Pullé, 1898. Full references to the other works of these authors, as well as of Calori, Lombroso, Helbig, Virchow, and others, will also be found in the Bibliography. Broca, 1874 b, in reviewing Nicolucci's work, gives a good summary of conclusions at that time, before the more recent methods of research were adopted.

stead of all three of the European racial types. In other words, the northern Teutonic blond race is debarred by the Alps. It does appear in a few places, as we shall take occasion to point out; but its influence is comparatively small. This leaves us, therefore, with only two rivals for supremacy—viz., the broad-headed Alpine type of central Europe and the true Mediterranean race in the south.

A second reason, no less potent than the first, for the simplicity of the ethnic problems presented in Italy, is, of course, its peninsular structure. All the outlying parts of Europe enjoy a similar isolation. The population of Spain is even more unified than the Italian. The former, as we shall see, is probably the most homogeneous in Europe, being almost entirely recruited from the Mediterranean long-headed stock. So entirely similar, in fact, are all the peoples which have invaded or, we had better say, populated the Iberian Peninsula, that we are unable to distinguish them anthropologically one from another. The Spaniards are akin to the Berbers in Morocco, Algiers, and Tunis. The division line of races lies sharply defined along the Pyrenees. In Italy a corresponding transition, anthropologically, from Europe to Africa takes place more gradually, perhaps, but no less surely. It divides the Italian nation into two equal parts, of entirely different racial descent.

Geographically, Italy is constituted of two distinct parts. The basin of the Po, between the Apennines and the Alps, is one of the best defined areas of characterization in Europe. The only place in all the periphery where its boundary is indistinct is on the southeast, from Bologna to Pesaro. Here, for a short distance, one of the little rivers which comes to the sea by Rimini, just north of Pesaro, is the artificial boundary.* It was the Rubicon of the ancients, the frontier chosen by the Emperor Augustus between Italy proper and Cisalpine Gaul. The second half of the kingdom, no less definitely characterized, lies south of this line in the peninsular portion. Here is where the true Italian language in purity begins, in

* Zampa, 1891 b, p. 177.

20

contradistinction to the Gallo-Italian in the north, as Bion-
delli [53] long ago proved.* The boundaries of this half are
clearly marked on the north along the crest of the Apennines,
away across to the frontier of France; for the modern prov-

PHYSICAL GEOGRAPHY
OF ITALY.

inces of Liguria (see map) belong in flora and fauna, and, as
we shall show, in the character of their population, to the
southern half of the country. It is this leg of the peninsula

* Gröber, 1888, p. 489; and Pullé, 1898, pp. 65–89, with maps.

below the knee which alone was called Italy by the ancient geographers; or, to be more precise, merely the portion south of Rome. Only by slow degrees was the term extended to cover the basin of the Po. The present political unity of all Italy, real though it be, is of course only a recent and, in a sense, an artificial product. It should not obscure our vision as to the ethnic realities of the case.

The topography and location of these two halves of the kingdom of Italy which we have outlined, have been of profound significance for their human history. In the main distinct politically, the ethnic fate of their several populations has been widely different.* In the Po Valley, the "cockpit of Europe," as Freeman termed it, every influence has been directed toward intermixture. Inviting in the extreme, especially as compared with the transalpine countries, it has been incessantly invaded from three points of the compass. The peninsula, on the other hand, has been much freer from ethnic interference; especially in the early days when navigation across seas was a hazardous proceeding. Only in the extreme south do we have occasion to note racial invasions along the coast. The absence of protected waters and especially of good harbours, all along the middle portion of the peninsula, has not invited a landing from foreigners. Open water ways have not enabled them to press far inland, even if they disembarked. These simple geographical facts explain much in the anthropological sense. They meant little after the full development of water transportation, because thereafter travel by sea was far simpler than by land. Our vision must, however, pierce the obscurity of early times before the great human invention of navigation had been perfected.

In order to give a summary view of the physical characteristics of the present population which constitutes the two halves of Italy above described, we have reproduced upon the following pages the three most important maps in Livi's great atlas. Based as they are upon detailed measurements made upon nearly three hundred thousand conscripts, they can not

---

* *Cf.* Livi, 1894 b.

fail to inspire confidence in the evidence they have to present. Especially is this true since their testimony is a perfect corroboration of the scattered researches of many observers since the classical work of Calori and Nicolucci thirty years ago. Researches at that time made upon crania collected from the cemeteries and crypts began to indicate a profound difference in head form between the populations of north and south. Then later, when Zampa, Lombroso, Pagliani, and Riccardi * took up the study of the living peoples, they revealed equally radical differences in the pigmentation and stature. It remained for Livi to present these new data, uniformly collected from every commune in the kingdom, to set all possible doubts at rest. It should be observed that our maps are all uniformly divided by white boundary lines into *compartimenti*, so called. These administrative districts correspond to the ancient historical divisions of the kingdom. Their names are all given upon our preceding map of physical geography. Being similar through the whole series, they facilitate comparisons between smaller districts in detail.

The basin of the Po is peopled by an ethnic type which is manifestly broad-headed. This Alpine racial characteristic is intensified all along the northern frontier. In proportion as one penetrates the mountains this phenomenon becomes more marked. It culminates in Piedmont along the frontier of France. Here, as we have already shown in our general map of Europe, is the purest representation of the Alpine race on the continent. It is identical with that of the Savoyards over the frontier not alone in physical type, but also over a considerable area in language as well; for Provençal French is spoken well over into this district in Italy.† Comparison of our portrait types, obtained through the courtesy of Dr. Livi, will emphasize this fact. Our first page exhibits the transition from north to south, which appears upon our map of cephalic index, as it appeals to the eye. The progressive narrowing of the face, coupled with the regular increase in the length of the head from front to back, can not fail to attract attention. The

---

* For a complete list of their works consult our Bibliography.
† Pullé, 1898, pp. 66 and 95, with map.

79.   PIEDMONT. Eyes and hair light brown. Index 91.3.   80.

81.   ISLAND OF ISCHIA. Eyes and hair dark brown. Index 83.6.   82.

83.   SASSARI, Sardinia. Deep brunet. Index 76.2.   84.

ITALY.

phenomenon is precisely similar to that which was illustrated in our first page of German portraits at pages 218 and 219; except that in this case dolichocephaly increases toward the south, not as in Germany toward the north. The upper portrait is de-

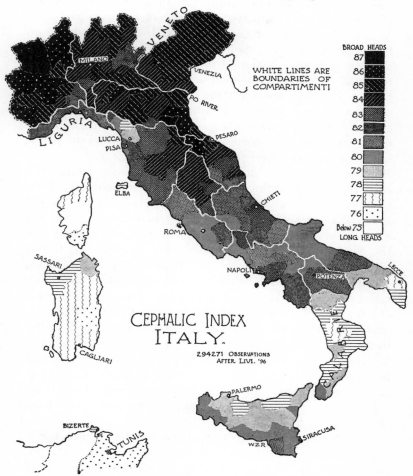

CEPHALIC INDEX
ITALY.

2.942.71 OBSERVATIONS
AFTER. LIVI. '96

WHITE LINES ARE
BOUNDARIES OF
COMPARTIMENTI

BROAD HEADS
87
86
85
84
83
82
81
80
79
78
77
76
Below 75
LONG. HEADS

scribed to me as peculiarly representative of a common type throughout Piedmont, although perhaps in this case the face is a trifle longer than is usual in the harmonic Alpine race.

This Alpine type in northern Italy is the most blond and the tallest in the kingdom. The upper types on both our portrait pages represent fairly the situation. The hair is not seldom of a lightish brown, with eyes of a corresponding shade. This, of course, does not imply that these are really a blond and tall people. Compared with those of our own parentage in northern Europe, these Italians still appear to be quite brunet; hair and eyes may be best described on the average as light chestnut. Standing in a normal company of Piedmontese, an Englishman could look straight across over their heads. For they average three to five inches less in bodily stature than we in England or America; yet, for Italy, they are certainly one of its tallest types. The traits we have mentioned disappear in exact proportion to the accessibility of the population to intermixture. The whole immediate valley of the Po, therefore, shows a distinct attenuation of each detail. We may in general distinguish such ethnic intermixture from either of two directions: from the north it has come by the influx of Teutonic tribes across the mountain passes; from the south by several channels of communication across or around the Apennines from the peninsula. For example, the transition from Alpine broad heads in Emilia to the longer-headed population over in Tuscany near Florence is rather sharp, because the mountains here are quite high and impassable, save at a few points. On the east, however, by Pesaro, where natural barriers fail, the northern element has penetrated farther to the south. It has overflowed into Umbria, Tuscany, and Marche, being there once more in possession of a congenial mountainous habitat. The same geographical isolation which, as Symonds asserts, fostered the pietism of Assisi, has enabled this northern type to hold its own against aggression from the south.

It is interesting to note the prevalence of the brachycephalic Alpine race in the mountainous parts of northern Italy; for nowhere else in the peninsula proper is there any evidence of that differentiation of the populations of the plains from those of the mountains which we have noted in other parts of Europe. Nor is a reason for the general absence of the phenomenon hard to find. If it be, indeed, an economic and social phenomenon, dependent upon differences in the economic possibilities of any given areas, there is little reason for its appearance elsewhere in Italy; since the Apennines do not form

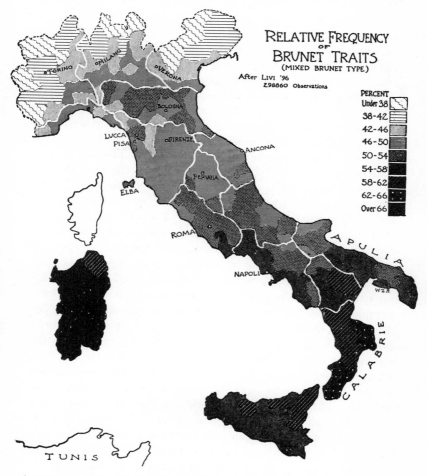

RELATIVE FREQUENCY
OF
BRUNET TRAITS
(MIXED BRUNET TYPE)
After Livi '96
298860 Observations

PERCENT
Under 38
38-42
42-46
46-50
50-54
54-58
58-62
62-66
Over 66

regions of economic unattractiveness, as their geology is favourable to agriculture, and their soil and climate are kind. In many places they are even more favourable habitats than the plains, by reason of a more plentiful rainfall.   It is indeed to-day accepted as a law by the archæologists that throughout central and southern Italy orderly settlement has first taken place in the mountains, extending gradually thence down into the plains.   The reason for this seems to be found in the greater salubrity of the upland climate, and also in the larger measure of security afforded in the mountains.*   The first of these considerations is certainly potent enough to-day, rendering the mountains more often preferable to the plains as a place of habitation.   The absence of anthropological contrasts coincident with a similar absence of economic differences is thus a point in favour of our general hypothesis.

Are there any vestiges in the population of northern Italy of that vast army of Teutonic invaders which all through the historic period and probably since a very early time has poured over the Alps and out into the rich valley of the Po?   Where are those gigantic, tawny-haired, " fiercely blue-eyed " barbarians, described by the ancient writers, who came from the far country north of the mountains?   Even of late there have been many of them—Cimbri, Goths, Ostrogoths, Visigoths, Saxons, Lombards.   Historians are inclined to overrate their numerical importance as an element in the present population.   On the other hand, many anthropologists, Virchow,† for example, have asserted that these barbarian invaders have completely disappeared from sight in the present population.   Truth lies intermediate between the two.   It is, of course, probable that ancient writers exaggerated the numbers in the immigrant hordes.   Modern scholars estimate their numbers to be relatively small.   Thus Zampa ('92) holds the invasion of the Lombards to have been the most considerable numerically, although their forces did not probably exceed sixty thousand, followed perhaps by twenty thousand Saxons.   Eighty thousand immigrants in the most thickly settled area in ancient Europe surely would not have diluted the population very greatly.   We can not expect too much evidence in this direction consequently, although there certainly is some.

* Von Duhn, 1896, p. 126.
† 1871 a.   Steub maintains that the Lombard influence was insignificant.

The relative purity of the Piedmont Alpine type compared with that of Veneto is probably to be ascribed to its greater inaccessibility to these Teutons. Wherever any of the historic passes debouch upon the plain of the Po there we find some

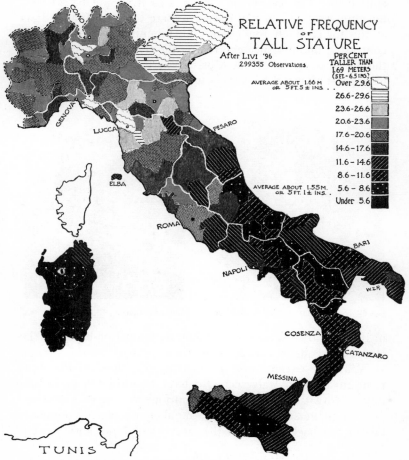

disturbance of the normal relations of physical traits one to another; as, for example, at Como, near Verona, and at the mouth of the Brenner in Veneto. The clearest indubitable case of Teutonic intermixture is in the population of Lom-

bardy about Milan.   Here, it will be observed on our maps, is
a distinct increase of stature; the people are at the same time
relatively blond.*   The extreme broad-headedness of Piedmont and Veneto is moderated.   Everything points to an
appreciable Teutonic blend.   This is as it should be.   Every
invading host would naturally gravitate toward Milan.   It is
at the focus of all roads ever the mountains.   Ratzel † has
contrasted the influence exerted by the trend of the valleys on
the different slopes of the Alps.   Whereas in France they all
diverge, spraying the invaders upon the quiescent population;

San Giacomo di Lusiana (*Sette Comuni*), Province of Vicenza. Blond. Index, 85.2.

in Italy all streams seem to concentrate upon Lombardy.   The
ethnic consequences are apparent there, perhaps for this reason.

With the exception of Lombardy, the blood of the Teutonic invaders in Italy seems to have been diluted to extinction.   Notwithstanding this, it is curious to note that the German language still survives in a number of isolated communities in the back waters of the streams of immigration.   Up

---

* Livi, 1896 a, p. 141 ; 1894 b, p. 156.

† Anthropo-Geographie, i, pp. 191–198. *Cf.* also Lenthéric, 1896, pp.
208 and 380, on the passes known and used by the ancients. They seem
to have been mainly the Brenner, by Turin across into Savoy, and along
the Corniche road. On Teutonic place names in Italy, see Taylor, Words
and Places, p. 98.

in the side valleys along the main highways over the Alps are still to be found German customs and folklore as well. Dr. Livi tells us that the peasants are not to be distinguished physically to-day from their true Italian-speaking neighbours.* Ranke,† however, makes the interesting observation concerning the people of the *Sette Comuni*, that the women still exhibit distinctive German traits, especially in relative blondness. And Dr. Beddoe likewise writes me that, according to his own view, Teutonic characteristics in facial features rather than in head form are quite noticeable in places. In this connection the accompanying portrait from one of the *Sette Comuni* can not fail to be of interest. Its Germanic appearance is strongly noticeable; even although, as should be observed, this individual retained no trace of Teutonic descent in his accentuated breadth of head. Of this man Dr. Livi, to whom I am indebted for the portrait, writes me that it is " a very good Venetian type." This seems at first sight improbable, even making allowance for the law that atavism is more characteristic of the female, since the Teutonic invasions more often brought warriors alone, who intermarried with the native women.

The southern Alps are also places of refuge for many other curious *membra disjecta*. Mendini ('90), for example, has studied in Piedmont with some detail, a little community of the Valdesi, descendants of the followers of Juan Valdès, the mediæval reformer. Here they have persisted in their heretical beliefs despite five hundred years of persecution and ostracism. In this case mutual repulsion seems to have produced real physical results, as the people of these villages seem to differ quite appreciably from the Catholic population in many important respects.

A word must be added before we pass to the discussion of middle Italy, as to the people of the provinces of Veneto. In many respects they seem not to be dissimilar physically from the Lombards or Piedmontese. The only trait by which they may be distinguished is in relative tallness. The light shad-

---

* Livi, 1896 a, pp. 137 and 146; Pulle, 1898, p. 83; Tappeiner, 1883; Galanti, 1885.

† Beiträge zur Anth. Bayerns, ii, 1879, p. 76.

ing upon our map of stature on page 255 surely denotes this.
A greater average height prevails than even in the Teutonized
parts of Lombardy, although no Teutonic invasions even over
the Brenner Pass can historically be held accountable for it.
Here, again, the data of physical anthropology serve to corroborate the ancient chroniclers and the historians. The Ve-
neti have been generally accepted as of Illyrian derivation.*
This explains the phenomenon, then; for around east of the
Adriatic we have found a secondary centre of giantism, especially marked all along the Dalmatian coast, in Bosnia and Albania. The present tallness of the Venetians directly points to
a relationship with this part of Europe.

The ethnic transition from the Alpine race in the Po valley to the Mediterranean race in Italy proper is particularly
sharp along the crest of the Apennines from the French frontier to Florence. The population of modern Liguria, the
long, narrow strip of country between the mountains and the
Gulf of Genoa, is distinctly allied to the south in all respects.
Especially does the Mediterranean long-headedness of this
region appear upon both of our maps of cephalic index. It
is curious to note how the sharpness of the ethnic boundary
is softened where the physical barriers against intercourse between north and south are modified. Thus north of Genoa
there is a decided break in the distinct racial frontier of the
province; for just here is, as our topographical map of the
country indicates, a broad opening in the mountains leading
over to the north. The pass is easily traversed by rail to-day.
Over it many invasions in either direction have served to confound the populations upon either side.

The individuality of the modern Ligurians culminates in
one of the most puzzling ethnic patches in Italy, viz., the people
of the district about Lucca, in the northwest corner of Tuscany. Consideration of our maps will show the strong relief
with which these people stand forth from their neighbours.
These peasants of Garfagnana and Lucchese seem to set all

* Arbois de Jubainville, 1889, p. 305 ; Von Duhn, 1896, p. 131 ; Pigorini,
1892 ; Sergi, 1897 b, p. 175 ; Pullé, 1898, p. 19. Moschen is perhaps the
best authority on the anthropology of this region. *Cf.* also Tedeschi, 1897.

ethnic probabilities at naught. They are as tall as the Venetians or any of the northern populations of Italy, yet in head form they are closely allied to the people of the extreme south. They are among the longest-headed in all the kingdom. They seem also to be considerably more brunet than any of their neighbours.* Nor are these peculiarities of modern origin,

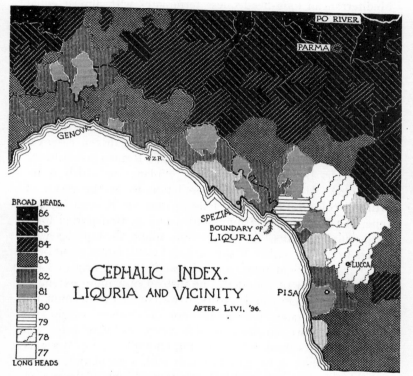

certainly not their stature, at all events; for Strabo tells us that the Romans were accustomed to recruit their legions here because of the massive physique of the people.

In order to make the reality of this curious patch more apparent, we have reproduced in our small map on this page a bit of the country in detail. It shows how suddenly the head

---

* Livi, 1896 a, p. 153.

form changes at the crest of the Apennines as we pass from the Po valley to the coast strip of Liguria. As we leave the river and rise slowly across Emilia toward the mountain range the heads gradually become less purely Alpine; and then suddenly as we cross the watershed we step into an entirely different population. On the southern edge this little spot of Mediterranean long-headedness terminates with almost equal sharpness, although geographical features remain quite uniform. This eliminates environment as an explanation for the phenomenon; we must seek the cause elsewhere.

All sorts of explanations for the peculiarities of this ethnic spot about Lucca have been presented. Lombroso,* who first discovered its tall stature, inclines to the belief that here is a last relic of the ancient and long-extinct Etruscan people penned in between some of the highest mountains in Italy and the sea. He holds that they were here driven to cover in this corner of Tuscany by the developed Roman power in the south. Dr. Beddoe gives another explanation which is interesting.† He believes this population to be the result of artificial colonization. Livy tells us that the Romans at one time, in pursuance of a long-settled policy, transported forty thousand Ligurians (?) to Samnium, filling their places with others from the south. If this artificial transplanting had been effected a sufficient number of times; if the Liguria of Livy had surely been this modern one instead of a more extended Alpine ancient one; and thirdly, if we could thus account for the tallness of stature, certainly not of southern origin, we might place more reliance upon this ingenious hypothesis. As it is, we can not think it far-reaching enough. To us it seems more likely that we have to do rather with a population highly individualized by geographical isolation. Much of the region is very fertile; it is densely populated; it is closely bounded by mountain and sea. It is an ideal spot for the perpetuation of primitive physical characteristics. Why may they not be found here, exhibiting merely a clearer persistency of many of the traits common all along the coast strip of the Gulf of

---

* 1878, p. 123; Rosa, 1882.　　　　† 1893, pp. 31 and 85.

Genoa? The people of the island of Elba off the coast are quite similar. Insularity explains their peculiar physical traits. Why not environmental isolation about Lucca as well?

Who were the Ligurians of the ancients, and where do we find their descendants to-day? This question has been scarcely less productive of controversy than that concerning the derivation and affinities of the Celts—believed to be their immediate successors historically. Arbois de Jubainville * assures us on the authority of the classical historians, that the Ligurians, some seven hundred years before Christ, occupied a large part of southwestern Europe, perhaps from the Po valley to Spain, and well toward northern Gaul.† Such extended domination, if, improbable as it seems, it ever existed in fact, became narrowed down at the early Roman period to the territory bounded by the Rhone on the west, the Mediterranean on the south, and the Po basin on the east. This geographical localization, it will be observed, at once complicates any attempt on the part of the physical anthropologist to identify this historic people with any living type to-day. For the area bounding upon the Mediterranean, comprised between the Rhone and the upper valley of the Po, has been just shown to contain two radically different populations. Throughout precisely this part of the Alps, on the one hand, extends our brachycephalic type in its maximum purity even for all western Europe. We proved this for Savoy and its vicinity in treating of France; and now we see it also to be true in Piedmont. Nevertheless, all around the Gulf of Genoa, along the Corniche road, closely hedged in by the mountains on the north, extends a narrow belt of population exhibiting all the physical characteristics, as we have seen, of our dolichocephalic Mediterranean race. Which of these two populations, both comprised within the ancient territory of that name, is entitled, then, to the name Ligurian? The Italian Government has settled the matter administratively, at least, by assigning the name Liguria to the littoral strip. For the modern

---

* 1890, pp. 153–161; and in his great work, 1889–'94, ii, pp. 205–215.
† Bertrand and Reinach, 1891, pp. 233–253, with map, discuss this fully. *Cf.* also Pullé, 1898, pp. 5–12; and Jacques, 1887, p. 222.

21

geographers these coast people are then Ligurians; but the word is used in a very different sense from that of the classical historians.

Anthropologists have long contended over the identification of this primitive people. The first disposition, a quarter of a century ago, was to assign the name unhesitatingly to the broad-headed population characteristic of the mountains; at that time, in fact, the existence of an entirely different coast population was not even suspected. Nicolucci,* Calori,† and all the older anthropologists asserted, therefore, that the Ligurians were brachycephalic, allied racially to the Celts in France, and that their lineal descendants still occupy the Maritime Alps in force. So clear did this seem that von Hölder,‡ in his great work on the anthropology of southern Germany, adopted the name Ligurian for the broad-headed type prevalent in that region and throughout central Europe.# On the other hand, the later Italians without exception have rejected this opinion, and agree with remarkable unanimity in identifying the present living dolichocephalic Ligurians with their historic predecessors.‖ The reason for this is plain. All over northern Italy a long-headed population has been proved to underlie the modern Alpine one.ᐃ Broad-headedness has in fact become more than two and a half times as prevalent as in the Neolithic period. The dolichocephalic coast strip of

---

* 1864; recently enunciated in 1888, pp. 4–10.

† 1868 and 1873.

‡ 1867, and 1876, p. 7.

This opinion was shared by most English authorities, following Davis, 1871. *Cf.* Rolleston's Scientific Papers and Addresses, 1884, ii, p. 232; Canon Taylor, 1890, p. 115. Quatrefages and Hamy, in their Crania Ethnica, 1882, adopt it. Lapouge (1889 a) and Olóriz (1894 a, p. 227) are the only later writers who adhere to this opinion.

‖ Livi, 1886, pp. 265 and 273; 1896 a, pp. 138 and 153; Sergi, 1883 b, pp. 125 and 132 *et seq.*; 1895 a, pp. 66 *et seq.*; Issel, 1892, ii, p. 331; Castelfranco, 1889, pp. 593 *et seq.*; Zampa, 1891 a and 1891 b. Ranke agrees in this view among Germans, Der Mensch., 1886, ii, p. 531; Collignon among the French, 1890 a, p. 13; and Dawkins among English, 1880, p. 328. *Cf.* also von Duhn, 1896, p. 132.

ᐃ Zampa, 1891 a, p. 77, and 1891 b, p. 175; Nicolucci, 1888, p. 2; Sergi, 1883 b, pp. 118 *et seq.*

modern Liguria is regarded, therefore, as merely a remnant of a once more widely extended race. The broad-headed type throughout the Alps, according to this view, represents not the Ligurians, but the Celts, who, as we know, succeeded them in central Europe. The true descendants of the ancient Ligurians inhabit the modern provinces of the same name.* The purest representatives of these people may still be found in the tall, dark, and exceedingly dolichocephalic population of the district about Lucca, whose peculiarities we have been at such pains to describe.†

The transition from an Alpine type of population in the Po basin to the purely Mediterranean race in the south does not occur at or even near the Rubicon, which marks, as we have said, the limits of the Italian language in purity. Turn again to our map of cephalic index on page 251 and observe how the brachycephaly of the north extends over and down into Umbria, into Marche by Pesaro, and over much of Tuscany. Every indication in that dark-tinted area upon our map suggests an intrusive wedge of the Alpine racial type of population with its point directed toward Rome.‡ Bearing in mind what we have already affirmed in speaking of the population of the Po valley—namely, that the entire peninsula was once peopled by a primitive long-headed (Ligurian) type, underlying the modern one—it appears that we must account for the characteristics of the present Umbrians on the supposition of an overflow of population from the north sufficient in magnitude to transform the entire character of the people by intermixture. Who could these immigrants have been? It is apparent at once what their physical characteristics were. They were certainly of a racial origin akin to that of the Celtic broad-headed type throughout central Europe. With whom,

---

* Arbois de Jubainville, 1890, p. 153, positively asserts that the ancient Ligurians have never been disturbed in modern Liguria, even by the Gauls.

† Pieroni, 1892. Such seems to be the view both of Sergi (1883 b, p. 136) and Livi (1896 a, p. 150).

‡ Livi, 1896 a, p. 156; Zampa, 1888, with map, at p. 183, finds a brachycephaly even more marked than does Livi. Cf. Calori, 1873, p. 156.

however, may they be identified historically? That is the
question at issue. They could not have been Gallic; for these
traits have persisted since long before the era of the Roman
wars. Two solutions have been proposed. Sergi * and Zampa † have most ably championed the claim of the ancient Umbrians, asserting from archæological evidence that this people
were of northern extraction, akin to that of the Celts. They
maintain that these Umbrians were of the first wave of the
Aryan invasion up along the Danube, of which the Celts were

only a succeeding por-
tion.‡ Their early oc-
cupation of the penin-
sula is indicated by
the little map on this
page, which we have
reproduced from Ser-
gi's recent brilliant
work. The correspond-
ence between the Um-
brian area marked with
small crosses and the
dark tints of broad-
headedness upon our
cephalic map is highly
significant.

Umbrian period.

This view just stated is in opposition to that of the older
school of anthropologists, represented by Calori # and Nicolucci.‖ They believed the Umbrians to have been the indigenous inhabitants of Italy, closely related to the Oscians
and Vituli (Itali) of classical antiquity. It will be seen at
once, however, that the theory of an Umbrian immigration
need in no wise disturb the serenity of the historians; for this

---

* 1898 a, pp. 75, 83, and 144. This represents a conversion from his
earlier view expressed in 1883 b, p. 126.

† Zampa, 1888, p. 193 ; and 1889, p. 128.

‡ Consult our chapter on European Origins for further details.

1873, p. 14.

‖ 1888, p. 10, where he clearly restates his first theory, propounded a
generation earlier.

immigration certainly antedated by many centuries the beginnings of recorded history and of Roman civilization. To this older school the intrusive element, responsible for the acknowledged broad-headedness of Umbria, was not readily explained. Archæological research still left in doubt the character of the only other possibly extraneous people in Italy—the Etruscans. Moreover, the territory assigned by archæology to the Etruscans is quite distinct from that of the Umbrians, lying to the west of it in the modern provinces of Tuscany and Roma. So much has this long-suffering people—the Etruscans—endured at the hands of ethnographers that we must treat of them a moment in more detail.

All that we know historically of the Etruscans is that at a very early period * they invaded the territory of the Umbrians, who certainly preceded them in the peninsula. Their advent was characterized by a highly evolved culture, from which that of the Romans developed. For the Etruscans were the real founders of the Eternal City. We know less of their language than of many other details of their existence—only enough to be assured that it was of an exceedingly primitive type. It was constructed upon as fundamentally different a system from the Aryan as is the Basque, described in a preceding chapter. It seems to have been, like the Basque, allied to the great family of languages which includes the Lapps, Finns, and Hungarians in modern Europe, and the aborigines of Asia and America. These unfortunate similarities led to all sorts of queer theories as to the racial origin of the people; as wild, many of them, as those invented for the Basques.† It never occurred to any one to differentiate race, language, and culture one from another, distinct as each of the trio may be in our eyes to-day. If a philologist found similarity in linguistic structure to the Lapp, he immediately jumped to the conclusion that the Etruscans were Lapps, and Lapland the

---

* 1100 B. C., according to Montelius, most authorities placing it considerably later. Zampa, 1892, p. 280, places it at 1200–1300 B. C. Varro states the invasion to have taken place in 1044 B. C. Sergi, 1898 a, p. 149, says 800 B. C.

† Calori, 1873, p. 29, gives a good summary of the various hypotheses.

primitive seat of their civilization. Thus Taylor,* in his early work, asserts an Asiatic origin akin to the Finns. Then Pauli and Deecke for a time independently traced them to the same Turanian source.† At last, when the Etruscan civilization began to be investigated in detail, authorities fell into either one of two groups. They both agree that the culture itself was of foreign origin. The Germans, with the sole exception of Pauli, Cuno, and von Duhn, are unanimous in the assertion that it is an immigrant from the Danube Valley and northern Europe.‡ Much of their testimony is derived from a supposed trade between the north and south of Europe at a very early period described by Genthe and Lindenschmidt. These authorities regard the Etruscan as an offshoot of the so-called Hallstatt civilization, which flourished at a very early period in this part of the continent. In a later chapter on the origins of culture we shall have occasion to speak of this relation more in detail. This school of writers declares the people racially to be of Rhætian or Alpine origin. Dennis tells us that the blond types among the Tuscan peasants are locally believed to be representatives of these Raseni.

The second school of archæologists is disposed to derive the Etruscan civilization from the southeast—generally Lydia in Asia Minor. The relation of the Etruscan to the Greek is by them held to be very close.# Much evidence is favourable to

---

* 1874, p. 30.

† Deecke abandoned in 1882 his earlier theory of Finnic origin, to which Pauli still adheres, while Corssen advocated the theory of Indo-Germanic affinity. Consult Fligier, 1882 a.

‡ Von Czoernig, Hoernes, Hochstetter (for a time), Koch, Müllenhoff, Niebuhr, Mommsen, Seemann, Steub, and Virchow (1871 a), together with the Roman school of archæologists, represented by Helbig and Pigorini. Von Duhn, 1896, p. 140, clearly rejects these hypotheses in favour of an Ionian derivation. Scholl, 1891, p. 37, discusses fully the relationship to the Rhætians.

The Italians, especially of the Bologna school, range on this side ; thus Nicolucci, 1869 and 1888 ; Brizo, 1885 ; Sergi, 1883 and 1895 a ; Lombroso ; and Zampa, 1891 b ; Arbois de Jubainville, 1889, i, p. 134 ; Montelius, 1897 ; Lefevre, 1891 and 1896 a ; A. J. Evans, and Hochstetter in his later work agree. Brinton, 1889 and 1890 c, advocates a Libyan origin ; Dawkins, 1880, p. 333, an Iberian affinity. Cf. Bertrand and Reinach, 1894 a, pp. 63 and 79. Nicolucci, 1888, p. 37, gives many other theories.

either side. To us it seems that Deecke * is more nearly correct than either, as such a division of eminent authority at once implies. He holds it to be probable that both centres of civilization contributed to the common product. In his opinion the Etruscans were crossed of the Tyrrhenians from Asia Minor and the Raseni from the Alps. Many of these views, it will be noted, making no distinction between physical type and culture, reason almost entirely from data of the latter kind. It is now time for us to examine the purely physical data at our disposition. Even supposing their culture to have been an immigrant from abroad, that need not imply a foreign ethnic derivation for the people themselves. Two classes of testimony are open to us, one consisting of the living population of Etruria, the other of crania from Etruscan tombs.

Inspection of our maps, in so far as they concern Etruria, convinces one that if the Etruscans were of entirely extra-Italian origin, their descendants have at the present time completely merged their identity in that of their neighbours, the Umbrians ; for no sudden transitions are anywhere apparent, either in respect of head form, stature, or pigmentation. On the whole, the trend of testimony appears to favour the German theory that the population of Tuscany must have made a descent upon Italy from the north; and that it was derived from the same source as the Rhætians, racial ancestors of the modern Swiss and other Alpine peoples.† Thus it will be observed that Tuscany, like Umbria, allies itself in head form to the north rather than the south. The difficulty is that the Etruscans really overlaid the Umbrians, as our second map from Sergi's work on the next page represents. It is impossible to separate the two elements in the modern population. Perhaps even Helbig is right in his contention that Umbrians and Etruscans were really one and the same. All that we can assert is that the modern Tuscans are strongly infused with

---

* Introduction to K. O. Müller, 1877.

† Rütimeyer and His, 1864 a, p. 30, seem to be doubtful on this ; but not till 1868 did Calori fully prove the prevalent brachycephaly of the modern Tuscans.

broad-headedness. Greek or Semitic racial intermixture would certainly have produced the opposite result from this; for, as we shall see, both of these are alike purely Mediterranean in physical type. To resolve the difficulty of both an Umbrian and an Etruscan intermixture throughout the same region we must turn to our second witness, that of crania from the ancient tombs.

Archæological research during the last few years has fully confirmed the first discoveries of a quarter century ago that the crania from the Etruscan tombs betray a very mixed people. This explains the variety of theories of ethnic origin, based upon the earliest investigations. Retzius [43], for example, had no difficulty in proving a common origin with the Lapps,

Etruscan period.

Basques, and Rhætians from a few broad-headed crania in his possession; and von Baer [60] as readily proved the opposite— of a relation to the dolichocephalic races.* Nicolucci [69] first established the fact of a great heterogeneity of cranial types in these tombs; confirmed by Zannetti [71], who found about one quarter of the heads to be brachycephalic, the remainder being allied to the elongated oval type indigenous to the peninsula. This relative proportion of the two is to-day confirmed by the best authority.† It indicates a population at this early period more purely Italian than that

---

* Lombroso, 1878, and Rosa, 1882, in their attempt to identify the Garfagnana population about Lucca with the Etruscans, represent this view.

† Calori, 1873, pp. 65 *seq.*; Sergi, 1883 b, p. 139; 1897 b, p. 169; 1898 a, pp. 108–114; Nicolucci, 1888, pp. 42–46; Zampa, 1891; pp. 48–56.

of modern Tuscany,* although the broad-headedness even to-day is less accentuated in Etruria proper than in Umbria, according to our map. Which of these two cranial forms unearthed in their tombs, one Mediterranean, one Alpine, represents the Etruscans proper, and which the population subjugated by them? To us it appears as if here, in the case of the Etruscans as of the Teutonic immigrants, there were reason to suspect that the ethnic importance of the invasion has been immensely overrated by historians and philologists. It seems quite probable that the Etruscan culture and language may have been determined by the decided impetus of a compact conquering class; and that the peasantry or lower orders of population remained relatively undisturbed.† If this be indeed so, one might expect that the minority representation of broad-headed Alpine types, which we have mentioned, was proof of a northern derivation of this ruling class. But then, again, there are those antecedent Umbrians to be considered. It is a difficult problem at best. Perhaps, and indeed it seems most probable, Sergi ‡ is right in asserting that the Etruscans were really compounded of two ethnic elements, one from the north bringing the Hallstatt civilization of the Danube Valley, the other Mediterranean both by race and by culture. The sudden outburst of a notable civilization may have been the result of the meeting of these two streams of human life at this point midway of the peninsula.

The Tiber River really marks the boundary between competitive Italy and isolated Italy, so to speak. Rome arose at this point, where Latium, protected by this river, repressed the successive invasions from the north.# It is curious to note that the present population of the city is precisely similar to its predecessor in classical times, so far as archæology can discover. The peninsula south of this point has little of special

---

* Nicolucci, 1888, pp. 12–17 ; Calori, 1873, p. 151.

† Livi, 1886, p. 273 ; 1896 a, p. 156. Nicolucci, 1869, agrees.

‡ 1898 a, pp. 113–125.

Von Duhn, 1896, p. 127. On Roman crania, consult Maggiorani ; Nicolucci, 1875 ; Sergi, 1895 d ; Moschen, 1893 a. On Pompeiian crania, Nicolucci, 1882.

interest to offer.   From the Alpine type of population in the north the transition to a purely Mediterranean one is at last fully accomplished.   The peasantry is strongly brunet with few exceptions; almost abnormally short-statured; and as universally dolichocephalic as the Spaniards or the Berbers in Africa.   Especially is this true in the mountains of Calabria, where geographical isolation is at an extreme.   On the other hand, all along the seacoast we find evidence of colonization from across the water.   It is curious to contrast the north and south of the peninsula in this respect.   North of Rome the immigrant populations all lie inland, while the aboriginal Ligurian is closely confined to the seacoast.   In the south, on the other hand, the conditions are exactly reversed.   Apulia from the heel of the peninsula north, being adjacent to the western coast of the Balkan Peninsula, contains a number of such foreign colonies from over seas.   Some of these are of especial interest as hailing from the extremely broad-headed country east of the Adriatic.   So persistently have these Albanians kept by themselves, that after four centuries of settlement they are still characterized by a cephalic index higher by four units than the pure long-headed Italians about them.*   Many Greek colonists have settled along these same coasts.   Greek dialects are still spoken at a number of places.   They, however, being of the same ethnic Mediterranean stock as the natives, are not physically distinguishable from them.†   Perhaps the strongly accentuated broad-headedness in Salerno, just south of Naples along the coast, may be due to a similar colonization from abroad.   Our portrait type for this district on the opposite page is certainly very different in head form from the purely Mediterranean Sardinian types, to which the normal south Italians tend.   And our recruit from Salerno justly represents the people of his district.   Colonization by sea rather than land would seem to be most probable.

In conclusion, let us for a moment compare the two islands of Sicily and Sardinia in respect of their popula-

---

* Zampa, 1886 a ;   and 1886 b, p. 636 ; Pullé, 1898, p. 86 ; Livi, 1896 a, pp. 167–177.

† Nicolucci, 1865 ; Zampa, 1886 a.

85.   B<small>ERGAMO</small>, Lombardy.   Blondish.   Index 82.5.   86.

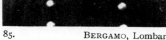

87.   S<small>ALERNO</small>, Campania.   Index 84.5.   88

89.   C<small>AMPIDANO D'ORISTANO</small>, Sardinia.   Index 69.   90.

ITALY.

tions.* With the latter we may rightly class Corsica, although it belongs to France politically. Our maps corroborate the historical evidence with surprising clearness. In the first place, the fertility and general climate of Sicily are in marked contrast to the volcanic, often unpropitious geological formations of the other islands. In respect of topography as well, the differences between the two are very great. Sardinia is as rugged as the Corsican nubble north of it. In accessibility and strategic importance Sicily is alike remarkable. Commanding both straits at the waist of the Mediterranean, it has been, as Freeman in his masterly description puts it, " the meeting place of the nations." Tempting, therefore, and accessible, this island has been incessantly overrun by invaders from all over Europe—Sicani, Siculi, Fenicii, Greeks, and Romans, followed by Albanians, Vandals, Goths, Saracens, Normans, and at last by the French and Spaniards. Is it any wonder that its people are less pure in physical type than the Sardinians or even the Calabrians on the mainland near by? Especially is this noticeable on its southern coasts, always more open to colonization than on the northern edge. Nor is it surprising, as Freeman rightly adds, that " for the very reason that Sicily has found dwelling places for so many nations, a Sicilian nation there never has been."

Sardinia and Corsica, on the other hand, are two of the most primitive and isolated spots on the European map; for they are islands a little off the main line. Feudal institutions of the middle ages still prevail to a large extent. The old wooden plough of the Romans is still in common use to-day. This geographical isolation is peculiarly marked in the interior and all along the eastern coasts, where almost no harbours are to be found. Here in Sardinia stature descends to the very lowest level in all Europe, almost in the world. Livi assures us that it is entirely a matter of race, a conclusion from which we have already taken exception in our chapter on Stature. To us it means, rather, that population has always gone out from

---

* Authorities on these are indexed in our supplementary Bibliography. On Sicily, Morselli, 1873, and Sergi, 1895, are best ; on Sardinia, Zannetti, 1878 ; Gillebert d'Hercourt, Niceforo, and Onnis. *Cf.* Livi, 1896 a, pp. 177 *et seq.*

the island and never in, thus leaving to-day nothing but the
dregs, so to speak.   At all events, whether a result of unfavourable environment or not, this trait is very widespread to-day.
It seems to have become truly hereditary.   It extends over
fertile and barren tracts alike.   In other details also there is
the greatest uniformity all over the island—a uniformity at an
extreme of human variation be it noted: for this population is
entirely free from all intermixture with the Alpine race so
prevalent in the north.   It betrays a number of strongly African characteristics, which are often apparent in the facial features.   The flattened nose, with open nostrils, thick lips, and
retreating foreheads are all notable in a remarkable series of
portraits, which Dr. Livi courteously placed at our disposition.
These details, with the long and narrow face, are represented
in our two portraits reproduced in this chapter.   Imagine the
black hair and eyes, with a stature scarcely above five feet, and
a very un-European appearance is presented.

We have now seen how gradual is the transition from one
half of Italy to the other.   The surprising fact in it all, is that
there should be as much uniformity as our maps indicate.
Despite all the overturns, the ups and downs of three thousand
years of recorded history and an unknown age precedent to it,
it is wonderful to observe how thoroughly all foreign ethnic
elements have been melted down into the general population.
The political unification of all Italy; the rapid extension of
means of communication; and, above all, the growth of great
city populations constantly recruited from the rural districts;
will speedily blot out all remaining trace of local differences
of origin.   Not so with the profound contrasts between the
extremes of north and south.   These must ever stand as witness to differences of physical origin as wide apart as Asia is
from Africa.   This is a question which we defer to a subsequent chapter, in which we shall seek to explain the wider
significance of the phenomenon both physically and in respect
of the origins of European civilization.

" Beyond the Pyrenees begins Africa."   Once that natural
barrier is crossed, the Mediterranean racial type in all its purity

confronts us. The human phenomenon is entirely parallel with the sudden transition to the flora and fauna of the south.* The Iberian populations, thus isolated from the rest of Europe, are allied in all important anthropological respects with the peoples inhabiting Africa north of the Sahara from the Red Sea to the Atlantic. These peoples are characterized, as we have seen, by a predominant long-headedness, in this respect quite like the Teutonic type in Scandinavia; by an accentuated darkness of hair and eyes; and by a medium stature inclining to short. The oval facial characteristics of this group have been already illustrated in our portraits in this chapter. A large area of such conspicuous purity of physical type as here exists over a vast extent of territory is rarely to be found.

The Iberian Peninsula itself is little differentiated geographically. It consists of a high plateau, too cold in winter for the Mediterranean flora and fauna, and too arid in summer for those of the middle temperate zone. As a consequence its human activities and its population are in the main necessarily located in the coastal strip along the seaboard. Of natural barriers or defensible positions in the form of mountains or important rivers there are none, save in the northwest, where in Galicia and Asturias a rugged and lofty region occurs. As a consequence of this geographical structure, the peninsula as a whole has been neither attractive to the colonist nor the invader. It has, it is true, formed the natural highway from Africa to Europe, and has been overrun at all times by extraneous peoples. These invasions have almost always been ephemeral in character, disappearing to leave little except ruins along the way. Thus the population still remains quite true to its original pattern; nearer, indeed, to the aboriginal European racial type than that of any other civilized land on the continent.

The homogeneity of the Iberian Peninsula is well expressed by our map of the head form on the next page.† A variation of

---

* Peschel, 1880, i, p. 33, aptly describes the geographical contrasts on the two Pyrenean slopes.

† Dr. F. Olóriz, Distributión geográfica del indice cefálico en España, Madrid, 1894; La talla humana en España, Madrid, 1896; Hoyos Sáinz

cephalic index, imperceptible to the eye, of scarcely four units
from the most dolichocephalic type in Europe is at once apparent.*   Only where the topography changes, in the northwestern corner, is there any considerable increase of broad-headedness, shown by our darker shading.†   This brachycephaly
closely follows the mountainous areas in many places.   It is
not a transitory phenomenon.   Crania from the earliest times

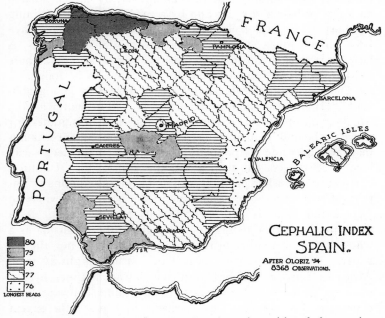

CEPHALIC INDEX
SPAIN.

AFTER OLORIZ '94
8368 OBSERVATIONS.

80
79
78
77
76
LONGEST HEADS

betoken the same tendency.‡   On the other side of the peninsula, the Catalan strip of coast about Valencia exhibits the
opposite extreme.   Portugal also is equally dolichocephalic,

and De Aranzadi, Un avance á la antropología de España, Madrid, 1892 ;
and Vorläufige Mittheilungen zur Anthropologie von Spanien, Archiv
für Anth., xxii, pp. 425–433., For Portugal, I have manuscript data most
courteously offered by Dr. Ferraz de Macedo, of Lisbon. On ethnology,
Lagneau, 1875, is best. See also index to our Bibliography.

   * Olóriz, 1894 a, p. 72.
   † Olóriz shows this strikingly by diagram at p. 83. Cf. also p. 163.
   ‡ Ibid., p. 259. Cf. Jacques, 1887, on the prehistoric archæology also.

as our map at page 53, in which Dr. Ferraz de Macedo's data for that country have been incorporated, exhibits. In discussing the linguistic geography of the peninsula (page 18) we took occasion to note that the political separation of Portugal from Spain is in no degree fundamental. Now, in respect of this physical characteristic of the head form, we are able to verify the same truth.

The first glance at our map of average stature would seem to indicate a variability strongly in contrast with the homogeneity of the people, so notable in the head form. This is largely due to the over-emphasized contrast of shading on our map. For the legend shows that in reality the extreme difference, according to provinces, is less than two inches. Its

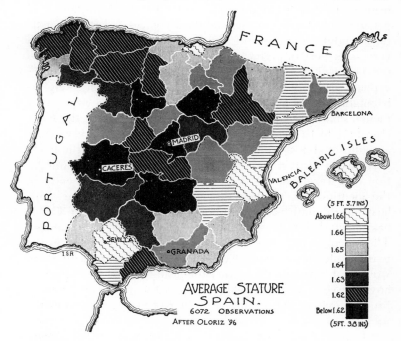

AVERAGE STATURE
SPAIN.
6072 OBSERVATIONS
AFTER OLORIZ '96

(5 FT. 5.7 INS)
Above 1.66
1.66
1.65
1.64
1.63
1.62
Below 1.62
(5FT. 3.8 INS)

distribution geographically has no great significance. Comparing this map with that of languages, on page 18, we observe perhaps that the Catalans as a whole are somewhat taller, while

22

the northwestern provinces are rather more diminutive, with the exception of those in the Basque country. As for Portugal, the data exhibited on our map at page 97 show it to be quite homogeneous in character with its larger neighbour. Taking the evidence as a whole, it would seem that a slight indication of the comparative prosperity of the coastal regions all about the peninsula was apparent in a somewhat taller population. The interior plateau, especially between Caceres and Madrid, represents perhaps the aridity and barrenness of the environment.

It is pertinent at this point to ask for an ethnological explanation of the physical phenomena which we have described. All authorities agree as to the primitive Iberians being the primary possessors of the soil. Whether the Ligurians ever penetrated as far as this, beyond the Pyrenees, is certainly matter for doubt.[*] Following the Ligurians came the Celts at a very early period, pretty certainly overrunning a large part of the peninsula.[†] To them does the still noticeable brachycephaly along the northern coast seem to be most likely attributable.[‡] The people of this region apparently betray many mental characteristics also, more or less peculiar to the Celts elsewhere in Europe. Tubino[#] comments upon their reserve, amounting almost to moroseness, as compared with the lively peasants in Murcia and Tarragona. As for the later inundation of Saracens and Moors, there is a profound difficulty in the identification of their descendants, owing to their similarity to the natives in all important respects. Canon Taylor has shown their extension by means of a study of place names.[||] They seem to have been in evidence everywhere except in the extreme north and northwest. But intermixture with them would not have modified either the head form or the stature in any degree. Aranzadi believes the very prevalent "honeybrown" eyes of the southwest quarter of Spain, near Granada,

---

[*] Jacques, 1887, denies Lagneau's assertion to this effect. Olóriz. 1894 a, p. 264, discusses these questions. See also page 262 *supra*.

[†] Arbois de Jubainville, 1893-'94 ; Mínguez, 1887.

[‡] Hoyos Sáinz and Aranzadi, 1892, p. 34.

[#] 1877, p. 105.   [||] Words and Places, p. 68.

to be due perhaps to strong Moorish influence.* And the effect of a Moorish cross is also apparent in producing a broader and more African nose, according to the same authority. Beyond this the permanent influence of the foreigner has been slight. The varied experiences of Portugal with the English and French invasions, seems to have left no permanent effects.† In fine, we may conclude that the present population is closely typical of that of the earliest prehistoric period. It is cranially not distinguishable either from the prehistoric Long Barrow type in the British Isles, or from that which prevailed throughout France anterior to its present broad-headed population of Celtic derivation.

We must describe the modern African population of Hamitic speech very briefly.‡ It falls into two great divisions— the Oriental and the Western. In the first are included the entire population of northeastern Africa from the Red Sea, throughout the Soudan, Abyssinia, the Nile Valley, and across the Sahara Desert as far as Tunis. The second or western group is the only one to-day in contact or close affinity with Europe, although both groups are a unit in physical characteristics.# All through them we have to distinguish in turn two elements—the nomadic Arabs and the sedentary or local population. It is the latter alone which concerns us in this place. Of the Arabs we shall have to speak in treating of the Jews and Semites. This sedentary population is comprehended in all the northwestern region under the generic name of Berbers, whence our geographical term Barbary States.

The physical traits of these Berbers are at once apparent by

---

* Archiv für Anth., xxii, 1894, p. 431, with maps showing the distribution of the eye colour.

† Da Silva Amada, Ethnogénie du Portugal, 1880.

‡ The best *résumé* of our knowledge of these peoples is by Sergi, Africa: Antropologia della Stirpe Camitica, Torino, 1897. Among the original authorities are Collignon, 1887 a and 1888; Bertholon, 1891 and 1897; Paulitschke and R. Hartmann (*q. v.*).

Cf. Sergi, 1897 a, p. 259, on their fundamental unity of cranial type since the earliest Egyptian times. Carette is best on ethnographical classification.

reason of their isolation from all admixture with the other ethnic types of Europe. The distinctively long, narrow face appears in most of our subjects, although the broad-faced, disharmonic Cro-Magnon type is quite generally represented (pages 45 and 173). In many cases the slightly concave nose in profile is characteristic, suggesting the negro. This frequently occurs among the Sardinians also. The hair of these people is the most African trait about them. Among all the Hamites from Abyssinia to Morocco it varies from the European wavy form to a crispy or curly variety. This may with certainty be ascribed to intermixture with the negro tribes south of the Sahara. Our Moor from Senegal, on the opposite portrait page, offers an illustration of this variety of hair. Upon the soft and wavy-haired European stock has surely been ingrafted a negro cross. By this characteristic alone may some of the Berbers be distinguished from Europeans, for the blackness of their hair and eyes is scarcely less accentuated than that of the Spanish and south Italians. Especially is this Europeanism true of the coast populations, the Riff Berbers in Morocco, for example, being decidedly European in appearance.* While local variations of type are common there can be no doubt of the entire unity and purity of this whole group.† An additional token of ethnic similarity among these people is that beards among the men are uniformly rare, and that the bodily habit is very seldom heavy. The slender and agile frame may be regarded as a distinctively Mediterranean trait.

The entire population of Africa and Europe north of the Sahara and south of the Alps and Pyrenees is overwhelmingly of a pure brunet type, as we have already shown.‡ Nevertheless, an appreciable element of blondness appears in Morocco, and especially in the Atlas Mountains. Tissot,# in fact, asserts that in some districts one third of the population is of this blond type. This, judging from the testimony of others, is an

---

* Sergi, 1897 a, p. 336. † *Op. cit.*, pp. 312–316.
‡ Page 71 *supra*.
# 1876, p. 390; Harris, 1897, p. 66; Gillebert d'Hercourt, 1868, p. 10; Andree, 1878, p. 337.

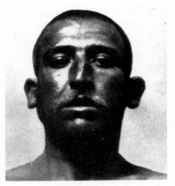

91.   Blond KABYLE.   Index 78.7.   Index 76.5.   MOOR, Senegal.   92.

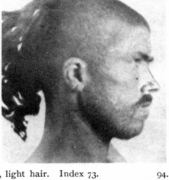

93.   KABYLE, Tunis.   Eyes blue, light hair.   Index 73.   94.

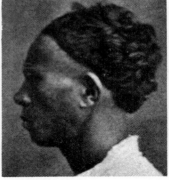

95.   BERBER, Tunis.   Eyes and hair black.   Index 70.   96.

NORTH AFRICA.

exaggeration, yet the existence of such blondness about Morocco can not be denied. It seems to become less frequent in western Tunis, finally becoming practically negligible as one goes east.* Our series of portraits herewith, courteously loaned by Dr. Bertholon of Tunis, shows two of these blond Kabyles.

Several explanations for this curious phenomenon of blondness in Africa have been presented. Brinton, and after him Keane, have, because of this appreciable blond element in northwestern Africa, attempted to make this region the original centre from which the blondness of Europe has emanated. This interesting hypothesis, seemingly based upon an attempt to reconcile the early origin of civilization in Africa with the Indo-Germanic Aryan theory, is controverted by all the facts concerning the relative brunetness of Europe, which we have heretofore outlined. Much more probable does it appear that this blondness is rather an immigrant offshoot from the north than a vestige of a primitive and overflowing source of it in Africa. Several attempts at historical explanations have been made, especially that the Vandals introduced this blondness during the historic period.† This theory was then rejected in favour of the view that it represented an immigrant which entered Africa from the north at a much earlier time, its path being marked by the occurrence of the dolmens all over France and Spain.‡ Its localization in the vicinity of the straits of Gibraltar certainly seemed to favour some such view of northern derivation, although the direct proof of its connection with any specific culture is problematical.# Perhaps these blonds were dolmen builders; they may have been of the same stock as the extinct Guanches of the Canary archipelago, or even of a Libyan origin, according to Brinton.‖ We will not venture to decide the matter. It would seem, from a recent study of the

---

* Collignon, 1887 a, p. 234, and 1888 ; Bertholon, 1892, pp. 14–41.

† Broca, 1876, refuted this.

‡ Faidherbe, 1854 ; and in Bull. Soc. d'Anth., 1869, p. 532 ; 1870, p. 48, and 1873, p. 602 ; Topinard, 1873, 1874, and 1881.

Verneau, 1886, p. 24.

‖ 1890 a, p. 116. Arbois de Jubainville insists on an Iberian affinity of these Libyans.

physical facts, that two separate centres of such blondness are distinguishable. The principal one is located in the fastnesses of the Atlas Mountains in the interior, while another exists along the Mediterranean coast among the Riff Berbers.* It is said that two fifths of these latter people are of blondish type. As for the coastal blonds, they might easily be accounted for on the ground of immigration, but such an explanation is obviously impossible for the Atlas group. Sergi † offers a suggestion, which had already occurred to me, which seems plausible enough. Why may not this blondness in the Atlas Mountains, surely indigenous to Africa, be of an environmental origin? In our chapter on Blonds and Brunets we have spoken at length of such influences. The case is parallel to that of the light-haired and blue-eyed Amorites of the mountains in Palestine, ‡ who since the earliest Egyptian monuments have been thus represented as a blond people. Perhaps in their case as well they are merely the local product of environmental causes; if not, one theory of immigration is as good as another so far as conclusive proof is concerned.

---

* Quedenfeldt, xxi, pp. 115 and 190. His denial of the Atlas blondness is controverted by all other observers. Collignon, 1888, finds a similar blondness along the coast of Tunis.

† 1897 a, p. 296. His treatment of these blonds is admirable at pp. 284–296.

‡ Sayce, 1888 a.

CHAPTER XI.

THE Alpine highlands of central Europe—Switzerland and
the Tyrol—while perfectly well determined in the main features of their racial constitution, abound in curious and interesting anthropological contrasts and contradictions.* This is
not alone due to their central geographical position, for that
by itself would long ago have entirely destroyed any ethnic
individuality which this little district might have possessed.
The constant passage to and fro across it of migrant peoples
from north, south, east, and west would have been fatal to
purity of physical type. Its dominant race has been preserved
for us by the rugged configuration of its surface alone. The
mountains offer us superb illustrations of the effect of geographical isolation upon man; this we have all been taught to
note in its social and political phenomena. And it is this two-
fold aspect of Switzerland and the Tyrol geographically which
also enables us to account for their physical contrasts. We
expect and we find almost absolute purity of type; but we are
not surprised to discover also radical contradictions on every
side.

The influence of the topography and central situation of this
mountainous region is well exemplified in the prevailing speech
of the people to-day. The three great languages—French,

---

* Prof. J. Kollmann, of Basel, is the best living authority on Switzerland. His most important contributions are those of 1881 a, 1881–'83,
1882 c,1885 a, whose titles are given in our Bibliography. His courtesy in
obtaining photographs and other material merits the sincerest gratitude. A second authority, classical although now obsolete, is Rütimeyer
and His, Crania Helvetica, Basel, 1864. Consult also the works of Drs.
Bedot, Studer, and others herein cited.

German, and Italian—come together along most irregular
boundaries. These are shown upon our maps at pages 101 and
284. Then, besides these, subdivided by the way into thirty-
five dialects of German, sixteen of French, and eight of Italian;
there are five varieties of the Romansch in the Grisons and
Tyrol. And all this, too, as Taylor * says, in a country but
twice the size of Wales. The Romansch is really a degenerate
and primitive Romance or Latin language. Under the several names of Ladino or Friaoulian it still persists in the most
isolated regions of Italy and Austria. Everywhere it is gradually receding before the official languages, which are pressing
upon it from every direction.

The head form throughout the Alps, as our general map
of Europe has proved, is in general at an extreme of broad-
headedness of the human species. Switzerland and the Tyrol,
according to this test, must be adjudged overwhelmingly of
the Alpine racial type. Von Baer's discovery of this in 1860
established one of the first landmarks in the anthropological
history of Europe; it has been confirmed by all observers
since that time.† Great local variations, however, occur.
Switzerland, especially the northern German-speaking half, is
far less pure than either the Tyrol or Savoy. Even Bavaria
seems to be of purer type.‡ A Teutonic long-headedness has
interpenetrated the entire middle region, seemingly having entered by the Rhine and the valley of the Aar. This will appear likewise from consideration of the other physical traits.
Whether the first Teutons were the Helvetians, who conquered
or drove the broad-headed Rhætians before them, is a matter
for historical identification.# The anthropologists incline to the

---

* Words and Places, p. 34.

† His and Rütimeyer, 1864; Kollmann, 1885 a; Beddoe, 1885, p. 81;
Scholl, 1891; Bedot, 1895; and Pitard, 1898, are best on Switzerland.
Their results, so far as they give averages at all, are shown on our map
of stature at page 285. Kollmann's results, among the best, do not,
unfortunately, give averages.

‡ A comparison of the two seriation curves on page 116 will prove this
at once. On Savoy see Hovelacque, 1877-'79, and Longuet.

Rütimeyer and His, 1864, at p. 32, and Scholl, 1891, at p. 32, discuss
historical probabilities. On the Ligurians and Etruscans, with their
affinities, consult our chapter on Italy.

opinion that the ancient Rhætians, whose language still persists in the Romansch, were so far influenced by Celtic-speaking invaders as for a time to adopt their speech and culture. Throughout all this time they remained faithful to what Rüti-meyer and His called the " Dissentis " type, because of its prevalence in the upper Rhine Valley. It conforms to our notion of the Alpine race. These people were the lineal descendants of the Lake Dwellers, who settled the Alps in the early stone age.* Their racial equilibrium was upset at a comparatively late period by the advent of the Helvetians, Burgundians, and other Teutonic tribes. These people came as conquerors from the north. It is significant that their physical type prevails even to-day more noticeably in the upper classes.† A result of the ethnic intermixture has been in many cases to produce a disharmonic head, with the brachycephalic cranium conjoined to a rather longish and narrow face. This type is exemplified in our two portraits from the Tyrol at pages 290 and 291. A fine pure Alpine head and face is illustrated by our type from Dissentis. The possibilities of pure Teutonic descent appear in the type from Basel.

The Teutonic racial influence invading Switzerland along its principal water course is clearly manifested by our map on the next page. Kollmann's researches proved the existence of a relatively blond zone across the middle, setting aside the Romansch-Italian and the French-speaking sections on the east and west as relatively brunet districts.‡ His results as to pure brunet types were confused by the widespread prevalence of an intermediate or neutral coloured eye among the Swiss. Beddoe, by charting the hair colour, alone seems to reach far more definite conclusions.# There can be little doubt that the more primitive substratum of the Alpine type has been rele-

---

* Studer and Bannwarth, 1894, p. 13. Sergi, 1898 a, pp. 61–68, in his attempt to prove the lake dwellers to be of Mediterranean descent, is, I think, in error.

† His, 1864, p. 870.

‡ Our map at page 222 shows his distribution of brunet types. His report, 1881 a, contains all original data.

At Beddoe, 1885, pp. 75–85, is perhaps the best brief summary of Swiss anthropology anywhere available.

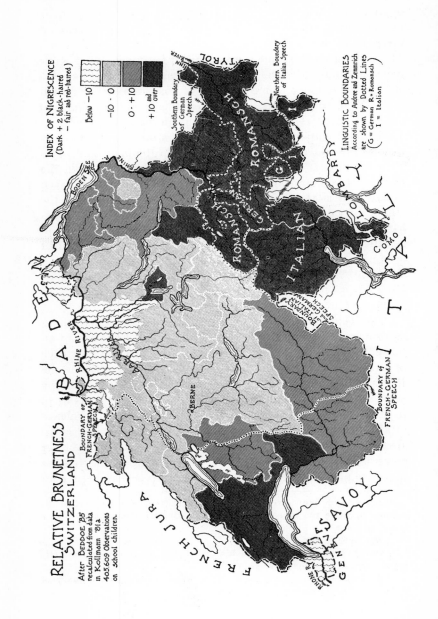

RELATIVE BRUNETNESS
SWITZERLAND

After BEDDOE '85
recalculated from data
in Kollmann '81a
405,609 Observations
on School children.

INDEX OF NIGRESCENCE
(Dark + 2 black-haired
— fair and red-haired)

Below −10
−10 · 0
0 · +10
+ 10 and over

LINGUISTIC BOUNDARIES
According to Andree and Zemmrich
are shown by Dotted Lines
(G = German R = Romansch
I = Italian)

gated to the southeast and southwest by a wave of advancing blondness from the north.   The extreme blondness of Geneva,

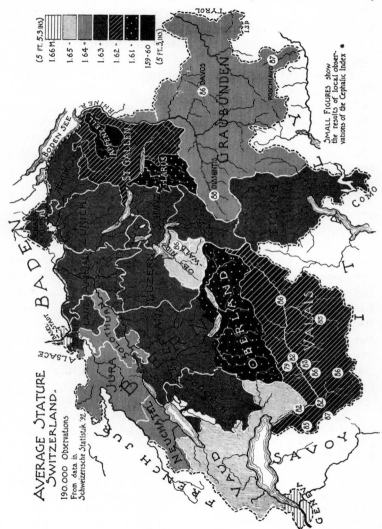

ancient capital of the Burgundian kingdom, may be of recent origin from this people.   Whether the gray iris, which is the most common shade among the peasantry, associated with a brownish colour of hair, is indeed a distinctive Alpine trait; or whether it is merely a result of the intermixture of blond and brunet varieties, is still matter of dispute. In any case, it is a marked peculiarity of the population all through the Alpine highlands.

Our map of stature in Switzerland, in which, as always, dark tints denote the populations of shorter bodily height, brings to light another of those curious contradictions in which this little country abounds. While its eastern and western extremes, as we have just shown, are in respect of the colour of hair and eyes divided by an intrusive wedge of relative blondness; now in stature this blondest girdle appears to be composed of the relatively shortest-statured population. To be sure, the differences are not great, but they are perfectly well proved by these data, here mapped for the first time. Confirmatory testimony comes from comparison with the statures of the surrounding countries.* Geneva, Vaud, Neufchâtel, the Bernese Jura, and, we may add, Savoy also, surely lie within the influence of a specific centre of tall stature which covers the Burgundian or northeastern corner of France. On the other hand, the canton of Graubünden marks the outermost concentric circle of a second core of tallness which culminates along the Adriatic Sea. This influence is equally apparent in northeastern Italy. It endows the Tyrolese, whose peculiarities of stature we have described upon page 101, with a marked superiority over the Swiss in this respect.†

---

* See maps on pages 149, 227, and 236. Livi, 1883, gives a map of stature in Italy by averages which invites comparison. Carret (1883) gives the average for 13,199 Savoyards of 1.649 metres. Lorenz and Bedot both confirm these data exactly for the Grisons and Valais.

† Schweizerische Statistik, 1892, p. 38, gives parallel data on the proportions of statures above 1.69 metres, by cantons, strictly comparable with our map of the Tyrol. Roughly speaking, a population with 30 per cent of statures superior to 1.69 metres seems to correspond to an average height of 1.66 metres; 20 to 25 per cent to an average of 1.63 metres; and 8 to 10 per cent to an average of 1.60 metres. Lorenz, 1895, confirms this. Even allowing for a difference in the age of recruits of two years, the Tyrol remains superior.

All this is indeed very confusing. It seems to confound all attempts at an ethnic explanation. The variations are slight, to be sure, but they are all contrary to racial probability. We are forced again to take refuge in purely environmental explanations. The law that areas of extreme elevation or infertility are unfavourable to the development of stature has already been discussed. We must invoke it here. Especially does it seem to fit the situation in the canton of Berne. Three zones of decreasing stature from the Jura to the Oberland are shown on our map. In this latter case the most widespread area of stunted population in Switzerland must, it seems to us, be due to the unfavourable influence of the habitat. If the Oberland were indeed, as Studer presumes because of its relative blondness, an area of late Teutonic colonization, it surely would be of greater average stature than it here appears. One other centre of relative shortness is clear in the Appenzells and Glarus. To test it I have traced it through a number of years of recruits. It appears in each contingent. Chalumeau's [96] map brings it into strong relief. Perhaps here again some local influence has been in play. A field for anthropological research of great interest in this quarter of the country is as yet almost untouched. Detailed analyses are, however, needed. Cantonal averages show very little, for they include all extremes of environment at once.

Another example of the competency of environment to confuse the phenomena of race is offered by a detailed study of the school children in the canton of Berne by Dr. Studer [80]. We have just examined the distribution of stature in this region, noting the depressing effect of the high Alps in this respect. Topographically this canton extends over three regions quite distinct in character. A middle strip along the valley of the Aar as far as the city of Berne consists of an elevated, not infertile table-land, with a rolling, hilly surface. This becomes gradually more rugged, until it terminates in the high mountains of the Bernese Oberland south of Interlaken. Here in this chain we have the most elevated portion of Switzerland; and, we may add, one of the most unpropitious for agriculture or industry. The peasantry hereabouts must live upon the

tourist or not at all. The northern third of Berne covers the
Jura Mountains, quite high, but of such geological formation
that the soil yields not ungraciously to agriculture. Thus
from the economic point of view we may divide the canton into
two parts, setting aside the southern third—the Oberland—
as decidedly inferior to the rest. The people of this region in

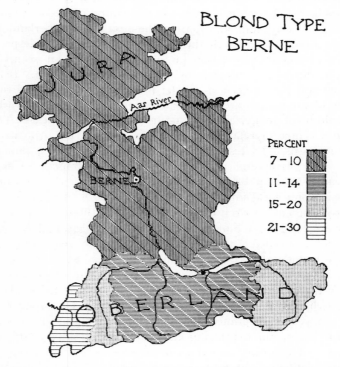

the ante-tourist era could not but be unfavourably affected by
their material environment.

Our map shows that this economic contrast is duplicated
in the anthropological sense by an appreciable increase of
blondness within the Oberland, which becomes more marked
as the fastnesses of the mountains are approached. North
of the city of Berne there are from seven to eleven per cent of
pure blonds; in the Oberland sometimes upward of three times

as many. Is it possible that this blondness in the mountains
may be due to race? If so, it must be Teutonic. We have
just seen that Switzerland is cut in halves at this point by an
intrusive strip of such Teutonic blondness. Dr. Studer explained the phenomenon on the assumption that this blondness
migrating to the south along the Rhine, and then up the Aar,
had heaped itself up, so to speak, against this great geographical barrier, by a colonization of lands hitherto unoccupied by
the native inhabitants. This supposition might be tenable
were not the evidence from all parts of Europe flatly opposed
to it. There is nothing to show that the law of segregation
of the Alpine type in the areas of isolation does not hold here
as in the Tyrol, in western Switzerland, and all over the continent. Central Switzerland was historically overrun by the
Helvetians, as we have said, who have been identified as Teutonic by race. The Rhætians were the more primitive Alpine
type. Every principle of human nature and ethnology opposes
the supposition that these conquering Helvetians would be
content to leave the darker Rhætians in full possession of the
fertile plain of the Aar while they betook themselves to the
barren valleys of the Oberland. Everywhere else in Europe
the rule is, " To the conquerors belong the plains, to the vanquished the hills." The blondness of the Oberland must therefore be regarded as racially anomalous. Another explanation
for it must be found in the influence of environment. It is, in
our opinion, traceable most probably to the effect upon the pigmental processes of the mountainous and infertile territory of
these high Alps. In an earlier chapter * the evidence upon
this point for Italy seemed to be quite clear. Further examples
will be mentioned later.

The broad-headed type not only forms the bulk of the population all through the Alps; it is so much more primitive than
all others that it lies closer to the soil. The racial character of
the population varies in direct relation with the physical geography of the country. The Tyrol is the most favoured spot in
which to study the succession of the long and the broad heads

---

* Page 75.

23

respectively.* It is the geographical centre of the continent. It holds strategically the great highway of communication—the Brenner Pass—between the north and the south of Europe. As our map on the next page shows, it is also the crest of the great European watershed. From it flow the Inn River and the Drave into the Danube, thence to the Baltic Sea on the east; the Adige is an affluent of the Po, running due south to the Adriatic; and on the west the branches of the Rhine carry its waters into the Atlantic. Each of these great river systems has marked a line of human immigration and has directed racial movement to this spot. By the Danube the Slavs have come, and by Innsbruck over the Brenner, the Teutons have passed across into the valley of the Adige and thence directly into the plain of Italy. Back over the same route have flowed many phases of Mediterranean culture into the north from the time of the Phœnicians to the present. The Tyrol, for these reasons, is the one spot in Europe in which racial competition has come to a focus. The population is exceedingly mixed. I have seen men of the purest Italian type speaking the German tongue; and at Botzen blond Teutons who made use of good Italian. Despite this circumstance of racial intermixture, there are within the Tyrol at the same time a number of areas of isolation which possess very marked individuality. We thus have the sharpest contrasts between mixed and pure populations. The Oetzthal Alps, in the very centre of the country, are as inaccessible as any part of Europe. So rugged is this latter district that the dialects differ from valley to valley, and the customs and social institutions as well.†

We have already discussed the variations of stature in this region (page 101). We have shown how sharp is the transition from a tall population north of the Alps to the stunted

---

* The literature upon the Tyrol is especially rich. The best *résumé* of the detailed researches of Holl, Tappeiner, Rabl-Rückhard, Zuckerkandl, and others will be found in Toldt, Zur Somatologie der Tiroler, Sitzungsb. Anth. Ges. Wien, xxiv, 1894, pp. 77–85. Our map is constructed from his data. On languages consult Bidermann, Schneller, and others.

† Tappeiner, 1878, p. 56, gives interesting examples.

97. TYROL. 98.

99. APPENZELL,
Brachycephalic disharmonic.

OBER-RHEINTHAL, 100.
Pure Dissentis type.

101. BASEL, Teutonic type. Cephalic Index 64. 102.

SWITZERLAND AND TYROL.

people of Italian speech in the valley of the Adige. A similar tendency toward brunetness is perfectly certain. The northern half of the country is distinctly German in its colouring, while the south becomes suddenly Italian.*

Turning now to the anthropological map of this region, based upon a measurement of over twelve thousand skulls, it

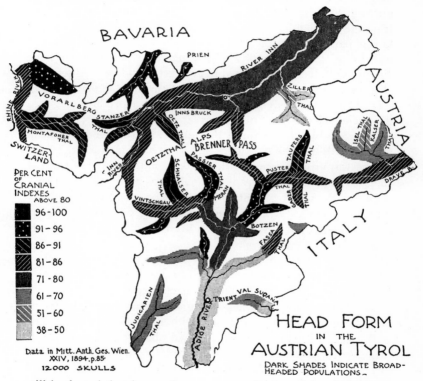

HEAD FORM
IN THE
AUSTRIAN TYROL

DARK SHADES INDICATE BROAD-
HEADED POPULATIONS.

PER CENT
OF
CRANIAL
INDEXES
ABOVE 80

96 - 100
91 - 96
86 - 91
81 - 86
71 - 80
61 - 70
51 - 60
38 - 50

Data in Mitt. Anth. Ges. Wien.
XXIV, 1894. p. 85.
12.000 SKULLS

will be found that in nearly every case the broad heads become numerous in direct proportion to the increase in altitude. In other words, the broad open valleys leading out toward the great river systems of Europe are relatively dolichocephalic; while the side branches in the Oetzthal Alps, isolated from foreign influences, show a marked preponderance of round-head-

---

* Moschen, 1892, with map; Tappeiner, 1878, p. 288.

edness.   Thus in the Stanzerthal and the valley of the Schnals, indicated upon our map by the solid black tint, are two of the broadest-headed spots in the world.   In the first almost seventy per cent, in the second over ninety per cent of the cranial indices were above 85.*   These both lie, it will be observed, well off the main line of travel, either by the Inn Valley or over the Brenner.   At their outlets they contain many heads of medium breadth, but these become less frequent as we penetrate the highlands.   Like them are nearly all the side valleys in this part of the Alps.   So closely, indeed, does this physical trait follow the topography that Ranke of Munich, as we have already said, has endeavoured to connect broad-headedness and altitude as cause and effect.   For us the true explanation of this phenomenon is entirely racial.†   It is a product of genuine social selection.   The two great branches of narrow-headedness, the blond Teuton at the north and the Mediterranean at the south with its dark eyes and hair, have invaded the Alps all the way from France to the Balkan states.   At the time of their coming a broad-headed population, as it would appear, occupied the whole mountain chain.   The result is that to-day its main peculiarity has become attenuated exactly in proportion to the degree to which it has been exposed to racial intermixture with the new-comers.

Here is an example, then, of purely human stratification. The Alpine type has been overlaid by the new-comers, or else has been gradually driven up and back into the areas of isolation.   Those who remained along the great routes of travel have been swamped in a flood of foreign intermixture.   The only exceptions to the rule we have observed of a primitive broad-headed layer of population isolated in the uplands are offered by the two valleys of the Ziller in the northeast and of the Isel and Kalserthals just across the main chain of the Alps by Linz.   In these places Holl ('84) has proved that the converse of our proposition is true, since, as one ascends the valleys the broad heads become less frequent.   No explanation for this has been offered; but I have a suspicion that it points to

---

* Rabl-Rückhard, 1879, p. 210.
† Moschen, 1892, p. 125, discusses this.

still a third layer of population. The Slavic peoples immigrating within the historic period are all very broad-headed. It is not impossible that this racial element which has overlaid the Teutons in parts of eastern Europe may have followed them into these valleys. Certain it is that Slavic skulls begin to occur in this region.* It may have happened in this way: When the long-headed Teutons came, they drove the primitive Alpine population into the side valleys. Then, when the Slavs followed the Teutons, these latter types drifted up and back as well, merging with the original broad-headed stock to produce an intermediate type of head form. This would obviously be less broad than the new Slavic type in relative purity along the main channels of immigration.

The evidence from the Tyrol that in the Alps the broad heads lie nearest the soil is sustained by similar testimony from the other end of the same mountain chain. Bedot and Pitard have studied in some detail the population of the Valais—the valley of the upper Rhone in western Switzerland. Their results appear on our map at page 285. Here, precisely as in the Tyrol, the side valleys are distinctly broader-headed than that of the Rhone itself. Wherever the foreigner has come he has lowered the cephalic index. Thus, for example, in the open valley of the Rhone the average index is but 82, while in the Gorge du Trient, leading over toward Savoy, it rises 87. Few of the villages investigated are as isolated to-day as those in the Oetztal valleys of the Tyrol; but in proportion as they lie off the main track the index rises appreciably. The evidence is indubitable that the broad-headed type is the oldest and most primitive all through the Alps.

The Netherlands are generally conceded to be Teutonic, just as Belgium is regarded as Gallic or French in its affinities. Religious differences seem to confirm the deduction. Historians—Motley, for example—assume the boundary between the Catholic and Protestant Low Countries to be dependent in large measure upon differences of physical descent. Nothing

---

* Zuckerkandl, 1884, p. 124.

could be more erroneous. We have already seen in Belgium, that the transition from an Alpine to a Teutonic population is entirely accomplished in passing from the Walloons to the Flemings.* In the Netherlands similar contrasts of population exist, although it is more difficult to correlate them exactly with the geographical character of the country. Nevertheless, the anthropology of this little nation is of exceeding interest, because it offers a clew to the problem of the origin of the curiously un-Teutonic populations which we have shown to exist in Denmark and southwestern Norway.

Linguistically, the Netherlands to-day is at bottom entirely Teutonic, but it is dialectically divided into several distinct parts.† The Frisian language, which since the very earliest times has occupied its present territory, is of interest as being perhaps nearest to modern Saxon English and Lowland Scotch of all the continental languages. It is spoken principally in the province of Friesland (see map on page 296), in the hook of Noord-Holland, and on the islands along the coast, even as far north as the southern boundary of Denmark.‡ The language is slowly giving way before the aggressive Low German speech. The Saxon has crowded it out of Gröningen and most of Drenthe, where it once prevailed. Frankish is crowding it back south of the Zuider Zee. Throughout Zeeland and south Holland a mixed Friso-Frankish language is spoken, which approaches the Flemish toward the Belgian frontier. Finally, in Limburg and parts of Noord-Brabant we come upon the Walloon linguistic influence, as an added element. Thus it will be seen that, despite the small size of this country, the greatest diversity of speech prevails. One is led to expect that conditions giving rise to such variety of language ought to be competent also to perpetuate racial peculiarities of importance. Such is indeed the case, although, curiously enough, such physical differences are quite independent of language in their distribution.

---

* Page 162 *supra*.

† For maps and data consult Kuyper, 1883, and especially Winkler, 1891.   Lubach, 1863 a, p. 424, with map, treats of it fully also.

‡ Hansen, 1892, maps it in Schleswig.

Very few anthropometric observations upon the living Dutch have been made; but research upon the cranial characteristics of the people has been ardently prosecuted for more than a generation.* The material is difficult to handle, since it has never been systematically co-ordinated. We have made an attempt to do this in our map on the next page, which represents as accurately as may be the present state of our knowledge concerning the head form of the people. It shows, as we might expect, that the greater portion of the country is entirely Teutonic in respect of this characteristic. The people are predominantly long-headed, oval-faced, tallish, and blond. These latter traits are expressed with great purity, especially in Friesland and the neighbouring provinces.† It is curious to note also, as Lubach observes, that while the townspeople seem to be slightly different from the peasantry, betraying greater intermixture, few traces of any diversity between the upper and lower classes exist. This he asserts to be a result of the political homogeneity of the people and the absence of any hereditary ruling class of foreign origin or descent. Little by little, as we go south from Friesland, the people become darker-complexioned, the most noticeable change being in the shorter stature and more stocky habit. This we might expect, indeed, from what we know of the Walloons, who are of Alpine racial descent.

---

* The standard authority upon the Netherlands is the late Dr. A. Sasse, of Zaandam. To his son, Dr. J. Sasse, who is ably continuing his father's investigations, I am indebted for much assistance. Dr. De Man, of Middelburg, is also an authority upon the especially interesting district of Zeeland. He has courteously placed much original matter at my disposition. In addition to these, Drs. Folmer, De Pauw, and Jacques have contributed to our knowledge of the country. Lists of their work will be found in our supplementary Bibliography. The best comprehensive works are D. Lubach, De Bevoners van Nederland, Haarlem, 1863 ; A. Sasse, Ethnologie van Nederland, Tijd. Aardrijkskundig Genootschap, 1879, pp. 323–331, with map ; J. Sasse, Over Zeeusche Schedels, Academisch Proefschrift, Amsterdam, 1891 ; and the later reports of Dr. A. Sasse as chairman of the Commissie voor de Ethnologie van Nederland in Ned. Tijd. voor Geneeskunde, especially 1893 and 1896.

† Lubach, 1863 a, pp. 420 *et seq.*, gives the best general description of the population. Beddoe, 1885, pp. 38–43, gives a good summary also.

Virchow injected an element of interest into the ethnology
of the Netherlands in 1876 by an attempt to prove craniologi-

Data for this map are corrected from the original skull measurements by adding two
units, to make them comparable with other maps based upon study of living
heads.

cally that the Frisians were in reality not Teutons at all, but
were of a more primitive or Neanderthaloid derivation.*   His

* Beiträge zur physischen Anthropologie der Deutschen, mit besonderer
Berücksichtigung der Friesen, Abh. K. Akad. Wiss., Berlin, aus dem

conclusions were based upon studies of a few crania from the islands of Urk and Marken, in the Zuider Zee. The Frisian skull, according to Virchow, was not only peculiar but atavistic by reason of its peculiarly low vault and flat, retreating forehead. In this respect it seemed to approach the ancient type of the so-called Neanderthal race.* He did not deny that in other respects the general proportions, especially as measured by the cranial index, were quite similar to those of the other Teutonic peoples. Subsequent investigation has, I think it may be fairly said, entirely shaken confidence in Virchow's inferences. When measured according to normal and well-accepted methods and in sufficient numbers to eliminate chance variation, the northern Dutch seem to be in their head form, as also in all their other physical characteristics, distinctly and purely Teutonic.

Having vindicated the right of the northern and eastern Dutch to the title of Teutons, we come to a different problem in the case of the people of the provinces of Holland and Zeeland. As our map shows, a sudden and violent rise of cephalic index betrays the presence of a large population of Alpine or broad-headed affinity. Even here all along the seacoast the Teutonic characteristics seem to have persisted, probably due to roving bands from the north, similar to those which have settled all along the *litus Saxonicum* in France. But on the inner islands, especially in Nord and Zuid Beveland, there is every indication of a broad-headed Alpine colony of considerable size. This is shown by the dark tints upon our map. An extreme brachycephaly has been proved here by Dr. De Man, who has most courteously sent me many photographs of crania from the region. We have already made use of two of these, at page 38, as illustrative of the limits of type variation within the continent of Europe.† The long-headed one is from

Jahre 1876. Its conclusions are ably contested by Dr. A. Sasse, 1879, and especially by Von Hölder, 1880; and J. Sasse, 1896, furnishes a good review of the controversy.

* *Op. cit.*, pp. 31, 75–109, 236, and 356.

† In addition to his other papers, those of 1865 and 1893 are especially important. Consult on the finds at Saaftingen also; Kemna, 1877; J. Sasse, 1891, pp. 45–54; and De Pauw, 1885.

the seacoast, where Teutonic characteristics prevail; the other
globular one is from a village in the middle of the brachycephalic area, submerged in the sixteenth century. These are
each typical; the contrast is too marked to need further comment. There can be no longer any doubt that in these islands
a settlement of the Alpine invaders took place at an early time.
Whether they actually antedated the Teutons, as Dr. J. Sasse
supposes,* or not, is matter for question. Müllenhof states
that the Celts occupied the Rhine delta as early as 400 B. C.; †
perhaps these broad-headed Zeelanders are a heritage of their
occupation. De Man ('93) certainly holds the brachycephaly

Alpine type, Zeeland.   Index, 86.   Teutonic type.   Blond.

to represent an immigrant type more recent than the long-
headed population on the coast. At all events, Lubach, nearly
forty years ago, long before any precise measurements were
taken, commented upon the brunetness, the stocky build, and
the round visage of the peasants of this district. In each of
these respects they have been proved to differ from the Fries-
landers farther north, who, as we have said, are Teutonic by
descent. Quite often the type is disharmonic, arising from a
cross of the two races, as in the case of the peasant illustrated
in our portrait herewith. The black hair of this man and his

* 1891, p. 84.   † Virchow, 1876 a, p. 364.

accentuated brachycephaly are in strong contrast with his elongated Teutonic face. The nearest blood relatives of these south Hollanders are the Walloons in Belgium * and the original broad-headed element in the Danish population. From which of these colonies the Round-Barrow type invading the British Isles came we may never determine; we only know that the Alpine race touched the western ocean at this spot, and has here persisted in remarkable purity to this day. It seems as if a race had here found refuge in this secluded spot against the aggression of the Teutonic type, just as the Walloons are sheltered in the wooded uplands of the Ardennes plateau in Belgium a little farther south.

---

* From Vanderkindere's data on the school children in Belgium, a tendency toward brunetness, more marked than usual in Flanders, becomes apparent in the direction of Zeeland. An Alpine racial occupation of this region would account for it.

CHAPTER XII.

THE BRITISH ISLES.

THE ethnic history of the British Isles turns upon two significant geographical facts, which have rendered their populations decidedly unique among the other states of western Europe.* The first of these is their insular position, midway off the coast between the north and south of the continent. That narrow silver streak between Calais and Dover which has insured the political security and material prosperity of England in

---

* For invaluable assistance I am deeply indebted to Dr. John Beddoe, F. R. S., late President of the Anthropological Institute of Great Britain, of Bradford-on-Avon, Wilts, not only for the loan of rare material for the illustration of this particular chapter, but for kindly criticism and interest throughout our whole series. To ex-President E. W. Brabrook, C. B., of the Anthropological Institute, London, also, I would acknowledge most gratefully my obligation. Recognition should be made of the courtesy of Mr. J. A. Webster, secretary, as well. The complete collection of photographs of the Institute has not only been opened to us ; a large part of it has even been subjected to the perils of transportation to America for our benefit. From these sources all of our portraits are derived.

Authorities comprehensively treating the anthropology of the British Isles are very few. Pre-eminent is Dr. John Beddoe's Races of Britain, Bristol and London, 1885 ; and his Stature and Bulk of Man in the British Isles, in Memoirs of the Anthropological Society of London, iii, 1869. A full list of his other valuable papers will be found in our Bibliography. The monumental work of Davis and Thurnam, Crania Britannica, two volumes, London, 1865, covers the whole subject of past and present populations. An essay, On Some Fixed Points in British Ethnology, by the late T. H. Huxley, in the Contemporary Review for 1871, is a convenient summary, with no attention to the evidence of craniology, however. Finally, the reports of the Anthropometric Committee of the British Association for the Advancement of Science, especially its last one in 1883, should not be omitted. Many other papers of local importance are named in our Bibliography above mentioned.

later times, has always profoundly affected her racial history. A partial bar against invasion by land, the fatal step once taken, it has immediately become an obstacle in the way of retreat. Invasion thus led inevitably to assimilation. Protected sufficiently against disturbance to assure that homogeneity of type which is attendant upon close contact, the islands at the same time could never suffer from the stagnation which utter isolation implies.

We are still further assured of the truth of this geographical generalization on comparison of the racial history of England with that of Ireland; for we thereby have opportunity to observe the effects of different degrees of such insularity. In the latter case, it has become a bit too pronounced to be a favourable element in the situation. Disregarding her modern political history—for we are dealing with races and not nations—it is indeed true, as Dr. Beddoe says, that Ireland " has always been a little behindhand." Ethnic invasions, if they took place at all, came late and with spent energy; most of them, as we shall see, whether of culture or of physical types, even if they succeeded in reaching England, failed to reach the Irish shores at all. These laws apply to all forms of life alike. Thus the same geographical isolation which excluded the snakes of the mainland from Ireland—we are speaking seriously of an established zoölogical fact and not a myth— was responsible for the absence of the peculiar race of men who brought the culture of bronze and other arts into England in prehistoric times. It also accounts for the relative scarcity of the Teutonic invaders afterward. As we may grade both the flora and fauna of the islands in variety of species from the continent westward, so also may we distinguish them anthropologically. In flora, Ireland has but two thirds of the species indigenous to England and Scotland; for the same reason her human population contains much less variety of human type.* Among the Irish peasantry there are no such contrasts as those we shall show to exist between the highland and the lowland Scotch, or between the Englishman in Cornwall and in Yorkshire.

---

* Sir A. Geikie, in Macmillan's Magazine, March, 1882, pp. 367 *et seq.*

A second geographical peculiarity of the British Isles has not been devoid of importance for us. The eastern island contains both extremes of fertility and accessibility. Ireland is far more uniform. Another point for us to note also is that

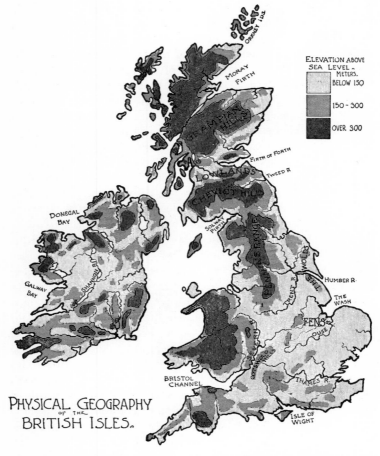

PHYSICAL GEOGRAPHY
OF THE
BRITISH ISLES.

the backbone of the larger island lies along the west coast. Both England and Scotland certainly present their best sides to the continent; all the way from Caithness to Kent either the most fertile lands, or the mouths of rivers leading to them,

103.   "Old Black Breed" Type.   104.

105.   "Old Black Breed" Type.   106.

107.   A Teutonic—Black Breed Cross.   108.

SHETLAND ISLANDS.

lie on the east. The same thing is partially true of Ireland, although more in respect of geology than topography, which latter is alone shown upon our map. The result, of course, is the accentuation of the contrasts between the populations of the east and west sides in either case. The best lands are at the same time nearest the mainland. All incentive to further invasion beyond a certain point ceases at once. The significance of this will appear in due time. We may realize its importance in advance, however, by supposing the situation reversed, with the goal of all invasions on the farther side of each island. Is there a doubt that Wales, the western Scottish Highlands, and farther Ireland would have been far more thoroughly infused with foreign blood than they are in reality to-day? It makes a great difference whether a district is on the hither or the hinter side of Canaan.

These truths, which we have here to apply to ethnic facts, hold good in social relations as well. Either extreme of heterogeneity or isolation is unfavourable to progress. This we may prove by applying the same laws to another country which in many respects is similar to the British Isles. Japan stands in much the same relation to Asia that Britain does to Europe. Like the British, her population is to-day quite well assimilated, although compounded of several ethnic types different from those of the mainland. Here again it is a modest degree of isolation which has left her to digest in comparative quiet the Mongol, the Malay, and the Polynesian elements in her population; and yet it is undoubtedly the very variety of these elements which makes the Japanese so apt in the ways of civilization.

The most remarkable trait of the population of the British Isles is its head form; and especially the uniformity in this respect which is everywhere manifested. The prevailing type is that of the long and narrow cranium, accompanied by an oval rather than broad or round face. This cephalic uniformity throughout Britain makes the task of illustrating types by means of portraits peculiarly difficult; for distinctions of race are reduced mainly to matters of feature and relative blondness, instead of the more fundamental characteristics. In this con-

24

nection, by the way, it should always be borne in mind that when we speak of broad or oval faces we refer to the proportions of the bony framework alone. We must look below the flesh, behind beard or whiskers, or else endless confusion will result. Full cheeks need not imply a broad face as we mean it. The width behind the malar bones is the crucial test.

CEPHALIC INDEX.
'BRITISH ISLES.
ABOUT 1200 OBSERVATIONS

Measured by the cephalic index—that is, the extreme breadth of the head expressed in percentage of its length from front to back—the uniformity in cranial type all through the British Isles is so perfect that it can not be represented by shaded maps as we have heretofore been accustomed to do.

Wherever heads have been measured, whether in the Aran Islands off the west coast of Ireland, the Hebrides and Scottish Highlands, Wales and Cornwall, or the counties about London, the results all agree within a few units. These figures, noted upon the localities where they were taken, are shown upon our little sketch map on page 304. It will be observed at once that the indexes all lie between 77 and 79, with the possible exception of the middle and western parts of Scotland, where they fall to 76.*

What do these dry statistics mean? In the first place, they indicate an invariability of cranial type even more noticeable than in Spain or Scandinavia. Compared with the results elsewhere in central Europe, they are remarkable. On the continent near by, the range of variation of averages of cephalic index in a given country is never less than ten points; in Italy and France it runs from 75 to 88. Oftentimes within a few miles it will drop five or six units suddenly. Here in the British Isles it is practically uniform from end to end. Highland and lowland, city or country, peasant or philosopher, all are practically alike in respect of this fundamental racial characteristic. Our second deduction from the data concerning the cephalic index is that here we have to do with a living population in which the round-headed Alpine race of central Europe is totally lacking; an ethnic element which, as we have already shown in our preceding chapters, constitutes a full half of the present population of every state of middle western Europe—that is to say, of France, Belgium, Italy, and Germany. We have already proved that this Alpine race is distinctively a denizen of mountainous regions; we christened it Alpine for that reason. It clings to the upland areas of isolation with a persistency which even the upheavals of the nineteenth century can not shake. Almost everywhere it appears to have yielded the seacoasts to its aggressive rivals, the Teutonic long-headed race

---

* Beddoe, 1885, pp. 231–233; 1893, p. 104, and 1894, is authority on England, primarily; Haddon and Browne are best on Ireland; Beddoe, 1887 a, on the Isle of Man; Gray, 1895 b, gives an average of 77 for 169 Scots on the east coast in Aberdeen. *Cf.* also Horton-Smith, 1896; MacLean, 1866; Venn, 1888, etc. Muffang, 1899, is fine.

in the north and the dolichocephalic Mediterranean one on the south. This curious absence of the broad-headed Alpine race in the British Isles therefore is merely another illustration of its essentially continental character.

Before we proceed to consider the other physical traits of the living population, we must draw in a background by a hasty summary of the facts which the science of archæology has to offer concerning the prehistoric human types in the islands. In the first place, it is certain that the earliest inhabitants were decidedly long-headed, even more so than any Europeans of to-day; far more so than the present British. The evidence concerning this most primitive stratum is carefully presented by Boyd Dawkins [80] in his Early Man in Britain. These men, whose remains have been unearthed in caves, and whose implements have been discovered in the river drift of the late Glacial epoch, were decidedly dolichocephalic. Both in the stage of culture attained and in head form they were so like the Eskimo of North America that Nilsson more than a half century ago suggested a common derivation for both. Boyd Dawkins lends his support to the same hypothesis, assuming that as the ice sheet withdrew to the north, these primitive folk followed it; just as we know to a certainty that the mammoth, mastodon, and other species of animals have done.* A former connection of Europe with Greenland would have made this migration an easy matter. Whether this interesting supposition be true or not, we know that the earliest type of man in Britain was as long-headed as either the African negro or the Eskimo—that is to say, presenting a more extreme type in this respect than any living European people to-day.

The second population to be distinguished in these islands was characterized by a considerably higher culture; but it was quite similar to the preceding one, although somewhat less extreme in physical type, so far as we can judge by the head form. This epoch, from the peculiarities of its mode of interment, is known as the Long-Barrow period.† The human

---

* 1880, p. 233 ; consult also his 1874 a and 1874 b.

† The best authorities upon this and the succeeding type are Canon

remains are found, often in considerable numbers, generally in more or less rudely constructed stone chambers covered with earth. These mounds, egg-shaped in plan, often several hundred feet long, are quite uniform in type. The bodies are found at the broader and higher end of the tumulus, which is more often toward the east, possibly a matter of religion, the entrance being upon this same end. These people were still in the pure stone age of culture; neither pottery nor metals seem to have been known. But a distinct advance is indicated by the skilfully fashioned stone implements. Such long barrows occur most frequently in the southwest of England, in the counties of Wilts and Gloucestershire, and especially in the bleak uplands of the Coteswold Hills; but they are also found much farther north as well. The people of this period were, as we have said, like their predecessors extremely long-headed. The cephalic index in the life was as low as 72, several units below any average in Europe to-day, save perhaps in parts of Corsica. It is worthy of note also that a remarkable purity of type in this respect was manifested; positively no broad crania with indexes above 80 have ever been found. These long-barrow men were also rather undersized, about five feet five inches—that is to say, an inch shorter than any English average to-day. Rolleston claims never to have found human remains characterized by a stature above five feet six inches. Beddoe [89] concedes it to have been a population shorter than any now living in Britain. The full significance of this important point will appear shortly. Finally, the evidence seems to bear out the conclusion that thus far we have to do with but one race type, which had, however, slowly acquired a low stage of culture by self-education.

This neolithic, or stone age, primitive type is still repre-

Greenwell's British Barrows, with its anthropological notes by Dr. Rolleston, 1877, at pages 627–718 ; the Crania Britannica above mentioned, but more especially the essays by Dr. Thurnam in Memoirs of the Anthropological Society of London, vol. i, pp. 120–168, 458–519, and vol. iii, pp. 41–75. Consult also Rolleston in Jour. Anth. Inst., London, v, pp. 120–172 ; Garson, 1883, and in Nature, November 15 and 22, 1894. The older authorities are Sir Daniel Wilson, 1851, pp. 160–189 ; Bateman, 1861 : also Laing and Huxley, 1866, especially pp. 100–120.

sented in the present population, according to the testimony of those best fitted to judge.   One of these neolithic types, judging by the combination of diminutiveness of stature, brunetness, and accentuated dolichocephaly, is represented by our number 137 at page 330.   Dr. Beddoe writes me that it is not confined to Devonshire, but is " common enough in other parts of England."

The next event in the prehistoric history of the British Isles —pardon the bull, it conveys our meaning—is of profound significance.   Often directly superposed upon the relics of the Long-Barrow period, and in other ways indicating a succession to it in time, occur the remains of an entirely different racial type.   This stratum represents the so-called Round-Barrow period, from the circumstance that the burial mounds are no longer ovoid or elongated in ground plan, but quite circular or bell-shaped.   The culture is greatly superior to that of its predecessor.   Pottery, well ornamented, occurs in abundance; and the metals are known.   Bronze implements are very common, and even a few traces of iron appear.   Now the dead are often buried in urns, showing that incineration must have been practised.   More remarkable than this advance in culture, and more directly concerning our present inquiry, the people were as broad-headed as the modern peasants of middle France.   The cephalic index was fully ten points on the average above that of the long-barrow men, averaging about 83 in the life.   The former type has not entirely disappeared, but it is in a decided minority.   So persistent is the difference that Dr. Thurnam's well-known axiom, " long-barrow, long skull; round-barrow, round head," is accepted as an ethnic law.   It is impossible to emphasize too strongly the radical change in human type which is hereby implied.   The contrast is every whit as marked as that between a modern Alpine peasant and a south Italian or Scandinavian.   The new population differed in still another important respect from the underlying one. This is known from scores of detailed measurements of skeletons.   The average stature was fully three inches greater, rising five feet eight inches.   The Round-Barrow population, therefore, attained a bodily height more respectable as com-

109. BRONZE AGE, Cumberland. 110.

111. BARLEY, Hertfordshire. 112.

113. Black hair and eyes. Eyes gray, hair dark brown. 114.

CORNWALL. Index 77.1.

OLD BRITISH TYPES.

115.   Anglian.   YORKSHIRE.   Danish.   116.

117.   YORKSHIRE.   SURREY.   118.

119.   SCOTTISH LOWLANDS.   Index 77.   SUSSEX.   120.

BLOND ANGLO–SAXON TYPES.

pared with the present living one than its stunted predecessor. Dr. Beddoe has selected our portrait Nos. 109 and
110 as representing this almost extinct broad-headed type
of the bronze age. It is said to be not uncommon in the re-
moter parts of Cumberland. Harrison * describes it best in
the life. It is above the average in height, strong-jawed, sometimes fair in complexion, though more often dark. The head
is broad and short, the face strongly developed at the cheek
bones, " frowning or beetle-browed," the development of the
brow ridges being especially noticeable in contrast with the
smooth, almost feminine softness of the Saxon forehead. Our
old British type from Barley, Herts (No. 111), would seem
to conform pretty well to this type. It is most prevalent
among the remnants of the now well-nigh extinct yeomanry
class. Another equally good example of this primitive old
British type is shown in our " old black-breed " man from
the Shetland Islands, shown at pages 302 and 303. These
people are to-day nearly extinct in the islands, I am informed
by Dr. Beddoe, being crowded out, as we shall see, by the Scandinavian invaders. The effect of a cross with the Norsemen is
clearly evident in our Nos. 107 and 108. On the mainland,
this " old black breed " is still numerous in west Caithness and
east Sutherland.

The generally accepted view among anthropologists to-day,
is that the Round-Barrow men came over from the mainland,
bringing with them a culture derived from the East. We can
never know with certainty whether they were Celtic immigrants from Brittany, where, as we have already shown, a
similar physical type prevails to-day—such is Thurnam's view:
or whether they were the vanguard of the invaders from Denmark, where a round-headed type was for a time well represented—an opinion to which Dr. Rolleston inclines. This
latter hypothesis is strengthened by study of the modern populations, both of Norway and the Danish peninsula. For example, turn for a moment to our map on page 206, showing
the head form in Scandinavia to-day. Notice how the tints

---

* 1882, p. 246; Beddoe, 1885, p. 15.

darken—that is to say, the heads broaden—in the southwest corner of Norway. The same thing is true just across the Skager Rack in Denmark proper, where the round-headed type is still more frequent than immediately to the south in Schleswig-Holstein and Hanover. This neighbourhood was once a distinct subcentre of distribution of this type. It might readily have come over to England from here, as the Jutes, Angles, and Saxons did a few centuries later. Differing in these details as to their precise geographical origin, all authorities are nevertheless agreed that the round-barrow men came from the continent somewhere. Any other derivation would have been an impossibility. We also know that this Alpine immigrant type overran all England and part of Scotland. It never reached Ireland because of its remoteness; with the result that greater homogeneity of type prevails, while at the same time the island was deprived of a powerful stimulus to advance in culture. This is the first indication of the geographical handicap under which Erin has always laboured. Finally, we have to note that this broad-headed invasion of the Round-Barrow period is the only case where such an ethnic element ever crossed the English Channel in numbers sufficient to affect the physical type of the aborigines. Even here its influence was but transitory; the energy of the invasion speedily dissipated; for at the opening of the historic period, judged by the sepulchral remains, the earlier types had considerably absorbed the newcomers.

The disappearance of the round-barrow men is the last event of the prehistoric period which we are able to distinguish. Coming, therefore, to the time of recorded history, we find that every influence was directed toward the complete submergence of this extraneous broad-headed type; for a great immigration from the northern mainland set in, which, after six hundred years of almost uninterrupted flow, completely changed the complexion of the islands—we speak literally as well as figuratively. The Teutonic invasions from Germany, Denmark, and Scandinavia are the final episodes in our chronicle. They bring us down to the present time. They offer us a brilliant example of a great ethnic conquest as well

as of a military or political occupation. The Romans * came
in considerable numbers; they walled cities and built roads;
they introduced new arts and customs; but when they abandoned the islands they left them racially as they were before.
For they appear to have formed a ruling caste, holding itself
aloof in the main from intermarriage with the natives. Not
even a heritage of Latin place names remains to any considerable degree. Kent and Essex were of all the counties perhaps
the most thoroughly Romanized; and yet the names of towns,
rivers, and hills were scarcely affected. The people manifest
no physical traits which we are justified in ascribing to them.
The Teutonic invasions, however, were of a different character. The invaders, coming perhaps in hopes of booty, yet
finding a country more agreeable for residence than their
barren northern land, cast in their lot with the natives, in many
districts forming the great majority of the population. We
find their descendants all over Britain to-day.

These Teutonic invaders were all alike in physical type,
roughly speaking. We can scarcely distinguish a Swede from
a Dane to-day, or either from a native of Schleswig-Holstein
or Friesland, the home of the Jutes, Angles, and Saxons. They
are all described to us by chroniclers, and our modern research
corroborates the testimony, as tall, tawny-haired, fiercely blue-
eyed barbarians. Evidence there is indeed that the Alpine
broad-headed race once effected a lodgment in southwest Norway, as we have already said. Our map of that country on
page 206 shows a persistence greatly attenuated of that trait
all along the coast. Archæology shows it to have invaded
Jutland also in early times; but it seems to be of secondary
importance there to-day. The Danes are somewhat broader-
headed than the Hanoverians perhaps; but in all other respects they are tall and blond Teutons.

Since we can not follow these invaders over Britain by
means of their head form, they being all alike and entirely
similar to the already prevailing type in the British Isles previous to their advent, we must have recourse to a contributory

* On the Romans consult the Crania Britannica, pp. 175 *et seq.*, and
Beddoe, 1885, pp. 30–37.

kind of evidence. We have at times made use of the testimony of place names heretofore; but it is nowhere else in Europe so clear or convincing as in this particular case. We may trace with some surety, each current of the great Teutonic inundation by means of them. Then, having done this and completed our historical treatment of the subject, we may once more take up the main thread of our argument by returning to the study of the living population. We shall thus have the key to the situation well in hand. The distribution of colour of hair and eyes and of stature will have a real significance.

Our map on the next page, adapted from Canon Taylor's exceedingly valuable little book entitled Words and Places, will serve as the mainstay of our summary. In choosing our shading for it, we had one object in mind, which we can not forbear from stating at the outset. The three shades denoting the Teutonic place names are quite similar in intensity, and sharply marked off from the Celtic areas, which we have made black. This is as it should be; for the whole matter involves a contrast of the three with the one which we know to be far more primitive and deep-seated. The witness of spoken language, to which we shall come shortly, would suffice to confirm this, even had we no history to which to turn. Our map shows at a glance, an island where once all the names of natural features of the landscape and of towns as well were Celtic. This primitive layer of names has been rolled back by pressure from the direction of the mainland. It is a unit opposed to the combined aggression of the Germanic tongues.*

The Jutes, Angles, and Saxons set the Teutonic ball a-rolling. They came from the northern coast of Germany, from the marshes and low-lying country of Friesland. These barbarians seem to have followed close upon the heels of the retiring Romans, making their appearance about the year 400 of our era. The whole island lay open to them, and they made haste to overrun the best of it. They avoided the fens and forests, to which the natives withdrew. Within two hundred

---

* Consult Beddoe, 1885, p. 66, for criticisms of evidence derived from place names.

PLACE NAMES
BRITISH ISLES.

AFTER TAYLOR '93 by Permission.

NORWEGIAN
DANISH
SAXON
CELTIC

HEBRIDES
ISLANDS
LEWIS
SKYE
MULL
ISLAY
CAITHNESS
Moray Firth
Firth of Forth
Tweed R.
Solway Firth
Tees R
LANCASTER
Humber R
The Wash
Thames R
Isle of Wight
I.S.R.
Bristol Channel
Pembroke
WATERFORD
DUBLIN
Galway Bay
Donegal Bay
SHETLAND ISLES

years their influence had extended even to the uttermost parts of Ireland, over the whole of which, as our map shows, Saxon village names sporadically occur.* From their widespread distribution it would seem, as Taylor suggests, that the invaders often avoided the settled places and founded entirely new settlements in virgin territory. The main centre of their occupation was in the southeast and middle of England, where, from their first landings in Kent and Essex, they transformed the entire country. Scotland also, south of Edinburgh, was infused with Saxon blood if we may judge from our map. This district, from the river Tees to the Forth, is in fact, as Taylor † says, as purely English as any part of the island. The Lothians were reputed English soil until the eleventh century. Scotland begins racially, not at the political boundary of the river Tweed and Solway Firth, but at the base of the Grampian Hills.‡ The correspondence between our maps of physical geography and of Celtic place names in Scotland shows undoubtedly a relation of cause and effect.

This first inoculation with Teutonic blood was an unwilling one. We have every evidence that the struggle was bitter to the end. The tale of Saint Guthlac, a devout Saxon, shows it. Disturbed in his meditations one night by a great uproar outside his hermit hut, he engaged himself in prayer for preservation until the morning. The chronicler tells us that he was much relieved at daybreak by the discovery that the midnight marauders were *only devils*, and not Welshmen.⁎ So strong was race antipathy that the laws forbade a Briton from drinking from a cup touched by a Saxon till it had been scoured with sand or ashes.‖ Two hundred years of such a

---

* Canon Taylor has personally offered one criticism of our map which is worthy of note. The Saxon spots throughout Ireland seldom represent but a single village name. They were of necessity made somewhat too large relatively, for purposes of identification. The island is really far more exclusively Celtic than this map makes it appear.

† *Op. cit.*, p. 112.   ‡ *Cf.* A. Geikie, 1887, p. 397.

⁎ Beddoe, 1885, p. 53.

‖ Davis and Thurnam give many other interesting examples. Gomme, in his Village Community in Britain, p. 240, gives testimony to the same effect from quite different sources.

struggle could not but modify the purity of the native stock, as we shall be able to prove. It is probable, indeed, that more than half the blood in the island was by this time Saxon.

About the year 850 came the second instalment of the Teutonic invasion at the hands of the Danes.* They put an end to the inroads of their Saxon predecessors by attacking them in the rear. Two contrasted kinds of expeditions seem to have been despatched against the island. Those which besieged London and skirted the southern coasts were mainly piratical; few names indicating any permanent settlement occur. These Danes were in search of booty alone. Farther north, especially in Lincolnshire and its vicinity, the character of the names betokens intentional colonization, and a very intensive one at that. Thus, nearly a quarter of all the village names in Lincolnshire terminate in " by," as Whitby, Derby, and the like. The Saxon equivalent for this Danish word for village is " ham " or " ton," as Buckingham and Huntington. The line of demarcation of Danish settlement on the south is very sharp. The fens deterred them from extending in this direction, for the marshes were long a stronghold of the Britons, as we have seen. From the Wash north over Yorkshire to the Tees they occupied and settled the country effectively.†
Three hundred years were necessary to accomplish this result.

The Norwegians, coming next, mainly confined their attention to the northern and western coasts of Scotland, shunning their vigorous competitors to the south. They attacked the island from the back side. The fringe of Norse place names upon our map is very striking. These Teutons rarely penetrated far inland in Scotland, especially along this west coast. For here the country is rugged; the only means of communication is by sea; so that the isolated colonies of " baysmen " were speedily absorbed. They dislodged the Gaelic speech in eastern Caithness entirely, so that the country has been Teutonic for upward of one thousand years. Pure Norse was spoken for a long time both in northern Ireland and Scotland.‡

---

* Taylor, *op. cit.*, pp. 103–122 ; Beddoe, 1885, pp. 86–92.
† *Vide* Beddoe, 1837, on Yorkshire.
‡ Noreen, 1890, p. 369.

On the islands—the Shetlands, Orkneys, and Hebrides—the case was much the same. Here the aborigines were often entirely replaced by a purely Scandinavian population. Such a family with strongly accentuated Norwegian peculiarities is depicted on this page. Its contrast with the aboriginal dark population, the "old black breed," needs no comment. Our

Scandinavian types.   Lewis, Hebrides Islands.

No. 138 at page 330 is another good example of a pure blond Scandinavian from this district. One reason for the Teutonization of these islands, which should be noted, is that they were really wintering stations and bases of supplies for the expeditions along the coasts of Scotland, Ireland, and Wales during the summer season. The only other district where Norse settlements occur in frequency is, as our map shows, in Lancashire and the lake district. This may also have been a centre whence expeditions all about the western coasts took place, planting little stations where opportunity offered. One of the most important of these was in Pembrokeshire, that strip of coast which, as Laws [88] has shown in detail, has been the seat of so many foreign occupations.

The Normans,* last of the Germanic series, came to the islands after they had become so infiltrated with Teutonic

---

* Davis and Thurnam, 1865, pp. 193 *et seq.* ; Beddoe, 1885, pp. 110–135.

121.   JUTISH TYPES, Kent.   122.

123.   BRUNET WELSH TYPE, Cardiganshire.   124.

125.   BRUNET WELSH TYPE, Montgomeryshire.   126.

settlements that but few traces of them separately can be detected. They did not come as they entered Normandy, as colonizers; but as political conquerors, a few thousand perhaps, forming a ruling class just as the Franks invaded south Germany or Burgundy. Their influence is most strongly shown in York and parts of Lancashire and Durham. Much of the land here they laid entirely waste; what they did with the native owners we can only surmise. At a later time a gradual influx of Norman blood made itself felt in the south and east of England, so that Dr. Beddoe concludes that by the time of Edward I perhaps a fifth of the population was of Norman descent more or less indirectly.

The Teutonic immigration had now run its course. The islands were saturated. Let us see what the anthropological effect has been, by returning once more to the consideration of physical characteristics alone.

We are now prepared to show why it is that in head form the population of the British Isles to-day is so homogeneous. The average cephalic index of 78 occurs nowhere else so uniformly distributed in Europe, nor does it anywhere else descend to so low a level, save at the two extremes of the continent in Scandinavia and Spain. We have already shown that in these two outlying members of Europe we have to do with relatively homogeneous populations in this respect. Other facts, already recited, prove that this uniformity of head form is the concomitant and index of two relatively pure, albeit widely different, ethnic types—Mediterranean in Spain, Teutonic in Scandinavia. Purity of descent in each case—that is to say, freedom from ethnic intermixture—is the direct and inevitable outcome of peninsular isolation. It is now proper to ask—and this is the crucial question, to whose elucidation all of our argument thus far has been contributory—whether we may make the same assumption of racial purity concerning the British populations. We have a case of insularity even more pronounced than in Spain or Scandinavia; we have cephalic uniformity. The interest of our problem intensifies at this juncture. If relatively pure, have we to do here in Britain with the type of the Teuton or of the Iberian race?

We are generally known as Teutonic by descent. Or is there some complex product here made up of both ethnic elements,

RELATIVE BRUNETNESS
BRITISH ISLES.

AFTER BEDDOE '85
13088 OBSERVATIONS

BOUNDARY OF
GAELIC CELTIC SPEECH.

INDEX OF NIGRESCENCE
(DARK + 2 BLACK HAIRED
— FAIR AND RED HAIRED)

MINUS

0 – 5

Over 5

" 10

" 15

" 20

EASTERN LIMIT OF
GAELIC CELTIC
SPEECH.

LIMIT OF
KYMRIC CELTIC
SPEECH.

CORRECTION.—Gaelic is spoken only in the western half of Caithness. The linguistic boundary should be continued across this county on our map.

in which case the apparent homogeneity revealed by the head form is entirely specious and misleading? As our mainstay in such matters, cephalic index, fails us utterly, since both north and south are precisely alike in this respect, we must rely upon the other, albeit less stable, physical traits. To these we turn next in order.

A glance at the accompanying map of relative brunetness suffices to show a curious increase of pigmentation from northeast to southwest, measured by the prevailing colour of the hair.* The map is almost the exact counterpart of our preceding one of place names. From our previous chapters we might have been led to expect such an increase from north to south; for that is the rule in every continental country we have studied. The phenomenon we found to be largely a matter of race; but that physical environment, notably climate, played an important part. Moreover, we proved that in elevated districts some factor conduced to increase the blondness, so that mountains more often contained a fairer population than the plains roundabout. Here is a surprising contradiction of that law, if law it be; for the Grampian Hills in Scotland, wild and mountainous Wales, and the hills of Connemara and Kerry in western Ireland, contain the heaviest contingent of brunet traits in the island. The gradation from east to west is in itself a flat denial of any climatic influence, for the only change in that direction is in the relative humidity induced by the Gulf Stream.

The darkest part of the population of these islands constitutes the northern outpost of that degree of pigmentation in Europe. Western Ireland, Cornwall, and Argyleshire in Scot-

---

* This map is constructed upon a system adopted by Dr. Beddoe as an index of pigmentation. It differs from others mainly in assigning especial importance to black hair as a measure of brunetness, on the assumption that a head of black hair betrays twice the tendency to melanosity of a dark brown one. Without accepting this argument as valid, the map in question seems to accord best with others constructed by the measurement of pure light and dark types on the German system. Dr. Beddoe regards this one as best illustrating the facts in the case. The maps of the Anthropometric Committee, 1883, working with the colour of hair and eyes combined, seem to be highly inconclusive.

land are about as dark, roughly speaking, as a strip across
Europe a little farther south, say from Normandy to Vienna.
Even in these most brunet areas pure dark types are not very
frequent.   No such extremes occur as Italy and southern
France present.   The prevailing combination is of dark hair
and grayish or hazel eyes.   Such is particularly the case among
the western Irish and southern Welsh.*   So striking is the
brunetness in the latter case that we find an early writer in
this century, the Rev. T. Price,[29] ascribing the prevalence
of black hair in Glamorganshire to the common use of coal
as fuel.   Such absurd hypotheses aside, we may be certain
of the strongly accentuated brunetness of the peasantry hereabouts.   All our Welsh types are decidedly dark in this way.
The opposite extreme of blondness corresponds, as nearly
as we can judge, to the continental populations in the latitude of Cologne.   Light hair and brown or blue eyes become common.   Perhaps the lightest part of Britain is in Lincolnshire—Dr. Beddoe states that the people here remind him
strongly of the peasantry about Antwerp.†   Portraits of a
number of these blond Anglo-Saxon types appear in our series
at page 308.   None of these men are quite as fair as the pure
Teutonic race in Scandinavia, although isolated examples indeed occur.   We shall probably not be far wrong in the statement that the extremes in the British Isles are about as far
separated from one another as Berlin is from Vienna.   In the
darkest regions pure brunet types are more frequent than the
blond by about fifteen per cent.   In the eastern and northern
counties, on the other hand, the blonds are in the majority
by an excess of about five per cent.   Everywhere, however,
all possible crossings of characteristics appear, proving that
the population is well on the road toward homogeneity.

Blondness in some districts often takes the peculiar form

---

* The recent work of Haddon and Browne, published in the Proceedings of the Royal Irish Academy, Dublin, since 1893, on the western
Irish, is our best recent authority on this people.   Thus in the Aran
Islands (1893, p. 784) while among the men only five per cent of fair hair
occurred, almost ninety per cent of the eyes were classed as light.

† Davis and Thurnam, 1865, p. 218 ; Beddoe, 1885, p. 252.

of freckled skin and red hair. We in America are familiar
with two types of Irish, for example; one thus constituted,
while the other is more often compounded of the black or dark
brown hair and steel-blue iris. This is known to the older
anthropologists as the " light Celtic eye." It seems, from
everyday observation, as if this latter variety were far more
common among the women in our immigrants from Ireland.
A similar contrast is remarkable in Scotland. Here, in fact,
in some districts red-headedness is more frequent than almost
anywhere else in the world, rising sometimes as high as eleven
per cent.* In our chapter on Scandinavia we have undertaken
to prove that this phenomenon is merely a variation of blondness.† At all events, investigation shows that red hair is most
frequent in the lightest parts of the continent. In Scotland
the same rule applies, so that the contrasts between east and
west still hold good. The Camerons and Frasers are as dark
as the Campbells are inclined to red-headedness.‡ As for the
Balliols and Sinclairs, we expect them to be light, as their
Norman names imply.

Seeking for the clew to this curious distribution of brunetness in the British Isles, we may make use for a moment of
the testimony of language. The Celtic speech is represented
to-day by Gaelic or Goidelic, which is in common use in parts
of Scotland and Ireland; and secondly by Kymric or Brythonic, which is spoken in Wales. It was also spoken in Cornwall until near the close of the last century, when it passed
into tradition. On our map of brunetness we have roughly
indicated the present boundaries of these two branches of the
Celtic-spoken language. It will be noted at once that the
darkest populations form the nucleus of each of the Celtic
language areas which now remain, especially when we recall
what we have just remarked about Cornwall. Leaving aside
for the moment the question whether this in any sense implies
that the original Celts were a dark people, let us be assured
that the local persistence of the Celtic speech is nothing more

---

* Gray, 1895 a and 1895 b, finds in Aberdeen from five to seven per
cent of this type.

† See page 206 *supra*.   ‡ Beddoe, 1867, p. 158.

nor less than a phenomenon of isolation to-day. The aggressive English language has been crowding its predecessor to the wall in every direction.* This has been proved beyond all possible doubt. In the nooks and corners, the swamps and hills, where the railroad and the newspaper are less important factors in everyday life, there we find a more primitive stratum of language. Is it not justifiable for us, from the observed parallel between speech and brunetness, to assume also that of the two the darkest type in the British Isles is the older? The women generally, conformably to a law of which we shall speak later, seem to be more persistent in their brunetness than the men.† This corroborates our view. Thus Gray,‡ among three thousand Scotch agricultural labourers in Aberdeenshire, found dark hair ten per cent more frequent among the women, while dark eyes occurred well-nigh twice as often. A hasty examination of Dr. Beddoe's tables indicates the same tendency all over the islands where the sexes are distinguished.# Pfitzner ‖ observed the same phenomenon in Alsace, where, as in Britain, a dark population has been overrun by a Teutonic one. So striking was the contrast here that he even ascribes it to a real sexual peculiarity.

One detail of our map confirms us in this opinion that a primitive dark population in these islands, now mainly of Celtic speech, has been overlaid by a lighter one. Notice the strongly marked island of brunetness just north of London. Two counties, Hertfordshire and Buckinghamshire, are as dark as Wales, and others north of them are nearly as unique. All investigation goes to show that this brunet outcrop is a reality. It is entirely severed from the main centre of dark eyes and hair in the west, by an intermediate zone as light as Sussex, Essex, or Hampshire (Hants). Our stature map on page 327 makes the people in this vicinity very much shorter than those about. This again betokens a British lineage. The explanation is simple. We have already shown that the south

---

* Ravenstein has mapped it in detail for different decades in the Journal of the Royal Statistical Society, London, vol. xlii, 1879, pp. 579–646.

† *Cf.* page 399 *infra.*   ‡ 1895 b, p. 21.

\# 1885, especially p. 186,   ‖ 1896, pp. 487–498.

Saxons entered England by the back door. They spread inland from the southern coast, prevented from following up the Thames by the presence of London. On the other side the same invaders pushed south from the Wash and the Humber. These two currents joined along the light intrusive zone. Our dark spot is the eddy of native traits, persistent because less overrun by the blond Teutons. The fens on the north, London on the south, with dense forests in early times, left this population relatively at peace. History teaches us this. Natural science corroborates it strikingly. The fen district particularly was long a refuge of the old British peoples, who made it a secure base of operations against the invaders.* In a later chapter, considering purely social phenomena, we shall show that peculiarities in suicide, land tenure, habits of the people, and other details of these counties, are likewise the concomitants of this same relative isolation. The fact is all the more striking because the district lies so close to the largest city of Europe. Another locality where there is reason to suspect that Teutonic intermixture was less intensive is in the region west of Lincoln, mainly in the counties of Notts and Derby.† Especially the northwestern corner of Derbyshire, lying in the Pennine hills. Taylor tells us the name is from the German "thier," a beast, so wild was the region. Nevertheless, the people seem to be quite light-haired, although they are very much shorter than the purely Teutonic people in Lincolnshire. Inspection of our several maps will make this clear.

The variation of brunetness in Britain shown by our map is not a modern phenomenon, nor is its discovery even of recent date. So early do we find attention called by the chroniclers to this contrast between northeast and southwest, that, while of course largely a result of the Teutonic invasions of historic times, we can not believe that it should be entirely ascribed to them. They have in all likelihood merely accentuated a condition already existing. This we assume from the testimony of Latin writers.‡ In fact Tacitus' statements, the

* Beddoe, 1867, p. 77 ; 1885, p. 53.
† Davis and Thurnam, 1865, p. 212 ; Beddoe, 1885, p. 253.
‡ Huxley, 1871, is good on this.

mainstay of the hypothesis of an Iberian substratum of population in Britain, prove that long before the advent of the
Saxons several distinct physical types coexisted in Roman
Britain. One of these, he tells us in the eleventh chapter of
his Agricola, was the Caledonian, " red-haired and tall "; the
other, that of the Silures in southern Wales, with " dark complexion and curly hair." He also notes the similarity in appearance between the southern Britons and the Gauls; and
suggests a Germanic origin for the Caledonians, an Iberian
one for the Welsh, and a Gallic one for the English. This
is positively all that he said upon the subject, never having
been in the 'country. Then Jornandes, an early Italian com-
mentator, added fuel to the flame by amending Tacitus' words
concerning the Silures of Wales, giving them not only " dark
complexions," but " *black*, curly hair." Such were the humble
beginnings of the Iberian hypothesis; notwithstanding which
it has passed current for generations as if founded upon the
broadest array of facts. What if we should conclude that the
assumption is correct in the light of modern research! It is
no justification for the positiveness with which the law has
been laid down by hosts of secondary writers. By such a tenu-
ous historical thread hangs many another ethnic generalization. May the day come when the science of anthropology
assumes its due prominence in the eyes of historians, and renders the final judgment in such disputed cases of physical
descent!

Many attempts have been made at a philological corroboration of this Iberian hypothesis, classical in origin, as we have
shown. We are told that even the word Britain is of such
derivation by as eminent an authority as Canon Taylor. More
recently, Rhys asserts that the word Brython merely meant
the " cloth-clad " people, as distinct from the aborigines, who
wore skins.* A play upon the words Iberia and Hibernia may
have given rise to the time-honoured Irish myths of such
proud descent.† It is curious to note, moreover, as Elton sug-

---

* Words and Places, second edition, p. 159; Rhys, 1884, pp. 210–214,
226.

† H. Martin. 1878, and Sir W. R. Wilde in Trans. Brit. Ass. Adv.
Science, 1874, p. 121. Elton, 1890, pp. 133–154, after an able summary of

127.   Braemar.   REDDISH BLOND TYPES.   Lochaber.   128.

129.   Edinburgh.   SHORT DARK BRUNET TYPES.   Argyleshire.   130.

131.   Moray.   TALL DARK TYPES.   Inverness.   132.

SCOTLAND.

gests, that the short, dark-haired Irish type, to which alone the physical anthropologist allows such ethnic derivation to-day, is the very one—the despised Firbolg—to whom the native historians positively denied it. Such are the accidents by which science controverts mythical history. The principal net result of philological investigation on this question, was to lead to the well-known and widely accepted opinion of a Basque substratum in the British Isles. The Iberian hypothesis of Tacitus was narrowed down to this. The argument was simple. In certain words were discovered traces of a primitive non-inflectional origin. The Basque speech to-day is the only agglutinative one in western Europe. Wilhelm von Humboldt long ago proved to his own satisfaction that Basque is the modern representative of the ancient Iberian language. Hence it was assumed as a matter of course that Tacitus' Silures must have been of Basque affinities. Thus nearly all writers on British ethnology are led to discover this pre-Celtic element in the islands. Even Dr. Beddoe regards a Basque-like physiognomy in parts of southern Wales as significant of possible relationship.* The linguistic identification was rendered particularly plausible anthropologically because the Basques, as we have already shown, contain two radically distinct physical types. We know to-day that they are a *people* and not a *race*. Hence in the past, writers could find almost any type of head form necessary to prove their philological theses. Recent expert linguistic testimony on the subject still discovers some slight Iberian elements in the islands, particularly in the now extinct dialects of the Picts; but the evidence is very inadequate.† Even were it more positive and definite, it would carry little weight with us in any case; for, as we must ever contend, language means often worse than nothing as to physical descent. Summing up the last two

---

this linguistic and mythical testimony, finds "hardly any affirmative evidence in its favour." Boyd Dawkins, 1880, pp. 330 *et seq.*, agrees. Davis and Thurnam, p. 52, were doubtful about it; as also Rolleston, 1877.

  * 1885, p. 26.

  † Rhys, 1892; Fita, 1893; Beddoe, 1893, p. 101; Academy, September 26, 1891.

26

paragraphs, then, we conclude that the sole evidence worth considering, of an Iberian or Mediterranean substratum in the British Isles is that derived from physical characteristics and geographical probabilities.

Professor Rhys, the best living authority, assents to this, being content " to leave the question of origin mainly to those who study skins and skulls." * Skulls are indeed Mediterranean in their dolichocephaly, but they are unfortunately just as much Teutonic. The difficulty is, as we have said, that all head forms in Britain to-day are similar. Skins—including therewith, of course, hair and eyes—supply the necessary proof; they suffice to render the Iberian theory highly probable. This, it should be observed, by no means implies any Basque affinities, for this little people is in no wise typical of any great racial group. The theory is far broader than that. Neither is Britain in any wise peculiar in this respect. All Europe, as we shall hope to prove, contains the same primitive Mediterranean substratum. It would be anomalous if in Britain any other condition prevailed.† This substratum is quite widely diffused, but it seems to be most clearly represented in the southern Welsh, the western (Firbolg) Irish, and possibly in the short and dark remnants throughout Scotland.

Thus far all has been plain sailing. It seems as if the case were clear. An Iberian brunet, long-headed substratum, still persistent in the western outposts of the islands, dating from the neolithic long-barrow period, or even earlier; and a Teutonic blond one, similar in head form, in all the eastern districts overrun from the continent, seem to be indicated. Now we have to undertake the addition of a third physical trait—stature—to the others, and the complexity of the problem appears. Our map on the opposite page shows that the British Isles contain variations in average of upward of four inches. Scotland, as we have shown elsewhere, contains positively the tallest population in Europe, and almost in the entire world.

---

* 1884, p. 217.   In his 1890–'91, xviii, p. 143, however, he reaffirms his belief in a neolithic " Ibero-Pictish " population.

† Sergi, 1895 a, pp. 78–84, discusses this. *Cf.* the map in his appendix ; as also A. J. Evans, 1896.

Even the average of five feet six inches and over in Wales and southwest England is not low; for this is greater than any on the continent south of the Alps. Broadly viewed, the facts

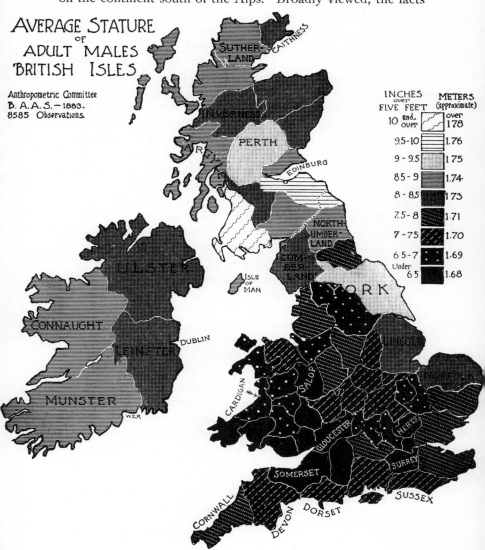

AVERAGE STATURE
of
ADULT MALES
BRITISH ISLES

Anthropometric Committee
B. A. A. S. — 1883.
8585 Observations.

INCHES over FIVE FEET | METERS (approximate)
10 and over | over 1.78
9.5 - 10 | 1.76
9 - 9.5 | 1.75
8.5 - 9 | 1.74
8 - 8.5 | 1.73
7.5 - 8 | 1.71
7 - 7.5 | 1.70
6.5 - 7 | 1.69
Under 6.5 | 1.68

in England alone seem to fit our hypothesis.   Here we observe the eastern counties relatively tall, with a steady decrease as we pass westward, culminating in southern Wales.*   The ancient Silures or their modern descendants are still relatively short, with an average stature but an inch or so greater than the long-barrow men of the stone age.†   For England, then, the maps of brunetness and of average stature agree remarkably well.   Our portraits of Welsh types clearly express the combination of brunetness with a size rather below the average.   Even the curious dark spot north of London, which we have already identified as an ancient British outcrop, appears clearly upon our map as a region of abnormally short population, particularly in Hertfordshire.   It seems to be nearly severed from the western short populations by an intermediate and seemingly intrusive zone of taller men.‡   As a rule, coast populations all over England are taller than inland ones. Even Ireland does not seriously embarrass our hypothesis of a primitive dark and short population.   The eastern half, to be sure, is shorter on this particular map than the western; but a variation of half an inch is not very much, and we know that the Irish are much more homogeneous than the English or Scotch in colour of hair and eyes.   The western half ought certainly to be shorter to fit our hypothesis exactly, for we know that the people are darker-complexioned.   Perhaps, indeed, it is in reality; for the Anthropometric Committee confesses that its observations for Ireland are " too few to be relied upon."

The distribution of stature in Scotland is the real stumbling-block in the way of entire consistency in an anthropological analysis of Britain.#   The physical traits seem to cross one another at right angles.   Inverness and Argyleshire, as brunet as any part of the British Isles, equalling even the Welsh in this trait, are relatively well toward the top in

---

* Pembrokeshire in Wales is of peculiar interest.   Consult Laws, 1888.
† *Vide* Beddoe, 1889, on this.
‡ Anthropometric Committee, 1883, p. 14.
# Read Lubbock, 1887, and Bryce for an indication of the differences of opinion concerning Scotch origins.

respect of stature. This is all the more remarkable since this mountainous and infertile region might normally be expected to exert a depressing influence. To class these Scotchmen, therefore, in the same Iberian or neolithic substratum with the Welsh and Irish is manifestly impossible. Tacitus was possibly right when he asserted that the Caledonians were Germans. The counties of southwestern Scotland, where stature culminates for all Europe, are also fairly dark. Only two explanations seem possible: Either some ethnic element, of which no pure trace remains, served to increase the stature of the western Highlanders without at the same time conducing to blondness; or else some local influences of natural selection or environment are responsible for it. Men with black hair are indeed shorter in many places, but the averages shown on our map belie any general law in that direction. We have no time to discuss the phenomenon further in this place. As Dr. Beddoe acknowledges, the difficulty is certainly a grave one. At all events, a profound contrast in respect of stature between this and the Welsh branch of the Celtic-speaking peoples is certain. The only comforting circumstance is that we find even within the same language some indication of a very early division of the Gael from the Brython. On the whole the Gaelic branch, the Irish and Scotch, seem to agree in stature, and to contrast alike with the Brythonic branch of the Welsh and Cornish. It is permissible to suppose that the absence of contact implied by these ancient linguistic differences, might allow of a separate modification of the Scottish wing to the end we have observed.

The phenomena of stature distribution are in general paralleled by the data concerning weight.* Taking averages by counties, the variations for adult males run from one hundred and eighty pounds in the vicinity of Edinburgh and in Argyleshire to a minimum forty pounds less than this in southwest England and Leinster in Ireland. The Welsh and southern English are of medium weight, from one hundred and fifty-five to one hundred and sixty pounds. The Teutonized eastern

* *Vide* Map 2 in the Report of the Anthropometric Committee for 1883. Dr. Beddoe's Stature and Bulk, 1867, is the standard authority.

counties, Lincoln, Norfolk, Suffolk, and the Anglian Scotch border counties are somewhat heavier. On the whole, the Scotch exceed the English by at least ten pounds, and the Irish by as much more. This is the normal relation. Tall people are generally heavy by reason of their stature. Whenever it is otherwise we are led to suspect some disturbing influence. The difficulty is that in the matter of weight environment is so predominant a factor that the characteristic is of little value in our ethnographic inquiry. An abundance of good food will speedily raise an Irishman from his normal class into that of the naturally heavy Scotchman, and *vice versa*. There is consequently little to claim our attention further respecting this trait. It is merely corroborative of the evidence of stature.

Enough portraits have now been presented to admit of a few hasty generalizations concerning the facial features peculiar to Britain. To be sure, all sorts of difficulties beset us at once. It is unfair to compare different ages, for example. The youthful countenance is less scarred by time. Nor, again, is it just to draw comparisons from different stations in life. In the same race the exposed farm labourer will differ from the well-fed and groomed country gentleman. Strongly marked racial differences between social classes exist all over the islands. The aristocracy everywhere tends toward the blond and tall type, as we should expect. We may, however, draw a few inferences from the data at our disposal, which seem to be well grounded in fact.*

The most characteristic facial feature of the old British populations, be they Scotch, Irish, Welsh, " old black breed," or bronze age, as compared with the Anglo-Saxon, is irregularity and ruggedness. The mouth is large, the upper lip broad, the cheek bones prominent. In the bronze-age type, as we have seen, the nose is large and prominent. In most of the other earlier types it is oftener merely broad at the nostrils, sometimes snubbed, as in our younger black-breed Shetlander

---

* On this Harrison, 1882 and 1883, is best in accurate description of facial types. *Vide* also Mackintosh, 1866 ; MacLean, 1866 and 1890 ; Davis and Thurnam, 1865, p. 206 *et seq.* ; and in the appendix to Beddoe, 1885.

133.   INISHMAAN, Ireland.   Index 82.3.   134.

135.   IRISH TYPES.   136.

137.   NEOLITHIC, Devon.   SCANDINAVIAN TYPE.   138.
Small dark type.   Hebrides.

at page 302; not often very delicately formed. Perhaps we may best classify them under what Bishop Whately, in his Notes on Noses, terms the "anti-cogitative" type.* Most peculiar and persistent of all in these old British faces, however, is the "overhanging pent-house brows," so noticeable in the Gael.† The eyes are deep-set beneath brow ridges in which the bony prominence is strikingly developed. This endows the face oftentimes with a certain ruggedness and strength which is gratifying to the eye. In the Scotch also, according to MacLean, other peculiarities of the face are the straightness of the brows, seen in our Nos. 128, 131, and 132 especially, as well as the great length of the lower jaw. The three main physical types in Scotland are well represented by our portraits at page 324. The upper pair, rawboned and red-headed, is familiar enough, as also the equally tall, heavily built but dark type illustrated in our Moray and Inverness subjects. The middle pair, the little dark men, are representative of probably the oldest element of all in Scotland. This corresponds closely to the Silures of Wales, or the small, dark Firbolgs west of the Shannon in Ireland. The curly hair, shown in both our examples, is, I am informed by Dr. Beddoe, very common among men of this type.

Nothing could be more convincing to the student of physiognomy than the contrast between many of these faces which we have just described, and those of the typical Anglo-Saxons at page 308. Of course by reason of their blondness, often really florid, and the portliness of their figures, we immediately recognise them as Teutonic. With equal certainty may we point to the smooth regularity of their faces, noticeably the absence of the heavy, bony, brow ridges. The face is smooth, almost soft in its regularity. No. 115 is, I am informed by Dr. Beddoe, "an extremely good typical specimen; he abounds in Yorkshire." Nos. 117 and 118 are characteristic of the

---

* Mackintosh, 1886, p. 14.

† Cf. Barnard Davis, 1867, p. 70, cited by Beddoe, 1870: "The most distinctive features of the western Irish are seen to be derived from the strongly marked superciliary ridges, extending across the nose, making a horizontal line, upon which the eyebrows are placed and overhanging the eyes and face."

British squire. The two young men represent the Englishman rather of the upper class. In many of these cases the finer mould of the features makes us suspect that they are not so much a matter of racial as of social or aristocratic selection, which is so constantly operative in these respects.

One more facial type needs to be mentioned. It is commonest in Kent and in the Isle of Wight. It is generally ascribed to a Jutish ancestry.* Our two upper portraits at page 316 represent this adequately enough. These people are darkish in complexion. The principal peculiarity is their convexity of profile from chin to forehead. The lips are rather thick; the nose is difficult to describe, unless we can agree to call it Jewish. Whether we may, indeed, accept it as Jutish, for we are accustomed to regard the Jutes as near relatives of the Anglo-Saxons, is matter of question. It is certainly a noticeable type in the south and east of England, where Jutish settlements were common.

A by no means negligible factor in the discussion as to the ethnic origin of the most primitive stratum of the populations of the British Isles is temperament. To treat of disposition thus as a racial characteristic is indeed to trench upon dangerous ground. Nevertheless, remembering how potent environment, social or material, may readily become in such matters, even the most superficial observer can not fail to notice the profound contrast which exists between the temperament of the Celtic-speaking and the Teutonic strains in these islands. These present almost the extremes of human development in such matters. They come to expression in every phase of religion or politics; they can no more mix than water and oil. The Irish and Welsh are as different from the stolid Englishman as indeed the Italian differs from the Swede.† Far be it from us to beg the question by implying necessarily any identity of origin by this comparison; yet we can not fail to call attention to these facts. There is some deep-founded reason for the utter irreconcilability of the Teu-

---

* Harrison, 1883..

† Read Frances Power Cobbe, The Celt of Wales and the Celt of Ireland, Cornhill Magazine, xxxvi, 1877, pp. 661–678.

tons and the so-called Celts. Our most staid and respectable
commentators, the authors of the Crania Britannica, never
weary of calling attention to it. Imagine an Englishman—
choosing one of their many examples of Celtic characteristics
—describing the emotional tumult of a marriage celebration in
Cornwall by declaring that he " had never see sic a wedding
before, it was just like a vuneral "!

The Welsh disposition or temperament is less familiar to
us in America than the Irish; it is the exact counterpart of
it. The keynote of this disposition lies in emotion. As vehe-
ment in speech as the Alpine Celt in Switzerland, France, or
Germany is taciturn; as buoyant and lively in spirits as the
Teutonic Englishman is reserved; the feelings rise quickly
to expression, giving the power of eloquence or its degenerate prototype loquacity. This mental type is keen in perception, not eminent for reasoning qualities; " a quick genius,"
as Matthew Arnold puts it, " checkmated for want of strenu-
ousness or else patience." As easily depressed as elated, this
temperament often leads, as Barnard Davis says, to " a tumult
followed by a state of collapse." Apt to fall into difficulty by
reason of impetuousness, it is readily extricated through quick
resourcefulness. In decision, leaning to the side of sentiment
rather than reason, " always ready," in the words of Henri
Martin, " to react against the despotism of fact." Compare
such an emotional constitution with the heavy-minded, lum-
bering but substantial English type. The Teutonic character
is perhaps most strongly expressed in the Yorkshireman; I
may quote Dr. Beddoe's words in this connection. It includes " the shrewdness, the truthfulness without candour, the
perseverance, energy, and industry of the lowland Scotch, but
little of their frugality, or of the theological instinct common
to the Welsh and Scotch, or of the imaginative genius or more
brilliant qualities which light up the Scottish character. The
sound judgment, the spirit of fair play, the love of comfort,
order, and cleanliness, and the fondness for heavy feeding, are
shared with the Saxon Englishman; but some of them are
still more strongly marked in the Yorkshireman, as is also
the bluff independence—a very fine quality when it does not

degenerate into selfish rudeness." Bearing all these traits in mind, one realizes the possible " clashing of a quick perception with a Germanic instinct for going steadily along close to the ground." Ascribe it all to a difference of diet, if you please, as the late Mr. Buckle might have done; derive the emotional temperament from potatoes, and the stolid one from beef; or invent any other excuse you please, the contrast is a real one. It points vaguely in the direction of a Mediterranean blend in the Welsh and Irish, even to a lesser degree in the Highland Scotch. More we dare not affirm.

CHAPTER XIII.

RUSSIA AND THE SLAVS.*

ON the east, the west, and the north, the boundaries of the Russian Empire are drawn with finality. Its territory ends where the land ends. The quarter of this empire which is comprised in Europe is defined with equal clearness on three sides and a half. Only along the line of contact with western Europe is debatable territory to be found. Even here a natural frontier runs for a long way on the crest of the Carpathian Mountains. To be sure, Galicia, for the moment, owes political allegiance to Austria-Hungary; but the Ruthenians, who constitute the major part of her population, are nowise distinguishable from the Russians, as we shall soon see. This leaves merely the two extremes of the Baltic-Black Sea frontier in question. The indefiniteness of the southern end of this line, from the Carpathians down, is one cause of that Russian itch for the control of the Bosporus which no number of international conventions can assuage. The Danube could never form a real boundary; a great river like that is rather a uni-

---

* To a number of eminent anthropologists I am especially indebted for assistance in the collection of original Slavic materials used as the basis of this chapter. Among these should be especially mentioned with grateful recognition of their invaluable aid : Prof. D. N. Anutschin, president of the Society of Friends of Natural Science, Ethnology, and Anthropology in the Imperial University at Moscow ; Prof. A. Taranetzki, of the Imperial Military Medical Academy, president of the Anthropological Society at St. Petersburg ; Prof. Lubor Niederle, of Prague ; Dr. Adam Zakrewski, chief of the Statistical Bureau at Warsaw ; Dr. Talko-Hryncewicz, now in Transbaikal, Siberia ; Dr. Wl. Olechnowicz, of Lublin ; Dr. H. Matiegka, of Prague ; and Prof. N. N. Kharuzin, of St. Petersburg. In the translation of the Slavic monographs I have been aided by Robert Sprague Hall, Esq., of the Suffolk bar, and Dr. Leo Wiener, of Harvard University.

fying factor in the life of nations than otherwise. Hence the
great problems of the Balkan Peninsula. From the Carpathians north to the Baltic Sea, likewise, no geographical line
of demarcation can be traced with surety. No water shed
worthy of the name between the Dnieper and Vistula exists,
although the waters of the one run east and the other west
not far from the present boundary of Poland and Russia. The
former country possesses no sharply defined area of characterization. The State of Texas has as clear a topographical title
to independent political life. The partition of Poland was in
a measure a direct result of geographical circumstances; and
these have condemned this unhappy country, despite the devoted patriotism of her people, to a nondescript political existence in the future. By language the Poles are affiliated with
Russia, not Germany; but in religion they are Occidental
rather than Byzantine. Thus Poland stands to-day, padded
with millions of politically inert Jews, as a buffer between
Russia and Teutonism. It is a case not unlike that of Alsace-
Lorraine. In both instances the absolute inflexibility of physical environment as a factor in political life is exemplified.

From the Carpathian Mountains, where, as we have said,
Russia naturally begins, a vast plain stretches away north and
east to the Arctic Ocean and to the confines of Asia; an expanse of territory in Europe eleven times as large as France.*
It is not limited to Europe alone. Precisely the same formation, save for a slight interruption at the Ural Mountains,
extends on across Asia, clear to the Pacific Ocean. European
Russia, only one quarter the size of Siberia, is, however, the
only part of immediate interest to us here. Nowhere in all its
vast expanse is there an elevation worthy the name mountain.
Even the most rugged portion, the Valdäi Hills in southern
Novgorod, are barely one thousand feet high; they are more
like a table-land than a geological uplift. Across this bound-
less plain, the last part of Europe to emerge from the sea, slug-
gishly meander some of the longest rivers on the globe. Some
conception of the flatness of the country may be gained from

---

* Leroy-Beaulieu, 1881–'89, gives a superb description of the country.
Its simple geology is shown by map in Petermann, xli, 1895, No. 6.

the statement that the projected new canal to connect the Baltic and Black Seas can be made available for navigation by the largest vessels from end to end by the construction of only two locks.

Whatever its local character, be it great peat swamps or barren steppe, the impression of the country is ever the same. Monotony in immensity; an endless uniformity of geographical environment, hardly to be equalled in any country inhabited by European peoples. Thus is the geographical environment of the Russian people determined in its first important respect. Their territory offers no obstacle whatever to expansion in any direction; the great rivers, navigable for thousands of miles, are, in fact, a distinct invitation to such migrations. On the other hand, this plain surface and the great rivers offer the same advantages to the foreigner as to the native; there is a complete absence of those natural barriers behind which a people may seek shelter from the incursions of others. The only natural protection which the region offers is in its dense forests and swamps. These, however, unlike mountains, offer no variety of conditions or natural products; they afford no stimulation to advance in culture; they retard civilization in the act of protecting it; they are better fitted to afford refuge to an exiled people than to encourage progress in a nascent one.

The second factor in determining a geographical area of characterization is its relative fertility. As we have observed before, this invites or discourages the movement of populations, in armies or in peaceful migration, just as much as the configuration of the surface makes this an easy or difficult matter. Judged by this second criterion, the territory of European Russia varies considerably. Leroy-Beaulieu divides it into three strips from north to south. The half lying north of a line from Kiev to Kazan (see map facing page 348), constituting the forest zone, is light soiled; it varies from heavy forest on the southern edge to the stunted growth of the arctic plains. South of the forest belt—south of a line, that is, from Kiev to Kazan—lies the prairie country. This is the flattest of all; over a territory several times the size of France, a hill of three hundred and fifty feet elevation is unknown. This prairie or woodless strip is of surpassing fertility—the so-called Black Mould belt, just south of the forests, rivalling the basin of the Mississippi in its natural richness of soil. From this the country gradually becomes less and less fertile with the decreasing rainfall, as we go south. This brings us at last to the third region, that of the barren steppes, or saline deserts, which centre about the Caspian Sea. These are found also less extensively north of the Crimean Peninsula, as far west as the lower Dnieper. Their major part lies south and east of the Don River. As Leroy-Beaulieu observes, the real boundary between Europe and Asia, viewed not cartographically but in respect of culture and anthropology, lies not at the Ural River and Mountains at all, where most of our geographies place it. Sedentary, civilized, racial Europe, roughly speaking, ends at a line, shown on our map, up the Don from its mouth to the knee of the Volga, thence up the latter and away to the northeast. This brings us to Asia, with its terrific extremes of continental climate, with its barren steppes, its slit-eyed Mongols, and its nomadic and imperfect culture.

Over this great territory population is very unevenly scattered. It conforms strictly in its density to the possibilities for support offered by the environment. The forest zone, with its thin soil and long winters, is well-nigh saturated with a population of fifteen to the square mile. Across the Black Mould strip population rises to a respectable European figure of sixty or even sometimes seventy-five to the square mile. An area about twice the size of France offers every advantage for the pursuit of agriculture. From this it falls to the figure of about two to the mile in the great Caspian depression, once the bed of an inland sea. The great aggregation of population is, of course, about the historic centres, Moscow and Kiev. The latter is the expression of matchless advantages of soil and climate, while Moscow is rather the centre of an industrial population. Its commercial advantages are no less marked, lying as it does just between the head waters of the western rivers and the great water way to Kazan and the east down the course of the Volga. Novgorod, former centre of

Russian civilization when fugitive in the forests of the north, at the time of the Mongol invasions, now is of little relative importance; and St. Petersburg, surrounded by Finnic swamps, is of course merely the artificial creation of an absolute monarch. With great rapidity the population is retracing its steps in this century, expanding toward the east and south. It is moving away from Europe. The marshes and swamps which lie all along the Baltic Sea and the German frontier offer no inducement in that direction. Western Russia is indeed but scantily populated for the same reason. This fact, together with the intermission of Poland, has isolated the Russians as a people. A population about twice that of the United States has been left to evolve its individuality in complete separation from the rest of Europe. From the Carpathians to the Ural chain on the east, and to the Caucasus on the south, this vigorous branch of the European races has expanded. It surely lags behind the rest of Europe in culture, as it has always done. But the fate of the Slav, lying on the outskirts of cultural or little Europe, has always been to bear the brunt of the barbarian Asiatic onslaughts. Such a task of guarding the " marches " of Europe, has not been borne without leaving a distinct impress upon the entire civilization of the country. The task before us is to inquire as to the original physical nature of this great nation; and then to investigate as to whether effects, analogous to those upon culture, have been produced by the peculiar geographical location and experience of Russia in the past.

A word must be said, before we proceed to the physical anthropology of Russia, as to the languages which are spoken there. The true Russians form about one half the population of the European portion of the country; the rest are Letto-Lithuanians, of whom we shall speak in a moment, Poles, Jews, Finns, and Mongols, with a sprinkling of Germans. The true Russians are divided into three groups of very unequal size.* These are said to differ not only in language,

---

* Rittich, 1878 b, has mapped their distribution in minute detail. His final work of 1885 is a model of cartographical completeness. Talko-Hryncewicz, 1893 and 1894, gives detailed maps of linguistic boundaries also. Velytchko, 1897, is the most recent.

27

but in temperament as well. About fifty of the seventy-odd millions of them, known as Great Russians, occupy the entire centre, north, and east of the country. These are the " Muscovites," their historic centre being in the ancient capital city of Moscow. Next in numbers come the people of Little Russia, or Ukraine, who, as our maps designate, inhabit the governments of the southwest, up against Galicia. They in turn centre politically in Kiev, covering a wedge-shaped territory, with its point lying to the east in Kharkov and Voronesh. The Cossacks, who extend down around the Sea of Azof into the Kuban, are linguistically Little Russians also. The third group, known as the White Russians, only four million souls in number, is found in the four governments shown on our map, extending from Poland up and around Lithuania. The White Russian territory is flat, swampy, and heavily forested, in strong contrast to the fertile, open Black Mould belt of Little Russia. In topography and in the meagreness of its soil, White Russia is akin to the sandy Baltic provinces from Lithuania north. Linguistically, the White and Great Russians are closely allied; the dialect of the Little Russians is considerably differentiated from them both. This is probably due to the Tatar invasions from the east across middle Russia. In face of these the Great Russians withdrew toward Moscow; the White Russians took refuge in their inhospitable swamps and forests; while the population of the Ukraine was left to itself at the south. We shall not attempt to discuss the question as to which of these represents the purest Russian. Bearing in mind the constant migration of the Great Russians across Mongolian and Finnic territory, and the inviting character of the Ukraine; one is disposed at once to adjudge with Leroy-Beaulieu that, of the three tribes, the White Russian in his forests and swamps, far removed from Oriental barbarian influences, " is certainly the one whose blood is purest." Whether this is borne out by purely anthropological testimony we shall see later.

Entirely distinct from the Slavs in language is the Letto-Lithuanian people, which, to the number of three million or more, occupies the territory between the White Russians and the Baltic Sea extending down into northern Prussia.* Their speech, in the comparative isolation of this inhospitable region —an isolation which made them the last people in Europe to accept Christianity—is the most archaic member of the great Aryan or inflectional family. Standing between Slavic and Teutonic, it is more primitive than either. Three tribes or peoples of them coexist here: Letts, Jmouds or Samogitians, and Lithuanians proper, as shown on our map. Contact with the Finnic-speaking peoples north of them—Esths, Livs, Tchouds, and Vods—has modified the purity of the Lettic speech considerably.† These Finns, in turn, speak a language like that of the Magyars in Hungary, and the Basques, which is not European at all. It is similar in structure to the primitive languages of Asia and of the aborigines of America. It represents a transitional stage of linguistic evolution, through which the Aryan family has probably passed in earlier times. But the language of the Letto-Lithuanians, while primitive in many respects, bears no relation structurally to the Finnic; it is as properly Aryan as the speech of the Slavs.

The perfect monotony and uniformity of environment of the Russian people is most clearly expressed anthropologically in their head form. Our results are shown graphically, it is believed for the first time, by the accompanying map of cephalic index.‡ Bearing in mind that the Poles and Letto-Lithua-

---

* Müschner and Virchow, 1891, have studied these Prussians.

† The Livonian speech is now extinct. Stieda, Correspondenzblatt, 1878, p. 126, states that in 1846 only twenty-two people still spoke it.

‡ Our data for this map may be found mainly in the original and excellent compilation of Niederle, 1896 a, pp. 54–57. Additional material of great value, especially from unpublished sources, is given in Deniker, 1897 and 1898 a ; while his announced work, *in extenso* (1898 b), promises to give the most notable results. It will be a contribution unsurpassed in comprehensiveness. We had, prior to the knowledge of these, independently collected data from the original sources, published in L'Anthropologie, vii, 1896, pp. 513–525 ; but these later authorities agree so perfectly with our own observations, that reference to them is sufficient. We can only add certain unpublished data on the Magyars from Dr. Janko, of Buda-Pesth ; Talko-Hryncewicz's (1897) recent observations in Podolia ; Vorob'ef on the population of Riazan ; N. N. Kharuzin on Esth-

nians along the Baltic Sea are not Russians properly, and excluding, of course, the Tatars of the Crimea, a moment's consideration of our map shows at once a great similarity of head form prevailing all over Europe from the Carpathian Mountains east and north. The cephalic index oscillates but two or three points about a centre of 82. This is about the head form of the northwestern French; appreciably broader, that is to say, than the standard for the Anglo-Saxon peoples. In places the breadth of head in Russia increases, especially among the Polesians isolated in the marshes of Pinsk and along the swamps of the Pripet River. These people are supposed to be infused with Polish blood, which may account for it,* as the southeastern Poles are known to be quite brachycephalic. At other times, as in southern Smolensk, the index falls to 80.† Our widest range of variation in Russia is about five units. Compare this with our former results

---

land, 1894, etc. In addition, in all that concerns Bohemia and its vicinity, we have had the benefit through the courtesy of Dr. Matiegka, of Prague, of unpublished maps, for comparison with our own.

On the whole, owing especially to the zeal of the younger school of Slavic anthropologists—by which we mean those who work from simple measurements on a large number of people rather than detailed descriptions of a few skulls in the laboratory—during the last five years, the main facts are perfectly well established. It remains to settle many points of detail, especially among the Hungarians and southern Slavs, but it is not likely that serious modification of the scheme will be necessary in Russia, at all events. Anutchin, Zograf, Talko-Hryncewicz, and their fellows have laid a solid foundation for future investigators.

* Talko-Hryncewicz, 1894, p. 159, on the anomalous position of the Polesians. Rittich, 1878 b, divides them dialectically between White and Little Russians. Talko-Hryncewicz, 1893, p. 133, and 1894, p. 172, gives his observations on head form. The seriation points to a strong brachycephaly.

The student of Slavic ethnology should carefully distinguish these Polesians from a number of other peoples of similar name. Thus there are also, besides the true Poles, the Podolians in the south Russian government of that name; the Podlachians, inhabiting a small district in the government of Grodno on the Polish frontier; and, finally, the Podhalians in the Carpathian Mountains. These last are best described by Lebon, 1881.

† Deniker asserts an index of 80.8 in southern Volhynia and of 86 in southern Kiev; but I am unable to confirm it by adequate data.

139.   VLADIMIR GOVERNMENT.   Cephalic Index 84.2.   140.

141.   VLADIMIR GOVERNMENT.   Cephalic Index 82.   142.

143.   VLADIMIR GOVERNMENT.   Cephalic Index 85.7.   144.

GREAT RUSSIAN TYPES.

for western Europe. In France, less than half the size of this portion of the Russian territory covered by our map, the cephalic index runs from 78 to 88. In Germany the limits are about the same; while in Italy, only one eighteenth the size of European Russia, the head form changes from an index of 75 in Sardinia to one of 89 in the Alps of Piedmont. These are almost the extremes of long- and broad-headedness presented by the human species; the Russian type is about midway between the two.

One cause of this unparalleled extension of a uniform type, measured by the proportions of the head—a variability, notwithstanding the size of the country, only about one third of that in the restricted countries of western Europe—is not far to seek. It lies in the monotony of the Russian territory, which we have emphasized above. Once more are we confronted with an example of the close relation which exists between man and the soil on which he lives. A variety of human types is the natural accompaniment of diversity in physical environment. Intermixture and comparative purity of race may coexist side by side. Switzerland and the Tyrol offer us violent contrasts of this sort. Russia, devoid of all obstacles in the way of fusion, presents a great mean or average type, about halfway between the two limits of variation of which the European races elsewhere can boast. But pass beyond the foothills of the Caucasus, and behold the change! A Babel of languages—no less than sixty-eight dialects, in fact—and half as many physical types, of all complexions, all head forms, and all sizes. Truly it seems to be a law that mountains are generators of physical individuality, while the plains are fatal to it.

The population of Russia is not alone made up of Russians. In a preceding paragraph we have expressly excluded the population of the Baltic provinces. For the Letto-Lithuanians are not Slavs, as we have already observed, and of course the Finnic peoples, Esths, Tchouds, and Vods, are still more distinct. Our map at once brings the peculiar head form of these groups into strong relief. All along the frontier of Germany, and away up to Finland, a strong tendency to long-headedness is manifested. This contrast is exemplified in our portraits distributed through this chapter. A narrow head generally is accompanied by a rather long and narrow face; our Mongol types, with their very round bullet heads, are characteristically broad and squarish-faced. This is partially due to the prominence of the cheek bones. It is this latter characteristic of our American aborigines which gives them their peculiar Mongol aspect. I have observed the very broad face to be one of the most persistent traits in the cross-breeds. Dr. Boas has proved it statistically. Even a trace of Indian blood will often cause this peculiarity. Now, the Russians express their relative broad-headedness, as compared with the Letto-Lithuanians, in the relatively squarish form of their faces.* Our portraits make this difference apparent at once.

The head form and facial proportions of the purest of the Letto-Lithuanians, it will be observed, approximate quite closely to our Anglo-Saxon model. The Russians impress the English traveller as being quite squarish-faced and heavy-featured for this reason. The British Isles, as we have shown, manifest a cephalic index of about 78. This is, as one would expect, the type of the primitive Anglo-Saxons. It appears all through northern and western Germany. Its main centre of dispersion is in the Scandinavian Peninsula, just across the narrow inland sea. The query at once suggests itself as to the origin of this similar long-headedness on the Baltic coast in Russia. If the eastern Prussians have been proved to be Slavonized Teutons in type, why not assume with equal surety that the western Poles are Slavs, Teutonized away from their original characteristics? Action and reaction in anthropology, as in physics, must always be equal and opposite in effect. Only thus can we account for the increased long-headedness in parts of Poland. And if it be Teutonic influence in this province, where shall we draw the line as we follow

---

* Talko-Hryncewicz, 1893, p. 169. Majer and Kopernicki, 1885, p. 59, show the round broad face of the Poles in Galicia, as compared with the Ruthenians. The Carpathian mountaineers seem to be anomalously long-faced. (Kopernicki, 1889, p. 49; and Lebon, 1881, p. 233.)

up the Baltic coast, over one language after another? Is there
a Teutonic cross in the Lithuanians? If so, why not in Letts
as well? And how about Esths and Tchouds? We shall see.

South and west of the Carpathian Mountains a second great
division of the Slavs exists. This includes the Poles, Czechs,
Slovaks, Moravians; and—divided from them by the intrusive
Magyars, who speak a Finnic language—the Slovenes, Serbo-
Croatians, and Bosnians in the south. This *congeries* of scattered Slavic nationalities seem to be, for some reason, politically adrift in Europe.* The Bulgars and Roumanians belong
to a still different class. For the former, while Slavic in
speech, is quite distinct in physical derivation; and the Roumanians, in origin probably allied to the Slavs, speak a corrupted Romance language. Matters are indeed becoming
mixed as we approach the Balkan Peninsula. This entire
group of southwestern Slavs is characterized by a very prevalent broad-headedness, much more marked than among the
Russians, as Weisbach has been proving for twenty-five years.†
Their brachycephaly is directly conjoined to that of the Alpine
highlands in the Tyrol, where we pass beyond the limits of
Slavdom, and enter the territory once occupied by the Celts.
Our map of head form points to a general broad-headedness
over all the present Austro-Hungarian Empire, from which a
spur seems to extend over into Little Russia, becoming lost in
an expanse of longer-headedness in the plains beyond. All the
mountainous regions are still characterized by brachycephaly;
it is a repetition of the law which holds good all over western
Europe. This brachycephaly is tempered only in those districts like Austria, where we know both from language and
history that the Teutonic influence has been strong. Other
physical traits will corroborate this deduction shortly. Yet
these Austrian Germans are to-day only distantly related to
the blond Scandinavian Germans along the Baltic. They resemble the Bavarians and Swabians, who are, as we know, a
cross between the blond Teutonic race and a thick-set, broad-
headed Alpine one. Leaving aside for the moment the long-

---

* *Cf.* page 411, *supra.*

† Our Bibliography gives a complete list of all his papers.

headed strip on the Black Sea, which will demand special consideration, we can not resist the final inference that all this part of Europe, now inhabited by the southern Slavs, is fundamentally Alpine in racial type; although eroded in places by Teutonic influences from the north, and disturbed by the volcanic irruption of the Finnic Magyars and the Turkish Bulgarians.

The word Russian is undoubtedly derived from a root meaning red. Our adjective rufous, and the name Ruthenian, applied to the inhabitants of Galicia, bear the same signification. The name is aptly applied: for the Russians, wherever found, are characterized by a distinct tendency toward what we would term a reddish blondness. Yantchuk, in the government of Minsk, in White Russia, found almost half his peasants to have hair of this shade.* It is not a real red. It might be called either a light chestnut, a dark flaxen, or an auburn tint. This shade of hair, combined with what Talko-Hryncewicz terms a " beer-coloured " eye, is the centre from which variation up or down occurs. This range of variation is very considerable. It seems to conform to the general law for all Europe, to which we have already called attention in our chapter on the subject. Brunetness increases regularly from north to south. In Russia the population also manifests a distinct tendency toward darker hair and eyes from west to east. The Baltic Sea is the centre of distribution for blondness, here as in Germany. The relations are well illustrated by the following table; statistics offer merely a scientific confirmation of the facts of common observation.

Percentage of types (hair, eyes, and skin combined).	476. Letto-Lithuanians.	961. White Russians.	252. Podolians.	2,610. Little Russians.	188. Ruthenian mountaineers.	22,682. Great Russians.
Blond..............	67	57	55	33	28	40
Mixed	28	31	29	46	32	40
Brunet	5	11	18	20	40	20

These figures show that the Letto-Lithuanians are the lightest people in the group. They are characterized most

---

* 1890 b, col. 69.

145. LITHUANIAN. 146.

147. WEST COAST FINN. Index 78. 148.

149. Index 84. WEST COAST FINNS. Index 75.2. 150.

FINNO–TEUTONIC TYPES (BLONDS).

frequently by a blue eye, and light hair which rivals the Swedish and Norwegian in its purity.* Two thirds of these Baltic peoples appear as pure blonds. The Poles are nearly as light, apparently. Majer and Kopernicki,† in fact, found more blond types among adults even than Virchow did among his German school children; and this, too, despite the fact that the blondness of the latter would surely decrease with growth. Next to the Poles and Letto-Lithuanians come the White Russians and the people of Podolia (see map facing page 340), with still a majority of blond types. The Great Russians are somewhat darker, but even they are appreciably lighter in complexion than the Little Russians in the southern governments. The latter—the Ukrainians—are still blue or lightish in eye, but betray a strong predisposition for dark-brown hair. This latter is here as common as the light brown.‡ The " beer-coloured " eye, in most frequent combination with really dark hair, brings us to the culmination of brunetness among the Galicians in the Carpathian Mountains. These Gorali, as our table indicates, in contrast with the Letto-Lithuanians, show the clear brunet at last outweighing the blond. The name " black Russians," applied to these mountaineers to distinguish them from the Ruthenians, or " red Russians," of the plains of Galicia, appears to be deserved. They seem to con-

---

* Talko-Hryncewicz is the only observer who has consistently applied a uniform system of observation to various localities. This table, arranged from his works of 1893, p. 112 ; 1894, p. 168 ; and 1897, p. 279, presents the best summary of his conclusions. He has covered Lithuania, White and Little Russia ; adding results from Majer and Kopernicki, 1877, p. 112, and 1885, p. 43, and Kopernicki, 1889, as to the Ruthenians and Poles in Galicia. We add, although not strictly comparable, Zograf's (1892 a, p. 165) results on the Great Russians. More definite comparisons, yielding, however, entirely parallel results, may be drawn from the colour of the hair alone. Thus we may include the Poles and even the southern Slavs as far as Bulgaria. To the tables in Talko-Hryncewicz's papers may then be directly added Weisbach's observations over a large field. Niederle, 1896 a, pp. 60 et seq., has done this most satisfactorily.

† 1877, pp. 90 and 112, and 1885, p. 34. Elkind's results (1896, col. 261) also show a marked blondness along the Vistula, though not quite so pronounced as in Galicia. Cf. also Schimmer, 1884, p. ix.

‡ Tschubinsky, 1878, p. 364, confirms these results.

tain twice as many clear brunet types as the Ukrainians, who
are in Russia accounted dark. Lebon ('81) has proved that
the Podhalians in these mountains are a local variety, being
considerably lighter. He found nearly one third of them
blond, while seventy per cent of them had light eyes. Elkind * found one third of the Poles along the Vistula to have
blue eyes and dark-red hair. The light type is less frequent,
however, than in Galicia, as Talko-Hryncewicz † proved. Beneath all these variations, however, underlies the rufous, or
rather auburn, tendency of which we have spoken. It distinguishes the Russian blondness from that of all other Europeans. We shall seek a cause for it when we come to consider the Finns and other pre-Slavic inhabitants of the country.

In this connection we can not resist calling attention to
the bearing of this testimony upon Poesche's ('78) celebrated
theory that the original centre of dispersion of the blond
Aryans (?) lay in the great Rokitno swamps about Pinsk and
along the Pripet in White Russia. We have seen that these
people are indeed blond. Mainof ‡ it was whose testimony to
this effect gave Poesche his cue. Since we have proved how
much less blond these White Russians are than their neighbours toward the Baltic, it would seem as if we had effectually
disposed of Poesche's theory at the same time.

In stature the Russians are of medium height, but they
betray the same susceptibility to the influences of environment
as other Europeans. Our map herewith illustrates this clearly.
This investigation of upward of two million recruits, by the
eminent anthropologist Anutchin, shows a considerable variation according to the fertility of the country. Thus in the
northern half, above Moscow and Kazan, the adult males are
two inches shorter than in the Ukraine about Kiev, which lies
in the heart of the Black Mould belt. The difference between
White and Little Russians is due to the same cause. Other
influences besides physical environment are, however, at work,
beyond question. This is especially the case in Poland. This
unhappy country is the adopted fatherland of millions of Jews.

---

* 1896, col. 261.   † 1890, p. 29.
‡ Cong. int. des sciences géographiques, Paris, 1878, p. 269.

STATURE
RUSSIA.

2.017 000
OBSERVATIONS.

AFTER
ANUTCH

BALTIC SEA

F

TA

ST. PETER

PRUSSIA

POLAND

CRACOW

GALICIA

	5 FT. 6.1 INS	
(dotted)		1.68 M
(wavy)		1.67
(horizontal lines)		1.66
(light)		1.65
(grey)		1.64
(black)		1.63
(diagonal)		1.61-2
	5 FT. 3.4 INS	

BL

There are almost more here than in all the rest of Europe put together. These Jews are one of the most stunted peoples in Europe. In how far this is the result of centuries of oppression, and in what degree it is an inherent ethnic trait, we need not stop to consider. It is an indisputably proved fact. The presence of this horde of Jews, often outnumbering the native Poles especially in the towns, is largely accountable for the short stature shown by our map. This does not exonerate the Poles by any means from the charge of relative diminutiveness.* The degree in which they are surpassed by their Slavic neighbours on the other side is shown by our map on page 350. Comparisons are facilitated by the uniformity of tints upon the two maps. Yet even here in Austria-Hungary the shortness of the Poles and Ruthenians, which together form the population of Galicia, may be partly attributable to the large contingent of Jews.

The clearest example of stature as an unmitigated ethnic trait, hereditary and persistent, is shown in the eastern half of Austria-Hungary (map on next page). Notice the lightness of shading among all the Germans (Deutsche) in Austria, in the Tyrol, and in the northwestern corner of Bohemia (Böhmen). These are just the districts where Teutonic infiltration from the north has been historically proved since early times. We have already mentioned it in our study of the head form. The German-speaking Austrians, then, are by nature and not by acquisition, an inch or two taller than many of the Slavic peoples subject to their political domination. It is the same phenomenon already so familiar to us in the case of the relatively gigantic Burgundian peasantry in France to-day; in the tallness of the people of Lombardy; and, above all, in the Teutonized eastern half of the British Isles. This latter example comes directly home to us, because we in America owe a large measure of our surpassing stature to the same ethnic cause. Never has a physical trait shown so surprising a persistency as in the height of these Teutonic peoples.

Just here a difficulty confronts us—one which no anthropologist has satisfactorily explained. Our second map shows

---

* Talko-Hryncewicz, 1895, p. 264. See our chapter on Jews.

a very tall population among the southern Slavs, the Slovenes, Serbo-Croatians, and Bosnians, contrasted with the short Poles, Ruthenians, and Slovaks in the northeast. This can not historically be traced to a Teutonic ancestry. Anthropologically it is even less probable, because these southern Slavs are all very dark in hair and eye, being in this respect as in head form the polar extreme from the Teutons of the north. A distinct subcentre of giantism, inexplicable but established

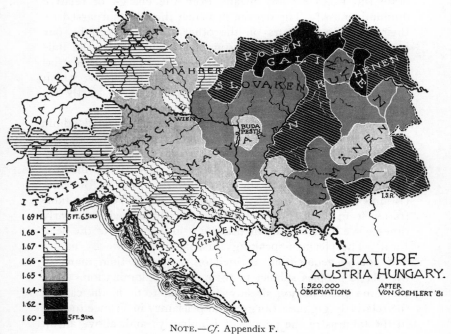

NOTE.—*Cf.* Appendix F.

beyond all doubt, exists just east of the Adriatic Sea. Its influence radiates through the Slovenes over into northeastern Italy. We find indication of it in the Rhætian parts of Switzerland. Deniker, in his recent classification of the anthropological types of Europe, carries it even further, under the definite name of the Adriatic or Dinaric race.* Who can affirm

* 1898 a, with map. We emphasized the same fact in our general stature map of Europe ; see page 97 *supra.*

that the tallness of the Tyrolese, who in their mountainous habitat, despite the depressing influence of their environment, surpass the Swiss, the Bavarians, the Austrians, and the Italians, may not possibly be due to a double ethnic source? At just this point in the Tyrol the Teutonic wave of tall stature from the north and the Adriatic one from the south come together. Thus, an exception to the law that, other things equal, the populations of mountains are unfavourably affected in stature by their environment may possibly be explained.

Turning back to our map of stature in Russia, facing page 348, we observe a distinctly lighter shading—that is to say, a taller stature along the coast of the Baltic Sea. This is merged in the mediocre stature of the Great Russians, a little east of Novgorod. Although unfortunately our map does not give the data for Finland, we know that a similar superiority of stature extends all across this province. All the Finns in this part of Russia are very tall. G. Retzius [76], Bonsdorff,* Hjelt [72], Elisyeef [87], and all observers agree in this.† An average height not a whit less than that of the pure Scandinavians in Norway and Sweden is proved. It lessens toward the north in contact with the Lapps, most stunted of men, at an average of only five feet for adult males. It decreases on the east among the Karelian Finns, falling rapidly to the Russian average. Bear in mind that in no other part of northern Europe, save in Scandinavia just across the Baltic Sea, is an average stature anywhere near that of the Finns to be found; that a cross with the Swedes in consequence is inadequate as an explanation for this tallness; that wherever there is contact with the Slav—precisely as in Austria-Hungary, where, as we have seen, an ethnic trait ran up against Slavdom—the bodily height falls to mediocrity: and draw the only inference possible both from geography and physical anthropology. We shall deal with the philologists later.

Summarizing our results thus far, we find two physical

---

* Cited by Topinard, Éléments, p. 494.

† On the Esths, Grube, 1878 ; A. N. Kharuzin, 1894. Waldhauer, 1879, on the Livs ; Waeber, 1879, on the Letts. Kollmann, 1881–'83, gives a fine *résumé* of this work.

28

types more or less clearly coexisting in the Russian people,
and throughout all the Slavs, too, for that matter. One is tall,
blondish, and long-headed; the other is brachycephalic, darker-
complexioned, and of medium height. The relative proportions of each vary greatly from one region to another. Among
Lithuanians and Poles, the former is more noticeable; in the
Ukraine the other type becomes more frequent; the Great
Russians stand between the two; while among the southern
Slavs the blond, long-headed variety entirely disappears.*
Not only do the relative proportions of these component types
vary from one region to another. Distinct differences in the
several social strata of the same locality appear. The tall
dolichocephalic blonds are more characteristic of the upper
classes as a rule, so far as the matter has been examined.†
Our results for western Europe are entirely harmonious with
this tendency. And, thirdly, it is curious to note that the relative proportions of these two ethnic types have changed entirely since prehistoric times. This point is of so great significance that we must examine it a bit more in detail.

Nowhere else in Europe is the complete submergence of
an old race by an intrusive one more clear than in the Slavic
portion of Europe. Bogdanof, founder of Russian archæology, devoted his entire life to proof of this fact in his own
country.‡ The first indications of this submerged aboriginal
population were given by crania from tumuli, which are
scattered all over Russia from the Carpathians almost to the
Ural chain, and even beyond in Siberia. These *Kurgans*, so
called, are merely large mounds of earth from twenty to fifty
feet high, sometimes single, sometimes arranged in series for

---

* Zograf, 1892 a, p. 173, describes these.   Lebon, 1881, p. 233, finds the
same two types in Podhalia.

† Olechnowicz, 1893, 1895 a, and 1897, has obtained some highly interesting results among the *petite noblesse* in Poland.   Talko-Hryncewicz,
1897 b, confirms it.

‡ The facts yielded by his first investigation in 1867 have been confirmed by every observation since.   We are fortunate in that a complete
summary of his life work was given by himself at the International Congress of Anthropology at Moscow in 1892.   Titles of all his monographs
will be found in our Bibliography.

miles. They are not unlike the simpler relics of our own mound builders. The dead level of the country makes them in the open prairies often of great service to herdsmen in tending their flocks. These tumuli were found for the most part to date from the stone age; no implements or ornaments of metal were unearthed in them. The absence of weapons or utensils of war in them also denoted a peaceable folk.* The population must have been considerable, for these tumuli are simply innumerable. The men of this *Kurgan* period betrayed a notable homogeneity of type, even more uniform than that of the modern living population. The crania were almost invariably of a pure, long-headed variety; the cephalic indexes ranging as low as or lower than that of the purest living Teutonic peoples to-day. Remembering that the modern Russians are well up among the moderately broad-headed Europeans, it will be seen what this discovery implied. Nothing else was known save that this extinct people were very tall, considerably above the standard of the Russian mujik to-day, and it seemed as if their hair betrayed a tendency toward red.† The most obvious explanation, in view of the fact that Finnic place names occurred all over Russia, was that these tumuli were the remains of an extinct substratum of Finns, driven out or absorbed by the incoming Slavs. Their civilization, made known to us by Uvarof ('75), and more recently by Inostranzef ('82), was definitely connected with that of the Merian people, so called by the historians.‡

Soon a new and significant point began to be noted. While the range of this primitive long-headed people so different from the living Russians, was distinctly set on the north and east, no definite limits could be set to it toward the southwest. In the meanwhile Kopernicki and others, from 1875 on, began to find evidence of the same dolichocephalic stratum of popu-

---

* Kohn and Mehlis, 1879, ii, p. 111, compare them with the Reihengräber in this respect. *Cf.* Zaborowski, Bull. Soc. d'Anth., 1898, pp. 73–111.

† Niederle, 1896 a, p. 88. Minakoff, 1898, has investigated this more fully, asserting the reddish cast to be due to the degeneration of age.

‡ Bogdanof, 1893, p. 2, gives a full list of the authorities, Karamsine, Solovief, Beliaef, Hatzouk, etc.

lation, underlying all the Slavs in Podolia and Galicia.* Their track has been followed, entirely antedating the modern Slavs, down into Bohemia and Moravia, by Niederle † and Matiegka,‡ and as far as Bosnia; where, in the great discoveries at Glasinac,# the existence of this same aboriginal population was abundantly proved. On the west, Lissauer followed it across Prussia beyond the Vistula.|| Thus on every side it was traced to the limits of Slavdom, and found to underlie it throughout. The next step taken by the archæologists was to examine the graves of the early historic period. Bogdanof △ investigated the ancient cemeteries at Moscow and elsewhere, and found that the brachycephaly of the living Russians in its present form is even more recent than history. Thus, while in the *Kurgan* stone age three fourths of the skulls were dolichocephalic, in the Slav period from the ninth to the thirteenth century only one half of them were of this form, and in purely modern cemeteries the proportion was ten per cent less even than this. Added confirmation of this proof of the extreme recency of the Russian broad-headedness was almost the last service rendered to science by the late lamented Professor Zograf.◊ In Bohemia Matiegka has done the same, showing that even as late as the sixth to the twelfth centuries the Czechs were less extremely broad-headed than to-day.↯ Two explanations were suggested for this widespread phenomenon. Bogdanof and a few others asserted that civilization implied an increased broad-headedness, and that a morphological change had taken place in the same people; while the majority of anthropologists found in it proof of an entire change of race since

---

* Kohn and Mehlis, 1879, give a complete *résumé* of Kopernicki's results in an excellent work which seems to be little known. See especially vol. ii, pp. 108–110, 152, 153.

† 1891 a, 1894 a, p. 277, and best of all in his masterly work of 1896 a, pp. 67–75, where he gives data for all Slavic countries in detail. His paper in French, at the Moscow Congress of 1892, gives a mere outline of the results obtained. Palliardi, 1894, deals with Moravia also.

‡ 1892 b and 1894 a.

Weisbach, 1895 a, p. 206; 1897 b, p. 575; also L'Anth., v, p. 567.

|| 1874–'78.   △ 1879 b, and 1880 g.

◊ 1896, p. 52.   ↯ 1891, pp. 133, 134.

the earliest times.* The first explanation, even granting that the brachycephalic races as a rule are endowed with a greater cranial capacity than the long-headed ones, could hardly be accorded a warm reception in any of the Anglo-Saxon countries like our own. To relegate long-headedness to an inferior cultural position would result not only in damning the entire Teutonic race, but that one also which produced the early Semitic, Greek, and Roman civilizations. No explanation for the recency of broad-headedness in the Slavic countries is, then, tenable for a moment, save that the brachycephalic contingent is a newcomer in the land.

Which of these two elements in the population, which have contended so long for mastery among the people of this part of Europe, represents the primitive Slavic type? It is a delicate matter, by no means free from national prejudice. The Germans have always looked down upon their eastern neighbours, by reason of their backwardness in culture. Our ignoble word "slave," originally signifying the illustrious or renowned, is a product of this disdain in Europe of the Slav.† To find the primitive Slavic type, therefore, in that variety, which accords so completely with our pattern of the Teutonic race, is as disheartening to the Germans as for the Slavs themselves; it runs counter to their distrust of modern aggressive Teutonism. Even science is not free to violate the provisions of the Triple Alliance with impunity.

The most generally accepted theory among anthropologists as to the physical relationship of the Slavs, is that they were always, as the majority of them are to-day, of the same stock as the broad-headed Alpine (Celtic) race. This latter occupies, as we have seen, all the central part of western Europe. It predominates among the north Italians, the French in Auvergne and Savoy, and the Swiss. It prevails in the Tyrol and all across southern Germany, in Alsace-Lorraine, Würtemberg, and Bavaria. The French anthropologists, especially Topinard, have emphasized the direct similarity in head

---

* *Vide* p. 40 *supra.*

† Consult Lefèvre, 1896 b, p. 351 ; Canon Taylor, Words and Places, p. 303, and Leroy-Beaulieu, 1893–'96, i, p. 97, on this.

form which exists between all these people and the Slavs. The name Celto-Slavic has been applied to broad-headed race by virtue of this fact.*　It was a logical deduction from the first discovery of broad-headedness among the Slavs by A. Retzius [43], von Baer [60], and Weisbach [64]. The main objection to it came from the philologists, who found the Slavic languages much nearer the Teutonic than the Celtic branch.†　This Celto-Slavic theory, affirmed by the French anthropologists mainly on the ground of similarity of head form, is generally sustained by the Germans on the basis of their investigations of relative brunetness among school children.　The Germans have consistently maintained the existence of a radical difference of origin between themselves and the Slavs.　The Slavic portions of Germany, such as Mecklenburg, Posen, and Brandenburg, as we have shown in an earlier chapter, are certainly darker in the colour of hair and eyes than the purely Teutonic ones, like Hanover and Schleswig-Holstein.　Schimmer ‡ has especially called attention to the contrast in Bohemia.　The Czechs and the Germans have always kept distinct from one another.　The relative brunetness of the former is very marked.　Children of Czech parentage betray about twice the tendency to brunetness of hair and eyes of the pupils in the purely German schools.　The Poles are almost the lightest of all the Slavs.　Their contrast with the Czechs in Austria-Hungary is also very marked.　Yet even they, blondest of the Slavs, are in Posen and Silesia, as Virchow's [86b] maps prove, relatively much darker than the Prussians.

Another trait which many of the German anthropologists, notably Kollmann [82b], hold to be Slavic, is the gray or greenish-gray eye, in contradistinction to the light blue of the pure

---

* Sergi, 1898 a, chapter vi, has perhaps best expressed and proved this relationship.　Hovelacque and Hervé, 1887, p. 564, assert that no Slavic type really exists in fact.

† Krek, 1887, is the leading authority.　Niederle, 1896 a, pp. 13 to 32, gives a fine review of all the linguistic data.　Schrader, 1890, p. 56, outlines all these theories.　Bopp, Zeuss, Grimm, Fick, and Schleicher all insist upon the affinity of the Slav and the Teuton.

‡ 1884, pp. 16 and 19.

Teuton or the distinct brown and black of southern Europe. This colour, so frequent among the Russians, is very common all through the Alpine highlands.* It corroborates the testimony of the head form as to the affinity of the Alpine (Celtic) type and the Slav; unless we agree with Kollmann and Virchow that this grayness of eye is merely the result of a cross between the blond and brunet varieties.† In this sense it is merely a neutral or intermediate characteristic. At all events, even denying validity to the witness of the gray eye, plenty of evidence remains to show that the modern Slavic population of eastern Europe is, in the same latitude, more inclined to brunetness than the Teuton. The presence among the Russian people themselves of a medium-statured, dark-complexioned, and broad-headed majority is acknowledged by all. That this represents the original Slavic stock is certainly the most logical direct inference. It is the opinion—tacitly at least —accepted by most of the English writers.‡ Direct evidence as to the former coloration of the Slavs is very scanty. The testimony of the old travellers like Ibrahim ibn Jacub as to the black hair and beards of the Czechs, contrasted with the Saxons, adduced by Dr. Beddoe* in favour of a dark Slavic origin, is contested by Niederle.‖ No such unanimity of testimony as is found from Tacitus, Martial, and a host of other Latin writers as to the blondness of the Teutons can be adduced. On the whole, the chroniclers leave the matter as unsettled as ever. The only reliable testimony is that of the living populations of Slavic speech.

The native anthropologists are divided in theory as to the type of their Slavic ancestors. No one pretends to question the facts in the case; the divergence of opinion is merely as to which stratum of population, which region, or which social class of the two we have described, is entitled to claim the honoured title. Thus Anutchin,ᴬ Taranetzki,◊ Talko-Hrynce-

---

* Studer, 1880, p. 70.

† Ranke, Der Mensch., ii, p. 253 ; also p. 267. *Cf*. Rhamm in Globus, lxxi, No. 20.

‡ Beddoe, 1893, p. 110, and Taylor, 1890, p. 104.   # 1893, p. 70.

‖ 1896 a, pp. 80–87, giving much historical testimony.

ᴬ 1893, pp. 279–281.   ◊ 1884, pp. 63–65.

wicz,[*] Olechnowicz,[†] Kopernicki,[‡] Píc,[#] Ikof,[||] and Yantchuk [△] identify the modern broad-headed population as a Slavic invader of originally Finnic territory; while Bogdanof,[◊] Zograf,[⸘] and especially Niederle,[⸘] represent the claims of the extinct *Kurgan* people to the honoured name of Slav. Leroy-Beaulieu seems to represent a popular tendency in favour of this latter view.[⸘] For our own part, we rather incline to agree with Matiegka that it is a question which the craniologists are not competent to settle.[**] That the Alpine (Celtic) racial type of western Europe is the best claimant for the honour seems to us to be the most logical inference, especially in the light of studies of the living aborigines of Russia, to which we must now turn.

Three ethnic elements are generally recognised as component parts of the Russian people—the Slav, the Finn, and the Mongol-Tatar. The last two lie linguistically outside the family of related peoples which we call Aryans, the only other non-Aryan language in Europe being the Basque.[††] In any classification according to physical characteristics, we must, however, set aside all the evidences of language as untrustworthy. To admit them as a basis of classification would involve us at once in inextricable confusion.[‡‡] These tribes have

---

* 1893, p. 171.   † 1893, p. 37; 1895, p. 70.

‡ Kohn and Mehlis, vol. ii, pp. 114, 153, and 164. In his 1869, p. 629, he asserts the Ruthenians to be nearest the original Slavic type.

Athenæum, Prague, viii, p. 193. || 1890, col. 103.

△ 1890 a, col. 202.   ◊ 1893, pp. 10 and 13.

⸘ 1896, p. 63.

⸘ 1891 a, 1892 a, and especially in his positively brilliant 1896 a, pp. 50 *et seq.* Consult his answer to criticisms, 1891 b, and in Globus, vol. lxxi, No. 24 also. His bibliography of the subject is superb.

⸘ 1893–'96, vol. i, pp. 96 and 108.   ** 1891, p. 152.

†† Consult Chapter VIII.

‡‡ The errors of such a classification are well exemplified in Leroy-Beaulieu's otherwise excellent work, in which his aborigines are utterly confused in relationship. Rittich in all his work, and Keane, 1886, as well as in his Ethnology, 1896, pp. 303 *et seq.*, are equally at sea. Since the days of Nilsson and Prichard, the philologists have befogged the questions of physical descent. Niederle, 1896 a, in his appendix upon the subject, seems to be very confused. *Cf.* Topinard, 1878, p. 465.

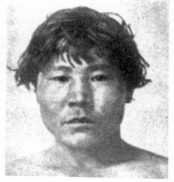
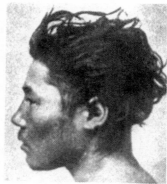

151.   SAMOYED.   Cephalic Index 86.8.   152.

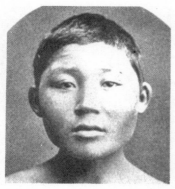
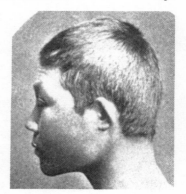

153.   KIRGHEZ, Horde of Bukee.   154.

155.   Cephalic Index 86.   KALMUCKS.   Cephalic Index 79.   156.

MONGOL TYPES.

all been more or less nomadic for ages in this great plain country; they have taken on and put off customs, language, and religion time and again, according to circumstances. The latter characteristic, religion, in fact, affords us a far better standard for ethnic classification than language; since the Finns have persisted in Christianity, the Turks and Tatars have held to Mohammedanism, and the Mongols proper to Buddhism, with a remarkable constancy. The varying proportions of barbarism in each group are well illustrated by this fact. For in race, as in religion, the Finns are truly indigenous to western Europe, the Tatar-Turks are Oriental, while the Mongols proper are Asiatic.

The evils incident to any linguistic classification of the aborigines in Russia are best illustrated by a comparison of the Lapps with the Livs, Esths, and Tchouds of the Baltic provinces; both groups alike speak Finnic languages; the philologists, therefore, from Castrén to Mikkola, class them as alike members of a Finnic " race," along with the Magyars or Hungarians, who are also Finnic in speech. Nothing could be more absurd than to assert a community of physical origin for the three. The Magyars, among the finest representatives of a west European type, are no more like the Lapps than the Australian bushmen; and the Baltic Finns are equally distinct. The Lapps, as our portraits at page 208 illustrate, are among the broadest-headed of men.[*] Their squat faces show it. In stature they are among the shortest of the human species. Virchow's[†] celebrated hypothesis that they are a " pathological race " seems excusable on this ground. Their hair and eyes are very dark brown, often black. Could any type of human beings be further removed from this than the Finns described to us by G. Retzius, Bonsdorff, Elisyeef, or Mainof? These latter Finns are among the tallest of men, with fair skin, flaxen or tow-coloured hair, and blue eyes. Turn to our map at page 362. It shows us among the Esths on the Baltic coast, through the Cheremiss on the Volga, and clear beyond

---

[*] Sommier, 1886 ; Kelsief, 1886 ; N. N. Kharuzin, 1890; Garson, 1886 a, and others have studied them in detail.

[†] 1875, a and b.

the Ural Mountains among Ostiäks and Voguls in Siberia, a long-headedness not a whit less pronounced than throughout Teutonic Germany. The contrast of tints on our map corresponds to a radical contrast of physical type.

The same utter confusion of racial—that is to say, of somatological—relations, incident to a linguistic division of the Finns, appears at once in any like attempt to classify the Turkish-speaking branch of the Asiatic peoples. For the Chouvaches, just across the Volga from the Cheremiss,* not in any important respect to be distinguished from them physically, as our map shows, have by chance adopted the language and religion of the neighbouring Tatars. It is as absurd to class them with the latter as Turks by race, as to jumble the broad-headed and brunet Samoyeds, who are quite like the Lapps, with the Zyrians just south of them; † or to confuse the Tatars as a class with the Kirghez. Comparison of our portraits of each will manifest this at once. The Tatars of the Crimea—whether, as the historians assert, because of early Gothic influence or otherwise—are in many cases entirely European. To class them as Mongols because being closely massed, somewhat isolated, and possessed of glorious traditions from the past, they have preserved their Asiatic speech, is a travesty upon science.

Turning to the Russian aborigines, then, with an eye single to their purely physical characteristics, we may relegate them to two groups, sharply distinguished in isolation, but intermixed along their lines of contact. Our map of cephalic index facing page 362 will roughly make the division clear. Our several pages of portraits (portraits, pp. 346 and 364) will strengthen the contrast. The first group is distinctly longheaded, with an index as low as 79 or 80, among the Livs, Esths, Cheremiss, Chouvaches, and Vogul-Ostiaks in Siberia.

---

* Nikolski, 1897.

† Keane calls the Samoyeds Finns, Ethnology, p. 305. To be sure they speak Finnic, but are really Mongols. Mainof is clearest, perhaps, in classing them as "black Finns." On the Samoyeds consult Szombathy in Mitt. Anth. Ges., Wien, xvi, pp. 25–34, and Virchow, Verh. Anth. Ges., ix, 1879, pp. 330–346.

These are all more or less clearly blond, with a distinctly rufous tendency, even among the extreme eastern tribes of Voguls and Ostiaks.* Sometimes, as among the Votiaks, whom Dr. Beddoe † inclines to identify with the Budini of the Greeks because of their red hair, we find this trait very marked, especially in the beard. It seems to be somewhat less pronounced along the Baltic, where the Livs, Esths, and Tchouds shade off imperceptibly into the pure blond Letto-Lithuanians. Here we discover the source of that peculiar reddish blondness of the modern Russians of which we have spoken, for a widespread admixture of blood in the Slav from this stock is recognised by all. In this first type we recognise the Finn, using the linguistic term guardedly, with the express reservation that not every tribe of Finnic speech is of this racial ancestry. These are the tall people who in the Eddas are called Jötuns, or giants. The word Tchoud applied by the Slavs to the Finns also means a giant.‡ Mythology confirms our anthropological deductions.

Our second physical type of the Russian aborigines is the polar extreme from this long-headed, red-blond one. We may follow it on our map by the black tints, indicating a prevalent broad-headedness. This is best exemplified at the two extremes of Russia, in the Lapp at the northwest and the Kalmuck and Kirghez hordes of the Caspian steppes. The Samoyeds are merely a continuation of the Lapp type toward Asia along the arctic.# These people correspond closely to what we popularly regard as Mongolian. They are all dark or black haired, with swarthy skins; they are peculiarly beardless (portraits, pp. 358 and 208). With the round face, bullet head, high cheek bones, squint eyes, and lank hair, they constitute

---

* Sommier, 1887, p. 104; 1888. The Ostiaks and Voguls are, according to Anutchin, 1893, the original Voguls, who were settled in Perm a few centuries ago. Their emigration across the Urals is of comparatively recent date. *Cf.* also Vámbéry, 1885, p. 62; and Zaborowski, Bull. Soc. d'Anth., 1898, pp. 73–111.

† 1893, p. 42. *Cf.* Topinard, Anthropology, p. 465.

‡ Taylor, 1888, p. 249.

Zograf's work on the Samoyeds is summarized in Revue d'Anth., série 2, iv, p. 296; Bogdanof's at ibid., p. 117.

an unmistakable type.* We may provisionally call it Mongol for want of a better word, but it must not be confused with the Turk or Tatar, which is nothing of the sort. Many of these people speak Finnic languages, so that in a sense it is still proper to class them as Finns. If so, they should be distinguished from the other variety. Mainof does this best by classing the two as " light " and " black " Finns respectively. This second group is not characterized by any peculiarity of stature, as the Finns seem to possess. From Yavorski's data † we note an extreme variability in this trait in both Mongols and Finns. The western Finns show a strong tendency to a very tall stature; the pure Mongols are also rather above medium height; but many of both stocks are exceedingly degenerate in this respect. The Lapps and Samoyeds could not but be stunted by their environment; ‡ and even the Ostiaks, Permiaks, Votiaks, and Cheremiss, driven from the valleys where alone the Russians can win a subsistence, to the sterile uplands on the upper river courses, have certainly been starved into relative diminutiveness. It is along the line of these tribes just named, and above all among the Bashkirs,# that we discover a variety of mongrels, compounded of Finn and Mongol, with a strong infusion of Tatar through the whole. Kazan, at the elbow of the Volga, is truly a meeting place of the tribes. The intermingling of strains of blood, of religions, customs, and of linguistic stocks may be observed here at a maximum. Especially among the Mordvins, widely disseminated in little groups, not aggregated in solid communities, as among Cheremiss or Chouvaches, has the infusion of Tatar traits taken place. An interesting fact in this ethnic intermixture is the extreme insidiousness of the Mongolian features. This is a fertile source of confusion of the Finn and the Asiatic tribes. Many long-headed, red-

---

* On the Kalmucks and Mongols, consult Ivanovski, 1893 and 1896; Metchnikoff, 1878; Schendrikovski, 1894; Deniker, 1883; Chantre, 1885–'87, iv, p. 250; and also Hovelacque, Études de Linguistique, 1878, pp. 271 et seq.

† 1897, p. 196.

‡ Yavorski, p. 196; N. N. Kharuzin, 1890 a, p. 155.

Weissenberg, 1892; Sommier, 1881; Nazarof, 1890.

SWEDEN

L A

BALTIC SEA

LIVS

RIGA

CHU

ESTI

TA

WRE

LITH
UANI

KOVNO

•VILNA

VISTULA
RIVER

GRODNO

MIN

FINN

POLAND

RU

•WARSAW

I

CRACOW

R

**CEPHALIC
INDEX**

PODOLI

LONG HEADS

	78
	79
	80
	81
	82
	83
	84
	85
	86·7

BESSARABIA

BROAD HEADS

H
FINN

blonds, as among the Ostiaks and Zyrians, who are surely Finnic at bottom, superficially resemble the Mongols in cast of countenance. Perhaps our dolichocephalic Kalmuck, depicted at page 358, is of some such mixed origin. His features are ultra-Mongolic. His head form is quite foreign to that racial type.* In the case of the Basques, we have explained how unreliable these facial features are as a test of physical descent; for, being distinctive and noticeable, they are immediately subject to the disturbing influences of artificial selection. They may thus wander far from their original type, becoming part of the local ideal of physical beauty prevalent among a primitive people. Only in this way can we explain the almond eyes, flat noses, and high cheek bones of tribes which by their blondness and head form betray unmistakably a Finnic descent. This combination of Mongol features and Finnic or dolichocephalic head form, occurs sporadically throughout western Asia, especially near the Himalayas, where the two extreme human types, both of face and head, are in close juxtaposition. Where intermixture has taken place, the resultant is often a curious blend between the Hindu and the Mongol.†

One objection to our ascription of the name Finn to a long-headed type is bound to arise. We must meet it squarely. If the Finns are of this stock, why is all Finland relatively so broad-headed as our map (facing page 362) makes it appear? Here is the largest single aggregation of Finnic-speaking people; ought we not to judge of the original type from their characteristics in this region? By no means, for Finland is the

---

* Cf. portraits of Ostiaks in Jour. Anth. Inst., 1894–'95. Talko-Hryncewicz, 1893, p. 171, remarks upon the effect of a Mongol cross to broaden the face, as among the Permiaks, Votiaks, and Esths. Bogdanof, 1893, p. 10, remarks upon this broad face of even the Kurgans of early times in eastern Russia. Cf. Beddoe, 1893, p. 40 ; Niederle, 1896 a, p. 147 ; Keane, 1896, p. 306.

† Cf. Ujfalvy, Les Aryens, etc., 1896, pp. 398–408, on the interpretation of cephalic index among Mongol peoples. His curious thesis that the Mongols are originally dolichocephalic, because such head forms, as among the Ladakis, are often conjoined with Mongolic facial traits, seems without foundation.

refuge of a great body of aborigines driven forth from Great
Russia by the advent of the Slavs, just as also all along the isolated peninsulas of the Baltic and in the Valdai Hills north of
Tver. But in Finland, in contradistinction to these other places
of refuge, the Finns were crowded in together against the
Lapps. Especially in the north we see clear evidence of intermixture. The Russian Lapps are very much less broad-headed
than their pure Scandinavian fellows, by reason of such a cross.*
Can we deny, contrariwise, that a similar rise of index in the
case of the Finns must have ensued for the same reason? The
Karels, further removed from the Lapps, are somewhat longer-
headed; the Baltic Finns, being quite free from their influence,
are much more so. Moreover, all along the southwest coast
of Finland the heads are much longer. Observations upon
twenty-eight Finns in the lumber camps of Wisconsin by my
friend Mr. David L. Wing, yielded an average index of only
78.9, while thirty-nine Swedes were two units lower. Granting that the infusion of Swedish blood all along this Baltic
coast must be reckoned as a factor, a distinct tendency to such
long-headedness among the Finns appears. Coupled with
the long-headedness of the Cheremiss, Vogul-Ostiaks, and
others, and especially the tendency of the mongrel Bashkirs
to dolichocephaly as we leave the Caspian Mongol influence
and approach the Ural Mountains, our affirmation of an original long-headedness of this type seems to be justified.

In assigning a relationship to these various peoples, let
us avoid the gratuitous assumption that because a people
speak a primitive type of language they are necessarily barbarians. Great injustice to an important constituent in the
Russian people will inevitably result. It may often happen
to be true; but in Russia, although both Finns and Tatars have
clung to a Ural-Altaic agglutinative language, they are not
all deficient in mentality. Nothing could be more contrary
to fact. Neither Basques nor Magyars are barbarians. The
Finnic languages, while a trifle clumsier perhaps, are powerful and rich in many respects. In culture also there are Finns

---

* Kelsief, 1886, and N. N. Kharuzin, 1890 a and b.

157.   Coast Tatars, Goursuf, Crimea.   158.

159.   Cheremiss, Volga Finn.   160.

161.   Mordvin, Volga.   162.

and Finns. To be sure, the whole eastern branch along the Volga and in Asia are truly aboriginal in civilization, as in the case of the Chouvaches and Votiaks. Expelled from all the lands worth cultivation, even as in the case of the Voguls and Ostiaks driven out of Europe altogether, it is a wonder that they are not less civilized than we find them. On the other hand, the Baltic Finns in their general standard of life, intellectually and morally, compare very favourably with the Russian " mujik." Helsingfors, capital of Finland, is one of the finest cities in Russia. Its university ranks high among those of Europe. Finnic scholars, poets, and musicians there have been of note. Once for all, then, let us fully disabuse ourselves of the notion that there is anything ignoble in a Finnish ancestry. Had Virchow and De Quatrefages fully done so, much of the acerbity in their celebrated controversy over the Finnic origin of the Prussians would have been avoided.*

If our original Finns are proved to be long-headed blonds, oftentimes very tall; if the Letto-Lithuanians, contrasted with the Russian Slavs, betray the same physical tendencies; if, just across the Baltic Sea, the main centre of this peculiar racial combination is surely located in Scandinavia; and, finally, if in every direction from the Baltic Sea, whether east across Russia or south into Germany, these traits vanish into the broader-headed, darker-complexioned, medium-statured, and stocky Alpine (Celtic?) type; how can we longer deny that Finns, Letto-Lithuanians, and Teutons are all offshoots from the same trunk? A direct physical relationship between the three, referring them all to a so-called Nordic race, is confirmed by the very latest and most competent authority; † and this in absolute independence of our own conclusions.

---

* *Cf.* page 219 *supra*.

† Consult Deniker's map of the races of Europe, 1898 a, reproduced in our Appendix D. Talko-Hryncewicz, 1893, p. 170, emphasizes the similarity of Letto-Lithuanians and Finns. Canon Taylor, 1888, in his brilliant revival of Diefenbach's (1861) theory of Aryan evolution from a blond Finnic ancestry, arrives at precisely the same conclusion. Kohn and Mehlis, vol. ii, pp. 108 and 153, acknowledged the similarity of Kopernicki's Kurgan people and the Teutonic Reihengräber; as does Bogdanof, 1893, pp. 19–21 also.

If it be established by further investigation, our theory goes far to simplify the entire problem of the physical anthropology of Europe. It is not a new idea. Diefenbach [61] and Europeaus [75] advanced it a generation ago on the basis of the then recent archæological discoveries of a long-headed, tall race in the tumuli of the stone age; although it never gained any acceptance at the time. A curious corollary of this theory is that De Quatrefages and Virchow, in their celebrated international controversy over the origin of the Prussians, were both partly in the right. Virchow resented the view of a Finnic origin of his people as an insult, because Lapps and Finns were then confused with one another, and he certainly was right in denying any affinity of Prussians with Lapps. De Quatrefages, in asserting that the Prussians were of Finnic ancestry, was equally in the right, if our theory be true; but he erred in supposing that this damned them as non-Teutonic. For us the Prussians, along with the Hanoverians and Scandinavians, are all at bottom Finnic. We would not stop here. We would agree absolutely with Europeaus in his further hypothesis—that these Finns of northern Europe are directly related with that primitive Mediterranean long-headed stock, sprung from the same root as the negro, which we have shown to underlie all the other races of Europe.* Its blondness is an acquired characteristic, due to the combined influences of climate and artificial or natural selection. From this centre in the north, invigorated by the conditions of its habitat, and speedily pressing upon the meagre subsistence afforded by Nature, this race has once again during the historic period retraced its steps far to the south, appearing among the other peoples of Europe as the politically dominant Teutonic race.†

The anthropological history of northeastern Europe is now clear. Leaving aside the question of the original centre of

---

* Cf. page 461 in this connection.

† See page 467 infra. This is in perfect accord with Sergi's most recent work in Centralblatt für Anthropologie, 1898, p. 2; and with Niederle's conclusions (1896 a, p. 131; and especially in Globus, vol. lxxi, No. 24). Cf. Taylor, 1888, criticised in Schrader and Jevons, 1890, p. 104.

dispersion of the Slavic languages, generally placed some-where along the upper Dnieper,* it would seem that the Slavs as a physical type penetrated Russia from the southwest, where they were physically an offshoot from the great Alpine race of central Europe. In so doing they forced a way in over a people primitive in culture, language, and physical type. This aboriginal substratum is represented to-day by the Finns, now scarcely to be found in purity, pushed aside into the nooks and corners by an intrusive people, possessed of a higher culture acquired in central Europe. Yet the Finn has not become extinct. His blood still flows in Russian veins, most notably in the Great and White Russian tribes. The former, in colonizing the great plain, has also been obliged to contend with the Asiatic barbarians pressing in from the east. Yet the impress of the Mongol-Tatar upon the physical type of the Great Russian, which constitutes the major part of the nation, has been relatively slight; for instead of amal-gamation or absorption as with the Finn, elimination, or what Leroy-Beaulieu calls "secretion," has taken place in the case of the Mongol hordes.† They still remain intact in the steppes about the Caspian; the Tatars are banished to the eastern governments as well, save for those in the Crimea. The Asi-atic influence has been perhaps more powerful in determining the Great Russian character than the physical type. A strug-gle for mastery of eastern Europe with the barbarians has made the great Russian more aggressive; vigour has to some degree developed at the expense of refinement. The result has been to generate a type well fitted to perform the arduous task of protecting the marches of Europe against barbarian onslaught, and at the same time capable of forcefully extend-ing European culture over the aborigines of Asia.

---

* Niederle, 1896 a, p. 77 ; Beddoe, 1893, p. 35.
† *Op. cit.*, i, pp. 71, 82, and 109.

CHAPTER XIV.

THE JEWS AND SEMITES.*

SOCIAL solidarity, the clearest expression of which to-day is nationality, is the resultant of a multitude of factors. Foremost among these stand unity of language, a common heritage of tradition and belief, and the permanent occupation of a definite territory. The first two are largely psychological in essence. The third, a material circumstance, is necessary rather to insure the stability of the others than for its own sake; although, as we know, attachment to the soil may in itself become a positive factor in patriotism. Two European peoples alone are there, which, although landless, have succeeded, notwithstanding, in a maintenance of their social consciousness, almost at the level of nationality. Both Gypsies and Jews are men without a country.† Of these, the latter offer perhaps the more remarkable example, for the Gypsies have never disbanded tribally. They still wander about eastern Europe and Asia Minor in organized bands, after the fashion of the nomad peoples of the East. The Jews, on the

---

* In the preparation of this article I have to acknowledge the courtesy of Mr. Joseph Jacobs, of London, whose works in this line are accepted as an authority. In its illustration I have derived invaluable assistance from Dr. S. Weissenberg, of Elizabethgrad, Russia, and Dr. L. Bertholon, of Tunis. Both of these gentlemen have loaned me a large number of original photographs of types from their respective countries. Dr. Bertholon has also taken several especially for use in this way. The more general works upon which we have relied are: R. Andree, Zur Volkskunde der Juden, Bielefeld, 1881; A. Leroy-Beaulieu, Les Juifs et l'Antisémitisme, Paris, 3e éd. 1893: and C. Lombroso, Gli Antisemitismo, Torino, 1894.

† Freeman, 1877 c, offers an interesting discussion of this. He adds the Parsees to this category of landless peoples.

other hand, have maintained their solidarity in all parts of the earth, even in individual isolation one from another. They wander not gregariously in tribes, often not even in families. Their seed is scattered like the plant spores of which the botanists tell us; which, driven by wind or sea, independently travel thousands of miles before striking root or becoming fecund. True, the Jews bunch wherever possible. This is often a necessity imposed for self-preservation; but in their enforced migrations their associations must change kaleidoscopically from place to place. Not all has been said even yet of the unique achievement of this landless people. That the Jews have preserved their individuality despite all mutations of environment goes without saying. They have done more. They have accomplished this without absolute unity of language. Forced of necessity to adopt the speech of their immediate neighbours, they have been able either to preserve or to evolve a distinctive speech only where congregated in large numbers. In Spain and the Balkan states they make use of Spanish; in Russia and Poland they speak a corrupt German; and in the interior of Morocco, Arabic. Nevertheless, despite these discouragements of every kind, they still constitute a distinctive social unit wherever they chance to be.

This social individuality of the Jews is of a peculiar sort. Bereft of linguistic and geographical support, it could not be political. The nineteenth century, says Anatole Leroy-Beaulieu, is the age of nationality; meaning obviously territorial nationality, the product of contiguity, not birth. To this, he says, the Jew is indifferent, typifying still the Oriental tribal idea. As a result he is out of harmony with his environment. An element of dislike of a political nature, on the part of the Christian is added to the irreconcilability of religious belief. It has ever been the Aryan *versus* the Semite in religion throughout all history, as Renan has observed; and to-day it has also become the people *versus* the nation, as well as the Jew *versus* the Christian. Granted that this political dissonance is largely the fault of the Gentile, its existence must be acknowledged, nevertheless.

How has this remarkable result been achieved? How, be-

reft of two out of three of the essentials of nationality, has the
Jew been enabled to perpetuate his social consciousness?   Is
the superior force of religion, perhaps abnormally developed,
alone able to account for it all?   Is it a case of compensatory
development, analogous in the body to a loss of eyesight reme-
died through greater delicacy of finger touch?   Or is there
some hidden, some unsuspected factor, which has contributed
to this result?   We have elsewhere shown that a fourth element of social solidarity is sometimes, though rarely, found
in a community of physical descent; that, in other words,
to the cementing bonds of speech, tradition, belief, and contiguity, is added the element of physical brotherhood—that
is to say, of race.   Can it be that herein is a partial explanation of the social individuality of the Jewish people?   It is
a question for the scientist alone.   Race, as we constantly
maintain despite the abuses of the word, really is to be measured only by physical characteristics.   The task before us is
to apply the criteria of anthropological science, therefore, to
the problems of Jewish derivation and descent.   Only incidentally and as matters of contributory interest, shall we consider the views of the linguists, the archæologists, and the
students of religious traditions.   Our testimony is derived from
those physical facts which alone are indicative of racial descent.
To these the geographer may add the probabilities derived from
present distribution in Europe.   No more do we need to settle
the primary racial facts.   Further speculations concerning matters rather than men belong to the historian and the philologist.

The number and geographical distribution of the chosen
people of Israel is of great significance in its bearing upon
the question of their origin.*   While, owing to their fluid

---

* Andree, 1881, pp. 194 *et seq.*, with tables appended ; Jacobs, 1886 a,
p. 24 ; and quite recently A. Leroy-Beaulieu, 1893, chapter i, are best on
this.   Tschubinsky, 1877, gives much detail at first hand on western
Russia.   In the Seventeenth Annual Report of the Anglo-Jewish Association, London, 1888, is a convenient census, together with a map of distribution for Europe.   On America, no official data of any kind exist.
The censuses have never attempted an enumeration of the Jews.   Schimmer's results from a census of 1880 in Austria-Hungary are given in
Statistische Monatsschrift, vii, pp. 489 *et seq.*

ubiquitousness, it is exceedingly difficult to enumerate them exactly, probability indicates that there are to-day, the world over, between eight and nine million Jews. Of these, six or seven million are inhabitants of Europe, the remainder being sparsely scattered over the whole earth, from one end to the other.

Their distribution in Europe, as our map opposite shows, is exceedingly uneven. Fully one half of these descendants of Jacob reside in Russia, there being four or five million Jews in that country alone. Austria-Hungary stands next in order, with two million-odd souls. After these two there is a wide gap. No other European country is comparable with them except it be Germany and Roumania with their six or seven hundred thousand each. The British Isles contain relatively few, possibly one hundred thousand, these being principally in London. They are very rare in Scotland and Ireland— only a thousand or fifteen hundred apiece. Holland contains also about a hundred thousand, half of them in the celebrated Ghetto at Amsterdam. Then follows France with eighty thousand more or less, and Italy with perhaps two thirds as many. From Scandinavia they have always been rigidly excluded; from Sweden till the beginning, and from Norway until nearly the middle, of this century. Spain, although we hear much of the Spanish Jew, contains practically no indigenous Israelites. It is estimated that there were once about a million there settled, but the persecutions of the fifteenth century drove them forth all over Europe, largely to the Balkan states and Africa. There are a good many along the Mediterranean shores of Africa, principally in Morocco and Tripoli. The number decreases as we approach Egypt and Palestine, the ancient centre of Jewish dispersion. As to America, it is estimated, although we know nothing certainly, that there are about half a million Jews scattered through our cities in the United States. New York city, according to the last census, contained about eighty thousand Poles and Russians, most of whom, it may be assumed, were Jews. But they have come since in ever-increasing numbers with the great exodus from Russia, at the rate of scores of thousands annually. A recent writer places their present number in New York city at a quarter of a million. The British provinces, on the other hand, do not seem to offer great attractions; as late as 1870, for example, the census in Nova Scotia did not discover a solitary Jew.

A more suggestive index of the problems of Jewish distribution is offered in the ratio of the number of Jews to the entire population. This is directly illustrated by our map. To be sure this represents the situation twenty years ago, but no great change in relativity is to be suspected since that time. Even the wholesale exodus from Russia of recent years, has not yet drawn off any large proportion of its vast body of population. Inspection of our map shows that the relative frequency of Jews increases in proportion to the progressive darkening of the tints. This brings out with startling clearness, the reason for the recent anti-Semitic uprising in both Russia, Austria, and the German Empire. A specific " centre of gravity " of the Jewish people, as Leroy-Beaulieu puts it, is at once indicated in western Russia. The highest proportion, fifteen per cent more or less, appears, moreover, to be entirely restricted to the Polish provinces, with the sole exception of the government of Grodno. About this core lies a second zone, including the other west Russian governments, as well as the province of Galicia in the Austro-Hungarian Empire. Germany, as it appears, is sharply divided from its eastern neighbours, all along the political frontier. Not even its former Polish territory, Posen, is to-day relatively thickly settled with Jews. Hostile legislation it is, beyond a doubt, which so rigidly holds back the Jew from immigration along this line. *Anti-Semitismus* is not to-day, therefore, to any great extent an uprising against an existing evil; rather does it appear to be a protest against a future possibility. Germany shudders at the dark and threatening cloud of population of the most ignorant and wretched description which overhangs her eastern frontier. Berlin must not, they say, be allowed to become a new Jerusalem for the horde of Russian exiles. That also is our American problem. This great Polish swamp of miserable human beings, terrific in its proportions, threatens to drain itself off into our country as

well, unless we restrict its ingress. As along the German frontier, so also toward the east, it is curious to note how rapidly the percentage of Jews decreases as we pass over into Great Russia. The governments of St. Petersburg, Novgorod, and Moscow have no greater Jewish contingent of population than has France or Italy; their Jewish problem is far less difficult than that of our own country is bound to be in the future. This clearly defined eastern boundary of *Juden-thum* is also the product of prohibitive legislation. The Jews are legally confined within certain provinces. A rigid law of settlement, intended to circumscribe their area of density closely, yields only to the persuasion of bribery. Not Russia, then, but southwestern Russia alone, is deeply concerned over the actual presence of this alien population. And it is the Jewish element in this small section of the country which constitutes such an industrial and social menace to the neighbouring empires of Germany and Austria. In the latter country the Jews seem to be increasing in numbers almost four times as rapidly as the native population.* The more elastic boundaries of Jewish density on the southeast, on the other hand, are indicative of the legislative tolerance which the Israelites there enjoy. Wherever the bars are lowered, there does this migratory human element at once expand.

The peculiar problems of Jewish distribution are only half realized until it is understood that, always and everywhere, the Israelites constitute pre-eminently the town populations.† They are not widely disseminated among the agricultural districts, but congregate in the commercial centres. It is an unalterable characteristic of this peculiar people. The Jew betrays an inherent dislike for violent manual or outdoor labour, as for physical exercise or exertion in any form. He prefers to live by brain, not brawn. Leroy-Beaulieu seems to consider this as an acquired characteristic due to mediæval prohibition of land ownership or to confinement within the Ghetto. To us it appears to be too constant a trait the world over, to

---

* Andree, *op. cit.*, p. 258.

† This is clearly shown by Schimmer in Statistische Monatsschrift, vii, pp. 489 *et seq.* See also Leroy-Beaulieu, i, p. 118 ; Andree, pp. 33 and 255.

justify such an hypothesis. Fully to appreciate, therefore, what
the Jewish question is in Polish Russia, we must always bear
this fact in mind. The result is that in many parts of Poland
the Jews form an actual majority of the population in the
towns. This is the danger for Germany also. Thus it is Berlin, not Prussia at large, which is threatened with an overload
of Jews from the country on the east. This aggregation in
urban centres becomes the more marked as the relative frequency for the whole country lessens. Thus in Saxony, which,
being industrial is not a favourite Jewish centre, four fifths
of all the Jewish residents are found in Dresden and Leipsic
alone.* This is probably also the reason for the lessened frequency of Jews all through the Alpine highlands, especially
in the Tyrol. These districts are so essentially agricultural
that few footholds for the Jew are to be found.

A small secondary centre of Jewish aggregation appears
upon our map to be manifested about Frankfort. It has a
peculiar significance. The Hebrew settlers in the Rhenish
cities date from the third century at least, having come there
over the early trade routes from the Mediterranean. Germany
being divided politically, and Russia interdicting them from
1110 A. D., a specific centre was established especially in Franconia, Frankfort being the focus of attraction. Then came
the fearful persecutions all over Europe, attendant upon the
religious fervour of the Crusades. The Polish kings, desiring
to encourage the growth of their city populations, offered
the rights of citizenship to all who would come, and an exodus in mass took place. They seem to have been welcomed,
till the proportions of the movement became so great as to
excite alarm. Its results appear upon our map. Thus we
know that many of the Jews of Poland came to Russia as a
troublesome legacy on the division of that kingdom. At the
end of the sixteenth century but three German cities remained open to them—namely, Frankfort, Worms, and Furth.†
Yet it was obviously impossible to uproot them entirely. To

---

* See also map in Kettler, 1880.

† J. C. Majer (1862, p. 355) ascribes the present shortness of stature in
Fürth and parts of Franconia to this Jewish influence.

their persistence in this part of Germany is probably due the small secondary centre of Jewish distribution, which we have mentioned, indicated by the darker tint about Frankfort, and including Alsace-Lorraine. Here is a relative frequency not even exceeded by Posen, although we generally conceive of this former Polish province as especially saturated with Jews. It is the only vestige remaining to indicate what was at one time the main focus of Jewish population in Europe. It affords us a striking example of what legislation may accomplish ethnically, when supplemented, or rather aggravated, by religious and economic motives.

Does it accord with geographical probability to derive our large dark area of present Jewish aggregation entirely from the small secondary one about Frankfort, which, as we have just said, is the relic of a mediæval centre of gravity? The question is a crucial one for the alleged purity of the Russian Jew; for the longer his migrations over the face of the map, the greater his chance of ethnic intermixture.

The original centre of Semitic origins linguistically has not yet been determined with any approach to certainty. The languages to be accounted for include Arabian, Hebrew, Syrian or Aramean, and the ancient Assyrian. Of these, the first is the only one now extant, spoken by the nomad Bedouins. Orientalists are not unanimous in their views.* Sayce, Schrader, and Sprenger say the family originated in central Arabia. Renan prefers a more northern focus. Guidi ('79), from comparison of the root words in its various members, traces it to Mesopotamia. Thus he finds a common root in all for " river," but various ones for " mountain." The original Semites, he also argues, must have dwelt near the sea, for a common root for this obtains. This would exclude Armenia. The absence of any common root for desert also eliminates Arabia, according to his view. But, on the other hand, how about Kremer's argument, based upon acquaintance with the camel, but not the ostrich? All this in any

---

* Guidi, 1879 ; Bertin, 1881 ; Goldstein, 1885, p. 650; Hommel, 1892 ; Schrader, 1890, p. 96 ; Brinton, 1890, p. 132 ; and Keane, 1896, p. 391, discuss it.

event, we observe, has to do with languages and not racial types. Few ancient remains have been found, owing to the widespread repugnance to embalming of the dead. The main problem for the somatologist is to have some clew as to whether the family is of Asiatic or African descent. So far as our data for living types are concerned, we get little comfort. Physical traits of the Arabs fully corroborate Brinton's and Jastrow's [90] hypothesis of African descent; but, on the other hand, many of the living Syrians of Semitic speech are, according to Chantre [95], as brachycephalic as the Armenians. This, as we shall see in our next chapter, would preclude such an African derivation. It seems most probable, in view of these facts, that the family of languages has spread since its origin over many widely variant racial groups. To identify the original one would be a difficult task.

A moot point among Jewish scholars is as to the extent of the exodus of their people from Germany into Poland. Bershadski has done much to show its real proportions in history. Talko-Hryncewicz * and Weissenberg † among anthropologists, seem to be inclined to derive this great body of Polish Jews from Palestine by way of the Rhone-Rhine-Frankfort route. They are, no doubt, partially in the right; but the mere geographer would rather be inclined to side with Jacques [91]. He doubts whether entirely artificial causes, even mediæval persecutions, would be quite competent for so large a contract. There is certainly some truth in Harkavy's theory, so ably championed by Ikof, that a goodly proportion of these Jews came into Poland by a direct route from the East.‡ Most Jewish scholars had placed their first appearance in southern and eastern Russia, coming around the Black Sea, as early as the eighth century. Ikof, however, finds them in the Caucasus and Armenia one or two centuries before Christ.# Then he follows them around, reaching Ruthenia in the tenth and eleventh centuries, arriving in Poland

---

　　* 1892.　　　　　　　　　　　　　　† 1895, p. 577.

　　‡ 1884, p. 383.　*Cf.* criticism by Talko-Hryncewicz, 1892, p. 61.

　　# On the Jews in the Caucasus, Seydlitz, 1881, p. 130 ; Chantre, 1885–'87, iv, p. 254.

from the twelfth to the fourteenth. The only difficulty with this theory is, of course, that it leaves the language of the Polish Jews out of consideration. This is, in both Poland and Galicia, a corrupted form of German, which in itself would seem to indicate a western origin. On the other hand, the probabilities, judging from our graphic representation, would certainly emphasize the theory of a more general eastern immigration directly from Palestine north of the Black and Caspian Seas. The only remaining mode of accounting for the large centre of gravity in Russia is to trace it to widespread conversions, as the historic one of the Khozars. Whichever one of these theories be correct—and there is probability of an equal division of truth among them all—enough has been said to lead us geographically to suspect the alleged purity of descent of the Ashkenazim Jew. Let us apply the tests of physical anthropology.

Stature.—A noted writer, speaking of the sons of Judah, observes: " It is the Ghetto which has produced the Jew and the Jewish race; the Jew is a creation of the European middle ages; he is the artificial product of hostile legislation." This statement is fully authenticated by a peculiarity of the Israelites which is everywhere noticeable. The European Jews are all undersized; not only this, they are more often absolutely stunted. In London they are about three inches shorter than the average for the city.* Whether they were always so, as in the days when the Book of Numbers (xiii, 33) described them " as grasshoppers in their own sight," as compared with the Amorites, sons of Anak, we leave an open question. We are certain, however, as to the modern Jew. He betrays a marked constancy in Europe at the bodily height of about five feet four inches (1.63 metres) for adult men. This, according to the data afforded by measurements of our recruits during the civil war, is about the average of American youth between the ages of fifteen and sixteen, who have still three, almost four, inches more to grow. In Bosnia, for example, where the natives range at about the American level—that

---

* Jacobs, 1890, p. 81.

is to say, among the very tallest in the world (1.73 metres)—
the Jews are nearly three inches and a half shorter on the
average.*   If we turn to northern Italy, where Lombroso ['94]
has recently investigated the matter, we apparently find the
Jew somewhat better favoured by comparison.   He is in
Turin less than an inch inferior to his Italian neighbours.

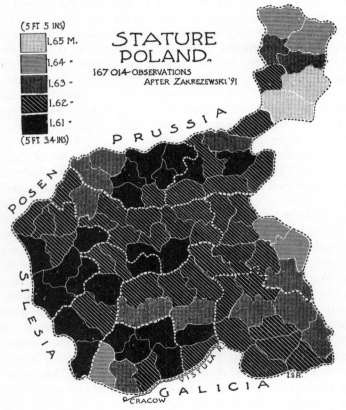

But why?   Not because taller than in the case of Bosnia, for
his stature in both places is the same.   The difference decreases, not because the Jew in Piedmont is taller, but solely
because the north Italians are only of modern height.   So it

---

goes all over Austria and Russia: the diminutiveness is plainly apparent.* There are in all Europe only two exceptions to the rule we have cited. Anutchin finds them in Odessa and Riga slightly to exceed the Christians, and Dr. Bertholon informs me that in Tunis the Jews are rather taller than the average. Everywhere else the testimony as to their shortness is unanimous. In order to emphasize this point it will repay us to consider the adopted fatherland of the chosen people a bit more in detail.

Our map on the opposite page shows the average stature of Poland by districts. This unhappy country appears to be populated by the shortest human beings north of the Alps; it is almost the most stunted in all Europe. The great majority of the districts, as our map shows, are characterized by a population whose adult men scarcely average five feet four inches (1.62 metres) in height. This is more than half a head shorter than the type of the British Isles or northern Germany. What is the meaning of this? Is it entirely the fault of the native Poles? We know that the northern Slavs are all merely mediocre in stature. But this depression is too serious to be accounted for in this way; and further analysis shows that the defect is largely due to the presence of the vast horde of Jews, whose physical peculiarity drags down the average for the entire population.† This has been proved directly. Perhaps the deepest pit in this great " misery spot," as we have termed such areas of dwarfed population elsewhere, is in the capital city of Warsaw, where Elkind found the average stature of two hundred male Jews to be less than five feet three inches and a half (1.61 metres).‡ The women were only four feet eleven inches tall on the average. Compare the little series of maps given on the next pages if further proof of this national peculiarity be needed. Two of these, it will be

---

* Majer and Kopernicki, 1877, p. 36, for Ruthenia ; Stieda, 1883 a, p. 70 ; Anutchin, 1889, p. 114 *et seq.*

† Zakrezewski, 1891, p. 38. *Cf.* map of Russia facing p. 348. It brings out the contrast very strongly.

‡ Centralblatt für Anthropologie, iii, p. 66. Uke, cited by Andree, 1881, p. 32, agrees.

30

observed, give the average height of Jews and Poles respectively, dividing the city into districts. The social status of these districts is shown upon our third map. Comparison of these three brings out a very interesting sociological fact, to which we have already called attention in our earlier chapter on the subject. The stature of men depends in a goodly measure upon their environment. In the wards of the city where prosperity resides, the material well-being tends to produce a stature distinctly above that of the slums. In both cases, Poles and Jews are shortest in the poorer sections of the city, dark tinted on the maps. The correspondence is not exact, for the

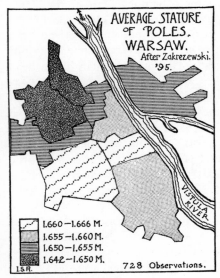

AVERAGE STATURE
of POLES.
WARSAW.
After Zakrezewski.
'95.

1.660 – 1.666 M.
1.655 – 1.660 M.
1.650 – 1.655 M.
1.642 – 1.650 M.
I.S.R.   728 Observations.

number of observations is relatively small; but it indicates beyond doubt a tendency commonly noticeable in great cities. But to return to our direct comparison of Poles and Jews. The deficiency of the latter, as a people, is perfectly apparent. The most highly favoured Jewish population socially in the whole city of Warsaw in fact, can not produce an average stature equal to that of the very poorest Poles; and this, too, in the most miserable section of the capital city of one of the most stunted countries in Europe.

We may assume it as proved, therefore, that the Jew is to-day a very defective type in stature. He seems to be susceptible to favourable influences, however; for in London, the West End prosperous Jews almost equal the English in height, while they at the same time surpass their East End brethren by more than three inches.* In Russia also they become taller

* Jacobs, 1889, p. 81.

as a class wherever the life conditions become less rigorously oppressive. They are taller in the fertile Ukraine than in sterile Lithuania; they sometimes boast of a few relatively tall men.* These facts all go to show that the Jew is short, not by heredity, but by force of circumstances; and that where he is given an even chance, he speedily recovers a part at least of the ground lost during many ages of social persecution. Jacobs mentions an interesting fact in this connection about his upper-class English Jews. Close analysis of the data

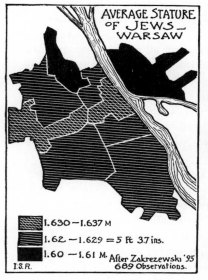
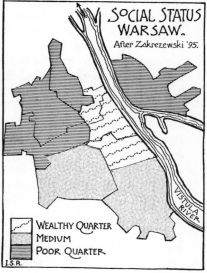

seems to show that, for the present at least, their physical development has been stretched nearly to the upper limit; for even in individual cases, the West End Jews of London manifest an inability to surpass the height of five feet nine inches. So many have been blessed by prosperity that the average has nearly reached that of the English; but it is a mean stature of which the very tall form no component part. Thus perhaps does the influence of heredity obstruct the temporary action of environment.

* Talko-Hryncewicz, 1892, pp. 7 and 58.

Whether the short stature of the Jew is a case of an acquired characteristic which has become hereditary, we are content to leave an open question. All we can say is that the modern Semites in Arabia and Africa are all of goodly size, far above the Jewish average.* This would tend to make us think that the harsh experiences of the past have subtracted several cubits from the stature of the people of Israel. In self-defence it must be said that the Christian is not entirely to blame for this physical disability. It is largely to be ascribed to the custom of early marriages among them. This has probably been an efficient cause of their present degeneracy in Russia, where Tschubinsky describes its alarming prevalence. Leroy-Beaulieu says that it is not at all uncommon to find the combined age of husband and wife, or even of father and mother, to be under thirty years. The *Shadchan*, or marriage broker, has undoubtedly been an enemy to the Jewish people within its own lines. In the United States, where the Jews are, on the other hand, on the up grade socially, there are indications that this age of marriage is being postponed, perhaps even unduly.†

A second indication in the case of the Jew of uncommonly hard usage in the past remains to be mentioned. These people are, anthropologically as well as proverbially, narrow-chested and deficient in lung capacity. Normally the chest girth of a well-developed man ought to equal or exceed one half his stature, yet in the case of the Jews as a class this is almost never the case. Majer and Kopernicki ‡ first established this in the case of the Galician Jews. Stieda # gives additional testimony to the same effect. Jacobs ‖ shows the English Jews distinctly inferior to Christians in lung capacity, which is generally an indication of vitality. In Bosnia, Glück ᐃ again refers to it as characteristic. Granted, with Weissenberg,◊ that it

---

* Collignon, 1887 a, pp. 211 and 326; and Bertholon, 1892, p. 41.

† Jacobs, 1891, p. 50, shows it to be less common in other parts of Europe. In the United States, Dr. Billings finds the marriage rate to be only 7.4 per 1,000—about one third that of the Northeastern States.

‡ 1877, p. 59.   # 1883, p. 71.   ‖ 1889, p. 84.

ᐃ 1896, p. 591.   ◊ 1895, p. 374.

is an acquired characteristic, the effect of long-continued sub-jection to unfavourable sanitary and social environment, it has none the less become a hereditary trait; for not even the per-haps relatively recent prosperity of Jacob's West End Jews has sufficed to bring them up to the level of their English brethren in capacity of the lungs.

At this point a surprising fact confronts us. Despite the appearances of physical degeneracy which we have noted, the Jew betrays an absolutely unprecedented tenacity of life. It far exceeds, especially in the United States, that of any other known people.* This we may illustrate by the following ex-ample: Suppose two groups of one hundred infants each, one Jewish, one of average American parentage (Massachusetts), to be born on the same day. In spite of all the disparity of social conditions in favour of the latter, the chances, deter-mined by statistical means, are that one half of the Americans will die within forty-seven years; while the first half of the Jews will not succumb to disease or accident before the ex-piration of seventy-one years. The death rate is really but little over half that of the average American population. This holds good in infancy as in middle age. Lombroso has put it in another way. Of one thousand Jews born, two hundred and seventeen die before the age of seven years; while four hundred and fifty-three Christians—more than twice as many —are likely to die within the same period. This remarkable tenacity of life is well illustrated by the table on the next page from a most suggestive article by Hoffmann.† We can not forbear from reproducing it in this place.

From this table it appears, despite the extreme poverty of the Russian and Polish Jews in the most densely crowded portions of New York; despite the unsanitary tenements, the overcrowding, the long hours in sweat shops; that neverthe-

---

* On Jewish demography, consult the special appendix in Lombroso, 1894 b; Andree, 1881, p. 70; Jacobs, 1891, p. 49. Dr. Billings, in Eleventh United States Census, 1890, Bulletin No. 19, gives data for our country. On pathology, see Buschan, 1895.

† The Jew as a Life Risk ; The Spectator (an actuarial journal), 1895, pp. 222–224, and 233, 234. Lagneau, 1861, p. 411, speaks of a viability in Algeria even higher than that of the natives.

*Death Rates per 1,000 Population in the Seventh, Tenth, and
Thirteenth Wards of New York City, 1890, by Place of Birth.*

AGES.	Total.	United States (includes coloured).	Ireland.	Germany.	Russia and Poland (mostly Jews)
Total............	26.25	45.18	36.04	22.14	16.71
Under 15 years ...	41.28	62.25	40.71	30.38	32.31
15 to 25 years.....	7.55	9.43	15.15	7.14	2.53
25 to 65 years.....	21.64	25.92	39.51	21.20	7.99
65 and over......	104.72	105.96	120.92	88.51	84.51

less, a viability is manifested which is simply unprecedented.
Tailoring is one of the most deadly occupations known; the
Jews of New York are principally engaged in this employment; and yet they contrive to live nearly twice as long on the
average as their neighbours, even those engaged in the outdoor occupations.

Is this tenacity of life despite every possible antagonistic
influence, an ethnic trait; or is it a result of peculiar customs
and habits of life? There is much which points to the latter
conclusion as the correct one. For example, analysis of the
causes of mortality shows an abnormally small proportion of
deaths from consumption and pneumonia, the dread diseases
which, as we know, are responsible for the largest proportion
of deaths in our American population. This immunity can
best be ascribed to the excellent system of meat inspection
prescribed by the Mosaic laws.* It is certainly not a result
of physical development, as we have just seen. Hoffmann
cites authority showing that in London often as much as a
third of the meats offered for sale are rejected as unfit for
consumption by Jews. Is not this a cogent argument in favour
of a more rigid enforcement of our laws providing for the
food inspection of the poor?

A second cause conducive to longevity is the sobriety of
the Jew, and his disinclination toward excessive indulgence
in alcoholic liquors. Drunkenness among Jews is very rare.
Temperate habits, a frugal diet, with a very moderate use
of spirits, render the proportion of Bright's disease and affec-

---

* Jacobs, 1886 a, p. 7, discusses these fully.

tions of the liver comparatively very small. In the infectious diseases, on the other hand, diphtheria and the fevers, no such immunity is betrayed. The long-current opinion that the Jews were immune from cholera and the other pestilences of the middle ages is not to-day accepted.* A third notable reason for this low death rate is also, as Hoffmann observes, the nature of the employment customary among Jews, which renders the proportion of deaths from accidental causes exceedingly small. In conclusion, it may be said that these people are prone to nervous and mental disorders; insanity, in fact, is fearfully prevalent among them. Lombroso asserts it to be four times as frequent among Italian Jews as among Christians. This may possibly be a result of close inbreeding in a country like Italy, where the Jewish communities are small. It does not, however, seem to lead to suicide, for this is extraordinarily rare among Jews, either from cowardice as Lombroso suggests, or more probably for the reason cited by Morselli—namely, the greater force of religion and other steadying moral factors.

Tradition has long divided the Jewish people into two distinct branches: the Sephardim or southern, and the Ashkenazim, or north European. Mediæval legend among the Jews themselves traced the descent of the first from the tribe of Judah; the second, from that of Benjamin. The Sephardim are mainly the remnants of the former Spanish and Portuguese Jews. They constitute in their own eyes an aristocracy of the nation. They are found primarily to-day in Africa; in the Balkan states, where they are known as Spagnuoli; less purely in France and Italy. A small colony in London and Amsterdam still holds itself aloof from all communion and intercourse with its brethren. The Ashkenazim branch is numerically far more important, for the German, Russian, and Polish Jews comprise over nine tenths of the people, as we have already seen.

Early observers all describe these two branches of the

---

* Buschan, 1895, p. 46.

Jews as very different in appearance. Vogt in his Lectures on Man assumes the Polish type to be descended from Hindu sources, while the Spanish alone he held to be truly Semitic. Weisbach * gives us the best description of the Sephardim Jew as to-day found at Constantinople. He is slender in habit, he says; almost without exception the head is "exquisitely" elongated and narrow, the face a long oval; the nose hooked and prominent, but thin and finely chiselled; hair and eyes generally dark, sometimes, however, tending to a reddish blond. This rufous tendency in the Oriental Jew is emphasized by many observers. Dr. Beddoe † found red hair as frequent in the Orient as in Saxon England, although later results do not fully bear it out.‡ This description of a reddish Oriental type corresponds certainly to the early representations of the Saviour; it is the type, in features perhaps rather than hair, painted by Rembrandt—the Sephardim in Amsterdam being familiar to him, and appealing to the artist in preference to the Ashkenazim type. This latter is said to be characterized by heavier features in every way. The mouth, it is alleged, is more apt to be large, the nose thickish at the end, less often clearly Jewish perhaps. The lips are full and sensual, offering an especial contrast to the thin lips of the Sephardim. The complexion is swarthy oftentimes, the hair and eyes very constantly dark, without the rufous tendency which appears in the other branch. The face is at the same time fuller, the breadth corresponding to a relatively short and round head.

Does this contrast of the traditional Sephardim and Ashkenazim facial types correspond to the anthropometric criteria by means of which we have analyzed the various populations of Europe? And, first of all, is there the difference of head form between the two which our descriptions imply? And, if so, which represents the primitive Semitic type of Palestine? The question is a crucial one. It involves the whole matter of the original physical derivation of the people, and the rival claims to purity of descent of the two branches of the nation.

---

* 1877, p. 214.　　　　　　　　† 1861 b, pp. 227 and 331.

‡ Glück, 1896 a. Jacobs, 1890, p. 82, did not find a trace of it in the Sephardim congregation in London. See Andree, 1878, in this connection.

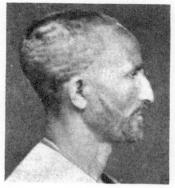 

163.   ARAB.   Index 76.   164.

165.   MUSSULMAN, Tunis.   Index 75.   166.

167.   JEW, Tunis.   Index 75.   168.

AFRICAN SEMITIC TYPES.

In preceding chapters we have learned that western Asia is quite uniformly characterized by an exceeding broad-headedness. This is especially marked in Asia Minor, where some of the broadest and shortest crania in the world are to be found. The Armenians, for example, are so peculiar in this respect that their heads appear almost deformed, so flattened are they at the back. A head of this description appears in the case of the Jew from Ferghanah in our second portrait series (page 394). On the other hand, the peoples of African or negroid derivation form a radical contrast, their heads being quite long and narrow, with indices ranging from 75 to 78. This is the type of the living Arab to-day. Its peculiarity appears in the prominence of the occipital region in our Arab and other African portraits. Scientific research upon these Arabs has invariably yielded harmonious results. From the Semites in the Canary Islands,* all across northern Africa,† to central Arabia itself,‡ the cephalic indices of the nomadic Arabs agree closely. They denote a head form closely allied to that of the long-headed Iberian race, typified in the modern Spaniards, south Italians, and Greeks. It was the head form of the ancient Phœnicians and Egyptians also, as has recently been proved beyond all question.# Thus does the European Mediterranean type shade off in head form, as in complexion also, into the primitive anthropological type of the negro. The situation being thus clearly defined, it should be relatively easy to trace our modern Jews; if, indeed, as has so long been assumed, they have remained a pure and undefiled race during the course of their incessant migrations. We should be able to trace their origin if they possess any distinctive head form, either to the one continent or the other, with comparative certainty.

During the last quarter of a century about twenty-five hundred Jews have submitted their heads to scientific measure-

---

* Verneau, 1881 a, p. 500.

† Pruner Bey, 1865 b ; Gillebert d'Hercourt, 1868, p. 9 ; and especially Collignon, 1887 a, pp. 326–339 ; Bertholon, 1892, p. 41 ; also Collignon, 1896 b.

‡ Elisyeef, 1883.

Bertholon, 1892, p. 43 ; Sergi, 1897 a, chapter i, and even more recently Fouquet, 1896 and 1897, on the basis of De Morgan's discoveries.

ment. These have naturally for the most part been taken
from the Great Russian and Polish branch; a few observers,
as Lombroso, Ikof, Jacobs, Glück, and Livi, have taken observations upon a more or less limited number from southern
Europe. For purposes of comparison we have reproduced
herewith a summary of all the results obtained thus far. In-

AUTHORITY.	Place.	Number.	Cephalic Index.
Lombroso 1894 a.	Turin, Italy.	112	82.0
Weisbach, '77....	Balkan states.	19	82.2
Majer and Koper-nicki, '77......	Galicia.	316	83.6
Blechmann, '82...	W. Russia.	100	83.21
Stieda, '83 a (Dy-bowski).......	Minsk, Russia.	67	82.2
Ikof, '84	Russia.	120	83.2
Ikof, '84	Constantinople.	17 crania.	74.5
Ikof, '84	Crimea.	30 crania (Karaim).	83.3
Majer and Koper-nicki, '85......	Galicia.	100	81.7
Jacobs, '90	England.	363	80.0
Jacobs, '90	England (Sephardim).	51	
Talko-Hrynce-wicz, '92	Lithuania.	713	
Deniker, '98 a ...	Caucasia.	53	85.2
Weissenberg, '95.	South Russia.	100	82.5
Weissenberg, '95.	South Russia.	50 women.	82.4
Glück, '96.......	Bosnia (Spagnuoli).	55	80.1
Livi, '96 a.......	Italy.	34	81.6
Elkind, '97......	Poland.	325	{ Men, 81.9 { Women, 82.9
Deniker, '98.....	Daghestan.	19	87.0
Ammon, '99.....	Baden.	207	83.5

spection of the table shows a surprising uniformity. Ikof's
limited series of Spagnuoli from Constantinople, and that of
the Jews from Caucasia and Daghestan, are the only ones
whose cephalic index lies outside the limits of 80 to 83. In
other words, the Jews wherever found in Europe betray a
remarkable similarity in head form, the crania being considerably broader than among the peoples of Teutonic descent.
As we know, the extremes of head form in Europe measured
by the cephalic index extend from 74 to 89; we thus observe
that the Jews take a place rather high in the European series.
They are about like the northern French and southern Germans. More important still, they seem to be generally very

closely akin in head form to the people among whom they reside. Thus in Russia and Poland scarcely an appreciable difference exists in this respect between Jews and Christians. The same is true in Turin, while in the direction of Asia our Jews are as bullet-headed as even the most typical Armenians and Caucasians round about them.

This surprising similarity of head form between the Jews of north and south Europe bears hard upon the long-accepted theory that the Sephardim is dolichocephalic, thereby remaining true to the original Semitic type borne to-day by the Arabs. It has quite universally been accepted that the two branches of the Jews differed most materially in head form. From the facial dissimilarity of the two a correlative difference in head form was a gratuitous inference. Dr. Beddoe observes that in Turkey the Spagnuoli " seemed " to him to be more dolichocephalic. A few years later Barnard Davis [67] " suspected " a diversity, but had only three Italian skulls to judge from, so that his testimony counts for little. Then Weisbach [77] referred to the " exquisitely " long heads of the Spagnuoli, but his data show a different result. Ikof with his small series of crania from Constantinople, is the only observer who got a result which accords in any degree with what we know of the head form of the modern Semitic peoples. On the other hand, Glück in Bosnia and Livi in Italy find no other sign of long-headedness than a slight drop in index of a point or two. Jacobs in England, whose methods, as Topinard has observed, are radically defective, gives no averages for his Sephardim, but they appear to include about eleven per cent less pure long-headed types than even their Ashkenazim brethren in London. This, it will be noted, is the exact opposite of what might normally be expected. This tedious summary forces us inevitably to the conclusion that, while a long-headed type of Sephardim Jews may exist, the law is very far from being satisfactorily established.

Thus, from a study of our primary characteristic—the proportions of the head—we find our modern Jews endowed with a relatively much broader head than that of the average Englishman, for example: while the best living representative of

the Semitic peoples, the Arab, has a head which is even longer
and narrower than our own type. It is in short one of the
longest known, being in every way distinctly African. The
only modern Jews who even approach this type would seem
to be those who actually reside to-day in Africa, as in the
case of our two portrait types from that region. Two possible
explanations are open to us: either the great body of the Jews
in Europe to-day—certainly all the Ashkenazim, who form
upward of ninety per cent of the nation, and quite probably
the Sephardim also, except possibly those in Africa—have
departed widely from the parental type in Palestine; or else the
original Semitic type was broad-headed, and by inference
distinctly Asiatic in derivation; in which case it is the modern
Arab which has deviated from its original pattern. Ikof is the
only authority who boldly faces this dilemma, and chooses
the Asiatic hypothesis with his eyes open.* Which, we leave
it to the reader to decide, would be the more likely to vary—
the wandering Jew, ever driven from place to place by constant persecution, and constantly exposed to the vicissitudes
of life in densely populated cities, the natural habitat of the
people, as we have said; or the equally nomadic Arab, who,
however, seems to be invariable in type whether in Algeria,
Morocco, or Arabia Felix itself? There can be but one answer, it seems to us. The original Semitic stock must have
been in origin strongly dolichocephalic—that is to say, African
as the Arabs are to-day; from which it follows naturally, that
about nine tenths of the living Jews are as widely different in
head form from the parent stock to-day as they well could
be. The boasted purity of descent of the Jews is, then, a
myth. Renan ('83) is right, after all, in his assertion that the
ethnographic significance of the word Jew, for the Russian
and Danubian branch at least, long ago ceased to exist. Or,
as Lombroso observes, the modern Jews are physically more
Aryan than Semitic, after all. They have unconsciously taken
on to a large extent the physical traits of the people among

---

* Compare Brinton, 1890 a, p. 132, and 1890 b, for interesting linguistic
data on the Semites.

whom their lot has been thrown. In Algiers they have remained long-headed like their neighbours; for, even if they
intermarried, no tendency to deviation in head form would
be provoked. If on the other hand they settled in Piedmont,
Austria, or Russia, with their moderately round-headed populations, they became in time assimilated to the type of these
neighbours as well.

Nothing is simpler than to substantiate the argument of
a constant intercourse and intermixture of Jews with the Christians about them all through history, from the original exodus
of the forty thousand (?) from Jerusalem after the destruction
of the second temple. At this time the Jewish nation as a
political entity ceased to exist. An important consideration
to be borne in mind in this connection, as Neubauer ('86) suggests very aptly, is that opposition to mixed marriages was
primarily a prejudice of religion and not of race. It was dissipated on the conversion of the Gentile to Judaism. In fact,
in the early days of Judaism marriage with a non-believer was
not invalid at all, as it afterward became, according to the
Jewish code. Thus Josephus, speaking of the Jews at Antioch,
mentions that they made many converts receiving them into
their community. An extraordinary number of conversions to
Judaism undoubtedly took place during the second century
after Christ. As to the extent of intermarriage which ensued
during the middle ages discussion is still rife. Renan, Neubauer, and others interpret the various rigid prohibitions
against intermarriage of Jews with Christians—as, for example, at the church councils of 538, 589 at Toledo, and of
743 at Rome—to mean the prevalent danger of such practices becoming general; while Jacobs, Andree, and others are
inclined to place a lower estimate upon their importance.
Two wholesale conversions are known to have taken place: the
classical one of the Khozars in South Russia during the reign
of Charlemagne, and that of the Falashas, who were neighbouring Arab tribes in Yemen. Jacobs has ably shown, however, the relatively slight importance of these. It is probable
that the greatest amount of infusion of Christian blood must
have taken place, in any event, not so much through such

striking conversions as insidiously through clandestine or irregular marriages.

We find, for example, much prohibitive legislation against
the employment of Christian servants by Jews.   This was directed against the danger of conversion to Judaism by the
master with consequent intermarriage.   It is not likely that
these prohibitions were of much avail, for despite stringent
laws in Hungary, for example, we find the archbishop of that
country reporting in 1229 that many Jews were illegally living with Christian wives, and that conversions by thousands
were taking place.   In any case, no protection for slaves was
ever afforded.   The confinement of the Jews strictly to the
Ghettos during the later centuries would naturally discourage
such intermixture of blood, as also the increasing popular
hatred between Jew and Christian; but, on the other hand, the
greater degree of tolerance enjoyed by the Israelites even during this present century would be competent speedily to produce great results.   Jacobs has strenuously, although perhaps
somewhat inconclusively, argued in favour of a substantial
purity of the Jews by means of a number of other data—such
as, for example, by a study of the relative frequency of Jewish
names, by the supposed relative infecundity of mixed marriages, and the like.   Recent statistics also point in this direction.   Thus in Germany about ninety-five per cent of the Jews
marry those of their own belief.*   Experience and the facts
of everyday observation, on the other hand, tend to confirm
us in the belief that racially no purity of descent is to be supposed for an instant.   Consider the evidence of names, for example.   We may admit a considerable purity, perhaps, to the
Cohns and Cohens, legitimate descendants of the *Cohanim*,
the sons of Aaron, early priests of the temple.   Their marital
relations were safeguarded against infusion of foreign blood
in every possible way.   The name is, perhaps, in its various
forms, the most frequent among Jews to-day.   But how shall
we account for the equally pure Jewish names in origin, such
as Davis, Harris, Phillips, and Hart?   How did they ever

* Pubs. American Statistical Association, iii, 1892–'93, p. 244, from
Zeits. Kön. preuss. stat. Bureaus, 1891.

stray so far from their original ethnic and religious significance, unless the marital bars were lowered to a large degree? Some of them certainly claim a foremost position numerically in our Christian English directories. We have an interesting case of indefinite Jewish delimitation in our portraits. The middle one at page 387 is certainly a Jewish type. Dr. Bertholon writes me that all who saw it immediately asserted it to be a Jew. Yet the man was a professed Mussulman in fact, even though his face was against him.

There is, as we have sought to prove, no single uniform type of head peculiar to the Jewish people which may be regarded as in any sense racially hereditary. Is this true also of the face? Our first statement encounters no popular disapproval; for most of us never, perhaps, happened to think of this head form as characteristic. But the face, the features! Is this another case of science running counter to popular belief?

The first characteristic to impress itself upon the layman is that the Jew is generally a brunet. All scientific observers corroborate this impression, agreeing that the dark hair and eyes of this people really constitute a distinct racial trait. About two thirds of the Ashkenazim branch in Galicia and Russia where the general population is relatively quite blond, is of the brunet type, this being especially marked in the darker colour of the hair. For example, Majer and Kopernicki,* in Galicia, found dark hair to be about twice as frequent as the light. Elkind,† in Warsaw, finds about three fifths of the men dark. In Bosnia, Glück's observations on the Sephardim type gave him only two light-haired men out of fifty-five. In Germany and Austria ‡ this brunet tendency is likewise strongly emphasized. Pure brunet types are twice as frequent in the latter country, and three times as frequent in Germany, among Jewish as among Christian school children. Ammon [99] finds black hair most frequent among Jews in Baden, all recruits showing a strong tendency in the same direction. Facts also

---

* 1877, pp. 88–90; 1885, p. 34.
† Centralblatt für Anthropologie, vol. iii, p. 66.
‡ Virchow, 1886 b, p. 364; Schimmer, 1884, p. xxiii.

31

seem to bear out the theory, to which we have already alluded, that the Oriental Jews betray a slightly greater blond tendency, thus inclining to rufous. In Germany also the blond tendency becomes more frequent in Alsace-Lorraine. This comparative blondness of the Alsatian Jew is not new, for in 1861 the origin of these same blonds was matter of controversy. Broca believed them to be of northern derivation, while Pruner Bey traced them from a blondish Eastern source. The English Jews seem also to be slightly lighter than their continental brethren, even despite their presumably greater proportion of Sephardim, who are supposed to be peculiarly dark. As to the relative red blondness of the Oriental Jew, the early observations of Dr. Beddoe, and those of Langerhans * as to the blue eyes and red-brown hair of the Druses of Lebanon, while substantiated by some observers, is controverted by Jacobs and others. Perhaps, as Dr. Beddoe suggests, a cross with the blond Amorites may account for the phenomenon. At all events, the living Semites are dark enough in type: and the evidence of the sacred books bears out the same theory of an original dark type. Thus " black " and " hair " are commonly synonymous in the early Semitic languages. In any case, whatever the colour in the past, we have seen that science corroborates the popular impression that the modern Jews are distinctively of a brunet type. This constitutes one of the principal traits by which they may be almost invariably identified. It is not without interest to notice that this brunetness is more accentuated oftentimes among the women, who are, the world over, persistent conservators of the primitive physical characteristics of a people.†

Secondly, as to the nose. Popularly the humped or hook nose constitutes the most distinctive feature of the Jewish face. Observations among the Jews in their most populous centres do not, however, bear out the theory. Thus Majer and Kopernicki [85], in their extended series, found only nine per cent of the hooked type—no greater frequency than among the

---

* 1873, p. 270.

† Weissenberg, 1895, p. 567, finds brunets twice as frequent among the south Russian Jewesses as among the men.

169.   FERGHANAH, Turkestan.   170.

171.   HÉRAULT, France.   ELIZABETHGRAD, Russia.   172.

173.   SPAGNUOLI, Bosnia.   ELIZABETHGRAD, Russia. 174.

JEWISH TYPES.

Poles; a fact which Weissenberg confirms as to the relative scarcity of the convex nose in profile among his South Russian Jews. He agrees, however, that the nose is often large, thick, and prominent. Weisbach [77] measured the facial features of nineteen Jews, and found the largest noses in a long series of people from all over the earth; exceeded in length, in fact, by the Patagonians alone. The hooked nose is, indeed, sometimes frequent outside the Jewish people. Olechnowicz found, for example, over a third of the noses of the gentry in southeast Poland to be of this hooked variety. Running the eye over our carefully chosen series of portraits, selected for us as typical from four quarters of Europe—Algeria, Russia, Bosnia, and the confines of Asia—representing the African, Balkan Spagnuoli, and Russian Ashkenazim varieties, visual impressions will also confirm our deduction. The Jewish nose is not so often truly convex in profile. Nevertheless, it must be confessed that it gives a hooked impression. This seems to be due to a peculiar "tucking up of the wings," as Dr. Beddoe expresses it. Herein lies the real distinctive quality about it, rather than in any convexity of outline. In fact, it often renders a nose concave in profile, immediately recognisable as Jewish. Jacobs * has ingeniously described this "nostrility," as he calls it, by the accompanying diagrams: Write, he says, a figure 6 with a long tail (Fig. 1); now remove the turn of the twist, and much of the Jewishness disappears;

Fig. 1.   *Fig. 2.*   *Fig. 3.*

and it vanishes entirely when we draw the lower continuation horizontally, as in Fig. 3. Behold the transformation! The Jew has turned Roman beyond a doubt. What have we proved, then? That there is in reality such a phenomenon as a Jewish nose, even though it be differently constituted from our first assumption. A moment's inspection of our series of portraits will convince the sceptic that this trait, next to the prevalent

---

* 1886 a, p. xxxii.

dark hair and eyes and the swarthy skin, is the most distinctive among the chosen people.

Another characteristic of the Jewish physiognomy is the eyes. The eyebrows, seemingly thick because of their darkness, appear to be nearer together than usual, arching smoothly into the lines of the nose. The lids are rather full, the eyes large, dark, and brilliant. A general impression of heaviness is apt to be given. In favourable cases this imparts a dreamy, melancholy, or thoughtful expression to the countenance; in others it degenerates into a blinking, drowsy type; or, again, with eyes half closed, it may suggest suppressed cunning. The particular adjective to be applied to this expression varies greatly according to the personal equation of the observer. Quite persistent also is a fulness of the lips, often amounting in the lower one almost to a pout. The chin in many cases is certainly rather pointed and receding, Jacobs to the contrary notwithstanding. A feature of my own observation, perhaps not fully justified, is a peculiar separation of the teeth, which seem to stand well apart from one another. But a truce to speculations. Entering into greater detail, the flat contradictions of different observers show that they are vainly generalizing from an all too narrow base of observations. Even the fancied differences in feature between the two great branches of the Hebrew people seem to us to be of doubtful existence. Our portraits do not bear it out. It seems rather that the two descriptions of the Ashkenazim and Sephardim types which we have quoted, denote rather the distinction between the faces of those of the upper and the lower classes. Enough for us to know that there is a something Jewish in these faces which we instantly detect. We recognise it in Rembrandt's Hermitage, or in Munkaczy's Christ before Pilate. Not invariable are these traits. Not even to the Jew himself are they always a sure criterion. Weissenberg gives an interesting example of this.* To a friend, a Jew in Elizabethgrad, he submitted two hundred and fifty photographs of Russian Jews and Christians in undistinctive costume. Seventy per

* 1895, p. 563.

cent of the Jews were rightly chosen, while but ten per cent of the Russians were wrongly classed as Jews. Of what concern is it whether this characterization be entirely featural, or in part a matter of expression? The first would be a matter of direct heredity, the second partakes more of the nature of a characteristic acquired from the social environment. Some one—Jacobs, I think—speaks of it as the "expression of the Ghetto." It certainly appears in the remarkable series of composite Jewish portraits published in his monograph. It would not be surprising to find this true. Continued hardship, persecution, a desperate struggle against an inexorable human environment as well as natural one, could not but write its lines upon the face. The impression of a dreary past is deep sunk in the bodily proportions, as we have seen. Why not in the face as well?

We are now prepared, in conclusion, to deal with what is perhaps the most interesting phase of our discussion. It is certainly, if true, of profound sociological importance. We have in these pages spoken at length of the head form—primary index of race; we have shown that there are Jews and Jews in this respect. Yet which was the real Jew it was not for us to decide; for the ninety-and-nine were broad-headed, while the Semite in the East is still, as ever, a long-headed member of the Africanoid races. This discouraged our hopes of proving the existence of a Jewish cephalic type as the result of purity of descent. It may indeed be affirmed with certainty that the Jews are by hereditary descent from early times no purer than most of their European neighbours. Then we discovered evidence that in this head form the Jews were often closely akin to the people among whom they lived. In long-headed Africa they were dolichocephalic. In brachycephalic Piedmont, though supposedly of Sephardim descent, they were quite like the Italians of Turin. And all over Slavic Europe no distinction in head form between Jew and Christian existed. In the Caucasus also they approximate closely the cranial characteristics of their neighbours. Hypnotic suggestion was not needed to find a connection here, especially since all history bore us out in the assumption of a large degree of intermixture of Gentile blood. Close upon this disproval of purity of type by descent, came evidence of a distinct uniformity of facial type. Even so impartial an observer as Weissenberg—certainly not prejudiced in favour of cephalic invariability—confesses this featural unity.

How shall we solve this enigma of ethnic purity and yet impurity of type? In this very apparent contradiction lies the grain of comfort for our sociological hypothesis. The Jew is radically mixed in the line of *racial descent;* he is, on the other hand, the legitimate heir to all Judaism as a matter of *choice.* It is for us a case of purely artificial selection, operative as ever only in those physical traits which appeal to the senses. It is precisely analogous to our example of the Basques in France and Spain. What we have said of them will apply with equal force here. Both Jews and Basques possessed in a high degree a "consciousness of kind"; they were keenly sensible of their social individuality. The Basques primarily owed theirs to geographical isolation and a peculiar language; that of the Jews was derived from the circumstances of social isolation, dependent upon the dictates of religion. Another case in point occurs to us in this connection. Chantre ('95), in a recent notable work, has shown the remarkable uniformity in physical type among the Armenians. They are so peculiar in head form that we in America recognise them at once by their foreshortened and sugar-loaf skulls, almost devoid of occiput. They too, like the Jews, have long been socially isolated in their religion. Thus in all these cases, Basques, Armenians, and Jews, we have a potent selective force at work. So far as in their power lay, the individuality of all these people was encouraged and perpetuated as one of their dearest possessions. It affected every detail of their lives. Why should it not also react upon their ideal of physical beauty? and why not influence their sexual preferences, as well as determine their choice in marriage? Its results became thus accentuated through heredity. But all this would be accomplished, be it especially noted, only in so far as the physical traits were consciously or unconsciously impressed upon them by the facts of observation. There arises at once the difference between artificial selection in the matter of the head form and that concerning the facial features. One is an unsuspected possession of individuality, the other is matter of common notice and, it may be, of report. What Jew or Christian, till he became anthropologist, ever stopped to consider the shape of his head, any more than the addition of a number of cubits to his stature? Who has not, on the other hand, early acquired a distinct concept of a Jewish face and of a distinctly Jewish type? Could such a patent fact escape observation for a moment?

We are confirmed in our belief in the potency of an artificial selection such as we have described, to perpetuate or to evolve a Jewish facial type by reason of another observation. The women among the Jews, as Jacobs * notes in confirmation of our own belief, betray far more constantly than the men the outward characteristics peculiar to the people. We have already cited Weissenberg's testimony that brunetness is twice as prevalent among Russian Jewesses as among the men. Of course this may be a matter of anabolism, pure and simple. This would be perhaps a competent explanation of the phenomenon for physiologists like Geddes and Thompson. For us this other cause may be more directly responsible. Artificial selection in a social group wherein the active choice of mates falls to the share of the male, might possibly tend in the direction of an accentuated type in that more passive sex on which the selective influence directly plays. At all events, observations from widely scattered sources verify the law that the facial individuality of a people is more often than otherwise expressed most clearly in the women. Thus, for example, Lagneau asserts this to be true of the Basques in France. The women betray the Mongol type more constantly than the men among the Asiatic tribes of eastern Russia, as well as among the Turkomans.† Mainof, best of authority, confirms the same tendency among those of Finnic descent.‡ The *Sette Comuni*

---

* 1886 a, p. xxviii.

† Sommier, 1887, reprint p. 116. Vámbéry, 1885, p. 404. *Cf.* Zograf, 1896, p. 50, on crania from the sixteenth century in Moscow ; and Ranke, 1897 a, p. 56, on the persistent brachycephaly of women in Munich.

‡ Congrès int. des sciences géographiques, Paris, 1875, p. 268.

in northern Italy still preserve their German language as evidence of a historic Teutonic descent. They seem to have lost their identity entirely in respect of the head form,* but Ranke †states that among the women the German facial type constantly reappears. A better example than this is offered among the Hamitic aborigines of Africa north of the Sahara. These peoples, from Abyssinia to Morocco, really belong to the white races of Europe. Among nearly all their tribes the negroid traits are far more accentuated among the women, according to Sergi.‡ In the .British Isles, as we have seen, a brunet substratum of population is overlaid by a Teutonic blond one. Darkness of hair, and particularly of eyes, is in many places characteristic of the women.# This is so noticeable in Alsace, where a similar supersession of a dark by a light population has occurred, that Pfitzner ‖ is led to affirm that abundant pigmentation constitutes a real sexual peculiarity among women. Another interesting case of this kind is offered by the Bulgarian women, who seem to represent a more primitive cranial type than the men.ᐃ It is not necessary to cite more specific testimony.◊ The law occupies a respected place among anthropologists. That the Jews confirm it, would seem to strengthen our hypothesis at every point.

Our final conclusion, then, is this: It is paradoxical, yet true, we affirm. The Jews are not a race, but only a people, after all. In their faces we read its confirmation: while in respect of their other traits we are convinced that such individuality as they possess—by no means inconsiderable—is of their own making from one generation to the next, rather than a product of an unprecedented purity of physical descent.

---

* Livi, 1896 a, pp. 137 and 146.

† Beiträge zur Anth. Bayerns, vol. ii, 1879, p. 75.

‡ Africa, Antropologia della Stirpe Camitica, Torino, 1897, p. 263.

Haddon and Browne, 1893, pp. 782–786 ; Gray, 1895 b, p. 21 ; Ellis, Man and Woman, p. 226.

‖ 1897, pp. 484–498.   ᐃ *Vide* page 427 *infra*.

◊ Havelock Ellis, Man and Woman, second edition, p. 367, gives other examples.

CHAPTER XV.

EASTERN EUROPE: THE GREEK, THE TURK, AND THE SLAV;
MAGYARS AND ROUMANIANS.

THE significant geography of the Balkan Peninsula may best be illustrated by comparing it with the other two south European ones, Italy and Spain.* The first point to notice is that it is divided from the mainland by rivers and not by a well-defined mountain chain. Iberia begins definitely at the Pyrenees, and Italy proper is cut off from Europe by the Apennine chain. On the other hand, it is along the line of the Danube and of its western affluent, the Save (see map at page 403) that we find the geographical limits of the Balkan Peninsula. This boundary, as will be observed, excludes the kingdom of Roumania, seeming to distinguish it from its trans-Danubian neighbour Bulgaria. This is highly proper, viewed both in respect of the character of its population as we shall see, and also from the standpoint of geography and topography as well. For Roumania is for the most part an extensive and rich alluvial plain; while the Balkan Peninsula, as soon as you leave the Bulgarian lowlands, is characteristically rugged, if not really mountainous.

From Adrianople west to the Adriatic, and from the Balkan Mountains and the Save River south to the plains of Epirus and Thessaly, extends an elevated region upward of two thousand feet above the sea, breaking up irregularly into peaks

---

* A very concise description of the geography of this region in its relation to man will be found in A. S. White (The Balkan States, Scottish Geographical Magazine, ii, 1886, pp. 657–676, with maps). Freeman's brilliant Essays, particularly those of 1877 and 1879, should be read in this connection.

often rising above five thousand feet.*   There is no system in
these mountains.   Here again is a contrast with other areas
of characterization in Europe.   In the main, in Albania, Montenegro, and Herzegovina the course of these chains is parallel
to the Adriatic; in its eastern half they are rather more at
right angles to the Black Sea; but definiteness of topography
is lacking throughout.   The land is rudely broken up into
a multitude of little " gateless amphitheatres," too isolated for
union, yet not inaccessible enough for individuality.   As White
observes, " if the peninsula, instead of being the highly mountainous and diversified district it is, had been a plateau, a very
different distribution of races would have obtained at the present day."   Nor can one doubt for a moment that this dis-
ordered topography has been an important element in the
racial history of the region.

In its other geographical characteristics this peninsula is
seemingly more favoured than either Spain or Italy.   More
varied than the former, especially in its union of the two flora
of north and south; far richer in contour, in the possession of
protected waters and good harbours than Italy; the Balkan
Peninsula nevertheless has been, humanly speaking, unfortunate from the start.   The reason is patent.   It lies in its central
or rather intermediate location.   It is betwixt and between;
neither one thing nor the other.   Surely a part of Europe, its
rivers all run to the east and south.   " By physical relief it
turns its back on Europe," continually inviting settlement from
the direction of Asia.   It is no anomaly that Asiatic religions,
Asiatic institutions, and Asiatic races should have possessed
and held it; nor that Europe, Christianity, and the Aryan-
speaking races should have resisted this invasion of territory,
which they regarded in a sense as their own.   In this pull and
haul between the social forces of the two continents we finally
discover the dominant influence, perhaps, which throughout
history has condemned this region to political disorder and
ethnic heterogeneity.

As little racial as of topographical system can we discover

---

* A good geological and topographical map will be found in Mitt.
Geog. Gesell., Wien, xxiii, 1889.

in the Balkan states. Only in one respect may we venture upon
a little generalization. This is suggested by the preliminary
bird's-eye view which we must take as to the languages spoken
in the peninsula. This was a favourite theme with the late
historian, Freeman.* It is developed in detail in his luminous
writings upon the Eastern question. The Slavs have in this
part of Europe played a rôle somewhat analogous to, although
less successful than, that of the Teutons in the west. They
have pressed in upon the territory of the classic civilizations
of Greece and Rome, ingrafting a new and physically vigorous
population upon the old and partially enervated one. From
some centre of dispersion up north toward Russia, Slavic-
speaking peoples have expanded until they have rendered all
eastern Europe Slavic from the Arctic Ocean to the Adriatic
and Ægean Seas. Only at one place is the continuity of Slavdom broken; but this interruption is sufficient to set off the
Slavs into two distinct groups at the present day. The northern one, of which we have already treated, consists of the
Russians, Poles, Czechs, and Slovaks. The southern group,
now before us, comprises the main body of the Balkan peoples from the Serbo-Croatians to the Bulgars, as shown upon
the accompanying map. Between these two groups of Slavs
—and herein is the significant point—is a broad belt of non-
Slavic population, composed of the Magyars, linguistically
now as always, Finns; and the Roumanians, who have become
Latin in speech within historic times. This intrusive, non-
Slavic belt lies along or near the Danube, that great highway
over which eastern peoples have penetrated Europe for centuries. The presence of this water way is distinctly the cause
of the linguistic phenomenon. Rome went east, and the Finns,
like the Huns, went west along it, with the result as described.
Linguistically speaking, therefore, the boundary of the southern Slavs and that of the Balkan Peninsula, beginning, as
we have said, at the Danube, are one and the same.

We may best begin our ethnic description by the appor-
tionment of the entire Balkan Peninsula into three linguistic

---

* 1877 d, pp. 382 *et seq.* especially.

divisions, viz., the Greeks, the Slavs, and the Tatar-Turks. Of these the second is numerically the most important, comprising the Serbo-Croatians, and, in a measure, the Bulgarians. As for the Albanians, the place of their language is still undetermined. Their distribution is manifested upon our map, to which we have already directed attention. These Slavs, with the Albanians, form not far from half the entire population.* Next in order come the Greeks, who constitute probably about a third of the total. As our map shows, this Greek contingent is closely confined to the seacoast, with the exception of Thessaly, which, as an old Hellenic territory, we are not surprised to find Greek in speech to-day. The Slavs contrasted with the Greeks, are primarily an inland population; the only place in all Europe, in fact, where they touch the sea is along the Adriatic coast. Even here the proportion of Greek intermixture is more considerable than our map would seem to imply. The interest of this fact is intensified because of the well-deserved reputation as admirable sailors which the modern Dalmatians possess. They are the only natural navigators of all the vast Slavic world. Everywhere else these peoples are noted rather for their aptitude for agriculture and allied pursuits. There is still another important point to be noted concerning the Greeks. They form not only the fringe of coast population in Asiatic as well as in European Turkey; they, with the Jews, monopolize the towns, devoting themselves to commerce as well as navigation. Jews and Greeks are the natural traders of the Orient. Thus is the linguistic segregation between Greek and Slav perpetuated, if not intensified, by seemingly natural aptitudes.

Perhaps the most surprising feature of our map of Turkey is the relative insignificance of the third element, the Turks. There were ten years ago, according to Couvreur [90], not above seven hundred and fifty thousand of them in all European Turkey. Bradaska [69] estimated that they were outnumbered by the Slavs seven to one. Our map shows that they form the dominant element in the population only in

---

* For statistics consult Sax, 1878; Lejean, 1882; White, 1886; Couvreur, 1890; or Behm and Wagner, serially in Petermann.

eastern Bulgaria, where they indeed constitute a solid and coherent body. Everywhere else they are disseminated as a small minority among the Greeks or Slavs. Even about Constantinople itself the Greeks far outnumber them. In this connection we must bear in mind that we are now judging of these peoples in no sense by their physical characteristics, but merely by the speech upon their lips. Nowhere else in Europe, as we shall soon see, is this criterion so fallacious as in the Balkan states. Religion enters also as a confusing element. Sax's original map, from which ours is derived, distinguishes these religious affiliations, as well as language. It was indeed the first to employ this additional test.* The maze of tangled languages and religions upon his map proved too complicated for our imitative abilities. We were obliged to limit our cartography to languages alone. The reader who would gain a true conception of the ethnic heterogeneity of Turkey should consult his original map.

The word Turk was for several centuries taken in a religious sense as synonymous with Mohammedan,† as in the Collect for Good Friday in its reference to "Jews, Turks, infidels, and heretics." Thus in Bosnia, where in the fifteenth century many Slavs were converted to Mohammedanism, their descendants are still known as Turks, especially where they use the Turkish speech in their religion. Obviously in this case no Turkish blood need flow in their veins. It is the religion of Islam, acting in this way, which has served to keep the Turks as distinct from the Slavs and Greeks as they are to-day. Freeman ‡ has drawn an instructive comparison in this connection between the fate of the Bulgars, who, as we shall see, are merely Slavonized Finns, and the Turks, who have steadily resisted all attempts at assimilation. The first came, he says, as "mere heathen savages (who) could be Christianized, Europeanized, assimilated" because no antip-

---

* Oppel, 1890, gives a good cartographical history of the Balkan states; more complete, however, in Sax, 1878, or Lejean, 1861 and 1882.

† Consult Taylor, 1864 (ed. 1893), p. 48; Von Luschan, 1889, p. 198; Sax, 1863, p. 97.

‡ 1877 d.

athy save that of race and speech had to be overcome. The
Turks, in contradistinction, came "burdened with the half-
truth of Islam, with the half-civilization of the East." By
the aid of these, especially the former, the Turk has been enabled to maintain an independent existence as "an unnatural
excrescence" on this corner of Europe.

Even using this word as in a measure synonymous with
religious affiliations, the Turks form but a small and decreasing minority in the Balkan Peninsula. Couvreur [('90)] again
affirms that not over one third of the population profess the
religion of Islam, all the remainder being Greek Catholics.
This being so, the query at once suggests itself as to the reason
for the continued political domination of this Turkish minority,
Asiatic alike in habits, in speech, and in religion. The answer
is certain. It depends upon that subtle principle, the balance
of power in Europe. Is it not clear that to allow the Turk
to go under, as numerically he ought to do, would mean to
add strength to the great Slavic majority, affiliated as it is
with Russia both by speech and religion? This, with the
consent of the Anglo-Saxon and other Teutonic rivals of the
Slav, could never be allowed. Thus does it come about that
the poor Greek is ground between the upper Turkish and
the nether Slavic millstone. "Unnatural disunion is the fate
of the whole land, and the cuckoo-cry about the independence and integrity of the Ottoman Empire means, among the
other evil things that it means, the continuance of this disunion." Let us turn from this distressing political spectacle
to observe what light, if any, anthropology may shed upon
the problem.

From the relative isolation of the Greeks at the extreme
southern point of the peninsula, and especially in the Peloponnesus, it would seem that they might be relatively free from
those ethnic disturbances which have worked such havoc elsewhere in the Orient. Nevertheless, Grecian history recounts
a continuous succession of inroads from the landward north,
as well as from the sea. It would transcend the limits of
our study to attempt any detailed analysis of the early eth-

nology of Greece.* Examination of the relationship of the Pelasgi to their contemporaries we leave to the philologists. Positively no anthropological data on the matter exist. We are sufficiently grateful for the hundred or more well-authenticated ancient Greek crania of any sort which remain to us. It is useless to attempt any inquiry as to their more definite ethnic origin within the tribal divisions of the country.† The testimony of these ancient Greek crania is perfectly harmonious. All authorities agree that the ancient Hellenes were decidedly long-headed, betraying in this respect their affinity to the Mediterranean race, which we have already traced throughout southern Europe and Africa.‡ Whether from Attica, from Schliemann's successive cities excavated upon the site of Troy, or from the coast of Asia Minor; at all times from 400 B. C. to the third century of our era, it would seem proved that the Greeks were of this dolichocephalic type. Stephanos * gives the average cranial index of them all as about 75.7, betokening a people like the present Calabrians in head form; and, for that matter, about as long-headed as the Anglo-Saxons in England and America. More than this concerning the physical traits of these ancient Greeks we can not establish with any certainty. No perfect skeletons from which we can ascertain their statures remain to us. Nor can we be more positive as to their brunetness. Their admiration for blondness in heroes and deities is well known. As Dr. Beddoe ⁽⁹³⁾ says, almost all of Homer's leaders were blond or chestnut-haired, as well as large and tall. Lapouge ‖ seems inclined to regard this as proof that the Greeks themselves

---

* Consult Fligier, 1881 a. Stephanos, 1884, p. 430, gives a complete bibliography of the older works. *Cf.* also Reinach, 1893 b, in his review of Hesselmeyer; and on the supposed Hittites, the works of Wright, De Cara, Conder, etc.

† Stephanos, 1884, p. 432, asserts the Pelasgi to have been brachycephalic, while Zampa, 1886 b, p. 639, as positively affirms the contrary view.

‡ Nicolucci, 1865 and 1867; Zaborowski, 1881; Virchow, 1882 and 1893; Lapouge, 1896 a, pp. 412–419; and Sergi, 1895 a, p. 75; are best on ancient Greek crania.

1884, p. 432.   ‖ 1896 a, p. 414.

32

were of this type, a broad interpretation which is scarcely justifiable.* As we shall see, every characteristic in their modern descendants and every analogy with the neighbouring
populations, leads us to the conclusion that the classical Hellenes were distinctly of the Mediterranean racial type, little
different from the Phœnicians, the Romans, or the Iberians.

Since the Christian era, as we have said, a successive downpour of foreigners from the north into Greece has ensued.†
In the sixth century came the Avars and the Slavs, bringing
death and disaster. A more potent and lasting influence upon
the country was probably produced by the slower and more
peaceful infiltration of the Slavs into Thessaly and Epirus from
the end of the seventh century onward. A result of this is that
Slavic place-names to-day occur all over the Peloponnesus in
the open country where settlements could readily be made.
The most important immigration of all is probably that of the
Albanians, who, from the thirteenth century until the advent of the Turks, incessantly overran the land. As a result
the Albanian language is spoken to-day over a considerable
part of the Peloponnesus, especially in its northeastern corner,
where it attaches to the mainland. Only one little district
has preserved, it may be added, anything like the original
classical Greek speech. The Tzakons, in a little isolated and
very rugged district on the eastern coast, include a number
of classical idioms in their language.‡ Everywhere else, either
in the names of rivers, mountains, and towns, or in borrowed
words, evidence of the powerful influence of foreign infiltration occurs. This has induced Fallmerayer, Philippson, and
others to assert that these foreigners have in fact submerged the
original Greeks entirely.# Explicit rebuttal of this is offered
by Hopf, Hertzberg, and Tozer, who admit the Slavic element,
but still declare the Greeks to be Greek. This is a matter

---

* Stephanos, 1884, p. 439.

† Philippson, Zur Ethnographie des Peloponnes ; Petermann, xxxvi.
1890, pp. 1–11, 33–41, with map, gives a good outline of these. Consult
also Stephanos, 1884, pp. 422 *et seq.*

‡ *Op. cit.*, p. 37.

Cf. Couvreur, 1890, p. 514 ; and Freeman, 1877 d, p. 401.

concerning which neither philologist nor geographer has a right to speak; the anthropological testimony is the only competent one.   To this we turn.

The modern Greeks are a very mixed people.   There can be no doubt of this fact from a review of their history.   In despite of this, they still remain distinctly true to their original Mediterranean ancestry.   This has been most convincingly proved in respect of their head form.*   The cephalic index of modern living Greeks ranges with great constancy about 81.   This, it should be observed, betokens an appreciably broader head than in the case of the ancient Hellenes. Stephanos,† who has measured several hundred recruits, finds dolichocephaly to be most prevalent in Thessaly and Attica; while broad-headedness, so characteristic, as we shall see, of the Albanians and southern Slavs, is more accentuated toward the north, especially in Epirus.   About Corinth also, where Albanian intermixture is common, the cephalic index rises above 83.   The Peloponnesus has probably best preserved its early dolichocephaly, as we should expect.   In Thessaly also are the modern Greeks as purely Mediterranean as in classic times.   It is most suggestive of the heterogeneity of these modern Greeks, despite their clearly Mediterranean affinities, to examine the seriation of these measurements. Turn, for example, to that remarkable curve of von Luschan's for the Greeks of southwestern Asia Minor, reproduced on page 116.   Its double apex, at two widely separated points, one denoting a pure Mediterranean dolichocephaly, the other a broader-headedness as great as that of the pure Albanians, we have already described.‡   There can be no doubt that in Asia Minor, at least, the word Greek is devoid of any racial

---

* Weisbach, 1882 ; Nicolucci, 1867 ; Apostolides in Bull. Soc. d'Anth., 1883, p. 614 ; Stephanos, 1884 ; Neophytos, 1891 ; Lapouge, 1896 a, p. 419. Von Luschan, 1889, p. 209, illustrates the similarity between the Greek and the Bedouin skull.

† 1884, p. 434.

‡ Von Luschan, 1889, p. 206 ; 1891, p. 39.   Stephanos's series, 1884, p. 435, has three distinct culminations, at 78, 82, and 84 respectively. Neophytos' series from northwest Asia Minor is equally irregular ; *op. cit.*, p. 29.

significance.   It merely denotes a man who speaks Greek, or
else one who is a Greek Catholic, converted from Mohammedanism.   Greek, like Turk, has become entirely a matter
of language and religion, as these people have intermingled.
Thus in the southwest of Asia Minor, where Semitic influences have been strong, von Luschan * makes the pregnant
observation that the Greeks often look like Jews, although they
speak Turkish.   The climax of physical heterogeneity is betrayed in Neophytos' series of Greeks from northwestern Asia
Minor, where he found not a single individual out of a hundred and fifty with a cephalic index below 80.   Here is proof
positive that no Greeks of pure Mediterranean descent remain
to represent the primitive Hellenic type in that region.

Whatever may be thought of the ancients, the modern
Greeks are strongly brunet in all respects.   Ornstein [79]
found less than ten per cent of light hair, although blue and
gray eyes were characteristic of rather more than a quarter
of his seventeen hundred and sixty-seven recruits.   This
accords with expectation; for among the Albanians, next
neighbours and most intrusive aliens in Greece, light eyes are
quite common.   Weisbach's [82] data confirm this, ninety-six
per cent of his Greeks being pure brunets.†   In stature these
people are intermediate between the Turks and the Albanians
and Dalmatians, which latter are among the tallest of Europeans.‡   In facial features Nicolucci's [67] early opinion seems
to be confirmed, that the Greek face is distinctively orthogna-
thous—that is to say, with a vertical profile, the lower parts of
the face being neither projecting nor prominent.   The face
is generally of a smooth oval, rather narrow and high, especially as compared with the round-faced Slavs.   The nose is
thin and high, perhaps more often finely chiselled and straight
in profile.   The facial features seem to be well demonstrated

---

* 1889, p. 209.

† Neophytos finds 82.5 per cent of dark-brown or black hair, only 5
per cent blond or red ; while 17 per cent of the eyes were dark among 200
individuals.

‡ Weisbach, 1882, p. 73, gives averages as follows : Greeks, 1.65 metres ;
Turks, 1.62 metres ; Albanians, 1.66 metres ; and Dalmatians, 1.69 metres.

175.   Greeks.   176.

177.   Roumanians, County Hunyad, Hungary.   178.

179.   Bulgarians, County Temes, Hungary.   180.

BALKAN STATES.

in the classic statuary, although it is curious, as Stephanos observes, that these ideal heads are distinctly brachycephalic. Either the ancient sculptors knew little of anthropology, or else we have again a confirmation of our assertion that, however conscious of their peculiar facial traits a people may be, the head form is a characteristic whose significance is rarely recognised.

Linguistically the pure Slavs in the Balkan states comprise only the Serbo-Croatians, who divide the ancient territory of Illyria with the Arnauts or Albanians. The western half of the peninsula, rugged and remote, has been relatively little exposed to the direct ravages of either Finnic or Turkish invaders. Especially is this true of Albania. Nearly all authorities since Hahn are agreed in identifying these latter people—who call themselves Skipetars, by the way—as the modern representatives of the ancient Illyrians.* They are said to have been partly Slavonized by the Serbo-Croatians, who have been generally regarded as descendants of the settlers brought by the Emperor Heraclius from beyond the Save. This he is said to have done in order to repopulate the lands devastated by the Avars and other Slavs who, Procopius informs us, first appeared in this region in the sixth century of our era. The settlers imported by Heraclius came, we are told, from two distant places: Old Servia, or Sorabia, placed by Freeman in modern Saxony; and Chrobatia, which, he says, lies in southwestern Poland.† According to this view, the Serbo-Croatians are an offshoot from the northern Slavs, being divided from them to-day by the intrusive Hungarians; while the Albanians alone are truly indigenous to the country.

The recent political fate of these Illyrian peoples has been quite various, the Albanians alone preserving their independence continually under the merely nominal rule of the Turks. Religion, also, has affected the Slavs in various ways. Servia

---

* Glück, 1897 a; Lejean, 1882, p. 628; Bradaska, 1869. On early ethnology, consult Fligier, 1876; Tomaschek, 1880 and 1893.

† Freeman, 1877 d, pp. 385, 404 *et seq.*; Lejean, 1882, pp. 216–222, and especially Howorth, 1878–'81.

owes much of its present peace and prosperity to the practical
elimination of the Moslems.   Bosnia is still largely Mohammedan, with about a third of its people, according to White [86],
still professing that religion.*   The significance of this is increased, it being mainly the upper classes in Bosnia, according
to Freeman, who embraced the religion of Islam in order to
preserve their power and estates.   The conversion was not
national, as in the case of the Albanians.   Thus social and religious segregation work together to produce discord.   With
multitudes of Jews monopolizing the commerce of the country and the people thus divided socially, as well as in religion, the political unrest in Bosnia certainly seems to require the strong arm of Austrian suzerainty to preserve order.
In this connection it is curious to note Sax's [63] observation
as to the physical peculiarities of these Mohammedans in Bosnia, who, as we have said, call themselves Turks.   According
to him a process of selection has evolved a purer " Caucasian "
type, greater regularity of features, along with other traits.
Certainly the force of religion as a factor in artificial selection
can not be denied, as in this case.

Whatever the theory of the historians as to origins may be,
to the anthropologist the modern Illyrians—Serbo-Croatians
and Albanians alike—are physically a unit.   More than this,
they constitute together a distinct type so well individualized
that Deniker [98], in his recent masterly analysis, honours them
as a separate Adriatic, or, as he calls it, " Dinaric " race.   Our
knowledge of the region, considering its remoteness, is quite
complete, owing especially to the zeal of Dr. Weisbach.†
Two physical characteristics render this ethnic group distinctive : first, that it comprises some of the tallest men in the
world, comparing favourably with the Scotch in this respect ;

---

* Von Schubert, 1893, p. 133, places the estimate much higher than this.

† To him I am grateful for the most courteous assistance both in the
collection of material and the loan of photographs.   On the Albanians,
consult Zampa, Anthropologie Illyrienne, 1886 b, and Glück, 1896 b and
1897 a ; on the Serbo-Croatians, including Dalmatia, Weisbach, 1877, 1884,
and 1895 a, the latter with especial reference to Bosnia ; on Herzegovina,
Weisbach, 1889 b.   For Servia by itself no separate data exist ; and the
same may be said of Montenegro.

and, secondly, that these Illyrians tend to be among the broad-est-headed people known.   In general, it would appear that the people of Herzegovina and northern Albania possess these traits to the most notable degree; while both in the direction of the Save and Danube and of the plains of Thessaly and Epirus they have been attenuated by intermixture.   Presumably also toward the east among the Bulgarians in Macedonia and Thrace these characteristics diminish in intensity.   Thus, for example, while the Herzegovinians, measured by Weis-bach, yielded an average stature of 5′ 9″ (1.75 metres), the Bosnians were appreciably shorter (1.72 metres),* and the Dalmatians and Albanians were even more so (1.68 metres). Nevertheless, as compared with the Greeks, Bulgars, Turks, or Roumanians, even the shortest of these Slavs stood high. The superiority in stature of the whole body of the southern Slavs over the Russians, Poles, and others of the northern group is very noticeable.   We have already spoken of it in another connection.†   It would apparently preclude the possi-bility of this as an imported Slavic trait; rather does it seem tò be indigenous to the country.   From this specific centre out-ward, especially around the head of the Adriatic Sea, over into Venetia, spreads the influence of this giantism.   It confirms, as we have said, the classical theory of an Illyrian cross among the Venetians, extending well up into the Tyrol.

As for the second trait, the exaggerated broad-headed-ness, it too, like the tallness of stature, seems to centre about Herzegovina and Montenegro.   Thus at Scutari, in the corner of Albania near this last-named country, Zampa ‡ found a cranial index of 89; in Herzegovina the index upon the living head ranges above 87.   It would be difficult to ex-ceed this brachycephaly anywhere in the world.   The square foreheads and broad faces of the people correspond in every way to the shape of the heads.   Its significance appears imme-diately on comparison with the long oval faces of the Greeks. This broad-headedness diminishes slightly toward the north, probably by reason of the Serbo-Croatian intermixture; * nev-

---

* Capus, 1895, confirms it.   † Pages 98 and 350 *supra*.
‡ 1886 b, p. 637.   # *Cf.* map at p. 340 *supra*.

ertheless, it still maintains the very respectable average of 85.7 among the 3,803 Bosnians measured by Weisbach.* It falls more rapidly in the direction of Greece, showing how strong is the influence of that Mediterranean element among the Illyro-Greeks about Epirus. It seems to be a persistent trait. The Albanian colonists, studied by Livi and Zampa † in Calabria, still, after four centuries of Italian residence and intermixture, cling to many of their primitive characteristics, notably their brachycephaly and their relative blondness. This persistency again leads us to regard these traits as properly indigenous to the land and the people, not lately acquired by infusion of foreign blood from abroad.

One more trait of the Balkan Slavs remains for us to note. The people are mainly pure brunets, as we might expect; but they seem to be less dark than either the Greeks or the Turks. Especially among the Albanians are light traits by no means infrequent. In this respect the contrast with the Greeks is apparent, as well as with the Dalmatians along the coast and the Italians in the same latitude across the Adriatic.‡ Weisbach # found nearly ten per cent of blond and red hair among his Bosnian soldiers, while about one third of the eyes were either gray or blue. The Herzegovinians are even lighter than the Bosnians, almost as much so as the Albanians. From consideration of these facts it would appear as if the harsh climate of these upland districts had been indeed influential in setting off the inland peoples from the Italian-speaking Dalmatians along the coast. For among the latter brunetness certainly increases from north to south,‖ conformably to the general rule for the rest of Europe; while in the interior, blondness apparently moves in the contrary direction, culminating in the mountain fastnesses of northern Albania and the vicinity. On the whole, we find also in this trait of brunetness com-

---

* 1895 a, p. 228. Glück's average for thirty Albanians is only 82.6. Weisbach, 1897 a, p. 84, finds the Bosnian brachycephaly to-day quite paralleled in crania from the early historic period.

† 1886 b and 1886 a, p. 174 respectively.

‡ Zampa, 1886 b, p. 636 ; Livi, 1896 a, p. 175.

1895 a, p. 210.   ‖ Weisbach, 1884.

petent evidence to connect these Illyrians with the great body of the Alpine race farther to the west. We have also another illustration of its determined predilection for a mountainous habitat, in which it stoutly resists all immigrant tendencies toward variation from its primitive type.

The Osmanli Turks, who politically dominate the Balkan Peninsula notwithstanding their numerical insignificance, are mainly distinctive among their neighbours by reason of their speech and religion.* Turkish is the westernmost representative of a great group of languages, best known, perhaps, as the Ural-Altaic family. This comprises all those of northern Asia even to the Pacific Ocean, together with that of the Finns in Russian Europe. Its members are by no means unified physically. All varieties of type are included within its boundaries, from the tall and blond one which we have preferred to call Finnic,† prevalent about the Baltic; to the squat and swarthy Kalmucks and Kirghez, to whom we have in a physical sense applied the term Mongols. The Turkish branch of this great family of languages is to-day represented in eastern Europe by two peoples, whom we may roughly distinguish as Turks and Tatars.‡ The term Tatar, it should be observed, is entirely of European invention, like the similar word Hungarian. The only name recognised by the Osmanli themselves is that of Turk. This, by the way, seems quite aptly to be derived from a native root meaning " brigand," according to Chantre (⁹⁵). They apply the word Tatar solely to the north Asiatic barbarians. By general usage this latter term, Tatar, has to-day become more specifically applied by ethnologists to the scattered peoples of Asiatic descent and Turkish speech who are mainly to be found in Russia and Asia Minor.#

---

* Lejean, 1882, p. 453, gives good descriptive material. Vámbéry, 1885, divides the Ural-Altaic family into five groups—viz., (1) Samoyed, (2) Tungus, (3) Finnic, (4) Mongolic, (5) Turkish or Tatar.

† Page 360 *supra*.

‡ On terminology consult Vámbéry, 1885, p. 60 ; Chantre, 1895, p. 199 ; Keane, 1897, p. 302.

Vámbéry's (1885) further classification of the Tatar-Turkish subdivision is as follows: (a) Siberian ; Yakuts, etc.; (b) Central Asiatic ;

Of the two principal physical types to-day comprised within the limits of the Ural-Altaic languages, the Turks and Tatars seem to be affiliated with the Mongol rather than the Finn, not physically alone, but in respect of language as well.* As a matter of fact they are much nearer other Europeans in original type than most people imagine. Their nearest relatives in Asia seem to be the Turkoman peoples, who, to the number of a million or more, inhabit the deserts and steppes of western Asia. It was from somewhere about this region, in fact, as we know, that the hordes of the Huns under Attila, and those of Genghis Khan and Tamerlane, set forth to the devastation of Europe. The physical type of these inhabitants of Turkestan has been fairly well established by anthropologists. It persists throughout a great multitude of tribes of various names, among whom the Kara-Kirghez, Uzbegs, and Kiptchaks are prominent.† At page 44 we have represented these Turkoman types. The most noticeable feature of the portraits is the absence of purely Mongol facial characteristics. Except in the Kara-Kirghez the features are distinctly European. There is no squint-eye; the nose is well formed; the cheek bones are not prominent, although the faces are broad; and, most important of all, the beard is abundantly developed, both in the Uzbeg and the Kiptchak. The Kara-Kirghez, on the other hand, betrays unmistakably his Mongol derivation in every one of these important respects. One common trait is possessed by all three: to wit, extreme brachycephaly, with an index ranging from 85 to 89.‡ The flatness of the occiput is very noticeable in our portraits in every case, giving what Hamy calls a "cuboid aspect" to the skull.#

Turkomans; (c) Volga: Chuvashes and Bashkirs; (d) Pontus: as in Crimean and Nogaï Tatars; (e) Western: Osmanli and Azerbeidjian.

* Vámbéry, 1885, p. 63.

† Complete data on these people will be found in Ujfalvy, 1878–'80, iii, pp. 7–50; Les Aryens, etc., 1896 a, pp. 51, 385–434: Bogdanof, 1888: Yavorski, 1897.

‡ Yavorski, 1897, p. 193, gets an index of 75.6 for his 191 observations; every other authority confirms the opposite tendency.

Considérations générales sur les races jaunes. L'Anth., vi, 1895, p. 247.

These portraits, if typical, should be enough to convince us that the Turkoman of the steppes about the Aral and Caspian Seas is far from being a pure Mongol, even in his native land, although a strain of Mongol blood is apparent in many of their tribes. He is not to be classed with the peoples depicted in our series at page 358, in other words.

The fact is that the Asiatic Turkomans, whence our Osmanli Turks are derived, are a highly composite type. A very important element in their composition is that of certain brachycephalic Himalayan peoples, the Galchas and Tadjiks, who are for all practical purposes identical with the Alpine type of western Europe. In their accentuated brachycephaly, their European facial features, their abundance of wavy hair and beard, and finally in their intermediate colour of hair and eyes,* these latter peoples in the Pamir resemble their European prototypes. So close is this affiliation that we shall see in our next chapter that the occurrence of this type in western Asia is the keystone in any argument for the Asiatic origin of the Alpine race of Europe. The significance of it for us in this connection, is that it explains the European affinity of many of the Turkoman tribes, who are more strongly Alpine than Mongol in their resemblances. It is highly important, we affirm, to fix this in mind; for the prevalent opinion seems to be that the Turks in Europe have departed widely from their ancestral Asiatic type, because of their present lack of Mongol characteristics, such as almond eyes, lank black hair, flat noses, and high cheek bones. The chances of physical resemblance really depend upon a decision as to the particular origin of the progenitors of these present Turks. If they are indeed directly derived from the pure Kirghez, as Vámbéry † asserts, we might expect all manner of Mongol

---

* Ujfalvy (Les Aryens, etc., 1896 a, p. 428) found chestnut hair most frequent, with 27 per cent of blondness, among some of the Tadjiks. The eyes are often greenish gray or blue (Ujfalvy, 1878–'80, iii, pp. 23–33. tables).

† 1885, p. 382. It is curious to notice that the nearest Asiatic language to the Turkish occurs among the Yakuts, in northern Siberia. They are unmistakable Mongols.

traits.   If, on the other hand, they originally were Turkomans, it would seem that we have no right to expect any such phenomena even in Asia itself; to say nothing of the Osmanli Turks who have for generations, through Circassian wives and slaves, bred into the type of the other peoples of eastern Europe.

Either the Osmanli Turks were never Mongols, or they have lost every trace of it by intermixture.   Our portraits on the opposite page give little indication of Asiatic derivation except in their accentuated short- and broad-headedness.   This is considerably more noticeable in Asia Minor than in European Turkey.*   West of the Bosporus the Turks differ but little from the surrounding Slavs in head form.   They have been bred down from their former extreme brachycephaly, which still rules to a greater degree in Asia Minor.   In our portraits from this region the absence of occipital prominence is very marked.   In addition to this, the Turks are everywhere, as Chantre [95] observes, " incontestably brunet." †   The hair is generally stiff and straight.   The beard is full.   This latter trait is fatal to any assumption of a persistence of Kirghez blood, or of any Mongolic extraction, in fact.   The nose is broad, but straight in profile.   The eyes are perfectly normal, the oblique Mongol type no more frequent than elsewhere.‡   In stature the Turks are rather tall, especially those observed by Chantre: #   but in this respect social conditions are undoubtedly of great effect.   On the whole, then, we may consider that the Turks have done fairly well in the preservation of their primitive characteristics.   Chantre especially finds them quite

---

* On the anthropology of European Turks, Weisbach, 1873, is the only authority.   He found an average cephalic index of 82.8 in 148 cases. Elisyeef, 1890-'91, and Chantre, 1895, pp. 206–211, have worked in Anatolia, with indices of 86 for 143 individuals, and 84.5 for 120 men, respectively.   Both Von Luschan and Chantre give a superb collection of portrait types in addition.

† Elisyeef's tables show a blondness by no means inconsiderable.

‡ Von Luschan, 1889, p. 212, finds less than one per cent in Lycia.   *Cf.* Chantre, 1895, p. 207.

1895, p. 208.   Over half of his 120 were above 1.70 metres ; the average 1.71 metres.   Elisyeef obtained a lower average of 1.67 metres.

181.   NOMAD IVERVEK, Lycia, Asia Minor.   182.

183.   TURK, Lycia, Asia Minor.   184.

185.   TURK, Lycia, Asia Minor.   186.

TURKS.

homogeneous, considering all the circumstances. They vary according to the people among whom their lot is cast. Among the Armenians they become broader-headed, while among the Iranian peoples—Kurds or Persians—the opposite influence of intermixture at once is apparent.

A sub-type of the Turk occurs among the nomads, who, under the name of Jurüks and Iverveks, still roam through central Anatolia. The name of these tribes signifies " wanderers." Little is known of them, save that they are of Turkish speech and have entered Asia Minor in late historic times.* One of these is depicted in our upper portraits herewith. A difficulty in the analysis of these peoples lies in the prevalence of customs of cranial deformation among them. All that is certain is that they are very brunet, but in no wise Mongoloid. Their resemblance to the Gypsies, of supposedly Hindoo extraction, is rather close, as comparison of our portraits in this series will make apparent. Another Gypsy of distinctly Indian type from Asia Minor is represented in the series at page 422.†

Before taking leave of the Turkish peoples a word should be added concerning the Tatars. No other people of Europe have scattered so far and wide, preserving an identity of language meanwhile. They fall, in the main, into three groups: One about Kazan in eastern Russia, known as the Volga Tatars (see map, page 362); a second in and about the Crimean peninsula; and, thirdly, that centreing about the Caucasus mountains. These last, in northern Caucasia, are known as Nogays or Koumyks; those in the south, constituting the Azerbeidjian or Iranian Tatars. The first are aggregated in a solid body; the second seem to be dispersed among a host of Armenians, Kurds, Persians, and other peoples. Their distribution is in part shown upon our map of Caucasia at page 439. This latter group of Tatars in Russian Armenia number to-day upward of a million souls. They are popularly sup-

---

* Vámbéry, 1885, p. 603: Von Luschan, 1889, pp. 213–217; Chantre, 1895, p. 200.

† Glück (1897 a), Von Luschan (1889), Schwicker (1883), describe these Gypsies and their languages and customs.

33

posed to represent an element which was left behind during
the historic invasions of the Seljukian Turks into Europe.*
The contrast between the two groups north and south of the
Caucasus is very marked. The Nogays and Koumyks, from
their proximity to the Kirghez and the Kalmucks, are strongly
Mongolian in aspect and in head form.† The Azerbeidjians,
on the other hand, have become much Iranized by contact with
the dolichocephalic peoples of this region. This endows them
with the long oval face and smooth features of the Persians
and Kurds.‡ Despite these differences, both Nogays and Azerbeidjians adhere closely to their primitive Tatar speech. Long-
continued separation has been powerless to affect them in this
respect.

The Crimean or Pontus Tatars offer us the same example
of a community of language, coupled with a great diversity
of physical type. Radde distinguishes three groups among
them: one in the steppes just north of the peninsula, which
still preserves many of its Asiatic characteristics; a second,
the so-called " hill Tatars," which is said to be more mixed;
and a third known as the coast Tatars. This last group has
become entirely Europeanized. Our portraits of these coast
Tatars at pages 364 and 422 make this apparent at once. We
must suppose strong admixture among them of Greek, Gypsy,
and possibly also of Gothic blood.# Similar contrasts occur
among the Volga Tatars, dependent upon the particular Finnic,
Mongol, or Russian element, with whom they happen to have
been thrown in contact.‖ As for the Tatars in the Dobrudsha
district at the mouth of the Danube, shown upon our map of
the Balkan states, we are unable to give information. Finally,
as a last and complete example of Europeanized Tatars, still

---

* Vámbéry, 1885, pp. 569–579; Chantre, 1885–'87, iv, pp. 248 *et seq.*, and
1895, pp. 177–189; as well as Wyrubof, 1890.

  † *Cf.* Sviderski, 1898, on the Koumyks.

  ‡ The cephalic index of the Nogays is about 86; of the Azerbeidjians,
78; of the Crimeans, 86; of the Don, 79. *Cf.* Yavorski's table, p. 193.

  # Consult A. N. Kharuzin, 1890 a, b, and d; and also Merezkovski,
1881.

  ‖ Benzengre, 1880, on the Tatars of Kassimof, is the only standard on
these peoples.

Turkish in speech, we may instance the small colony in Lithu-ania. Even less of the Mongol remains in this case than among the shore Tatars of the Crimea.* The utter futility of attempting to correlate physical characteristics and language are again illustrated for us among these people to an extreme degree.

The Bulgarians are of interest because of their traditional Finnic origin and subsequent Europeanization. This has en-sued through conversion to Christianity and the adoption of a Slavic speech. Our earliest mention of these Bulgars would seem to locate them between the Ural Mountains and the Volga.† The district was, in fact, known as Old Bulgaria till the Russians took it in the fifteenth century. As to which of the many existing tribes of the Volga Finns (see map, page 362) represent the ancestors of these Bulgarians, no one is, I think, competent to speak. Pruner Bey seems to think they were the Ostiaks and Voguls, since emigrated across the Urals into Asia; ‡ the still older view of Edwards and Klaproth made them Huns; * Obédénare, according to Virchow (’86), said they were Samoyeds or Tungus; while Howorth and Beddoe claim the honour for the Chuvashes.|| These citations are enough to prove that nobody knows very much about it in detail. All that can be affirmed is that a tribe of Finnic-speaking people crossed the Danube toward the end of the seventh century and possessed themselves of territory near its mouth. Remain-ing heathen for two hundred odd years, they finally adopted Christianity and under their great leaders, Simeon and Samuel, became during the tenth century a power in the land. Their rulers, styling themselves " Emperors of the Slavs," fought the Germans; conquered the Magyars as well as their neighbours in Thrace, receiving tribute from Byzantium; became allies of Charlemagne; and then subsided under the rule of the

---

* Superb portraits of these are given in the Dnevnik, Society of Friends of Natural Science, etc., Moscow, 1890, at column 63.

† Read Pruner-Bey, 1860 b ; Obédénare ; Howorth, 1881 ; and espe-cially Kanitz, 1875, for historic details.

‡ See note, p. 361 *supra*.　　　　* *Cf.* Vámbéry, 1882, pp. 50–60.

|| 1881, p. 223, and 1893, p. 49, respectively.

Turks. Since the practical demise of this latter power they have again taken courage, and in their semi-political independence in Bulgaria and northern Roumelia rejoice in an ever-rich and growing literature and sense of nationality.

Bulgarian is spoken, as our map at page 403 indicates, far outside the present political limits of the principality—indeed, over about two thirds of European Turkey. Gopčević * has made a brilliant attempt to prove that Macedonia, shown by our map and commonly believed to be at bottom Bulgarian, is in reality populated mainly by Serbs. The weakness of this contention was speedily laid bare by his critics. Political motives, especially the ardent desire of the Servians to make good a title to Macedonia before the disruption of the Ottoman Empire, can scarcely be denied. Servia needs an outlet on the Mediterranean too obviously to cloak such an attempted ethnic usurpation. As a fact, Macedonia, even before the late Greco-Turkish war, was in a sad state of anarchy. The purest Bulgarian is certainly spoken in the Rhodope Mountains; there are many Roumanians of Latin speech; the Greeks predominate all along the sea and throughout the three-toed peninsula of Salonica; while the Turks are sparsely disseminated everywhere. And as for religion—well, besides the severally orthodox Greeks and Turks, there are in addition the Moslem and apostate Bulgarians, known as Pomaks, who have nothing in common with their Greek Catholic fellow-Bulgars, together with the scattering Pindus Roumanians and Albanians in addition. This interesting field of ethnographic investigation is, even at this late day, practically unworked. As Dr. Beddoe [93] writes—and his remarks are equally applicable to Americans—" here are fine opportunities for any enterprising Englishman with money and a taste for travel and with sufficient brains to be able to pick up a language. But, alas! such men usually seem to care for nothing but ' killing something.' "

The Roumanians, or Moldo-Wallachians, are not confined within the limits of that country alone. Their language and

---

* 1889 a, with map, in Petermann, 1889 b. *Cf.* criticism of his contention by Oppel, 1890; Couvreur, 1890, p. 523; and Ghennadiéff, 1890, p. 663.

187.   COAST TATARS, Goursuf, Crimea.   188.

189.   GYPSY, Lycia, Asia Minor.   190.

191.   GYPSY, Lycia, Asia Minor.   192.

nationality cover not only the plains along the Danube and the Black Sea; but their speech extends beyond the Carpathian Mountains over the entire southeastern quarter of Hungary and up into the Bukovina. (See map at page 429.) Transylvania is merely a German and Magyar islet in the vast extent of the Roumanian nation. There are more than a third as many Roumanians, according to the census of 1890, as there are Magyars in the Hungarian kingdom.* Politically it thus happens that these people are pretty well split up in their allegiance. Nor can this be other than permanent. For the Carpathian Mountains, in their great circle about the Hungarian basin, cut directly through the middle of the nation. as measured by language. This curious circumstance can be accounted for only on the supposition that the disorder in the direction of the Balkan Peninsula incident upon the Turkish invasion, forced the growing nation to expand toward the northwest, even over the natural barrier interposed between Roumania proper and Hungary. Geographical law, more powerful than human will, ordains that this latter natural area of characterization—the great plain basin of Hungary—should be the seat of a single political unit. There is no resource but that the Roumanians should in Hungary accept the division from their fellows over the mountains as final for all political purposes.†

The native name of these people is Vlach, Wallach, or Wallachian. Various origins for the name have been assigned. Lejean [82] asserts that it designates a nomad shepherd, in distinction from a tiller of the soil or a dweller in towns. Picot [75] voices the native view as to ethnic origins by deriving the word Wallach from the same root as Wales, Walloon, etc., applied by the Slavs and Germans to the Celtic peoples as "foreigners." ‡ This theory is now generally discountenanced. Obédénare's [76] attempt to prove such a

---

* Jekelfalussy, 1897, with his map of nationalities, 1885, is the best authority. *Cf.* also Auerbach, 1898, pp. 285–297.

† Auerbach, 1898, p. 286, gives a full summary of the rival controversy between Roumanians and Hungarians as to priority of title in Transylvania.

‡ *Cf.* Taylor, Words and Places, p. 42.

Celtic relationship has met with little favour.* The western name Roumanian springs from a similarly exploded hypothesis concerning the Latin origin of these people. To be sure, Roumanian is distinctly allied to the other Romance languages in structure. It is an anomaly in the eastern Slavic half of Europe. The most plausible explanation for this phenomenon, and one long accepted, was that the modern Roumanians were descendants of the two hundred and forty thousand colonists whom the Emperor Trajan is said to have sent into the conquered province of Dacia. The earlier inhabitants of the territory were believed to have been the original Thracians. Since no two were agreed as to what the Thracians were like, this did not amount to much. Modern common sense has finally prevailed over attempts to display philological erudition in such matters. Freeman † expresses this clearly. Roumania, as he says, lay directly in the path of invasion from the East; the hold of the Romans upon Dacia was never firm; the province was the first to break away from the Empire; and finally proof of a Latinization only at the late date of the thirteenth century is not wanting.‡ The truth seems to be that two forces were contending for the control of eastern Europe. The Latin could prevail only in those regions which were beyond the potent influence of Greece. Dacia being remote and barbarian, this Latin element had a fighting chance for survival, and succeeded.

Our ethnic map at page 403 shows a curious islet of Roumanian language in the heart of the Greek-speaking territory of Thessaly. There is little sympathy between the two peoples, according to Hellène [90]. The occurrence of this Roumanian colony, so far removed from its base, has long puzzled ethnographers. Some believe the peoples were separately Romanized *in situ;* others that they were colonists from Dacia in the ninth and tenth centuries. At all events, these Pindus Roumanians are too numerous—over a million souls—to be

---

* *Cf.* Picot, 1883, in his review of Tocilescu ; and Rosny, 1885, p. 83.

† 1879, p. 217. *Cf.* also Auerbach, 1898, p. 286.

‡ *Cf.* Obédénare, 1876, p. 350 ; Slavici, 1881, p. 43 ; Rosny, 1885, p. 27 ; Hellène, 1890, p. 190.

neglected in any theory as to the origin of their language.*
Another islet of quasi-Roumanian speech occurs in Istria, on
the Adriatic coast. Its origin is equally obscure.†

It is no contradiction that, in spite of the fact of our exclusion of Roumania from the Balkan Peninsula owing to its
Latin affinities, thereby seeming to differentiate it sharply from
Bulgaria, the latter of Finnic origin; that we now proceed
to treat of the physical characteristics of the two nationalities,
Roumanian and Bulgarian, together. Here is another example of the superficiality of language, of social and political
institutions. They do not concern the fundamental physical
facts of race in the least. At the same time we again emphasize the necessity of a powerful corrective, based upon
purely natural phenomena, for the tendency of philologists
and ethnographers to follow their pet theories far afield, giving
precedence to analogies of language and customs over all the
patent facts of geographical probability. Let us look at it in
this light. Is there any chance that, on the opposite sides of
the Danube, a few Finns and a few Romans respectively inter-
spersed among the dense population which so fertile an area
must have possessed, even at an early time, could be in any wise
competent to make different types of the two? There is nothing in our confessedly scanty anthropological data to show it,
at all events. We must treat the lower Danubian plain as a
unit, irrespective of the bounds of language, religion, or nationality.

It was long believed that the Bulgarians were distinctive
among the other peoples of eastern Europe by reason of their
long-headedness. All the investigations upon limited series of
crania pointed in this direction.‡ This naturally was interpreted as a confirmation of the historic data as to a Finnic
Bulgarian origin very distinct from that of the broad-headed
Slavs. Several recent discoveries have put a new face upon
the matter. In the first place, researches of Dr. Bassanovič,
of Varna, upon several thousand recruits from western Bul-

---

* Picot, 1875, pp. 390 *et seq.*   † Auerbach, 1898, p. 211.
‡ Kopernicki, 1875 b. Beddoe, 1879; Virchow, 1886 a; Malief, in his
Catalogue of 1888, gives details for thirty-eight Bulgarian crania also.

garia yielded an average cephalic index of 85.* This is
nearly ten units above the results of the earlier observers. It
proves that the west Bulgarians at least even outdo many
of the Balkan Slavs in their broad-headedness. At the same
time it appears that the older authorities were right, after all,
in respect of the eastern Bulgarians. Among them, and also
over in eastern Roumelia, the cephalic index ranges as low
as 78. Our map at page 340 expresses this relation. The
long oval-faced Bulgarians among our portraits are probably of this dolichocephalic type. Their contrast facially with
the broad-headed Roumanians is very marked. Thus it is established that the Bulgarian nation is by no means a unit in
its head form. We should add also that, although not definitely proved as yet, it is highly probable that similar variations
occur in Roumania. In the Bukovina brachycephaly certainly
prevails. Our square-faced Roumanians facing page 410 may
presumably be taken to represent this type. This broad-
headedness decreases apparently toward the east as we leave
the Carpathian Mountains, until along the Black Sea it seems,
as in Bulgaria, to give way to a real dolichocephaly.†

How are we to account for the occurrence of so extended
an area of long-headedness all over the great lower Danubian
plain? Our study of the northern Slavs has shown that no
such phenomenon occurs there among the Russians. It certainly finds no counterpart among the southern Slavs or the
Turks. The only other people who resemble these Bulgars in
long-headedness are the Greeks. Even they are far separated;
and, in any event, very impure representatives of the type.
What shall we say? Two explanations seem to be possible, as
Dr. Beddoe observes.‡ Either this dolichocephaly is due to the
Finnicism of the original Bulgars; or else it represents a characteristic of the pre-Bulgarian population of the Danube basin.
He inclines with moderation to the former view. The other

---

* 1891, p. 30. Dr. Bassanovič has most courteously sent me a sketch
map showing the results of these researches. Deniker, 1897, p. 203, and
1898 a, describes them also.

† Deniker, 1898 a, p. 122 ; Weisbach, 1877, p. 238 ; Rosny, 1885, p. 85.

‡ 1879, p. 233.

horn of the dilemma is chosen by Anutchin * in a brilliant paper at the late Anthropological Congress at Moscow. According to his view—and we assent most heartily to it—this dolichocephaly along the Black Sea represents the last survival of a most persistent trait of the primitive inhabitants of eastern Europe. Referring again to our study of Russia,† we would call attention to the occurrence of a similar long-headed race underlying all the modern Slavic population. We shall be able to prove also that such a primitive substratum occurs over nearly all Europe. It has been unearthed not far from here, for example, at Glasinac in Bosnia.‡ When archæological research is extended farther to the east, new light upon this point may be expected. It will be asked at once why this primitive population should still lie bare upon the surface, here along the lower Danube, when it has been submerged everywhere else in central Europe. Our answer is ready. Here in this rich alluvial plain population might, expectedly, be dense at a very early period. As we have observed before, such a population, if solidly massed, opposes an enormous resistance to absorption by new-comers. A few thousand Bulgarian invaders would be a mere drop in the bucket of such an aggregation of men. We are strengthened in this hypothesis that the dolichocephaly of the Danubian plain is primitive, by reason of another significant fact brought out by Bassanovič.# Long-headedness is overwhelmingly more prevalent among women than among men. The former represent more often what Bassanovič calls the "dolichocephalic Thracian type." The oval-faced Bulgarian woman among our portraits would seem to be one of these. Now, in the preceding chapter, we have sought to illustrate the principle that in any population the primitive type persists more often in the women. The bearing of such a law in the case of the Bulgars would seem to

---

* 1893, p. 282.

† Page 352 *supra*. *Cf.* especially Bogdanof, 1893, p. 1.

‡ *Vide* p. 463 *infra*.

1891, p. 31. Women dolicho-, 25 per cent; meso-, 42 per cent; brachycephalic, 30 per cent; while among men the percentages are 3, 16, and 81 ± per cent respectively.

be definite.   Their long-headedness, where it occurs, must date
from a far more remote period than the historic advent of the
few thousand immigrants who have given the name Bulgaria
to the country.

As for the other physical traits of the Bulgarians and Roumanians there is little to be added.   It goes without saying
that they are both deep brunets.   Obédénare [76] says the
Roumanians are very difficult to distinguish from the modern
Spaniards and Italians.   This is probably true in respect of
brunetness.   The Oriental caste of features of our portraits, on
the other hand, can not fail to attract attention.   More than
two thirds of Bassanovič's nineteen hundred and fifty-five
Bulgarians were very dark-haired.   Light eyes were of course
more frequent, nearly forty per cent being classed as blue or
greenish.   A few—about five per cent—were yellow or tawny-
haired, these individuals being at the same time blue-eyed.
This was probably Procopius' excuse for the assertion that
the Bulgars were of fair complexion.   He also affirmed that
they were of goodly stature.   This is not true of either the
modern Roumanians or Bulgars.   They average less than five
feet five inches in height,* being considerably shorter than
the Turks, and positively diminutive beside the Bosnians and
other southern Slavs.   The Bulgarians especially are correspondingly stocky, heavily boned and built.   We may add that
there is a real difference in temperament between the two nationalities, built up, as we assert, from the same foundation.
The Wallachians are said to be more emotional and responsive;
the Bulgarians inclined to heaviness and stolidity.   Both are
pre-eminently industrious and contented cultivators of the soil,
with little aptitude for commerce, so it is said.   We hesitate
to pass judgment in respect of their further aptitudes until fuller
data can be provided than are available at the present time.

At almost no point are the Hungarian people permitted

---

* Bassanovič's series of 1,955 individuals averages only 1.638 metres.
Op. cit., p. 30.   Auerbach, 1898, p. 259, gives an average of 1.63 metres
for 880 Wallachians in Transylvania.   Obédénare, 1876, p. 374, states
brown eyes to be most frequent in Roumania.

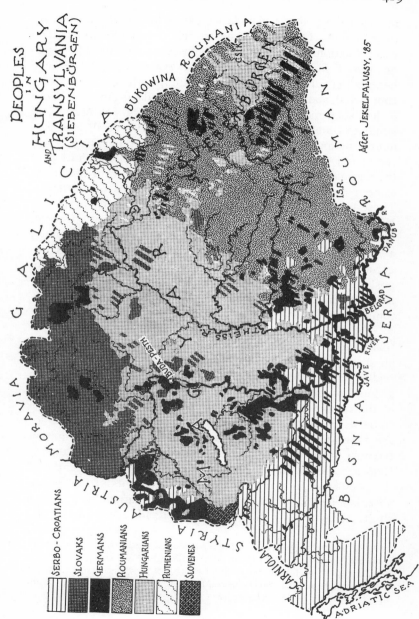

PEOPLES
IN
HUNGARY
AND
TRANSYLVANIA
(SIEBENBÜRGEN)

After JEKELFALUSSY, '85

SERBO-CROATIANS
SLOVAKS
GERMANS
ROUMANIANS
HUNGARIANS
RUTHENIANS
SLOVENES

to touch the political boundaries of the kingdom which bears
their name.* Our map illustrates this peculiar relation. The
various nationalities are indeed disposed, as Auerbach ('98) suggests, as if in order of battle, the Magyars in a state of siege
beset upon all sides. This dominant people are principally
compacted about the historic city of Buda-Pesth in a more
or less solid mass. In upon them from every side press rival
languages and peoples. The Slovaks to the north are both
numerous and united. Moravia, it will be remembered, was
conquered by the Magyars only through the co-operation of
the Germans. More than half of the population in the entire
eastern half of the monarchy are Roumanians or Wallachs.
These people have, as our map shows, penetrated so far into
Hungary as to cut off a considerable area of Magyar speech in
Transylvania (Siebenbürgen) from the great body of the nation
about Buda-Pesth. A number of connecting islets of Hungarian survivals still exist between the two. This is proof
positive that the Roumanians have come in later than the
first Magyar possession, submerging their language and customs thereby.

The Transylvanian Magyars on the slopes of the Carpathians are known as *Szeklers*, or "borderers," although we
are disposed to think that it is the western Hungarians who are
really best entitled to that name. At all events, this eastern
group, though smaller, is far more compact. The main body
of the nation in the west is interpenetrated by multitudes of
colonists from the outside, especially by the Germans. As for
the Serbo-Croatians, who have encroached upon Hungarian
territory from the south, they seem, unlike the Germans, to
form a coherent and clannish people. Almost nine tenths of
the population in many places within the limits of the Serbo-
Croatian language are in reality of this nationality. In no
single Magyar district, on the other hand, according to the

---

* On the demography of Hungary consult especially the official com-
pendium published in English, The Millennium of Hungary and its
People, edited by Jekelfalussy, Buda-Pesth, 1897. Auerbach, Les Races
et Nationalités en Autriche-Hongrie, Paris, 1898, is also excellent, Hunfalvy, 1877 and 1881, is a classic authority.

census of 1880, is there more than seventy per cent of Hungarians.*

By this time it will have been noted that Hungary is by no means solidly Magyar. Only about four tenths of the 17,500,000 inhabitants of the monarchy are of this nationality.† This minority, to be sure, outnumbers the total of the Germans, Slovaks, and Roumanians combined, but it is still a minority nevertheless. There are two good reasons why these people are entitled to rule; for, of course, we assume it to be a self-evident geographical proposition that but one single political unit should abide in this Danubian plain. It is one of the most clearly defined areas of characterization in Europe. The prior claim in behalf of Magyar sovereignty is based upon numerical preponderance. This is becoming strengthened continually, for it is certain that the Magyar speech is gaining ground more rapidly than any of its competitors. This is partly because the Hungarians are increasing faster than the other peoples about them. It is also due in a measure to the adoption of the official language by many who are of foreign birth. The second reason why the Magyars are entitled to rule all Hungary is because these people seem to be pre-eminent intellectually. They form the large mass of the city populations, the Slavs being natural cultivators of the soil. The liberal professions seem to be recruited from the Magyars also in the main.‡ Our data are drawn from Hungarian statistics, which naturally would not underestimate the ability of their own nationality. Even making due allowance for this, their representation in the intellectual classes is very marked. Certainly no better title to sovereignty could be urged.

---

* Jekelfalussy, 1885. The census of 1890 shows the same relative compactness of the Serbo-Croatians, although for some reason the percentages are considerably lower. Jekelfalussy, 1897, p. 417.

† Jekelfalussy, 1897, p. 417, gives census returns for 1890. The proportions are as follows: Hungarians, 42.8 per cent; Germans, 12.1 per cent; Slovaks, 11 per cent; Wallachs, 14.9 per cent; Ruthenians, 2.2 per cent; Croats, 9 per cent; Servians, 6.1 per cent. This, of course, is for Hungary alone, not for the Austro-Hungarian Empire.

‡ Cf. Jekelfalussy, 1897, p. 418, and Auerbach, 1898, p. 252.

The definite origin of the Magyars has long been a matter of controversy. Historically, they displaced the Avars, who had reduced the country to a state of anarchy in the last decade of the ninth century.* They seem to have come in from the northeast. For a while they were encamped in the plains between the Don and the lower Dnieper in Russia. The Bulgars seemingly pressed upon them here from behind, until they, to the number possibly of a few hundred thousand, crossed the Carpathians. They seem to have met with little opposition in effecting a settlement along the Danube, except in Moravia. Whence they came before their appearance in southern Russia no man knows with any approach to certainty. The only evidence is linguistic rather than historical.

Two centuries ago Fogel discovered a number of points of similarity between the Magyar language and that of the Lapps and Finns.† Closer analysis thereafter appeared to connect it most definitely with the speech of the Volga branch of this Finnic family, especially the Ostiaks and Voguls. A number of Turkish words seemed also to be related to the language of the Chouvashes. Vámbéry ‡ has made a determined and able effort to prove that both the Hungarian culture and language are Turkish rather than Finnic in origin. The nearest " poor relations " of the Hungarians are the Bashkirs, according to him; an opinion in which Sommier [81] seems to acquiesce. As for the Byzantine chroniclers, they called them Turks, Huns, and Ungars indiscriminately. On the whole, the trend of opinion seems to favour the Finnic hypothesis, making due allowance for the chance of borrowing from the Turkish peoples during the course of their long migrations. For our more general purposes all these theories lead to the same result. We may be fairly certain that we have to do with an immigrant people, originating in some part of Russia entirely beyond the sphere of the Aryan or inflectional languages.

---

* Hunfalvy, 1877, pp. 145–179.

† Simonyi gives an excellent chapter on this, in Jekelfalussy, 1897, pp. 143–165. *Cf.* also Hunfalvy, p. 146, and Pruner Bey, 1865.

‡ 1882, pp. 235–257. Auerbach, 1898, p. 230, discusses it ably. Obermüller's (1871) fantastic theory of a Caucasian Kabardian derivation may be mentioned.

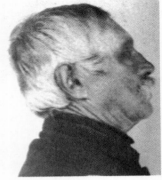

193.   SZEKLER, Torda-Aranyos.   Blue eyes, chestnut hair.   Index 89.   194.

195.   SZEKLER, Torda-Aranyos.   Blue eyes, chestnut hair.   Index 91.   196.

197.   County Csik.   TRANSYLVANIA.   County Borsod.   198.

HUNGARIAN TYPES.

The physical characteristics of the Magyars have been but little investigated scientifically. We know less of them than of almost any other great European people. On the one hand, Topinard [78] assures us that they form to-day "one of the most beautiful types in Europe"; on the other, we have it from Lefèvre * that our word "ogre" is a derivative from *ougre* or Hungar, so outlandish were these people to their new neighbours in Europe. Perhaps this may indeed have been so, although even the present Volga Finns shown in our portraits at page 358 are by no means Mongols or even ogres, in personal appearance. The modern Hungarians are certainly not un-European in any respect. Through the courtesy of Dr. Janko, custos of the National Museum at Buda-Pesth, we are able to present authentic portraits of perhaps the purest of the Magyars. Our types on the opposite page, and the additional one at page 228, are all representative of the Szeklers of Transylvania. From their isolation and the compactness of their settlement one might expect them to have retained their primitive features in some purity.

From these portraits and from our other data it appears that the Magyars are a strikingly fine-looking and well-developed people. The facial features are regular, the nose and mouth well formed. There is nothing Asiatic or Mongol to be seen. Perhaps, indeed, they have, as Dr. Beddoe writes me, an Oriental type of beauty, with somewhat prominent "semi-Tatar" cheek bones. Nevertheless, we find no trace of the "coarse Mongoloid features" which Keane [96] describes among these *Szeklers*, whom he rightly seems to regard as the purest representatives of their race. Nor are they even very dark, these Hungarians. Brunets are in a majority, to be sure, but this is true of all southeastern Europe. The most prevalent combination is of blue eyes and chestnut hair, judging by the data from Dr. Janko's observations. Nearly every one of our portrait types were thus constituted.† Ac-

---

* 1896 b, p. 367. *Cf.* Jekelfalussy, 1898, p. 402.

† Of 81 Szeklers, 35 had blue eyes, 34 brown, 9 gray, and 3 light brown. As to hair colour, 20 were blond, 44 chestnut-brown, 13 black, 1 red, and 3 light brown.

cording to this, the Magyars differ but slightly from the Austrian Germans. Their blondish proclivities would tend to confirm the theory of Finnic rather than Turkish origin; for, as we have already shown, the Volga Finns, and even the Ostiaks and Voguls over in Siberia, are still quite light in type.

As for the head form of the Hungarians, the data are very scanty and defective. The eighty-four *Szeklers* of Janko's series gave an index of 84.5, from which it would appear that the purest of Magyars are pretty broad-headed. Weisbach's [77] and Lenhossek's * results are not far from these, although Deniker † gives some indication of a longer-headedness. Rashly generalizing from this scanty material, we have ventured to predict a distribution of head form as shown on our map at page 340. This would indicate a natural cephalic index of about 84, falling toward the west by reason of German intermixture. In this respect, then, we find Turkish rather than Volga Finnic affinities, for the Volga Finns are all quite long-headed (see map, page 360). Finally, in stature our evidence in the matter of Finnic or Turkish origins is equally inconclusive. Janko's *Szeklers* were all very tall (1.70 metres), but others do not confirm this as a characteristic trait of the nation.‡ Most observers agree that the Magyars are only of average height; taller than the Poles, but shorter than the Serbo-Croatians. It is to be hoped that this most interesting field of investigation may not long remain unworked.[#] So far as our knowledge goes, it tends to confirm us in the view that the historians and ethnographers have immensely overestimated the importance of the original Finnic immigration, with a corresponding neglect of the population which existed in Hungary before their advent. These earlier inhabitants, while adopting the language of their conquerors, have succeeded in almost entirely obliterating the original traits of the Magyars as a race. If they were originally Finns and related to the Ostiaks and Voguls, the direction of their intermixture

---

* Revue d'Anth., série i, v, p. 552 ; Hunfalvy, 1877, p. 273.

† 1898 a, p. 120.   ‡ *Cf.* map, page 350 *supra*, with appendix.

[#] On the state of archæology, *vide* Pulszky, 1891.

has all been toward that of the Alpine race. This latter has been proved an early possessor of the soil of central Europe. The present traits of the Hungarians seem to lend force to the hypothesis that the same race was also firmly rooted in the great Danubian plain before their appearance. According to this view, they would be, roughly speaking, perhaps one eighth Finnic and seven eighths Alpine by racial descent.

CHAPTER XVI.

WESTERN ASIA: CAUCASIA, ASIA MINOR, PERSIA, AND INDIA.

THE utter absurdity of the misnomer Caucasian, as applied to the blue-eyed and fair-headed " Aryan " (?) race of western Europe, is revealed by two indisputable facts. In the first place, this ideal blond type does not occur within many hundred miles of Caucasia; and, secondly, nowhere along the great Caucasian chain is there a single native tribe making use of a purely inflectional or Aryan language. In the days of Brosset and Bopp we were taught that the Georgians, most noted of the Caucasian tribes, spoke such a tongue. Blumenbach is said to have given the name Caucasian to his white race after seeing a fine specimen of such a Georgian skull. We know better to-day, thanks to the labours of Uslar and others. Even the Ossetes, whose language alone is possibly inflectional, have not had their claims to the honour of Aryan made positively clear as yet.* And even if Ossetian be Aryan, there is every reason to regard the people as immigrants from the direction of Iran, not indigenous Caucasians at all. Their head form, together with their occupation of territory along the only highway—the Pass of Dariel—across the chain from the south, give tenability to the hypothesis.† At all events, whether the Ossetes be Aryan or not, they little deserve preeminence among the other peoples about them. They are lacking both in the physical beauty ‡ for which this region is justly famous, and in courage as well, if we may judge by their reputation in yielding abjectly and without shadow of resistance to the Russians.

---

* Smirnof, 1878, gives full discussion. *Cf.* Seydlitz, 1881, p. 98.
† Houssay, 1887, p. 106 ; Seydlitz, 1881, p. 125.
‡ Chantre, 1895, iv, p. 156.

We mention these apparently irrelevant facts because it is undeniable that a large measure of the popularity of the name Caucasian has had its origin in the traditional physical perfection and chivalrous spirit of the natives of this part of the world. Byzantine harem tales of Circassian beauty have not failed to influence opinion upon the subject of European origins. Not even the charm of mystery remains in support of a Caucasian race theory to-day. In the present state of our knowledge, it is therefore difficult to excuse the statement of a recent authority, who still persists in the title *Homo Caucasicus* as applied to the peoples of Europe. It is not true that any of these Caucasians are even " somewhat typical." * As a fact, they could never be typical of anything. The name covers nearly every physical type and family of language of the Eur-Asian continent, except, as we have said, that blond, tall, " Aryan "-speaking one to which the name has been specifically applied. It is all false; not only improbable, but absurd. The Caucasus is not a cradle—it is rather a grave—of peoples, of languages, of customs, and of physical types.† Let us be assured of that point at the outset.

Nowhere else in the world probably is so heterogeneous a lot of people, languages, and religions gathered together in one place as along the chain of the Caucasus mountains.‡ Herodotus and the Plinys were well aware of this. The number of dialects is reckoned in the neighbourhood of sixty-eight. These represent all stages of development. One—that of the Ossetes—is possibly Aryan; it is but very primitively European, to say the least. A second, the Circassian—Kabardian and Abkhasian—is incorporative. It is so like the American Indian languages in structure that we find Cruel # using it as proof of a primitive American Indian substratum of population over Europe. May the day come when philologists shall have an eye to the common decencies of geographical and

---

* Keane, Ethnology, p. 226.   † Smirnof, 1878, p. 241.
‡ On the ethnography, mainly linguistic, of the Caucasus, the principal authorities are Smirnof, 1878 ; Seydlitz, 1881 and 1885 ; and Chantre, 1885. Our map, after Rittich, 1878, has been corrected from the results of the later authorities.   # 1883, pp. 166–173.

physical possibility! Then again, there are the purely agglutinative languages—Asiatic in their affinities—of the Koumyks, Kalmucks, and Tatars. To all these we may add a fourth great linguistic family, the Semitic, represented by the Armenians and the omnipresent Jews. Over all and through all is what Bryce calls a "top dressing" of Europeans, speaking the most highly evolved languages peculiar to western or civilized Europe. Thus it happens, as Uslar long ago proved, that greater differences exist within the Caucasus between its linguistic "microcosms" than between the most widely separated members of the Aryan family in Europe. In other words, for example, the Avars differ more from the Ossetes or the Kabardians in language than the Lithuanians differ from the Spaniards. In the former case it is a matter of structure; in the latter merely of deviation from a common type or stem by a transmutation of root words.

The geographical character and location of the Caucasian mountains offer a patent explanation for this phenomenon of heterogeneity. Four distinct currents of language with their concomitant physical types, have swept up to the base of this insuperable physical barrier. We use the term insuperable advisedly, for there is in reality only one break in the entire chain from the Black Sea to the Caspian. This is the famous Pass of Dariel—eight thousand feet high—lying in the territory of the Ossetes. It explains why this people alone among all its neighbours is able to occupy both slopes of the mountains. All the other tribes and languages lie either on one side or the other. The Tatars, to be sure, are both north and south of the mountains; they seem to be about everywhere. Yet we have already shown (page 419) that where they have crossed the chain they have been entirely transformed physically by isolation. Up against such a mountain system as this, have swept great currents of human life from every quarter of the eastern hemisphere. They have not blended. There has been contiguous isolation, to coin a phrase, ample in supply for all. Thus has it been possible for each language to preserve and perhaps still further to develop its peculiarities *in situ*. Linguistic isolation has again served to intensify the geo-

graphical segregation due to physical environment. The effect
of all this in the matter of race could not be other than to cause

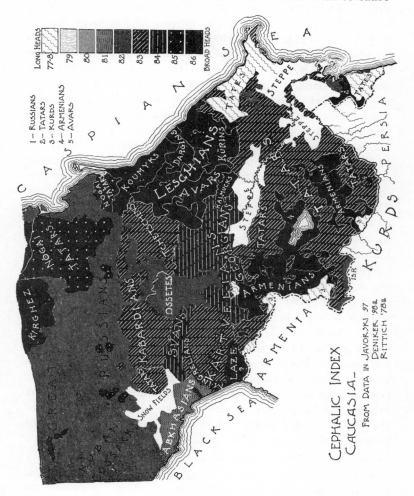

a heterogeneity of physical types quite without parallel elsewhere in the world.

It would lead us too far astray from the main line of our
interests to attempt a detailed description of the physical types

peculiar to all the Caucasian tribes.*   Our principal object is
negative—viz., to show what these people are not; that is to
say, to divest this region of the fanciful importance which has
so long been assigned to it by students of European origins.
A glance at our map of cephalic index of Caucasia will make
its physical heterogeneity apparent, even excluding the Armenians, Kurds, and Azerbeidjian Tatars who lie entirely outside the mountain chain.   The first impression conveyed by
the map, next to that of heterogeneity, is of a prevalent broad-
headedness.   In this respect the Caucasians as a whole are
distinct both from the Russian Slavs on the north, and from
the Iranian peoples—Tates or Tadjiks, Kurds, and Persians—
in the opposite direction.   Among the mountaineers themselves, the Lesghian tribes betray an accentuated brachycephaly equal to that of the pure Mongols about the Caspian.
The Kartvelian tribes, numerically most important of all, seem
to become somewhat longer-headed from east to west.†   As
for the principal remnant of the Tscherkesses or Circassians,
known as Kabardians, they are not very different from their
neighbours; but the Abkhasians along the Black Sea belonging to the same family, whom, by the way, Bryce ‡ calls " the
most unmitigated rogues and thieves in all Caucasia," are
slightly more dolichocephalic than even the Russians.   The
fourth group—the Ossetes—appear on our map to be quite
different from all the other Caucasians, except the Abkhasians
just named.   The difference between them and the Lesghians
in head form is exemplified by comparison of the two lower
types in our series near by.   The round and occipitally short
head of the Lesghian is at one extreme; the long oval one of
the Ossete at the other.   Their faces are as differently proportioned also as are their skulls.

---

* Chantre's monumental work, Recherches Anthropologiques dans le
Caucase, 4 vols., Atlas, Paris, 1885–'87, is a standard.   In addition, the
detailed researches of Russian observers should be consulted, such as Pan-
tyuckhof, 1893, on the Georgians ; Vyschogrod, 1895, on the Kabardians ;
Gilchenko, 1897, on the Ossetes ; Sviderski, 1898, on the Koumyks, etc.

† Cf. table in Chantre, 1885, iv, p. 272.

‡ Transcaucasia and Ararat, 1897.

199. MINGRELIAN. 200.

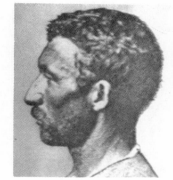

201. LAZE, Batum. 202.

203. OSSETE, Koban. 204.

CAUCASIA.

205. TSCHETSCHEN. Cephalic Index 82.3. 206.

207. INGOUCHE (Tschetschen group). Cephalic Index 84.4. 208.

209. LESGHIAN from Gounib. 210.

CAUCASUS MOUNTAINS.

An important fact must be noted at this point—viz., that customs of cranial deformation are exceedingly prevalent all through Caucasia and Asia Minor. This renders all study of the head form quite uncertain. Thus the Laze about Batum practise this deformation most persistently; their foreshortened heads and their long oval faces are in corresponding disharmony.* Our portrait type from this tribe is apparently normal in head form. The occiput shows no sign of artificial depression. That their brachycephaly is real is much to be doubted. Among the Abkhasians, on the other hand, the rare phenomenon of lateral compression of the skull may account for their striking long-headedness.† On the whole, making due allowance for this uncertainty, it would seem that the Caucasians are pretty strongly inclined to be broad-headed. The Lesghians and the Svans are the wildest and most isolated. They are most brachycephalic. The Ossetes are on the highway of transmigration. They have either deviated from the original pattern, or else, as we have suggested above, they are immigrants, not indigenous at all.

Our series of portraits illustrates the facts concerning the facial features of these tribes. Their classic beauty is well represented in our Mingrelian, whom we may assume as typical of the Georgian group. It is, however, a perfectly formal, cold, and unintelligent beauty, in no wise expressive of character, as Chantre observes. The Mingrelians, despite their warm and fertile country, are, according to Bryce, persistently "ne'er-do-weels." The Lesghian group, and also the Tchetchen, are described as less regularly featured than the Circassians or Georgians. The faces bear evident traces of the hardship to which not only their rigorous environment exposes them, but also of the continual struggle against the Mongols, who incessantly threaten them from the north. Their contrast in temperament with the characteristically gay and dance-loving Georgians is very marked. The renowned beauties of the Caucasus are, of course, the Tscherkessen or Circassians. The Kabardians are less pure than the Adighe or

---

* Chantre, 1885, iv, p. 91.   † *Op. cit.*, iv, p. 130.

Circassians proper, but even among them the broad shoulders and erect carriage, with the oval face, brilliant brown eyes, and fine chestnut hair, are predominant. In character these Circassians are also pre-eminent. Amiable, talkative, and inquisitive to a degree, they are also brave, chivalrous, and hospitable. To be sure, their name may be derived from the Turkish words meaning " to cut the road." Nevertheless, though given to brigandage, they are faithful to their friends. Their wholesale preference of exile to Russian domination, more than four fifths of them having emigrated to Turkey in the sixties, is evidence of a not inconsiderable moral stamina. The Ossetes, who by the way call themselves Ir or Irons, stand at the other extreme as regards both face and character. They are tall, but lack suppleness, elegance, and dignity; the features are said to be irregular and angular. Our portrait is a good type. Many Jewish features occur, as among the Circassians also, for that matter. In character they are deficient in bravery, their prompt acquiescence in the Russian military rule, as we have said, being characteristic. One physical peculiarity of importance remains to be noted. Chantre * found among the Ossetes above thirty per cent of blonds. This is thrice as great as among the Georgians. Nearly all the other Caucasians are of a relatively dark type, chestnut hair and dark-brown eyes prevailing, although black is quite common.†
Even among the Laze, whose whiteness of skin is remarkable, Chantre found the hair of a third of them black. Thus we are easily able to dispose of any theory of a blond Caucasian race in the light of these facts.

A large area, indefinitely bounded by the Mediterranean Sea, Caucasia, the Red Sea, and the Pamir, remains to be described. Obviously, Asia Minor, Mesopotamia, and Persia can not be left out of account in our review of the Oriental peoples of Europe. This region has been the seat of the oldest known civilizations. It possesses a far better claim to our

---

* *Op. cit.*, iv, p. 170. *Cf.* Khanykoff, 1886, p. 113.

† Vyschogrod, for example, found forty-seven per cent of black hair among the Kabardians.

attention as a possible centre of human or cultural evolution than Caucasia. Two difficulties confront us at the outset in an analysis of its racial types. One is the kaleidoscopic changes ever taking place in the character of its nomad populations; the other is the intricacy of the problem due to the central location of the district. To it have converged from every direction great currents of immigration or invasion: Turkish-Tatar, from the steppes of Asia; European, from Greece; African, from Egypt. In the convergence of these currents upon this point we find, of course, a plausible explanation for its early pre-eminence in civilization. Corresponding difficulty in distinguishing the several ethnic elements is a necessary corollary of this fact.

The distribution of language offers positively no clew to the problem. The Azerbeidjian Tatars, forming a major element in the population of Persia, are positively Iranian in every trait, although their language is Turkish. Our portrait of one of these at page 449 reveals no symptom of Turkon an blood. Notwithstanding this, no other alternative is offered to the linguist than to class these people as Turks. The Kurds, on the other hand, are mainly inhabitants of Asiatic Turkey, but they are Iranian in their affinities, both linguistic and physical. The Armenians, judging by their language which seems to be Aryan,* might reasonably be expected to stand between the Greeks and the Persians. As a matter of fact, they are far more closely related physically to the Turkomans than to these other Aryan-speaking peoples. Language fails utterly to describe the racial situation.

This extensive region is to-day occupied by two distinct racial types, roughly corresponding to two of the three races which we have so painfully followed over Europe.† The first of these in this part of the world we may provisionally call the Iranian. It includes the Persians and Kurds, possibly the Ossetes in the Caucasus, and farther to the east a large

---

* *Cf.* note in Keane's Ethnology, p. 411. Whether Armenian be Iranic, Semitic, or unique, it is surely Aryan.

† Chantre's monumental Recherches dans l'Asie Occidentale, Lyon, 1895, is our authority. *Cf.* especially his summary at pp. 234–244.

35

number of Asiatic tribes, from the Afghans to the Hindus. These peoples are all primarily long-headed and dark brunets. They incline to slenderness of habit, although varying in stature according to circumstances. In them we recognise at once undoubted congeners of our Mediterranean race in Europe. The area of their extension runs off into Africa, through the Egyptians, who are clearly of the same race. Not only the modern peoples, but the ancient Egyptians and the Phœnicians also have been traced to the same source.* By far the larger portion of this part of western Asia is inhabited by this eastern branch of the Mediterranean race.

The second racial type in this borderland between Europe and Asia we may safely follow Chantre in calling Armenoid, because the Armenians most clearly represent it to-day. It is less widely distributed than the Iranian racial type. Outside of Asia Minor, it occurs sporadically among a few ethnic remnants in Syria and Mesopotamia. Throughout the Anatolian peninsula it forms the underlying substratum of population, far more primitive than any occupation by the Turks. This type is possessed of a most peculiar head form, known to somatologists as hypsi-brachycephaly. It is illustrated by our accompanying portrait page. The head is abnormally flattened at the back. It rises sharply from the neck, while, as if at the expense of this foreshortening, the height of the skull is greatly increased. This disguises, of course, the real breadth of face peculiar to this type, as contrasted with the Iranians. Artificial compression is at once suggested by such head forms as these. It is undoubtedly present, either consciously performed or else as a product of the hard cradles. That the shortness of the head is not entirely artificial can not be doubted, or else we have a case of inheritance of acquired characteristics. For even in absence of such deformation the same sugar-loaf cranial form occurs.† Along with this peculiarity of head form are other bodily characteristics differentiating these people from the Iranian type. The body is heavier built, with an inclination—among the Armenians at least—to

---

* Page 387 *supra*.　　　† Chantre, 1895, pp. 38–67.

211.   Armenian.   212.

213.   Tachtadsky, Lycia, Asia Minor.   214.

215. Tachtadsky, Lycia, Asia Minor. Stature 1.71 m. Index 86. 216.

ARMENOID TYPES.

obesity. There are not very great differences in pigmentation between the two racial types. Both are overwhelmingly brunet. The rare blonds of the Caucasus are even more scarce hereabouts; although Chantre found eleven per cent of blonds among them, the great majority were very dark. Only as we enter the Himalayan highlands, among Galchas and their fellows, do lighter traits in hair and eyes appear.

Two rival peoples—Kurds and Armenians—contend for the mastery of eastern Asia Minor. The first of these, the Kurds, are difficult to classify culturally. The lower classes are sedentary dwelling in villages, while the chiefs live in tents wandering at will. There are nearly two million of them in all, two thirds in Asiatic Turkey, the rest in Persia, with a few thousand in Caucasia. The Armenians claim that these Kurds are of Median origin, but the better opinion is that they are descendants of the Chaldeans. Their affinity to the Syrian Arabs can not be doubted.* These Kurds have remained relatively untouched by the Mongol or Turkish invasions in the retirement afforded by the mountains of Kurdistan. Both in their language and their physical traits they are Iranian. Chantre,† studying them in Asia Minor, reports as to their hard features and savage aspect. Their own derivation of " Kurd " is from a word meaning " excellent "; but the Turkish equivalent for it, " wolf," seems more aptly to describe their character. They are very dark, with eyes of a deep-brown tint; the women darker, as a rule. Our portrait at page 449 is fairly typical. The nose is straight or convex; rarely concave. The head is long and exceedingly narrow (index 78.5), with a face corresponding in its dimensions. The effects of lateral compression of the skull are plainly apparent in our portrait. In stature they are of moderate height. As a whole, owing to their wide extension, nomadic habits, and lack of social solidarity, these Kurds are a heterogeneous people. They lack the strong cementing bonds either of religion or of a national literature.

---

* Chantre, 1885, ii, p. 214.

† 1895, pp. 75 *et seq.*; with data on 332 subjects. Nasonof, 1890, is also good.

Even aside from their persistence in Christianity despite all manner of oppression, the Armenians are by far the most interesting people of Asia Minor. Of all the Orientals, they are the most intelligent, industrious, and peaceful. In many traits of character they resemble the Jews, especially in their aptitude for commercial pursuits and in their characteristic frugality, inclining to parsimony. There are about five million of these Armenians in all, somewhat over half of them being inhabitants of Turkey, with the remainder in Russian Caucasia and Persia. Anthropologically, these people are of supreme importance as an example of purity of physical type, resulting from a notable social and religious solidarity. They rival the Jews again in this respect. One of this nation can almost invariably be detected at once by means of his peculiar head form, which we have already described.[*] Even in places where they have been isolated from the main body of the nation for centuries they adhere to this primitive type. Houssay,[†] for example, finds the Armenian colonists near Ispahan in Persia settled there in 1605, still strongly individualized physically.

It is not without significance, we believe, that Chantre,[‡] remarking upon the purity of the Armenian type, adds that it is " more homogeneous in appearance than in reality." There is good evidence to show that their unity of type, being largely a product of social selection, is defective in those details of which the people themselves are not conscious. It would appear that in their head form, differently from most people, they fully realize their own peculiarities. Deformation of the skull so commonly practised, seems often, as Chantre says, to " exaggerate the brachycephaly common to them." The Kurds, on the other hand, being naturally dolichocephalic, make their heads appear longer than they really are by artificial means.[#] The deadly enmity between Kurds and Armenians is well known. Can it be that these opposing customs of cranial de-

---

* On the Armenians, consult Chantre, 1895, pp. 37 *et seq.* ; Von Luschan, 1889, p. 212 ; Khanykoff, 1866, pp. 112 ; and Tvaryanovitch, 1897.

† 1887, p. 120.   ‡ 1895, pp. 238, 341.

Op. cit., pp. 51 and 113.

formation are an expression of it to some degree? We venture to suggest it as a partial explanation.

That the Armenoid or hypsi-brachycephalic racial type of Asia Minor is not entirely a matter of artificial selection would appear from its prevalence in out-of-the-way places all over Asia Minor. It occurs far outside the Armenian territory. It is more fundamental than the social consciousness of a nation. Von Luschan * finds it among a number of primitive tribes in Anatolia, noticeably among the so-called Tachtadsky. These people, now few in numbers, inhabit the mountainous and remote districts in Lycia. Their name, " woodcutters," designates the occupation in which they are mainly engaged. They are only superficially Mohammedans, their real cult being entirely secret, and probably pagan. Living in rude shelters at elevations of three or four thousand feet above the sea, they appear in the towns only at rare intervals. The necessity of selling their wares overcomes their dread of the tax-gatherer and of army service. Quite like the Tachtadsky physically are another people, known as the Bektasch, or " half Christians," who form the town population in some regions. Down in the mountains of northern Syria the same stratum of population crops out among the Ansariés, or " little Christians." According to Chantre,† these people are anthropologically indistinguishable from the other Armenoid types. Generally speaking, all these peoples are found only in regions of isolation— in marshy, mountainous, or remote districts. On the coast and in the larger towns a type akin to the long-headed Greek is more apt to prevail. For these reasons, von Luschan ('89) concludes that the Armenoid type is the more primitive, and that it represents the earliest inhabitants of the peninsula. That it is older than the Turks no one can doubt. Yet we are inclined to agree with Sergi ‡ that it is not necessarily the very earliest. In fact, there is evidence to show a still more ancient type, like that found in the Greek necropoli. This latter is quite Mediterranean in its racial affinities; probably of the

---

* 1889, pp. 198–213. *Cf.* also Vámbéry, 1885, p. 607.
† 1895, pp. 139–148.   ‡ 1895 a, p. 58.

same origin as the dolichocephalic Iranian peoples who still predominate to the south and west.

Summarizing the anthropological history of Asia Minor, we draw the following conclusions: First, that the Mediterranean or Iranian racial type represents the oldest layer of population in this part of the world. This, as we shall see in the next chapter, is true of all Europe also. A second racial element, subsequently superposed, is that of the Armenoid or brachycephalic type. The similarity of this to our Alpine races of western Europe has been especially emphasized by the most competent authority, von Luschan.* Finally, on top of all has come the modern layer of immigrant and more or less nomadic Turks and their fellows. The possibility of connecting one of these, our second or Armenoid type, with the ancient Hittites can not fail to suggest itself.† Possibly it was Pelasgic. Von Luschan [92] suggests it. Sergi [95] believes the Pelasgi and Hittites were both Asiatic in origin. Who knows? It would be of interest to examine the question further had we sufficient time. For our immediate purposes the importance of the Armenoid group is derived from the fact that it, with the Caucasian one, is the only connecting link between the Alpine racial type of western Europe and its prototype, or perhaps we had better say merely its congener, in the highlands of western Asia. The tenuity of the connecting link between the two is greatest at this point. Were it not for the potent selective influences of religion, complete rupture by the invading Tatar-Turks might conceivably have taken place. As it is, the continuity of the Alpine race across Asia Minor can not be doubted.

In Persia there is no such clear segregation of racial types as we have observed between Armenians and Kurds, who are as impossible of intermixture as oil and water. We have passed beyond the outermost sphere of European religion, Christianity. Marked topographical features are also lacking on the great

---

* 1889, p. 212.

† On Hittite ethnography consult De Cara, Gli Hethei-Pelasgi, Roma, 1894 ; Sergi, 1895 a, p. 54 ; and the works of Wright (1884), Bertin (1888), Tomkins (1889), Sayce (1891), and Conder (1898).

217.   KURD, Asia Minor.   218.

219.   AZERBEIDJIAN, Persian Tatar.   Index 77.7.   220.

221.   SUZIAN, South Persia.   Index 74.7.   222.

IRANIAN TYPES.

plateau of Iran. A wholesale blending of types has consequently ensued among the modern Persians.* Three distinct ethnic influences have been at work, however, producing what we may call varieties, or subtypes, of the pure Iranian. This latter is found only in two limited districts: one among the Farsis about Persepolis, just northeast of the Persian Gulf; the other among the Loris, or "mountaineers," somewhat farther to the west, over against the Kurds. Of these, the former are the ideal Aryans (?) of the earlier philologists. Their skin is described as fair. They are slender but finely formed. This trait is quite noticeable in comparing them with the Turkomans or Tatars. The hair and beard are abundant, of a dark chestnut colour. Thus they are blonds, only by comparison with their darker neighbours on every side. Real blonds, with blue eyes, are very rare; we have Houssay's word for that. The Loris are taller and much darker, often with black hair. Let us add that they are also acutely dolichocephalic, with smoothly oval faces and regular features, thus in every detail corresponding to the criteria necessary to adjudge them Mediterranean by race.

Three subvarieties of this ideal Persian type lie in the several directions of Africa, central Asia, and India. The first of these is Semitic. It occurs all along the line of contact with the Arabs, producing as a natural consequence a distinctly darker population toward the southwest. The second subvariety forms the great mass of the nation. It results from an intermixture with the pure Iranian of a Turkoman or Tatar strain. Such are the Hadjémis and Tadjiks, for example, who predominate in the east and northeast. The Azerbeidjian Tatars, whom we have already described,† also fall within this class. Although they speak Turkish, they are in reality distinctly Iranian by race. Our portrait on the opposite page, reproduced from Danilof's monograph, is fairly typical. The hair is coarser,

---

* Authorities are Duhousset, Les Populations de la Perse, 1859 ; Khanykoff, Mémoire sur l'Ethnographie de la Perse, 1866 ; Houssay, Les Peuples Actuels de la Perse, Bull. Soc. d'Anth., Lyon, pp. 101–148, with map ; and Danilof's work of 1894 in Russian, especially cols. 10–20. This we have had translated ; our portraits are from the same source.

† Page 419 *supra*.

inclining to black; the face is broader, with greater prominence of the cheek bones, than in the pure Iranian. The heads at the same time become broader, especially toward the northeast; and what Bryce calls the "slim, lithe, stealthy, and catlike Persian," is transformed into the bigger and more robust Turkoman. Instead of Turkoman, dare we say an Alpine strain of blood is here apparent? We shall see. Finally, our third subtype of the Persian occurs toward the southeast, among the so-called Suzians, about the mouth of the Persian Gulf. Look at our portrait of one of these on the preceding page. Is not the strain of negroid blood at once apparent? Notice the flattened and open nose, the thick lips and the black hair and eyes. We have reached the confines of India. Here we meet the first traces of the aboriginal population underlying the Hindoos. It includes all the native Indian hill tribes, and extends away off over seas into Melanesia. We are entering upon a new zoölogical realm. Our tedious descriptive task for European peoples is nearly completed.

East of Persia the several racial types which have almost imperceptibly blended into the modern population of that country divide at the western base of the central Asiatic highlands. This great barrier, as we have already pointed out in our chapter on the head form, marks one of the most sudden racial transitions in the world. At its eastern end along the Himalayas, it divides the pure Mongols in Thibet from the Hindoos and the negroid hill tribes of India. Farther to the west, the Hindu-Koosh Mountains in Afghanistan have forced apart the two racial types which we have traced all the way here from Europe. North of the mountains in Turkestan one racial type—the Alpine—occurs among the Turkomans. We can not too strongly emphasize the fact that these peoples in the Aral-Caspian Sea depression are by no means Mongol as a whole. South of the Hindu-Koosh extends the eastern branch of the Mediterranean race, among the Afghans and Hindoos. Space forbids a description of these Indo-Europeans in detail.* We are all familiar with the type, especially as it

---

* Anthropological authorities on the Hindoos are less abundant than for the native or Dravidian peoples. Risley, 1891, is the most compre-

is emphasized by inbreeding and selection among the Brahmans.* There can be no doubt of their racial affiliation with our Berbers, Greeks, Italians, and Spaniards. They are all members of the same race, at once the widest in its geographical extension, the most populous, and the most primitive of our three European types.

In our former description of the Turkomans of the Aral-Caspian Sea depression we have left little doubt as to their affinity to the Alpine race of Europe. In the mountaineers of the Pamir this resemblance becomes perfect. Topinard's immediate recognition of this fact twenty years ago, on the basis of Ujfalvy's discoveries, has never been disputed.† More than that, in the highlands of the Pamir among the Galchas a little west of Samarcand, linguistic research has proved that the European or inflectional type of languages prevails over a large area.‡ These Galcha tribes, or mountain Tadjiks, differ in several ways from the great body of the nomadic Turkomans in the Caspian steppes. In every detail they tend toward the Alpine type, as if by reason of their isolation in the mountains, a primitive population had been preserved in relative purity. For all practical purposes, our two upper portraits at page 45 may be taken as representative of this easternmost member of the brachycephalic, gray-eyed, and heavily built race of central Europe. These people are not blonds, nor even as blond as the Tadjiks in the plains.# They are even more brachycephalic, however, almost establishing a world's record in this respect. In this connection it is curious to note

---

hensive. *Cf.* also Mantegazza, 1883-'84; Crooke, 1890; and the works of Oppert, Rousselet, and others.

* Johnston, Race et Caste dans l'Inde; L'Anth., vi, 1895, pp. 176–181, discusses the skin colour. Kollmann, Internationales Archiv für Ethnographie, vi, 1893, p. 51, shows the differences in head form; the Brahmans being apparently more brachycephalic.

† Rev. d'Anth., 1878, p. 706. *Cf.* note, p. 417 *supra*. Ujfalvy, in Bull. Soc. d'Anth., 1887, p. 15, describes the progress of opinion in this direction.

‡ Ujfalvy, 1896 a, pp. 44 *et seq.* Van den Gheyn (1884); also Tomaschek and others, cited by Keane, Ethnology, p. 411.

Ujfalvy, 1896 a, pp. 53, 428, and 485.

that among the peoples north of the Hindu-Koosh broad-headedness increases as one penetrates the mountains, while on their southern slopes the opposite rule obtains.* From either side, therefore, purity of types—and these, too, of a very different sort—increase toward the watershed which lies between them. How different a phenomenon from that afforded by the gradual transitions of type on the Iranian plateau! Can it longer be affirmed that in approaching the highlands of Asia we are tracing our European racial types back to a common trunk? Facts all belie the assumption. Two at least, of the racial elements in the peoples of Europe are as fundamentally different here in the heart of Asia as all through central Europe. In other words, in our progress from Europe eastward, instead of proceeding toward the trunk, rather does it appear that we have been pushing out to the farthest branches of two fundamentally distinct human types.

---

* *Op. cit.*, p. 52.

CHAPTER XVII.

In our school days most of us were brought up to regard
Asia as the mother of European peoples. We were told that
an ideal race of men swarmed forth from the Himalayan highlands, disseminating culture right and left as they spread
through the barbarous West. The primitive language, parent
to all of the varieties of speech—Romance, Teutonic, Slavic,
Persian, or Hindustanee—spoken by the so-called Caucasian
or white race, was called Aryan. By inference this name was
shifted to the shoulders of the people themselves, who were
known as the Aryan race. In the days when such symmetrical
generalizations held sway there was no science of physical
anthropology; prehistoric archæology was not yet. Shem,
Ham, and Japhet were still the patriarchal founders of the
great racial varieties of the genus *Homo*. A new science of
philology dazzled the intelligent world by its brilliant discoveries, and its words were law. Since 1860 these early inductions
have completely broken down in the light of modern research;
and even to-day greater uncertainty prevails in many phases
of the question that would have been admitted possible twenty
years ago. The great difficulty is to approach the matter in
a calm and entirely judicial spirit; for it may justly be affirmed
that no other scientific question, with the exception, perhaps,
of the doctrine of evolution, was ever so bitterly discussed or
so infernally confounded at the hands of Chauvinistic or otherwise biassed writers.

At the very outset let us rigidly distinguish the phenomena, principles, and conclusions concerning race from those
of language and culture, and each of these in turn from the

453

other. Archæology, to be sure, may sometimes combine the data of human remains with those of an attendant civilization; but philology has, in our present state of knowledge, no possible bond of union in the study of European origins with either of the other two sciences. All attempts, therefore, to correlate linguistic data with those derived from the study of physical characteristics are not only illogical and unscientific; they are at the same time impossible and absurd, as we shall hope to show. They involve an entire misconception of the just principles and limitations of scientific research.

Two antagonistic opinions, respectively characteristic of the rival French and German schools of anthropology, have obtained widespread popular currency through neglect to observe the rule laid down in the preceding paragraph. The first of these is that the " Aryan race " was somehow blond, long-headed, and tall—in other words, that the ancestors of the modern Teutonic type were the original civilizers of Europe. For civilization and Aryanism were indissolubly considered as one and the same; all plausible enough, to be sure, until you look the matter squarely in the face. It is easy to see how this gratuitous assumption of a tall, blond " Aryan race " originated. The sacred books of the East suggested that the chosen people were " white men." This is not surprising, in view of the fact that the aboriginal inhabitants of India, among whom they came, were veritably then, as they are to-day, negroes. Johnston ('95) has shown us how clearly a blond skin is an index of caste among the Brahmans even at this late day. After the Vedas the Greeks took it up, and represented their ideal types after the same blond fashion.* The coincidence that many of the most distinctive Aryan-speaking Europeans to-day are blonds compared with the Basques, Magyars, Turks, and Mongols, who lie outside the Aryan pale, apparently gave scientific voucher to the view. The Indo-Germanic languages—note the adjective—were essentially European; the Teutonic type was the only real *Homo Europæus*. Hence *Homo Europæus* was the original Aryan. A logical

---

* *Cf.* Lapouge, 1889 a ; Sergi, 1895 a, p. 19.

leap in the dark! This did not prevent it from being taken. The idea gained in prestige year by year, especially as the racial Teutonism of the upper classes all over Europe was definitely established. What wonder that the blondness, tallness —nay, even the necessary long-headedness—of the " Aryan race " rose about the need of proof? At the hands of Wilser,* Poesche ('78), Penka ('86), Zaborowski,† Lapouge ('89), and their disciples it has attained the rank of law!

The scientific heresy of attempting to locate a linguistic centre through appeal to physical characteristics has created its greatest devastation among the ranks of the philologists; even Sayce ('87), Rhys,‡ and Rendall ('89) seem to have been deceived by its apparent plausibility. Some of the older anthropologists were certainly tainted with the notion. Schaffhausen, Ecker, and von Hölder are all cited in its favour by Penka.# The notion crops out all along through the memorable discussions over the Aryan question in the Société d'Anthropologie at Paris in 1864.‖ Latterly, with clearer light upon the subject, few authorities upon either side hesitate to condemn any and all such attempts to correlate the data of two entirely incompatible and independent sciences. Virchow, for example, styles such a theory of an " Aryan race " as " pure fiction." Reinach ('92) stigmatizes Penka's hypothesis that the Aryans were Scandinavians as a " prehistoric romance." Few somatologists would even agree with Huxley △ to-day that blondness of the Aryans is a " fair working hypothesis "; or assume with Keane that " nevertheless, all things considered, it seems probable enough." Max Müller ('88), making heroic reparation for the errors of his youth, hits much nearer the mark when he writes: " To me, an ethnologist who speaks of an Aryan race, Aryan blood, Aryan eyes and hair, is as great a sinner as a linguist who speaks of a dolichocephalic dictionary or a brachycephalic grammar. It is worse than a Baby-

---

* 1885, p. 77.   † 1898, p. 62.   ‡ 1890–'91, p. 251.

Von Hölder, 1876, p. 32, expressly denies the possibility of any racial proof.

‖ *Résumé* by Reinach, 1892, pp. 38–46. See also Aryans in index to our supplementary Bibliography.   △ 1890, p. 297.

Ionian confusion of tongues—it is downright theft. . . . If I say Aryas, I mean neither blood, nor bones, nor hair, nor skull. I mean simply those who speak an Aryan language."

We have shown what havoc may be wrought in clear thinking by attempted correlations between physical anthropology and linguistics. A second error against which we must be on our guard is that of confusing the data of archæology with those of the science of language. Because a people early hit upon the knowledge of bronze and learned how to tame horses and milk cows, it does not follow that they also invented the declension of nouns and the conjugation of verbs. Such an assumption is scarcely less unwarranted than that a man's hair must be blond and his eyes blue because he is inflectional in his speech. Nevertheless, this is the basis upon which many anthropologists of the Gallic school * have sought to identify the Alpine race—a predominant element in the French nation, be it observed—as the only and original Aryans. Whether they are justified, in the first place, in their claim that this race really bore an Oriental culture into western Europe will be food for our further discussion.† But, even assuming for a moment's peace that they did, it does not and can not prove anything further respecting the language which was upon their lips. Unless reasoning can be held well aloof from any such assumptions, the question of European origins will never cease to be an arena in which heads are wildly broken to no scientific avail.

In order that we may conscientiously distinguish between the positively proved and the merely hypothetical, we shall advance by propositions, keeping them in martial order. We are entering debatable territory. One great advantage alone we may claim. As Americans, we should be endowed with "the serene impartiality of a mongrel," as the late Professor

---

* De Mortillet, 1879 ; Ujfalvy, 1884 b, p. 437 ; Sergi, 1898 a, p. 141 ; Zampa, 1891 a, p. 77. Canon Taylor's reasoning is also prejudiced by this assumption (1890, p. 295). Zaborowski, 1881, asserts that Henri Martin among Frenchmen alone dissents from this view. He should have added Lapouge, 1889 a. *Cf.* Reinach, 1892, p. 59 ; and the renewed discussion of the Aryan question in the Société d'Anthropologie in 1879.

† Page 486 *infra*.

Huxley put it. No logical conclusion has terror for us. Whether the noble Aryan be proved Teuton, Celt, or Iberian, it is all the same. We have no monopoly of inheritance in it in any case.

Concerning **race,** first of all, we may hold four propositions to be fairly susceptible of proof. They are as follows:

I. *The European races, as a whole, show signs of a secondary or derived origin; certain characteristics, especially the texture of the hair, lead us to class them as intermediate between the extreme primary types of the Asiatic and the negro races respectively.*

From what we have seen of the head form, complexion, and stature of the population of Europe, we might be led to expect that in other physical traits as well this little continent contained all extremes of human variation. We have been surprised, perhaps, at the exceeding diversity of forms occurring within so restricted an area, and in a human group which most of us have perhaps been taught to regard as homogeneous. One physical characteristic alone affords justification for this hypothesis of ethnic homogeneity. This is the form and texture of the hair. Only in this respect, not in its colour, the hair is quite uniform all over Europe, and even far into Hindustan, where Aryan languages have migrated. At the same time, however, this texture in itself indicates a secondary origin—that is to say, it denotes a human type derived from the crossing of others which we may class as primary. The population of Europe, in other words, should be numbered among the secondary races of the earth. What its constituent elements may have been we shall discuss somewhat later.

The two extremes of hair texture in the human species are the crisp curly variety so familiar to us in the African negro; and the stiff, wiry, straight hair of the Asiatic and the American aborigines. These traits are exceedingly persistent; they persevere oftentimes through generations of ethnic intermixture. It has been shown by Pruner Bey and others that this outward contrast in texture is due to, or at all events coincident with, real morphological differences in structure. The

curly hair is almost always of a flattened, ribbon-like form
in cross section, as examined microscopically; while, cut
squarely across, the straight hair more often inclines to a fully
rounded or cylindrical shape. It may be coarse, or fine, or of
any colour, but the texture remains quite constant in the same
individual and the same race. Moreover, this peculiarity in
cross section may often be detected in any crossing of these
extreme types. The result of such intermixture is to impart
a more or less wavy appearance to the hair, and to produce
a cross section intermediate between a flattened oval and a
circle. Roughly speaking, the more pronounced the flatness

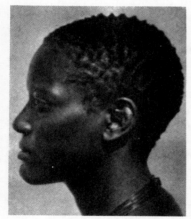

Negro type; Uganda. (From Buchta, Die oberen Nil-Länder, 1881.)

the greater is the tendency toward waviness or curling, and
the reverse.

Our map, after Gerland ('92), shows the geographical distribution of these several varieties of hair texture among the races
of the earth. As in all our preceding world maps, we have to
do with the aboriginal and not the imported peoples. Our
data for North America apply to the Indians alone, before the
advent of either the whites or negroes. These latter depart
in no wise physically from the types whence they were derived. It appears that most of Asia and both the Americas
are quite uniformly straight-haired. At the other extreme

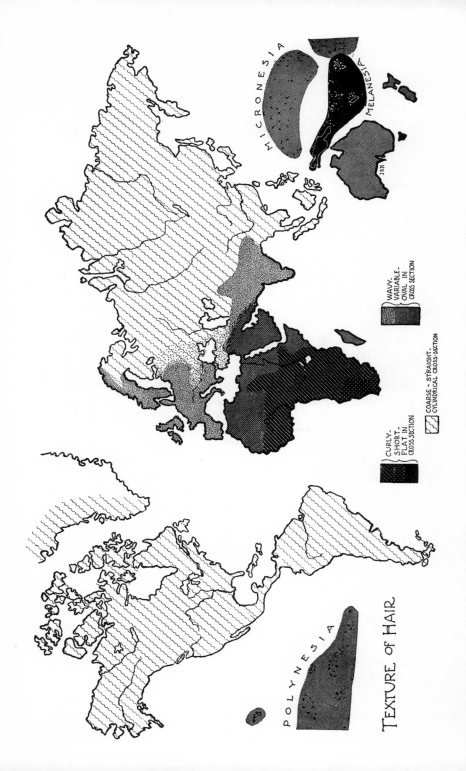

TEXTURE OF HAIR

POLYNESIA

MICRONESIA

MELANESIA

CURLY-
SHORT-
FLAT IN
CROSS SECTION

WAVY-
VARIABLE-
OVAL IN
CROSS SECTION

COARSE - STRAIGHT-
CYLINDRICAL CROSS-SECTION

stands Africa, and especially Papua and the archipelago to the southeast of it, which as far as the Fiji group is known as Melanesia, or the " black islands." According to Keane [96], the name Papua is derived from a Malay word, meaning " frizzled." This map strikingly corroborates the evidence presented by our other world maps, showing the distribution of the head form and the skin colour. Generally speaking, the aphorism holds that the round-headed people are also round-haired. The black-skinned races are, on the other hand, generally long-headed and characterized by hair of an elongated oval in cross section. Physical anthropologists, to be sure, distinguish several subvarieties of this curly hair. Thus, among the Bushmen and Hottentots at the southern tip of Africa, the spirals are so tight that the hair aggregates in little nubbles over the scalp, leaving what were long supposed to be entirely bald spots between. This is known as the peppercorn type, from its resemblance to such grains scattered over the head. And in Melanesia the texture is not quite like that of the main body of the Africans; but for all practical purposes they may all be classed together.

The remaining tints upon our map denote the extension of the wavy textured hair, which is generally intermediate in cross section, varying from ribbonlike to nearly cylindrical shape. There are three separate subdivisions under this head. Two of these, the Polynesian and the Australian, are most certainly wavy-haired mongrels, derived from intermixture of the straight-haired Asiatic races with the extreme frizzled type of Melanesia. This latter is by all authorities regarded as the primitive occupant of the Pacific archipelago, and of Indonesia as well. Among the Malays, and such hybrids as the Japanese, the Asiatic type preponderates; in the Australian peoples the other element is more strongly represented. Tasmania is quite distinct from its neighbouring continent. Isolation perhaps has kept it true to its primitive type. The Polynesians and Micronesians seem to be compounded of about equal proportions of each. Of course, all sorts of variations are common. The peoples of the Pacific are peculiarly aberrant in this respect. Some islands are characterized by quite lank and coarse-haired types; some have the frizzled hair stiffened just enough to make it stand on end, producing those surprising shocks familiar to us in our school-geography illustrations of the Fiji islanders.

What shall we say of the European races, the third of our intermediate types? Here also all individual variations occur, seemingly in utter defiance of any law. The Italian is as apt to be straight-haired as the Norwegian; in either nation the curly variety seems to occur sporadically. Yet common observation, to say nothing of microscopical examination, would naturally class the population of Europe among the fine-textured, wavy-haired races of the earth. One never sees the wiry form so familiar in the American Indian, or the frizzle of the full-blooded negro. Are we to infer from this that the people of Europe, therefore, are, like the Polynesians and Australians, the result of an ethnic cross between other more primary types? Certainly the study of the head form, with every extreme known to man within the confines of the single continent, seems to discredit this possibility. The only alternative is to consider this texture of hair to be a more liquid characteristic, so to speak, than the shape of the head; in other words, to assume that a few drops of alien blood might suffice to produce an intermediate texture of the hair, and yet not be adequate to modify the head form. If this were indeed so, then we might imagine that, even while our three European races have kept reasonably distinct in head form, intermixture has nevertheless taken place to some extent in every nook and corner of the continent; and that this infinitesimal crossing has been enough to modify the hair texture. But we are now wandering off into vague hypothesis. There is yet enough that is positively known to demand our attention without indulging in speculation. We have stated the situation; let the reader draw his own conclusions.

II. *The earliest and lowest strata of population in Europe were extremely long-headed; probability points to the living Mediterranean race as most nearly representative of it to-day.*

Of the most primitive types, coexisting with a fauna and flora now extinct or migrated with change of climate from central and western Europe, oftentimes no remains exist except the skulls by which to judge of their ethnic affinities. We know more, in fact, concerning their culture than their physical type in the earlier stone age at least; but it is nevertheless established beyond all question that they were dolichocephalic, and that, too, to a remarkable degree. This feature characterized all subdivisions of the populations of this epoch. Many varieties have been identified by specialists, such as the stocky, short-statured Neanderthal type and the taller and more finely moulded Cro-Magnon race. The classification of each nation differs in minor details, but they all agree in this, that the population both of the early and the late stone age was long-headed to an extreme.

The present unanimity of opinion among archæologists concerning this earliest dolichocephalic population is all the more remarkable because it represents a complete reversal of the earliest theories on the subject. Retzius, in 1842, from a comparison of the Scandinavians with the Lapps and Finns, propounded the hypothesis that the latter broad-headed brunet types were the relics of a pre-Aryan population of Europe. The comparative barbarism of the Lapps confirmed him in this view. It seemed to be plain that this Mongoloid or Asiatic variety of man had been repressed to this remote northern region by an immigrant blond, long-headed race from the southwest. That this is in a measure true for Scandinavia can not be denied. Arbo's researches show a Lapp substratum considerably outside their present restricted territory. That is a very different matter from the affirmation that such a brachycephalic (" Turanian ") race once inhabited all Europe before the Aryan advent. Such was, however, the current opinion. To show its popularity, it is only necessary to cite the names of its leading exponents.* Nilsson and Steenstrup first took it up, and then afterward Schaffhausen, Nicolucci, Thurnam, Lubach, Busk, and Carter Blake. Its leading exponents in France were Pruner Bey and De Quatrefages. Edwards and Belloguét assumed it as proved in all their generalizations.

* Cf. Hamy, 1884, p. 44 ; and Virchow, 1874 a ; Ranke, Mensch., ii, pp. 445, 528–530 ; Schaffhausen, 1889.

Then began the discoveries of abundant prehistoric remains all over Europe, particularly in France. These with one accord tended to show that the European aborigines of the stone age were not Mongoloid like the Lapps after all, but the exact opposite. In every detail they resembled rather the dolichocephalic negroes of Africa. The only other races approaching them in long-headedness are either the Eskimos, whom Boyd Dawkins believes to be a relic of this early European·people, or else the Australians. Huxley, in turn, long ago asserted these latter savages to be our human progenitors. We need not stop to discuss either of these radical opinions. It is sufficient for us that Broca finally dealt the death blow to the older view in 1868 by the evidence from the caves of Périgord; the very district where our living Cro-Magnon type still survives, as we have already shown.

This dolichocephalic substratum has been traced all over Europe with much detail in the neolithic or late stone age; by which time the geography and the flora and fauna of the continent had assumed in great measure their present conditions. We know that the long-headed type, now predominating on the northern and southern outskirts of Europe, in Spain, southern Italy, the British Isles, and Scandinavia, once occupied territory close up to the foot of the high Alps on every side. Remains of it have not yet been found in the mountains themselves, although closely hedging them in on every side. For example, Zampa, Nicolucci, and Sergi have alike collected evidence to prove that the whole basin of the Po River, now a strongly brachycephalic centre, was in the neolithic period populated by this long-headed type.* In other words, Italy, from end to end, was once uniform anthropologically in the head form of its people; in the south it is to-day still true to the primitive and aboriginal type. As far north as Rome no change can be detected between the modern and the most ancient skulls.† For France, a recent summary of the human remains of the late stone age, based upon nearly seven hundred skeletons or skulls, shows an overwhelming preponder-

---

* *Vide* page 262 *supra*.   † Calori, 1868, p. 205; Nicolucci, 1875.

ance of this long-headed type.* The round-heads were almost
entirely absent in the beginning, as we showed them heretofore
to have been in the British Isles during the same epoch.†
France was apparently very unevenly populated. In all the
uplands, especially the central plateau of Auvergne, human
remains are less abundant, although when occurring being of
the same decidedly long-headed type ‡—this, be it remembered, in the same district where to-day one of the roundest-
headed populations in the world resides. For Germany, investigation all points the same way. Ranke # has exhibited
the chronological development with great clearness for Bavaria. This region corresponds to northern Italy in its proximity to the main core of the living Alpine type. In Bavaria,
now like the Po basin the seat of a purely brachycephalic
population, the paleolithic inhabitants were exclusively long-
headed. The average index of seven crania of this most ancient epoch Ranke finds to be 76. At the time of the early
metal period a large part of the racial substitution had apparently taken place, broad-headedness being quite prevalent.
After a diminution of the cranial index, during the period of
the *Völkerwanderung*, it again rose to its present figure (83),
as it appears in the modern broad-headed Bavarians. This
agrees even in details all too closely with the independently
discovered data for France to be a mere coincidence.

As for the outlying parts of Europe, the same law holds
good without exception. Thus in Spain, whether judged by
crania from the caves and dolmens or from the kitchen middens
of Mugem, the modern population is almost an exact counterpart of the most ancient one.‖ A slight increase in breadth

* Salmon, 1895. *Vide* seriation curve on p. 116 *supra*. G. de Mortillet,
1878 and 1897, p. 275 ; Reinach, 1889, ii ; and Hervé, 1892, give convenient
summaries also.   † Page 306 *supra*.

‡ Durand and De Lapouge, 1897-'98, reprint pp. 13 and 57.

1897 a, pp. 58–65. *Cf.* Kollmann, 1881–'83 and 1882 a ; Virchow,
1872 b ; Ammon, 1893, p. 66. Ecker, 1865, p. 79, said mixed ; but von
Hölder, 1876, p. 20, found purer. For Alsace-Lorraine, also true ; Blind,
1898, p. 4.

‖ Oliviera, in Cartailhac, 1886, pp. 305–316 ; Jacques, in Siret, 1887, pp.
273–396 ; and also 1888, p. 221 ; Olóriz, 1894 a, pp. 259–262 ; and Antón, 1897.

of head is noticeable, for even the long-headed Spaniards, like the French as well, scarcely equal the absolutely negroid head form of the earliest inhabitants. The same fact confronts us in Scandinavia. Long-headed as the people are to-day, they constitute a less pronounced type than their prehistoric ancestors. All authorities agree upon this point.* Turning next toward the east, we have already cited the testimony for the Slavic countries.† It admits of no possible doubt. And, last of all, even as far as the Caucasus, beneath its present brachycephalic population there is evidence that the aboriginal inhabitants were clearly long-headed.‡ Thus we have covered every part of Europe, emphasizing the same indubitable fact. Only in one place—in the highest Alps—is this law unverified. It seems as if this inhospitable region had remained uninhabited until a later time.

Assuming it as proved, therefore, that the first population of Europe was of this quite uniform type of head form, what do we know of its other physical characteristics? This concerns the second half of our primary proposition. That is to say, may we decide to which branch of the living long-headed race it belonged; that of the tall, blond Teuton or of the shorter-statured, dark-complexioned Mediterranean type? It is a matter of no small moment to settle this if possible. Unfortunately, we can prove nothing directly concerning the complexion, for of course all traces of hair have long since disappeared from the graves of this early period. Presumptively, the type was rather brunet than blond, for in the dark colour of hair and eye it would approach the foundation tints of all the rest of the human race. The light hair and blue eye of northern Europe are nowhere found in any appreciable proportion elsewhere, save perhaps among the Ainos in Japan, an insignificant people, too few in numbers and too remote to affect the generalization. If, therefore, as all consistent students of natural history hold to-day, the human races have evolved in the past from some common root type, this pre-

---

* Von Dueben, 1876; A. Retzius, 1843; Arbo, 1882; Montelius, 1895 b, p. 31; Barth, 1896. † Page 352 *supra*.

‡ Chantre, 1887, ii, p. 181.

dominant dark colour must be regarded as the more primitive.* It is not permissible for an instant to suppose that ninety-nine per cent of the human species has varied from a blond ancestry, while the flaxen-haired Teutonic type alone has remained true to its primitive characteristics.

We are strengthened in this assumption that the earliest Europeans were not only long-headed, but also dark-complexioned, by various points in our inquiry thus far. We have proved the prehistoric antiquity of the living Cro-Magnon type in southwestern France; and we saw that among these peasants the prevalence of black hair and eyes is very striking. And comparing types in the British Isles, we saw that everything tended to show that the brunet populations of Wales, Ireland, and Scotland constituted the most primitive stratum of population in Britain. Furthermore, in that curious spot in Garfagnana, where a survival of the ancient Ligurian population of northern Italy is indicated, there also are the people characteristically dark.† Judged, therefore, either in the light of general principles or of local details, it would seem as if this earliest race in Europe must have been very dark. It was Mediterranean in its pigmental affinities, and not Scandinavian.‡

As to stature, a trait in which the Teuton and the Iberian differ markedly from one another to-day, we have abundant evidence that this neolithic population was more akin to the medium-statured French than to the relatively gigantic Germans and Scandinavians.# The men of this epoch were not, to be sure, as diminutive as the modern south Italians or the Spaniards; they seem rather to approximate the medium height of the inhabitants of northern Africa. These Berbers and their fellows, in fact, shading off as they do into the negro race south of the Sahara, we must regard as having least departed from the aboriginal European type. And in Europe proper, the brunet long-headed Mediterranean race is but slightly aberrant from it. It may have become stunted by too

---

* *Cf.* Schaffhausen, 1889, p. 70.   † Livi, 1896 a, p. 153.

‡ This flatly contradicts Keane's affirmation (Ethnology, p. 376), based upon antiquated data from De Quatrefages.

Cf. page 307 *supra*, for example.

protracted civilization; it may have changed somewhat in facial proportions; but, on the whole, it has remained true to its ancestral image. Call it " Atlanto-Mediterranean " with Deniker, or " Ibero-Pictish " with Rhys [90], belief that a single fairly uniform physical type once prevailed throughout western Europe " from Gibraltar to Denmark " is daily growing in favour.

III. *It is highly probable that the Teutonic race of northern Europe is merely a variety of this primitive long-headed type of the stone age; both its distinctive blondness and its remarkable stature having been acquired in the relative isolation of Scandinavia through the modifying influences of environment and of artificial selection.*

This theory of a unity of origin of the two long-headed races of Europe is not entirely novel. Europaeus [76] proposed it twenty years ago. Only within the last decade has it attained widespread acceptance among the very best authorities: from the status of a remote possibility attaining the dignity of a well-nigh proved fact.* We affirm it as the best working hypothesis possible in the light of recent investigations. It will be seen at once that this theorem rests upon the assumption that the head form is a decidedly more permanent racial characteristic than pigmentation. In so doing it relegates to a secondary position the colour of the hair and eyes, which so eminent an anthropologist as Huxley has made the basis of his whole scheme of classification of European peoples. Brinton and even Virchow [96] have likewise relied upon these latter traits in preference to the phenomena of craniology in their racial classifications. Nevertheless, with all due respect to these distinguished authorities, we do not hesitate to affirm that the research of the last ten years has turned the scales in favour of the cranium, if properly studied, as the most reliable test of race. Tomaschek † is surely right in applying Linnæus' cau-

---

* Bogdanof, 1893, p. 23 : Niederle, 1896 a, p. 131 ; and in Globus, lxxi, No. 24 : Sergi, 1895 a, p. 87 ; 1898 a, chap. ix, and 1898 b especially : A. J. Evans, 1896. To Lapouge (1889 a, p. 187) apparently belongs credit for prior statement. Canon Taylor (1890, p. 123) hints at it. The wide extension of the Cro-Magnon race, already traced (p. 177 *supra*), fully bears out the theory. *Cf.* de Lapouge, 1899, p. 36 *et seq.*

† Cited by O. Schrader, 1890, p. 102.

tion concerning the lower animals to man, *Nimium ne crede colori*. We know that brunetness varies with age in the same individual—that is one proof of its impermanence. In a preceding chapter we have devoted much attention to proving also that there is a factor of the environment in mountainous or infertile regions which operates to increase the proportion of blond traits among men. We did not seek in these cases to determine whether such changes were due to climate alone or to the defective nutrition which too often attends a poverty of environment. It is a well-recognised law in the geographical distribution of lower forms of life that two hundred and fifty feet increase in altitude is equivalent to one degree's remove in latitude from the equator. If this be true applied to man, it would lead us to expect a steady increase of blondness toward the north of Europe, a fact which all our maps have substantiated fully. Experience in colonizing Africa to-day indicates that this adaptation of the Teutonic race to a northern climate constitutes a serious bar to its re-entry into the equatorial regions. May not this change physiologically be correlated in some way with the modified pigmentation? * We may assume, in other words, that as the primitive dark type of the stone age gradually spread over northern Europe, environmental influences slowly, very slowly, through scores of generations, have induced a blond subvariety to emerge. Its differentiation would in such an event be commensurate with the distance from its original southern centre of migration. In so far as this process is concerned, leaving other details open for the severest criticism later, Penka and his disciples seem to have been in the right. This is the thought clearly stated by Marshall in his Biological Lectures, that " the white man and the negro have been differentiated through the long-continued action of selection and environment." †

Climate as an explanation for the derived blondness of the Teutonic race is not sufficient by itself to account for the phenomenon. Its blondness is something more than a direct product of the fogs of the German Ocean. This is proved at once by

---

* Page 558 *infra*. *Cf.* also Beddoe, 1893, p. 10.
† Cited by Keane, 1896, p. 375.

a significant fact on which we laid emphasis in an earlier chapter—viz., that blondness not only decreases as we proceed southward from Scandinavia, but in an easterly direction as well. In other words, the Russians at the latitude of Norway and Sweden are far more brunet in type than the Scandinavians. How shall we reconcile this with our environmental hypothesis? In the first place, the hordes speaking the Slavic languages are comparatively recent immigrants in that part of Europe; they are physically allied to the broad-headed Alpine type. For this reason, comparisons between Scandinavia and the lands directly east of it are vitiated at once. But there is yet another reason why we may expect these Teutons to be notable even in their own latitude by reason of their blondness. It is this: that the trait has for some reason become so distinctive of a dominant race all over Europe that it has been rendered susceptible to the influence of artificial selection. Thus a powerful agent is allied to climate to exaggerate what may once have been an insignificant trait. Were there space we might adduce abundant evidence to prove that the upper classes in France, Germany, Austria, and the British Isles are distinctly lighter in hair and eyes than the peasantry.* It is no coincidence that *caste* and *colour* are of common derivation in the Sanscrit language. The classical Latin writers abound in testimony to this effect. The Teutonic conquerors of prehistoric times, the *Reihengräber* for example, were of this type. Both tall stature and blondness together constitute insignia of noble descent. Since the time of the Eddas, the servile ones have always been described as short brunets, according to von Hölder [76]. Borrow tells us in his Bible in Spain that "negro" is an opprobrious epithet even in that dark country. Gummere has collected some interesting materials from mediæval literature on this point.† The thrall or churl is invariably a dark type, the opposite of the flaxen-haired, blue-eyed jarl or earl. The rule has been effective in painting. Christ a blond,

---

* Von Hölder, 1876, p. 15 ; Beddoe, 1870, p. 177, and 1885, p. 187, comparing different classes in Cork, Ireland ; Taylor, 1889, p. 244 ; Mackintosh, 1866. *Cf.* pages 283, 295, and 352 *supra* for examples.

† Germanic Origins, pp. 62 *seq. Cf.* Beddoe, 1893, p. 13.

the two thieves as notably dark, was long the invariable rule in artistic composition.* Let us suppose, then, that such an opinion concerning nobility became widespread; suppose that it were intensified by the splendid military and political expansion of the Teutons in historic times all over the continent; suppose it to have become the priceless heritage of people more or less isolated in a corner of Europe! Is there any doubt that, entirely apart from any natural choice exerted by the physical environment, an artificial selective process would have been engendered, which in time would become mighty in its results? Is it not permissible to ascribe in some measure both the patent blondness of this Teutonic race and its unique stature as well to this cause? This is our hypothesis at all events.

IV. *It is certain that, after the partial occupation of western Europe by a dolichocephalic Africanoid type in the stone age, an invasion by a broad-headed race of decidedly Asiatic affinities took place. This intrusive element is represented to-day by the Alpine type of central Europe.*

We know that the broad-headed layer of population was not contemporary with the earliest stratum we have described above, because its remains are often found directly superposed upon it geologically. From all over western Europe comes testimony to this effect. We have seen in preceding chapters how clear the distinction was in Britain, Russia, and northern Italy.† France gives us the clearest proof of it. Oftentimes where several layers of human remains are found in caves or other burial places, the long-headed type is quite unmixed in the lowest stratum; gradually the other type becomes more frequent; until it outnumbers its predecessor utterly. It appears as if in Gaul the Alpine type first entered over two routes, and it is curious to note that these did not in any way follow the usual channels of immigration; for the broad-headed race seems to have come by infiltration, so to speak, following along the upland districts and the mountain chains. Sal-

---

* Jacobs, 1886 a, p. xxvi, reprint; also Beddoe, 1861 b, p. 186, who affirms that till the second century Christ was depicted as dark.

† Pages 262 and 308 *supra*, and 499 *infra*.

mon,* who has traced this movement archæologically in great detail, finds the first appearance of the new-comers in the vicinity of the Ardennes plateau, coming into France from the northeast. Their second avenue of approach was directly from the high Alps, crossing the Rhone, and thence over Auvergne toward the southwest.† This central plateau, in fact, like the Alps, seems to have been first settled at this period. The whole basin of the Seine was overflowed, and the incoming human tide swept clear out to the point of Brittany, where it has so completely held its own even to this day in relative purity. Topinard [97] perhaps slightly overstates the case when he ascribes the cast of eyes among certain Breton types to an Asiatic descent. But current opinion about the Oriental origin of the brachycephalic type in western Europe is based upon competent testimony of this kind.‡

The intensity of the supersession of an old race by a new one becomes more marked in proportion as we approach the Alps, the present stronghold of the Alpine broad-headed race. Nevertheless, in the mountains themselves, as we have already said, no displacement of an earlier population seems to have been necessary; for from Switzerland, Auvergne in south central France, and the German Alps eastward, the inhospitable highlands seem to have been but sparsely if at all occupied by the earlier long-headed races. At all events, it is certain that in these restricted areas the broad-headed type is the most primitive.# There it has remained in relative purity ever since. From the earliest remains of the lake dwellers; before bronze or iron were known; before many of the simpler arts of agriculture or domestication of animals were developed; man has in these Alps remained perfectly true to his ancestral

---

* 1895. *Cf.* Topinard, Anthropology, 1890, p. 441, for succinct statement; · as also Hervé, 1894 b, and 1896; Houzé, 1883; and Collignon, 1881–'82.

† Collignon, 1894 b, p. 69; Lapouge and Durand, 1897–'98.

‡ Collignon, 1894 a, p. 9. Sergi's later work, 1898 a, chapter vi.

Ranke, 1897 a, is particularly good on this. While in middle Bavaria a great increase of brachycephaly has taken place; in the southern part broad-headedness is certainly aboriginal. *Cf.* also von Hölder, 1880.

37

type.* We can add art after art to his culture, but we can not till very recent times detect any movement of population, after the first occupation in a state of relative savagery by this broad-headed race.† It is a surprising instance of the persistency of physical types.

The extent of this first occupation of Europe by the Alpine race was once much broader than it is to-day. Evidence accumulates to show that it spread widely at first, but that it was afterward obliged to recede from its first extravagant claims to possess all Europe. In a former chapter we saw that all along the southwest coast of Norway clear evidence of inter-mixture with this broad-headed type appears. The peasantry show a distinct tendency in this direction. In Denmark the same thing is true; the people are not as pure Teutons as in Hanover, farther to the south. We also know that this race invaded Britain for a time, but was exterminated or absorbed before reaching Ireland.‡ A very peculiar colony of these Alpine invaders seems also to have so firmly intrenched itself in the Netherlands that its influence is apparent even to this day. There can be little doubt that the modern Zeelanders date from this remote period.# They may be considered as a link in the chain connecting the Alpine type in Scandinavia and Denmark with its kind in the central European highlands. In the opposite direction the intrusive type seems also to have with difficulty entered Spain; for, as we have shown, the population of the mountainous northwest provinces is even at this present day less purely Iberian in type by reason of it.‖ One spot alone south of the Mediterranean Sea was perceptibly affected by it; recent evidence from the island of Gerba off Tunis proving such colonization to have taken place.△ In the eastern half of Europe the occupation was more or less complete, with the sole exception, as we have seen, of the lower Danubian plain. Apparently, also, this type seems to have been unable

---

* Studer and Bannwarth, 1894, pp. 13 *et seq.* ; Rütimeyer and His, 1864, p. 41 ; Zuckerkandl, 1883 ; Kollmann and Hagenbach, 1885 a.

† Page 501 *infra.*

‡ Page 308 *supra.*   Garson, 1883, p. 81, finds it in the Orkneys, however.   # Page 297 *supra.*

‖ Page 274 *supra.*   △ Bertholon, 1897. *Cf.* Collignon, 1887 a, p. 218.

to hold its own in eastern Russia. The only bond of union of the race with its congeners in Asia is by way of Asia Minor, over the primitive population now overlaid by the Turks. If it entered Europe from the East, as is generally assumed, it surely must have come by this route, for no signs of an entry north of the Caspian are anywhere visible.

What right have we for the assertion that this infiltration of population from the East—it was not a conquest, everything points to it as a gradual peaceful immigration, often merely the settlement of unoccupied territory—marks the advent of an overflow from the direction of Asia? The proof of this rests largely upon our knowledge of the people of that continent, especially of the Pamir region, the western Himalayan highlands. Just here on the "roof of the world," where Max Müller and the early philologists placed the primitive home of Aryan civilization, a human type prevails which tallies almost exactly with our ideal Alpine or Celtic European race. The researches of De Ujfalvy,[*] Topinard, and others localize its peculiar traits over a vast territory hereabouts. The Galchas, mountain Tadjiks, and their fellows are gray-eyed, dark-haired, stocky in build, with cephalic indexes ranging above 86 for the most part. From this region a long chain of peoples of a similar physical type extends uninterruptedly westward over Asia Minor and into Europe.

The only point which the discovery of a broad area in western Asia occupied by an ideal Alpine type settles, is that it emphasizes the affinities of this peculiar race. It is no proof of direct immigration from Asia at all, as Tappeiner [†] observes. It does, however, lead us to turn our eyes eastward when we seek for the origin of the broad-headed type. Things vaguely point to an original ethnic base of supplies somewhere in this direction. It could not lie westward, for everywhere along the Atlantic the race slowly disappears, so to speak. That the Alpine type approaches all the other human millions on the Asiatic continent, in the head form especially, but in hair colour and stature as well, also prejudices us in the matter; just as

---

* Page 451 *supra*.   † 1894, p. 36.   *Cf.* de Lapouge, 1899, p. 16.

the increasing long-headedness and extreme brunetness of our Mediterranean race led us previously to derive it from some type parent to that of the African negro. These points are then fixed: the roots of the Alpine race run eastward; those of the Mediterranean type toward the south.

Before we leave this question we must clear up a peculiar difficulty. If the Alpine broad-headed race entered western Europe with sufficient momentum to carry it clear across to the British Isles, up into Norway, and down into Spain, intruding between and finally separating the more primitive long-headed population into two distinct groups, why is it everywhere to-day so relegated to the mountainous and infertile areas? This is especially true wherever it comes in contact with the Teutonic race in the north. It is one of the most striking results of our entire inquiry thus far, this localization of the Alpine type in what we have termed areas of isolation. One is at a loss to account for this apparent turning back of a tide of prehistoric immigration. The original, more primitive races must once have yielded ground before the invader; our prehistoric stratification shows it. Why have they now turned the tables and reoccupied all the more desirable territory, driving their intrusive competitor to the wall? Were there proof that the original invasion of our Alpine race from the East had been a forcible one, an answer to this would be afforded by a study of culture; for it is now accepted generally, as we shall seek to show, that many arts of civilization have entered western Europe from the East. Hence if, as we say, the invasion by the broad-headed race had been by force of arms, every advantage would have been on the side of the more civilized race against the primitive possessors of the soil. The clew to the situation would have lain in the relative order in which culture was acquired by the competing populations. It would then have been possible that the Alpine invaders, penetrating far to the west by reason of their equipment of civilization, would have lost their advantage so soon as their rivals learned from them the practical arts of metallurgy and the like. Unfortunately for this supposition, the movement of population was rather an infiltration than a conquest. How may we explain this?

Our solution of the problem as to the temporary supersession of the primitive population of Europe by an invading race, followed by so active a reassertion of rights as to have now relegated the intruder almost entirely to the upland areas of isolation, is rather economic than military or cultural. It rests upon the fundamental laws which regulate density of population in any given area. Our supposition—it is nothing more—is this: that the north of Europe, the region peculiar to the Teutonic race to-day, is by Nature unfitted to provide sustenance to a large and increasing population. In that prehistoric period when a steady influx of population from the East took place, there was yet room for the primitive inhabitants to yield ground to the invader. A time was bound to come when the natural increase of population would saturate that northern part of Europe, so to speak. A migration of population toward the south, where Nature offered the possibilities of continued existence, consequently ensued. This may have at times taken a military form. It undoubtedly did in the great Teutonic expansion of historic times. Yet it may also have been a gradual expansion—a drifting or swarming forth, ever trending toward the south. We know that such a migration is now taking place. Germans are pressing into northern France as they have always done. Swiss and Austrians are colonizing northern Italy; Danish immigration into Germany is common enough. Wherever we turn we discover a constantly increasing population seeking an outlet southward. The ethnic result has been therefore this: that to-day the Teuton overlies the Alpine race, while it in turn encroaches upon, submerges the Mediterranean type. Thus do economic laws, viewed in a broader way, come to the support of ethnic facts. Other problems concerning population are immediately suggested. These we shall consider in a succeeding chapter.

Language in its bearing upon the question of European origins may be studied from two distinct points of view. These must be carefully distinguished from one another. The first we may term structural analysis. By this we mean study of the relationships existing between the various members of the great inflectional family from Sanscrit to English or Celtic. Geographical probabilities, based upon the present distribution of these several languages in Asia and Europe, form a not inconsiderable element in this first philological mode of study. Thus, for example, the present contiguity of the Teutonic, Lithuanian, and Slavic languages in Europe is strongly corroborative of their close structural affinity. The second kind of analysis has been aptly called " linguistic palæontology." It is a study of root words, not in and for themselves philologically, but rather as indications of a knowledge of the things which they denote. Thus a Sanscrit word for " lion " implies acquaintance with that mammal, even as a word for " father-in-law " might denote the existence of definite domestic relationships among those who used the Sanscrit language. This second mode of study is thus mainly concerned with words as indicative of things; while the first has to do primarily with grammatical structure. The relative value of these two kinds of linguistic investigation as applied to the study of European origins is very different. The first is by far the more important and trustworthy in every respect. The second is more seductive in its attractiveness for those who have a thesis to prove. Only a master of the science of philology is competent to make use of the first. The second has long been the plaything of *dilettanti*, both linguistic and anthropological.

More than a century has now elapsed since the first discovery by Sir William Jones of a distant relationship between Sanscrit and the classic languages of Europe. Definite proof of this was first afforded by Bopp in 1835, since which time the bonds of structural affinity have been drawn continually closer by the continued researches of the masters of philology.* It is now accepted as proved beyond all doubt that not only all the languages of Europe, except the Finnic, Basque, Magyar,

---

* The foremost authority who has summarized the progress of this work is Otto Schrader, Sprachvergleichung und Urgeschichte, Jena, 1883. The second edition, translated by Jevons, as Prehistoric Antiquities of the Aryan People, London, 1890, is a standard work. Canon Taylor, 1890, gives a succinct abbreviation of this. Reinach, 1892, does the same, with many valuable additions from French sources. *Vide* Index under " Aryans " for a list of other writers.

and Turkish, but many of those of Persia, India, and western Asia, are derivatives from a common source. That the location of this parent language must have been in Asia was suggested by two considerations: First, that the more primitive languages, and, secondly, that the more primitive peoples and civilizations lay in this part of the world. Such were the assumptions upon which the earlier philologists proceeded, in all their attempts to discover the source of this most highly evolved type of language. Pictet, in 1859 and 1877, was the first to give extended currency to this view of Asiatic derivation. Max Müller in his lectures on the Science of Language in 1861, became its ardent exponent. By him the term Aryan, invented to designate the whole inflectional family of languages, was also indiscriminatingly applied to an ideal " Aryan race." This eminent authority has lived to repent of his ways in so doing, as we shall see; but for more than a generation the entire question of physical origins was prejudiced by his untoward assumption. The conclusions of the philologists gained ready and wide acceptance among historians and students of culture, Mommsen, Lenormant, and others serving as ready examples, followed by a host of others of lesser importance.

Purely philological considerations, entirely apart from anthropological and cultural ones, of which we shall speak separately, have done much of late to weaken the Asiatic hypothesis. Foremost among these, with Whitney and Spiegel, was the discovery of highly archaic features, structurally, in several other members of the family, notably in Lithuanian, Armenian, and Icelandic. Judged by the standard of archaism in structure, even Greek, says Sayce,* is entitled to priority over Sanscrit. This at once undermined the entire argument based upon the supposed primitiveness of the sacred languages of the East. Furthermore, it was justly argued that a comparison between modern speech and ancient and extinct classical documents was entirely fallacious. Either modern Persian or Hindustanee should be compared with Keltic or German, or else parallels should be drawn between the most

---

* 1887, p. 172.

ancient records from the west of Europe and their contemporaries in the Orient. Since the sacred books of the East immeasurably antedate any written records in Europe, it was but natural, these objectors urged, that they should be more archaic. The fact that, even making due allowances for the difference of time, Lithuanian should still be distinctly primitive in its formation, did much to cast doubt upon the older view of Asiatic origins therefore.*

Purely philological evidence in favour of European Aryan origins of a different order were advanced by Omalius d'Halloy and Latham. In calling attention to the archaic features of the Lithuanian language, Latham followed the course of reasoning already described in the preceding paragraphs. To this he added another argument largely based upon geographical probability. We may give the gist of it in his own words, from an edition of the Germania in 1851: † " When we have two branches which belong to the same family, and are separated from each other, one of which covers a larger area and shows the greater number of varieties, while the other possesses a narrower range and greater homogeneity, it is to be assumed that the latter is derived from the former, and not the reverse. To derive the Indo-Europeans of Europe from the Indo-Europeans of Asia is the same thing in ethnology as if in herpetology one were to derive the reptiles of Great Britain from those of Ireland."

One of the most suggestive lines of purely philological inquiry is that employed by two leading authorities in English— Canon Taylor [88] and our own Dr. Brinton.‡ The argument is as follows: The highly evolved Aryan languages did not spring fully armed, Minerva-like, from the head of Zeus. They must have had more humble linguistic predecessors. The primary question, therefore, is a search not for Aryan origins, but for suitable ancestors from which to derive them. Their most probable source must have been in a member of the great

---

* Max Müller, in his Biography of Words, 1888, p. 94, offers but a weak denial of this archaism of Lithuanian. It is recognised by all experts in philology to-day. † Schrader, 1890, p. 86.

‡ Races and Peoples, 1890, pp. 148 et seq.

agglutinative family of languages now prevalent over Asia and Africa. In Europe the only representatives of this more primitive non-inflectional type still extant—exclusive of Turkish and Magyar, which we know to be recent immigrants— are the Basque, the Finnic, and the Berber. Brinton is inclined to derive the Aryan from this third source: the languages of the Hamitic peoples of northern Africa. Keane,* following out this thought, is inclined to regard the Basque as another European relic of the same primitive stock. This theory of an Afro-European origin of the Aryan speech has much to recommend it, especially in view of the undoubtedly negroid physical affinities of the most primitive substratum of European population. Its principal defect as yet is the extreme tenuity of the proof of any linguistic relation not only between Basque and Berber, but also between Hamito-Semitic and Aryan. Von der Gabelentz has many powerful opponents in his attempted confirmation of this first relationship. The second affinity underlying Dr. Brinton's suggestive hypothesis, is likewise discredited by many philologists of note,† although supported by a few ardent advocates.

Proof that of all the primitive languages of Europe, Finnic has the best right to consideration as a direct ancestor, or perhaps, we had better say, an elder brother in the Aryan family, is not wanting. This theory of Canon Taylor's,‡ based upon Weske's data, certainly has by far the most geographical probability upon its side. We necessarily, of course, deny absolutely all validity to any of Taylor's attempted anthropological proof, for reasons which have already been given. He too, like so many others, seems somehow to mix up the Aryan languages with the idea of blondness. The seductiveness of Penka and Pösche is indeed difficult to withstand. But, entirely apart from this, his philological argument is a taking one. That Lithuanian is the most archaic of the west European languages gives it weight at the outset. Geiger's [78] proof of a very ancient contact between Aryan and Finnic, on which

---

* Ethnology, pp. 205 and 376.

† Sayce, 1887, p. 171; Max Müller, 1888, p. 111; and Schrader, *op. cit.*, p. 96.   ‡ 1888 and 1890, pp. 285–295.

he based his theory of Baltic origins, has never been effectively gainsaid. Even if we ascribe the similarities to mere borrowing, the evidence of contact thereby necessarily implied, still remains. It may possibly have been contact with the eastern Finns, as Tomaschek * tried to prove, which would bring our scene of evolution out upon the steppes, where Schrader, from entirely different considerations, is disposed to place it. Other matters of importance forbid our further discussion of this interesting Finnic hypothesis. Granting with Reinach that it still rests upon somewhat " fragile evidence," † its tenability as a working hypothesis is well summarized by Schrader in styling it " a dream, without, however, denying that in the course of deeper research, especially in the region of Finnic, it may possibly prove to be true."

The most serious attack of a philological character upon the Asiatic hypothesis comes from Schmidt [('72)]. Until his time the simple theory prevailed of a swarming forth of languages from a common hive. This made it feasible to hope for the construction of a genealogical tree, whose topmost branches should be the highly evolved languages of western Europe, and whose trunk and roots should spring from a single hypothetical parent tongue. One insuperable difficulty soon appeared. Time brought no agreement among philologists either as to the root or the ramifications of such a tree.‡ No two could agree, for example, as to whether Greek stood between Latin and Sanscrit, or whether Slavonic lay nearer the root than Teutonic. That in each case the two were related could not be questioned, yet none could prove that the affinity was not merely collateral rather than along any line of direct descent. Schmidt placed the whole matter in a new light by a positive denial that any such genealogical tree could ever be constructed conformably to fact. According to his view, a series of local phonetic disturbances arose at some time in the dim past within the great undifferentiated body of a

---

* 1883. *Cf.* also Schrader, *op. cit.*, p. 104 ; Niederle, 1896 b ; and the works of Mikkola, Krek, Castrén, and Miklosich.   † 1892, p. 96.

‡ Schrader, 1890, pp. 49–73, discusses this fully. *Cf.* the diagrammatic tree in Keane, Ethnology, p. 380.

parent speech. From these local centres, each the core of future languages, spread ever-widening circles of variation. It was obviously necessary, he continued, that interference of one with another should speedily take place, resulting in coalescence or the appearance of affinity along their lines of contact. Thus both Greek and Latin, separately evolving from the primeval linguistic protoplasm, must of necessity mutually react upon one another in time. The resultant similarities would mean nothing more than merely collateral relationship. They would not in the least imply a derivation of one from the other. Schmidt's destructive criticism was tempered somewhat by Leskien, who nevertheless fully recognised the force of his objection to the old-fashioned theory. Delbrück, last of this series, even went so far as to deny that any single parent Aryan language ever existed in fact. Leaving this an open question for philological wranglers, the sobering effect of the whole attack upon the direct pedigree theory can not be doubted.

As a net result of the discussions above described, the present status of the Aryan question among philologists is somewhat as follows: Some—Delbrück, for example—deny that any parent language ever was; some, like Whitney, refuse to believe that its centre of origin can ever be located; some, with Fick and Hoefer, still adhere to Pictet's old theory of Asiatic derivation; some, notably Sayce, have been converted from this to the European hypothesis; Max Müller is wavering; while Brinton and Keane urge the claims of northern Africa; and some, following Latham and Schrader, have never found good cause for denying the honour to Europe from the first. Most of those who render a decision in this difficult matter do so upon far different philological grounds than those structural and fundamental ones with which we have heretofore been concerned. This leads us to consider our second group of philological reasonings, based upon the study of roots rather than grammar.

Linguistic palæontology—that second department of pure philology, concerning itself with root-words as symbols of primitive ideas rather than with grammar or linguistic structure

—has endeavoured to compass two distinct ends. Of these, the first has been to reconstruct the culture of the ideal undivided Aryan-speaking people; the second, to locate their primitive civilization geographically. It has without doubt been highly successful, in conjunction with prehistoric archæology, in accomplishing the first of these tasks.* In our subsequent consideration of culture we shall have occasion to compare its results with those yielded by other cognate sciences. As to the second phase of its interests—geographical localization—the value of its inductions is highly questionable.

Benfey, in 1868, was perhaps the first to apply this mode of research to flora and fauna.. From similar root-words for the bear, the wolf, the oak tree, the beech, and the fir, combined with the absence of others for the tiger and the palm, a European origin for the parent Aryan language was reasoned as a necessity. Difficulties soon presented themselves. Thus the Latin and Gothic root for " beech " is traced to a Greek word designating an " oak." Geiger and Fick interpret this as proof of a migration of language from a land of beeches to one of oaks—viz., from northwestern Europe to the south. Beech trees not being indigenous east of a line from Königsberg to the Crimea, the Aryan homestead is indicated, according to this view, with considerable precision.†

Perhaps the best way to give an adequate idea of the scientific limitations of any attempt to locate the supposedly undivided Aryan language by any such process of linguistic palæontology as this, will be to outline a few conclusions based entirely upon a comparison of root-words. We have already eliminated those quasi-linguistic theories which are tainted with anthropological considerations. Asia and Europe are about equally popular. Pictet [77], Van den Gheyn [81], and Biddulph [80] still find an Aryan home in the plateau of Pamir, in the vicinity of the Hindu-Koosh; Hehn [73] locates it in the Aral-Caspian Sea depression; Fick, " between the Ural, Bolor, and the Hindu-Koosh "; for Piétrement [79], says Schrader,

---

* Cf. Schrader, op. cit., pp. 148, 149.

† On the interminable " beech" controversy cf. Schrader, 1883 b ; Sayce, 1888 a ; Penka, 1888 ; and Taylor, 1889.

" it was reserved to refer our forefathers to a place their de-
parture from which certainly calls for no explanation—that is,
Siberia " (latitude 49° 20'). Following slowly west, we next
come upon Brünnhofer's Aryan centre in Armenia, which
brings us to Europe. Two parts of this continent seem to answer equally well to the pre-requisites for an ideal Aryan home
—viz., the steppes of southern Russia and the plains of northern Germany. To the first we are brought by Benfey [('69)], by
Spiegel [('71)], by Fr. Müller [('79)], and by Otto Schrader [('90)];
to the Baltic plains by Lazarus Geiger [('78)], von Loeher [('83)],
and Hirt [('92)]. All northern Europe, from the Urals to the
Atlantic, between latitudes 45° and 60°, is none too extensive
an area to suit Cuno [('71)]. This is about as definite as Max
Müller's [('88)] conversion from the highlands of the Pamir to
" somewhere in Asia." And all these variant and conflicting conclusions are drawn from the same source of information. Is it any wonder that the reader becomes sceptical?

Fully convinced, as we have said, of the great value of
" Iinguistic palæontology " in any study of the origin or development of civilization, we submit that the above summary
of conclusions as to the Aryan " bee-hive " is fully sufficient
to show its worthlessness when applied to the solution of its
geographical phases. Schrader, head and shoulders above
any of his contemporaries, seems to be fully conscious of this.
Even in the second edition of his great work, having ventured
no guesses as to the Aryan homestead in his first edition,
he justifies his choice of the Volga basin in Russia as follows:
" It is plain that theoretically there is no reason why this must
necessarily be sought in our quarter of the globe. It is, however, also clear, that if there can be found in it a locality which
satisfies all requirements, that is the place to which we must
look in the first instance."

What are these " requisites " for an Aryan homestead,
judging by the root-words still common to most members of
the inflectional family of European languages? They are not
many. Would that they were more consistent with one another! *Snow* and *cold* are indispensable. Here we see why the
Aryan cradle was necessarily swung in the first instance upon

the plateau of Pamir—"the roof of the world"—rather than either in India or Persia proper. We must also have *heat* and a quick alternation of seasons. No *spring* or *autumn* need apply. Add to this, *water*—a *river;* no *mountains;* few *trees;* a *wolf*—possibly a *lion;* surely a *bear* to climb said *trees;* no agriculture; most of the domesticated animals; *bees; grasshoppers;* and a few birds. As for social institutions, the "little paradise" of Justi and Fick, "penetrated with good sense and sound morality," has not materialized, according to the most rigid linguistic canons. A fairly definite patriarchal organization seems to be about all that can be assumed. Not much here, surely, from which to orient one's self in seeking the old homestead. And yet what labour has been expended upon the unprofitable—nay, we affirm, the scientifically impossible—task. The impossibility of any sure location of this original centre of Aryan linguistic dispersion arises from two facts: First, the extreme poverty of the data; and, secondly, that both phenomena which must be correlated are entirely independent variables. For while, on the one hand, there is every chance of great change in word meanings—"new wine being put into old bottles"—on the other, most of the things designated by the root-words are migratory in themselves; either with man, as in the case of the domestic animals, or of their own initiative, as in the natural flora and fauna. Thus even if we allow with Pauli that the lion was known to the primitive Aryan-speaking people, who shall say that there were never lions in Europe? Times may have changed for lions as well as men since that far-distant epoch. As Max Müller [88] rightly observes, it is "almost impossible to discover any animal or any plant that is peculiar to the north of Europe and is not found sporadically in Asia also." Eliminating these doubly variable factors, but little is left except purely general concepts—air, water, heat, and cold—too indefinite and common to warrant any conclusions. It is unnecessary to emphasize these considerations further. The masters of philological research have all admitted their cogency and force. Max Müller,* in his later

---

* 1888, pp. 100–118.

more humble mood, confesses that " the evidence is so pliant that it is possible to make out a more or less plausible case " for any part of the world. It is only the lesser lights who still deal with roots as if they were mathematical symbols. Unfortunately, this confessed inadequacy of philology by and of itself to settle the interesting question as to European origins has induced a most mischievous commingling of physical anthropology and linguistics, which has been dire in its unscientific results. No greater unanimity as to conclusions has resulted, as might have been expected; and two formerly self-respecting and respected sciences have been plunged into an ill-merited disrepute thereby.

CHAPTER XVIII.

Prehistoric archæology is possessed of a distinct advantage over linguistics in the investigation of racial problems; for, as we have already observed, human remains are often discovered in connection with the implements, utensils, or trinkets by which the civilization of an extinct people is archæologically determined. To attempt even an outline of the cultural history of Europe would be obviously impossible in this place. It would fill a complete volume by itself alone. Furthermore, the short span of forty years since the inception of archæological science has not sufficed to produce complete unanimity of opinion among the leading authorities. Many important questions, especially concerning eastern Europe, are still awaiting settlement. All that we can hope to do is to describe what may be termed a few fixed points in European cultural history. This, as in our discussion of physical origins, we shall attempt to do by means of definite propositions, concerning which there is now substantial agreement.

I. *In western and southern Europe an entirely indigenous culture gradually evolved during the later stone age. This was characterized by great technical advance in fashioning implements, carvings, and designs in stone, bone, ivory, and copper; by the construction of dolmens and habitations of stone; by pottery-making; and possibly even by a primitive system of writing.*

A marked reaction has taken place during the last ten years among archæologists respecting the course of cultural development in France. It was long believed that after the first crude attempts of the palæolithic epoch an extended *hiatus* ensued, followed by the sudden appearance of a more highly developed civilization, brought by an immigrant broad-headed race from the East. Two waves of invasion were described: the first bringing polished stone, a later one introducing bronze, cereals, agriculture, and the domestication of animals. Not even credit for the construction of the great stone dolmen tombs was granted to the natives in Gaul, for these were all ascribed to an invasion from the North. The undoubted submergence of the primitive long-headed population of France by a brachycephalic type from the East, to which we have already adverted, was held accountable for a radical advance in civilization. Even the existence of a bronze age was denied to this country by Bertrand, for example, it being maintained that the introduction of bronze was retarded until both metals came in together from the Orient in the hands of the cultural deliverers of the land. The absence of a distinct bronze age was speedily disproved by Chantre's [75] remarkable researches in the Rhone Valley; but the view that France and western Europe were saved from barbarism only by a new race from the East still held sway. It is represented by the classical school of G. de Mortillet,* Bertrand,† and Topinard,‡ followed by Lenormant # and a host of minor disciples. The new school, holding that a steady and uninterrupted development of culture *in situ* was taking place, is represented notably by Reinach ‖ in France and by Sergi ᴬ in Italy. Their proof of this seems to be unanswerable. Granting that it is easier to borrow culture than to evolve it, a proposition underlying the older view; it seems, nevertheless, that the West has too long been denied its rightful share in the history of European civilization.

---

* 1875, 1879 a, and 1883, and all through his Matériaux, etc.

† *Cf.* 1891, pp. 122, 163, and 195–231.

‡ Eléménts, p. 400, for example.

Les Premières Civilisations, etc., 1874.

‖ Le Mirage Orientale, 1893 a ; and in his admirable outline of sculptural origins in Europe (1894–'96).

ᴬ Arii e Italici, Torino, 1898, especially pp. 199–220. *Cf.* his earlier 1895 a, pp. 25–32, for criticism of Reinach, holding that the Mediterranean basin and not midwestern Europe is entitled to the main credit for this indigenous culture.

38

A notable advance in the line of culture entirely indigenous to southwestern Europe has been lately revealed by the interesting discoveries by Piette at the station of Brassempuoy and

Neolithic Ivory Carving.   Mas d'Azil.   (After Piette.*)

in the grotto of Mas d'Azil.† Carvings in ivory, designs upon bone, evidence of a numerical system, of settled habitations,‡ and, most important of all, of a domestication of the reindeer, of the horse, and the ox in the pure stone age occur ; # and that. too, in the uttermost southwestern corner of Europe.   In the lake dwellings of Switzerland, as also in Scandinavia, a knowledge of agriculture, pottery, and the domestication of animals is evinced, likewise as a native discovery.   From other quarters of the continent in the stone age comes similar testimony to a marked advance of man culturally.   The justly celebrated carving from Thayngen,‖ on the opposite page, almost worthy of a modern craftsman, betrays no mean artistic ability.   The man who drew it was far from being a savage, even if he knew no metals, and buried his dead, instead of cremating them.

A system of writing seems also to have been invented in western Europe as far back as the stone age.△   Letourneau and Bordier have advanced good evidence to this effect, al-

---

* By special permission.   Further reproduction prohibited.

† Annex A of Bertrand and Reinach, 1891 ; and in L'Anthropologie, v and vi, 1894 and 1895, with supplement.   ‡ Siret, 1887, p. 255.

Op. cit., p. 284.   De Candolle and Sanson trace from the East.   *Cf.* De Mortillet, 1879 b and 1879 c.   Montelius, 1895 b, p. 30, finds evidence of the horse, ox, sheep, and swine.   ‖ Heim, 1874, and Merk, 1875.

△ Reinach, 1893 a, p. 543–548.   G. de Mortillet, 1897, denies the claim.

though it is not yet incontestably proved. The Phœnicians were perhaps antedated in their noted invention by the dolmen builders, by the lake dwellers of the earliest times, and, according to Sergi, also by the people of the Villanova pre-Etruscan culture in Italy. In an earlier time still in the Po Valley, as far back as the stone-age *Terramare* period, of which we shall speak later, pottery was made, and that, too, of a very decent sort. And all this time there is not the slightest evidence of contact with or knowledge of the East. As Reinach says, in no dolmen, no lake station, no excavation of the stone age is there any trace of an Assyrian or Babylonian cylinder, or even of an Egyptian amulet. Even the jade and nephrite found in western Europe from Switzerland to Norway, which has so long been regarded as proof of early commerce with the East, he denies as evidence of such contact. The case thus put may perhaps be over-strenuously stated, yet one can not but realize from it that western Europe has too long been libelled in respect of its native aptitude for civilization. This

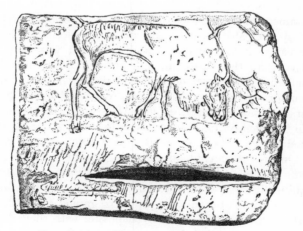

Bone Carving. Thayngen. (After Bertrand, '91.)

is not constituted of bronze alone, nor is its trade-mark cremation. Thus, while an intensive outbreak of culture of a high order may not have arisen west of the Alps, it can no longer be denied that the general standard of intelligence was surely rising of its own native volition.

II. *Throughout the eastern Alpine highlands a culture far more highly evolved than the neolithic one in the West, and betraying certain Oriental affinities, appears at a very early time, a thousand years or more before the Christian era. This prehistoric civilization represents a transitional stage between bronze and iron.*

In a secluded valley in Upper Austria, close to the border line of Salzburg, by the little Alpine hamlet of Hallstatt, a remarkable necropolis was discovered more than a half century ago, which marked an epoch in archæological research. Excavations at this place alone, far from any present considerable seat of population, have already revealed more than three thousand graves. The primitive culture here unearthed, represented by all kinds of weapons, implements, and ornaments, bore no resemblance to any of the then known classical ones of the Mediterranean basin. Its graves contained no Roman coins or relics. There was nothing Greek about it. It contained no trace either of writing or chronology. It was obviously prehistoric; there was no suggestion of a likeness to the early civilizations in Scandinavia. It was even more primitive than the Etruscan, and entirely different from it, especially in its lack of the beautiful pottery known to these predecessors of the Romans. Little wonder that von Sacken, who first adequately described it in 1868, and Hochstetter, who worthily carried on his researches, believed that Hallstatt represented an entirely indigenous and extinct Alpine civilization. On the other hand, so exceedingly rich and varied were the finds in this out-of-the-way corner of Europe, that another and quite different view seemed justifiable. Might this not be an entirely exotic culture, products gained by trade from all parts of the world being here depositel with their dead by a people who controlled the great and very ancient salt mines hereabouts? Neither of these interpretations of this find at Hallstatt have been exactly verified by later researches, and yet its importance has not lessened in the least. By later discoveries all over eastern Europe south of the Danube, from the Tyrol over to the Balkan peninsula, as well as throughout northern Italy, Würtemberg, and even over into northeastern France, the wide extension of this civilization * proves that it must in a large measure have developed upon the spot, and not come as an importation from abroad. On the other hand, its affinity in many details with the cultures both of Italy and Greece proved that it had made heavy drafts upon each of these, profiting greatly thereby. The best opinion to-day is that it constitutes a link in the chain of culture between eastern and western Europe. As such it is of primary importance in any study of European origins.

The primitive stage of European civilization, to which the term Hallstatt is specifically applied by archæologists, is characterized by a knowledge both of bronze and iron, although the latter is relatively insignificant. Its rarity indicates that we have to do with the very beginnings of its use. In this early combination of bronze and iron the Hallstatt culture is in strong contrast with the rest of Europe. Almost everywhere else, as in Hungary, for example, a pure bronze age—sometimes one even of copper also—intervenes between the use of stone and iron. Here, however, the two metals, bronze and iron, appear simultaneously. There is no evidence of a use of bronze alone. Bearing in mind what we shall subsequently emphasize in the case of Scandinavia, that in that remote part of Europe man had to put up with the inferior metal for close upon a thousand years before the acquisition of a better substitute, it will be seen that in the case of Hallstatt a remarkable foreshortening of cultural evolution had ensued. Iron, as we have said, was still comparatively rare. Only in the case of small objects, less often in the blades of bronze-handled swords, does this more precious metal appear. But it is far

---

* Chantre, 1884 ; Hoernes, 1892 ; Bertrand and Reinach, 1894 a ; Sergi, 1898 a ; and Orsi (Bull. Paletnologia Italiana, xi, 1885, p. 1 *et seq.*) are best authorities. See also Hallstatt in the subject index of our supplementary Bibliography. Naue, 1895, describes it in Bavaria. Care should be taken, however, to distinguish two uses of the word, Hallstatt. One is generalized to denote any mixed or transition stage between bronze and iron. The other is applied to the particular local type, akin to that of Hallstatt in detail.

more common than in the earliest Greek civilizations made known to us by Schliemann and others.

Pages of description would not give so clear an idea of this early civilization as the pictures of their lives, which the Hallstatt people have fortunately left to us. These are found in *repoussé* upon their bronzes, and particularly upon their little *situlæ*, or metallic pails. These *situlæ* are, in fact, the most distinctive feature among all the objects which they have left to us.* By means of them their civilization has been most accurately traced and identified geographically. On the opposite page we have reproduced the design upon the most celebrated of these *situlæ*, discovered by Deschmann in 1882 at Watsch in the Tyrol.† Another from Bologna, typical of the pre-Etruscan Italian time, will be found upon a later page. Upon each of these the skill manifested in the representations of men and animals is no less remarkable than the civilization which is depicted. The upper zone of this *situla* from Watsch apparently shows a festal procession, possibly a wedding, for a lady rides in the second chariot. The grooms and outriders betoken a party of distinction. As for the second zone, doubt as to its exact interpretation prevails. Hochstetter declares it to be a banquet, food and entertainment being offered to the personages seated upon chairs at the left. Bertrand is disposed to give it more of a religious interpretation. As for the contest between gladiators armed with the cestus, all is plain. The spectators, judges, even the ram and the helmet for reward of the victor, are all shown in detail. It is not necessary for us to cite more evidence. A civilization already far from primitive is surely depicted. As for its date, all are agreed that it is at least as early as ten centuries before Christ; ‡ not far, that is to say, from the supposed Homeric epoch in Greece.

---

* Bertrand and Reinach, 1894, pp. 96 *et seq.*, give a complete summary, description, and bibliography of the *situlæ* thus far discovered. Chantre, 1885, vol. ii, and Montelius, 1895 a, give many reproductions of their designs.

† Hochstetter, 1883, p. 170 *et seq.*, gives the best original description of it. Our reproduction is taken from this source.

‡ Hoernes, 1892, p. 529 ; Bertrand, 1876 a, second edition, pp. 207–216, fixes about 800 B. C. ; but 1894 a, p. 80, carries it back to 1200–1300 B. C.

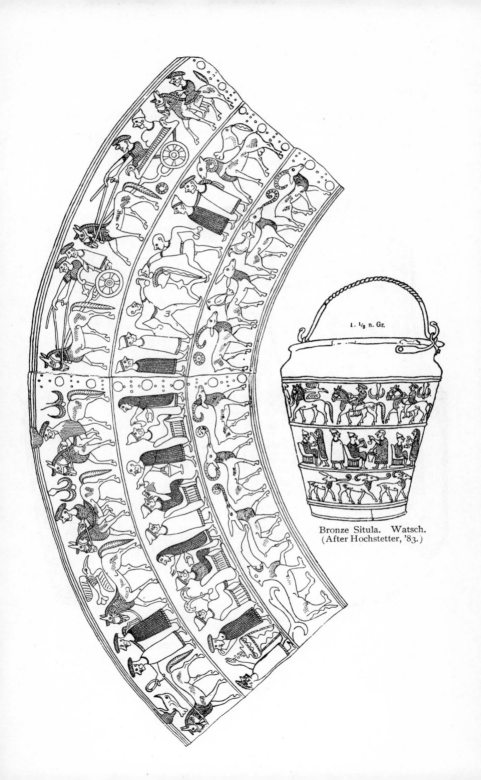

Bronze Situla. Watsch.
(After Hochstetter, '83.)

The Hallstatt civilization betrays unmistakable affinities with three other prehistoric European cultures, widely separated from one another. It contains many early Greek elements; it is very similar to a notable prehistoric culture in the Cau-

Bronze Breastplate. Olympia. (After Furtwaengler.)

casus Mountains; and it resembles most nearly of all perhaps the pre-Etruscan civilization in Italy. With the third of these —the Italian—it seems to have been most nearly upon terms of equality, each borrowing from the other, after a fashion of which we shall have occasion to speak shortly.* On the other hand, the relation of the Hallstatt culture to that of Greece and Caucasia seems to be somewhat more filial rather than fraternal. In describing the area of this civilization we have seen how firmly it is intrenched all through the southern part of Austria-Hungary and well over into the north of the Balkan peninsula. A comparison of Furtwaengler's magnificent collection of objects from Olympia † with those of Hallstatt instantly reveals their similarities. To make this clear, we have reproduced one of the Olympian breastplates, ornamented with figures which at once suggest those upon the *situla* from Watsch above described. This design is doubly interesting. It shows us a slightly higher stage of the art of figural representation, as well as of conventional design. Not only the men and horses, but the borders, are far better drawn. More than this, we begin to detect a distinctly Oriental motive in other details. The bulls and the lions—lions are not indigenous to Europe nowadays—at once remind us of their Babylonian and Assyrian prototypes. We have entered the sphere of Asiatic artistic influence, albeit very indistinctly. This design here represented, it should be said, is rather above the average of the Olympian finds of the earlier epoch. Many of the other objects, especially the little votive figures of beasts and men, are much more crude, although always, as Hoernes observes, characteristic and rudely artistic in many ways. Through this Olympian stage of culture we pass transitionally on to the Mycenean, which brings up into the full bloom of the classic Greek civilization.‡

The Oriental affinities of the Hallstatt culture have been especially emphasized by the recent archæological discoveries at Koban, in the Caucasian territory of the Ossetes.# A stage

---

* *Cf.* Hochstetter, 1883, p. 199; Hoernes, 1889 and 1890.

† Die Bronzen und die übrigen kleineren Funde von Olympia, Berlin, 1892.

‡ *Cf.* Sophus Mueller, 1884; Reinach in L'Anthropologie, i, 1890, pp. 552–565; ibid., iv, p. 610; Montelius, 1892; Tsountas and Manett, Perrot and Chippiez, and the classical archæologists. A. J. Evans, 1896, contains much of interest in this connection.

Described and superbly illustrated by Virchow, 1883 a, and Chantre, 1885–'87, especially ii, p. 187. *Cf.* also J. de Morgan, 1889, ii, chapter i.

of culture, transitional between bronze and iron, almost exactly equivalent to that of the eastern Alps, is revealed. Similarities in little objects, like fibulæ, might easily be accounted for as having passed in trade, but the relationship is too intimate to be thus explained. Hungary forms the connecting link

between the two. In many respects its bronze age is different from that of Hallstatt, notably in that the latter seems to have acquired the knowledge of iron and of bronze at about the same time. In Hungary the pure bronze age lasted a long time, and attained a full maturity. A characteristic piece is represented

Bronze Vessel. Hungary. (After Hampel.)

herewith.* In respect of the representation of figures of animals such as these, Hallstatt, Hungary, and Koban are quite alike.

Have we proved that bronze culture came from Asia by reason of these recent finds in the Caucasus? Great stress has been laid upon them in the discussion of European origins. Are we justified in agreeing with Chantre † that two currents of culture have swept from Asia into Europe—one by the Cau-

Bronze Chariot. Glasinac. (After Chantre, '85–'7.)

---

* On Hungary, Hampel, C. R. Congrès int. d'anth., session 8, Buda-Pesth, ii ; and Hoernes, 1888 and 1889–'90, best ; cf. also his 1892, pp. 405–411.　　　　　　　　　　　　† 1884, p. 315.

casus north of the Black Sea and up the Danube; the other across Asia Minor and into the Balkan peninsula, thence joining the first in the main centre of Hallstatt civilization, east of the Alps? The point seems by no means proved. Relationship does not necessitate parentage. Far more likely does it appear, as Reinach says,* that the Koban culture is a relic or an offshoot, rather than a cradle of bronze civilization. And even Chantre,† ardent advocate as he is of Oriental derivations, seems to feel the force of this in his later writings; for he confesses that Koban is rather from Mediterranean European sources than that Europe is from Koban. Most probable of all is it that both Hallstatt and Koban are alike derived from a common root in the neighbourhood of Chaldea.

III. *The Hallstatt (or Celtic?) civilization of bronze and iron roughly overlies the present area occupied by the brachycephalic Alpine race; yet this type is not always identified with the Oriental culture. It seems to have appeared in Europe in a far lower stage of civilization, and to have subsequently made progress culturally upon the spot.*

To trace any definite connection between race and civilization in Europe is rendered extremely hazardous scientifically, by reason of the appearance along with bronze of the custom of burning instead of burying the dead—their ashes being disposed in cinerary urns, jars, or other receptacles. By this procedure all possible clew to the physical type of the people is, of course, annihilated at once. It has become almost an axiom among archæologists that bronze culture and incineration are constant companions. Wherever one appears, the other may confidently be looked for. Together they have long been supposed to be the special and peculiar attributes of the new broad-headed immigrant race from the East. To prove this conclusively is, of course, absolutely impossible, for the above-mentioned reason. Of the two, it seems as if incineration would be a more reliable test of race than a knowledge of bronze; for burial customs, involving as they do the most sacred instincts and traditions of a people, would be most

---

* 1893 a, p. 561.   † 1885-'87, ii, p. 189.

persistently maintained, even throughout long-continued migrations.* The use of bronze, on the other hand, being a matter of obvious utility, and capable of widespread dissemination commercially, is seemingly of far less ethnic significance.

To indicate the uncertainty of proof in these matters, let us suppose that the Hallstatt civilization, for example, is the result of an immigration of a brachycephalic Oriental civilized race overlying a primitive native long-headed one. That seems best to conform to the data which northern Italy, at least, affords. Suppose the new people—call them Celts with the best authorities, if you please—brought not only bronze and iron, but the custom of incineration. Prior to their appearance inhumation was the rule. What would be the result if one attempted to determine the physical character of that people from a study of remains in their necropoli? All the crania to be found in the graves with the precious objects of bronze would in no wise represent the people who brought that bronze. They burned their bridges behind them at death, and disappeared for good and all. And the remains left to the archæologist would represent precisely that class in the population which had nothing to do with the main characteristics of its civilization. And then again, we must bear in mind that the interments in these necropoli as a whole, both with burned or buried dead, constitute a selected type. Neither Hallstatt, Watsch, nor any of the burial places of their type were open to the great mass of the common people. They were sacred spots, far removed among the mountains from any centres of population. Only the rich or powerful presumably had access to them. They are no more typical of the Hallstatt people, therefore, than interments in Westminster Abbey are representative of the English masses. All our data are necessarily drawn from a class within a class. Inductions from them must be very gingerly handled.

The situation above described seems to prevail almost everywhere in the Hallstatt cultural area. Two distinct burial customs denote possibly two separate peoples, the inhumers

---

* Bertrand, 1891, p. 196, has some interesting notes on this. *Cf.* Ranke, Der Mensch., ii, p. 543.

being certainly the older. In the Hallstatt necropolis, for example, about one third of the graves once contained human remains, all the others containing merely ashes. So ancient are these graves that only eight crania from the hundreds of interments of the first class are available for study. These are of a pronounced long-headed type.* The modern populations of this part of Europe are, as we have seen, among the broadest-headed people in the world, as are also all the modern Illyrians. Yet from the great necropolis at Glasinac in Bosnia, with its twenty thousand tumuli, the meagre Hallstatt returns are amply corroborated.† The ancient inhabitants were as long-headed as they are pronouncedly of the opposite type to-day. Up in Bohemia and Moravia also, according to Niederle,‡ the first bronze-age people, such as we know them, were still dolichocephalic quite like their predecessors in the pure stone age. And here also is incineration just about frequent enough to make it uncertain whether the human remains are typical of the whole population or not.

Under these circumstances, three suppositions are open to us. We may hold that these long-headed crania of the Hallstatt people are worthless for any anthropological purposes at all. This one would certainly be tempted to do were the testimony, such as it is, not so unanimous. Or, secondly, we may assume that these long-headed Hallstatt people belonged to a period subsequent to the appearance of our Alpine type in western Europe. If we do so, we place them in the same class with the Teutonic race which so certainly appears overlying the Alpine one in the later iron age in Switzerland and throughout southern Germany. For the Helvetians and the *Reihengräber* conquerors from the north surely imposed a novel culture, albeit a militant one, upon the long-settled Alpine people, racially speaking. The Hallstatt civilization is immeasurably too early to permit of this hypothesis. At this

---

* Zuckerkandl, 1883, p. 96. On page 93 he gives data for the modern Hallstatt people. *Cf.* also Hochstetter, 1878, p. 319 ; Hoernes, 1892, p. 618 ; Weisbach, 1894, p. 241.

† Weisbach, 1897 b, and Radimsky, 1891. ‡ 1892 a, p. 78.

time the long-headed Teutonic peoples about Scandinavia were
certainly vastly inferior in culture, as we shall attempt to prove
shortly. Thus we are forced to the third conclusion if we
admit the competency of our cranial evidence—namely, that
the Hallstatt people in this early bloom of civilization in Europe were allied to the Mediterranean type of the south. No
other source for such a dolichocephalic population is possible.
Our stock of types of this kind is exhausted.

It does not require a great credulity to admit of this hypothesis, that the Hallstatt people were of Mediterranean type.
Were not the Greeks, the Phœnicians, and the Egyptians all
members of this same race? One single difficulty presents
itself. Over in Italy throughout the valley of the Po an entirely analogous civilization to that of the eastern Alps occurs.
Hallstatt and Villanova, Watsch and Bologna, are almost identical culturally. And yet over here in Italy the new culture of
bronze and of incineration seems to be borne by a broad-
headed people of the same type as the modern one. Thus,
for example, at Novilara so long as the bodies were all in-
humed the people were of the long-headed Mediterranean
type once indigenous to the whole of Italy, now surviving,
as we have seen, only in the southern half. On the other hand,
when incineration begins to appear in this place, the human
remains still left to us are of a mixed and far more broad-
headed type.* It would seem admissible to assume that when
the modern brachycephalic Alpine race submerged the native
one it brought new elements of civilization with it. Many Italian authorities, at all events, agree in ascribing the new culture—call it Umbrian with Sergi, or proto-Etruscan with
Helbig—to a new race of Veneto-Illyrian or Alpine physical
proclivities.† What they have not definitely proved, however,
is that any necessary connection between race and culture
exists. There is much to show that the broad-headed race
came in some time before the introduction of the new arts.
Even in the later *Terramare* period preceding the Italian
Hallstatt culture, when stone and copper only are in evidence,

---

* Sergi, 1898 a, pp. 122–129.
† Zampa, 1891 a, p. 77 ; Sergi, 1898 a, p. 138.

a change of physical type in the people apparently begins, just as also in France in the neolithic period.*

The most indubitable testimony that the Alpine race did not appear in western Europe, armed *cap-à-pie* with bronze and other attributes of culture, is afforded by the lake dwellings of Switzerland.† Here in the pile-built villages of the Swiss lakes we can trace an uninterrupted development of civilization from the pure stone age through bronze and into iron. Beginning at a stage of civilization, as Schrader in his great linguistic work observes, about equal to that of the ancient Aryan-speaking peoples judged by the root-words known to us; not only knowledge of the metals, but of agriculture, of the domestication of animals, and of the finer arts of domestic life, have little by little been acquired. Equally certain is it that no change of physical type has occurred among these primitive Swiss, at least until the irruptions of the Teutonic Helvetians and others at the opening of the historic period. From the very earliest times in the stone age a broad-headedness no less pronounced than that of the modern Swiss prevailed among these people.‡ Here would seem to be pretty conclusive proof that the Alpine race entered Europe long before the culture with which its name has been all too intimately associated.

In the outlying parts of Europe, perhaps even in Gaul, it is extremely doubtful whether any closer connection between race and culture exists than in the Alps. It has long been maintained that the brachycephalic people of the Round Barrows introduced bronze into Britain. Surely, as we have already shown, things point to that conclusion. Beddoe,# Dawkins,‖

---

* Hervé, 1894 b.

† Keller's reports since 1858 are the main source. Munro, 1890, is best in English. *Cf.* also the works of Gross and others, in our supplementary Bibliography, under "Lake Dwellings."

‡ This fact has been established beyond doubt by the recent great work of Studer and Bannwarth, Crania Helvetica Antiqua, 1894. *Vide* p. 13. Sergi's attempt to interpet the data otherwise (1898 a, p. 67) is entirely erroneous. Gross's data apparently refer entirely to the later period of Teutonic invasions in the iron age (1883, p. 106). *Cf.* Munro, pp. 537 and 541.   # 1893, p. 29.   ‖ 1880, p. 342.

and other authorities maintain it at all events. Yet Canon Taylor * makes it pretty evident that the new race arrived in Britain, as it certainly did in Gaul,† considerably in advance of any knowledge of the metals. As for Scandinavia, much the same relation holds true. Both race and culture, as we shall see, came from the south; but it is by no means clear that they arrived at the same time or that one brought the other.‡ In Spain, Siret # has asserted that bronze came in the hands of a new immigrant broad-headed race, but the more authoritative opinion of Cartailhac [86] discovers no direct evidence to this effect.

The final conclusions which would seem to follow from our tedious summary is this: That the nearly contemporaneous appearance of the Alpine race and the first knowledge of metals, indicative of Oriental cultural influences in western Europe, is more or less a coincidence. The first civilized peoples of the Hallstatt period seem to have been closely allied, both in physical type and culture, with the Greeks and other peoples of the classic East. Among them, perhaps over them, swept the representatives of our broad-headed Alpine type who came from the direction of Asia. These invaders may have been the Scythians, although the matter is incapable of proof. Pressure from this direction set both culture and population in motion toward the west, in much the same way that the fall of Constantinople in the fifteenth century induced the Renaissance in Italy.

IV. *The remarkable prehistoric civilization of Italy is due to the union of two cultures: one from the Hallstatt region, having entered Europe by way of the Danube, the other coming from the southeast by sea, being distinctly Mediterranean. From these evolved the Umbrian and the Etruscan civilizations, followed in the historic period by the early Latin.*

The earliest culture in Italy worthy the name is found in the *palafitti* or pile dwellings in the northern lakes, and in the so-called *terramare* settlements in the valley of the Po.||

---

* 1890, p. 79.　　　　　　　　　　† Hervé, 1894 b.
‡ S. O. Mueller, 1897, p. 307.　　　　# 1887, p. 265.
　|| *Vide* map on page 264 *supra*. Sergi, 1898 a, gives a full description of them. For original data consult files of Bulletino di Paletnologia Italiana.

The former are not distinguishable from similar structures in the Swiss lake dwellings, but the *terramare* are entirely peculiar to Italy. Their like is not found anywhere else in Europe. Briefly described, they were villages built upon raised platforms of earth, encircled by a moat, and generally having a ditch or small pond in the middle, in which an altar is erected. These complicated structures were built upon the low, marshy, alluvial plains along the Po, but show many points of similarity with the true pile dwellings. The people of this early period were in the pure stone age, with few arts save that of making the coarser kinds of pottery. From their osseous remains, they seem to have been of a long-headed type, quite like their predecessors, who were cave dwellers. After a time, without any modification of the modes of construction of their settlements, new elements appear among these *terramare* people, bringing bronze and introducing cremation. At about the same period, as we have said, the Alpine broad-headed race begins its submergence of the primitive Ligurian type, leading to the formation of the north Italian population as we see it to-day.* This type surely invaded Italy from the north and northeast.

From the foregoing considerations it will appear that there were two constituent streams of culture and also of men here uniting in the valley of the Po and on the northern slopes of the Apennines.† Possibly, as Chantre affirms, these two streams were from a common Oriental source, here being reunited after long and independent migrations.‡ At all events, a remarkable advance in culture speedily ensued, superior to either of those from which its elements were derived. For the civilization unearthed at Villanova, in the Certosa at Bologna, at Este, and elsewhere, while in much of its bronze work similar to the Hallstatt types, contained a number of added features, obviously either indigenous or brought directly from the south. The Hallstatt affinities are especially revealed in the *situlæ* to which we have already called attention. That of Arnoaldi discovered at Bologna, betrays much

---

* *Cf.* p. 262 *supra.*

† On the Danube as a pathway of cultural immigration, *cf.* Bertrand, 1891, p. 256.   ‡ Chantre, 1884, p. 316.   *Cf.* p. 266 *supra.*

39

the same grade of skill in manufacture as the one from Watsch.
Its flat development is shown by the accompanying cut.   The

Arnoaldi Situla. Bologna.
(From Revue Archéologique, '85.)

scenes represented are not dissimilar. The boxers armed with the cestus, the chariots, and horses closely resemble one another. No doubt of a close intercourse between the two regions of Bologna and Austria can possibly exist.

The influence of the second or native element in prehistoric Italian civilization appears most clearly in the Etruscan period. Etruria, lying south of the Apennines, was more essentially Italian, as we might expect, than the region about Bologna, where the Umbro-Hallstatt, or continental, culture flourished. It is easy to note the superiority in the former case. It is most clearly indicated in the pottery. Here we

| Early Etruscan. | Pure Etruscan, Middle Period. |

find an art which is truly indigenous to the climate and soil of the Mediterranean.

Popularly, the word " Etruscan " at once suggests the ceramic art; the progress effected in a short time was certainly startling. To give an idea of the sudden change, we have reproduced upon this page illustrations of typical bits of Italian pottery.* The first vase, prior to the full Etruscan culture, shows its crudity at once, both in its defects of form and the plainness and simplicity of its ornamentation. Such a vessel might have been made in Mexico or even by our own Pueblo Indians. In a century or two some teacher made it possible to produce the sample depicted in the next cut. Perfect in

* From Montelius, 1897.

form, notably graceful in outline, its decoration is most effective; yet it betrays greater skill in geometrical design than in the representation of animate life. The dog drawn on the girdle is still far from lifelike. Then come—probably after inspiration from Greek art—the possibilities in complex ornamentation represented by our third specimen. Not more pleasing in form; perhaps less truly artistic because of its ornateness, it manifests much skill in the delineation of human and animal forms.

The advance in culture typified by our vases was equalled in all the details of life.* The people built strongly walled cities; they constructed roads and bridges; their architecture,

Greek Etruscan.

true predecessor of the Roman, was unique and highly evolved. All the plain and good things of life were known to these people, and their civilization was rich in its luxury, its culture and art as well. In costumes, jewelry, the paraphernalia of war, in painting and statuary they were alike distinguished. Their mythology was very complex, much of the Roman being derived from it. Most of our knowledge of them is derived from the rich discoveries in their chambered tombs, scattered all over Italy from Rome to Bologna. There can be no doubt of a very high type of civilization attained long before the Christian era. Roman history is merged in the obscurity of time, five or six hundred years later than this. The high antiquity of the Etruscan is therefore beyond question. But its highly evolved art and culture show that we have passed beyond the stage of European origins; to discuss it further would lead us to trench upon the field of classical rather than prehistoric archæology.

---

* A good recent *résumé* of Etruscan culture is given by Lefèvre, 1891 and 1896 a. *Cf.* " Etruscans " in our Bibliography.

V. *The northwestern corner of Europe, including Scandinavia, Denmark, and the Baltic plain of Germany, throughout the prehistoric period has been characterized by backwardness of culture as compared with the rest of Europe. It was populated from the south, deriving a large part of such primitive civilization as it possessed from the south and the southeast as well.*

That this region was necessarily uninhabited during the Glacial epoch, long after the advent of man in southern Europe, is indubitable. It is proved by the extent of the glaciated area, which extends on the mainland as far south as Hamburg, Berlin, and Posen, and over the entire British Isles at the same time.* It was by the melting of this vast sheet of ice that those high level river terraces in France and Belgium were formed, in which the most ancient and primitive implements of human manufacture occur. In the area beneath this ice sheet no trace of human occupation until long after this time occurs. This fact of itself, of course, proves nothing; for glaciation would have obliterated all traces of anterior habitation or activity. As to the possibility of a tertiary population before the Glacial epoch, it presents too remote a contingency for us to consider, although we do not deny its possibility. It too far antedates prehistory, so to speak.

At the notable International Congress of Anthropology and Prehistoric Archæology at Stockholm in 1874 a landmark in these sciences was established by substantial agreement among the leading authorities from all over Europe upon the proposition now before us.† First of all, every one subscribed to the view that the palæolithic or oldest stone age was entirely unrepresented in Sweden. The earliest and simplest stone implements discovered in the southern part of that country betray a degree of skill and culture far above that so long prevalent in France and Germany. Stone is not only rubbed and

---

* *Cf.* maps and data in J. Geikie, 1894; Penck, 1884; and Niederle, 1893, p. 25.

† Bertrand, 1876 a and 1876 b, gives a full account of it. The best recent authorities upon Scandinavian culture are Sophus Mueller, 1897, and Montelius, 1895 b. Other works of reference are those of Worsaae, Nilsson, Hildebrand, Madsen and Rygh, titles being given in our supplementary Bibliography.

polished into shape, but the complicated art of boring holes in it has been learned. Norway also seems to be lacking in similar evidence of a human population in the very lowest stage of civilization. Stone implements anterior to the discovery of the art of rubbing or polishing are almost unknown. Only about Christiania have any finds at all been made. In Denmark some few very rude implements have been found. They are so scarce as to suggest that they are mere rejects

Flint Dagger. Scandinavia.
(After Montelius, '95 b.)

Stone Axe. Scandinavia.
(After Montelius, '95 b.)

or half-finished ones of a later type. The kitchen middens, or shell heaps of Jutland, for which the region is most notable, as described by Steenstrup, abound in stone implements. They all represent man in the neolithic age. Polished stones are as abundant as the rudely hammered ones are rare. From the absence of all such very early stone implements, and from the sudden appearance of others of a far more finished type, the possibility of a gradual evolution of culture about Scandinavia *in situ* is denied on all hands. The art of working stone has surely been introduced from some more favoured region. The only place to look for the source of this culture is to the south.

Tardy in its human occupation and its stone culture, Scandinavia was still more backward, as compared with the rest of Europe, in its transition to the age of bronze. This is all the more remarkable in view of the rich store of raw materials on every hand. Nowhere else in Europe does the pure stone age seem to have been so unduly protracted. A necessary consequence of this was that stone-working reached a higher stage of evolution here than anywhere else in the world save in America. In other parts of Europe the discovery of metal-working, of course, immediately put an end to all progress in this direction. The ultimate degree of skill to which they attained is represented in the accompanying cuts. The first, a flint poniard, shows the possibilities, both in the line of form and finish, of manufacture by the chipping process. To equal this example one must look to the most skilful of the American Indians, as in Tennessee, where they were too remote from mines of native copper to make use of a ready substitute for stone. Our second implement is an axe hammer, made of diorite. To shape, sharpen, bore, and polish a piece of stone like this certainly required a long apprenticeship in the art.

Bronze culture, when it did at last appear in this remote part of Europe, came upon the scene suddenly and in full maturity. Whether this was as early as the eighth to the tenth century B. C., as Montelius [95] avers, is disputed by many. All are nevertheless agreed that evidence is absolutely lacking that the art was of indigenous origin. From what part of the world this knowledge of bronze ultimately came, we leave an open question, as also whether it came with Phœnician traders * or direct from Greece as Worsaae affirms. It was certainly introduced into Sweden, making its way into Norway about the same time, directly from the peninsula of Jutland. Its first appearance is in a highly evolved state. Such crude attempts at manufacture as Chantre finds so long prevalent along the Rhone Valley, for example, are entirely absent.

---

* Nilsson and Lindenschmidt, Wiberg, 1867, is good on this.

Both in form and ornamentation the hand of the master is apparent. This bronze age, like that of stone, lasted a very long time—far longer than anywhere else on the continent. Central Europe passed through three stages of metallic progress while Scandinavia was evolving two. Not until the second or third century of our era—not until the time of the Romans, it would appear—did iron begin to supplant bronze. History repeats itself. The excessive duration of the bronze age, as in the case of stone antecedently, led to the attainment of a remarkable skill. The two accompanying cuts are typical of the best work of this time. In the one case, merely superficial ornament, especially the skilful use of the spiral; in the other, real beauty of form in the bracelet, are clearly apparent. Possessed of such skill in the working of bronze, it is small wonder that the need of a better metal was not felt. Only when fashioned into weapons of war does iron reveal its supremacy over bronze. This, of course, with the campaigns of historical times, brings us to the end of our chronicle.

Bronze Axe. Scandinavia. (After Montelius, '95 b.)

Bronze Armring. Vestermanland. (After Montelius, '95 b.)

The prehistoric experience of metal-working in Scandinavia is typical of the other details of its cultural evolution. In its earliest epoch no trace of domestic animals is present. It is rather a remarkable fact that even the reindeer seems to have been unknown.* What can Penka say to this in his positive affirmation that the original Aryans got up into Scandinavia, having followed the reindeer from central Europe

* Bertrand, 1876 b, p. 40.

north after the retreat of the ice sheet. The fact is, archæologically speaking from the evidence furnished by the kitchen
middens, that if they ever did this " they left a fine country,
where deer were plenty, to subsist upon shellfish on the foggy
coasts of Denmark." *   Quite early, however, even in the
stone age, do evidences of domestic animals occur, to the dog
being added the ox, horse, swine, and sheep.† Pottery in a
rude form also follows. Finally, and in apparent coincidence
with the bronze culture, comes a new custom of incineration.
The dead are no longer buried, but burned. A profound modification of religious ideas is hereby implied. It seems to have
been at about this time also that our Alpine racial type entered Scandinavia from Denmark; although, as we have already
observed, it is yet far from certain that the new race was the
active agent in introducing the new elements of culture. All
that we know is that they both came from the south, and
reached this remote region at about the same time.

That Aryan matters in Europe are certainly mixed would
seem to be about the only warrantable conclusion to be drawn
from our extended discussion in these chapters. They have
an iconoclastic tone. Yet we would not leave the matter entirely in the air; nor would we agree with Mantegazza [84] in
his conclusion that " Ignoramus " sums up our entire knowledge of the subject. There is some comfort to be drawn even
from this mass of conflicting opinions. Our final destructive
aim has been achieved if we have emphasized the danger of
correlating data drawn from several distinct sciences, whose
only bond of unity is that they are all concerned with the same
object—man. The positive contribution which we would seek
to make is that the whole matter of European origins is by
no means so simple as it has too often been made to appear.
It is not in the least imperative that conclusions from all
contributory sciences should be susceptible of interweaving
into a simple scheme of common origins for all. The order
of races, for example, need mean nothing as respects priority

---

* Reinach, 1892, pp. 72–78, for severe criticism of Penka's hypotheses.
† Montelius, 1895 b, p. 30.

of culture.   Nor do the two sciences, philology and archæology, involve one another's conclusions so far as civilization is concerned.   Language and industrial culture may have had very different sources; their migrations need stand in no relation to one another in the least.   Each science is fully justified in its own deductions, but must be content to leave the results of others in peace.   Such is the ultimate conclusion to which all the latest authority is tending.   Only by a careful comparison of data from each sphere of investigation may we finally hope to combine them all in a composite whole, as many-sided and complex as the life and nature of man itself.

CHAPTER XIX.

SOCIAL PROBLEMS: ENVIRONMENT *VERSUS* RACE.

Has the intricate racial composition of the population of Europe, which we have been at so much pains to analyze, any significance for the student of social problems? Is there any reason why those who would rightly interpret sociological phenomena should first thoroughly acquaint themselves with the nature of the human stuff of which populations are compounded? Or have our conclusions, thus far, value merely as branches of investigation in pure science, a matter of academic interest alone? Such are the questions awaiting resolution at our hands in this chapter.

Let us begin by distinguishing between two equally competent and yet radically opposite explanations for any human phenomenon. One ascribes its origin to heredity, an internal factor; the other makes it a product of outward conditions— that is to say, of environment, social it may be, or physical. Thus the tall stature or blondness of an individual, a social class, or a people, may conceivably be due either to an inherited tendency from preceding generations, or else to the modifying influence of outer circumstances operative during a recent period. Considering a single individual alone, a third factor—viz., chance variation—must needs be taken into account; but viewing men by wholesale, in large masses, this matter takes care of itself. Thus an odd drunkard, social reject, or criminal here and there in a community may be nothing more than an aberrant type; but if we discover a goodly proportion of such bad men, we are led to suspect a more fundamental cause. Chance does not work thus by wholesale, steadily in any given direction. Quetelet discovered this fact years ago. Confronted by any such phenomenon existing in appreciable proportions in any society, as revealed by statistical examination, we are therefore at once called upon to decide between our two original explanations. One runs it to earth on the environmental theory; the other trees it in genealogical hypothesis. In plain English, it becomes a question of outward circumstances or else of inherited tendencies.* On the first supposition the phenomenon is of purely modern origin; in the second its roots are imbedded in the past. When the explanation thus becomes retrospective, if the people be in any wise homogeneous in characteristics, customs, or speech, we substitute another shorter word for inheritance. The whole matter simmers down to a decision between environment and race. Our problem in this chapter is to adjudge a few such difficulties, whereby we may subserve a double purpose. We may discover what are the distinctive social peculiarities of the three races whose history we have been outlining; and we may form a definite idea of the class of remedies necessary to meet the peculiar needs of each community. For it is quite obvious that social evils due to inherited tendencies require very different treatment from those which are of recent origin, the product of local circumstances.

Purely environmental factors in social phenomena have been all too largely neglected by investigators in the past. At times they rise paramount to all other circumstances. One of the most striking instances of the influence of climate, for example, upon the distribution of population is offered by the present location of the cotton mills of Lancashire along the west coast of England. Why were these mills all set up about the city of Manchester, nearly a century ago? Why were they not placed where plenty of labour was at hand—viz., in the south and west, at that time the most densely populated district in England? The mills were not moved up into Lancashire, far from the crowd, because of the proximity to coal or iron. That may have in part induced them to remain there, when the choice had once been made. But before the days

---

* *Cf.* page 7 *supra.*

of the steam engine, coal had no influence upon the selection of sites. Neither population nor coal being important elements, it is certain that climate was all-powerful in its attractiveness. Here along the west coast, where the warm, moist Gulf-Stream winds blow steadily landward, is the most humid district in all England. In such an atmosphere the cotton fibre becomes naturally pliant and supple, rendering the spinning of thread a comparatively simple task. So considerable an element was this, that all sorts of devices were adopted for securing permanent benefit from the natural climatic endowment. Building sites were chosen on the western hill slopes, just where the humidity from the rising currents of air was greatest. Oldham and other towns above Manchester were located in accordance with it. Artificial ponds were made just west of the mills, so that the gentle winds blowing over them might become duly dampened. So subtle was this advantage that potted plants in the windows sometimes sufficed to humidify the air to just the right amount. Even to-day, with all the artificial devices for supplanting Nature's aid, we are told by a manufacturer that a change of wind from east to west often makes a difference of seven or eight per cent in the product of a weaving shed.* To secure the precious humidity, factories have even at times been built half under ground, emulating the example of the Oriental makers of Dacca muslin, or " woven wind," who work sitting in holes in the ground, so that their delicate fabrics may be rendered supple by the moisture of the earth. Thus, perhaps, acting in this way, has the factor of climate been able to overcome the inertia of the large population once centering in southern England; for it has been compelled to transfer itself to the spot marked out by Nature for the industry.

To decide between race and environment as the efficient cause of any social phenomenon is a matter of singular interest at this time. A school of sociological writers, dazzled by the recent brilliant discoveries in European ethnology, show a

---

* For interesting data upon this point consult Transactions of the New England Cotton Manufacturers' Association, No. 57, pp. 185 *et seq.* ; Edward Atkinson, in the Popular Science Monthly, 1890, pp. 306 *et seq.*

decided inclination to sink the racial explanation up to the handle in every possible phase of social life in Europe. It must be confessed that there is provocation for it. So persistent have the physical characteristics of the people shown themselves, that it is not surprising to find theories of a corresponding inheritance of mental attributes in great favour. Yet it seems to be high time to call a halt when this " vulgar theory of race," as Cliffe-Leslie termed it, is made sponsor for nearly every conceivable form of social, political, or economic virtues or ills, as the case may be.

This racial school of social philosophers derives much of its data from French sources. For this reason, and also because our anthropological knowledge of that country is more complete than for any other part of Europe, we shall confine our attention primarily to France. Let us refresh our memories of the subject. For this purpose we must once again refer to our map on page 138, showing the distribution of the head form. This we hold to be the best expression of the racial facts. On this map the dark tints show the localization in the unattractive upland areas of isolation, of the Alpine broad-headed race common to central Europe. The light tints at the north, extending down in a broad belt diagonally as far as Limoges and along the coast of Brittany, denote intermixture with the blond, long-headed Teutonic race; while the similar light strip along the southern coast, penetrating up the Rhone Valley, measures the extension of the equally long-headed but brunet Mediterranean stock. The dotted area about Périgueux in the southwest, we have surely identified as a bit of the prehistoric Cro-Magnon race persisting here in relative purity. These ethnic facts correspond to physical ones; three areas of geographical isolation, dark-coloured, are distinct centres of distribution of the Alpine race. These differ in intensity. The high Alps of Savoy are the most isolated of all; Auvergne, the south central plateau, follows next in order. These two are populated by quite pure Alpine types. Brittany, most accessible of the three, contains only an attenuation of this broad-headed race, the Teutons having infiltrated through it quite generally.

The organization of the family is the surest criterion of the stage of social evolution attained by a people. No other phase of human association is so many-sided, so fundamental, so pregnant for the future. For this reason we may properly begin our study by an examination of a phenomenon which directly concerns the stability of the domestic institution—viz., divorce. What are the facts as to its distribution in France?

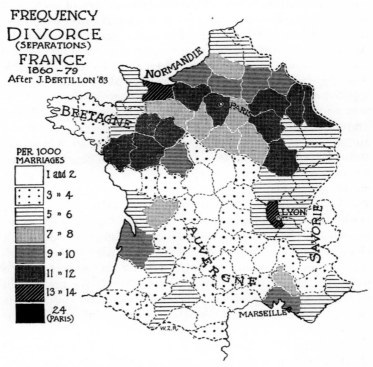

FREQUENCY
DIVORCE
(SEPARATIONS)
FRANCE
1860 – 79
After J. BERTILLON '83

NORMANDIE

BRETAGNE

PARIS

PER 1000
MARRIAGES

	I and 2
	3 " 4
	5 " 6
	7 " 8
	9 " 10
	11 " 12
	13 " 14
	24 (PARIS)

LYON

SAVORIE

AUVERGNE

MARSEILLE

W.Z.R.

Owing to the influence of the Catholic Church, no actual divorces were allowed by law in that country prior to 1884; but what were known as "*séparations de corps*," or judicial separations, were regularly granted. From data derived from the best authorities, we have prepared the map on this page, showing its relative frequency in different parts of the country. The dark tints correspond to the areas where it is most common.

From this map it appears that marked variations between different districts occur. Paris is at one extreme; Corsica, as always, at the other.* Of singular interest to us is the parallel which at once appears between this distribution of divorce and that of head form. The areas of isolation peopled by the Alpine race are characterized by almost complete absence of legal severance of domestic relations between husband and wife. Savoy and Auvergne certainly show infrequency of such judicial separations on this map, a social characteristic which extends clear to the Pyrenees, in just the same way that the Alpine broad-headedness occupies the same country. The correspondence appears to be defective in Brittany, but this is largely because of arbitrary departmental boundaries. It is highly important to observe the radical contrast between Brittany and Normandy. It will be verified in almost every demographic detail. A slightly increased tendency toward divorce appears in the narrow coast strip along the Mediterranean Riviera. The fertile valley of the Garonne is clearly outlined by increased frequency of separations, in marked contrast to the highlands on either side. This is, of course, partly due to the concentration of population in cities along the river; for divorce is always more frequent in urban than in rural communities. The same consideration may also be important along the Mediterranean coast, for a large part of the population is here aggregated in cities, for peculiar reasons which will appear in due time.† Even more strikingly the great basin of the Seine, centre of Teutonic racial characteristics, stands sharply marked off from the whole south. This is most important of all.

Do the facts instanced above have any ethnic significance? Do they mean that the Alpine type, as a race, holds more tenaciously than does the Teuton to its family traditions, resenting thereby the interference of the state in its domestic institutions?

---

* *Cf.* Demolins' (1897) description of domestic organization in Corsica and the Pyrenees, pp. 11 and 178. Turquan, in Soc. Normande de Géog., xvii, 1895, p. 203, gives another fine map.

† *Cf.* Demolins, 1897, pp. 119, 146.

A foremost statistical authority,* Jacques Bertillon, has devoted considerable space to proving that some relation between the two exists. Confronted by the preceding facts, his explanation is this: that the people of the southern departments, inconstant perhaps, and fickle, nevertheless are quickly pacified after a passionate outbreak of any kind. Husband and wife may quarrel, but the estrangement is dissipated before recourse to the law can take place. On the other hand, the Norman or the Champenois peasant, Teutonic by race, cold and reserved, nurses his grievances for a long time; they abide with him, smouldering but persistent. " Words and even blows terminate quarrels quickly in the south; in the north they are settled by the judge." From similar comparisons in other European countries, M. Bertillon draws the final conclusion that the Teutonic race betrays a singular preference for this remedy for domestic ills. It becomes for him an ethnic trait.

Another social phenomenon has been laid at the door of the Teutonic race of northern Europe; one which even more than divorce is directly the concomitant of modern intellectual and economic progress. We refer to suicide. Morselli devotes a chapter of his interesting treatise upon this subject † to proving that " the purer the German race—that is to say, the stronger the Germanism (e. g., Teutonism) of a country—the more it reveals in its psychical character an extraordinary propensity to self-destruction." On the other hand, the Slavic peoples seem to him to be relatively immune. These conclusions he draws from detailed comparison of the distribution of suicide in the various countries of western Europe, and it must be confessed that he has collected data for a very plausible case. There can be no doubt that in Germany the phenomenon culminates in frequency for all Europe, and that it tends to dis-

---

* Étude démographique du divorce, etc., Paris, 1883, pp. 42 *et seq*. Turquan, in l'Économiste Français, xvii, 1889, pp. 505–507, gives parallel results for the first five years of the new divorce law of 1884.

† Suicide, in the International Scientific Series, New York, 1882. A. M. Guerry, Statistique Morale, etc., Paris, 1864, shows precisely the same thing. Durkheim, Le Suicide, 1897, pp. 58 *et seq.*, effectually demolishes the ethnic argument from still another point of view.

40

appear in almost direct proportion to the attenuation of the
Teutonic racial characteristics elsewhere.

Consider for a moment our map on this page showing the
relative frequency of suicide, with the one on page 138, which
we have already described as illustrating the ethnic composition of France. The parallel between the two is almost exact
in every detail. There are again our three areas of Alpine
racial occupation—Savoy, Auvergne, and Brittany—in which
suicide falls annually below seventy-five per million inhabitants. There, again, is the Rhone Valley, and the broad, diag-

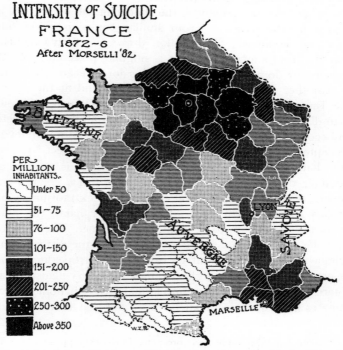

INTENSITY OF SUICIDE
FRANCE
1872–6
After MORSELLI '82

PER
MILLION
INHABITANTS.

Under 50
51–75
76–100
101–150
151–200
201–250
250–300
Above 350

onal strip from Paris to Bordeaux, characterized alike by
strong infusion of Teutonic traits and relative frequency of the
same social phenomenon. The great Seine basin is sharply
differentiated from the highlands along the eastern frontier;
and even the Mediterranean coast strip, distinct from the Al-

pine and Auvergnat highlands, is indicated. Inspection of these maps betrays at once either a relation of cause and effect or else an extraordinary coincidence.

The distribution of suicide in England apparently lends still greater force to Morselli's generalization. Herewith is a

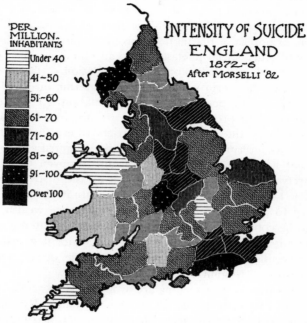

PER MILLION INHABITANTS

Under 40

41-50

51-60

61-70

71-80

81-90

91-100

Over 100

INTENSITY OF SUICIDE
ENGLAND
1872-6
After MORSELLI '82

map of its variations. Observe how Wales and Cornwall are set apart from all the rest of the island. Were the map more extensive, we should discover the Scottish Highlands, the third stronghold of the ancient Briton types, characterized by an equal infrequency of suicide. Most remarkable of all is the little light-coloured area, just north of London, comprising the counties of Hertfordshire, Bedford, and Huntingdon. This district we were at great pains to emphasize in our chapter upon the British Isles as a region where the physical characteristics of the pre-Teutonic invaders of the island were still represented in comparative purity.* We saw that the conquer-

---

* Page 322 *supra.*

ing Teutons entered England from two sides, avoiding London and the impenetrable fen district, and thereby passed over this region, leaving it notably brunet in physical type to this day. Here, again, in nearly every detail of our map would seem to be a corroboration of Morselli's law. For suicide diminishes in direct proportion to the absence of Teutonic intermixture.*

Divorce and suicide, which we have just discussed, will serve as examples of the mode of proof adopted for tracing a number of other social phenomena to an ethnic origin. Thus Lapouge attributes the notorious depopulation of large areas in France to the sterility incident upon intermixture between the several racial types of which the population is constituted. This he seeks to prove from the occurrence of a decreasing birth rate in all the open, fertile districts where the Teutonic element has intermingled with the native population.† The argument has been advanced a stage further even than this; for purely economic phenomena, such as the distribution of property, tax-paying faculty, and the like, are in the same way ascribed to purely racial peculiarities.‡ Because wealth happens to be concentrated in the fertile areas of Teutonic occupation, it is again assumed that this coincidence demonstrates either a peculiar acquisitive aptitude in this race, or else a superior measure of frugality.

By this time our suspicions are aroused. The argument is too simple. Its conclusions are too far-reaching. By this we do not mean to deny the facts of geographical distribution in the least. It is only the validity of the ethnic explanation

---

* The same temperament which drives the German to self-destruction is by Bannister and Hektoen (1888) recognised in the melancholic form which insanity takes among them. In Italians, as in negroes, acute mania is far more likely to occur than nervous depression.

† Lapouge, 1895–'96, criticised by us in Ripley, 1896 c. Von Hölder (1876, p. 14) noted a similar occurrence of higher birth rates in the areas of Alpine racial occupation in Germany. The facts are, perhaps, incontestable; their interpretation is the only point of criticism. *Cf.* for example Turquan's suggestive map in Bull. Soc. Normande de Géog., xvii, 1895, p. 205 ; and Dumont, Dépopulation et Civilisation, Paris, 1890, as also his Natalité et Démocratie, Paris, 1898.

‡ Corrélations Financières de l'Indice Céphalique, Revue d'Économie Politique, 1897, pp. 257–279. See also Closson, 1897.

which we deny. We can do better for our races than even its best friends along such lines of proof. With the data at our disposition there is no end to the racial attributes which we might saddle upon our ethnic types. Thus, judging from mere comparison of our map of head form with others of social statistics, it would appear that the Alpine type in its sterile areas of isolation was the land-hungry one described by Zola in his powerful novels. For, roughly speaking, individual land-holdings are larger in them on the average than among the Teutonic populations.* Peasant proprietorship is more common also; there are fewer tenant farmers. Crime in the two areas assumes a different aspect. We find that among populations of Alpine type in the isolated uplands, offences against the person predominate in the criminal calendar. In the Seine basin, along the Rhone Valley, wherever the Teuton is in evidence, on the other hand, there is less respect for property; so that offences against the person, such as assault, murder, and rape, give place to embezzlements, burglary, and arson.† It might just as well be argued that the Teuton shows a predilection for offences against property; the native Celt an equal propensity for crimes against the person. Or, again, why does not the Alpine type appear through statistical eyes as endowed with a peculiar aptitude for migration? For the sterile upland areas of his habitation are almost invariably characterized by emigration to the lowlands and to the cities.‡ The persistence of a higher birth rate in these districts makes such relief to an ever-increasing population necessary. Finally, why not apply the same mode of proof to the artistic or literary attributes of population? Turquan # has recently mapped the awards made by the *Salon*, at Paris, according to the place of

---

* Demolins, 1897, p. 295.

† For maps showing the distribution of all these, consult A. M. Guerry, Statistique Morale, etc., Paris, 1864. Fletcher, Jour. Royal Stat. Society, London, xii, 1849, pp. 151–335, gives many interesting maps for England. See also Yvernes, in Jour. Soc. de Statistique, Paris, xxxvi, 1895, pp. 314–325.

‡ *Cf.* Topinard, Éléments, p. 449 ; and Demolins, 1897, p. 365.

La Statistique aux Salons, Revue Politique et Littéraire, Paris, série 4, vi, 1896, pp. 207–210.

birth of the artists. We reproduce this directly herewith, not because it proves anything racially, but because it might as well be adduced as proof of the artistic bent of Teutonism in France as many another map above mentioned. For, broadly

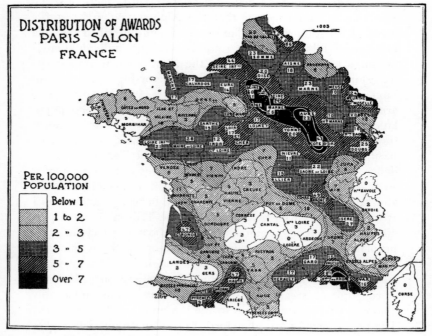

viewed, the artistic instinct, measured by the canons of the *Salon's* judges, seems to cling persistently, as Turquan concludes, to the fertile river basins, which are the great centres of Teutonic populations. In precisely the same way, judging by parallels between physical traits and the distribution of marked intellectual superiority in France, would Jacoby * be equally justified in ascribing genius to the Teutonic race as its special and peculiar attribute. Odin's † suggestive study of the

---

* Études sur la Sélection, Paris,1881, pp. 460–475 and 535–554. Lombroso, 1888, pp. 118–127, traces the parallel in France between stature and genius on the basis of his data.

† 1895, i, pp. 439–464.

distribution of intellectual notables in France points in the same direction, as a moment's consideration of the accompanying map will demonstrate. The principal areas of isolation are conspicuously deficient in men of distinction in the world of letters, which Odin takes as a criterion of general intellectuality. Nevertheless we are convinced with him, despite the geographical correspondence with our anthropological maps, that it is not the factor of race, but rather of social environment—

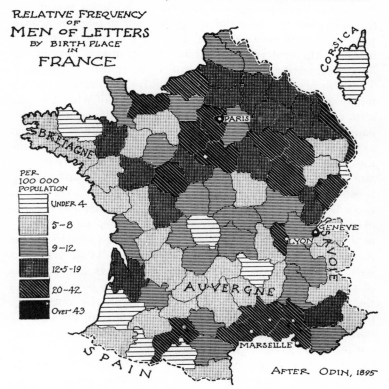

RELATIVE FREQUENCY
OF
MEN OF LETTERS
BY BIRTH PLACE
IN
FRANCE

PER
100 000
POPULATION

UNDER 4
5 – 8
9 – 12
12·5 – 19
20 – 42
Over 43

AFTER ODIN, 1895

education and the inspiration of contiguous culture—which is really the responsible agent in the case.

Italy is even simpler in its geographical, ethnic, and social phenomena than France. We may profitably correlate all these for this country as we have done for France. The regular and gradual transition from a pure Alpine racial type in the Po Valley to a Mediterranean one in the south is already familiar to us. Precisely such a gradation of demographic phenomena occurs. Pullé [98] has conveniently mapped these for us. In the northern half of the kingdom we have, first of all, far less illiteracy. This is accompanied by more frequent suicides. Crime varies not only in intensity but in kind. The greater tendency to lawlessness in the south is particularly manifested in crimes against the person—homicide, assault, and the like; while northern Italy more abounds in offences against property—theft, embezzlement, and fraud. The southern provinces are the centres of prostitution, illegitimacy, juvenile delinquency, terrific mortality, and the other spawn of ignorance. The contrary phenomena of progressive civilization characteristic of the north are indicated by means of what we may term psychological statistics. For example, the relative abundance of periodical literature is mapped by Pullé as an index of the higher standard of intelligence in the northern half of the kingdom. Intellectuality has been measured by others in various ways. One of the most ingenious is that applied by Lombroso and Cougnet * in tracing the distribution of men of note according to their places of birth. The overwhelming preponderance of that part of Italy north of Rome, and especially in the Po Valley, in its intellectual life at once appears. This is true to-day: it has been the rule throughout Italian history as well. Bellio † has distributed the poets, painters, and sculptors of antiquity, according to their place of birth, over a map of that country. The effect has been to emphasize once more the enormous preponderance of artistic genius all through the north, from Tuscany to the Alps. How does this coincide with our previous deduction concerning France? It seems, perhaps, to corroborate the relation of Teutonism to art, until we recall the fact that all northern Italy is overwhelmingly Alpine by race, as compared with the artistically sterile south. Couple

---

* La geografia degli artisti in Italia e degli scienziati in Francia in rapporto ai pazzi, Archivio di Psichiatria, ii, 1881, pp. 460–465, with maps.

† Rapporti fra l'etnografia antica dell' Italia e la sua produttività artistica, Boll. Soc. geog. Italiana, Roma, xxiii, 1886, pp. 261–279, maps.

with this the fact that in reality Teutonism is a negligible factor in Italy, physically speaking, and that precisely the same ethnic type which is so fecund culturally in Italy, is in France the one localized wherever art is not; and all doubt as to the predominant cause of the phenomenon is dissipated. We see immediately that the artistic fruitfulness in either case is the concomitant and derivative product of a highly developed centre of population. Contact of mind with mind is the real cause of the phenomenon. It is not race but the physical and social environment which must be taken into account.*

This mode of destructive criticism—namely, appeal to the social geography of other countries wherein the ethnic balance of power is differently distributed—may be directed against almost any of the phenomena we have instanced in France as seemingly of racial derivation. In the case either of suicide or divorce, if we turn from France to Italy or Germany, we instantly perceive all sorts of contradictions. The ethnic type which is so immune from propensity to self-destruction or domestic disruption in France, becomes in Italy most prone to either mode of escape from temporary earthly ills. For each phenomenon culminates in frequency in the northern half of the latter country, stronghold of the Alpine race. Nor is there an appreciable infusion of Teutonism, physically speaking, herein, to account for the change of heart. Of course, it might be urged that this merely shows that the Mediterranean race of southern Italy is as much less inclined to the phenomenon than the Alpine race in these respects, as it in turn lags behind the Teuton. For it must be confessed that even in Italy neither divorce nor suicide is so frequent anywhere as in Teutonic northern France. Well, then, turn to Germany. Compare its two halves in these respects again. The northern half of the empire is most purely Teutonic by race; the southern is not distinguishable ethnically, as we have sought to prove, from central France. Bavaria, Baden, and Würtemberg are scarcely more Teutonic by race than Auvergne. Do we find differences in suicide, for example, fol-

---

* Sergi, 1898 a, pp. 190 *et seq.*, in an attempt to explain these phenomena, on an ethnic.basis, seems to be entirely neglectful of this.

lowing racial boundaries here? Far from it; for Saxony is its culminating centre; and Saxony, as we know, is really half Slavic at heart, as is also eastern Prussia. Suicide should be most frequent in Schleswig-Holstein and Hanover, if racial causes were appreciably operative. The argument, in fact, falls to pieces of its own weight, as Durkheim [97] has shown. His conclusion is thus stated: " If the Germans are more addicted to suicide, it is not because of the blood in their veins, but of the civilization in which they have been raised."

A summary view of the class of social phenomena seemingly characteristic of the distinct races in France, if we extend our field of vision to cover all Europe, suggests an explanation for the curious coincidences and parallelisms above noted, which is the exact opposite of the racial one. In every population we may distinguish two modes of increase or evolution, which vary according to economic opportunity for advancement. One community grows from its own loins; children born in it remain there, grow up to maturity, and transmit their mental and physical peculiarities unaltered to the next generation. Such a group of population develops from within, mentally as well as physically, by inheritance. Such is the type of the average rural community. Its evolution is surely " monotypic," to borrow a biological term from Romanes. It is conservative in all respects, holding to the past with an unalterable tenacity. Compare with that a community which grows almost entirely by immigration. Stress of competition is severe. There is no time for rearing children; nor is it deemed desirable, for every child is a handicap upon further social advancement. Marriage even, unless it be deferred until late in life, is an expensive luxury. Population grows, nevertheless; but how? By the steady influx of outsiders. Such is the type known to us in the modern great city. Between these two extremes are all gradations between the progressive and the conservative type of population. To the former are peculiar all those social ills which, as Giddings has rightly urged, are the price paid for such progress.* Suicide is a

---

* *Cf.* Principles of Sociology, pp. 325–340.

correlative of education; frequency of divorce is an inevitable concomitant of equality of rights between the sexes, and the decline of the religious sanction of *patria potestas*. Marriage, no longer a sacrament, becomes merely a legal contract, terminable at the will of the parties concerned. The character of social control changes with its institutions. The individual will is of necessity subordinated to that of the body politic. Crime changes in character, becoming a matter more of business or necessity, and less of impulse. A decreasing birth rate almost always attends social advancement. To prevent such a fall in the birth rate, and at the same time to overcome the devastations of disease, is held by many to be the demographic ideal to which all states should aspire. Not postponed marriages, not childless families, not a high proportion of celibates; not, on the other hand, reckless and improvident unions with a terrific infant mortality as a penalty therefor; but a self-restrained and steady birth rate in which a high percentage survives the perils of infancy. " Civilization is the baptism of the passions. In the cloister neither does the mother die of fever nor the child of croup; but outside the cloister to find both mothers and children, and bring both well through fever and croup—that is civilization." * Could we for France apply this last-named criterion of progress, I doubt not we should find it to accord with all the facts we have instanced above. To ascribe them to racial causes is to lose sight of the primary factors in social evolution.

Our theory, then, is this: that most of the social phenomena we have noted as peculiar to the areas occupied by the Alpine type, are the necessary outcome, not of racial proclivities but rather of the geographical and social isolation characteristic of the habitat of this race. The ethnic type is still pure for the very same reason that social phenomena are primitive. Wooden ploughs pointed with stone, blood revenge, an undiminished birth rate, and relative purity of physical type are all alike derivatives from a common cause, isolation, directly physical and coincidently social. We discover,

* From a very suggestive paper, A Measure of Civilization, in Journal of the Royal Statistical Society, London, lx, 1897, pp. 148–161.

primarily, an influence of environment where others perceive phenomena of ethnic inheritance. In the preceding paragraph we have referred to the apparently disintegrating influence of social evolution upon domestic institutions. Let us for a moment turn to another phase of family life in France, in order to illustrate the complex forces which play upon it to-day. The danger of rashly generalizing from inadequate data will be immediately apparent.

An index of the solidarity of the family is afforded by the degree to which it resents the interference of the state in its domestic affairs. A similar expression of the force of family feeling is often rendered through the tenacity with which it holds itself aloof from the intrusion of strangers not allied by blood or adoption to the other members of the naturally close corporation. In other words, statistics of what we may call " home families," or families occupying an entire dwelling by themselves, give us a clew to the cohesiveness of the institution. It is the question of the boarding house and the tenement *versus* the home. Any direct comparison in this respect between different parts of the same country is of course entirely worthless, unless we take account of the relative proportions of city population in each; for, always and everywhere, it is in the crowded city that the " home " is superseded by its degenerate prototypes. Fortunately, we possess for France data upon this subject, with the necessary elimination of this cause of error. The accompanying map shows the proportion of families occupying each a whole house to itself, and with the exclusion of all cities of upward of two thousand inhabitants in every case. In other words, we have before our eyes statistics of the separately existing families among the French peasantry.

Inspection of this map of " home families " shows the widest range of variation. Some parts of France, notably Brittany, exhibit twice the degree of domestic intermixture, so to speak, that prevails in other regions. On the whole, the northwest manifests a weaker opposition to the intrusion of strangers in the family circle than does the south and east. In some respects this agrees with the testimony of divorce, as to the

cohesiveness of the domestic institutions. So far as Savoy,
Auvergne, and Alsace-Lorraine—the principal areas occupied
by the Alpine or Celtic race—are concerned, the parallel with
the map of divorce is quite close.   In the first two of these,
upward of seventy per cent of the families occupy an entire
dwelling independently. On the other hand, the Mediterranean
coast strip, nay even the intrusive zone up the Rhone Valley,
are indicated as areas where the family is less cohesive than in

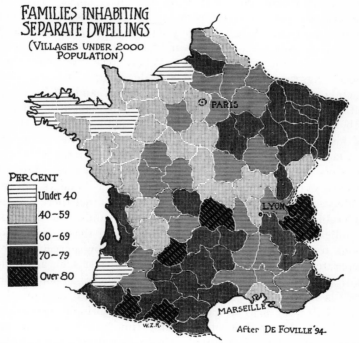

FAMILIES INHABITING
SEPARATE DWELLINGS
(VILLAGES UNDER 2000
POPULATION)

PARIS

PER-CENT
Under 40
40-59
60-69
70-79
Over 80

LYON

MARSEILLE

W.Z.R.

After DE FOVILLE '94

the upland areas of isolation.*   But what shall we say about
Brittany?   Racially and in stability of the family as well, it
belongs with Savoy and Auvergne as an area of isolation,
characterized by comparatively backward social phenomena.
Nevertheless, inspection of our map shows it to be the region

* Demolins, 1897, p. 130, comments upon this instability.   The early
age of marriage possible in this highly favoured region, where the struggle
for existence is reduced to a minimum, must also be taken into account.

where such "home intermixture" is exceedingly prevalent. Less than one half the families live under entirely separate roofs, whereas in the other areas of Alpine racial occupation the proportion of independent families is about twice as great.

This peculiar anomaly in the case of Brittany is all the more notable as this region is one of the most conservative in all France, judged by the character of its social phenomena. Some disturbing factor is evidently at work. It seems to be purely environmental. Surprising as it may appear, this exaggerated "home intermixture" in the Armorican peninsula is apparently to a large degree referable to its geological and climatic peculiarities. Levasseur makes some interesting observations upon this subject.* Where peasant houses are closely aggregated or bunched in little villages, it is easy for each family to maintain its separate dwelling, and yet for them all to co-operate with one another in daily labour. On the other hand, the peasant whose house is quite apart from those of his neighbours, placed squarely, perhaps, in the centre of his landed property, must of necessity take his farm labourers into his own household. Thus, where population is scattered evenly over a district, not in closely built hamlets but in widely separated houses, it generally happens that there is considerable "home intermixture." Several families or parts of families live under the same roof. Applying these considerations to Brittany, it seems as if the very low percentage of separate "home families" were a result of just such a broadcast distribution of population. This absence of hamlets in turn is a direct result of geology and climate. In Brittany the rainfall is very heavy; water courses and springs abound on all sides. The soil is at the same time thin, overlying an impervious granite formation. This makes it possible to build houses wherever convenient, without anxiety concerning water supply.† The exact opposite of this occurs along the dry Mediterranean coast, where water is a marketable commodity;

---

* Bulletin de l'Institut International de Statistique, iii, 1888, pp. 70 et seq. Cf., however, Demolins, 1897, page 405.

† The same thing is true in the Charolais mountains, according to Gallois, 1894. Cf. also, on soil and population, Frech, 1889.

and in those departments with a permeable chalk soil, where water disappears rapidly in subterranean streams. In these latter cases houses inevitably collect about the water courses and springs, and a high proportion of aggregated population at once is manifested, with all that is thereby implied, socially speaking. One of the first results would be that each family in such a hamlet might occupy its own dwelling exclusively.

Another factor is the relative poverty of the environment, and the intensity of the struggle for existence. The effect of the rigours of environment is thus apparent in the age at which marriage can be contracted. In Brittany and Auvergne late marriages are of necessity the rule, while on the Mediterranean coast, as in Italy, the natural beneficence of the habitat permits of very early and too often unstable matrimonial alliances.* Such is the close interrelation of social phenomena and physical circumstances.

Geographical factors have also operated in still another way in Brittany to discourage the growth of closely built villages. This region is so remote from any of the routes of military invasion from the east, that no necessity has ever arisen for compacting the population in villages capable of ready defence. Levasseur gives this as an important element in producing the contrasts in the proportion of urban population between the different parts of France. In all of our areas of isolation, the Alps, Auvergne, or Brittany, protected by Nature against intrusion of enemies, the population can safely scatter as it will. It is not only free to live in isolation: it is forced to do so because the thin and barren soil will not permit of communal life. Thus Demolins † observes that the necessity of living where an eye can be kept upon the cattle is an efficient factor in the wide distribution of population in Brittany. In any case, as we have said, the effect upon the family, especially in all that concerns its separate existence under a roof by itself, is very patent.

If the geographical isolation peculiar to the areas occupied by the Alpine race is thus potent in the way we have

---

* Jour. Société de Statistique, Paris, xxxviii, 1896, p. 228. *Cf.* also Demolins, 1897, p. 406. † *Op. cit.*, p. 415.

indicated, why may it not appear in political as well as in social affairs? Conservatism should be its motto. To test this we have studied minutely the results of a general election of deputies from all over France, held in 1885. We chose this example for the reason that this important political event was the last supreme effort, the expiring gasp of the monarchical party in France. It is the last time that the conservative element obtained any formidable representation in the Chambers at Paris. From ninety-five deputies standing for a return to the old *régime* in the preceding Chambers, the number advanced to one hundred and eighty-three; it nearly doubled, in other words. Three million three hundred thousand conservative votes, in a total suffrage of 7,500,000, was a very respectable, even formidable, showing. This remarkable overturn was due to a fortuitous conjuncture of events. The Ferry Republican ministry had been recklessly extravagant; its policy in Tonquin was unpopular. Disturbing local issues were, however, rare, so that the main questions at home were calculated to appeal directly to any intellectual or moral prejudices which happened to be abroad. The Radical party stood for the separation of Church and State; universal suffrage in senatorial and presidential elections was a leading issue. It was an exceptional occasion in every respect for reviving the smouldering fires of conservatism, while at the same time affording opportunity for the fullest expression of progressive ideas, wherever they were present. The election, therefore, was squarely a question of the old *versus* the new. By analysis of its results, we may perhaps gain an inkling of the temper of the people.

Our map herewith denotes by its lightest shades the areas of most advanced modern ideas where the radicalism of the nineteenth-century type had cut itself loose from all bonds with the past. The opposite extreme, where both politics and religion combined to rejuvenate the conservative party, is tinted black. The intermediate gradation of sentiment is demonstrated by the degrees of light or dark shading. Inspection of this map reveals a certain parallelism with all those that we have studied heretofore. Especially do we note the conservatism of Brittany, Auvergne, and the southwest. It should be said that the apparent conservatism of the most northern departments was due to the local protection-and-free-trade issue, complicated by the Boulanger episode. For this reason these manufacturing centres should be eliminated from our comparison. Savoy and the high Alpine departments also were strongly affected by their proximity to the republican institutions in Switzerland. We must allow for that fact also.

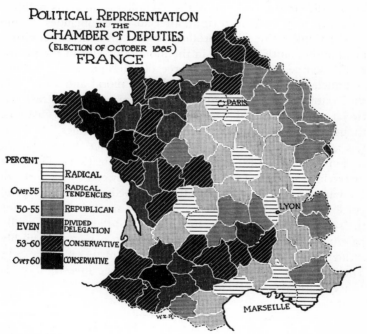

A curious contrast, ever persistent in all our ethnic or social maps, is that which is manifested between the coast strip along the Mediterranean and the mountains north of it. A light strip of radicalism extends all along the sea and up the Rhone Valley, setting apart Auvergne from Savoy. Whether this radicalism bears any relation to the high percentage of urban population hereabouts—a product partly of climate, as we have seen, although in some degree a heritage from Roman

41

rule—or whether it is an expression of the innate impulsiveness of the Mediterranean race, we leave it to others to decide. It is a fact, at all events.*

Having made allowance for all the disturbing factors above named, it is roughly true that the areas of Alpine racial occupation manifest a distinct tendency toward conservatism in politics. We incline to the belief that here, again, is the influence of physical circumstances appreciable. Cliffe-Leslie [74], keenly alive to the weakness of the old dollars-and-cents political economy, may have been right, after all. He concludes: " One may, I think, point with certainty to the difference of environment and conditions of life in the mountains and in the plains, as the source of the superior force of religion, family feeling, and ancient usage in the former. On its moral and social side the contrast between mountain and plain is the contrast between the old world and the new; between the customs, thoughts, and feelings of ancient and modern times." † Politics at one extreme, anthropology at the other, have afforded us constant proof of the truth of this generalization. The close interrelation which of necessity exists between every form of human phenomena in a naturally developed society is a second corollary from the same law. Of profound significance for the sociologist, however, is the fact that to-day we are rapidly passing from such natural organization to a new and highly artificial one. Problems of city life confront us on every side. They are not devoid of ethnic importance; investigation is concentrating upon them. They must engage our attention at once.

---

* *Cf*. Demolins, 1897, pp. 109 and 141, on the political aptitude of the natives of Provence and on the influence of the *petite culture* of the olive and vine upon social temperament.

† *Cf*. Antonini, Sulla distribuzione topografica della degenerazione psichica nella provincia di Bergamo ; Archivio di Psichiatria, ser. 2, pt. 1, xvii., 1896, pp. 143–147, maps.

CHAPTER XX.

SOCIAL PROBLEMS (*continued*): ETHNIC STRATIFICATION AND URBAN SELECTION.

THE extreme fluidity of our heterogeneous population is impressed upon us by every phenomenon of social life here in America. We imagine the people of Europe, on the other hand, after scores of generations of stable habitation, to have settled themselves permanently and contentedly into place. This is an entirely erroneous assumption. As a matter of fact, they are almost as mobile as our own American types. There are two ways in which demographic crystallization may have taken place. A people may have become rigid horizontally, divided into castes, or social strata; or it may be geographically segregated into localized communities, varying in size all the way from the isolated hamlet to the highly individualized nation. Both of these forms of crystallization are breaking down to-day under the pressure of modern industrialism and democracy, in Europe as well as in America. Nor is it true that the recency of our American social life has made the phenomena of change more marked here than abroad. In fact, with the relics of the old *régime* on every hand, the present tendencies in Europe are the more startling of the two by reason of the immediate contrast. Demographic processes are at work which promise mighty results for the future. These are not cataclysmic, like the French Revolution; but being well-nigh universal, the fact that they are slow-moving should not blind us to their ultimate effects. Such movements threaten to break up, not only the horizontal social stratification, but the vertical geographical cleavage of locality and nationality as well. Obviously any disturbance of these at once involves destruction of the racial individuality of the continent at the same time. For this reason, many phases of social analysis appertain directly to the sphere of natural science. The anthropologist and sociologist alike are called upon to take cognizance of the same phenomena. The physical and social sciences are equally involved in the determination of their laws. Certain problems of city life are foremost among these questions which lie on the border line between what were once widely separated sciences.

The most conservative societies in Europe are really to-day a seething mass of moving particles, viewed with the statistical eye. To borrow a familiar figure, a great population almost anywhere is like the atmosphere; even when apparently most quiescent, in the sunlight of investigation revealing itself surcharged with myriad motes in ceaseless agitation. These particles, microscopic or human, as the case may be, are swept along in currents determined both in their direction and intensity by definite causes.* With men, the impelling forces are reducible mainly to economic and social factors. Most powerful of these movements of population to-day is the constant trend from the rural districts to the city. Its origin is perfectly apparent. Economically it is induced by the advantages of co-operation in labour; perhaps it would be nearer the truth to say, by the necessity of aggregation imposed by nineteenth-century industrialism. This economic incentive to migration to the towns is strengthened by the social advantages of urban life, the attractions of the crowd; often potent enough in themselves, as we know, to hold people to the tenement despite the opportunity for advancement, expansion, or superior comfort afforded elsewhere outside the city walls. The effect of these two combined motives, the economic plus the social, is to produce a steady drift of population toward the towns. This has a double significance. It promises to dissolve the bonds of geographical individuality—nay, even of nationality; for a political frontier is no bar against such

---

* *Vide* maps for England by Ravenstein, 1885 : for Austria, by Rauchberg, 1893 : for France, by Turquan, Soc. Normande de Géog., xvii, 1895, p. 218 ; and La Réforme Sociale, xxix, 1895, pp. 150–169, 308–321, and 392–410 : for Germany, von Mayr, Jour. Soc. de Stat., Paris, xxxv, 1894, pp. 463–476.

immigration, provided the incentive be keen enough. At the same time it opens the way for an upheaval of the horizontal or social stratification of population; since in the city, advancement or degradation in the scale of living are alike possible, as nowhere else in the quiet life of the country.

The sudden growth of great cities is the first result of the phenomenon of migration which we have to note. We think of this as essentially an American problem. We comfort ourselves in our failures of municipal administration with that thought. This is a grievous deception. Most of the European cities have increased in population more rapidly than in America. Shaw has emphasized the same fact in his brilliant work on Municipal Government in Europe. This is particularly true of great German urban centres.* Berlin has outgrown our own metropolis, New York, in less than a generation, having in twenty-five years added as many actual new residents as Chicago, and twice as many as Philadelphia. Hamburg has gained twice as many in population since 1875 as Boston; Leipsic has distanced St. Louis. The same demographic outburst has occurred in the smaller German cities as well. Cologne has gained the lead over Cleveland, Buffalo, and Pittsburg, although in 1880 it was the smallest of the four. Magdeburg has grown faster than Providence in the last ten years. Düsseldorf has likewise outgrown St. Paul. Beyond the confines of the German Empire, from Norway to Italy, the same is true. Stockholm has doubled its population; Copenhagen has increased two and one half times; Christiania has trebled its numbers—in a generation. Rome has increased from 184,000 in 1860 to 450,000 in 1894. Vienna, including its suburbs, has grown three times over within the same period. Paris from 1881 to 1891 absorbed four fifths of the total increase of population for all of France within the same decade.

Contemporaneously with this marvellous growth of urban centres, we observe a progressive depopulation of the rural

---

* N. Brückner. Die Entwickelung der grossstädtischen Bevölkerung im Gebiete des deutschen Reichs. Allgem. stat. Archiv, Tübingen, i, 1890, pp. 135–184. *Cf.* A. F. Weber; Studies in History, Economics, etc., Columbia University, N. Y., xi., 1899.

districts. What is going on in our New England States, especially in Massachusetts, is entirely characteristic of large areas
in Europe. Take France, for example. Most of us are aware
of the distressing demographic condition of affairs in that
country. One of the finest populations in Europe is almost
at a standstill numerically; nay, some years show an actual
decrease of population. This is not due to emigration abroad,
for the French are notably backward in this respect. Nor
can it be ascribed to a heavy mortality. The death rate has
appreciably fallen during this century, in conformity with the
great advances made in hygiene and sanitation. The marriage rate is not lower than usual. Yet for some reason children do not come to cheer the land. The practical result is
that Germany, the great political rival, seems destined to control the European military situation in future.* Such is the
condition, viewing the country as a whole. Studying it in
detail, the evil is still more magnified; for, with a stationary
population for the entire country, the cities continue to grow,
draining the life blood of the rural districts year by year, with
ever-increasing vigour. The towns are absorbing even more
than the natural increment of country population; they are
drawing off the middle-aged as well as the young. Thus great
areas are being actually depopulated. For example, in the
decade from 1881 to 1891, the French cities of thirty thousand
inhabitants or over added to their respective numbers more
than three times as many as the total increase of population
for the entire country. Even their due proportion of the abnormally slow increase was denied to the rural districts; the
ten years left them less densely populated than before. In
1846 almost half of the eighty-eight departments in France
had a larger population than they have to-day. Paris alone,
the metropolis, has, as we have already observed, absorbed
four fifths of the entire increase of the land during the decade
to 1891; the remainder was added to the other large cities in
proportion to their size. The British Isles exemplify the same
tendency. More than half of the English towns with popula-

---

* We have analyzed certain of these details in French demography in
Pubs. American Stat. Ass., iii, 1892, pp. 248 *et seq.* *Cf.* p. 522 *supra.*

tions over twenty-five thousand are the product of this century. Sixty out of one hundred and five of these cities have arisen since 1825. This is, of course, due to the extension of the factory system in great measure. The same depopulation of the rural districts is noted. Ten rural counties in England and Wales alone have fewer inhabitants than in 1851. The fact is that western Europe is being gradually transformed into a huge factory town. It is being fed less and less from the products of its own territory. The wheat fields of the Americas, India, and Australia are contributing what formerly was raised by the peasantry at home. It is not surprising that the trend is toward the cities; were it even more marked it would be no marvel.

This growth of city populations has, then, taken place largely at the expense of the country. It must be so, for the urban birth rates are not enough in excess of the mortality, save in a few cases, to account for more than a small part of the wonderful growth which we have instanced. The towns are being constantly recruited from without. Nor is it an indiscriminate flocking cityward which is taking place. A process of selection is at work on a grand scale. The great majority to-day who are pouring into the cities are those who, like the emigrants to the United States in the old days of natural migration, come because they have the physical equipment and the mental disposition to seek a betterment of their fortunes away from home. Of course, an appreciable contingent of such migrant types is composed of the merely discontented, of the restless, and the adventurous; but in the main the best blood of the land it is which feeds into the arteries of city life.

Another more certain mode of proof is possible for demonstrating that the population of cities is largely made up either of direct immigrants from the country or of their immediate descendants. Dr. Ammon, of Carlsruhe, in a most suggestive work which we have constantly cited in these pages,* has

---

* Die natürliche Auslese beim Menschen, Jena, 1893. His, 1896 d, gives an excellent summary of the progress of opinion. In a new work, now in press, 1899, we are promised a fuller analysis based upon a far

carefully analyzed in detail the populations of certain representative cities in Baden.   In Carlsruhe and Freiburg, for
example, he found that among the conscripts examined for
military service an overwhelming proportion of the residents
were either immigrants themselves or else the children of immigrants. Less than eight per cent, in fact, were the children
of city-born parents—that is to say, were the outcome of three
generations of continued urban residence.   In a similar investigation of other German cities, Hansen ('89) found that nearly
one half their residents were of direct country descent.   In
London it has been shown that over one third of its population are immigrants; and in Paris the same is true. For thirty
of the principal cities of Europe it has been calculated that
only about one fifth of their increase is from the loins of their
own people, the overwhelming majority being of country birth.
One direct result of this state of affairs is that cities as a rule
contain more than their due proportion of middle-aged adults.
They do not immigrate until they have attained majority;
they do not marry till comparatively late in life, so that children and young persons form an unusually small percentage
of the entire population.*   The aged, moreover, often betake
themselves to the country after the stress of life is abated.
They return to their place of birth, there to spend the last
days in peace.   These latter, together with those who are
driven back to their homes by the fierce competitions of city
life, constitute a certain feeble counter current of migration
from the city outward. Yet this is insignificant compared with
the inflowing tide.   Thousands are yearly pouring into the
towns, while those who emerge may be numbered by hundreds,
perhaps even by scores. The fact is that the great majority
of these immigrants either fall by the way: or else their line,
lacking vitality, dwindling in numbers either through late
marriages and few children, or perhaps the opposite extreme
of overproduction and abnormal mortality, comes to naught

---

larger number of observations.   Lapouge, in a brilliant series of monographs, has also outlined his results. Kuczynski, 1897, pp. 118 *et seq.*,
gives an extended criticism of these views.

* *Cf.* Lapouge, 1896 a, p. 387 *et seq.*

in a few generations. Thus the steady influx of immigration goes on. Truly, cities are, as has been observed, " consumers of population." Our problem here is to determine whether such consumption is being applied equally to all our racial types; if not, the future of Europe, ethnically, can not but be profoundly affected. The future character of European peoples will be largely determined by this circumstance. From the point of view of relative increase, the German nation is undoubtedly in the lead, especially as compared with the French. Equally important, however, is it to consider the relative destruction which is annually being waged. If, as is asserted, these prolific Teutons are pre-eminently a city type, and if thereby they lay themselves open to decimation, the future balance of power in Europe may not be so completely disturbed after all.

These various social phenomena have been most ably correlated in a rather suggestive broad-line sketch of a mode of social selection given by Hansen.* Basing his hypothesis upon data derived in the main from the cities of Germany, he distinguishes in any given population what he designates as three degrees of vital and psychic capacity respectively. The vitality is measured in each class by the ratio of the birth to the death rate. The first vitality rank consists of the well-to-do country people, leading a tranquil existence, healthy in mind and body, free alike from dread or aspiration. This class increases rapidly by birth, and loses relatively few by premature mortality. It has enough and to spare in numbers. Both country and city alike depend upon it for future growth. Below this is a second vitality rank, composed of the middle classes in the towns. Herein we find a somewhat lower birth rate; ambition and possibility of social advancement become effective in limiting the size of families. Coincident with this is a low death rate, owing to material comfort and a goodly intelligence. This class holds its own in numbers, perhaps contributes slightly to swell the census returns from year to year. Below this lies the third vitality rank, composed of the great

---

* Die drei Bevölkerungsstufen, München, 1889.

mass of the urban populations, the unskilled labour and the poorer artisans. Here occur an abnormally high birth rate, little self-restraint, and, through ignorance and poverty, an inordinately high rate of mortality. This is the portion of the city population continually recruited from the country or through rejects from the superior classes—those, that is to say, who fail in the intense competition of the upper grades of society. Measured by vitality alone, it would appear that the first rank we have described—the average country population—were the ideal one. Applying, however, the tests of intellectual capacity, Hansen discovers curious cross-cleavages. For the country population is being continually drained of its best blood; those who are energetic or ambitious in the majority of cases leaving their homes to seek success in the city. Thus an intellectual residuum is left on the soil, representing merely the average intelligence; perhaps, if near a great metropolis, even falling below the normal in this respect. Those in their turn who emigrate to the towns are speedily sorted by inexorable fate. Some achieve success; the majority perhaps go to swell the other middle classes; or else, entirely worsted in the struggle, land in a generation or two in the lowest ranks of all. Thus a continual tide of migration becomes necessary to insure stability in numbers in the entire population. This ingenious scheme, too simple of course to be entirely correct, as Giddings has suggestively pointed out,* does nevertheless contain a germ of truth. Our problem is to test its applicability to modern conditions by a study of purely anthropological facts.

The first physical characteristic of urban populations, as compared with those of country districts, which we have to note, is their tendency toward that shape of head characteristic of two of our racial types, Teutonic and Mediterranean respectively. It seems as if for some reason the broad-headed Alpine race was distinctly a rural type. This we might have expected from the persistency with which it clings, as we have seen all over Europe, to the mountainous or otherwise isolated areas.

---

* Principles of Sociology, pp. 342 *et seq.*

Thirty years ago an observer in the ethnically Alpine district of south central France noted an appreciable difference between town and country in the head form of the people.* In a half dozen of the smaller cities his observations pointed to a greater prevalence of the long-headed type than in the country round about. In the same year, in the city of Modena in Italy, investigations of the town and country populations, instituted for entirely different purposes, brought the same peculiarity to light.† These facts escaped notice, however, for about a quarter of a century. In entire ignorance of them, in 1889 a gifted young professor in the university at Montpellier in southern France, having for some years been occupied in outlining various theories of social selection, stumbled upon a surprising natural phenomenon.‡ On examination of a considerable series of skulls, dating from various periods in the last two hundred years, which had been preserved in crypts at Montpellier, he found that the upper classes as compared with the plebeian population, contained a much larger percentage of long-headed crania. These crania of the aristocracy, in other words, seemed to conform much more nearly to the head form of the Teutonic race than those of the common people. Additional interest was awakened in the following year by the researches of Dr. Ammon of Carlsruhe, who, working again in entire independence upon measurements of thousands of conscripts of the Grand Duchy of Baden, discovered radical differences here between the head form in city and country, and between the upper and lower classes in the larger towns.# Several explanations for this were possible. The direct influence of urban life might conceivably have brought it about, acting through superior education, habits of life, and the like. There was no psychological basis for this assumption. Another tenable hypothesis was that in these cities, situated, as we have endeavoured to show, in a land where two racial types of population were existing side by

---

* Durand de Gros, 1868 and 1869.

† Calori, 1868 ; Lombroso, 1878, p. 123 ; Riccardi, 1883 a ; and Livi, 1886, p. 274, have since confirmed it.

‡ Lapouge, 1889 b.   # Ammon, 1890 ; and 1893, p. 72.

side, the city for some reason exerted superior powers of attraction upon the long-headed race. If this were true, then by a combined process of social and racial selection, Carlsruhe, Freiburg, Mannheim, and the other towns would be continually drawing unto themselves that tall and blond Teutonic type of population which, as history teaches us, has dominated social and political affairs in Europe for centuries. This suggested itself as the probable solution of the question; and investigations all over Europe during the last five years have been directed to the further analysis of the matter. This was not an entirely new discovery even for Germany; the same fact had been previously noted in Würtemberg, that the peasantry were noticeably rounder-headed than the upper classes.* Yet Ammon undoubtedly first gave detailed proof of its existence, basing it upon a great number of physical measurements; and he undoubtedly first recognised its profound significance for the future. To him belongs the honour of the discovery of the so-called " Ammon's law," that the Teutonic race betrays almost everywhere a marked *penchant* for city life. This is all the more surprising as Tacitus tells us that the ancient Germans, unlike the Italians, were strongly imbued with a hatred of communal existence. We have no time to give in detail all the evidence which has been accumulated in favour of its validity. The fact of greater frequency of the long-headed type in town populations, as compared with rural districts, has been established by Lapouge in a great number of investigations all through central and southern France,† and in Brittany his data are being confirmed by Muffang.‡ Collignon, foremost authority upon the physical anthropology of France, gives in his adherence to it as a general rule, finding it applicable to Bordeaux and nearly all the cities of the southwest.# It is true of Paris and Lyons especially, the department of the Seine being well below the average for France

---

* Von Hölder, 1876, p. 15.

† Lapouge, 1894 a, p. 483 ; 1896 a, p. 401 ; 1897 b.   Closson has presented his work most acceptably to English readers.

‡ Lapouge, 1896 b, p. 91 ; Muffang, 1897.

1895, pp. 123–125 ; see also table in 1894 b, p. 19, on Limoges.

and for the neighbouring departments.* It seems to hold true in Vienna, which with its suburbs forms a little islet of Teutonic long-headedness in Austria,† and Ranke has proved the same for Munich.‡ In northern Italy the long-headedness is almost universally more prevalent in all the cities, although the opposite is more often true south of Rome.# In Spain the only indication of the law is offered by Madrid, where nearly seven hundred conscripts have been measured in detail.‖ In this latter country, as in the British Isles,△ in southern Italy, as we have observed, and in Scandinavia ◊—everywhere, in fact, on the outskirts of Europe where the Alpine broad-headed race is but sparsely represented, we find the contrasts in head form between city and country absent in great measure. Observations on nearly five hundred American college students have not yielded me any differences in this respect. Only where the Alpine race forms an appreciable element in the population does "Ammon's law" appear to hold true.

The circumstance which we have mentioned, that only in those portions of Europe where the Alpine broad-headed type is strongly in evidence do we find a more prevalent long-headedness in the city populations, suggests a criticism, first made by Livi ('96) in his superb monograph on Italy, upon the somewhat extravagant claims to the universality of "Ammon's law" made by ardent disciples of the school of so-called "anthropo-sociologists." It is this: City populations are the inevitable result of great intermixture of blood; they of necessity contain a hodge-podge of all the ethnic elements which lie within the territory tributary to them, which, in other words, lie within what Lapouge has aptly termed their "spheres of attraction." ‡ As a whole, one should not expect to find the extreme individuality of type in the cities which can persist

---

* Lapouge, 1897 b, p. 70.   † Weisbach, 1895 b, p. 77, map.
‡ 1897 a, p. 56.   The index seems to be falling, moreover.
# Livi, 1896 a, pp. 87–89, 147, 148, 151, 159, and 187.
‖ Olóriz, 1894 b, pp. 47 and 279; also pp. 173 and 224.
△ Beddoe, 1894, p. 664 ; and L'Anthropologie, x, 1899, pp. 21–41.
◊ Hultkrantz, 1897, p. 16.
‡ Pubs. Américan Stat. Ass., v, 1896, pp. 37 *et seq.*

alone in the isolated areas free from ethnic intermixture. If, as in Baden, in Brittany, or along the Rhone Valley, an extremely broad-headed type of population is localized in the mountains, as we know it is all over Europe; while along the rivers and on the seacoast are found many representatives of an immigrant Teutonic long-headed people; it would not be surprising that cities located on the border line of the two areas should contain a majority of human types intermediate between the two extremes on either side. These city populations would naturally be longer-headed than the pure Alpine race behind them in the mountains, and coincidently broader-headed than the pure Teutons along the rivers and on the seacoast. The experience of Italy is instructive. In this country the transition from a pure Alpine broad-headed population in the north to an equally pure and long-headed Mediterranean type in the south is perfectly regular, as our maps in a preceding chapter upon Italy have made manifest. It has been established that while the cities in the north are less broad-headed than the country, in mid-Italy no appreciable difference between the two exists; and in the south, the cities being ever nearer the mean for the country as a whole, actually contain fewer long-headed individuals than the rural districts. This consideration, which no statistician can fail to keep in mind, seems, however, to be insufficient to account for the entire phenomenon, especially north of the Alps. We are forced to the conclusion, in other words, that there is some mental characteristic of the long-headed race or types, either their energy, ambition, or hardiness, which makes them peculiarly prone to migrate from the country to the city; or else, what would compass the same result, a peculiar disinclination on the part of the broad-headed Alpine race of central Europe thus to betake itself to the towns. The result in either case would be to leave the fate of the urban populations to be determined more and more by the long-headed type.

A second mode of proof of the peculiar tendency of the long-headed type to gravitate toward the city, is based upon the detailed study of individuals, tracing each person from his place of birth, or from generation to generation from the rural origin to the final urban residence. Dr. Ammon * divided his conscripts into three classes: The *urban*, those whose fathers were of city birth, as well as themselves; the *semi-urban*, comprising those born in cities, but whose fathers were immigrants from the country; and, thirdly, the *semi-rural* class, who, born in the country, had themselves taken up an abode in the city. Comparing these three classes with those who were still domiciled in the country, a regularly increasing long-headedness was apparent in each generation. Lapouge and his disciples in France are now collecting much valuable information upon this point which can not fail to be suggestive when accumulated in sufficient amount. Everything goes to prove a slight but quite general tendency toward this peculiar physical characteristic in the town populations, or in the migratory class, which has either the courage, the energy, or the physical ability to seek its fortunes at a distance from its rural birthplace.

Is this phenomenon, the segregation of a long-headed physical type in city populations, merely the manifestation of a restless tendency on the part of the Teutonic race to reassert itself in the new phases of nineteenth-century competition? All through history this type has been characteristic of the dominant classes, especially in military and political, perhaps rather than purely intellectual, affairs. All the leading dynasties of Europe have long been recruited from its ranks. The contrast of this type, whose energy has carried it all over Europe, with the persistently sedentary Alpine race is very marked. A certain passivity, or patience, is characteristic of the Alpine peasantry. This is true all the way from northwestern Spain, where Tubino [77] notes its degeneration into morosity in the peasantry, as far as Russia, where the great inert Slavic horde of northeastern Europe submits with abject resignation to the political despotism of the house of the Romanoffs. Ordinarily a negative factor in politics, always socially conservative, this race when once aroused becomes irresistible. As a rule, not characterized by the domineering spirit of the Teuton, this Alpine type makes a comfortable

---

* 1893, p. 76 : also, 1899, pp. 431–439 ; 614–642.

and contented neighbour, a resigned and peaceful subject. Whether this rather negative character of the Alpine race is entirely innate: or whether it is in part, like many of its social phenomena, merely a reflection from the almost invariably inhospitable habitat in which it has long been isolated, we may not pretend to decide.

The peculiar temperament of the Alpine population comes to the surface in political affairs, being attested by great conservatism. This reactionary instinct is in the long run far more common to all human nature, I believe, than is generally supposed; in the Alpine Celt it is developed or conserved, if you please, to a marked degree. Socially, the peculiarities of disposition we have mentioned are of even greater importance, as we sought to impress in the preceding chapter. In fact, the future of the type depends largely upon this circumstance. The most persistent attribute of the Alpine Celt is his extreme attachment to the soil, or, perhaps, better, to locality. He seems to be a sedentary type *par excellence;* he seldom migrates, except after great provocation; so that, once settled, he clings to his patrimony through all persecution, climatic or human. If he migrates to the cities, as does the " mobile " Teuton, he generally returns home to the country to spend his last days in peace. Such re-emigration of the Alpine type late in life is in fact offered by Collignon * as the main explanation for the prevalence of the long-headed variety in the towns to-day. He inclines to this view rather than to the theory that it is due to the greater number of the immigrant Teutons, as Ammon and Lapouge are disposed to maintain. At all events, whichever explanation be true, the fact that mental differences between our racial types exist, if they become accentuated with the ever-increasing pressure of civilization, can not but profoundly affect the future complexion of European populations. A phase of racial or social competition of such magnitude that we hesitate to predict its possible effects, is at once suggested.

Let us now for a moment take up the consideration of a

---

* 1895, p. 125. *Cf.* Lapouge, 1896 a, p. 407.

second physical characteristic of city populations—viz., stature. Some interesting points are concerned herein. The apparently contradictory testimony in this respect becomes in itself highly suggestive, I think, for the student of social problems. A few of the older observers found that city populations sometimes surpassed those of the country in the average of bodily height. Thus Quetelet [69] and Villermé [29] discovered such a superiority of stature in the Belgian cities, amounting to several centimetres. From this coincidence Quetelet derived a law to the effect that the superior advantages of urban residence were directly reflected in the physical development of the people. This hypothesis is now definitely disproved by nearly all the data available. Ammon * in Baden, to be sure, finds a higher average stature in the larger towns of that duchy. He ascribes it to a greater frequency of the tall Teutonic type. Switzerland, also, has the taller populations, as a rule, in its cities. Thus Berne, Lucerne, Zurich, Basle, Lausanne, and Neuchâtel all yield average statures appreciably above those in their respective cantons.† In Basle the superiority of the townsmen is upward of three centimetres—that is to say, about an inch and a quarter. With the sole exception of these two countries, and of three cities in Hungary,‡ the exact opposite of this rule is demonstrated by all the later investigations. If there be a law at all in respect of average statures, it demonstrates rather the depressing effects of city life than the reverse. For example, Hamburg is far below the average for Germany; # Dunant [67] finds it true in Geneva; Pagliani observed it in Turin. The city of Madrid contains almost the shortest male population in all Spain; only one province, Valladolid, standing slightly below it. Residents of its poorer quarters are absolutely the shortest in the entire peninsula.‖ From Franconia, Bavaria,△ and Alsace-Lorraine ◊ comes corroborative testimony to the same

---

* 1893, p. 116.

† Schweizerische Statistik, Lief. 85, 1892, Tab. ix. *Cf.* also Chalumeau, 1895.　　　　　‡ Scheiber, 1881, p. 255.

Meisner, 1889, p. 116. Reischel, 1889, pp. 139–142, notes it of smaller cities, as in Erfurt.　　　　　‖ Olóriz, 1896, pp. 42 and 60.

△ Ranke, 1881, p. 4.　　　　　◊ Brandt, 1898, p. 14.

42

effect. All over Britain there are indications of this law, that town populations are on the average comparatively short of stature. The townsmen of Glasgow and Edinburgh are four inches or more shorter than the country folk roundabout, and thirty-six pounds on the average lighter in weight.* Dr. Beddoe, the great authority upon this subject, concludes his investigation of the population of Great Britain thus: " It may therefore be taken as *proved* that the stature of men in the large towns of Britain is lowered considerably below the standard of the nation, and as *probable* that such degradation is hereditary and progressive." † This is not an invariable rule; as, for example, in Saxony ‡ and parts of France,# where investigators have discovered no differences at all between city and country. Nevertheless, the trend of testimony is in favour of Beddoe's view, as a rule; especially when applied to the great modern factory towns, where contributory influences, such as professional selection and the like, come into operation.‖

A most important point in this connection is the great variability of city populations in size. All observers comment upon this. It is of profound significance. The people of the west and east ends in each city differ widely. The population of the aristocratic quarters is often found to exceed in stature the people of the tenement districts. This is clearly demonstrated by our maps of the city of Warsaw on page 381. In this case, both among Jews and Poles, variations in stature corresponding to those of social condition were proved beyond doubt. Manouvrier ('88) has analyzed the Parisians most suggestively in much the same way, showing the similar tendency upon his map. In Madrid also it appears that the well-to-do people are nearly two inches taller on the average than the residents of the poorer quarters.△ We should expect this, of course, as a direct result of the depressing influence of un-

---

* British Association, Anthropometric Committee Report, 1883, pp. 273 *circa*.

† 1867–'69 a, p. 180.   ‡ Levasseur, 1889, i, p. 383.

Carlier, 1892, p. 330.

‖ Page 89 *supra*.   △ Olóriz, 1896, pp. 42 and 61.

favourable environment. Yet there is apparently another factor underlying that—viz., social selection. While cities contain so large a proportion of degenerate physical types as on the average to fall below the surrounding country in stature, nevertheless they also are found to include an inordinately large number of very tall and well-developed individuals. In other words, compared with the rural districts where all men are subject to the same conditions of life, we discover in the city that the population has differentiated into the very tall and the very short. This is true in Hamburg; * it holds good in many of the cities of Franconia, as Majer † long ago established. Brandt ‡ has just proved the same in Alsace-Lorraine. Here, also, while the average statures in city and country are equal, the composition of each contingent is very different; for the relatively homogeneous suburban type is replaced in the cities by two components, one superior and one defective in height. Of these, the first is more conspicuous. Its presence has been oftener noted by observers.# It is scarcely apparent in towns of minor importance, but the phenomenon becomes exaggerated in proportion to the size of the city. Anutchin's || data for Russia brings this into strong relief. It is only in capital cities—St. Petersburg, Moscow, Kazan, and Sebastopol—that the excess of taller men raises the average above that of the surrounding country. In other cities no such superiority can be detected. This perhaps is why Collignon [(95)] finds Bordeaux above the average for Gironde, while La Rochelle, being a smaller place, is precisely like its department.

The explanation for this phenomenon is simple. Yet it is not direct, as in Topinard's ᐃ suggestion that it is a matter

---

* Meisner, 1889, p. 120.   † 1862, p. 355.

‡ 1898, p. 15. Ammon, 1899, page 456, in his masterly analysis of the population of Baden, shows the same tendency.

In Modena, by Riccardi, 1882, pp. 249–253. In Bavaria, by Ranke, Beiträge, iv, 1881, p. 4. *Cf*. Galton, 1875.

|| 1889, p. 165. *Cf*. also Erismann, 1888, p. 129. Kronstadt is low because of its sailors. Odessa is scarcely above its government, because the general stature thereabouts is already very great. This seems also to be true for the relative inferiority of Geneva, its suburbs being already far above the average.   ᐃ Topinard, Éléments, pp. 445, 451, 492.

of race or that a change of environment operates to stimulate growth. Rather does it appear that it is the growth which suggests the change. The tall men are in the main those vigorous, mettlesome, presumably healthy individuals, who have themselves, or in the person of their fathers, come to the city in search of the prizes which urban life has to offer to the successful. On the other hand, the degenerate, the stunted, those who entirely outnumber the others so far as to drag the average for the city as a whole below the normal, are the grist turned out by the city mill. They are the product of the tenement, the sweat shop, vice, and crime. Of course, normally developed men, as ever, constitute the main bulk of the population; but these two widely divergent classes attain a very considerable representation. As an example of the influence of such selection, Dr. Beddoe remarks upon the noticeably short stature of all the agricultural counties about London, being even less than in the metropolis itself.* On the other hand, the Anthropometric Committee,† measuring more among the upper classes in London, found them to exceed both in height and weight the peasantry in Hertfordshire, near by. This need not disprove Dr. Beddoe's assertion. In fact, the contradictory evidence is very valuable for that reason. The only way to account for it is to suppose that the constant draught upon these suburban populations for their most powerful men, for service in the neighbouring city as policemen, porters, firemen, and in other picked professions, has depleted the land of all its best specimens. Such an inflowing current always tends cityward. Everything points to the conclusion, on the other hand, that the final product of the continued residence of such sorted populations in the city is to divide them into the chosen few who succeed and rise socially, and the many who descend, in the social scale as well as in stature, until their line becomes extinct. As they differentiate thus, they migrate within the city. The few drift toward the West End, toward the Champs Elysées or Fifth Avenue, where they maintain the high physical standard of the quar-

---

* 1867-'69 a, p. 178.   † 1883, p. 20.

ter; the others gravitate no less irresistibly toward Whitechapel and the Bowery.

We have seen thus far that evidence seems to point to an aggregation of the Teutonic long-headed population in the urban centres of Europe. Perhaps a part of the tall stature in some cities may be due to such racial causes. This was Topinard's explanation of it in part. A curious anomaly now remains, however, to be noted. City populations appear to manifest a distinct tendency toward brunetness—that is to say, they seem to comprise an abnormal proportion of brunet traits, as compared with the neighbouring rural districts. The first notice of this is due to Mayr,* who, studying some seven hundred and sixty thousand school children in Bavaria, stumbled upon it unexpectedly. Although blonds were in a very decided majority in the kingdom as a whole, the cities all contained a noticeable preponderance of brunet traits. This tendency was strikingly shown to characterize the entire German Empire when its six million school children were examined under Virchow's direction.† In twenty-five out of thirty-three of the larger cities were the brunet traits more frequent than in the country. In Metz alone was there a decided preponderance of blonds, due perhaps to the recent Germanization of Alsace-Lorraine as a result of political circumstances. Broadly viewed, all the larger cities, dating from the period prior to 1850, showed this brunet peculiarity in their school children. Quite independently, and in fact as early as 1865, Dr. Beddoe refers to the same fact as a matter of common report, finding it to hold good in the Rhine cities. His conclusions, however, were based entirely upon adults.‡ Here again, as in the case of the head form, we must reckon with the fact that city populations are always by reason of intermixture a mean, intermediate between the extremes presented by the country at large. So in northern blond Hanover the cities should contain more dark traits than the country; in Bavaria, on the contrary, we should expect them, for this same reason, to be

---

* 1875, pp. 299 and 305, with tables.

† 1885 and 1886 b, pp. 320 *et seq.* Beddoe, 1893, p. 113, gives a fine summary of it. ‡ 1885, p. 211.

somewhat more blond. Nevertheless, this would not account for the dark hair in certain Prussian cities, which contain more than twice as many dark as there are light traits; and in Bavaria, as we have seen, the actual condition is exactly the reverse of what might have been statistically expected.

Austria offers confirmation of the same tendency toward brunetness in twenty-four out of its thirty-three principal cities.* Farther south, in Italy, it was noted much earlier that cities contained fewer blonds than were common in the rural districts roundabout.† The rule has been corroborated for the greater part of the country, since Livi ‡ finds that even in the thirty-two darkest provinces, where towns tending toward the mean for the country should contain more blonds than the suburban districts, twenty-one of the capital cities show the reverse relation, while only nine conform to statistical probability. For Switzerland the evidence is conflicting.# Applying the rule to the cities of the British Isles, Dr. Beddoe finds it to hold good especially in the colour of the hair.‖ Ammon in his detailed researches discovers a tendency toward brunetness in the cities of Baden.△ So uniform is the testimony that those who, like Lapouge,◊ have ascribed the long-headedness of city populations to a predominance of the Teutonic racial type, now acknowledge this tendency toward brunetness in spite, in this case, of ethnic probabilities to the contrary. The relative frequency, in fact, of long-headedness and coincidently of brunet characteristics induced Lapouge to designate this combination the "foreordained urban type." ‡ In conclusion, let us add, not as additional testimony for the data are too defective, that among five hundred American students at the Institute of Technology in Boston, roughly classified, there were nine per cent of pure brunet type among those of country

---

* Schimmer, 1884, p. xiii. For Tyrol, see comparative table in Toldt, 1894, and Virchow, 1886 b, p. 379.

† Raseri, 1879, p. 118. 　　　　　　　　‡ 1896 a, pp. 70 *et seq.*

Studer, 1880, p. 59, says it holds good as a rule. Kollmann, 1881, p. 17, and Chalumeau, 1896, p. 8, affirm the cities to be more blond.

‖ 1893, p. 114. See also tables in 1885, p. 160.

△ 1899, pp. 472 and 642. *Cf.* his 1893, pp. 93–99. 　◊ 1897 b, p. 85.

‡ Collignon, 1895, p. 123, apparently acquiesces in this view.

birth and training, while among those of urban birth and parentage the percentage of such brunet type rose as high as fifteen. The arbitrary limit of twenty thousand inhabitants was here adopted as distinguishing city from suburban populations. Dark hair was noticeably more frequent in the group drawn from the larger towns.

It is not improbable that there is in brunetness, in the dark hair and eye, some indication of vital superiority. If this were so, it would serve as a partial explanation for the social phenomena which we have been at so much pains to describe. If in the same community there were a slight vital advantage in brunetness, we should expect to find that type slowly aggregating in the cities; for it requires energy and courage, physical as well as mental, not only to break the ties of home and migrate, but also to maintain one's self afterward under the stress of urban life. Selection thus would be doubly operative. It would determine the character both of the urban immigrants and, to coin a phrase, of the urban *persistents* as well. The idea is worth developing a bit.

Eminent authority stands sponsor for the theorem that pigmentation in the lower animals is an important factor in the great struggle for survival.* One proof of this is that albinos in all species are apt to be defective in keenness of sense, thereby being placed at a great disadvantage in the competition for existence with their fellows. Pigmentation, especially in the organs of sense, seems to be essential to their full development. As a result, with the coincident disadvantage due to their conspicuous colour, such albinos are ruthlessly weeded out by the processes of natural selection; their non-existence in a state of Nature is noticeable. Darwin and others cite numerous examples of the defective senses of such non-pigmented animals. Thus, in Virginia the white pigs of the colonists perished miserably by partaking of certain poisonous roots which the dark-coloured hogs avoided by reason of keener sense discrimination. In Italy, the same exemption of black sheep from accidental poisoning, to which

---

* Dr. William Ogle, in Medico-Chirurgical Transactions, liii, 1870, pp. 263 *et seq.* *Cf.* de Lapouge, 1899, pp. 70–79.

their white companions were subject, has been noted. Animals so far removed from one another as the horse and the rhinoceros are said to suffer from a defective sense of smell when they are of the albino type. It is a fact of common observation that white cats with blue eyes are quite often deaf. Other examples might be cited of similar import. They all tend to justify Alfred Russel Wallace's conclusion that pigmentation, if not absolutely necessary, at least conduces to acuteness of sense; and that where abundantly present it is often an index of vitality.* This eminent naturalist even ventures to connect the aggressiveness of the male sex among the lower animals with its brilliancy of colouring.

Applying these considerations to man, evidence is not entirely wanting to support De Candolle's ('87) thesis that "pigmentation is an index of force." Disease often produces a change in the direction of blondness, as Dr. Beddoe has observed; asserting, as he does, that this trait in general is due to a defect of secretion. The case of the negro, cited by Ogle, whose depigmentation was accompanied by a loss of the sense of smell, is a pertinent one. The phenomenon of light-haired childhood and of gray-haired senility points to the same conclusion. A million soldiers observed during our civil war afforded data for Baxter's † assertion that the brunet type, on the whole, opposed a greater resistance to disease, and offered more hope of recovery from injuries in the field. Darwin long ago suggested a relationship of pigmentation to the similar resistant power of the dark races in the tropics,‡ although he had to deal with much conflicting evidence. Dr. Beddoe finds in Bristol that the dark-haired children are more tenacious of life, and asserts a distinct superiority of the brunet type in the severe competitions induced by urban life.# Havelock Ellis ‖ marshals some interesting testimony to the end that the apparently greater pigmentation in woman is correlated with its greater resistant power in the matter of disease.

---

* Address in Transactions of the British Association for the Advancement of Science, 1876, pp. 100 *et seq.*   † 1875, i, pp. 61 and 72.

‡ Descent of Man, i, pp. 235 *et seq.*   # 1885, p. 223, and 1893, p. 115.

‖ Man and Woman, pp. 224–229.

More recently Pfitzner [97] has investigated the same subject, although it is not certain, as we have already observed,* that the greater brunetness of his Alsatian women is a phenomenon of race rather than of sex. It is not for us to settle the matter here and now. The solution belongs to the physiologist. As statisticians it behooves us to note facts, leaving choice of explanations to others more competent to judge. It must be said in conclusion, however, that present tendencies certainly point in the direction of some relation between pigmentation and general physiological and mental vigour. If this be established, it will go far to explain some of these curious differences between country and city which we have noted.

From the preceding formidable array of testimony it appears that the tendency of urban populations is certainly not toward the pure blond, long-headed, and tall Teutonic type. The phenomenon of urban selection is something more complex than a mere migration of a single racial element in the population toward the cities. The physical characteristics of townsmen are too contradictory for ethnic explanations alone. A process of physiological and social rather than of ethnic selection seems to be at work in addition. To be sure, the tendencies are slight; we are not even certain of their universal existence at all. We are merely watching for their verification or disproof. There is, however, nothing improbable in the phenomena we have noted. Naturalists have always turned to the environment for the final solution of many of the great problems of nature. In this case we have to do with one of the most sudden and radical changes of environment known to man. Every condition of city life, mental as well as physical, is at the polar extreme from those which prevail in the country. To deny that great modifications in human structure and functions may be effected by a change from one to the other is to gainsay all the facts of natural history.

---

* *Cf.* page 400 *supra.*

CHAPTER XXI.

ACCLIMATIZATION: THE GEOGRAPHICAL FUTURE OF THE EUROPEAN RACES.

Footnotes in this chapter refer to a special Bibliography of the subject on pages 589, 590.

THERE is no question of greater significance for European civilization than the one which concerns the possibility of its extension over that major part of the earth which is yet the home of barbarism or savagery. The rapid increase of its populations is more and more forcing this to the forefront as a great economic problem. No longer is it merely a scientific and abstract problem of secondary importance as contributory to the theories of the unity or plurality of the human race. Even the United States, with its newly imposed colonial policy, through the acquisition of the Philippine Islands and Porto Rico, is called upon to deal with the problem. It has to-day become a matter of peculiar significance for the present generation of men, and the old abstractions which did so much to confuse its students, are laid aside.* The substantial unity of the species having become an accepted fact along with the doctrine of evolution, the migration and consequent acclimatization of the various branches of the parent stock follow as a matter of course.

The modern problem plainly stated is this: First, can a single generation of European emigrants live? and, secondly, living, can they perpetuate their kind in the equatorial regions of the earth? Finally, if able permanently so to sustain themselves, will they still be able to preserve their peculiar Euro-

---

* The French distinction between "acclimatement" and "acclimatation" is practically an illustration of these two phases of the question. Bull. Soc. d'Anth., v, 1864, pp. 780–809.

pean civilization in these lands; or must they revert to the barbarian stage of modern slavery—of a servile native population, which alone in those climates can work and live? An area of fertile lands six times as great as that cultivated by the people of Europe to-day stands waiting to absorb its surplus population.* But its point of saturation will obviously soon be reached if traders and superintendents of native labour are the only colonists who can live there. Moreover, the problem of acclimatization has a great political importance; for if any one of these European nations be possessed of a special physiological immunity in face of the perils of tropical colonization, the balance of power may be seriously disturbed. Or a great menace to the feeble attempts of Europeans to colonize the tropics may exist in the surpassing aptitude of the great Mongol horde, which is perhaps the most gifted race of all in its power of accommodation to new climatic conditions.† Africa, Polynesia, and all parts of the earth have now been divided among the nations of Europe. What will they be able to do with them, now that the explorer has finished his work? ‡ Because the problem pertains to the sciences of physiology and of anthropology, in no wise lessens its concrete importance for the economist and the statesman.

Before we are in a position to measure even approximately the influence of a change of climate upon the human body and its functions, a number of subordinate confusing factors must be eliminated. Neglect to observe this rule vitiates much of the testimony of observers in the field. In the first place, a change of residence in itself always tends to upset the regular habits of the soldier or the colonist. The temperate youth

---

* Ravenstein, Proc. Royal Geog. Soc., xiii, 1891, pp. 27–32, with map. Also Felkin, 1891, with map; as also Hahn, in Petermann's Geog. Mitt., xxxviii, 1892, p. 8, with map.

† This theme is ably discussed by Ratzel, in Kolonization, Breslau, 1876. It forms the groundwork of the pessimistic plaint in Pearson's National Life and Character. Cf. also Dilke, Problems of Greater Britain.

‡ This was the great question before the International Geographical Congress at London, in August, 1895.

in England becomes a heavy drinker in the barracks of India;
and the Portuguese and Spanish races, predisposed to the use
of light wines—ready even to give up the habit if need be—
suffer from the disorders incident to alcoholism far less than
the English.* Inflammation of the liver is indigenous to the
tropics; and yet the ofttimes sixfold deadliness of hepatitis
among English soldiers in India, compared with the mortality
among the native troops from the same disease, is probably
due more to the consumption of alcoholic drinks than to the
influence of the climate.† To this fact is also due a certain
immunity of the wives and children of soldiers in this regard.
A moderate amount of alcoholic stimulant undoubtedly has
a beneficent action.‡ Clarke [56] even asserts that light wine
is an indispensable part of a hygienic diet; but the abuse of the
drinking habit is a factor in the comparative immunities of all
races in the tropics not to be neglected.

Alcoholism and sexual immorality go hand in hand. Newly
acquired vicious habits, unknown amid the restraints of home
life, would speedily cause physical prostration in any climate.
An engineer in Algeria testifies that " a Sunday will put more
men in the hospital than three days in the hot sun." # One of
the most subtle physiological effects of a tropical climate is a
surexcitation of the sexual organs,|| which in the presence of a
native servile and morally undeveloped population often leads
to excesses even at a tender age.ᐃ The elimination of this
factor becomes especially important in dealing with the crossing of races and the effects of climate upon fecundity. It is
invariably true that the mulatto—a social as well as an ethnic
hybrid—suffers from a loss of caste which exposes this class
to many temptations. The effect of this upon morbidity, as
Corre [82] justly observes, can not but be very great in face
of the peculiarly weakened physical resistance. Among the
imported and liberated negroes in the West Indies, indeed, im-

---

* Montano, 1878, and St. Vel, 1872, insist upon the necessity of ab-
stemiousness.

† Davidson, 1892, i, p. 455.   ‡ Science, xvii, 1891, p. 3.

De Quatrefages, 1879, p. 236. || Jousset, 1884, p. 229.

ᐃ Beyfuss, Verh. Berliner Ges. f. Anth., 1886, pp. 88–92.

morality rises to a climax almost sufficient to outweigh every other consideration.*

The influence of national habits in the choice of food is a third element to be eliminated. One of the immediate effects of a tropical climate is a stimulation of the appetite,† which too often leads to over-indulgence. On the other hand, it seems to be rather the kind than the quality of food which is the decisive factor. Dr. Felkin advises an increase in the daily allowance, provided it be of the right sort.‡ In this regard the Teutonic nations are especially handicapped in competition with the Mediterranean peoples. The English and Germans insist upon their usual allowance of meat, where the Spaniards or Italians are content with cereals or lighter food. The Chinese are especially favoured in accommodation to a new tropical climate by reason of their simple diet of rice.

More important even than food, as a correction to be applied, is the effect of daily habits of life and of profession upon the physiological processes. An indolent life always and everywhere tends to superinduce a multitude of disorders. De Quatrefages has pointed out that in the West Indies the wealthy and idle creoles, and not the " petit blancs," swell the death rate of the white population above the average.# Gentle and regular exercise, then, must be accounted one of the most important hygienic precautions to be observed. Worse than lack of exercise, however, is overexertion, especially if it be coupled with exposure to the hot sun or to miasmatic exhalations. Statistics for the Jewish race, confining all its activities to shops in the towns, must be corrected, therefore, for this circumstance, before they are compared with statistics for the Germans, who as colonists take up the ever-deadly cultivation of the soil. The Boers, who thrive as herders, would undoubtedly suffer were they to stir up the soil as husbandmen.‖ Most

---

* Pubs. Amer. Stat. Ass., iv, 1895, p. 195.

† Jousset, *op. cit.*, p. 211 ; St. Vel., p. 29.

‡ The physiological effects of diet are discussed in Proc. British Ass: Adv. Science, 1889, p. 787. *Vide* also Archiv für Anth., xxiii, 1894, p. 467. Foster (Elements of Physiology, p. 843) agrees with Dr. Felkin.

1879, p. 236.　　　　　‖ Verh. Berliner Ges. f. Anth., 1885, p. 258.

favoured of all is that nationality which is seafaring by nature. The apparently high vitality of the Italians and Maltese in Algeria is in part because they are mainly sailors and fishermen.* In consonance with this principle is the relative immunity, already cited, of the wives and children of soldiers in India.† In some cases, however, the mortality of adult women is higher, as in the island of St. Louis, according to Corre (*²). Slavery also always produces a terrific death rate which vitiates all comparison between the statistics for the white and the negro.‡ It should be noted, moreover, that such an institution exercises a selective choice upon the negro; for the survivors of such severe treatment will generally be a picked lot, which ought to exhibit vitality to a marked degree, all the weaklings having been removed.# Racial comparisons are also invalidated by the fact that hygiene and sanitation are generally confined to the European populations, so that, other things being equal, a higher death rate among the natives would be most natural.

.   .   .   .

In any scientific discussion of the effect of climate upon the human body the racial element must always be considered; and correction must be made for ethnic peculiarities before any definite conclusions become possible.||

Three diseases are peculiar to the white race and to civilization—namely, consumption, syphilis, and alcoholism,△ there being marked differences in the predisposition of each of the barbarous races for them, which often vary inversely with the degree of civilization they have attained; so that their widely

---

* Jousset, *op. cit.*, p. 291.

† *Vide* also Verh. Berliner Ges. f. Anth., 1886, p. 90.

‡ De Quatrefages, 1879, p. 234.

The bearing of this in Algeria is discussed by Corre, 1882.

|| Bordier, 1878, 1881, and 1884; Corre, 1882; and Montano, 1878. *Cf.* also Mazaé Azéma, Rev. d'Anth., série 2, ii, 1879, p. 135; and Buchner in Corr-blatt deut. Ges. f. Anth., xviii, p. 17; and Sammlung gemeinverst. wissenschaft. Vorträge, 1886, No. 42.

△ Whether nervous affections belong to this category is a matter of present controversy. *Vide* Science, December 16 and 30, 1892. Suicide as an ethnic disease we have discussed elsewhere.

varying liability to contract these diseases becomes an important consideration in the ingrafting of any degree of culture or of artificial life upon the native inhabitants of a colonial possession.

The European races in their liability to consumption stand midway between the Mongol and the negro, climatic conditions being equal. The immunity of the Ural-Altaic stock in this respect is very remarkable. The Kirghis of the steppes, exposed to severe climatic changes, are rarely affected with this disease,[*] and the pure Mongolian stock seems to be almost exempt from its ravages.[†] This may be one reason why the Chinese are able to colonize in many places even in the tropics where the negro can not live, since it is well known that a tropical climate is fatal to all persons with a consumptive tendency.[‡] The Chinese succeed in Guiana, where the white can not live ;[#] and they thrive from Siberia, where the mean temperature is below freezing, to Singapore on the equator.[||] That their immunity from phthisis is due in large measure to race, and not to climatic circumstances, seems to be indicated by the results of ethnic intermixture. The Japanese apparently derive a liability to it from their Malay blood, which not even their Mongolian descent can counteract.[△] The Malays, a mixed race, seem to lack vitality in many other respects as well, in all of which the Japanese share to some extent. Their liability to consumption seems to be akin to that *penchant* for alcoholism, which is lacking among the Chinese because of the national opium habit.

The negro even in the tropics is especially subject to all affections of the lungs, a fact which constitutes a serious bar to his wide extension over what has been designated by Dr. Fuchs the catarrhal zone, in contradistinction to the dysenteric zone of the tropics.[◊] The black races have in general less

---

* Rev. d'Anth., série 3, i, p. 77.   † Rev. d'Anth., série 3, iv, p. 238.

‡ Jousset, *op. cit.*, p. 300.   # Bordier, 1884, p. 472.

|| *Cf.* Bordier, 1878, with mortality tables, as also De Quatrefages, 1879, p. 235.

△ Bordier, 1881, p. 238 ; also Bull. Soc. d'Anth., 1881, p. 733.

◊ Rey, 1878, has fully discussed this.

fully developed chests * and less respiratory power † than the
European race. They perspire less freely,‡ and their skin is
thicker, or at least more dense, so that oxygenation by the
lungs alone is more necessary. They are consequently exceedingly sensitive to atmospheric changes, and are severely
handicapped in any migration for this reason. Buchner # distinguishes between " ectogenous " and " endogenous " diseases: the former due to environment, as malaria; the latter
from within, as in tuberculosis. He avers that the white races
more easily fall a prey to the first, the negroes to the second.
Certain facts, notably the relative immunity of the African
aborigines from septicæmia, seem to give probability to this.
Almost invariably, where the European succumbs to bilious or
intestinal disorders, the negro falls a victim to diseases of the
lungs even in the tropics. An interesting case is instanced ‖
of a caravan in Senegal, composed of ninety-five negroes and
ninety Europeans, in which the average mortality for each of
the two contingents was exactly equal for two years. Yet
only one of the whites was affected with disease of the lungs,
while five of the eleven negroes who died succumbed to diseases of this class. Similar to the effect of change of climate
upon the negro in inducing respiratory derangement, is the
influence exerted by altitude, which will be discussed in another place.

An interesting reason has been suggested for the predisposition of the negro for consumption—namely, that the broad,
open nostril of the race is unfitted to perform the necessary
service of warming the air before its entrance into the lungs.△
Leptorrhinism, it is asserted, may be due to natural selection,
which has fixed upon that form of nose as most suitable to
the temperate zone; and the negro, deprived of this advantage, suffers from disease of the lungs at once he is transferred

---

* Jousset, p. 85.
† Idem, p. 88.   The same point is startlingly proved by the statistics
of the civil war of Gould, 1869, and Baxter, 1875.
‡ Jousset, p. 111.
# Corr-blatt deutschen Ges. f. Anth., xviii, p. 17.
‖ Corre, 1882.   △ Science, xxi, 1893, p. 169.

to that part of the earth. It is not inconceivable that this may indeed serve as a partial explanation, but how, then, can we account for the equally open nostril of the Mongolian stock so immune from consumption? Or how can this theory be made to square with the predisposition of the Polynesian for the same class of diseases, especially when the leptorrhinism of this latter race is taken into account? * At all events, this element of race must be reckoned with in every comparison of the statistics of different localities.

In the geographical distribution of diseases there is no more uncertain factor than the ethnic peculiarities of syphilis. It can therefore never be neglected in any project for acclimatization by crossing with the natives, since its relation to fertility is so important. Probably brought by Europeans to America † and to New Guinea,‡ and by them disseminated in Polynesia, this disease seems to be as yet unknown in Central Africa to any extent.# In fact, it dies out naturally in the interior of that continent even when introduced, while it kills the American aborigines at sight.‖ The American negroes, however, are seemingly very prone to it in its worst forms, according to authorities cited by Hoffmann.△ From this dread disease the Chinese are especially exempt; for if contracted, it speedily becomes benign, in marked contrast to the Japanese, who betray their Malay blood in this respect.◊ Everywhere syphilis follows the Malay stock even in crossing with other races, like the negroid, which by nature is immune, as has been said. In Madagascar, where five sixths of a certain population was infected, Hirsch declares that the Malagasy (negroid) element is quite free from it, the Hovas (Malay cross) having it in the severest form.⟊ These ethnic peculiarities of

---

* Cf. Bordier, 1878, and De Quatrefages, 1877.

† Rev. d'Anth., série 2, i, 1878, p. 81. Cf. Hirsch, op. cit., ii, pp. 67 and 74.

‡ Rev. d'Anth., série 2, vi, 1883, p. 497.

Lombard, op. cit., iv, p. 485 ; and Hirsch, ii, p. 77.

‖ Livingstone, Travels, p. 128 ; and Hirsch, ii, p. 82.

△ 1896, p. 87 et seq.

◊ Bordier, 1881, p. 238 ; also Bull. Soc. d'Anth., 1867, p. 543, and 1881, p. 733. ⟊ Op. cit., ii, p. 77 ; Corre, 1882, p. 56.

43

syphilis are of the greatest importance, therefore; since this disease is likely to prevail among exactly those classes in a colonial population where ethnic crossing would be most likely to occur. Intermixture as a remedy for acclimatization would consequently be much more difficult of application in the East Indies or in South America than in Cochin China or the Congo Valley; for where this malady strikes down the first cross—the mulatto or the half-breed—all further assimilation of the races is at an end.

The list of ethnic diseases might be greatly extended, but enough has perhaps been said to indicate the importance of eliminating it before entering upon the discussion of acclimatization *per se*. The predisposition of the negro for elephantiasis * and tetanus,† his sole liability to the sleeping sickness, so severe that in some localities the black is utterly useless as a soldier,‡ his immunity from cancer # and his liability to skin diseases in general,|| together with his immunity from yellow fever and bilious disorders, are well-recognised facts in anthropology. The Mongolian type appears to be likewise free from inflammatory diseases,△ and oftentimes from cholera to some extent; ◊ as well as from beri-beri, which is so peculiar to the Malay stock that it may be traced in the Japanese *kakké*.‡ The Polynesians are immune from scarlet fever,‡ and it is said that the Japanese can not even be inoculated with it.‡ This again is an illustration of the same persistence of pathological predispositions, since the partial affinity of the Japanese to the Polynesian race is well established. Recent investigation is bringing out similar examples of the constancy of racial diseases among the modern peoples of Europe. Dr. Chibret affirms that the Celtic or Alpine type is immune from " tra-

---

* De Quatrefages, 1879, p. 426.   † Bordier, 1881, p. 243.

‡ Hirsch, iii, p. 595 ; Montano, 1878, p. 444.

Not universal, however.   Bull. Soc. d'Anth., 1879, p. 390.   The frequency of tumours among negroes in the United States is a peculiar fact. || Clarke, 1859, p. 67.

△ Bordier, 1881, p. 237.

◊ *Cf.* tables in Bordier, 1878, p. 87.   *Cf.* De Quatrefages, 1879, p. 235.

‡ Rev. d'Anth., série 3, iv, p. 206.

‡ Corre, 1882, p. 31.   ‡ Science, xix, 1892, p. 343.

choma," or epidemic granular conjunctivitis, which has often seriously ravaged the rest of Europe.* Spreading in the Belgian army, it passed over the Walloons; and in the central plateau of France attacking strangers alone, it passed over southern Bavaria, even when contracted by a Celt, speedily becoming benign. The only exception to this racial immunity is that of the Piedmontese, otherwise it never extends above the two hundred metre Celtic boundary.† In America it appears to be more probably a filth disease. Always, in accounting for such a phenomenon, two factors are to be considered—race and environment. Hence, in our study of climatic circumstances the first must be carefully eliminated before proceeding to study the second.

Finally, the effects of ethnic intermarriage or crossing must in every case be taken into account. It is present as a complication in almost all colonial populations, and is by far the most subtle and difficult of all eliminations to be made. Notwithstanding the objection that accommodation to climate by intermarriage is in reality not acclimatization at all, but the formation of an entirely new type, the two are continually confused; and crossing with native stocks is persistently brought forward as a mode and policy of action. As an element in colonization, and a devious means of avoiding the necessity of acclimatization, it arises to complicate the situation. Intermarriage is said by Silva Amada ('80) to be the secret of Spanish and Portuguese success; in Mexico this has also apparently been the case, as well as in the Philippines.‡ Bordier states that the Spanish and southern French are more prolific than others in marriage with negroes;# and concludes that the only hope for the future of French colonization in Cochin China lies in such crossing with the natives.‖ The efficacy of this remedy is to-day accepted quite generally by anthro-

---

* C. R. deuxième Congrès int. des Sciences médicales, Berlin, 1891.

† The geographical distribution of *caries* also indicates an ethnic predisposition. *Cf.* Ripley, 1895, p. 644, note.

‡ Bull. American Geog. Soc., 1883, No. 2.

1884, p. 285. An example is also given in Revue d'Anth., série 2, viii, p. 190. ‖ 1884, p. 397.

pologists. Topinard agrees with Ten Kate that half-breeds resist climatic changes better than pure whites,[*] and other authorities concede the same.[†] Desmartis has even proposed to inoculate the British troops in India with Hindu blood as a preventive of tropical disorders.[‡]

On the other hand, a cross between races is too often apt to be a weakling, sharing in the pathological predispositions of each of its parent stocks, while enjoying but imperfectly their several immunities. Mulattoes in any climate lack vitality; and, unless a continual supply of white blood is kept up, they tend to degenerate.[#] Dr. Gould [(69)] notices this lack of vitality among mulattoes as very marked in the Union army. For this reason intermixture is by many regarded as a doubtful remedy. Corre [(82)] especially, whose data for the hybrid peoples of South America is very full, acquiesces in this opinion. Neither the Malay nor the Japanese mixed races, according to Bordier [(81)], have the vitality of the Chinese. Jousset affirms that in many cases crossing increases the liability to attacks of fever.[||] It is said that in Guiana the negroes thrive, but the mulattoes suffer from the climate.[Δ] Bérenger-Féraud states that the mulatto in Senegal so far degenerates as to become infertile after three generations;[◊] and Westermarck [(94)], while acknowledging that many statements of this kind are exaggerated, inclines to the view that crossing may be unfavourable to fertility. Be this as it may, it is certain that mulattoes are pathologically intermediate between the white and the negro; they rarely have yellow fever, and are less liable to malaria than the Europeans; and they are not predisposed to

---

[*] Éléments, p. 204.

[†] Proc. British Ass. Adv. Science, xxix, p. 178. "Bertillon's principle" is accepted by Landowsky in Bull. Ass. fr. Av. Sciences, 1878, p. 817. [‡] Hunt, 1861, p. 143.

[#] Hoffmann, 1896, pp. 177 *et seq.*, discusses this question.

[||] 1884, pp. 150-154.

[Δ] Walther (Revue d'Anth., série 2, i, 1878, p. 76) gives, for example, the following rates of mortality from cholera in Guadeloupe in 1865 : Chinese, 2.7 per cent ; negro, 3.44 ; Hindu, 3.87 ; European, 4.31 ; mulatto, 6.32. The particularly high vitality of the Chinese is as marked as the weakness of the half-breed.   [◊] Rev. Anth., série 2, ii, pp. 577-588.

bilious disorders. But they have all the diseases to which the negro is alone liable—namely, elephantiasis, leprosy, phthisis, and even the dreaded sleeping sickness (*mal de sommeil*).* Finally, it may be added that many of the most successful examples of acclimatization have occurred where there has been a complete absence of crossing, as in the island of Réunion; † with the Boers in South Africa, according to Wallace [90]; and in many parts of South America as well. The Jews are the most remarkable people in this respect. Montano [78] affirms that they thrive in South America; and we know from Wallace [90] that they are increasing, in the uttermost parts of Russia, even faster than the natives. Felkin [86] goes even further in suggesting that a little Semitic blood is always a help in acclimatization. Although this may certainly be doubted, the cosmopolitan adaptive aptitudes of these people has never been denied from the time of Boudin [57] to that of Bordier [78].

The physical elements of climate, ranged in the order of their importance, are humidity, heat, and lack of variety.

Heat by itself, when unaccompanied by excessive humidity, does not seriously affect human health except when unduly extended.‡ The ranges of temperature to which the human body may become accustomed are very broad, so that the limitations to the dispersion of the race seem to be set by the food supply rather than the degree of heat or cold. All authorities agree, therefore, that the regions where acclimatization is most difficult are to be found in the areas of excessive humidity, or, roughly, where there is the maximum rainfall.# For this reason the successful examples adduced in favour of the view that acclimatization in the tropics is possible, should always be examined in the light of this consideration.

---

* Bordier, 1884; Corre, 1882; Bérenger-Feraud, *op. cit.*

† De Quatrefages, 1879, p. 236.

‡ Jousset, p. 37; Ratzel, 1882, i, p. 308; Virchow in Verh. Berliner Ges. f. Anth., 1885, p. 208.

A comparison of Hahn's map of the extension of the plantation system in Petermann, xxxviii, No. 1, p. 8, with a map of the distribution of rainfall will illustrate this relation.

A traveller in northern Africa has noted this in his observation, that " where there is water and something can grow, there the climate is murderous; where the climate is healthy, there is no water and nothing can grow." * In this sense, the boasted acclimatization of the French in Algeria is merely accommodation to one element of climate, after all. With this limitation it will be generally conceded that the success of the French in their African possessions along the Mediterranean is assured.† The mortality of soldiers and sailors in Algeria was seventy-seven *pro mille* from 1837 to 1848, so that Boudin, Bertillon, and Knox doubted if the French could ever colonize there. At the present time the birth rate even exceeds that in France itself; ‡ and the death rate is but little above the normal. In Tunis also the birth rate was 35.6 *pro mille* in 1890-'92, greatly exceeding the ruling death rate of 25.7 per thousand.# In America it is in the uplands of Mexico, Peru, and Bolivia, or along the arid coast of the Pacific, and not in the real tropical climate of Brazil, where the Spaniards have succeeded most fully. They have also done well in Cuba, to be sure, but the cases are entirely dissimilar. And to reason, from the French success in Algeria, as Ravenstein [91] says, that the same would ensue in the Congo basin, in Madagascar, or in Cochin China, is totally to misconceive the real limitations of a tropical climate. The relative difficulties to be encountered in these several cases may be roughly indicated by the mortality of soldiers. In Cochin China it is almost exactly double that in Tunis; || and this is, roughly speaking, a measure of the difference between a mere torrid climate as distinguished from one which is very humid as well as hot, for humidity means that malaria is superadded to all the other difficulties inherent in climate alone.

---

* Max Nordau, Rabies Africana, in Asiatic Quarterly Review, second series, ii, p. 76.

† *Cf.* Bertholon, Bull. Soc. d'Anth., 1897, pp. 509-536. Also Landowsky, in Bull. Ass. fr. Av. Sciences, 1878, p. 817.

‡ Levasseur, 1889-'92, iii, p. 432 ; and De Quatrefages, 1879, p. 229.

Cf. Review of Bertholon in L'Anth., v, p. 731.

|| Revue d'Anth., série 3, iv, 1889, p. 346.

The heat in a tropical climate becomes important but indirectly, because it is the cause of humidity and generally accompanies it. In the temperate regions humidity goes with cool weather except in the dog days, while within the tropics heat prevails just when radiation through perspiration is most retarded by moisture in the atmosphere. This, in combination with the enforced lack of exercise and its attendant excretion, forms the double cause of physiologic disturbances. The blood is not properly purified and anæmia ensues, if the more immediate effects do not manifest themselves in intestinal disorders.

Everything which conduces to give a variety to the climate of the tropics affords relief. The alternating sea and land breezes of islands make them more amenable to European civilization.* Especially when these islands are volcanic or mountainous is the strength of these tempering elements increased. This, in fact, is the only alleviating circumstance in Jamaica, where the fierce sea breezes by day, reversing at night, have made life for the English possible. Singapore owes its prosperity to the fact that it is the only place in the East Indies where malaria is completely unknown. Similarly, wherever there are alternating seasons of heat and cold, the chance of acclimatization becomes greater.† One advantage possessed by Cuba over the Philippine Islands seems, according to Bordier [78], to be the relief climatically which comes in winter. It is curious to note, however, that this is the season most fatal to the negroes in the island. Here we perceive one advantage of the climate of plateaus in the tropics, since both daily and seasonal variations are very great. Even in the major part of the African plateau, however, the elevation can not overset the monotony of the tropical climate, the seasonal variations ranging much lower than ours, while the mean temperature is fifty per cent higher.‡

Altitude, while giving at least temporary relief to the white race,# seems to exert a peculiarly baneful effect upon the negro

---

* Jousset, p. 50.   † Jousset, p. 62.   ‡ Cf. p. 586 infra.
# Jousset, p. 57 ; Montano, 1878, p. 434. Topinard, Anthropologie, p. 392, analyzes Bertillon's views in this regard.

and the Indian. Dr. Spruce, cited by Wallace [(90)], gives an interesting example of great economic distress produced by it in South America. Coffee grows in the zone from four thousand to six thousand feet, and the demand for native labour is very great. Indians coming from above die of dysentery, while if they come from the coast they succumb to respiratory diseases, so that the planters are severely hampered. It is said in our Southern States that the negro can not go from the hill country to the plains without great physiologic disturbance.* Jousset declares that the elevation of three thousand to forty-five hundred feet proves fatal to the negro in Africa.† This, of course, is due in part to the greater sensitiveness of all primitive peoples to climatic changes, and partly due to lack of hygiene. But that the negro by nature really lacks a power of accommodation, even in the tropics, in this respect is conceded by most observers; ‡ for by change of habitat he loses the immunities he once enjoyed, and does not thereby gain any new ones.# A project to import twenty thousand negroes from Alabama and Mississippi into the State of Durango in Mexico has been definitely abandoned, after the payment of over one hundred thousand dollars for freight charges alone. The land companies will introduce Chinamen instead, and the outlook is correspondingly brighter. Every experiment but demonstrates more clearly that the negro is useless as a colonist, even for reintroduction into the tropics.‖

What is the first effect of a tropical climate upon the human body and its functions? The respiration becomes more rapid for a time, although it soon tends toward the normal; the pulse beats more quickly; the appetite is stimulated; and a

---

* Nation, New York, October 12, 1893. *Cf.* also Corre, 1882.

† *Op. cit.*, p. 341.

‡ Bull. Soc. d'Anth., i, 1860, p. 528 ; Hunt, 1861, p. 131 ; Jousset, p. 148 ; Ratzel, 1882, i, p. 304. *Cf.* the case of Apaches in Alabama given in Pubs. Amer. Stat. Ass., iii, 1893, p. 426.

Jousset, p. 279. Waitz and others agree that the negro returning to Africa from America becomes liable to fevers from which his predecessors were immune.

‖ *Vide* letter in Boston Transcript, dated Mexico, August 11, 1895.

surexcitation of the kidneys and the sexual organs ensues; the individual as a rule becomes thinner; * the liver tends to increase in size, which is perhaps the cause of a certain sallowness of skin; † and in females menstruation is often disturbed, the age of puberty being sooner reached.‡ A very important change, which has not perhaps been fully investigated as yet, is a temporary rise of temperature, which often lasts for some time after the individual leaves the tropics.# Sir Humphry Davy was the first to note, on a voyage to Ceylon, that the temperature of travellers tended to rise in this way,‖ and Guegnen confirms his conclusions, although he shows that the rise is less than had been supposed.ᐃ Maurel concludes that it varies from 0.3° to 0.5°.◊ Observations on Europeans between Khartoum and the equator showed that for those who had been there less than two years the average was 99.5°, or nearly a degree above the normal. Those who had been there longer than four years exhibited a lower temperature of 99.1°, still a half degree over the average in Europe.‡

It is not impossible that these delicate variations of temperature may bear some relation to the racial pathological predispositions which we have noted, as well as to the liability of the newcomer in the tropics to contract fevers and other zymotic diseases from which the natives and the fully acclimated whites—such as the creoles, for example—are immune. Darwin indirectly hinted at such a solution many years ago, and suggested at the same time a study of the relation of the complexion to immunity from fevers. But no one appears to

---

* Jousset, pp. 139, 160, 197, 208–211, 221, and 229. *Cf.* also Montano, 1878, and Revue d'Anth., série 2, ii, 1879, p. 134. Healthy Europeans in the tropics are lighter in weight than the same class at home (Archiv für pathologische Anatomie, etc., cxix, p. 254).

† Hirsch, *op. cit.*, iii, pp. 388: *cf.* Peschel, 1894, p. 92.

‡ Revue d'Anth., série 2, v, p. 373.

Jousset, *op. cit.* pp. 201, 207, 259, 391.

‖ Proceedings of the Royal Society, London, 1814, civ, 1825.

ᐃ Archives de Médecine navale, January, 1878.

◊ Bull. Soc. d'Anth., 1884, pp. 371–390.

‡ Proc. British Ass. Adv. Science, 1889, p. 787.

have followed it up.* The recent development of the science of hydro-therapeutics certainly points to this conclusion. Several observers have already noted a permanent difference in the normal mouth temperature of the different races. Glogner has shown that the temperature of the Malay is slightly lower than that of Europeans, the brown skin radiating heat more freely.† The Mongolian race more nearly approaches the European than does the negro, whose norm is considerably lower.‡ Dr. Felkin # gives observations to show that the average mouth temperature of six hundred negroes between the equator and 10° north latitude was 97.8° F., the European normal being 98.6°. Higher than either were the Soudanese, whose average was 99°. In the European coming to the tropics, therefore, the temporary rise of body temperature increases still more the difference between his own and the indigenous normal in most cases. It has, indeed, been suggested that this is the cause of malarial fever in the tropics, but the matter has never been fully investigated, especially in its relation to other zymotic diseases.

Among animals the connection between minute variations of body temperature and the liability to contract diseases due to micro-organisms is well established. A fowl, whose normal temperature is considerably above that of the horse, the dog, or the rabbit, is immune from splenic fever, to which these other animals are liable; and yet Pasteur, by reducing its blood heat to their level, by immersing its legs in cold water, was able successfully to inoculate it with the anthrax bacillus.|| And other fowls were cured of the fever so contracted, by artificially raising their temperature to a point at which the bacillus could no longer thrive. For the same reason tuberculosis does not flourish in frogs or other cold-blooded animals, unless their blood temperature is sufficiently raised to permit of its germination. It is too early to assert that the same law will

---

* Descent of Man, i, p. 233 *et seq.*
† Archiv f. pathologische Anatomie, cxvi, p. 540; and cxix, p. 256.
‡ Bull. Soc. d'Anth., 1884, p. 380; Jousset, *op. cit.*, p. 100.
# Proc. British Ass. Adv. Science, 1889, p. 787.
|| Sutton, Evolution and Disease, London, 1890, p. 253.

apply to the " traumatic " diseases of the tropics; but one point is certain, that newcomers in those regions are particularly liable to zymotic diseases during that period when their temperature is most above the native normal; and that immunity from attack, or at least a more benign form of the disorder, often comes with that fall in temperature which is perhaps the surest sign of true acclimatization. Finally, it will be noted that even when this temperature falls once more to the European normal, it is still higher than that of the natives. And if there were any truth in this theory, the perfect accommodation to the environment which the natives of the tropics enjoy, would be attained only when the normal temperature of the European had been reduced to their level. But the persistence of physiological ethnic traits is a well-known fact; the Hindu to-day, despite his long sojourn in the tropics, has a temperature merely reduced to his own racial normal—to reduce it still further to the level of the negro would require ages of time.*

Acclimatization in this physiological sense of a gradual approach and approximation to the normal type of the natives, must of necessity be an exceedingly slow process, involving many generations of men. Yet in every respect except of temperature it appears that the first effects of a sojourn in the tropics is to induce symptoms which point toward the peculiarities of the native type. Thus the increase in the size of the liver indicates the operation of those causes which have finally made the negro's liver normally larger than that of the European.† The only present difficulty is that an unusual strain is suddenly put upon the various organs in this process of gradual adaptation which is often too severe; as, for ex-

---

* Jousset, *op. cit.*, p. 105.

† Jousset, p. 108. The physiological characteristics of the negro are well described as follows : A weakly developed chest (p. 85), less respiratory power and lung capacity (p. 88), more rapid pulse (p. 95), diminished muscular tension (p. 100), lower temperature (p. 107), less perspiration (p. 111), and a tendency toward slimness (p. 139). The lessened vitality and power of endurance are also to be noted (p. 144). Pruner Bey confirms these results in his studies of the vascular system of the negro. *Vide* also De Quatrefages, 1879, p. 407. Gould, 1869; Baxter, 1875 ; and Hoffmann, 1896, all agree in these details.

ample, the high mortality among Europeans from derangement of the liver, such as hepatitis, bilious fever, abscesses, and the like, which indicates that some physiological change has taken place which has entailed an excessive demand upon the activities of this organ. Similarly the extreme liability of the negro to diseases of the lungs in the temperate zone may be due to his lack of physiological accommodation to those circumstances which have in hundreds of generations produced the European type. To expect that man can in a single generation compass the ends which Nature takes an age to perform is the height of folly. The exact nature of the physiological processes induced by the tropics is, however, so imperfectly known that we must in general rely upon concrete experience for our further conclusions.

RESULTS OF HYGIENE.—Hygiene and sanitation have accomplished wonderful results in assisting the individual to withstand those immediate effects of climatic change which, as we have said, are so often fatal.* The yearly loss at one time in India, according to Felkin [91], was eighty for each regiment of one thousand men. In 1856 it had been reduced to sixty-nine; from 1870 to 1879 it ranged about sixty-two; and in 1888 the annual loss was only fifty, including deaths and invaliding. The loss in Cochin China per regiment was one hundred and fifteen in 1861; the actual deaths have now been reduced to twenty-two, although a much higher figure would be needed to include invaliding. The terrific annual loss of one hundred and forty-eight per thousand in Senegal from 1832 to 1837 is now reduced to about seventy-three. In this last case, however, one hundred and fifty per thousand are returned for sickness every year.† A large proportion of these

---

* Discussed by Hunt, 1861, p. 140, and by Montano, 1878, p. 8 *et seq.*; by Davidson, 1892, for India ; and by Dr. Farr, in Jour. Royal Stat. Soc., xxiv, p. 472. *Vide* also, for statistical information, ibid., iv, p. 1 ; viii, pp. 77, 193 ; ix, p. 157 ; x, p. 100 ; xiv, p. 109 ; xv, p. 100. Tables of the comparative mortality of British troops in various countries are conveniently given in Revue d'Anth., série 2, iv, p. 175. Tulloch, Statistical Report on the Sickness and Mortality of Troops, London, 1838, gives a vast amount of information.

† Revue d'Anth., série 3, iv, 1889, p. 346.

would undoubtedly die if not removed immediately. One may indeed be hopeful from such results that, with further advance in the science of prevention, these figures may be yet further reduced. The system of vacations,* of strict regulation of diet, the avoidance of excessive fatigue and exposure, and especially of all forms of agricultural labour, together with the extension of the hill-station system, will do much in this respect; so that it is conceded by most candid observers that, with few exceptions, such as Cochin China and the coast of Africa, robust individuals by great care stand a fair chance of good health in the tropics. Nevertheless, this should never be allowed to conceal the real fact that the English to-day are no nearer true acclimatization in India than they were in 1840. To tolerate a climate is one thing, to become independent of it is quite a different matter. The securing of a permanent footing in the tropics depends upon factors of a totally different nature.

FERTILITY.—Passing now from the consideration of the individual to that of the race, the keynote of the matter rests in the much-controverted question of the influence of change of climate upon fertility. For, however well the individual may be enabled, by artificial means or otherwise, to exist, the race will never accommodate itself permanently unless the birth rate exceeds the death rate.† Here we must first carefully eliminate the effects of ethnic crosses with natives of the tropics; for a fatal mistake of many observers has been the neglect to distinguish the possible sterility induced by intermixtures of race from that caused by a change of climate and of life conditions; or statements of one have been accepted by tyros as equivalent to the other. It has been confidently asserted for so many years that sterility of the white race

---

* In Cochin China one year in three is the allowance. The improvement in Senegal is largely due to the brief sojourn of the troops, who are relieved at short intervals. This system now prevails also in India, in sharp contrast to the old practice of keeping the soldiers there for long terms, in the hope of forcing acclimatization in that way.

† *Vide* Virchow on this point in Verh. Berliner Ges. f. Anth., 1885, p. 202.

ensues after three generations in the tropics that it has become a household word in anthropology.*

The result of comparative study of the lower forms of life is suggestive in this connection. Wallace [90] treats of this most suggestively. With plants and animals a sudden change of habitat will often produce a temporary sterility, which disappears only after a series of chance variations. The chrysanthemum remained infertile for sixty years after its introduction into France from China, so that continued importation of the seed was necessary. Finally, in 1852 a few plants developed seeds; and from these others were raised, until to-day the species is self-sustaining in Europe. A similar experience with corn at Sierra Leone, with the goose at Bogotá, and with European poultry in America, is instanced by De Quatrefages [79]. His rather optimistic argument with regard to the future of acclimatization is based, indeed, upon the study of animals and plants, rather than of man. He reasons by analogy that if fertility becomes re-established by spontaneous variation in this sphere, it may be likewise affirmed to be true for man, thus giving countenance to the view that climatic changes do indeed produce infertility.

Despite the authorities who hold on general principles that sterility in man follows—or at least that it ought to follow—a sudden change of climate, direct proof for it is very hard to find. Broca has indeed affirmed that the Mamelukes in Egypt became infertile for that reason; † but in his case, as in all others, no attempt is made to eliminate a number of other factors. Jousset declares, on the contrary, that no direct effect upon fecundity can be traced to climate.‡ Dr. Fritsch con-

---

* Many examples of acceptance of this theory of infertility will be found in popular works. Pearson (National Life and Character, p. 89) bases his whole argument upon it. Even Virchow, *op. cit.*, p. 213, asserts it to be true. It was at the bottom of the exploded theory of Knox and Brace with respect to the decreasing birth-rate in America. *Cf.* Carlier in Mém. Soc. d'Anth., iii, 1868, p. 25.

† Human Hybridity. *Cf.* the case of the creoles in the island of St. Louis, cited by Corre, 1882.

‡ *Op. cit.*, p. 231. The superior health of women, due to less exposure, has already been noted.

cedes that, although sterility may result, there is as yet no direct evidence to prove it.* The difficulty, it will be observed, is to eliminate the effects of crossing with the natives, or else of marriage with newly arrived immigrants. A physician of twenty-seven years' experience in the Dutch Indies has never known a European family to keep its blood unmixed in this way for the necessary period of three generations. Only one example of pure isolation is known, in the island of Kisser, and sterility there is by no means certain. Sterility from climate as a single cause in this part of the world, then, can neither be affirmed nor denied, from utter lack of evidence.†

On the contrary, a number of examples of continued fertility might be given. Brace affirms the Jews to be fertile even in Cochin-China, and Joest says that Europeans in Africa often bear children.‡ The Spanish women in Guayaquil, on the authority of Dr. Spruce, cited by Wallace ('90), in a climate where the temperature is seldom below 83° F., and in the complete absence of intermarriage with the natives, are the finest along the coast; and the white population is exceedingly prolific. The experience of Algeria, so far at least as heat is concerned, seems to bear out the same conclusion, the birth rate being higher even than in France.# De Quatrefages ('79), despite his inference of a temporary infertility, certainly takes a hopeful view for the other French colonies. Some remarkable examples of fecundity, indeed, are not lacking. Some years ago, an English woman, never out of India, not even taking a vacation in the hills, died at the age of ninety-seven, leaving eighteen children.‖ Nearly all authorities, however, deny that the English in general can ever become acclimated there. Sterility, of course, while most important, is not the only element in the acclimatization of the race. Even if we could affirm that sterility did not result, the perpetuation of a people in the tropics would not necessarily follow; for the mother may seldom survive childbirth, as in the East Indies and on the

---

* Verh. Berliner Ges. f. Anth., 1885, p. 258.
† Ibid., 1886, pp. 89–92.
‡ Ibid., 1885, p. 473.   # Levasseur, 1889, iii, p. 432.
‖ Verh. Berliner Ges. f. Anth., 1885, p. 379.

Zambesi,* or the children may seldom live,† the age of six, according to Wallace ('⁹⁰), being often a critical period. But these facts have no connection with sterility or the reverse, although they may produce the same negative result in the end. The final word upon this subject awaits more carefully sifted evidence than any we now possess.

COMPARATIVE APTITUDES OF EUROPEAN NATIONS.—The future political destiny of Africa is not unlikely to be dominated by a remarkable fact—namely, the severe handicap against which the Teutonic stock, and especially the Anglo-Saxon branch, struggles in the attempt permanently to colonize the tropics. And this is peculiarly unfortunate, as Levasseur ('⁸⁹) says, since these are the very peoples who find population pressing most severely upon the soil at home. The Latin nations, of course, are the ones who lay most stress upon this comparative disability of their rivals; but in justice to the French, it must be added that they have generally recognised that the Spaniards and Italians possess as great an advantage over them as they in turn do over the Germans.‡ The experience of Algeria affords a good illustration of this point. The year 1854 marks the first excess of births over deaths in this colony; and the following table shows the relative disabilities of the Europeans for 1855–'56 : #

	Births *pro mille.*	Deaths *pro mille.*
Spaniards...............................	46	30
Maltese	44	30
Italians...........................	39	28
French	41	43
Germans................................	31	56

Dr. Ricoux ‖ gives the following death rates per thousand for children under one year: Spaniards, 180; Maltese, 178;

---

* Peschel, Wallace, De Quatrefages.

† Jousset, *op. cit.*, p. 314. *Cf.* Verh. Berliner Ges. f. Anth., 1885, p. 258, on Egypt.   ‡ Revue d'Anth., série 2, viii, 1885, p. 190.

Bull. Soc. d'Anth., 1886, p. 269 ; *cf.* L'Anthropologie, vi, p. 120. The small number of Germans weakens the force of the evidence somewhat.

‖ Annales de Démographie, vi, p. 14. *Cf.* De Quatrefages, *op. cit.*, p. 230, and Bordier, 1884, p. 184.

Italians, 194; French, 225.2; and Germans, 273. This disability of the Germans is confessed by all their most able and candid authorities.* The only north Europeans ever successful are the Dutch in southern Africa and the East Indies. All writers, even in France, acknowledge that the Mediterranean natives possess a peculiar aptitude in this respect.† Moreover, the French nation is further divided against itself. That the Provençals succeed better than the Teutonic French in the tropics is generally conceded; ‡ and the bulk of French emigration to-day comes from the Rhone Valley, Corsica, and Provence.# This makes the fact still more curious that these same Provençals endured the hardships of Napoleon's Moscow campaign far better than their comrades from Normandy and Champagne.|| Can it, indeed, be due to an admixture of Semitic blood, as Wallace suggests?

This disability of the Anglo-Saxon stock does not seem to indicate any less vitality, but rather the reverse.△ Bordier [78] assures us that the Crimean War apparently showed the English to be possessed of a peculiar advantage over the French in their ability to recover speedily from severe wounds.

---

* Ratzel, 1882, i, p. 304 ; Virchow, Fritsch, and Joest in Verh. Berliner Ges. f. Anth., 1885, pp. 211, 474, etc. It will have been noted that nearly all references in German fall within the years 1885–'87. The question drifted into politics—out of the hands of scientists into those of pamphleteers. *Vide* Max Nordau, Rabies Africana, in Asiatic Quarterly Review, second series, ii, p. 76 ; and G. A. Fischer, Mehr Licht im dunkeln Welttheil, Berlin, 1886. A blue-book on the subject was promised, but the attention of the Colonial Society was for some reason diverted. Tropical hygiene was fully discussed, but the broader scientific aspect of the matter was neglected (Verh., 1889, p. 732). As late as 1890 no definite government report had been issued except Mähly's work. The Germans apparently do not dare to handle it without gloves, and their views are unique in their optimism (Kohlstock, in Science, 1891, p. 3 ; and Finckelnburg, in Handbuch der Staatswissenschaft).

† Ratzel, *loc. cit.* ; Jousset, p. 292 ; Montano, 1878 ; Felkin, 1886 ; Bordier, 1884, pp. 185, 493 ; Levasseur, 1889, ii, p. 431.

‡ De Quatrefages, *op. cit.*, p. 230 ; Jousset, p. 192 ; Montano, p. 449 ; and Levasseur, ii, p. 431.   # L'Anthropologie, v, p. 253.

|| Bull. Soc. d'Anth., i, p. 326 ; and Bordier, 1878.

△ Dr. Beddoe, 1885, p. 224, gives some exceedingly interesting observations upon this point.

44

In fact, the mortality after capital operations in English hospitals is only about half that among the French.* We have already observed that primitive peoples, while showing a relative immunity from septic disorders, still remain peculiarly sensitive to all changes of climate. The stupendous failure of the project of colonizing the Mexican State of Durango, to which we have already referred,† is a case in point. And the case of the Anglo-Saxon stock is analogous to it in this respect, having a higher recuperative power conjoined to disability in becoming acclimatized; ‡ for Felkin and all the English authorities are agreed that the Teutonic peoples are exceedingly unelastic in power of adaptation to tropical climates. This is undoubtedly in part due to national habits, but it also appears to be rooted in race. In peopling the new lands of the earth, therefore, we observe a curious complication; for it is precisely those people who need the colonies most, and who are bending all their political energies to that end, who labour under the severest disabilities. A popular opinion is abroad that Africa is to be dominated by the English and German nations. If there be any virtue in prediction, it would rather appear that their activities will be less successful as soon as the pioneering stage gives way to the necessity for actual colonists, who with their families are to live, labour, and propagate in the new lands.

Summarizing the views of authorities upon this subject, the almost universal opinion seems to be that true colonization in the tropics by the white race is impossible.# The only writers who express themselves favourably are Crawford,|| whose hopes for India have certainly not been fulfilled; Armand ^ and Rattray,◊ Livingstone and Bishop Hannington, according to Felkin ('91a), and the physicians assembled at the Medical

---

* Topinard, Éléments, p. 412.

† Page 574 *supra* ; *cf*. Brinton, 1890, p. 40.

‡ Montano, 1878, p. 447 ; Corre, 1882, p. 74.

The most definite as well as the latest expression of expert opinion fully agrees with this. *Vide* Proceedings of the International Geographical Congress at London, 1895.

|| Trans. Ethnological Society, London, new series, i, p. 89.

^ Traité de Climatologie, Paris, 1873.   ◊ Jousset, p. 426.

Congress at Berlin in 1890,* with the Society for the Advancement of Medical Science in the Dutch Indian Settlements.† All these authorities may now be classed as antiquated, except the last, and moreover the first one represents that nation which is notoriously unsuccessful in acclimatization. The opinion of the Dutch physicians who have been fairly successful may be met by as good testimony from their own number on the opposite side.

Authorities in favour of the view that complete acclimatization of Europeans in the tropics is impossible might be multiplied indefinitely. Among the earlier writers of this opinion are Knox ('50), Prichard ('45), and Hunt ('61). The best German authority concedes it, including Virchow, Fritsch, Joest, Fischer,‡ with Buchner # and Hirsch.‖ The French, who have studied it more scientifically than any other nation, hold to this opinion with no exception.△ Jousset declares that recruiting stations never effect a permanent recovery, the only remedy being to leave the tropics altogether. This opinion is also shared by many of the Dutch, who dissent from the favourable views of their countrymen already quoted. Van der Burg ◊ expresses it well when he states that, after all precautions have been taken, " a settlement ought to be continually supported by new supplies from the European continent in order to have a chance of healthy existence." The English writers of this opinion include Ravenstein,‡ Sir William Moore,‡ and Tilt.‡ Dr. Felkin alone holds to a slightly more

---

* Proc. Royal Geog. Soc., January, 1891, p. 30.

† Proc. Seventh Int. Congress of Demography and Hygiene, London, x, pp. 170–178.

‡ Felkin, 1891, p. 647, and Verh. Berliner Ges. f. Anth., 1885, pp. 210, 257, 474. Virchow distinguishes between malaria and climate, which is generally called a distinction without a difference in the tropics.

Correspondenzblatt, xviii, p. 17.

‖ Verh. Berliner Ges. f. Anth., 1886, p. 164.

△ Rey, 1878 ; Jousset, pp. 426–434, cites many authorities ; to these may be added L. A. Bertillon and Bordier in all their work.

◊ Trans. Seventh Int. Congress of Demography and Hygiene, p. 170.

‡ Proc. Royal Geog. Soc., xiii, 1891, p. 30, and Proc. British Ass. Adv. Science, 1894.　　‡ Edinburgh Medical Journal, xxxi, part ii, p. 852.

‡ Trans. Seventh Int. Congress of Demography and Hygiene.

favourable view of colonization in Africa, although he qualifies it by requiring an unlimited amount of time; and he finds comfort in the thought that Central Africa is no worse than India. He finally concedes, however, that in this latter colony the hill districts are the only ones where the English can remain in health. For some years the hopes for Africa as a field for colonization were based upon the altitude of the inland plateau. But expert opinion on this seems to show that, with the sole exception of Matabele-land, the country is impossible for European colonists.* And even Stanley declares that cautious pioneering is all that can be expected for the future in the Congo basin—that colonization was never anticipated at all.† In the face of such testimony there can be but one conclusion: to urge the emigration of women, children, or of any save those in the most robust health to the tropics may not be to murder in the first degree, but it should be classed, to put it mildly, as incitement to it.

It must not be understood that by this is meant that the white man can not live in the tropics. Hygienic precautions and great care can often render a prolonged sojourn in these regions perfectly harmless. But, as Wallace ('90) observes, the Englishman who can spend a summer in Rome in safety only by sleeping in a tower and by never venturing forth at night, can not be truly said to be acclimated. A colony can never approximate even to the civilization of Europe until it can abolish or assimilate the native servile population; and yet, one of the many things which are expressly forbidden to all colonists in the tropics is agricultural labour. It would be a waste of energy to give citations to prove this, for every work on acclimatization insists upon the necessity of this precaution. Let it be understood, then, that a colonial policy in the tropics means a permanent servile native population, which is

---

* This was fully discussed at the Seventh Int. Congress of Demography and Hygiene, at London. Felkin and Markham took a hopeful view, while Ravenstein asserted that only a portion of the plateau was available. *Cf.* Jousset, p. 341.

† Proc. Int. Geographical Congress, London, 1895; *cf.* especially Scottish Geog. Mag., xi, 1895, p. 512.

manifestly inconsistent with political independence, or with any approach to republican institutions.

Such being our conclusions from a comparison of authorities, what shall we say about the broader question of original racial acclimatization? And what policy, if any, should be modelled upon the theories with regard to the way in which this undisputed operation once took place—for, as we have said, the substantial unity of the human race, followed by extensive migrations, is an accepted fact. Even in the absence of direct proof, to deny it would be to neglect all the evidence for the same phenomenon among plants and animals so ably set forth by Wallace, Agassiz, Drude, and other writers. Fortunately, however, the researches of ethnologists to-day are continually bringing new evidence to show that such widespread migration has indeed taken place. Two radically different policies are advocated by the adherents of one or the other of the two opposing factions in biological theory. For accommodation to climatic conditions may take place either by variation and natural selection or by habitual adaptation transmitted by inheritance.* Weissmann,† Wallace, De Quatrefages, and apparently Brinton,‡ rely upon natural selection, which they assert, directly or by inference, takes place in the following way: A large body of men (plants or animals) is transported to the new habitat at once—the larger the number the better—from which by elimination a few fortunate variations survive. Thus, after a long time, and enormous sacrifice of life, a new type, immune to some degree, becomes established. All that the state need do, therefore, is to keep up the supply of immigrants long enough, and leave the climate to do the rest.

What state policy may we adopt if we hold to the biological theory of adaptation and heredity? This school includes Virchow and Buchner,# who firmly defended it at the Natural Science Congress at Strasburg, and by Jousset as well.‖ Their

---

* Discussed by Wallace, 1890.
† Correspondenzblatt deutschen Ges. f. Anth., xviii, 1887, p. 18.
‡ 1890, p. 283.   # Correspondenzblatt, xviii, 1887, p. 18.
‖ Op. cit., p. 244—outlined in his general argument.

policy would be to imitate the operations of natural ethnic migrations; they would rely upon the utilization of the natural aptitudes of various nationalities, which we have mentioned— perhaps themselves the fruit of ages of sojourn in certain climates—until finally a great drifting movement toward the equator would take place. In other words, the peoples of the Mediterranean basin, learning of their aptitude for a southward migration, would perhaps move to Algeria, displacing the people of the Soudan and the Semitic stocks toward the equator. To fill the place thus left vacant, the people of northern France slowly drift to the Rhone Valley and Provence for a generation or two, and their place is taken by Germans and Belgians.

That this is a tendency at the present time can not be doubted.* Each generation adapting itself quietly would produce succeeding ones with an inherited immunity. Unfortunately, this most reasonable let-alone policy has two fatal objections: in the first place, it requires a policy of non-interference; and, more potent still, it absolutely neglects the political factor. To suppose that France would quietly allow her people to be dispossessed by Germans, even though she aided her colonial policy thereby, or that Germany would quietly leave Africa to her Gallic neighbour, is not to be supposed for a moment. Nevertheless, it will be probably the only policy which will finally produce a new immune type in the regions of the equator. Of course, England is by fate condemned to follow the first policy we have outlined. France, indeed, is the only one of the European states which extends over the two contrasted European climates; a large measure of her success is probably due to that fact; while all the nations north of the Alps must traverse her territory or that of Italy on the way to these newly discovered lands. Great political results are therefore not impossible, if the prognosis we have indicated prove to be correct. At all events, enough has perhaps

---

* Bull. Institut International de Statistique, iii, trois liv., 1888, p. 36; this fact is noticeably prominent. The destination of French emigrants is given in L'Anthropologie, v, p. 253. *Vide* also Transactions of the International Congress of Demography and Hygiene, pp. 131 *et seq.*

been said to show that great problems for science remain to be solved before the statesman can safely proceed to people those tropical regions of the earth so lately apportioned among European states.

SPECIAL LIST OF AUTHORITIES ON ACCLIMATIZATION.

BERTILLON, A. L. A.
    1887. Acclimatement; acclimatation.
        (In Dictionnaire encyclopédique des sciences médicales.)
BORDIER, A.
    1878. De l'anthropologie pathologique.
        (Revue d'anth., série 2, i, pp. 76–89.)
    1881. Japonais et Malais.
        (Revue d'anth., série 2, iv, pp. 236–246.)
    1884 a. La colonisation scientifique et les colonies françaises. Paris.
    1884 b. La géographie médicale. Paris.
CORRE, A.
    1882. De l'acclimatement dans la race noire Africaine.
        (Revue d'anth., série 2, v, pp. 31–97.)
DAVIDSON, A.
    1892. Geographical pathology. Edinburgh. 2 v.
FELKIN, R. W.
    1886. Can Europeans become acclimatized in tropical Africa?
        (Scottish geog. magazine, ii, pp. 647–657.)
    1889. On the geographical distribution of some tropical diseases, and their relation to physical phenomena. Maps. Edinburgh.
    1891 a. On acclimatization.
        (Scottish geog. magazine, vii, pp. 647–656.)
    1891 b. Tropical highlands : their suitability for European settlement.
        (Trans. seventh international congress of demography and hygiene, x, pp. 155–170.)
HIRSCH, A.
    1860–'64. Handbuch der historisch-geographischen Pathologie. Erlangen. 2 v.
    1883–'86. Translated as Handbook of geographical and historical pathology. 3 vols. London.
HOFFMANN, F. L.
    1896. Race traits and tendencies of the American negro.
        (Pub. Amer. economic ass., xi, pp. 1–329.)

HUNT, J.
    1861. On ethno-climatology, etc.
        (British ass. adv. of science, Manchester, pp. 129–150.)
JOUSSET, A.
    1884. Traité de l'acclimatement et de l'acclimatation. Paris.
LOMBARD, H. C.
    1877. Traité de climatologie médicale, etc. Paris. 3 v.
    1880. Atlas de la distribution géographique des maladies dans leur
        rapports avec les climats. Paris.
MONTANO, J.
    1878. L'hygiène et les tropiques.
        (Bull. soc. de géog., série 6, xv, pp. 418–451.)
NOVICOW, J.
    1893. Les luttes entre sociétés humaines et leurs phases succes-
        sives. Paris.
    1897. L'avenir de la race blanche. Paris.
ORGEAS, J.
    1886. La pathologie des races humaines et le problème de la coloni-
        sation. Paris.
REY, H.
    1878. Notes sur la géographie médicale de la côte occidentale
        d'Afrique.
        (Bull. soc. de géog., série 6, xv, pp. 38–71, 155–183, 229–246.)
SAINT-VEL, O.
    1872. Hygiène des Européens dans les climats tropicaux, etc.
        Paris.
WALLACE, A. R.
    1890. Acclimatization.
        (In Encyclopædia Britannica, 9th ed.)

Appendix A.

The Cephalic Index.

WHILE the cephalic index is generally recognised to-day by all authorities as the mainstay of the science of craniometry, a number of objections to its use have been urged at various times. The primary one—that it is not an expression of ethnic peculiarities at all, the relation of breadth to length being a mere matter of chance variation—is so fully answered by the data herewith presented in all our maps and references that we need not attempt to answer it otherwise than by appeal to these. No claim is made, even by its most earnest advocates, that it is indubitable in every case. Large numbers of parallel observations are always necessary to eliminate the effect of purely individual variation. The day when one could, like Retzius, formulate an entire theory as to the origin of European types by the study of two crania alone is happily past. Modern craniometry must rest for its justification upon a few simple measurements, taken, however, upon large numbers of subjects. Virchow's [96] relegation of it to a subordinate position as a racial test is based upon the shortcomings of the older system of detailed observations upon a very few crania, revived, for example, by von Török and others. Even properly taken, however, it must be confessed that certain parts of the earth yield as yet but meagre results. The Americas particularly, as studied by Boas and Ehrenreich (Anthropologische Studien über die Urbewohner Brasiliens, Braunschweig, 1897), seem to give rather discordant indexes, whether from the relatively small number of observations or because of chaotic ethnic conditions. This is the exception. Europe fully vindicates the cephalic index in every way, as we shall hope to prove.

Another objection to the cephalic index as an ethnic criterion has also been made—that it is merely a *relation*, and not expressive of any *absolute quantity* whatever. This may be granted, it seems, without in the least detracting from its value; for nearly every morphological test, either in zoölogy or anthropology, partakes of the nature of such a relation. It is not the absolute length of the frog's hind leg or of the negro's arm which determines the type; that length varies with growth, without lessening the possibility of immediate identification. It is really the relative length of that leg or arm to the spinal column, or to some other member, which is determinant. (*Cf.* Flower on Size of Teeth as a Character of Race, in Jour. Anth. Inst., xiv, p. 183.) The marked constancy of the relation, then, of the length of the head to its breadth from infancy to old age, despite the continued change of the absolute measurements, is a sufficient answer in this case. (Consult Boas, 1896, and Ripley, 1896 d, on the cephalic index and growth.)

A number of attempts have been made to substitute other cranial peculiarities than the relation of length to breadth as a primary test of racial origin. Most notable is that of the brilliant anthropologist Sergi, at Rome. (See Sergi, 1893; Moschen, 1895, etc.) His so-called " natural system " of classification is based upon the shape of the cranium rather than upon the mere ratio between its two diameters. There can be no doubt that this shape, as viewed from above, must often be taken into account. Only thus can the distinction between a false and a true type be detected. (Durand-Lapouge, 1897–'98, p. 305, and Lapouge, 1891 b, deal with this especially; see also Broca, 1872 a and 1872 b.) Nevertheless, by itself alone the mere shape of the skull does not seem to yield very satisfactory results. It is too liable to the influences of chance variation, as tested by Elkind [97] and others. Even Sergi himself [98b] confesses that the cephalic index is superior to it for general purposes. Of course, it is not omniscient. Dr. Beddoe (1893, p. 40) has well touched upon its defects. The school of so-called anthropo-sociologists has undoubtedly overestimated its significance. Nevertheless, for the continent of Europe at least, the results afforded by its use at the hands of its most ardent and skilful advocates, Broca, Collignon, Livi, Topinard, Weisbach, and a host of others, fully justifies our use of it as a primary test. (*Cf.* Niederle, 1896 a, p. 41.)

A number of technical points have to be considered in the correction and co-ordination of results from different parts of Europe. The most important is the distinction between the German and the French systems, otherwise called those of Broca and von Ihering respectively. The Germans, led by Virchow, Ranke, and Kollmann measure, not the maximum length of the skull as the French do, but its length in a horizontal plane, parallel to the normal plane of vision. Their indexes are thus appreciably higher than those in which the greatest length, wherever found, is measured. (Garson, 1884 and 1886 b, is good on this; see also the index to our Bibliography under Craniometry and Methods.) A correction of one to the other is, however, possible, as we have shown. (Ripley, 1896 a). Ammon [96], measuring several thousand heads on both systems, finds the difference to be 0.47 of one unit. We have, therefore, in rough accordance with his results, everywhere deducted one-half unit from the horizontal cephalic index to reduce it to a base comparable with the French data. The system of the latter certainly seems to be the more natural one; it is adopted in every country of Europe except Germany. Even the younger Swiss anthropologists, some in Germany and most of those in Austria, makes use of this French system.

Finally, anthropologists distinguish between the relative proportions of the head, measured over all the soft tissues, and those taken upon the skull divested of all the fleshy parts. The first is called the *cephalic*, in contradistinction to the second or *cranial* index. All sorts of corrections have been suggested for reducing one to the other. Experience seems to show that the cephalic index is generally about two units above that taken on the cranium. In other words, the living head seems to be relatively broader than the cranium by about three per cent. It is probable, as my friend Dr. Beddoe has suggested to me in correspondence, that the correction to be made will differ according to the degree of dolichocephaly, being greater

in the relatively long heads. He suggests a correction of two
units in the purely dolichocephalic types, decreasing succes-
sively to about one and one half in mesocephaly, and to somewhat less than one in the broadest-headed types. Thus alone
can we reconcile the results obtained by different students
(Ripley, 1896 a) in various parts of Europe. We have, however, to avoid complications, uniformly adopted in the construction of our maps the customary correction of two units;
adding two units, in other words, to the cranial index to obtain the cephalic proportions.

We have discussed the merits of the statistical systems of
average *versus* seriation in our chapter on the " Three European Races " (*q. v.*). For reasons there given, our maps represent average indexes unless otherwise stated.

Appendix B.

Blonds and Brunets.

For technical details concerning the divers methods, both
of observation and classification, the following references will
be useful: Virchow, 1886 b, on the German system; Topinard,
1886 b, 1887, and 1889 c; Livi, 1896 a, p. 52. Beddoe, 1885,
p. 76, gives an especially good criticism of the German system
as compared with his own. Collignon, 1888, and in all his
recent work, uses a modification of Topinard's scheme, both
alike rejecting all neutral shades. Livi, in the Atlas, 1896 a,
shows the parallelism of the maps of types and of traits. Our
method employed in reducing the widely differing systems
to a common base, so that comparisons may properly be drawn,
is simple. In many areas along the border line of systems the
same population has been studied from each side. Thus, in
the Tyrol, Tappeiner (1878, p. 269) has studied adults, so that
his results may be correlated with those of Livi in Italy. At
the same time Schimmer has studied the children of this region,
so that his data from the same people may bind them to the
German-Austrian populations. Weisbach, from adults in Austria, also works near by (1895 b, p. 73). Dr. Beddoe, in his

monumental work, The Races of Britain, with results of personal observation from all over Europe, gives data for international comparison, showing, for example, that southern England equals Alsace, and that Zurich equals London (p. 73, *seq.*). In another place he gives opportunity for comparison with the French system (1882 b). Topinard (Eléments, pp. 338, 339), from the same observations, has shown that Normandy, Vienna, and Cornwall are about equally pigmented, and that the Walloons and the Bretons are about alike in this respect. Knowing from Vanderkindere, Virchow, and Schimmer how the Walloons are related to the rest of central Europe, the way is clear. For Spain we have the merest hint from study of the eyes alone (Archiv für Anthropologie, xxii, p. 431), but Dr. Ferraz de Macedo has kindly placed his data for two thousand Portuguese at our disposition since this map was made. It confirms the prevalent brunetness completely. Other references for the various countries will be found in their respective chapters. Weisbach (1884) gives data for southeast Europe.

Appendix C.

Stature.

The data for this map are sufficiently indicated by our references in the following pages, wherein nearly every country is treated in detail. A comprehensive summary by Deniker, with a map on a large scale, is about to appear in Mém. Soc. d'Anth. It confirms our results fully so far as any details have been published.

A point of especial importance to note is that no correction for differences of age has been made. The practice of different countries varies; in some, conscriptions taking place at the age of nineteen years, in others being deferred to twenty or even twenty-one. Full growth not being attained until several years later even than this, the result of different observers will vary accordingly. It has seemed best, however, to give the results exactly as taken, since no correction will probably amount to much more than a centimetre. Practically the only country which differs considerably is Norway, for which Arbo's results are given at twenty-two years. All others lie between nineteen and twenty-one. Our statures for the British Isles are also unduly high by comparison, because they are taken independently upon fully adult men. The effect of this has been, of course, slightly to exaggerate the superiority of both these Teutonic peoples on our map. It was thought better, however, to avoid confusion by giving averages exactly as taken, making no correction for age differences whatever.

Many serious technical difficulties have to be overcome in making an exact comparison of the data respecting stature in different countries. It is important to distinguish statures taken on the entire male population from those taken in the army alone; for all degenerate types have been eliminated from the latter by the examining surgeons. Deniker (1897, p. 292) is probably right in asserting that correction for this selection just about counterbalances the deficiency of stature due to immaturity, which we have mentioned in the preceding paragraph. This affords another reason for mapping the results exactly as given by the measurements.

A third difficulty consists in the systems adopted for comparing different districts. Some observers adopt the average as best conforming to fact; others work by percentages or percentage groups. It is almost impossible to draw direct comparisons between the two, although perfectly parallel results are generally given by each. Our two maps of stature in France, in accordance with the two methods respectively, will prove this. Only in details or where the population is far from homogeneous do marked divergencies occur. (Collignon, 1894 b, p. 13, discusses it.) Percentage grades are often useful for revealing selective processes. The main difficulty is that no international agreement as to the divisions to be adopted exists. Most Germanic countries have now adopted 1.70 metres and over as a designation for the very tall; but Myrdacz in Austria-Hungary, for example, uses an entirely different one. His data are entirely useless for detailed comparison in consequence.

Appendix D.

Deniker's Classification of the Races of Europe.

(Condensed from Jour. Anth. Institute, N. S. i, 1898, pp. 166–173.)

A most notable work upon the physical characteristics of the races of Europe by Dr. J. Deniker, Librarian of the Muséum d'Histoire Naturelle, at Paris, is about to appear. Its character and general conclusions he has already made known to us in two preliminary articles (1897 and 1898 a). Their interest and value prompt us to take note of their contents even in advance of the final publication of the whole work.

Deniker's raw materials—his data as to cephalic index, colour of hair and eyes, and stature—differ only in slight detail from our own, albeit they were apparently collected in entire independence of one another. Nevertheless, from almost entire agreement as to the distribution of the three principal characteristics *each* by *itself*, Deniker reaches widely different conclusions as to their *combination* into racial types from nearly every standard authority in Europe. We have in a general summary of the evidence, found no occasion to differ from the opinions of Beddoe, Broca, Collignon, Livi, Topinard, and a host of others. These anthropologists all affirm the existence of our three main racial types. Deniker differs from all others in combining his three separate physical traits into six principal races and four or more sub-races. At least two of his combinations are like the commonly accepted ones. His "Nordic" type corresponds to the classical Teutonic; his "Occidental" or "Cévenole" is the Celtic or Alpine type. He has, however, a good name (Adriatic or Dinaric) for the tall variety of the brachycephalic population of the northwest Balkan Peninsula, which seems well adapted to it. As to his other seven, they are merely subdivisions of the three classical races. Thus, for example, Deniker splits the classic Mediterranean race into two groups (and we freely confess the fact of an existing difference of stature between them)—one tall, which he calls Atlanto-Mediterranean; and one short, named the Ibero-Insular. Thus it goes. There is a "sub-Nordic," a

"Vistulan," a "Nord-Occidental," and so on. Fortunately, it is not necessary for us to attempt a comparison of these in detail.

The fact that from the same data such widely variant racial conclusions may be drawn is, at first sight, calculated to shake one's confidence in the whole attempt at a systematic somatological classification of the population of Europe. This we believe to be an unjustifiable inference. Deniker is too well equipped an anthropologist to go astray in such matters; and certainly the eminent names which we have just cited in favour of a simple tripartite division of races preclude the chance of their being in error. What, then, is the matter? After examination of Deniker's scheme, we claim to be able to reconcile both views. Unless this can be done, scientifically, some one must be proved in serious error.

The controversy involves, it seems to us, a question which has been much discussed of late by naturalists concerning the definition of the word "type." For in anthropology the term "race"—alas! so often lightly used—corresponds in many respects to the word "type" in zoölogy.

Deniker's elaborate scheme of six main and four secondary races is, in reality, not a classification of "races" at all, in the sense in which Topinard and others have so clearly defined it. It is rather a classification of *existing varieties*. We have already quoted Topinard's (1879) definition of the word "race." It is "in the present state of things an abstract conception, a notion of continuity in discontinuity, of unity in diversity. It is the rehabilitation of a real but directly unattainable thing." Apply this criterion to Deniker's six "races" and four "subraces." Is there any ideality about them? Is there any "unity" in his scheme? If you think there may be, glance for a moment at his map. Italy is resolved into no less than five distinct "races." Norway, simple and retiring peninsula that it is, comprises four of these, exclusive of the Lapps. What say Livi and Arbo to this? And the British Isles! How can we describe their intricate maze of "Nordic," "sub-Nordic," and "Nord-Occidental," with nearly all Scotland and half of Ireland indicated as "unknown"? Dr. Beddoe, where is

he? and Davis and Thurnam, the Anthropometric Committee,
and all the rest?   Does this prove our author in error, then?

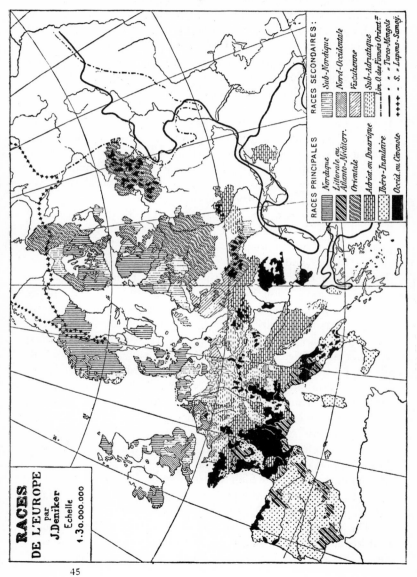

RACES
DE L'EUROPE
par
J.Deniker
Echelle
1.30.000.000

45

With equal positiveness, no. His so-called " races," as we now see, are real, actual, living combinations of traits as they exist in Europe to-day. You may safely take Deniker's map in hand, and, going to any region you please, you will surely find the population there to be outwardly just as he describes it. No surer guide could be found. That is why the map and the schematization is so elaborate; why it seems to lack that " unity in diversity " which we should seek. You are not discovering " races," in fact, at all. You are viewing *existent* types ; but not *ideal* ones, which may once have existed but may be now dissolved in a generalized mean. You are in possession of a living picture of the population of Europe *as it stands,* with all its complexities, its contradictions, and anomalies; but you will find no key to the relations of the several parts revealed, nor any idea of their possible origins.

How, then, are we to discover this ideal, this elusive " racial type "? How are we to reach the conclusions of the great body of anthropologists in Europe as to the existence of three " races," and no more? The process seems to us simple. Three steps must be taken; three, which Deniker, in laying his superb foundation for future use, has not yet had opportunity to take. These are: First, to eliminate all disturbing factors, thus being sure that no elements save those of hereditary descent are in evidence; secondly, to seek for similarities, and not diversities of traits, turning the pages of the book of life backward—making use, that is to say, of the data both of historical ethnology and prehistoric archæology; and, thirdly, utilizing the probabilities of geography in seeking the affinities between divergent types. Only thus may we boil his " races " down. In this wise alone may we attain that " unity in diversity " which we seek; and we may thus pass imperceptibly from the real existent type to that of the " abstract " and " unattainable " concept, which we term race. And we see that, after all, both Deniker and his opponents are right in fact; they differ only in their use of this single word.

The primary reason why, we affirm, Deniker has not carried his analysis far enough really to have discovered " races " lies in his neglect to eliminate all the modifying influences of environment, physical or social; of selection in its various phases; and of those other disturbing factors, which, together with the direct and perhaps predominant influences of heredity, constitute the figure of man as he stands. Wherever Deniker has spied a more or less stable combination of traits, he has hit upon it as a race, to paraphrase a well-known injunction. It is a case of too devoted attachment to the school of Broca; to the neglect of the admonitions of the followers of Villermé. If a certain group of men be discovered short of stature, they are at once assumed to be so by virtue of heredity. This is not always the case. For example, on Deniker's map of races, a " Vistulan " subtype, so called because of its prevalence among the Poles, is set apart because of its very short stature, from the main body of the Russians, who are termed " Oriental " by race. Is this justifiable? We have already sought to show that the apparent short stature of the Poles is largely due to the presence of a vast horde of Jews, who by their intermarriage have depressed the average for the country unduly. Is this mere political chance, the result of a few decrees of the Polish kings, to be allowed to father even a " sub-race "? Make allowance for this, and the Poles, it seems to us, fall at once into their proper place among the other Slavs.

A number of modifying factors are competent to effect a change of stature in a group of men. Deniker disregards this fact. Because of local differences of stature all through the brachycephalic middle zone of Europe, this great population, which has more and more universally been recognised as fundamentally a unit by descent from a broad-headed Celtic (?) ancestry, is by Deniker broken up into a number of subtypes. Wherever the broad-heads happen to be tall, they are set apart from the " Occidental " (Alpine) race by our author, and attributed to the " Adriatic " race, that darkish, very broad-headed, but, in contradistinction to the other brachycephals of central Europe, *very tall* type which certainly prevails in Bosnia, Servia, and Dalmatia. Thus the proverbially tall population in the Rhone-Saône Valley, which all other anthropologists since Broca have been content to consider tall by reason of an infusion of Teutonic blood from a Burgundian ancestry, is by Deniker attributed to the presence of this far-distant "Adriatic" or "sub-Adriatic" type. This is in utter defiance of geographical probability; it sets aside all historical evidence thus to herd the Burgundian and the Bosnian together. What if both are tall, brachycephalic, and darkish in complexion? Is there no other explanation in natural science to be found? The Adriatic type is thus scattered broadcast all over Europe by our author wherever a darkish and broad-headed contingent happens to be tall. One bit lies isolated just east of the Black Sea; a second in south central Russia; and again in the lower Loire Valley, in Provence, in Switzerland, in northern Italy. Call these "combinations," as we have said, if you please. Far be it from us to deny that they exist where indicated on the map. But who can say that the originally broad-headed peasantry in Burgundy are not tall because of the surpassing fertility and material prosperity of the Côte d'Or, with the addition perhaps of a strain of tall Teutonic blood, just as the Poles are stunted because of the intermixture with Jews? The two local anomalies are perfectly explicable by other means than to resort to the theory of race. That is the explanation to be adopted only when all environmental or other disturbing factors have been eliminated.

Just a word of minor criticism by way of interlude. Our author's map of the distribution of "races" seems to us a bit too minutely detailed to merit the fullest confidence. A little generalizing where specific data are not over-abundant would seem to yield a nearer approximation to the truth. Minute detail for outlying parts of the continent, where observations have been by scores and not by thousands, awakens distrust. Our author is fully acquainted with the best that is known; but even that is often little. His division of "races" is a bit too arbitrary, even if we view them only, as we have said, as "existent types." Thus his map of Spain shows the larger part to be constituted of his "Ibero-Insular" race—that is to say, brunet, dolichocephalic, and undersized in stature. But his map shows also a number of regions in Spain where an entirely distinct one of his six main "races"—his "Atlanto-

Mediterranean "—is indicated. Where is the division line drawn between " Ibero-Insular " and " Atlanto-Mediterranean "? Judging by the tints of the map, they are as different as their names. But compare this with Olóriz's map of stature (page 275 *supra*) in Spain. At once it appears that all provinces whose average stature falls below 1.65 are dubbed " Ibero-Insular "—classed, that is, with Sardinia, Corsica, and Calabria—while all regions quite the same in head form and pigmentation, characterized by a stature above this arbitrary line, become at once " Atlanto-Mediterranean." Thus the continuity of type of the tallish population of Catalonia, along the east coast, is rudely interrupted in this way, as our map shows; and an appearance of heterogeneity, which not even Deniker himself would acknowledge to exist, is imparted to his map. One has no right to violate geographical probability in this way; a little healthy generalization would not have been amiss. In this connection, however, it should be said that our author has done well to emphasize elsewhere the radical difference in stature between these two varieties of what we have termed the Mediterranean " race." It is not easy to explain why the Corsican, Sardinian, and Spaniard should be so many centimetres shorter than the Berber, when they all resemble one another so closely in other respects. Nevertheless, we find agreement among all the best authorities in affirming a substantial unity of origin of the two. Whether the divergence of stature be due, as we hold, to a degeneration attendant upon a too protracted civilization in Europe, to the evil effects of a long-continued survival of the unfittest through military selection, or to the depressing influences of malaria, and an unfavourable environment in Corsica, Spain, and southern Italy, no man can say with surety. We admit the fact of differences of stature, then; but we object to drawing the line at precisely 1,65 metres, and we believe the inclusion of both groups in a single all-embracing Mediterranean or Iberian " race " to be justified by the facts.

In eliminating all efficient factors save heredity, and in keeping an eye upon geographical probabilities, we have taken two of the three steps toward the scientific constitution of real

"races" from Deniker's "existing varieties" of man. Now
for the last. A "race" has been defined as an "hereditary
type." Has our author neglected this factor of heredity? Or
has he merely hit upon transitory compounds of human traits?
He is too keen for that. Fortunately, also, men considered
in the mass are never fickle in this respect. They betray a
marked persistency, even in their minor combinations. But
it seems to us, nevertheless, that Deniker might have simplified his scheme by going back, even of his *immediately* hereditary combinations, to the consideration of at least penultimate
derivation. We may rid ourselves of troublesome compounds
of traits oftentimes in this way. Thus in Alsace-Lorraine there
certainly is a peculiar persistence of a very tall, blondish, but
anomalously broad-headed population. This is so marked that
Dr. Collignon, prime authority upon the region, dubs it, with
reservations, a Lothringian sub-race. Heredity is at work,
for we know that this type has lasted in this locality for a
number of generations at least, with some approach to constancy. But the consistent evolutionist must go behind this
evidence. He must somewhere find an origin for this combination. It is not enough to affirm that it exists to-day. That
is merely to dodge the issue of descent entirely. To stop here
is to imitate Agassiz and the early systematists. We must
cast about for affinities. Here we touch, as it seems to us,
the tap-root of Deniker's evil. The eye has been blurred by
the vision of anthropometric divergencies, so that it has failed
to note similarities. Wherein, for example, does this peculiar
type of Alsace-Lorraine touch the neighbouring ones? Do
not query yet as to the amount of its difference from its neighbours. Does it not in its tallness of stature show a distinct
affinity with the "Nordic" or Teutonic type? Forget for the
moment that it differs from it in head form and less so in pigmentation. Turn, on the other hand, toward central Europe;
there you find a distinct *point d'appui* in the broad heads and
gray eyes of the Alpine peoples. Collignon finds an explanation for the Lothringian type in a cross of this kind between
two primary races. One confers its stature more largely than
other characteristics; it betrays a distinct persistency in this

respect. The other primal element has endowed the cross with its peculiarities of head form. Unless, in this way, we turn the pages of the book backward, we are speedily confronted with the endless varieties of the mere systematist. The broader our range of observation, the less do we clearly see. This, then, is perhaps the real fault of our author in his magnificent contribution. He certainly gives us one of the most complete pictures which we yet possess of the present anthropologic composition of Europe; but he leaves us more in the dark than ever as to the primary relation of the various parts to each other. Of course, if one be willing to accept the views of certain authorities as to the absolute immutability of certain morphological types, this scheme of Deniker's needs no further simplification. Those, however, it seems to us, are at variance with the whole evolutionary hypothesis.

Analyze our author's scheme in the way we have indicated, and we may, it seems to us, greatly simplify his elaborate classification. Even in the course of this hasty criticism we have incidentally stated what seem to us to be sufficient reasons for merging his " Vistulan " race in the " Oriental "; and for combining his " Ibero-insular " and his " Atlanto-Mediterranean " into one. This reduces the number of his races to eight. Combine his Nordic and sub-Nordic, his Adriatic and sub-Adriatic, and we come quite near the three, or, as we have said, more probably three and one half races, whose existence is acknowledged by the great majority of the best authorities to-day. It is comparatively simple to dispose of the rest in like fashion, especially in the light of recent archæological research; to discover such intimate relationships as to quiet our minds as to their primary derivation from the common sources. Only one great, insurmountable obstacle stands in the way of the ardent evolutionist who would finally run even the three primary types to earth in the far-distant past. How shall we ever reconcile the polar difference in every respect between the broad-headed Asiatic type of central Europe and its two dolichocephalic neighbours on the north and south. Suppose, as we have done, that even these last two finally are traceable to a common African source, are we to confess the existence of two distinct and primary forms of the *genus Homo* —one Asiatic and one African? are we to deny, in other words, the fundamental unity of the human species? We are entering upon the field of speculation pure and simple. Only by the establishment of a broad and secure base of intellectual supplies in the detailed analysis of the present living populations can we hope to assure the safety of such expeditions into the remote past. We need, first of all, a complete knowledge of the living populations of the earth, with all their variations. Deniker promises to afford this more thoroughly perhaps than any anthropologist heretofore for Europe. He has certainly cleared the way for all future investigators. To him all scientists should be duly grateful for this service.

APPENDIX E.

Traits as combined into Types.

Having treated of the relation between stature and blondness in individuals, two other possible combinations of our three main physical characteristics remain for consideration— namely, the relations between the head form and stature and between head form and blondness respectively in the same person. In both cases it appears that while normal associations of these traits—corresponding, that is to say, to our constitution of three ideal racial types—occur in the outskirts of Europe, no clear evidence of the law is offered in its central and most complicated part. Thus, respecting *head form and stature*, Arbo (1895 b, p. 51; 1897, p. 57) in Norway finds the dolichocephalic individuals generally taller; and in Italy, Livi (1896 a, p. 92) asserts that the dolichocephalic individuals are shorter. In each of these cases, it will be noted, the associations are normal, since the long-headed type in Italy, if Mediterranean in type, ought to be less tall. Weisbach (1895 b, p. 79), in Austria, and Salzburg also discover a normal Teutonic combination, the long-headed men being somewhat taller. The same is less clearly true in Poland (Elkind, 1896, col. 363), in Aveyron (Lapouge-Durand, 1897–'98, reprint, p. 27), and in Valais (Bedot, 1895, p. 493). In Baden, Ammon (1890, p. 14) at first found his dolichocephalic men taller as a rule, but his later work (1899, pp. 112 *et seq.*) fails to confirm it. Among other observers, Ranke (Beiträge, v, 1883, p. 199) in Bavaria; Anutchin (1893, p. 285) in Russia; Collignon (1883, reprint, pp. 57–59) in France; and Olóriz (1894 a, p. 52) in Spain; discover no relation whatever between the two traits in the same individual. Eichholz (1896, p. 101) for Russia is also doubtful, and his data are in any case too limited to give reliable results in this matter.

Turning finally to the association of *head form and pigmentation*, again we find Arbo asserting a normal Teutonic relation in Norway (1895 b, p. 55, and 1898, p. 68). Dr. Livi (1896 a, p. 95) also finds his dolichocephalic men of Mediterranean type darker in complexion, or rather in colour of hair, as they ought normally to be. Von Hölder (1876, p. 6) and Regel (1892–'96, iv, p. 600) give evidence for Würtemberg and Thuringia respectively to the same effect—viz., that their long-headed individuals more often than otherwise tend to be relatively light. Ammon, however, in his latest work (1899, pp. 189–191), finds almost no indication of it in Baden. Carret (1883, p. 106) asserts it of the Savoyards, but gives no precise data to verify the statement. In Moravia, Matiegka's figures (1892 a) for three hundred and ninety-five individuals show too slight a tendency to be of value. Most other observers discover no relation whatever between the two traits, dolichocephalic individuals being as apt to be light as dark. Among these are Ranke, for Bavaria (Beiträge, v, 1883, p. 199); Anutchin, for Russia (1893, p. 285); Majer and Kopernicki, for Galicia (1877, i, p. 132); Elkind, for Poland (1896, col. 362); Eichholz, for Russia (1896, p. 107); and Bedot, for Switzerland (1895, p. 493). Two observers, on the other hand, Weisbach in Austria (1895 b, p. 76), and Emme in Russia (1886)—the latter, however, with a very limited series of forty-one persons only—find their dark individuals rather more long-headed.

Appendix F.

This map seems to give average statures slightly lower than those of other observers, like Weisbach, Korösi, and Janko; but, on the other hand, they are corroborated by Scheiber, Majer and Kopernicki, and Zuckerkandl. In all cases the relativity of the various districts is precisely the same; it is confirmed by the maps for the empire by Le Monnier and Myrdacz. It seems to fit perfectly the results for neighbouring countries, given by Livi, Zakrezewski, and Anutchin.

INDEX.